Cisco CallManager Fundamentals

Second Edition

John Alexander
Chris Pearce
Anne Smith
Delon Whetten

Cisco Press

800 East 96th Street
Indianapolis, IN 46240 USA

Cisco CallManager Fundamentals, Second Edition

John Alexander

Chris Pearce

Anne Smith

Delon Whetten

Copyright© 2006 Cisco Systems, Inc.

Cisco Press logo is a trademark of Cisco Systems, Inc.

Published by:
Cisco Press
800 East 96th Street
Indianapolis, IN 46240 USA

Printed in the United States of America   4 5 6 7 8 9 0

Fourth Printing November 2007

Library of Congress Cataloging-in-Publication Number: 2003116869

ISBN: 1-58705-192-3

Warning and Disclaimer

This book is designed to provide information about Cisco CallManager release 4.1(2). Every effort has been made to make this book as complete and as accurate as possible, but no warranty or fitness is implied.

The information is provided on an "as is" basis. The authors, Cisco Press, and Cisco Systems, Inc. shall have neither liability nor responsibility to any person or entity with respect to any loss or damages arising from the information contained in this book or from the use of the discs or programs that may accompany it.

The opinions expressed in this book belong to the author and are not necessarily those of Cisco Systems, Inc.

Feedback Information

At Cisco Press, our goal is to create in-depth technical books of the highest quality and value. Each book is crafted with care and precision, undergoing rigorous development that involves the unique expertise of members from the professional technical community.

Reader feedback is a natural continuation of this process. If you have any comments regarding how we could improve the quality of this book, or otherwise alter it to better suit your needs, you can contact us through email at feedback@ciscopress.com. Please make sure to include the book title and ISBN in your message.

We greatly appreciate your assistance.

Trademark Acknowledgments

All terms mentioned in this book that are known to be trademarks or service marks have been appropriately capitalized. Cisco Press or Cisco Systems, Inc. cannot attest to the accuracy of this information. Use of a term in this book should not be regarded as affecting the validity of any trademark or service mark.

Publisher: John Wait

Editor-in-Chief: John Kane

Cisco Representative: Anthony Wolfenden

Cisco Press Program Manager: Jeff Brady

Executive Editor: Jim Schachterle

Production Manager: Patrick Kanouse

Senior Development Editor: Christopher Cleveland

Copy Editor: Keith Cline

Technical Editors: Marc Ayres, Ho Bao, Luc Bouchard, Thomas Chan, Gerardo Chaves, Joanna Chen, Lijun Chen, R. Vicky Chen, CT Chou, Darrick Deel, Mike Dybka, Clint Entrop, Mike Gallucci, Stefano Giorcelli, Paul Giralt, Dave Goodwin, Graham Gudgin, James He, Cullen Jennings, Stawan Kadepurkar, Jackie Lee, Kevin McMenamy, Hakim Mehmood, Larry Michalewicz, Aruna Muvvala, Kevin Nash, Ping Ni, Joe Pinkus, Tom Qian, John Restrick, Herb Sayre, Rohit Srivastava, David Staudt, Murat Tiryakioglu, Huot Tran, Satyam Tyagi, Henry Wang, Xi Zha

Team Coordinator: Raina Han

Cover and Book Designer: Louisa Adair

Composition: Mark Shirar

Indexer: Tim Wright

Proofreader: Tonya Cupp

CISCO SYSTEMS

Corporate Headquarters
Cisco Systems, Inc.
170 West Tasman Drive
San Jose, CA 95134-1706
USA
www.cisco.com
Tel: 408 526-4000
      800 553-NETS (6387)
Fax: 408 526-4100

European Headquarters
Cisco Systems International BV
Haarlerbergpark
Haarlerbergweg 13-19
1101 CH Amsterdam
The Netherlands
www-europe.cisco.com
Tel: 31 0 20 357 1000
Fax: 31 0 20 357 1100

Americas Headquarters
Cisco Systems, Inc.
170 West Tasman Drive
San Jose, CA 95134-1706
USA
www.cisco.com
Tel: 408 526-7660
Fax: 408 527-0883

Asia Pacific Headquarters
Cisco Systems, Inc.
Capital Tower
168 Robinson Road
#22-01 to #29-01
Singapore 068912
www.cisco.com
Tel: +65 6317 7777
Fax: +65 6317 7799

Cisco Systems has more than 200 offices in the following countries and regions. Addresses, phone numbers, and fax numbers are listed on the
C i s c o . c o m   W e b   s i t e   a t   w w w . c i s c o . c o m / g o / o f f i c e s .

Argentina • Australia • Austria • Belgium • Brazil • Bulgaria • Canada • Chile • China PRC • Colombia • Costa Rica • Croatia • Czech Republic
Denmark • Dubai, UAE • Finland • France • Germany • Greece • Hong Kong SAR • Hungary • India • Indonesia • Ireland • Israel • Italy
Japan • Korea • Luxembourg • Malaysia • Mexico • The Netherlands • New Zealand • Norway • Peru • Philippines • Poland • Portugal
Puerto Rico • Romania • Russia • Saudi Arabia • Scotland • Singapore • Slovakia • Slovenia • South Africa • Spain • Sweden
Switzerland • Taiwan • Thailand • Turkey • Ukraine • United Kingdom • United States • Venezuela • Vietnam • Zimbabwe

About the Authors

John Alexander is a director of CallManager software development at Cisco Systems, Inc. He has more than 35 years of experience in software development, including more than 25 years of management experience. His experience is primarily in the field of voice communications, including call processing, voice messaging, call center, and switching systems. John was a member of the team that developed and implemented the CallManager software from its early stages.

Chris Pearce is a Cisco distinguished engineer in the CallManager software development group at Cisco Systems, Inc. He has 14 years of experience in telecommunications. His primary areas of expertise include call routing, call control, and telephone features. Chris was a member of the team that developed and implemented the CallManager software from its early stages, and he was and continues to be directly involved in developing the system architecture and design.

Anne Smith is a technical writer in the CallManager support group at Cisco Systems. She has 12 years of documentation experience and was a member of the team that developed the CallManager documentation from its early stages. She currently writes engineering and customer-seen documents for CallManager, IP Phones, and other Cisco IP Communications products. She holds a B.A. in language and literature and is a coauthor of *Cisco CallManager Best Practices* (ISBN: 1-58705-139-7), *Troubleshooting Cisco IP Telephony* (ISBN: 1-58705-075-7), and *Developing Cisco IP Phone Services* (ISBN: 1-58705-060-9).

Delon Whetten is a senior manager of the core call processing team in the CallManager software development group at Cisco Systems, Inc. He has more than 28 years of software development experience. His experience centers on communication systems and includes the design and development of message switching, voice messaging, video teleconferencing, and VoIP call processing systems. Delon was a member of the team that developed and implemented the CallManager software from its early stages, and he was directly involved in developing the system architecture and design.

About the Contributing Author

Paul Giralt, **CCIE No. 4793**, is an escalation engineer at the Cisco Systems Technical Assistance Center in Research Triangle Park, North Carolina, where he has worked since 1998. He has been troubleshooting complex IP Telephony networks since the release of CallManager 3.0 as a TAC engineer, a technical leader for the Enterprise Voice team, and now as an escalation engineer supporting the complete Cisco line of IP Communications products. Paul has troubleshot problems in some of the largest Cisco IP Communications deployments and has provided training for TAC teams around the globe. He holds a B.S. in computer engineering from the University of Miami and is a coauthor of *Troubleshooting Cisco IP Telephony* (ISBN: 1-58705-075-7).

About the Technical Reviewers

Marc Ayres is a senior product manager in the IP Communications business unit at Cisco Systems, responsible for CallManager releases that will provide expanded SIP support and additional operating systems. He has more than 19 years of experience in voice and video communications. Marc joined Cisco in 2000.

Ho Bao is a technical leader in the CallManager software development group. He has led many protocol development projects in CallManager including SIP, MGCP, and H.323. Ho has worked as a software engineer for 15 years, with the past six years at Cisco Systems.

Luc Bouchard is a technical marketing engineer working in the Voice Technology group at Cisco Systems. He holds a B.S. in electrical engineering from Université Laval, Québec, Canada. A five-year Cisco employee, Luc has been designing and deploying networks for the past 15 years. Luc and his (much) better half Barb live and work in Silicon Valley and as Canadians still struggle with the lack of snow on the roads, Chardonnay being served at Shark's games, and barbequing in February. They hope to adapt soon.

Thomas Chan is a manager responsible for Cisco CallManager CTI (Computer Telephony Integration), JTAPI (Java Telephony Application Programming Interface), and TAPI (Telephony Application Programming Interface) software development. He has been at Cisco for five years and has worked in the telecom industry for 17 years. He holds an M.S. in computer science and a B.S. in biochemistry from the University of California, Davis.

Gerardo Chaves is a marketing product manager for CallManager. Prior to his current position, he was a software engineer in the IP Communications business unit developing voice applications. Gerardo has been with Cisco for seven years working on various IP Telephony projects. He holds a B.S. in computer science.

Joanna Chen is a technical leader in the CallManager software development group at Cisco Systems. For the past five years she has focused on call processing and has worked for Cisco since 1999. Joanna holds a B.S. in electrical engineering from Shanghai Jiao Tong University (China) and an M.S. in electrical engineering from China Academy of Posts and Telecommunication.

Lijun Chen is a software engineer in the CallManager software development group at Cisco Systems. He is a key module owner of MGCP/PRI/BRI components. Lijun has been at Cisco for five years. He holds an M.S. in electrical and computer engineering from the University of Texas at Austin.

R. Vicky Chen is a technical leader in the CallManager software development group at Cisco Systems. Her primary responsibility is CallManager media components. Vicky has been at Cisco for more than seven years and has worked as a software engineer for more than 12 years.

CT Chou is a technical leader in the CallManager Serviceability team at Cisco Systems. He has been at Cisco for six years. CT holds an M.S. in computer science from the University of Iowa.

Darrick Deel is a software engineer in the IP Communications business unit at Cisco Systems. He is the primary designer for the XML Services interface, which is used to create the services and directory infrastructure on Cisco IP Phones. He is a coauthor of *Developing Cisco IP Phone Services* (ISBN: 1-58705-060-9).

Mike Dybka, CCIE No. 1413, is a technical marketing engineer in the Cisco Voice Technology group. He provides design guidance for voice solutions to enterprise customers, the Cisco sales force, and Cisco partners. During the past nine years at Cisco, Mike has held various roles assisting customers design their network solutions. His career as a network engineer spans 14 years.

Clint Entrop is a manager in the CallManager call processing development team. Clint and his team develop enhancements to the core CallManager call processing engine to meet product requirements. Clint joined Cisco in early 1999. Prior to Cisco, he worked as an engineer in the telecom industry. He holds a B.S. in electrical engineering from Texas A&M University.

Mike Gallucci is a technical lead in the CallManager software development group at Cisco Systems. Mike has worked on feature development, scalability, and platform development. Prior to joining Cisco in 2000, he developed telephony software at AT&T/Lucent Technologies and was a software manager for the Space Environment Laboratory at the U.S. Department of Commerce. Mike holds M.S. degrees in both mathematics and computer science and a Ph.D. in computer science from the University of Colorado.

Stefano Giorcelli is a technical marketing engineer in the Voice Technology group at Cisco Systems. In this role, he works closely with engineering and product management, and focuses on assisting Cisco technical salespeople, partners, and customers to design IP Communications networks. He has contributed to numerous design guides, application notes, and technical white papers on various topics related to IP Communications, and regularly gives technical presentations at public conferences and internal training events. Stefano holds an M.S. in telecommunications engineering from the Politecnico di Torino, Italy.

Dave Goodwin, Routing & Switching and Voice CCIE No. 4992, is a customer support engineer for the Cisco TAC. He is responsible for providing escalation support to the Cisco TAC voice teams worldwide, as well as discovering and resolving issues in new and emerging Cisco IP Communications products. He also works closely with Cisco engineering teams and is actively involved in the field trials of new products. Dave has been with Cisco for 7 years and has worked as a network engineer for 10 years.

Graham Gudgin, CCIE No. 2370, is a technical marketing engineer in the Voice Systems Engineering group at Cisco Systems. He is a member of the team responsible for IP Communications system designs and the creation of Solution Reference Network Designs posted at http://www.cisco.com/go/srnd. Previously, Graham worked in the field and Cisco TAC specializing in the development and design of packet, cell, and TDM- and voice-based systems.

James He is a hardware engineer in the Data Center, Switch, and Wireless group at Cisco Systems. James worked in the wireless industry for CDMA and GSM before joining Cisco in 1999. In his first two years at Cisco, he helped develop VoIP and VoATM compliance testing capabilities on IOS. For the past four years, James has focused on developing VoIP compliance capabilities for CallManager. He holds an M.S. in electrical engineering from Cornell University.

Dr. Cullen Jennings is a distinguished engineer in the Voice Technology group at Cisco Systems. He is currently focusing on rich media, conferencing, security, and firewall and NAT traversal. Cullen is a co-chair of the IETF IP Telephone working group. He has worked with many of Cisco's key customers to help craft their voice security solutions and is a frequent speaker at major voice and security conferences. Cullen is an author of the book *Practical VoIP*, published by O'Reilly.

Stawan Kadepurkar is a software development manager with Infosys Technologies Ltd. He has worked on CallManager for the past six years and helps design and develop some of the features and applications. He works closely with the CallManager development, QA, and TAC/field support teams. Stawan has been working in this industry for the past 10 years.

Jackie Lee is a manager in the CallManager software development group at Cisco Systems. She holds an M.S. in electrical engineering and computer science from the University of California and has worked for Cisco Systems since 1999.

Kevin McMenamy is a senior technical marketing engineer in the Cisco IP Communications business unit. His responsibilities include technical marketing for CallManager and IP Phones and contributing to the design and development of various other key architectural areas such as quality of service (QoS); core voice and video signaling protocols such as H.323, SIP, and SCCP; and security. He is a coauthor of Cisco IP Video Telephony Solutions Reference Network Design (SRND) and has contributed to several other SRNDs, white papers, application notes, and magazine articles. Kevin is currently focused on the design and development of CallManager release 5.x and the next generation of SIP-based IP Phones and applications.

Hakim Mehmood is a software engineer in the Voice Technology group at Cisco Systems. In this role, he works on software development and focuses on protocols and call control. He has contributed in the areas of signaling protocol development, most recently Annex M1. In his career, Hakim has worked mostly on Voice over Packet (VoATM and VoIP) as well as legacy PSTN signaling (SS7/ISDN).

Larry Michalewicz is a software development manager in the Enterprise Voice Hardware Engineering group at Cisco Systems. He has managed the third-generation phone-quality team for one year, and previously worked as an engineer and manager on the CallManager sustaining/critical accounts team for five years. Larry has worked with CallManager since release 1.0 and has worked for Cisco Systems for 12 years. He holds a B.S. in computer science from the University of North Texas and is the author of three patents.

Aruna Muvvala is a software development manager in the Network Management Technology group at Cisco Systems. His group is responsible for IP Telephony management applications, which include CiscoWorks IP Telephony Environment Monitor. Aruna has been at Cisco for more than 9 years and has worked in networking software development for more than 10 years.

Kevin Nash is a software engineer in the CallManager software development group at Cisco Systems. He has been working on product development in VoIP technologies for the past 12 years and has worked in the telecommunications field for 20 years. Kevin has been employed at Cisco Systems for the past five years.

Ping Ni, Ph.D., is a technical leader for Cisco CallManager. She is currently the lead engineer for the development of various supplementary services for CallManager. Ping has been involved in the development of various components inside CallManager software during the past six years.

Joe Pinkus is a diagnostic engineer for the Advanced Engineering Services group at Cisco Systems. He is responsible for helping customers design, implement, and troubleshoot IP Communications solutions in their environment. He has been with Cisco as a TAC engineer for more than six years.

Tom Qian is a technical marketing engineer in the Voice Technology group at Cisco Systems. He provides design guidance for voice solutions to enterprise customers, the Cisco sales force, and Cisco partners. During the last four years at Cisco, he has held various roles assisting customers design their network solutions.

John Restrick is a manager in the CallManager software development group at Cisco Systems. He was named a Cisco Innovator for his work introducing video telephony in CallManager. In addition to video, John works in voice protocol interoperability, media, and security. He holds a B.A. from the University of California at Berkeley in statistics and has been with Cisco since 2001.

Herb Sayre, **MCSE #1332518**, is a software engineer in the CallManager software development group at Cisco Systems. He has 14 years of experience in software design and development. Herb has worked at Cisco since 1999 and has spent the last five years focused on CallManager software development.

Rohit Srivastava is a consultant from Infosys Technologies Ltd., and has worked with Cisco Systems since 1999. He has more than five years of experience in Cisco VoIP solutions and specializes in bulk system configuration. He holds a B.S. in electronics and power from REC, Maharashtra, India.

David Staudt is an engineer in the CallManager Developer Support group, with 10 years of experience in telephony application development. He has worked for Cisco Systems developer services since 2000.

Murat Tiryakioglu, **Routing & Switching and Voice CCIE No. 7611**, is an escalation engineer at Cisco Systems EMEA TAC. He provides resolution to critical business-impacting issues, author technical documentation, and creates and delivers training to TAC engineers, Cisco partners in EMEA, and customers. Murat has been in the industry for nine years focusing on Cisco IP Telephony for the past six years.

Huot Tran is a software engineer in the CallManager software development group at Cisco Systems. His primary focus is call distribution, immediate divert, and redirection (3xx) primitive features in CallManager. Prior to joining Cisco in 2000, Huot worked in the defense industry from 1993 to 1997 and in telecommunications since 1997. He has been a software engineer for 12 years. Huot holds an M.S. in computer engineering from the University of New Mexico and an M.S. in telecommunications from Southern Methodist University, Dallas.

Satyam Tyagi is a software development engineer at Sipera Systems. He works on innovative technology to detect, mitigate, and prevent attacks on VoIP and network infrastructure. Previously he was a software engineer in the CallManager software development group at Cisco Systems for four years. He worked in areas such as MLPP, MGCP, QSIG, PRI/CAS, and other gateway protocols. Satyam holds an M.S. in computer science from the University of North Texas and a B.S. in computer engineering from the Institute of Technology, Banaras Hindu University.

Henry Wang is a technical leader for CallManager Serviceability research and development at Cisco Systems. He is responsible for the development of billing, statistics, and reporting tools. Henry has been at Cisco for more than six years and also has worked for other companies in networking and telecommunication industries for many years.

Xi Zha is a network engineer and software programmer at Cisco Systems. He holds M.S. degrees in computer science and telecommunication engineering. He has years of experience in software development and network design. For the past four years, he has focused on serviceability for Cisco CallManager.

Dedications

John Alexander

This book is dedicated to my wife, Lee. Without her patience and support, I could not have contributed to the book.

Chris Pearce

To all of my teachers; to Mom and Dad; and, especially, to Clay.

Anne Smith

To my parents: Mom for teaching me strength, focus, and endurance; Dad for teaching me to be smart and always try harder. Dad, it's not Michener but at least it's 1000 pages.

To Herb, best friend, partner, lover, and husband, for his support, patience, and love.

To Vaughn and Eadlin for bringing so much laughter, wonder, and joy to our lives.

Delon Whetten

To my wife, Loraine, for her encouragement and support.

Paul Giralt

I dedicate this book to my wonderful wife, Archana, and my son, Rohen.

Acknowledgments

Chris Pearce would like to thank the following people for their superb help on this edition: Joanna Chen, Clint Entrop, and Cullen Jennings for helpful comments in the overview; Mike Gallucci and Kevin Nash for extensive help with new routing behavior; Hakim Mehmood for help with QSIG details; Ho Bao for detailed information about CallManager trunk protocols; Kevin McMenamy for help with Cisco gateway components and H.323; Luc Bouchard, Stawan Kadepurkar, and James He for routing expertise; Murat Tiryakioglu for extensive comments throughout; Anne Smith, Graham Gudgin, and Paul Giralt for their encyclopedic systems knowledge of CallManager and other Cisco components; Chris Cleveland at Cisco Press for extensive attention to detail throughout and an emphasis on consistency and clarity; and John Kane at Cisco Press for accommodating ever-slipping deadlines from his overwhelmed writers.

Anne Smith would like to thank the following people in particular: Scott Veibell for being an excellent boss and offering his constant encouragement, counsel, guidance, and support; Paul Giralt for his extensive knowledge of everything IP Communications and the never-closing late-night IM window; Darrick Deel for providing critical short-notice, last-minute additions to the XML sections in Appendix C and patiently answering countless phone-related questions; Richard Platt for his vision; Kevin McMenamy for his continuing work on the Feature List, leveraged in Appendix A; John Restrick for help with last-minute DSCP additions; and Gurdeep Kaur for explaining the mystery of CAPF service parameters. I also thank Delon, Chris, Paul, and John for making this book possible and making the experience an enjoyable one with teamwork, high standards of excellence, and dedication.

Paul Giralt would like to thank all the technical reviewers for their valuable feedback on Chapter 6.

The authors acknowledge the contribution of the following people for their valuable assistance on this book: Paul Adams, Nitika Agarwal, Tripti Agarwal, Mohammad Al-Taraireh, Faraz Aladin, Steve Anderson, Shivaji Apte, Gene Arantowicz, Ho Bao, Roger Beathard, Bob Bell, Karen Bissani, Luc Bouchard, Barry Bruxvoort, Thomas Chan, Tej Chadha, Gerardo Chaves, Ed Chen, Joanna Chen, Lijun Chen, Rongxuan Chen, Yun-Chung Chen, Bae-Sik Chon, Rita Chow, Yau-Fun Choy, Tony Collins, Craig Cotton, Bret Cullivan, Darrick Deel, Abhijit Dey, David Doherty, Ted Doty, Jay Du, Joe Duffy, Clint Entrop, Abid Fazal, Bill Forsythe, Alex Garbuz, Paul Giralt, Mike Greil, Moises Gonzalez, Manish Gupta, Vikram Gururaj, Addis Hallmark, James He, Scott Henning, Kathryn Holland, John Houston, Grace Hu-Morley, Feng Huang, He Huang, Lee Ji, Joanna Jiang, Vipin Kamra, Devinder Kathuria, Vinod Katkam, Gurdeep Kaur, Holli Kearns, David Kelly, Parameswaran Kumaraswamy, Mohan Kunnamkalath, Jackie Lee, Ron Lewis, Cheryl Li, Shipeng Li, William Liang, Ran Liu, Man Loh, Mark Loney, Zishan Lu, Rex McAnally, Terry McKeon, Kevin McMenamy, Hakim Mehmood, Adam Mermel, Chandra Mulpuri, Charlie Munro, Teresa Newell, Thang Nguyen, Thu Nguyen, Ping Ni, Mariano O'Kon, Jeff Ou, Arvind Patel, Padma Penmetsa, Shamim Pirzada, Richard Platt, Steve Pomeroy, Joe Porcheddu, Arun Ragunathan, Santosh Ransubhe, John Restrick, Chris Rigg, Jan Willem Ruys, Vishwanathan Sahasranamam, Mike Sandman (www.sandman.com/telhist.html), Stephen Sanoff, Susan Sauter, Herb Sayre, Brian Sedgley, Wes Sisk, Eddie Soliman, Chris Spain, James M Stormes, Steve Sun, James Tighe, Steve Toteda, Huot Tran, Ba Trinh, Todd Truitt, Satyam Tyagi, Manoshi Vasudevan, Sohil Virani, Triston Whetten, Martin Wu, Wei Yu, Tony Zhu, Jamie Zhuang.

To the folks at Cisco Press, we thank you. We especially thank Chris Cleveland, John Kane, Jim Schachterle, and Patrick Kanouse for their hard work and dedication to this title: Chris for his attention to detail and quick turnaround; John for keeping us on track and helping manage a difficult schedule; Jim for his professionalism and patience; and Patrick for working so hard to ensure a quality book and buying us the time we needed to get it right.

We also owe our thanks to everyone in the following groups for their contribution to the Cisco IP Communications technology: IPCBU Engineering, Quality Assurance, Integration, Test, CAP, Cisco TAC, Project Management, Technical Marketing, Product Management, Documentation, and Marketing.

This Book Is Safari Enabled

The Safari® Enabled icon on the cover of your favorite technology book means the book is available through Safari Bookshelf. When you buy this book, you get free access to the online edition for 45 days.

Safari Bookshelf is an electronic reference library that lets you easily search thousands of technical books, find code samples, download chapters, and access technical information whenever and wherever you need it.

To gain 45-day Safari Enabled access to this book:

- Go to http://www.ciscopress.com/safarienabled
- Complete the brief registration form
- Enter the coupon code MNGJ-32PF-DAX7-QKF3-MMSI

If you have difficulty registering on Safari Bookshelf or accessing the online edition, please e-mail customer-service@safaribooksonline.com.

Contents at a Glance

Contents

Command Syntax Conventions

The conventions used to present command syntax in this book are the same conventions used in the IOS Command Reference. The Command Reference describes these conventions as follows:

- **Boldface** indicates commands and keywords that are entered literally as shown. In actual configuration examples and output (not general command syntax), boldface indicates commands that are manually input by the user (such as a **show** command).
- *Italics* indicate arguments for which you supply actual values.
- Vertical bars | separate alternative, mutually exclusive elements.
- Square brackets [ ] indicate optional elements.
- Braces { } indicate a required choice.
- Braces within brackets [{ }] indicate a required choice within an optional element.

Icons Used in This Book

Throughout this book, you will see a number of icons used to designate Cisco-specific and general networking devices, peripherals, and other items. The following icon legend explains what these icons represent.

Network Device Icons

CallManager

IP Phone

Cisco IP Phone 7970

Stations

Used for:
Application Server
DHCP
DNS
MOH Server
MTP
SW Conference Bridge
Voice Mail Server

7985 Phone

Tandberg SCCP Video Endpoint

Cisco VT Advantage

Router

Switch

Gateway or 3rd-Party H.323 Server

SIP Proxy

Used for:
HW Conference Bridge
Transcoder
Voice-Enabled Switch

Used for:
Analog Gateway
H.323 Gateway
Gatekeeper
Gateway
Transcoder

SRST Router

PC

POTS Phone

PBX (small)

PBX/PSTN Switch

Server

Laptop

Access Server

Layer 3 switch

ATM Switch

Cisco Directory Server

Local Director

Relational Database

Fax machine

PC w/software

Modem

PIX Firewall

DAT Tape

Foreword

This second edition of *Cisco CallManager Fundamentals* introduces several key additions as well as major revisions to one of the most successful books ever published related to IP telephony in general and Cisco CallManager in particular.

Since the first edition was published, the industry has continued to move at Internet speeds in spite of a downturn in the economy. Cisco Systems now generates more than $1B in revenues from IP telephony and regularly ships 200,000+ phones per month (as of late 2004). Development, test, and support staff has more than doubled.

In July of 1997, the engineering group from Selsius Systems, a small start-up in Dallas, Texas, cofounded by David Tucker and me, connected two normal-appearing phones into a 10-Mbps Ethernet LAN. On one of the phones in the lab, I dialed a four-digit extension in a very ordinary way, which in turn caused the second phone to ring in a very ordinary way on David's desk. He answered the phone with the customary "Hello," and I replied with an uncustomary response, "Can you hear me?!" Thus began the third technology evolution in the long history of the telephone. Although the "phone call" appeared ordinary on the outside, everything inside was vastly different from the first generation of analog telephony and substantially different from the second generation of TDM digital telephony. This was the first time that a telephone call had been made entirely with Internet technology consisting of a true IP phone (connected over Ethernet), over an IP network, managed by an IP-connected server appropriately named the CallManager.

There are many components that comprise the Cisco IP Communications solution; nevertheless, Cisco CallManager is the heart of the solution. The content of this book is the first (now the second) public glimpse into the core of CallManager. The authors carefully discuss the fundamental design, its evolution, and the motives behind the current architecture. Over the course of its 11-year life, CallManager has undergone several major transitions. This is perhaps its key to success: the ability to adapt and change at Internet speed. The fundamental philosophy has remained intact; however, much of the underlying architecture has either evolved or been redesigned, resulting in a system that supports tens of thousands of devices and is deployed in thousands of companies all over the world.

Three of the authors of this book, John Alexander, Chris Pearce, and Delon Whetten, are three of the original designers of CallManager. Anne Smith was one of the original writers of the CallManager documentation. Today, John's role is director for Cisco CallManager development. Chris continues as the lead architect. Delon manages the core group of call processing. And Anne leads much of the supporting documentation effort. My association with the authors and the Cisco CallManager product spans more than a decade, but in Internet time, the equivalent is closer to 50 years.

While much has changed since the first edition, the applicability and usability of this book has not changed. The first edition can be found in labs, in data centers, and on engineers' desks with well-worn pages, coffee spills, dog-eared pages, and highlights. It was well used then and this second edition will be well used now as the IP telephony revolution continues its juggernaut march down the telecommunications lane.

Richard B. Platt
VP of Development
Cisco Systems, Inc.

Introduction

In October 2004, Cisco Systems released Cisco CallManager 4.1(2). CallManager, the heart of the Cisco IP Communications solution, provides administrators a platform by which they can manage their enterprise's voice communications over the same network on which they manage their enterprise's data communications. It enables devices that speak dozens of different protocols to communicate together with seeming effortlessness and supports both enterprise and endpoint applications.

We, the writers of this book, have been intimately involved with CallManager since its inception in 1997. And as the years have gone by, we've watched as both the capability and the complexity of the product have increased. Features that seemed obvious to us during CallManager development have sometimes proved less than obvious to those who have actually deployed CallManager. Furthermore, although the Cisco CallManager System Administration and Features and Services Guide is very good at telling you how to accomplish specific tasks, it isn't always as good at telling you why you need to accomplish a specific task, or in providing you with a framework for understanding how different CallManager concepts work together, or the underlying architecture of the product itself.

Therefore, we have tried to distill our knowledge of CallManager into these many hundred pages in the hopes that you will find here what you might not have found elsewhere: a blueprint that reveals order amid the dozens of devices and the hundreds of features that CallManager supports.

Target Release: Cisco CallManager 4.1

This book targets CallManager release 4.1(2), released in October 2004. Most of the material this book presents should apply for future releases as well. Long printing lead times and subsequent 4.1(x) releases might render some of this information out-of-date, but we have tried to protect against that wherever possible by foreseeing those changes.

The first edition of this book was applicable for many releases beyond the target release, and we expect similar performance for this edition. The architectural information presented in this edition should be useful for years to come. Generally, when new features and protocols are added, the existing architecture gets expanded rather than replaced, so the applicability of the information presented here should continue to be useful even as CallManager experiences ongoing major (first digit, such as 5.x) and minor (second digit, such as x.2) revisions.

Comments for the Authors

The authors are interested in your comments and suggestions about this book. Please send feedback to the following address:

cmfundamentals@external.cisco.com

Goals and Methods

This book provides a view of the Cisco IP Communications solution that centers on CallManager. This information helps you put together in your mind the various pieces of CallManager so that you can better understand how to design and implement your own CallManager system. By learning how CallManager processes information, you can configure and troubleshoot your system more effectively.

Who Should Read This Book?

This book is directed to CallManager system administrators who are responsible for configuring CallManager, integrating it into their networks, and maintaining it. This book is also appropriate for network architects looking to integrate Cisco IP Communications with third-party applications and for people interested in the nuts and bolts of a VoIP solution.

Book Features and Text Conventions

Each chapter provides basic information about the subject matter, followed by more detailed information. Chapter 1 includes a block diagram of CallManager's internal components. This diagram is subsequently presented in the introduction of each chapter of the book. The CallManager components that are covered in a particular chapter are highlighted in this diagram. Every chapter ends with a summary section that highlights the critical information that the chapter presents.

If you are new to CallManager, you should be able to get a feel for the information just by reading the first few sections of each chapter. Then you can return to read the more detailed sections as your knowledge of the product increases and you find yourself looking for more answers. For the "old-timers" out there who have been working with CallManager since 1997, the deeper you go into the sections, the more rewarded with information you will be.

This book uses the following formatting conventions to convey additional meaning:

- Key terms are italicized the first time they are used and defined.
- Notes emphasize information of a noteworthy or unusual nature.
- Sidebars provide additional information about important or interesting topics.
- Tips are handy information bits about the subject.
- Cautions provide critical information.

How This Book Is Organized

This book is meant to complement the information already available on Cisco.com and in the CallManager documentation. This book does not provide detailed configuration information or step-by-step instructions. The chapters in this book address the following topics:

- **Chapter 1, "Cisco CallManager Architecture,"** provides an overview of VoIP telephony and describes the evolution of CallManager. It describes the hardware and software components that make up Cisco IP Communications and outlines several methods for deploying a Cisco IP Communications solution.

- **Chapter 2, "Call Routing,"** discusses the fundamental building blocks of the CallManager call routing infrastructure and describes how you can apply these building blocks to solve complex routing problems that most enterprises face.

- **Chapter 3, "Station Devices,"** describes the station devices supported by CallManager. It categorizes them by protocol and then subdivides them by device capabilities.

- **Chapter 4, "Trunk Devices,"** details the gateway protocols supported by CallManager, including H.323, Media Gateway Control Protocol (MGCP), QSIG, and Session Initiation Protocol (SIP). It describes how the protocols signal to gateways, to other CallManager clusters, and to gatekeepers where applicable.

- **Chapter 5, "Media Processing,"** discusses allocation and control of media processing resources, such as conference bridges, transcoders, annunciator, and music on hold (MOH) servers. It explains media connection processing and call preservation.

- **Chapter 6, "Manageability and Monitoring,"** describes tools that you can use to make CallManager easier to manage. It explains in some detail the plug-ins and applications that work with CallManager to assist with system monitoring.

- **Chapter 7, "Call Detail Records,"** describes the facilities provided for controlling the generation and storage of call detail records (CDR) and call management records (CMR), and it provides information on how to access, interpret, and use the stored data.

- **Appendix A, "Feature List,"** provides a list of CallManager and Cisco IP Phone features through release 4.1(2).

- **Appendix B, "Cisco Integrated Solutions,"** details Cisco-developed solutions that can be used in conjunction with CallManager or other components in the Cisco IP Communications system.

- **Appendix C, "Protocol Details,"** provides information about call signaling for the following protocols: H.323, SCCP, QSIG, and SIP. It also describes JTAPI packages and provides details on how you can write your own Cisco IP Phone services.

Further Reading

The authors recommend the following sources for more information.

Cisco Documentation

You should be familiar with and regularly using the documentation that is provided with the Cisco IP Communications system to supplement the information in this book.

You can find Cisco IP Communications documentation by searching for a specific product on Cisco.com or by starting at the following link:

http://www.cisco.com/univercd/cc/td/doc/product/ipcvoice.htm

Cisco CallManager Best Practices

Learn best practices for deploying, maintaining, managing, and monitoring CallManager and related components. Hundreds of best practices are offered in the following areas: centralized call processing deployments, installation, backup and restoration, upgrades and patches, security, system configuration, dial plan, features, IP phones, gateways, tools and applications, services and parameters, directory integration, CDRs, manageability and monitoring, Multilevel Administration (MLA), and Real-Time Monitoring Tool (RTMT). You can examine this book (ISBN: 1-58705-139-7) at your favorite local or online bookseller.

Troubleshooting Cisco IP Telephony

Discover extensive troubleshooting information and troubleshooting methodology. All parts of a Cisco IP Telephony solution are examined, with particularly excellent information about reading traces, the many troubleshooting tools available to you (including a few special ones available for download with the book), voice quality, and gateways. You can examine this book (ISBN: 1-58705-075-7) at your favorite local or online bookseller.

Developing Cisco IP Phone Services

Find instructions and tools for creating custom phone services and directories for Cisco IP Phones in the book *Developing Cisco IP Phone Services* (ISBN: 1-58705-060-9). You can examine this book at your favorite local or online bookseller.

Cisco IP Telephony: Planning, Design, Implementation, Operation, and Optimization

Enjoy real-world examples and explanations with technical details, design tips, network illustrations, and sample configurations that guide you through the stages of planning a large-scale IP Telephony network, choosing the right architecture and deployment model, implementing, operating, and finally optimizing the deployment. You can examine this book (ISBN: 1-58705-157-5) at your favorite local or online bookseller.

Integrating Voice and Data Networks

Find information on how to integrate and configure packetized voice networks in the book *Integrating Voice and Data Networks* (ISBN: 1-57870-196-1). You can examine this book at your favorite local or online bookseller.

CHAPTER 1

Cisco CallManager Architecture

A Cisco IP Communications network is a suite of components that includes Internet Protocol (IP) telephony communications. Cisco CallManager is a core component of a Cisco IP Communications network, the primary function of which is to serve as the call routing and signaling component for IP telephony.

The term *IP telephony* describes telephone systems that place calls over the same type of data network that makes up the Internet. Although strictly speaking, IP telephony primarily enables users to have voice conversations, CallManager also has the capability to enable users with PCs associated with their phones, users with video-only endpoints, and users with H.323-based video systems to have end-to-end video conversations.

Telephone systems have been around for more than 100 years. Small, medium, and large businesses use them to provide voice communications between employees within the business and to customers outside the business. The public telephone system itself is a very large network of interconnected telephone systems.

What makes IP telephony systems in general, and CallManager in particular, different is that they place calls over a computer network. The phones that CallManager controls plug directly into the same IP network as your PC, rather than into a phone jack connected to a telephones-only network.

Phone calls placed over an IP network differ fundamentally from those placed over a traditional telephone network. To understand how IP calls differ, you must first understand how a traditional telephone network works.

In many ways, traditional telephone networks have advanced enormously since Alexander Graham Bell invented the first telephone in 1876. Fundamentally, the traditional telephone network is about connecting a long, dedicated circuit between two telephones.

Traditional telephone networks fall into the following four categories:

- Key systems
- Private Branch Exchanges (PBX)

- Class 5 switches

- Class 1 to 4 switches

A *key system* is a small-scale telephone system designed to handle telephone communications for a small office of 1 to 25 users. Key systems can be either analog, which means they use the same 100-year-old technology of your home phone, or digital, which means they use the 30-year-old technology of a standard office phone.

A *PBX* is a corporate telephone office system. These systems scale from the small office of 20 people to large campuses (and distributed sites) of 30,000 people. However, because of the nature of the typical circuit-based architecture, no PBX vendor manufactures a single system that scales throughout the entire range. Customers must replace major portions of their infrastructure if they grow past their PBX limits.

A *Class 5 switch* is a national telephone system operated by a local telephone company (called a local exchange carrier [LEC]). These systems scale from about 2000 to 100,000 users and serve the public at large.

Long distance companies and national carriers (called *interexchange carriers* [IEC or IXC]) use *Class 1 to 4 switches*. They process truly mammoth levels of calls and connect calls from one Class 5 switch to another.

Despite the large disparity in the number of users supported by these types of traditional networks, the core technology is circuit-based. Consider an old-time telephone operator. He or she sits in front of a large plugboard with hundreds of metal sockets and plugs. (Figure 1-1 shows a picture of an early PBX.) When a subscriber goes off-hook, a light illuminates on the plugboard. The operator plugs in the headset and requests the number of the party from the caller. After getting the number of the called party and finding the called party's socket, the operator checks to see whether the called party is busy. If the called party is not busy, the operator connects the sockets of the calling and called parties with a call cable, thus completing a circuit between them. The circuit provides a conduit for the conversation between the caller and the called party.

Today's central switching office—specifically, its call processing software—is simply a computerized replacement for the old-time telephone operator. Obeying a complex script of rules, the call processing software directs the collection of the number of the called party, looks for the circuit dedicated to the called party, checks to see whether the line is busy, and then completes the circuit between the calling and called parties.

Figure 1-1 *An Early PBX*

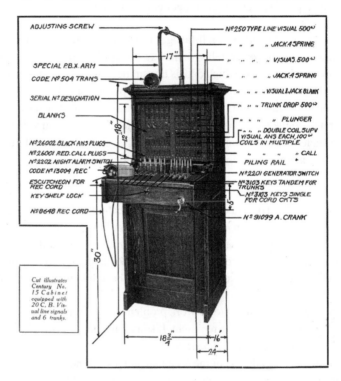

In the past, this circuit was an analog circuit from end to end. The voice energy of the speaker was converted into an electrical wave that traveled to the listener, where it was converted back again into a sound wave. Even today, the vast majority of residential telephone users still have an analog circuit that runs from their phone to the phone company's central switching office, whereas digital circuits run between central switching offices.

This reliance on circuits characterizes traditional telephone systems and gives rise to the term *circuit switching*. A characteristic of circuit switching is that after the telephone system collects the number of the called party, and establishes the circuit from the calling party to the called party, this circuit is dedicated to the conversation between those calling and called parties. The resources allocated to the conversation cannot be reused for other purposes, even if the calling and called parties are silent on the call. Furthermore, if something happens to disrupt the circuit between the calling and called parties, they can no longer communicate.

Like the central switching office, CallManager is a computerized replacement for a human operator. CallManager, however, relies on packet switching to transmit conversations. *Packet switching* is the mechanism by which data is transmitted through the Internet, which encapsulates packets according to the Internet Protocol (IP). Web pages, e-mail, and instant messaging are all conveyed through the fabric of the Internet by packet switching. The term *voice over IP (VoIP)* specifically refers to the use of packet switching using IP to establish voice communications between IP-enabled endpoints on LANs and IP WANs, as well as the Internet (although CallManager is generally not deployed in configurations that route voice traffic over the Internet).

In packet switching, information to be conveyed is digitally encoded and broken down into small units called *packets*. Each packet consists of a header section and the encoded information. Among the pieces of header information is the network address of the recipient of the information. Packets are then placed on a router-connected network. Each router looks at the address information in each packet and decides where to send the packet. The recipient of the information can then reassemble the packets and convert the encoded data back into the original information.

Packet switching is more resilient to network problems than circuit switching because each packet contains the network address of the recipient. If something happens to the connection between two routers, a router with a redundant connection can forward the information to a secondary router, which in turn looks at the address of the recipient and determines how to reach it. Furthermore, if the sender and recipient are not communicating, the resources of the network are available to other users of the network.

In circuit-switched voice communications, an entire circuit is consumed when a conversation is established between two people. The system encodes the voice in a variety of manners, but the standard for voice encoding in the circuit-switched world is *pulse code modulation (PCM)*. Because PCM is the de facto standard for voice communications in the circuit-switched world, it comes as no surprise that a single voice circuit has been defined as the amount of bandwidth required to carry a single PCM-encoded voice stream.

Video communications require that significantly more information be sent from one end of a connection to another. In circuit-switched video communications, multiple circuits are usually simultaneously reserved for a single call to allow endpoints to exchange high-quality video.

An interesting complication involving voice encoding is introduced by packet-switched communications. Even if circuit-switched systems encode the voice stream according to a more efficient scheme, little incentive exists to do so, because, in most instances, a circuit is fully reserved no matter how little data you place on it. In the packet-switched world, however, a more efficient encoding scheme means that for the same amount of voice traffic, you can place smaller packets on the network, which in turn means that the same network can carry a larger number of conversations. As a result, the packet-switched world has given rise to several different encoding schemes called *codecs*.

Different types of voice encoding offer different benefits, but generally the more high fidelity the voice quality, the more bandwidth the resulting media stream requires. As the amount of bandwidth that you are willing to permit the voice stream to consume decreases, the more clever and complex the codec must become to maintain voice quality. The codecs that attempt to minimize the bandwidth required for a voice stream require complex mathematical calculations that attempt to predict in advance information about the volume and frequency level of an utterance. Such codecs are highly optimized for the spoken voice. Furthermore, these calculations are often so computationally intensive that software cannot perform them quickly enough; only specialized hardware with digital signal processors (DSP) can handle the computations efficiently. As a result, codec support often differs substantially from device to device in the VoIP network, because devices that do not incorporate DSPs can generally support only easy-to-encode and easy-to-decode codecs such as G.711.

Because not all network devices understand all codecs, an important part of establishing a packet voice call is the negotiation of a voice codec to be used for the conversation. This codec negotiation is a part of a packet-switched call that does not assume nearly the same importance on a circuit-switched call. Chapter 5, "Media Processing," discusses codecs in more detail.

The information contained in a video call is also encoded using a particular codec; unlike voice codecs, however, of which a handful of variants must be interworked, for interactive video-conferencing, video in the IP world has widely adopted H.263 to encode end-to-end video information (although most products are moving toward H.264).

The rest of this chapter discusses the following topics:

- Circuit-switched systems

- Cisco IP Communications networks

- Enterprise deployment of CallManager clusters

Circuit-Switched Systems

A *circuit-switched system* is typically a vertically integrated, monolithic computer system. A mainframe cabinet houses a proprietary processor, often along with a redundant processor, which in turn is connected with a bus to cabinets containing switch cards, line cards, and trunk cards.

Line cards control station devices (usually phones), and trunk cards control trunk devices (connections to other telephone systems). A wire runs from a station into a line card and carries both the call signaling and the encoded voice of the station device. Similarly, wires called *trunks* connect circuit-switched systems together with trunk cards. Line and trunk cards forward received call signaling to the call processing software, while the encoded media is available to the switch cards. Figure 1-2 demonstrates this architecture.

Figure 1-2 *Traditional Circuit-Switched Architecture*

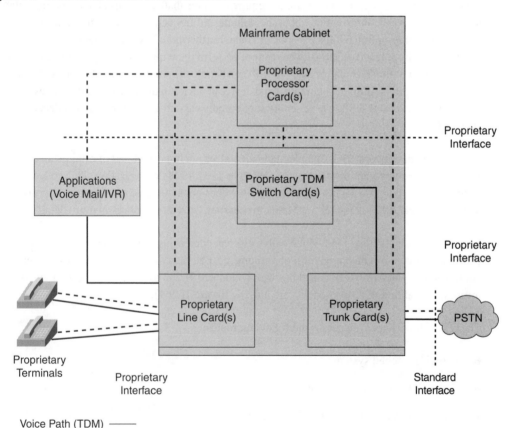

Call Establishment in a Circuit-Switched Telephone System

Call establishment with a circuit-switched system consists of two phases: a session establishment phase and a media exchange phase.

The session establishment phase is the phase in which the telephone system attempts to establish a conversation. During this phase, the telephone system finds out that the caller wants to talk to someone, locates and alerts the called party, and waits for the called party to accept the call. As part of the call establishment, the telephone system also establishes a circuit back from the telephone switch closest to the caller to the caller itself. This circuit permits the caller to hear a ringback tone in the earpiece of the handset and also ensures that, if the called party answers, the end-to-end circuit can be connected as quickly as possible. This optimization eliminates *clipping*, a condition that occurs when the called party speaks before the circuit is completely formed, causing the caller to miss the initial utterance.

As soon as the telephone system determines that the called party wants to take the call, it completes the end-to-end circuit between the caller and called user, which permits them to begin the media exchange phase. The media exchange phase is the phase in which the endpoints actually converse over the connection that the session establishment phase forges.

Session establishment is the purview of *call signaling protocols*. Call signaling protocol is just a fancy term for the methods that coordinate the events required for a caller to tell the network to place a call, provide the telephone number of the destination, ring the destination, and connect the circuits when the destination answers. The following represent just a sample of the dozens of call signaling protocols:

- Rudimentary indications that can be provided over analog interfaces

- Proprietary digital methods

- Various versions of ISDN Basic Rate Interface (BRI), which are implementations of ITU-T Q.931

- Various versions of ISDN Primary Rate Interface (PRI), which are also implementations of ITU-T Q.931

- Integrated Services User Part (ISUP), which is part of Signaling System 7 (SS7)

All of these protocols serve the purpose of coordinating the establishment of a communications session between calling and called users.

As part of the session establishment phase, the telephone network reserves and connects circuits from the caller to the called user. Circuit-switched systems establish circuits with commands to their switch cards. Switch cards are responsible for bridging the media from one line or trunk card to another card in response to directives from the call processing software.

After a circuit-switched system forges an end-to-end connection, the end devices (also called *endpoints*) can begin the media exchange phase. In the media exchange phase, the endpoints encode the spoken word into a data stream. By virtue of the circuit connection, a data stream encoded by one endpoint travels to the other endpoint, which decodes it.

One feature to note is that in a circuit-switched system, the telephone network's switches are directly involved in both the call signaling and the media exchange. The telephone system must process the events from the caller and called user as part of the session establishment, and then it issues commands to its switch cards to bridge the media. Both the call signaling and the media follow the same path.

Call signaling protocols sometimes embed information about the voice-encoding method to be used to ensure that the endpoints communicate using a common encoding scheme. For voice communications, however, this media negotiation does not assume the importance it does in a packet-based system, in which endpoints generally have more voice-encoding schemes from which to choose.

In summary, a circuit-switched system goes through the following steps (abstracted for clarity) to establish a call:

Step 1   **Call signaling**—Using events received from the line and trunk cards, the telephone system detects an off-hook event and dialed digits from the caller, uses the dialed digits to locate a destination, establishes a circuit between a ringback tone generator and the caller, offers the call to the called user, and waits for the called user to answer. When the called user answers, the telephone system fully connects a circuit between the caller and called user.

Step 2   **Media exchange**—By virtue of their connected circuit, the calling and called users can converse. The calling user's phone encodes the caller's speech into a data stream. The switch cards in the telephone system forward the data stream along the circuit until the called user's phone receives and decodes it. Both the call signaling and the media follow a nearly identical path.

Cisco IP Communications Networks

A Cisco IP Communications network is a packet-based system. CallManager is a member of a class of systems called *softswitches*. In a softswitch-based system, the call signaling components and device controllers are not separated by a hardware bus running a proprietary protocol but instead are separate boxes connected over an IP network and talking through open and standards-based protocols.

CallManager provides the overall framework for communication within the corporate enterprise environment. CallManager handles the signaling for calls within the network and calls that originate or terminate outside the enterprise network. In addition to call signaling, CallManager provides call feature capabilities, the capability for voice mail interaction, and an application programming interface (API) for applications. Among such applications are Cisco Unity, Cisco IP Communicator, Cisco IP Contact Center (IPCC) Enterprise edition, Cisco CallManager Attendant Console, Cisco IP Manager Assistant (IPMA), Cisco Emergency Responder (CER), Cisco Personal Assistant (PA), Cisco MeetingPlace, Cisco IP Queue Manager, and a variety of third-party applications.

A Cisco IP Communications network is by nature more open and distributed than a traditional telephone system. It consists of a set number of servers that maintain static provisioned information, provide initialization, and process calls on behalf of a larger number of client devices. Servers cooperate with each other in a manner termed *clustering*, which presents administrators with a single point of provisioning, offers users the illusion that their calls are all being served by the same CallManager node, and enables the system to scale and provide reliability.

The remainder of this section discusses the following topics:

- "CallManager History" presents a short history of CallManager.

- "Cisco-Certified Servers for Running Cisco IP Communications" describes the Windows 2000 servers that CallManager runs on.

- "Windows 2000 Services and Tomcat Services on Cisco IP Communications Servers" presents the services that run on the server devices in a Cisco IP Communications network.

- "Client Devices That CallManager Supports" presents the station, trunking, and media devices that CallManager supports.

- "Call Establishment in a Cisco IP Communications Network" describes how a Cisco IP Communications system places telephone calls.

- "Cisco IP Communications Clustering" describes the concept of clustering servers in a Cisco IP Communications system.

CallManager History

There have been several releases of the software that would become CallManager release 4.1. It started in 1994 as a point-to-point video product, but it was recast as an IP-based telephony system in 1997. By 2004, CallManager could support, via multiple clusters, hundreds of thousands of users with a full suite of enterprise-class features.

1994—Multimedia Manager

The application that would become CallManager release 4.1 began in 1994 as Multimedia Manager 1.0. Multimedia Manager was the signaling controller for a point-to-point video product. Multimedia Manager was developed under HP-UX in the language SDL-88.

Specification and Description Language (SDL) is an International Telecommunication Union (ITU)-standard (Z.100) graphical and textual language that many telecommunications specifications use to describe their protocols. An SDL system consists of many independent state machines, which communicate with other state machines solely through message passing and are thus object-oriented. Furthermore, because SDL is specifically designed for the modeling of real-time behavior, it is extremely suitable for call processing software.

Although Multimedia Manager 1.0 was developed in HP-UX, it was produced to run on Microsoft Windows NT 3.51. Each Multimedia Manager server served only as a call signaling source and destination. Multimedia Manager 1.0 managed connections by sending commands to network hubs, which contained the matrix for the video connections. Each hub contained 12 hybrid Ethernet/time-division multiplexing (TDM) ports. Each port could serve either a PC running videoconferencing software or a subhub that managed four PRI interfaces for calls across the public network. In addition, hubs could be chained together using hybrid Ethernet/TDM trunks. At that point in time, the software was somewhat of a hybrid system; Multimedia Manager, running on a Microsoft Windows NT Server 3.51, handled the call signaling and media control over IP like a softswitch, but the media connections were still essentially circuit-based in the network hubs.

Figure 1-3 depicts CallManager as it existed in 1994.

Figure 1-3 *CallManager in 1994*

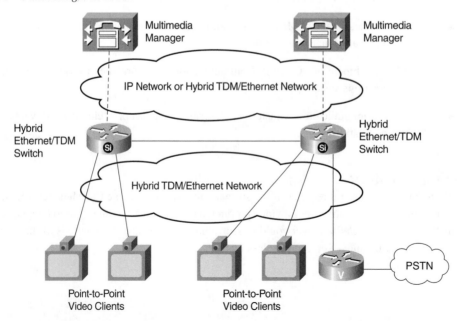

1997—Selsius-CallManager

Although Multimedia Manager 1.0 worked wonderfully, by 1997 it was clear that Multimedia Manager was not succeeding in the marketplace. Customers were reluctant to replace their Ethernet-only network infrastructure with the hybrid Ethernet/TDM hubs required to switch the bandwidth-hungry video applications. At that point, Multimedia Manager 1.0 changed from a videoconferencing solution to a system designed to route voice calls over an IP network. Unlike the hybrid solution, which required intervening hubs to connect a virtual circuit between endpoints, media signaling traveled over the IP infrastructure directly from station to station. In other words, the system became a packet-switched telephone system.

The change required the development of IP phones and IP gateways. The database, which had been a software application running under Windows NT, became a set of web pages connected to a Microsoft Access database. The new interface permitted administrators to modify the network configuration from any remote machine's web browser.

The call processing software changed, too. It incorporated new code to control the IP phones and gateways. For this purpose, the Skinny Client Control Protocol (SCCP) and Skinny Gateway Control Protocol (SGCP) were invented. In addition, the software supported Microsoft NetMeeting, an application that uses the H.323 protocol to support PC-to-PC packet voice calls.

At the same time, the call processing software had finally outgrown the SDL development tools. To ensure that the code base could continue to grow, the pure SDL code was converted into an SDL application engine based on C++ that duplicated all of the benefits that the previous pure SDL environment had provided.

Selsius-CallManager 1.0 was born. It permitted SCCP station-to-station and station-to-trunk calls. Each Selsius-CallManager supported 200-feature phones with features such as transfer and call forward.

Figure 1-4 depicts CallManager as it existed in 1997.

Figure 1-4   *CallManager in 1997*

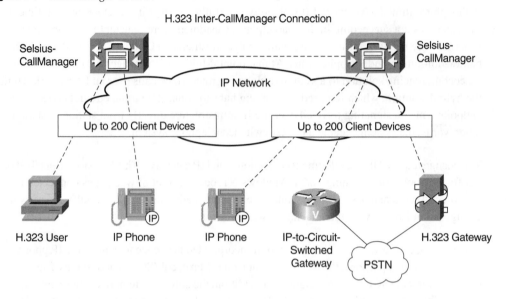

2000—Cisco CallManager Release 3.0

CallManager received a great deal of attention from the marketplace. By 1998, Selsius-CallManager 2.0 had been released, and Cisco Systems, Inc., had become interested in the potential of the product.

After acquiring the CallManager product as a result of its acquisition of Selsius Systems in 1998, Cisco concentrated on enhancing the product. Cisco also simultaneously undertook a huge design and re-engineering effort to provide both scalability and redundancy to the system. Clustering was introduced, and the SDL engine became the Signal Distribution Layer (SDL) engine, which permits the sending of signals directly from one CallManager to another. A redundancy scheme allowed stations to connect to any CallManager in a cluster and operate as if they were connected to their primary CallManager. Support for Media Gateway Control Protocol (MGCP) was added, as was the Cisco IP Phones 7910, 7940, and 7960, which provided a large display, softkeys (virtual buttons on the phone's display), and access to voice mail, phone settings, network directories, and services.

By mid-2000, Cisco CallManager release 3.0 was complete. It permitted feature-rich calls between H.323 stations and gateways, MGCP gateways, and SCCP stations and gateways. Each cluster supported up to 10,000 endpoints, and multiple cluster configurations permitted the configuration of up to 100,000 endpoints.

Figure 1-5 depicts CallManager release 3.0.

Figure 1-5 *CallManager in 2000*

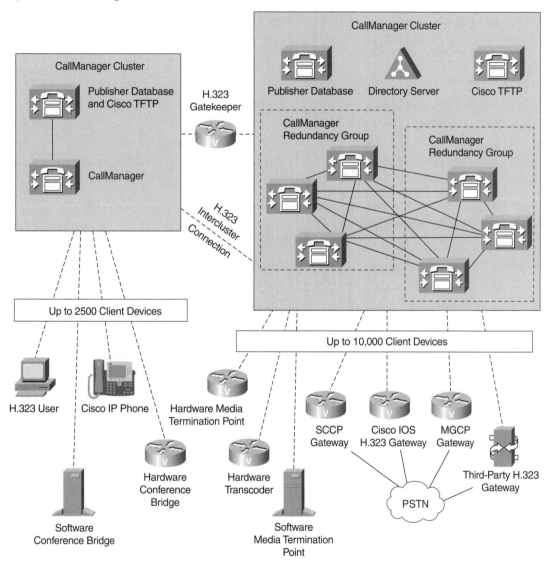

2001—Cisco CallManager Release 3.1

CallManager release 3.1 built on the foundation of CallManager 3.0. The platform supported more gateway devices and station devices, added enhancements to serviceability, and added more features. Among the specific enhancements were the following:

- Music on hold (MOH)

- Media resource devices available to the cluster, rather than to individual CallManager servers

- Support for digital interfaces on MGCP gateways

- Call preservation between IP phones and MGCP gateways on server failure

- Database support for third-party devices

- Extension mobility

- ISDN overlap sending and T1-CAS support in a variety of VoIP gateways

- Support for Extensible Markup Language (XML) and HTML applications in Cisco IP Phones

- Support for telephony applications through Telephony Application Programming Interface (TAPI) and Java TAPI (JTAPI) and JTAPI/TAPI call processing redundancy support

2001—Cisco CallManager Release 3.2

CallManager 3.2 was a small-scale release that improved the following areas:

- **Scalability**—Improvements to support up to 20,000 IP phone endpoints per cluster, to improve the number of simultaneous H.323 calls, and to permit CallManager to simultaneously connect to multiple voice messaging systems

- **Language**—Localization of end-user–visible interfaces, such as phones, end-user applications, gateways, and user-accessible configuration pages to U.K. English and many non-English language and tone sets

- **Supported devices**—Support for station-oriented analog gateways such as the VG224 and VG248, as well as the Cisco IP Phone 7905

- **Features**—Auto-answer at destination IP phone for hands-free intercom service, Automated Alternate Routing (AAR) to route calls over the Public Switched Telephone Network (PSTN) when network bandwidth is no longer available, the ability to drop the most recently joined conference participant from an Ad Hoc conference, consultation transfer from applications, and message waiting enhancements

2002—Cisco CallManager Release 3.3

Like CallManager 3.2, CallManager 3.3 was a reasonably small-scale release, but which improved the following areas:

- **Scalability**—Improvements to support up to 30,000 IP phones per cluster and hundreds of thousands of IP phones using multiple clusters with an H.323 gatekeeper

- **H.323 support**—Improved ability to support H.323 gatekeeper-controlled connections between CallManager nodes and better scalability and redundancy through support for multiple gatekeepers and alternate H.323 gateways

- **Application improvements**—Support for Cisco IP Manager/Assistant and Cisco Call Back on Busy applications

- **QSIG support**—Support for basic call and line identification services using QSIG, a protocol designed to foster feature transparency between different PBXs

- **Feature improvements**—Distinctive ring per line appearance and configurable call waiting tones for consecutive calls

2004—Cisco CallManager Release 4.0

CallManager 4.0 was a large-scale release that focused quite strongly on features. Chief among the feature changes was a fundamental change in the way that Cisco IP Phones could manage calls. Prior to CallManager 4.0, Cisco IP Phones abided by two main restrictions:

- For any given line appearance, a Cisco IP Phone could have at most two calls, of which one could be actively streaming voice.

- When a Cisco IP Phone was actively streaming voice, other Cisco IP Phones that shared a directory number with the active Cisco IP Phone could not place or receive calls on the shared directory number (although their other directory numbers, if any, could be used to place and receive calls).

In CallManager release 4.0, Cisco IP Phones are no longer restricted to at most two calls per line appearance. Instead, the maximum number of calls per line appearance is configurable, although phones are still restricted to at most one actively streaming call. (An exception is models such as the Cisco IP Phone 7905, 7910, and 7912, which lack a display that would permit a user to efficiently manage more than two calls—these devices are still limited to, at most, two calls.)

Furthermore, in CallManager 4.0, devices that share line appearances are no longer restricted from placing and receiving calls if other devices that share the directory number are actively streaming voice on a call. A phone can continue to place and receive calls until it reaches the maximum threshold (up to 200 calls) configured by the system administrator.

In addition to continuing to support end-user features provided by earlier releases (transfer, Ad Hoc conference, Meet-Me conference, drop the last conference party, call park, call pickup, group call pickup, call back on busy, redial, speed dials, and others), CallManager 4.0 added the following features to Cisco IP Phones:

- **Call join**—Allows a user to select several calls from the same line on a Cisco IP Phone and conference them all at once.

- **Direct transfer**—Allows a user to select two calls from the same line on a Cisco IP Phone and transfer (connect) them together.

- **Barge and cBarge**—Allow a user at one IP phone (the "barger") to automatically conference himself or herself into a call with two other conversing parties, one of which shares a line with the barger. cBarge relies on an external conference bridge resource; barge mixes the voice on IP phones that contain a built-in bridge, namely the Cisco IP Phones 7940, 7941, 7960, 7961, 7970, and 7971.

- **Privacy**—Allows a user at one Cisco IP Phone to prevent other users who share a line appearance from viewing the connected name and number identification of parties with which he or she is conversing.

- **Abbreviated dialing**—Permits a user to quickly dial preconfigured numbers by entering a one- or two-digit index code that represents the speed dial number.

- **Conference drop any party**—Permits a user who has created a conference to select from a list of currently connected parties and drop one from the conference.

- **Immediate diversion**—Permits a user who is receiving or already conversing on a call to divert the caller to the diverter's voice mailbox.

- **Malicious call identification**—Permits a user to press a button on an active or recently terminated call to notify the system administrator (and service provider) that a harassing or threatening call has been received.

- **Multilevel Precedence and Preemption**—Permits users to preempt lower priority calls already occurring at the called number with calls designated as higher priority. This feature is used primarily by the military.

- **Hunt groups**—Native hunt group capability in CallManager. Hunt groups support broadcast (ring all members), top down, circular, and longest idle hunting. A ring no answer timer can be applied to determine the time to wait before proceeding to the next point.

You can learn more about these features in Chapter 3, "Station Devices." Learn more about hunt groups in Chapter 2, "Call Routing."

In addition to focusing on features, CallManager 4.0 improved the following areas:

- **QSIG support**—Addition of QSIG supplementary services for call diversion and call transfer to permit display updates when calls across multiple PBXs are transferred or forwarded and to support delivery of message waiting indications between PBXs

- **Video support**—Addition of media control capabilities to support the establishment of video calls from either video-enabled Cisco IP Phones, third-party SCCP video endpoints, H.323-based video endpoints, and audio-only Cisco IP Phones that have an associated PC for video display

- **Security**—Support for signaling authentication of Cisco IP Phones to prevent rogue phones from registering with CallManager or impersonating other devices, support for Cisco IP Phone signaling, support for media encryption between phones, and integrated support for multiple levels of administrator access

- **SIP support**—Addition of the Session Initiation Protocol (SIP) call signaling protocol specifically for connections to phone systems outside of a CallManager cluster

2004—Cisco CallManager Release 4.1

CallManager 4.1 continues to focus on support for new features. The following list summarizes the new additions:

- **QSIG enhancements**—CallManager continued implementing the QSIG protocol for feature transparency with other PBXs.

  - **Path replacement** optimizes the path between two parties to remove circuit hairpins that form when one party transfers a call to another party.

  - **Call forward by rerouting** prevents circuit hairpins from forming when a phone on one system forwards a call to a phone on another system.

  - **Call back on no reply and call back on busy** allow a caller to set a monitor on a called number that has not accepted a call and receive a prompt to redial the called number when it becomes available.

  - **Called name** allows a calling user to see the name of the party he or she is calling, even when the called party is served by a different call agent.

- **Dialed number analyzer** is a service that allows you to enter dial strings on behalf of calling devices and analyze how the call may route.

- **Time of day routing** provides a flexible mechanism by which you can activate and deactivate route partitions according to a schedule. Chapter 2, describes this feature in more detail.

- **Client matter codes** allow you to define post-dial strings that are associated with specific clients that users can dial to attribute the cost of the call to the client. The codes show up in call detail records to achieve billing traceability.

- **Forced authorization codes** allow you to define post-dial strings that users must dial to reach their destinations.

Figure 1-6 depicts CallManager release 4.1.

Figure 1-6 *CallManager in 2005*

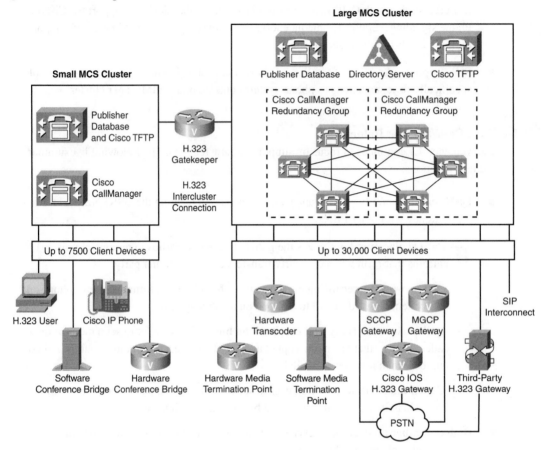

Cisco-Certified Servers for Running Cisco IP Communications

CallManager and its associated services run on a Windows 2000 server. Because voice applications are so critical to an enterprise's function, however, Cisco Systems requires that CallManager be installed only on certified server platforms.

Cisco Systems provides a suite of certified servers called Media Convergence Servers (MCS). In addition to these servers, Cisco allows users to install Cisco IP Communications software on servers offered by HP and IBM. Customer-provided servers must match exact server configurations provided by Cisco, because any deviations from the specifications might result in an incomplete install and an unsupported system.

> **NOTE**   At times, this book uses the term *server* and, at other times, it uses the term *node*, particularly when describing CallManager clustering.
>
> A CallManager cluster consists of networked *servers* running a variety of services that together provide an enterprise VoIP system. Some of these servers in the cluster are generally dedicated to the CallManager database or TFTP service. Others run CallManager, the call processing component of a Cisco IP Communications system.
>
> This book uses the term *node* to refer specifically to the servers in a CallManager cluster that are running the CallManager service. It's not uncommon to read a sentence referencing both *nodes* and *servers*. For example, it's consistent to state both that a CallManager cluster can consist of a maximum of 20 servers and that it can consist of a maximum of 8 nodes, because the 12 non-call processing servers handle services such as the Publisher database, TFTP, Cisco IP Voice Media Streaming App, and applications.

The current list, as of the release of 4.1, of MCSs that Cisco ships are as follows:

- Cisco MCS 7815I-2000

- Cisco MCS 7825H-3000

- Cisco MCS 7835H-3000

- Cisco MCS 7835I-3000

- Cisco MCS 7845H-3000

- Cisco MCS 7845I-3000

In addition to MCS, users can build Cisco IP Communications systems based off of the following HP and IBM platforms. (You can find the latest system information and specific parts lists on Cisco.com at http://www.cisco.com/go/swonly.)

- Compaq DL320-G2 Pentium 4 3060 MHz

- Compaq DL320 Pentium III 800 MHz

- Compaq DL320 Pentium III 1133 MHz

- Compaq DL320-G2 Pentium 4 2.26 GHz

- Compaq DL380 Pentium III 1000 MHz

- Compaq DL380 G2 Pentium III 1266 MHz

- HP DL380-G3 Xeon 3060 MHz

- HP DL380-G3 Dual Xeon 3.06 GHz

- HP DL380-G2 Pentium III 1400 MHz

- HP DL380-G2 Pentium III 1400 MHz

- HP DL380-G3 Xeon 2400 MHz

- HP DL380-G2 Dual Pentium III 1400 MHz

- HP DL380-G3 Dual Xeon 2.4 GHz

- IBM xSeries 306 Single-Processor 3.06 GHz

- IBM xSeries 346 Single-Processor 3.4 GHz

- IBM xSeries 346 Dual-Processor 3.4 GHz

Cisco MCS ships with an installation disk that contains all of the Windows 2000 services that are required to create a working IP telephony network. The HP and IBM servers are hardware-only; you must order a software-only version of CallManager (and the Windows 2000 installation) from Cisco to install on these servers.

Cisco IP Communications consists of a suite of applications that you can provision in numerous ways for flexibility. For example, although a server contains applications for managing the database, device initialization, device control, software conferencing, and voice mail, you might decide to reserve an entire server for just one of these functions in a large, differentiated Cisco IP Communications deployment. Servers that perform a sole function are called *dedicated servers*. For an overview of the services CallManager supports, see the section "Windows 2000 and Tomcat Services on Cisco IP Communications Servers."

The following list describes Cisco MCS 7800 series servers (two other servers, the MCS-7855-1500 and MCS-7865I-1500, are Cisco Unity-specific).

- **MCS-7815I-2000 server**—The only tower system that Cisco ships. It is suitable for smaller installations and can be configured to run CallManager, Unity, or Unity Bridge. This server can support up to 300 Cisco IP Phones. MCS 7815 server can only be deployed in the minimal cluster configuration, with one MCS running a Publisher database, Cisco TFTP, and backup CallManager and with the other MCS handling active call processing services.

- **MCS-7825H-3000 server**—A rack-mountable system, requiring a single rack space. This system can be configured to run CallManager, Cisco Conference Connection (CCC), Cisco Emergency Responder (CER), Cisco IPCC Express (Integrated Contact Distribution [ICD]), Cisco IP Interactive Voice Response (IP IVR), Cisco Personal Assistant, Cisco Queue Manager, and Cisco Unity Unified Messaging. This server can support up to 1000 IP phones or, via clustering, up to 4000 IP phones.

■ **MCS-7835H-3000 and MCS-7835I-3000 servers**—Rack-mountable systems that require two rack spaces and have a single 3.06-GHz processor. These servers can be configured to run CallManager, Cisco Conference Connection (CCC), Cisco Emergency Responder (CER), Cisco IPCC Express (ICD), Cisco IP Interactive Voice Response (Cisco IP IVR), Cisco Personal Assistant, Cisco Queue Manager, and Cisco Unity Unified Messaging. These servers can support up to 2500 IP phones or, via clustering, up to 10,000 IP phones.

■ **MCS-7845H-3000 and MCS-7845I-3000 servers**—Rack-mountable systems that require two rack spaces and have dual 3.06-GHz processors. These servers can be configured to run CallManager, Cisco Conference Connection (CCC), Cisco Emergency Responder (CER), Cisco Internet Service Node (ISN), Cisco IPCC Express (ICD), Cisco IP Interactive Voice Response (Cisco IP IVR), Cisco Personal Assistant, Cisco Queue Manager, and Cisco Unity Unified Messaging. These servers can support up to 7500 IP phones or, via clustering, up to 30,000 IP phones.

Windows 2000 and Tomcat Services on Cisco IP Communications Servers

Cisco IP Communications relies on several Windows 2000 services, of which Cisco CallManager is only one. Cisco IP Communications uses the Windows 2000 services described in Table 1-1.

Table 1-1   *Windows 2000 Services That Run on a Cisco IP Communications Server*

Service	Description
Cisco CallManager	Provides call signaling and media control signaling for up to 7500 devices. You can have up to eight instances of the CallManager service per cluster.
Cisco Certificate Authority Proxy Function	Manages security certificates for Cisco IP Phones such as the Cisco 7940 and 7960 that do not directly support installed certificates.
Cisco CTIManager	Provides support for the TAPI and JTAPI application interfaces.
Cisco IP Voice Media Streaming App	Provides media termination, RFC 2833 tone interworking, inband tone services for SIP, MOH, and G.711 media mixing capabilities.
Cisco Messaging Interface	Permits Simple Message Desk Interface (SMDI) communications to voice messaging systems over an RS-232 connection.
Cisco MOH Audio Translator	Converts any audio file format compatible with DirectShow and converts it to G.711, G.729a, and wideband codec for MOH to IP telephony endpoints.
Cisco RIS Data Collector	Collects serviceability information from all cluster members for improved administration.
Cisco Telephony Call Dispatcher	Allows users such as receptionists and attendants to receive and quickly transfer calls to other users in the organization; provides automated routing capabilities.

continues

Table 1-1 *Windows 2000 Services That Run on a Cisco IP Communications Server (Continued)*

Service	Description
Cisco TFTP	Provides preregistration information to devices, including a list of CallManager nodes with which the devices are permitted to register, firmware loads, and device configuration files.
Cisco Database Layer Monitor (provides database notification)	A change notification server and watchdog process that ensures that all Cisco IP Communications applications on a server are working properly.
Publisher database	Serves as the primary read-write data repository for all Cisco IP Communications applications in the cluster. The Publisher database replicates database updates to all Subscriber databases in the cluster.
Subscriber database	Serves as a backup read-only database for Cisco IP Communications applications running on the server, should the applications lose connectivity to the Publisher database.
Cisco CDR Insert	Periodically scans local call detail record (CDR) files logged by CallManager nodes and inserts them into the CDR database.
Cisco CTL Provider	Accepts connections from the CTL Client utility, which allows you to change the cluster security mode and update the cluster's Certificate Trust List (CTL).
Cisco Extended Functions	Provides the Quality Reporting Tool service, which allows users to report problems with their phone via the **QRT** softkey.
Cisco Serviceability Reporter	Generates a daily serviceability summary report for the cluster, including server performance, alerts generated by system, call activities, and other information.

While Table 1-1 indicates native Windows 2000 services that provide call-related services, Cisco IP Communications also supports applications that run as Java servlets hosted by the Apache plug-in Tomcat. Table 1-2 lists the Tomcat applications that Cisco IP Communications supports in the 4.1 release.

Table 1-2 *Tomcat Applications That Run on a Cisco IP Communications Server*

Name	Description
Cisco Web Dialer	Allows corporate directories to support click-to-dial functionality in which a user viewing a directory page can click a link to have his or her IP phone automatically call the selected person.
Cisco IP Manager Assistant	Provides an enhanced suite of services especially suited for managing the relationship between managers and assistants. This suite includes call filtering, immediate diversion, and send all calls functions.
Cisco Extension Mobility	Allows a user at a Cisco IP Phone to provide a user ID and password to log in to the phone and retrieve his or her extension and customized line settings.

Client Devices That CallManager Supports

In a Cisco IP Communications network, CallManager is the telephone operator, and it places calls on behalf of many different endpoint devices. These devices can be classified into the following categories:

- **Station devices**—Station devices are generally, but not always, telephone sets. CallManager offers a variety of sets, which it controls with SCCP.

  Cisco IP Phone 7902 is a cost-effective, single-line, entry-level station with no display.

  Cisco IP Phones 7905G and 7912G are single-line, entry-level phones (with a format different from the Cisco IP Phone 7910G) with a graphical display.

  Cisco IP Phone 7920 is a mobile 802.11b phone that enables voice communications over wireless LANs.

  Cisco IP Phone 7935 and 7936 are console speakerphones with softkey displays designed for use in conference rooms. They do not support inline power and do not have a switch for supporting an associated PC.

  Cisco IP Phone 7940G supports two line/feature buttons and offers a nine-line display with softkeys and status lines.

  Cisco IP Phone 7941G supports two line/feature buttons with lighted keys and offers a high-resolution display with softkeys and status lines.

  Cisco IP Phone 7960G supports six line/feature buttons and has the same display as the Cisco IP Phone 7940G.

  Cisco IP Phone 7961G supports up to six line/feature buttons with lighted keys and has the same display as the Cisco IP Phone 7941G.

  Cisco IP Phone 7970G offers eight line/feature buttons and an 11-line backlit, high-resolution color display with touch screen and additional softkeys.

  Cisco IP Phone 7971G-GE provides unconstrained bandwidth to desktop applica-tions via Gigabit Ethernet (GE) and features eight line/feature buttons and an 11-line backlit, high-resolution color display with touch screen and additional softkeys.

  Cisco IP Phone 7914 expansion modules can be added to Cisco IP Phone 7960G. Each expansion module adds 14 buttons and up to 2 modules can be added to a Cisco IP Phone.

  Station devices need not be physical handsets. CallManager also supports H.323 user clients, such as the following:

— NetMeeting, which runs as a software application on a user's PC

— Cisco IP Communicator, a software-based phone that connects to CallManager using SCCP

— Cisco IP SoftPhone, which connects to CallManager using the TAPI application interface

Chapter 3 goes into more detail about station devices.

■   **Gateway devices**—Gateways provide a bridge between two end users whose endpoints utilize different protocols. Gateways allow IP phones to interact with the billions of already deployed phones in the world.

Gateway devices generally provide one of two types of interconnections. One type of interconnection is from one telephone system to another. This access can be from one network of CallManager nodes to another, from a CallManager network to a PBX or from a CallManager network to a public network such as a Class 4 or Class 5 switch. (But note that intercluster H.323 trunks provide an alternative for connecting CallManager networks together without requiring a gateway device.)

Gateways do not necessarily need to provide access to other networks, however. Gateways can also be used to interwork VoIP directly with traditional telephones (POTS phones).

CallManager controls gateways via three protocols: H.323, MGCP, and the legacy Skinny Gateway Control Protocol (SGCP). On their circuit interfaces, gateways provide both digital—for example, BRI, T1/E1 Channel Associated Signaling (CAS) and T1/E1 Primary Rate Interface (PRI)—and analog (the same type of telephone interface that probably runs into your home) interfaces.

Cisco gateways fall into three general categories:

— Cisco IOS integrated routers are gateways that provide IP routing in addition to their gateway services. These can be viewed as IP routers that just happen to provide support for analog phones or for analog or digital trunk interfaces. Cisco IOS routers accept voice interface cards (VIC) and voice/WAN interface cards (VWIC) that can provide connectivity to the PSTN using many telephony protocols (as well as media services such as transcoding, media termination, and conference mixing).

— Cisco standalone voice gateways operate solely as end devices; they do not route IP traffic from network to network. The Cisco ATA 186, ATA 188, VG224, and VG248 provide CallManager with gateway services from its IP phones to analog phones or trunks.

— Cisco Catalyst voice gateway modules also operate solely as end devices. These modules are inserted into the Cisco Catalyst 6xxx chassis. Cisco Catalyst 6xxx can accept the Communication Media Module (CMM), the 6608 module, and the 6624 module. The CMM, in turn, can take port adapters that support the T1, E1, or FXS telephony interfaces.

Chapter 4, "Trunk Devices," goes into more detail about trunk devices.

- **Media processing devices**—Media processing devices perform codec conversion, media mixing, and media termination functions. CallManager controls media processing devices using SCCP. Five types of media processing devices exist.

  — **Transcoding resources**—These exist to perform codec conversions between devices that otherwise could not communicate because they do not encode voice conversations using a common encoding scheme. If CallManager detects that two endpoints cannot interpret each other's voice-encoding schemes, it inserts a transcoder into the conversation. Transcoders serve as interpreters. When CallManager introduces a transcoder into a conversation, it tells the endpoints in the conversation to send their voice streams to the transcoder instead of to each other. The transcoder translates an incoming voice stream from the codec that the sender uses into the codec that the recipient uses, and then forwards the voice stream to the recipient. The Catalyst 6xxx platform offers a blade that performs transcoding functions and the NM-HDV, NM-HDV2, and NM-HD-2VE modules support transcoding functions for IOS gateways.

  — **Unicast conferencing devices**—These exist to permit Ad Hoc and Meet-Me conferencing. When an endpoint wants to start a multiple-party conversation, all the other parties in the conversation need to receive a copy of its voice stream. If several parties are speaking at once in a conversation, some component in the conversation needs to combine the independent voice streams present at a particular instant into a single burst of sound to be played through the telephone handset.

  Unicast conferencing devices perform the functions of both copying a conference participant's voice stream to other participants in the conference and mixing the voice streams into a single stream. When you initiate a conference, CallManager looks for an available Unicast conferencing device and dynamically redirects all participants' voice streams through the device. The Catalyst 6xxx platform offers a blade that performs mixing functions, and NM-HDV, NM-HDV2, and NM-HD-2VE modules support mixing functions for Cisco IOS gateways. In addition, the Cisco IP Voice Media Streaming App is a software application that can mix media streams encoded according to the G.711 codec.

  — **Media termination point (MTP) resources**—These devices exist to allow users to invoke features such as hold and transfer, even when the person they are conversing with is using an H.323 endpoint such as NetMeeting. Devices that are only H.323v1-compatible do not tolerate interruptions in their media sessions very well. Attempts to place these devices on hold will cause them to terminate their active call. A media termination device serves as a proxy for these old H.323 devices and allows them to be placed on hold as part of feature operation.

CallManager also uses MTPs to interwork with SIP networks. SIP networks generally encode DTMF tones directly in the RTP stream using RFC 2833, while CallManager typically encodes tones directly in the signaling stream. An MTP can provide the interworking between these different types of tones as well as provide inband ringback when a Cisco IP Phone transfers a SIP caller.

The Catalyst 6xxx platform offers modules that perform media termination functions, and modules that provide media termination functions also exist for Cisco IOS routers. Furthermore, the Cisco IP Voice Media Streaming App is a software application that can perform media termination functions for calls that use the G.711 codec.

— **Music on Hold (MOH) resources**—These exist to provide users a music source when you place them on hold. When you place a user on hold, CallManager renegotiates the media session between the party you place on hold and the MOH device. For as long as you keep the user on hold, the MOH device transmits its audio stream to the held party. When you remove the user from hold, CallManager renegotiates the media stream between your device and the user.

— **Annunciator resources**—These exist to provide users audio announcements when error conditions occur such as preemption due to higher-priority calls, invalid dialed digit strings, or other problems CallManager encounters when placing calls.

Table 1-3 provides a comprehensive list of the Cisco IP Phones that CallManager supports.

Table 1-3 *Cisco IP Phones That CallManager Supports*

Name	Description
Cisco IP Phone 12SP+	Legacy phone with 12 feature buttons and 2-line text display
Cisco IP Phone 30VIP	Legacy phone with 30 feature buttons and 2-line text display
Cisco IP Phone 7902	Single-line appearance phone with no display
Cisco IP Phone 7905G	Single-line appearance phone with 2-line graphical display
Cisco IP Phone 7910G	Legacy single-line appearance phone with 2-line black-and-white alphanumeric display
Cisco IP Phone 7912G	Single-line appearance phone with 2-line graphical display
Cisco IP Phone 7920	6-line appearance wireless LAN phone (802.11b) with 9-line grayscale graphical display
Cisco IP Phone 7935	Speakerphone console with alphanumeric display designed for use in conference rooms
Cisco IP Phone 7940G	Dual-line appearance phone with 9-line grayscale graphical display
Cisco IP Phone 7941G	Lighted button, dual-line appearance phone with high resolution graphical display
Cisco IP Phone 7960G	6-line appearance phone with 9-line grayscale graphical display

Table 1-3 *Cisco IP Phones That CallManager Supports (Continued)*

Name	Description
Cisco IP Phone 7961G	Lighted button, 6-line appearance phone with high resolution grayscale graphical display
Cisco IP Phone 7970G	Lighted button, 8-line appearance phone with 9-line color graphical touch screen display
Cisco IP Phone 7971G-GE	Gigabit Ethernet lighted button 8-line appearance phone and 9-line color graphical touch screen display
Microsoft NetMeeting	Windows-based H.323 software client application
Cisco IP SoftPhone	Windows-based JTAPI software client application
Cisco IP Communicator	Windows-based SCCP software client application

Table 1-4 provides a list of the gateway devices that CallManager supports.

Table 1-4 *Cisco Gateways That CallManager Supports*

Gateway Model	Gateway Control Protocol	Trunk Interface	Port Types
Cisco IOS Integrated Routers			
Cisco 1750	H.323	FXS FXO	Loop start or ground start
Cisco 1751 Cisco 1760	MGCP H.323 SIP	FXS FXO T1/E1 PRI T1 CAS E1 CAS R2	Loop start or ground start E&M T1 PRI E1 PRI
Cisco 2600 series Cisco 2800 series	MGCP H.323 SIP (Only MGCP supports QSIG.) (Only H.323 supports E1 CAS R2.)	FXS FXO BRI T1/E1 PRI T1 CAS E1 CAS R2 QSIG (Not all Cisco 2600 series gateways support QSIG. Refer to your gateway documentation.)	Loop start or ground start T1/E1 PRI E&M

continues

Table 1-4 *Cisco Gateways That CallManager Supports (Continued)*

Gateway Model	Gateway Control Protocol	Trunk Interface	Port Types
Cisco 3600 series Cisco 3700 series Cisco 3800 series	MGCP H.323 SIP (Only MGCP supports QSIG.) (Only H.323 supports E1 CAS R2.)	FXS FXO BRI T1/E1 PRI T1 CAS E1 CAS R2 QSIG (Not all Cisco 3600 series gateways support QSIG. Refer to your gateway documentation.)	Loop start or ground start T1/E1 PRI E&M T1/E1 PRI
Cisco 7200 series Cisco 7500 series	MGCP H.323 SIP	T1/E1 CAS T1/E1 PRI QSIG	T1/E1 CAS T1/E1 PRI
Cisco AS5300 Cisco AS5350 Cisco AS5400	H.323	T1/E1 CAS T1/E1 PRI	T1/E1 CAS T1/E1 PRI
Cisco Standalone Voice Gateways			
Cisco Voice Gateway 200 (VG200)	MGCP or H.323 (Only MGCP supports QSIG.)	FXO FXS T1/E1 PRI T1 CAS QSIG	Loop start or ground start T1/E1 PRI E&M T1/E1 PRI
Cisco Voice Gateway 224 (VG224)	MGCP or SCCP	FXS	FXS
Cisco Access Digital Trunk Gateway DE-30+	MGCP	E1 PRI QSIG	E1 PRI E1 PRI
Cisco Access Digital Trunk Gateway DT-24+	MGCP	T1 PRI T1 CAS FXO QSIG	T1 PRI E&M Loop start or ground start T1 PRI
Cisco Access Analog Trunk Gateway (AT-2, AT-4, AT-8)	Skinny Gateway Control Protocol	FXO	Loop start
Cisco Access Analog Station Gateway (AS-2, AS-4, AS-8)	Skinny Gateway Control Protocol	FXS	Loop start

Table 1-4   *Cisco Gateways That CallManager Supports (Continued)*

Gateway Model	Gateway Control Protocol	Trunk Interface	Port Types
Cisco VG248 Analog Phone Gateway	SCCP	FXS	Loop start
Cisco IAD2420	MGCP	FXS FXO T1 PRI T1 CAS QSIG	Loop start or ground start T1 PRI E&M T1 PRI
Cisco Catalyst Voice Gateway Modules			
Cisco Catalyst 4000 Access Gateway Module (WS-X4604-GWY)	MGCP or H.323 (Only MGCP supports QSIG.)	FXS FXO T1 CAS T1/E1 PRI QSIG	POTS Loop start or ground start E&M T1/E1 PRI T1/E1 PRI
Cisco Catalyst 4224 Voice Gateway Switch	MGCP or H.323 (Only MGCP supports QSIG.)	FXS FXO T1/E1 PRI T1 CAS QSIG	POTS Loop start or ground start T1/E1 PRI E&M T1/E1 PRI
Cisco Catalyst 6000 8-Port Voice T1/E1 and Services Module (WS-X6608-T1) (WS-X6608-E1)	MGCP	T1/E1 PRI T1 CAS QSIG	T1/E1 PRI E&M, loop start, ground start T1/E1 PRI
Cisco Catalyst 6000 24-Port FXS Analog Interface Module (WS-X6624-FXS)	MGCP	FXS	POTS
Cisco Communication Media Module (WS-X6600-24FXS)	MGCP	FXS	POTS
Cisco Communication Media Module (WS-X6600-24FXS)	MGCP	T1 PRI T1 CAS E1 PRI	T1 PRI E&M E1 PRI

Call Establishment in a Cisco IP Communications Network

Call establishment between circuit-switched and VoIP systems is more similar than different. While a circuit-switched system relies on a two-phase process that consists of a call signaling phase (into which commands to connect circuits are included) and a media exchange phase, a VoIP system usually deconstructs call establishment into the following three phases:

Step 1 **Call signaling**—Like a circuit-switched call, VoIP systems need to coordinate the placing, offering, and answering of a call; that is, given a person named Alice who wants to call another person named Bob, the call signaling step answers the question, "Do Alice and Bob want to talk?"

Step 2 **Media control**—Unlike traditional circuit-switched systems, however, VoIP systems enable the endpoints to talk directly to each other over the IP infrastructure. While a circuit-switched system has a sort of tacit media control phase in which it asks the switching fabric to join two circuits, a VoIP system uses a more robust phase to enable the endpoints in the call to exchange IP and port information so that the endpoints can connect themselves. In this respect, the media control step answers the question, "How should Alice and Bob talk?"

> **NOTE** SIP and MGCP combine the exchange of media control information with the call signaling phase, although this behavior doesn't change the underlying fact that the endpoints are ultimately connecting themselves. H.323 also supports an integrated signaling and media control phase via its optional fast start procedure.

Step 3 **Media exchange**—After IP and port information has been exchanged, the endpoints encode information into Real-Time Transport Protocol (RTP) or Secure Real-Time Transport Protocol (SRTP) packets, which they stream directly to each other over the IP infrastructure. In the case of CallManager, this means that, although CallManager is handling the call signaling and media control phases, CallManager has nothing to do with the actual exchange of the conversation, which is a function of the phones and the IP routers that connect them. The media exchange phase answers the real important questions—questions such as "How about we go out for pizza Friday?"

Figure 1-7 shows a comparison between the circuit-switched and packet-switched call models.

Figure 1-7 *Circuit-Switched Call Versus Packet-Switched Call*

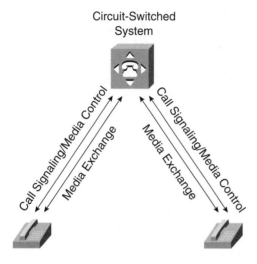

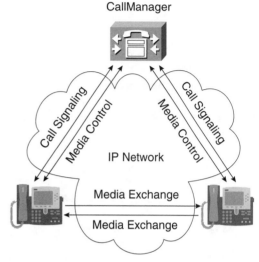

Phones are connected directly into the circuit-switched system.

1 Call signaling: The system detects a call request and extends the call to the destination. Negotiation of the type of connection usually occurs as part of the call signaling itself.

2 Media exchange: When the call is answered, the circuit-switched system must bridge the voice stream. Both call signaling and media exchange are centralized.

Phones connect to CallManager through a network of routers.

1 Call signaling: CallManager detects a call request and extends the call to the destination.

2 Media control (sometimes, but not always, part of call signaling): When the destination answers, the endpoints must negotiate a codec and exchange addresses for purposes of exchanging media.

3 Media exchange: The phones exchange media directly with each other. The media often follows a completely different set of routers than the call signaling. Call signaling and media control are centrally managed, but the high-bandwidth media is distributed.

Using the IP network as a virtual matrix offers some remarkable benefits. The Internet is an IP network that spans the globe. A computer on the Internet can talk to its neighbor as easily as it talks to a computer located 1000 miles away. Similarly, without the need to connect circuits one leg at a time across long distances, one CallManager can connect calls between IP phones separated by area codes or even country codes as easily as it can connect two IP phones in the same building.

Furthermore, IP networks are distributed by their nature. A traditional circuit-based solution requires that all the wires for your voice network run into the same wiring closet. This means that the telephone system can intercept events from the line and trunk cards and gain access to the media information that the devices send to connect them in the matrix. CallManager can communicate with devices by establishing virtual wires through the fabric of the IP network, and the devices themselves establish virtual wires with each other when they start exchanging media. This feature makes CallManager more scalable than traditional circuit-switched systems. Figure 1-8 offers a comparison.

Figure 1-8 *Cisco IP Communications (IPC) Scalability*

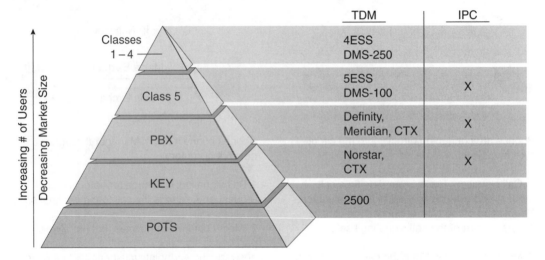

Another major benefit of CallManager is that it resides on the same network as your data applications. The Cisco IP Communications model is a traditional Internet client/server model. CallManager is simply a software application running on your data network with which clients (telephones and gateways) request services using IP interfaces. This co-residency between your voice and data applications allows you to integrate traditional data applications (such as web servers and directories) into the interface of your voice devices. The use of standard Internet protocols for such applications (HTML and XML) means that the skills for developing such applications are readily available, if you want to customize the services available to your voice devices.

Finally, CallManager interacts with IP devices on the network using call signaling protocols, which allows you to mix and match equipment from other vendors when building your voice network. For devices, CallManager supports SCCP to phones, gateways, and transcoding devices; MGCP to gateway devices; H.323 to user and gateway devices; and SIP to other SIP networks. For CTI applications, CallManager supports TAPI and JTAPI.

Cisco IP Communications Clustering

A traditional telephone system tends to come packaged in a large cabinet with racks of outlying cabinets to house the switch cards, line cards, and trunk cards. A Cisco IP Communications network, however, is composed of a larger number of smaller, more specialized components. This allows you to more closely tailor your telephone network to your organization's needs.

This focus on the combined power of small components extends to CallManager, the call processing component of a Cisco IP Communications network. Within a cluster, up to eight servers can be dedicated to running the CallManager service to handle the call routing, signaling, and media control for the enterprise, with other servers dedicated to providing database services, TFTP, applications, and media services such as conferencing, media termination, music on hold, or annunciation. Such a set of networked servers is called a *CallManager cluster.* Clustering helps provide the wide scalability of a Cisco IP Communications network, redundancy in the case of network problems, ease of use for administrators, and feature transparency between users.

Clustering allows for flexibility and growth of the network. In release 4.1, clusters can contain up to eight call processing nodes, which together can support 30,000 endpoints. If your network serves a smaller number of users, you can buy fewer servers. (Using multiple clusters served by an H.323 gatekeeper, CallManager can support larger networks—up to hundreds of thousands of phones.) As your network grows, you can simply add more servers. Clustering allows you to expand your network seamlessly.

The idea behind a cluster is that of a virtual telephone system. A cluster allows administrators to provision much of their network from a central point. Cluster cooperation works so effectively that users might not realize that more than one CallManager node handles their calls. A guiding philosophy of clustered operation is that if a user's primary CallManager node experiences an outage, the user cannot distinguish any change in phone operation when it registers with a secondary or tertiary CallManager. Thus, to the users and the administrators, the individual nodes in the cluster appear as one large telephone system, even if your users reside in completely different geographical regions.

CallManager cluster members do not need to be co-resident. In fact, geographically separating the cluster members can provide even greater device survivability. If a disaster occurs in one geographic site (if, for instance, the CallManager system administrator receives one too many special executive requests and takes a fire ax to the Media Convergence Servers), nodes in other geographic sites can take over the phones. Separating CallManager cluster members in this fashion is called *clustering over the WAN*.

Clustering over the WAN currently requires a high-performance network between the cluster members. The following list summarizes the guidelines:

■   At most a 40-ms round-trip packet delay between any two CallManager nodes

■   At most four active CallManager nodes (with four standby CallManager nodes for failover)

■ 900 kbps per each 10,000 Busy Hour Call Attempts (BHCA) in the cluster (with more bandwidth required if you want to support device failover across the WAN)

If your network doesn't meet the guidelines for clustering over the WAN, deployment options are still available to you:

■ Remote sites should run independent clusters—a model called *distributed call processing*.

■ Devices in remote sites should be managed by a cluster of servers that reside in a central site, a model called *centralized call processing*.

■ Both the centralized and distributed models should be used in a combined model.

Large networks tend to deploy a combination of distributed and centralized call processing systems.

Because performance characteristics and supported deployment models change from release to release, be sure to check http://www.cisco.com/go/srnd for current models and additional information.

Clustering and Reliability

Clustering provides for high reliability of a Cisco IP Communications network. In a traditional telephone network, a fixed association exists between a telephone and the call processing software that serves it. Traditional telephone vendors provide reliability through the use of redundant components installed in the same chassis. Table 1-5 draws a comparison between a traditional telephone system's redundant components and Cisco IP Communications redundancy.

Table 1-5 *Comparison Between Traditional Telephone System Redundancy and Cisco IP Communications Redundancy*

Function	PBX	Cisco IP Communications
Processor unit	Redundant	Up to eight call processing nodes (running CallManager) with one Publisher database, up to two TFTP servers, and other application and media servers as needed
Media switching	Redundant TDM switch	Distributed IP network (multiple path)
Intercabinet interfaces	Redundant	Distributed IP interfaces (multiple path)
Intracabinet buses	Redundant TDM bus	Redundant Ethernet buses
Power supplies	Redundant	Redundant
Line cards	Single (usually 24)	Not applicable

Table 1-5   *Comparison Between Traditional Telephone System Redundancy and Cisco IP Communications Redundancy (Continued)*

Function	PBX	Cisco IP Communications
Power to phones	Inline (phantom)	Inline (phantom), third pair, or external
Phones	Single interface	Capable of registering with up to three CallManagers and one SRST for retention of service during network outages

CallManager redundancy works differently. The redundancy model differs by Cisco IP Communications component. Clustering has one meaning with regard to the database, another meaning with regard to CallManager nodes, and a third meaning with regard to the client devices.

Database Clustering

To serve calls for client devices, CallManager needs to retrieve settings for those devices. In addition, the database is the repository for information such as service parameters, features, and the route plan. The database layer is a set of dynamic link libraries (DLL) that provide a common access point for data insertion, retrieval, and modification of the database. The database itself is Microsoft SQL 2000.

If the database were to reside on a single machine, the phone network would be vulnerable to a machine or network outage. Therefore, the database uses a replication strategy to ensure that every server can access important provisioning information even if the network fails.

Each CallManager cluster consists of a set of networked databases. One database, the Publisher, provides read and write access for database administrators and for CallManager nodes themselves. For large installations, it is recommended that the Publisher reside on a separate server to prevent database updates from impacting the real-time processing that CallManager does as part of processing calls.

In normal operations, all CallManager nodes in a cluster retrieve information from the Publisher. However, the Publisher maintains a TCP connection to each node in the cluster that runs a CallManager. When database changes occur, the Publisher database replicates the changed information to Subscriber databases on each of these connected nodes. The Publisher replicates all information other than Publisher call detail records (CDR). In addition, the Publisher serves as a repository for CDRs written by all CallManager nodes in the cluster.

In a large campus deployment, a server is often dedicated to handling the Publisher database. This server is often a high-availability system with hardware redundancy, such as dual power supply and Redundant Array of Independent Disks (RAID) disk arrays.

Subscriber databases are read-only. CallManager nodes access the Subscriber databases only in cases when the Publisher is not available. Even so, CallManager nodes continue operating with almost no degradation. If the Publisher is not available, Subscriber nodes write CDRs locally and replicate them to the Publisher when it becomes available again. Figure 1-9 shows database clustering.

Figure 1-9 *Database Clustering*

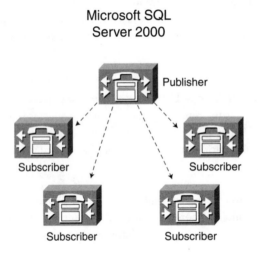

Microsoft SQL
Server 2000

Publisher

Subscriber

Subscriber

Subscriber

Subscriber

CallManager Clustering

Although the database replicates nearly all information in a star topology (one Publisher, many Subscribers), CallManager nodes replicate a limited amount of information in a fully-meshed topology (every node publishes information to every other node).

CallManager uses a fully-meshed topology rather than a star topology because it needs to be able to respond dynamically and robustly to changes in the network. Database information changes relatively rarely, and the information in the database is static in nature. For example, the database allows you to specify which CallManager nodes can serve a particular device, but the information does not specifically indicate to which node a device is currently registered. Therefore, a star topology that prevents database updates but permits continued operation if the Publisher database is unreachable serves nicely.

CallManager, on the other hand, must respond to the dynamic information of where devices are currently registered. Furthermore, because processing speed is paramount to CallManager, it must store this dynamic information locally to minimize network activity. Should a node fail or the network have problems, a fully-meshed topology allows devices to locate and register with backup CallManager nodes. It also permits the surviving reachable CallManager nodes to update their routing information to extend calls to the devices at their new locations.

Figure 1-10 shows the connections between CallManager nodes in a cluster.

Figure 1-10 *CallManager Clustering*

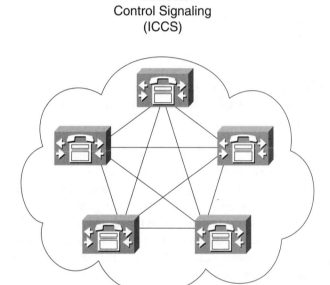

When devices initialize, they register with a particular CallManager node. The CallManager node to which a device registers must get involved in calls to and from that device. Each device has an address, either a directory number or a route pattern. (See Chapter 2 for more information about call routing). The essence of the inter-CallManager replication is the advertisement of the addresses of newly registering devices from one CallManager to another. This advertisement of address information minimizes the amount of database administration required for a Cisco IP Communications network. Instead of having to provision specific ranges of directory numbers for trunks between particular CallManager nodes in the cluster, the cluster as a whole can automatically detect the addition of a new device and route calls accordingly.

The other type of communication between CallManager nodes in a cluster is not related to locating registered devices. Rather, it occurs when a device controlled by one CallManager node calls a device controlled by a different CallManager node. One CallManager node must signal the other to ring the destination device. The second type of communication is hard to define. For lack of a better term, it is called Intracluster Control Signaling (ICCS).

Understanding this messaging requires knowing more about CallManager architecture. CallManager is roughly divided into six layers:

- Link
- Protocol
- Aggregator
- Media Control
- Call Control
- Supplementary Service

Figure 1-11 depicts this architecture. At the beginning of each subsequent chapter of this book, there is a copy of this figure with shading to indicate the components of CallManager that are covered in that particular chapter.

The Link Layer is the most basic. Its function is to ensure that if a device sends a packet of information to CallManager, or CallManager sends a packet of information to a device, the sent packet is received. CallManager uses two methods of communication. The Transmission Control Protocol (TCP) is by far the most commonly used. TCP underlies much communication on the Internet. It provides for reliable communication between peers using the Internet Protocol. CallManager uses TCP for call signaling and media control with CallManager nodes, media devices, IP phones, H.323 gateways, and ISDN call signaling originating from MGCP gateways. The User Datagram Protocol is a protocol in which a sent packet is not guaranteed to be received. CallManager uses UDP for communication with MGCP gateways and SIP proxies. Although UDP itself is not reliable, MGCP or SIP is designed to handle instances where the IP network loses the message; in such a case, MGCP or SIP retransmit its last message.

The Protocol Layer includes the logic that CallManager uses to manage the different types of devices that it supports. These devices include media devices, trunk devices, and station devices. The Protocol Layer also supports third-party integration with CallManager through the TAPI and JTAPI protocols.

The Aggregator Layer allows CallManager to properly handle the interactions between groups of related devices. The media resource manager, for example, permits one CallManager node to locate available media devices, even if they are registered to other CallManager nodes. The route list performs a similar function for gateways. Line control permits CallManager to handle IP phones that share a line appearance, even if the IP phones are registered with different CallManager nodes.

Figure 1-11 *Layers Within CallManager*

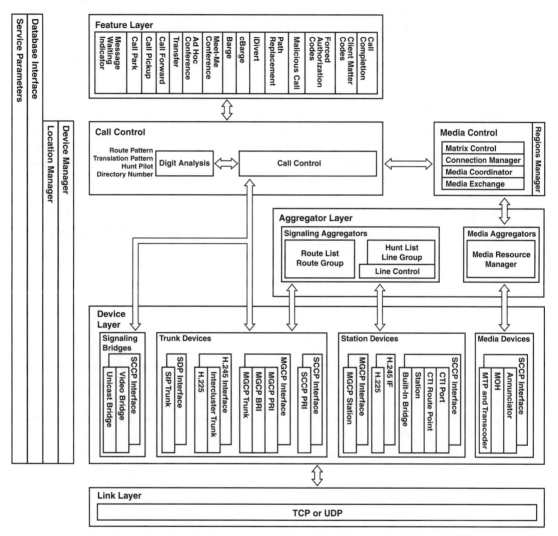

The Media Control Layer handles the actual media connections between devices. It handles the media control portion of setting up a call, but it also handles more complicated tasks. For instance, sometimes CallManager must introduce a transcoding device to serve as an interpreter for two devices that don't communicate via the same codec. In this case, one call between two devices consists of multiple media hops through the network. The Media Control Layer coordinates all the media connections.

The Call Control layer handles the basic call processing of the system. It locates the destination that a caller dials and coordinates the Media Control, Aggregator, and Protocol Layers. Furthermore, it provides the primitives that the Supplementary Service Layer uses to relate independent calls. The Supplementary Service Layer relates independent calls together as part of user-requested features such as transfer, conference, and call forwarding.

Within each layer, the SDL application engine manages *state machines*, which are essentially small event-driven processes, but they do not show up on the Microsoft Windows 2000 Task Manager. Rather, the SDL application engine manages state machine tasks. These state machines each handle a small bit of the responsibility of placing calls in a CallManager network. For example, one kind of state machine is responsible for handling station devices, whereas another type is responsible for handling individual calls on station devices.

These state machines perform work through the exchange of proprietary messages. Before CallManager release 3.0 was created, these messages were strictly internal to CallManager. With the 3.0 release, these messages could travel from a state machine in one CallManager node directly to another state machine managed by a different CallManager node. This mechanism is, in fact, what allows a CallManager cluster to operate with perfect feature transparency. The same signaling that occurs when a call is placed between two devices managed by the same CallManager node occurs when a call is placed between two devices managed by different CallManager nodes.

Architecturally, intracluster communication tends to occur at the architectural boundaries listed in Figure 1-11. Take, for example, the situation that occurs when two devices that share a line appearance register with different CallManager nodes. When someone dials the directory number of the line appearance, both devices ring. Even though the state machine responsible for managing each station is on its own CallManager node, both of these state machines are associated with a single state machine that is responsible for managing line appearances. (These can reside on one of the two CallManager nodes in question, or possibly on a third CallManager node.) The ICCS, however, guarantees that the feature operates the same, no matter how many CallManager nodes are handling a call.

The architectural layers are rather loosely coupled. In theory, a call between two devices registered to different CallManager nodes in the cluster could involve up to seven CallManager nodes, although in practice, only two are required.

Device Redundancy

In a traditional telephone system, the phone is a slave to the call processing logic in the cabinet; it is unaware of the operating condition of its master. Consequently, the secondary master must maintain the state of the endpoint. For this reason, traditional telephone system architectures are redundant architectures rather than distributed architectures: Maintaining state across more than a single backup processor is excessively complex and difficult. In the Cisco IP Communications architecture, the endpoint is aware of the operational status of the server, as well as its own connectivity states. As a result, the endpoints determine which CallManager nodes serve them. You can provision each endpoint with a list of candidate nodes. If the node to which an endpoint is registered has a software problem, or a network connectivity glitch prevents the endpoint from contacting the node, the endpoints move their registration to a secondary or even tertiary CallManager. Phones in active conversations, assuming that the media path is not interrupted, maintain their audio connection to the party to which they are streaming. However, because CallManager is not available to the phone during this interim, users cannot access features on the preserved call. When the call terminates and the phone reregisters, the phone regains access to CallManager features.

Figure 1-12 shows an example of this behavior in action. On Step 1 on the left, three phones are homed to CallManager SanJoseC in a cluster, and each has multiple CallManager nodes configured for redundancy. In Step 2, CallManager SanJoseC fails. As a result, Step 3 shows that all phones that were registered with CallManager SanJoseC switch over to their secondary CallManagers. One phone moves to CallManager SanJoseB, and the other phones move to CallManager SanJoseA.

Figure 1-12 *Device Redundancy*

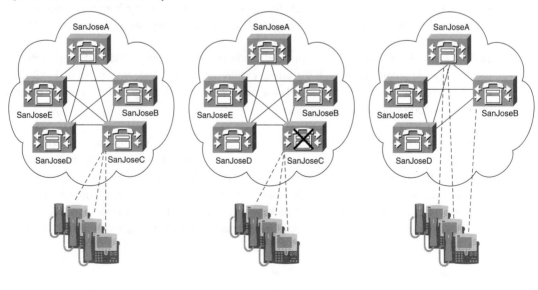

Deployment of Servers Within a CallManager Cluster

Each CallManager node in a cluster can support up to 7500 phones. A CallManager cluster can support up to 30,000 phones. Adding multiple clusters permits as many phones as you need. Within a cluster, several strategies exist for deployment of servers. Servers can be arranged into clusters, built up of small "molecular" (for lack of a better word) units. Any individual cluster contains at most one Publisher database. Every non-Publisher server in the cluster contains a Subscriber database. Furthermore, each cluster must contain at least one TFTP server to provide Cisco IP Phones and gateways their configurations.

Often, a cluster needs to contain individual servers that run applications or media services (for annunciation or music on hold). From a call agent architectural standpoint, these servers are more akin to end devices than direct participants in the clustering model.

Any single cluster must be composed according to the following rules:

■ A cluster can contain at most 20 servers.

■ A cluster can contain at most eight nodes running CallManager.

■ A cluster must have a Publisher database.

■ A cluster must have at least one TFTP service running.

For survivability purposes, a given cluster must contain at least two CallManager nodes. In case one node fails, IP phones and gateways can fail over to the backup node for call processing services. Cisco recommends two models for call processing redundancy. You can compose a cluster using a combination of the two models, but, in general, only one of the two is employed.

In the 1:1 model, you can have either one node entirely in reserve or split the load evenly between the primary and secondary node. If the primary node should fail, all devices registered to it fail over to the secondary node. A 1:1 redundancy model allows you to support the maximum number of phones—7500—per individual node.

In the 2:1 model, you hold one node in reserve for every two nodes that host active devices. If either primary node should fail, the devices registered to that node fail over to the backup node. Because both primary nodes could, in theory fail, causing all devices on both primary nodes to rehome to the secondary node, any individual primary node cannot host the maximum number of devices without unduly stressing the secondary node should both primary nodes fail. Therefore, a 2:1 model allows you to support 5000 phones per primary node, yielding a total of 10,000 per 2:1 redundancy group.

The following sections describe and depict the different configurations.

Minimum Configuration—Up to 1250 Users

The minimum configuration consists of merely two servers. However, because these servers must host a primary CallManager, backup CallManager, Publisher and Subscriber databases, and TFTP server, the maximum number of Cisco IP Phones and gateways that can be supported is 1250.

In this model, one server houses the Publisher and Cisco TFTP, and it serves as a backup CallManager. The other server houses a primary CallManager. Under normal operating conditions, all devices in the cluster register to the second server, but if the second server is unavailable, the first server takes over CallManager responsibilities. Figure 1-13 shows this deployment model.

Figure 1-13   *Deployment Model 1 for up to 1250 Users*

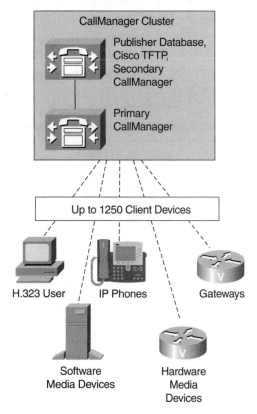

1:1 Redundancy—Up to 7500 Users

To support more than 1250 users, you must dedicate at least one server to both a Publisher database and Cisco TFTP server. When the data management services are offloaded onto a separate server, you can dedicate servers specifically to call processing.

In a 1:1 redundancy group, one server acts as a primary call processing server, with a second server prepared to take over call processing services should the primary server fail. This model also permits load sharing—you can spread your users across both servers. Should a server fail, you can permit users served by the failed CallManager server to fail to the other server. Figure 1-14 shows this deployment model.

Figure 1-14   *1:1 Redundancy Group with Separate Publisher and TFTP Server (7500 Users)*

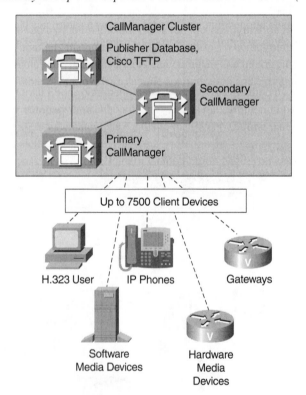

2:1 Redundancy—Up to 10,000 Users

To support more than 1250 users, you must dedicate at least one server to both a Publisher database and Cisco TFTP server. When the data management services are offloaded onto a separate server, you can dedicate servers specifically to call processing.

In a 2:1 redundancy group, two servers act as primary call processing nodes with one server reserved to take over call processing services should one or both primaries fail. The backup call processing node must be prepared to take the devices handled by both active call processing nodes. To prevent overloading the secondary nodes in case both primaries fail, the maximum number of devices that any primary can support must be reduced from 7500 to 5000, yielding a maximum load on the secondary of 10,000 devices should both primary nodes fail.

Figure 1-15 shows this deployment model.

Figure 1-15   *2:1 Redundancy Model with Separate Publisher and TFTP Server (10,000 Users)*

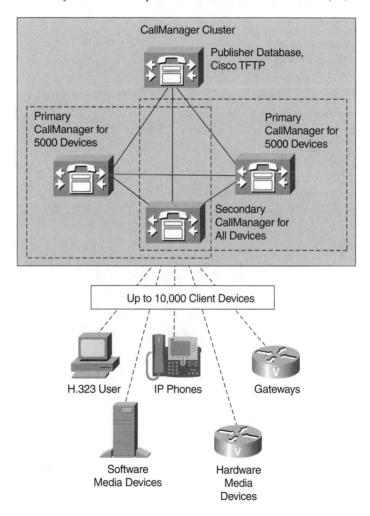

Separating the Publisher and TFTP server from the call processing nodes has the advantage of eliminating the risk that database activity on the Publisher node degrades performance of CallManager if the primary CallManager is unavailable.

Up to 30,000 Users

When you exceed 7500 users, it is advisable to configure one server as the Publisher database and one as a TFTP server.

After doing so, you can construct a cluster using either the 1:1 redundancy model or 2:1 redundancy model for call processing nodes.

The 1:1 redundancy model permits you to achieve the cluster maximum of 30,000 IP phones, with 1 server dedicated for a Publisher database, at least one server dedicated for TFTP, and four 1:1 redundancy groups. If you have 7500 IP phones per group, that yields 30,000 IP phones for each of 4 primary servers.

Figure 1-16 shows this deployment model.

Figure 1-16 *Deployment Model for 15,000 to 30,000 Users*

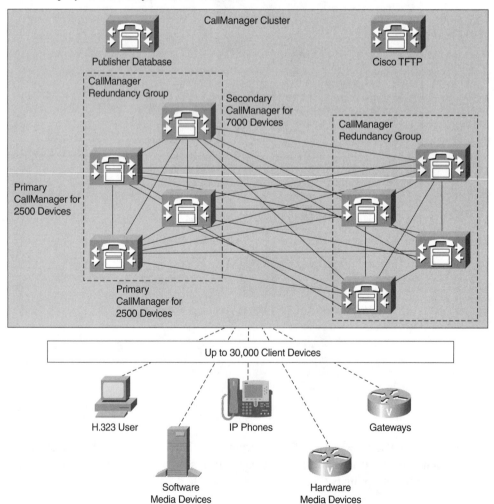

More than 30,000 Users

When the number of users climbs above 30,000, a single cluster cannot manage all devices. However, you can connect CallManager clusters together through either gateways or direct CallManager-to-CallManager connections called *intercluster trunks*. Intercluster trunks run a variant of the H.323 protocol. Figure 1-17 shows this configuration.

Between clusters, you can achieve dial plan management either by configuring your route plan to route calls across the appropriate intercluster trunks or through the use of an H.323 gatekeeper. If you need admissions control, you achieve it through the use of an H.323 gatekeeper.

Figure 1-17 *Deployment Model for More than 30,000 Users*

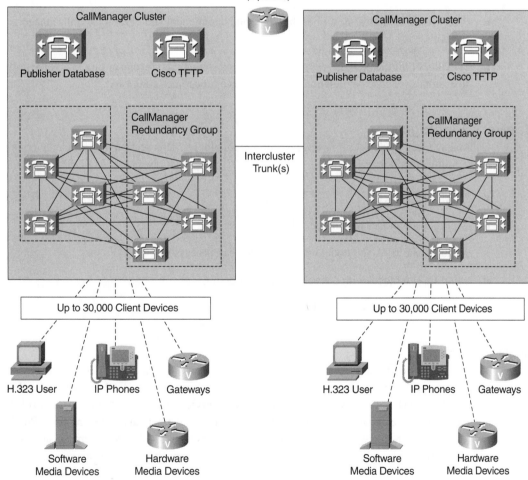

Enterprise Deployment of CallManager Clusters

This section provides an overview of the ways in which you can deploy CallManager throughout your enterprise. It addresses network infrastructure, admissions control, and supported CallManager topologies.

The excellent Cisco Solutions Reference Network Design guide "IP Telephony SRND," available at http://www.cisco.com/go/srnd, addresses all of the content in this section in far greater detail. The contents of this section have been stolen shamelessly from it. If you are already thoroughly acquainted with the aforementioned Cisco document, you might want to skip the rest of this chapter. In any case, we strongly recommend you read the document to supplement the information contained here.

This section covers two main topics:

- "Network Topologies" describes the supported deployment strategies for a CallManager network.

- "Quality of Service (QoS)" describes the methods by which you can ensure that voice traffic does not experience degradation when the network becomes congested.

Network Topologies

CallManager can be deployed in several different topologies. This section provides an overview of the following topologies:

- Single-site model

- Multiple-site model with independent call processing

- Multiple-site IP WAN model with distributed call processing

- Multiple-site model with centralized call processing

- Combined multiple-site model

Single-Site Model

The single-site model consists of a single site or campus served by a LAN. A cluster of up to ten servers (one dedicated to the Publisher database, one dedicated to the TFTP service, and eight running the CallManager service) provides telephony service to up to 30,000 IP-enabled voice devices within the campus. Calls outside of the campus environment are served by IP-to-Public Switched Telephone Network (PSTN) gateways. Because bandwidth is often overprovisioned and undersubscribed on the LAN, there is usually no need to worry about admissions control.

Figure 1-18 depicts the single-site model.

Figure 1-18   *Single-Site Model*

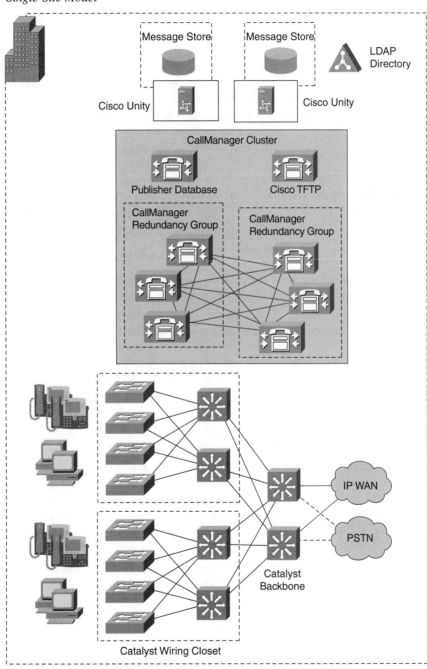

Multiple-Site Model with Independent Call Processing

The multiple-site model consists of multiple sites or campuses, each of which runs an independent cluster of up to ten servers. Each cluster provides telephony service for up to 30,000 IP-enabled voice devices within a site. Because bandwidth is often overprovisioned and undersubscribed on the LAN, there's usually no need to worry about admissions control.

IP-to-PSTN gateways handle calls outside or between each site. The multiple-site model with independent call processing allows you to use the same infrastructure for both your voice and data. However, because of the absence of an IP WAN, you cannot take advantage of the economies of placing voice calls on your existing WAN, because these calls must pass through the PSTN.

Figure 1-19 depicts the multiple-site model with independent call processing.

Multiple-Site IP WAN Model with Distributed Call Processing

From CallManager's point of view, the multiple-site IP WAN model with distributed call processing is identical to the multiple site model with independent call processing. From a practical point of view, they differ markedly.

Whereas the multiple-site model with independent call processing uses only the PSTN for carrying voice calls, the multiple-site IP WAN model with distributed call processing uses the IP WAN for carrying voice calls when sufficient bandwidth is available. This allows you to take advantage of the economies of routing calls over the IP WAN rather than the PSTN.

In such a case, you can set up each site with its own CallManager cluster and interconnect the sites with PSTN-enabled H.323 routers, such as Cisco 2600, 3600, and 5300 series routers. Each cluster provides telephony service for up to 30,000 IP-enabled voice devices. You can add other clusters, which allows your network to support vast numbers of users.

This type of deployment allows you to bypass the public toll network when possible and guarantees that remote sites retain survivability should the IP WAN fail. Using an H.323 gatekeeper allows you to implement a QoS policy that guarantees the quality of voice calls between sites. The same voice codec must apply to all intersite calls. Two chief drawbacks of this approach are increased complexity of administration, because each remote site requires its own database, and less feature transparency between sites.

Because each site is an independent cluster, for all users to have access to conference bridges, MOH, and transcoders, you must deploy these resources in each site. Figure 1-20 presents a picture of the multiple-site IP WAN model with distributed call processing.

Figure 1-19 *Multiple-Site Model with Independent Call Processing*

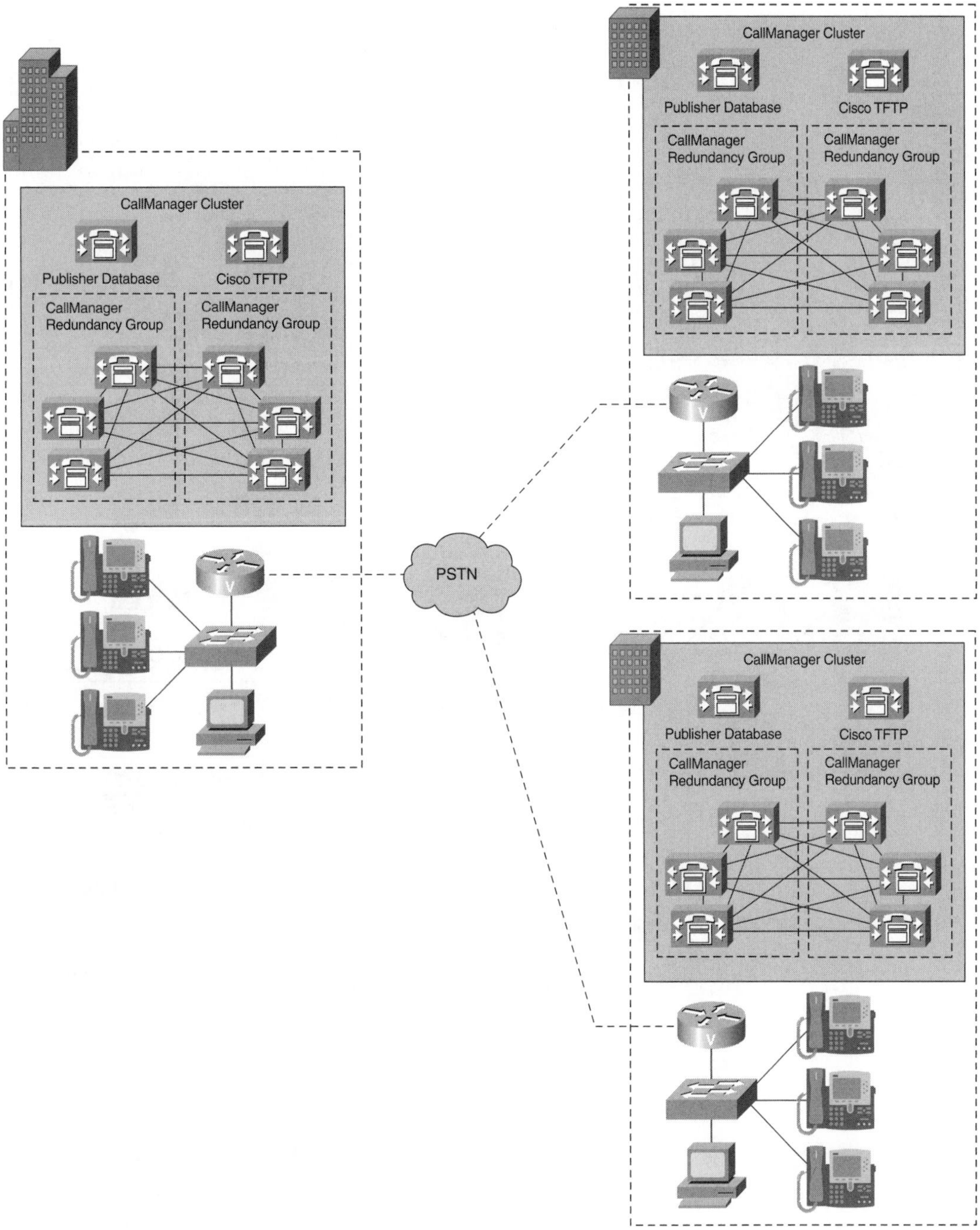

Figure 1-20 *Multiple-Site IP WAN Model with Distributed Call Processing*

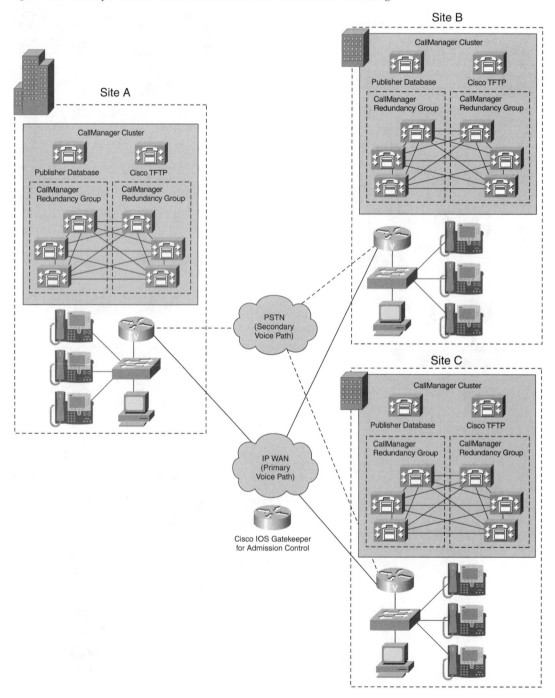

Multiple-Site Model with Centralized Call Processing

In a multiple-site model with centralized call processing, a CallManager cluster in a centralized campus processes calls placed by IP telephony devices both in the centralized campus and in remote sites connected by an IP WAN. This type of topology is called a *hub-and-spoke topology*: The centralized campus is the hub, and the branch offices sit at the end of IP WAN spokes radiating from the campus.

To CallManager, the multiple-site model with centralized call processing is nearly identical to the single-site model. However, guaranteeing voice quality between branch sites and the centralized site requires the use of a QoS policy that integrates the locations feature of CallManager.

Deploying a multiple-site model with centralized call processing offers easier administration and true feature transparency between the centralized and remote sites.

Because all sites are served by one cluster, you need to deploy only voice mail, conference bridges, and transcoders in the central site, and all remote sites can access these features. Figure 1-21 depicts the multiple-site model with centralized call processing.

Figure 1-21   *Multiple-Site Model with Centralized Call Processing*

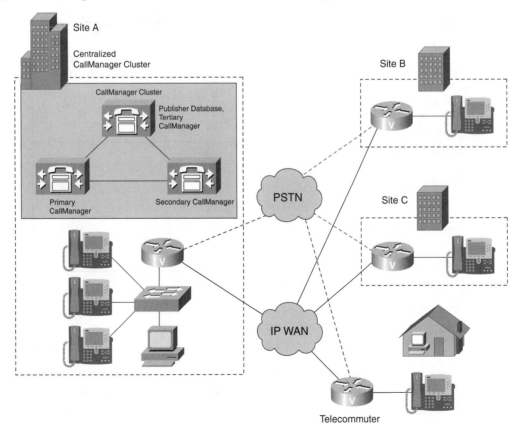

If the IP WAN should fail, Cisco Survivable Remote Site Telephony (SRST) can ensure that the phones in remote sites can continue to place and receive calls to each other and to the PSTN. SRST is a feature of Cisco IOS that allows a Cisco router to act as a CallManager when the primary or secondary CallManager nodes are not reachable. SRST requires minimal configuration because it derives most of its settings from the CallManager database.

When the IP WAN is available, SRST acts as a data router for Cisco IP Phones (and outbound PSTN gateway for local calls) and simply ensures connectivity between the branch office devices and CallManager. If the IP WAN fails, however, SRST takes over control of the phones, allowing them to call each other and the PSTN. While phones are registered to SRST, they have access to a reduced feature set. When the IP WAN again becomes available, the phones reconnect to the CallManager cluster.

Table 1-6 shows the router platforms that support SRST and the maximum number of phones that each supports.

Table 1-6   *Routers That Support SRST*

Router	Number of Phones Supported
Cisco 1751-V	24
Cisco 1760	
Cisco 1760-V	
Cisco 2801	
Cisco 2600XM	36
Cisco 2811	
Cisco 2650XM	48
Cisco 2651XM	
Cisco 2821	
Cisco 2691	72
Cisco 3640	
Cisco 3640A	
Cisco 2851	96
Cisco 3725	144
Cisco 3660	240

Table 1-6   *Routers That Support SRST (Continued)*

Router	Number of Phones Supported
Cisco 3825	336
Cisco 3745 Catalyst 6500 CMM	480
Cisco 3845	720

Combined Multiple-Site Model

You can deploy the centralized and distributed models in tandem. If you have several large sites with a few smaller branch offices all connected by the IP WAN, for example, you can connect the large sites using a distributed model, while serving the smaller branch offices from one of your main campuses using the centralized model. This hybrid model relies on complementary use of the locations feature of CallManager and gatekeepers for call admission control. Figure 1-22 depicts the combined multiple-site model.

Quality of Service (QoS)

Your network's available bandwidth ultimately determines the number of VoIP calls that your network can handle. As the amount of traffic on an IP network increases, individual data streams suffer packet loss and packet latency. In the case of voice traffic, this can mean clipped, choppy, and garbled voice. QoS mechanisms safeguard your network from such conditions.

Unlike data traffic, voice traffic can survive some loss of information. Humans are good at extracting information from an incomplete data stream, whereas computers are not. Data traffic, on the other hand, can deal with delayed transmission, whereas delayed transmission can destroy the intelligibility of a conversation. *Traffic classification permits* you to categorize your traffic into different types. Traffic classification is a prerequisite to *traffic prioritization*, the process of applying preferential treatment to certain types of traffic. Traffic prioritization allows you to minimize the latency that a voice connection experiences at the expense of the latency that a data connection experiences.

The design guide "Enterprise Quality of Service SRND" at http://www.cisco.com/go/srnd covers QoS in a Cisco IP Communications network in much greater detail than this section, which just provides an overview.

Call admission control (CAC) mechanisms prevent an IP network from becoming clogged with traffic to the point of being unusable. When a network's capacity is consumed, admissions control mechanisms prevent new traffic from being added to the network.

Figure 1-22 *Combined Multiple-Site Model*

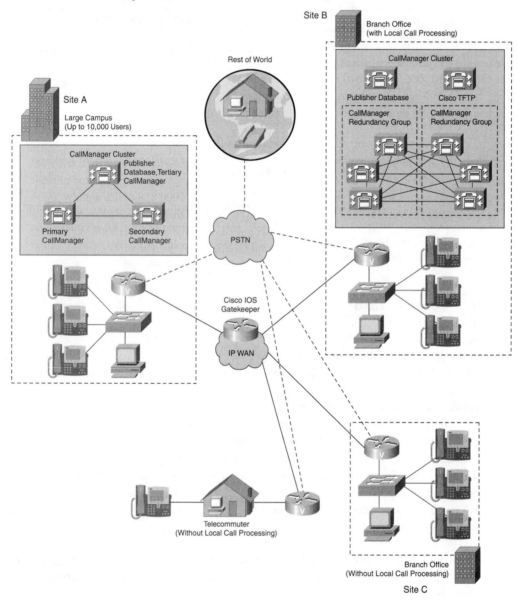

When calls traverse the WAN, admissions control assumes paramount importance. Within the LAN, on a switched network, life is good; if you classified your information properly, then either you have enough bandwidth or you do not. Links to remote sites across the IP WAN, however, can be a scarce resource. A 10-Mbps or 100-Mbps Ethernet connection can support hundreds of voice calls, but a 64-kbps ISDN link can route only a few calls before becoming overwhelmed.

This section describes the mechanisms that CallManager uses to enhance voice traffic on the network. It covers the following topics:

- "Traffic Marking" discusses traffic classification and traffic prioritization, features that enable you to give voice communications preferential treatment on your network.

- "Regions" discusses how you can conserve network bandwidth over bandwidth-starved IP WAN connections.

- "CallManager Locations" describes a method of call admissions control that functions within CallManager clusters.

- "H.323 Gatekeeper" describes a method of call admissions control that functions between CallManager clusters.

Traffic Marking

Traffic marking is important in configuring your VoIP network. By assigning voice traffic a routing priority higher than data traffic, you can ensure that latency-intolerant voice packets are passed through your IP fabric more readily than latency-tolerant data packets.

Routers that detect marked packets can place them in higher-priority queues for servicing before lower-priority packets. This strategy ensures that latency-sensitive voice and video traffic does not encounter undue delay between the endpoints. Marking voice and video streams at the highest priority helps ensure that users do not experience drops or delays in the end-to-end media stream. Marking call signaling higher than best-effort data helps ensure that users do not experience undue delay in receiving dial tone upon going off-hook.

CallManager supports two types of traffic marking. *IP Precedence* is the older type of traffic marking. In CallManager 4.0, a type of marking called Differentiated Services (or DiffServ), which is backward compatible with the older style of traffic marking, has essentially replaced it.

IP Precedence

The Cisco 79*xx* series phones (as well as the older Cisco 12SP+ and 30 VIP phones) all send out 802.1Q packets with the type of service field set to 5 for the voice stream and 3 for the signaling streams. CallManager permits you to set its type of service field to 3. In contrast, most data devices encode either no 802.1Q information or a default value of 0 for the type of service field.

When present, the type of service field permits the routers in your IP network to place incoming packets into processing queues according to the priority values encoded in the packet. By more quickly servicing queues into which higher-priority packets are placed, a router can guarantee that higher-priority packets experience less delay. Because all Cisco IP Phones encode their packets with a type of service value of 5 and data devices do not, in effect, the type of service and class of service fields permit you to classify the type of data passing through your network. This allows you to ensure that voice transmissions experience less latency. Figure 1-23 presents an example.

Figure 1-23 *IP Precedence Example*

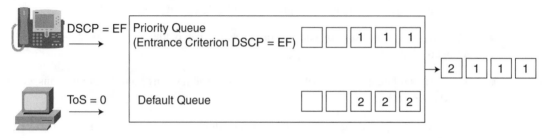

Figure 1-23 depicts two devices that send information through a network router. The Cisco IP Phone 7960 categorizes its traffic with type of service 5, while the PC categorizes its traffic with type of service 0. The router reads packets from both devices from the network and places them in queues based on the type of service field. Packets classified with type of service 5 go on a priority queue; other packets go on the default queue.

When the router decides to forward the packet out to the network again, it sends packets from the priority queue in preference to those on the default queue. Therefore, even if the Cisco IP Phone 7960 and PC send their packets to the router at the same time, the router forwards all of the packets sent by the IP Phone before forwarding any of the packets from the PC. This minimizes the latency (or end-to-end trip time) required for packets from the IP Phone, but increases the latency experienced by the PC. Thus, the router properly handles the latency-intolerant voice packets.

Differentiated Services

Differentiated Services (or DiffServ) is a traffic classification method that has essentially superseded the older IP Precedence traffic classification method. It permits a finer granularity classification than IP Precedence.

When a particular packet is marked, what is actually occurring is that a field in the IP packet header is being tagged with a particular value. The older IP Precedence field is 3 bits long, which permits IP Precedence values ranging from 0 to 7. The newer Differentiated Service Code Point (DSCP) values are 6 bits long, but they use, as the high-order bits of the DSCP, the original 3 bits set aside for the Type of Service field in the IP header. Therefore, routers that do not pay attention to the newer method of traffic classification can still provide voice and video traffic preferential treatment, because the high-order bits of this DSCP-marked traffic roughly correspond with the older IP Precedence values.

Table 1-7   *Comparison Between Traffic Classification Values*

3 High-Order Bits	IP Precedence	CallManager-Settable DSCP Values	Comment
000	Default	Default	Best-effort traffic
001	IP Prec 1	CS1 (001000) AF11 (001010) AF12 (001100) AF13 (001110)	
010	IP Prec 2	CS2 (010000) AF21 (010010) AF22 (010100) AF23 (010110)	
011	IP Prec 3	CS3 (011000) AF31 (011010) AF32 (011100) AF33 (011110)	Recommended call signaling
100	IP Prec 4	CS4 (100000) AF41 (100010) AF42 (100100) AF43 (100110)	Recommended video
101	IP Prec 5	EF (101110)	Recommended voice
110	IP Prec 6		Reserved
111	IP Prec 7		Reserved

Regions

Like IP precedence, regions play an important role in ensuring the quality of voice calls within your network. Regions allow you to constrain the codecs selected when one device calls another. Most often, you use regions to limit the bandwidth used when calls are placed between devices connected by an IP WAN. However, you can also use regions as a way of providing higher voice quality at the expense of network bandwidth for a preferred class of users.

When you define a new region, Cisco CallManager Administration asks you to define the compression type used for calls between devices within the region. You also define, on a region-by-region basis, compression types used for calls between the region you are creating and all other regions.

You associate regions with device pools. All devices contained in a given device pool belong to the region associated with that device pool. When an endpoint in one device pool calls an endpoint in another, the codec used is constrained to what is defined in the region. If, for some reason, one of the endpoints in the call cannot encode the voice stream according to the specified codec, CallManager attempts to introduce a transcoder (see Chapter 5) to allow the endpoints to communicate.

Figure 1-24 depicts a configuration that uses three regions to constrain bandwidth between end devices. Phones 1000 and 2000 are in the main campus; phone 3000 is in a branch office. Calls within the main campus use the G.711 codec, as do calls from phone 1000 to phone 3000. Calls between phone 2000 and phone 3000 use the G.729 codec.

Figure 1-24 *Regions Overview*

	Region 1	Region 2	Region 3
Region 1	G.711		
Region 2	G.711	G.711	
Region 3	G.711	G.729	G.711

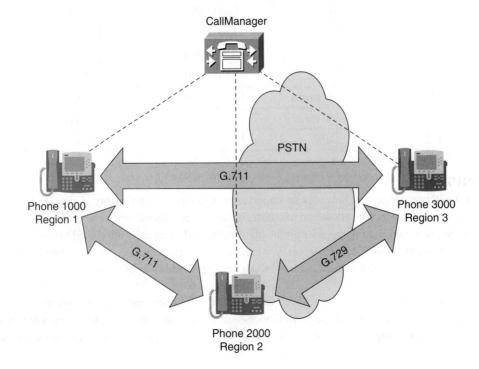

CallManager Locations-Based Call Admissions Control

Locations represent a form of admissions control. A location defines a topological area connected to other areas by links of limited bandwidth. With each location, you specify the amount of bandwidth available between users in that location and other locations in your network.

CallManager allows users to place an unlimited number of calls between devices within the same location; when a user places a call to another location however, CallManager temporarily deducts the bandwidth associated with the selected codec from the interlocation bandwidth remaining. When a user's call terminates, CallManager returns the allocated bandwidth to the pool of available bandwidth.

Users who attempt to place a call when no more bandwidth is available receive a fast busy tone (also called reorder tone), unless you enable a feature called Automated Alternate Routing (AAR). If AAR is properly configured, then instead of rejecting calls when the bandwidth between locations is oversubscribed, if the dialed destination has a PSTN number, CallManager automatically redials it to send the call to the local branch gateway for routing the call over the public network.

You must consider several design caveats before using locations-based CAC.

- Locations-based CAC requires that you deploy your voice network in a hub-and-spoke topology. Although locations allow you to configure admissions control, the locations mechanism is topologically ignorant. Having only one bandwidth counter for all interlocation calls means that all calls from one location to any other location must traverse only one logical network link, which limits deployment strictly to hub-and-spoke topologies. Figure 1-25 elaborates.

- When CallManager connects a call on behalf of a device that requires an MTP, CallManager does not account for the bandwidth between the device and the MTP. As a result, you must co-locate MTPs with the devices that require them and set up Media Resource Group Lists (MRGL) to use them.

Figure 1-25   *Hub-and-Spoke Topology Restriction*

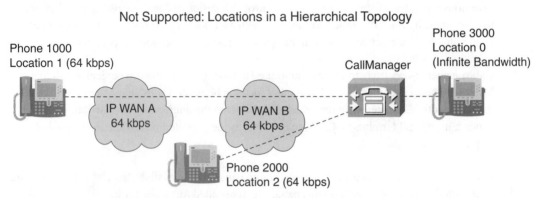

Not Supported: Locations in a Hierarchical Topology

Phone 1000
Location 1 (64 kbps)

CallManager

Phone 3000
Location 0
(Infinite Bandwidth)

IP WAN A
64 kbps

IP WAN B
64 kbps

Phone 2000
Location 2 (64 kbps)

Wrong: Calls from Phone 1000 to Phone 3000 decrement Location 1's bandwidth counter but not Location 2's. CallManager allows 64 kbps of calls from Location 1 to Location 0 and, at the same time, 64 kbps of calls from Location 2 to Location 0. IP WAN B is overwhelmed.

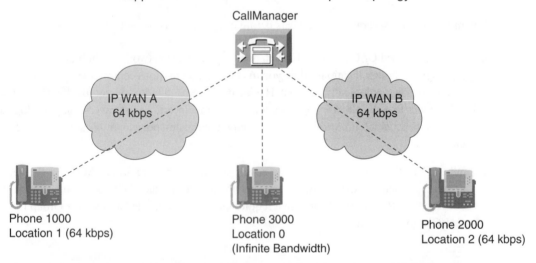

Supported: Locations in a Hub-and-Spoke Topology

CallManager

IP WAN A
64 kbps

IP WAN B
64 kbps

Phone 1000
Location 1 (64 kbps)

Phone 3000
Location 0
(Infinite Bandwidth)

Phone 2000
Location 2 (64 kbps)

Right: Calls from Phone 1000 to Phone 2000 decrement both Location 1 and Location 2's bandwidth counts. Calls from Phone 1000 to Phone 3000 decrement Location 1's bandwidth count, allowing Phone 2000 to call Location 0 if necessary. The IP WAN is never overwhelmed.

H.323 Gatekeeper

CallManager can be configured to use an H.323 gatekeeper for call admissions control between CallManager clusters. Before placing an H.323 call, a gatekeeper-enabled CallManager makes a Registration, Admissions, and Status (RAS) protocol admissions request (ARQ) to the H.323 gatekeeper.

The H.323 gatekeeper associates the requesting CallManager with a zone and can track calls that come into and go out of the zone. If the bandwidth allocated for a particular zone is exceeded, the H.323 gatekeeper denies the call attempt, and the caller hears a fast busy tone. (Alternatively, using route lists, you can configure CallManager to offer the call to a local PSTN gateway if the gatekeeper denies the call.) Essentially, an H.323 gatekeeper provides a locations-like functionality for the H.323 domain. Figure 1-26 depicts a gatekeeper-enabled configuration.

Figure 1-26 *H.323 Gatekeeper-Based Call Admissions Control*

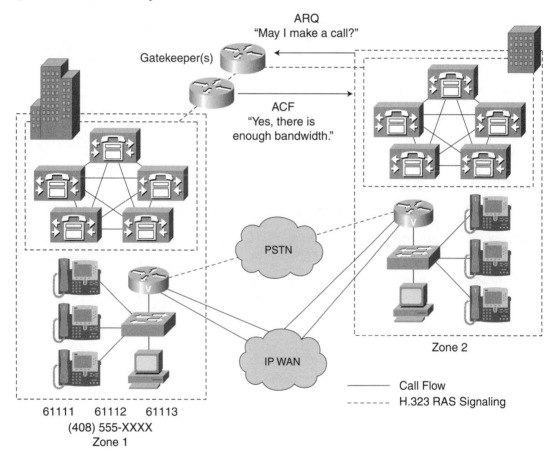

To configure fallback through the PSTN, you must configure the route plan to choose an alternate route if the gatekeeper rejects the call attempt. To configure PSTN fallback, you must configure a route list that contains two route groups. The first route group contains the intercluster trunk that routes outgoing calls over the IP WAN. If insufficient bandwidth is available, however, the H.323 gatekeeper rejects this outgoing call attempt. This call rejection triggers the alternate route associated with the route list. When CallManager selects this alternate route, it transforms the dialed digits to the destination's address as seen from the PSTN's point of view and offers the call to the PSTN gateway. Figure 1-26 demonstrates fallback routing through the PSTN.

Figure 1-27 *Fallback Routing Through the PSTN*

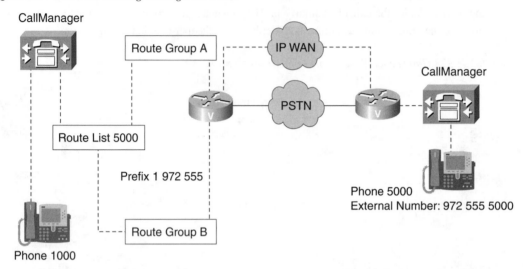

A call from Phone 1000 to Phone 5000 first attempts to route across the IP WAN. If the gatekeeper denies the call attempt, the route list modifies the dialed number and again offers the call to the gateway, which routes the call across the PSTN.

Chapter 2 discusses call routing in much more detail.

Summary

This chapter provided an overview of Cisco IP Communications, including VoIP and how Cisco IP Communications differs from traditional telephone systems, and how you can use VoIP to achieve savings by routing your telephone calls over the IP WAN.

You also learned about CallManager, the heart of Cisco IP Communications, including a short history of how CallManager has evolved and the following components of a Cisco IP Communications network:

- Cisco-certified servers on which CallManager runs

- Windows 2000 and Tomcat services that provide IP telephony in a Cisco IP Communications network

- Client devices that CallManager supports

Also discussed were the phases that CallManager goes through to set up a call and CallManager's clustering strategy for providing high availability and scalability. Several different deployment models for CallManagers within a cluster were also described, including several methods of deploying clusters to serve both campuses and campuses with remote offices. QoS, including traffic classification, traffic prioritization, and call admissions control (both locations-based and gatekeeper-controlled) by which you can guarantee good voice quality in your network were also discussed.

Call Routing

CallManager provides an extremely flexible set of tools with which you can control call routing in your enterprise, but this flexibility comes with a price: complexity. This chapter covers routing from the very beginning. It discusses the route pattern, which is CallManager's central routing concept, and it discusses wildcards, which are the basic building blocks of the route pattern. It discusses how CallManager uses route patterns to select destinations based on the digits that users dial.

From this foundation, the chapter delves further into ever more complex topics. This chapter consists of the following sections:

- "The Three Responsibilities of Call Routing" briefly discusses the tasks that CallManager's routing logic must accomplish.

- "The Seven Fundamentals of Call Routing" elaborates on the seven basic features—route patterns, route filters, dialing transformations, translation patterns, route lists, calling search spaces, and partitions—that CallManager uses to solve call routing problems.

- "Route Patterns and Route Filters" talks about the route pattern, CallManager's fundamental call routing concept, by which you can assign addresses to devices in your network.

- "Dialing Transformations" discusses the mechanisms by which you can alter the calling and called numbers as CallManager routes them during calls.

- "Translation Patterns" defines a method by which you can assign aliases to other route patterns. This method is often called on to resolve thorny call routing problems.

- "Call Hunting Constructs" describes two technologies that allow you to configure CallManager to intelligently route a call—route lists and hunt lists. Route lists allow you to organize your gateways into ordered lists so that you can ensure both that your gateways are fully utilized and that you use them in the most cost-efficient manner. Hunt lists allow you to serially or simultaneously offer calls to a group of related phones.

- "Calling Search Spaces and Partitions" defines a method by which you can customize routing on a device-by-device basis to accomplish complex tasks, such as routing calls by the type or the geographic location of the calling user. Partitions can also be associated with time schedules to provide time-of-day routing.

- "Case Studies" provides some extensive examples by which you can see how all the call routing concepts work together to solve complex problems.

- "Miscellaneous Solutions" provides specific solutions for call routing problems that administrators are commonly called on to solve. The solutions in this section often did not fit nicely in other sections of this chapter.

- "International Numbering Plans" covers how CallManager knows how to route calls for which you have selected a numbering plan. This section also describes how you can download additional country-specific numbering plans.

- "Troubleshooting" covers some common problems that administrators encounter when configuring their enterprise dial plans.

Figure 2-1 shows the block structure of CallManager. The shaded parts of Figure 2-1 are covered in this chapter.

This chapter is sprinkled with numerous examples throughout. These examples might be difficult to wade through, but they provide solutions to many common problems. By fully understanding how the examples work, you will be able both to improve on them and to discover solutions to problems that this chapter does not fully address.

The Three Responsibilities of Call Routing

The call routing component of CallManager has three main responsibilities:

- To determine which endpoint CallManager should ring based on the digits you dial

- To perform address translation

- To support individualized routing

Figure 2-1 *CallManager Block Structure Diagram*

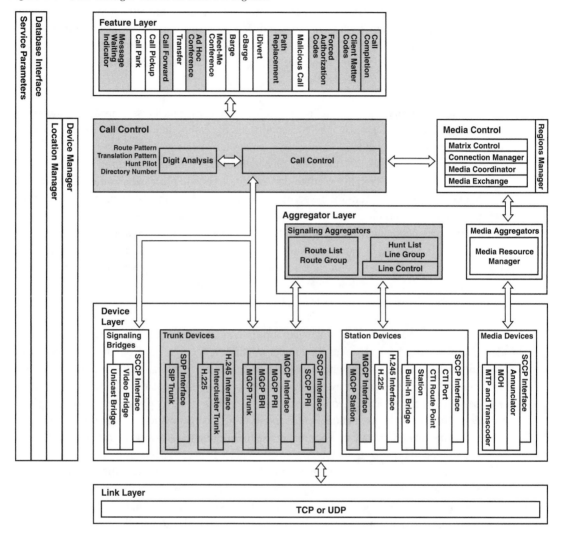

The first responsibility is to determine which endpoint CallManager should ring based on the digits you dial. These endpoints are often other IP phones, but they could just as easily be numbers controlled by other systems, such as the Public Switched Telephone Network (PSTN), other Private Branch Exchanges (PBX), or other CallManager clusters. Furthermore, the digits you dial can sometimes not even correspond to a physical destination at all. Numbers such as call park codes, Meet-Me conference codes, and translation patterns (the section "Translation Patterns" describes the way to provide aliases for numbers) do not cause any specific device to ring. Rather, they allow CallManager to treat your call in special ways, depending on the type of number. For example, dialing a call park code allows you to retrieve a party who has been held from another station; dialing a Meet-Me conference code allows you to join a multiparty conversation; dialing a translation pattern can redirect your call to a different destination; and dialing a Computer Telephony Interface (CTI) route point can pass control of your call to an application such as an automated attendant. Call routing concepts, such as route patterns, underlie CallManager's treatment of all of these virtual endpoints.

The call routing component's second responsibility is to perform address translation. Address translation allows you to modify the dialed digits and the calling number as the call propagates through a network. Such address translation is important when a network must pass a call from a private network with its private numbering plan to the PSTN with a standardized numbering plan. For example, most PBXs require users to dial an access code to place calls to the PSTN. If CallManager does not first remove the access code before offering the call to the PSTN, the PSTN rejects the call attempt. Imagine what happens if you dial an access code of 9 for calls you make from your home phone; most likely, the PSTN plays an announcement that you have composed your number incorrectly, or worse, it routes your call to a completely different destination. CallManager's address translation capabilities allow you to enforce a private numbering plan while simultaneously reconciling it against the PSTN's numbering plan. The section "Dialing Transformations" discusses address translation in more detail.

CallManager's third responsibility is to support individualized routing, which means that the destination you reach when you dial a number might differ completely from the destination your neighbor reaches when your neighbor dials the same number. This capability is useful to support routing by class of calling user, by organization, or by geographic location. For example, routing by class of calling user permits you to restrict calls made from lobby phones while allowing your executives full access to international numbers. Routing by organization permits you to route calls made by different departments in your enterprise to different locations, so calls from engineers to a technical support organization route to a different place than calls made by marketing executives. Taken to an extreme, routing by organization allows you to control entirely different enterprises using a single CallManager. Routing by geographic location allows you to deploy a single CallManager in one geographic location that controls phones in different geographic locations. Customizing the call routing for users in different geographic locations allows you to deploy multiple sites with an identical number to reach the receptionist: callers in New York reach the New York receptionist when dialing 0; users in Chicago reach the Chicago receptionist when dialing the same number. You can also control costs by routing calls across your IP network instead of the PSTN, a process called *toll bypass* or *toll restriction*.

The Seven Fundamentals of Call Routing

Cisco CallManager Administration presents several items in the Route Plan menu related to routing. However, this chapter describes routing concepts, not particular pages in CallManager

Administration. By understanding the underlying concepts, you can better develop your enterprise's call routing infrastructure. For example, the Route Pattern Configuration page (shown in Figure 2-2) incorporates several routing concepts: route patterns, route filters, transformations, route lists, and partitions. This chapter does not directly deal with the Route Pattern Configuration page, but when you understand the components that make up the Route Pattern Configuration page, building an individual route pattern is straightforward. Figure 2-2 demonstrates how an excerpt from a single page—the Route Pattern Configuration page in this case—incorporates several (but not all) routing concepts.

Figure 2-2   *Route Pattern Configuration Page*

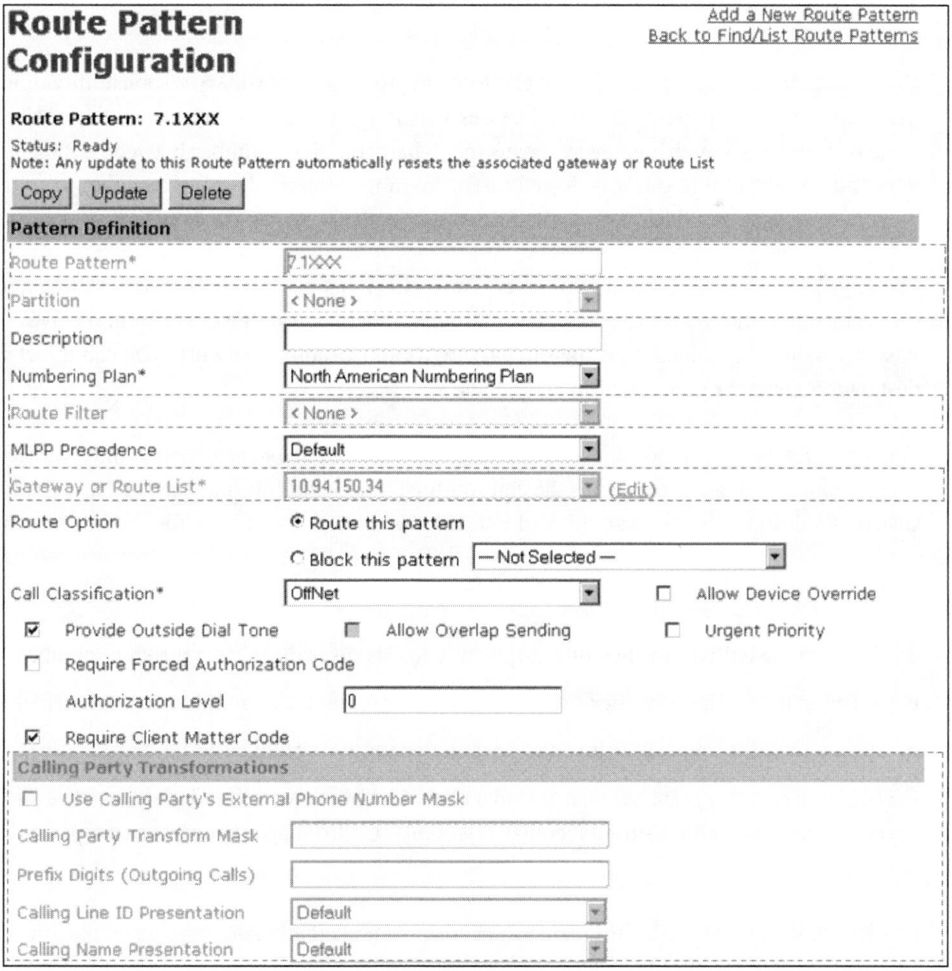

CallManager uses seven major concepts to fulfill its responsibilities:

- Route patterns

- Route filters

- Dialing transformations

- Translation patterns

- Call hunting constructs

- Calling search spaces

- Partitions

Route patterns and *route filters* permit CallManager to fulfill its primary responsibility of locating a destination. Route patterns are the addresses you assign to devices. For instance, associating the route pattern 8XXX with a gateway means that when you dial a number between 8000 and 8999, your call routes out that gateway. Route filters are more esoteric. Used in conjunction with the special route pattern wildcard @, route filters restrict the scope of the @ wildcard.

Dialing transformations, along with several miscellaneous gateway and system settings, permit CallManager to modify dialed digits and calling numbers before the destination receives a call. Also, by modifying dialed digits before passing a call to another network, you can affect which destination the other network ultimately dials.

Translation patterns provide a level of routing indirection that can resolve complicated scenarios. They are another feature that helps the call routing component fulfill its primary responsibility of selecting a destination. You can think of a translation pattern as an alias for another route pattern.

Translation patterns allow you to do the following:

- Change the **called number** of a call from what the user dialed to a different number

- Change the **calling number** of a call from the original user's number to another identity

- Route the resulting call as it is had been dialed with different call routing rules.

Call hunting constructs are mechanisms that allow CallManager to intelligently route a single call to several devices—either simultaneously or serially. CallManager supports two types of hunting constructs:

- **Route lists**—Enable CallManager to choose from available gateways when placing a call to another network. Route lists are composed of route groups, which in turn are composed of gateways. When CallManager selects a route list as the destination for a call, it begins searching serially, according to the specified search order, for an available gateway from among the gateways that the route list's route groups contain. If a gateway is busy, temporarily unreachable, or nonexistent, CallManager chooses another gateway to which to route the call.

■ **Hunt lists**—Enable CallManager to offer calls to IP phones, either simultaneously or serially. When CallManager selects a hunt list as a destination for a call, it looks at the hunting algorithm associated with the hunt list for an available line from among the lines that the hunt list's line groups contain. Hunt lists provide a variety of ways to treat calls when a particular line is busy or not available.

Calling search spaces and *partitions* allow CallManager to provide individualized routing. These features allow you to configure networks to use toll restriction, enforce calling restrictions by user, or configure networks that serve independent organizations with fully or partially segregated routing plans.

Route Patterns and Route Filters

This section introduces the basic building blocks of call routing—route patterns and route filters.

A route pattern is an address, much like your mailing address. When a user dials a number, CallManager tries to figure out to which destination to deliver the call. It performs this function by looking at all the route patterns you have configured and then figuring out which route pattern is the best fit for the number the user has dialed. CallManager then attempts to offer the call to the endpoint that you have associated with the route pattern.

Do not confuse the concept of route pattern that this section discusses with the Route Pattern Configuration page in CallManager Administration. The Route Pattern Configuration page allows you to associate an address with a destination and contains other settings that let you modify the calling and called numbers. One of the fields on the Route Pattern Configuration page takes a route pattern as input; so does one of the fields on the Translation Pattern Configuration page, as does the Hunt Pilot Configuration page. Figure 2-3 shows the field on the Translation Pattern Configuration page that takes a route pattern as input.

Figure 2-3 *Route Pattern Field in the Translation Pattern Configuration Page*

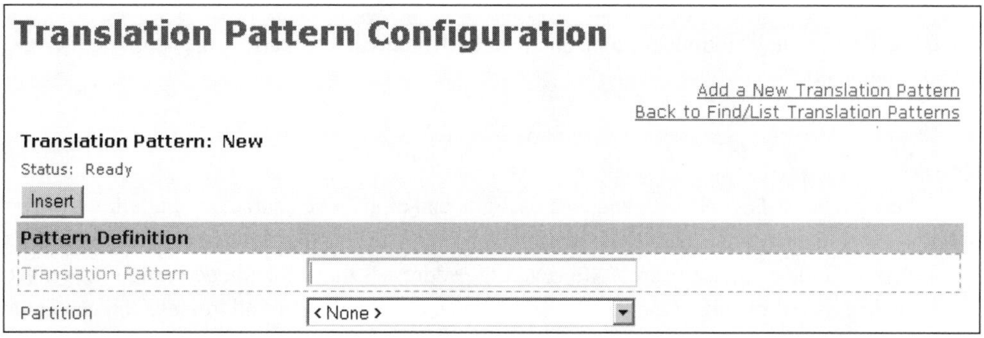

Many different CallManager Administration pages allow you to enter route patterns. For example, the directory numbers you assign to phones are actually route patterns, as are Meet-Me conference numbers, message waiting on/off numbers, call park numbers, call pickup group numbers, translation patterns, and hunt pilots.

A *route pattern* is a sequence of digits and other alphanumeric characters. When the digits are all numeric, as is usually the case with directory numbers, CallManager rings the device with which you have associated the route pattern only when a user dials the exact numerical sequence. By including non-numeric characters called *wildcards* in a route pattern, you tell CallManager to ring the associated device for a range of dialed numbers. For instance, if you assign the route pattern 8XXX to a device, CallManager rings the device when users dial numbers in the range from 8000 to 8999.

Route filters are a special range-refining mechanism. You use route filters with route patterns that contain the special @ wildcard. The @ wildcard allows you to represent the PSTN with a single route pattern. When you must limit the types of PSTN calls (such as emergency, local, long distance, and international) that users can place, route filters limit the scope of the @ wildcard.

This section discusses the following topics:

- "Wildcards" describes the building blocks out of which you build route patterns.

- "Dialing Behavior" describes how CallManager processes digits from a calling user and selects a destination.

- "Dialing Behavior Refinements" elaborates on the basic procedure discussed in the section "Dialing Behavior" by introducing the Urgent Priority check box and explaining the logic that underlies outside dial tone.

- "Other Wildcards (@ and .)" revisits some complex wildcards that the section "Wildcards" introduces but only glosses over.

- "Route Filters" introduces a mechanism by which you can narrow the scope of the @ wildcard.

Wildcards

A house address is a specific sequence of digits and alphabetic characters that allows the postal service to identify a package's destination. A route pattern is like a house address for a callable endpoint; unlike a house address, however, the addresses that a telephone system uses must provide a means by which the administrator can specify a range of addresses. You can enter individual addresses for every phone your network manages, but if users need to dial out of a gateway to the PSTN, the number of individual addresses becomes too vast to configure. Clearly, requiring the configuration of every single telephone number in the PSTN is not reasonable.

Route patterns use wildcards, which are digit placeholders that permit you to specify quickly a range of matching digits. For example, instead of configuring every individual number from 7000 to 7999 to route a call across a gateway to another network, by configuring 7XXX, you can tell CallManager to send all calls that begin with the digit 7 and are followed by three digits (in the range 0 to 9) to the gateway.

There is more to it, but first look at the basic wildcards, which Table 2-1 summarizes.

Table 2-1   *Wildcard Summary*

Wildcard	Description
0, 1, 2, 3, 4, 5, 6, 7, 8, 9, *, #	These look like digits, but they are actually simple wildcards. Each matches exactly one occurrence of the corresponding digit in a dialed digit string.
[xyz...]	This notation allows you to specify a set of matching digits. For example, [357] matches one occurrence of either the digit 3, 5, or 7.
[...x-y...]	Placing a hyphen between any two digits within square brackets causes one occurrence of any digits within the range to match, including the digits themselves. You can use range notation along with set notation. For example, [3-69] matches one occurrence of a digit 3, 4, 5, 6, or 9.
[^x-y]	If the first character after the open angle bracket is a carat, the expression matches one occurrence of any digit (including * and #) except those specified. For example, [^1-8] matches one occurrence of a digit 9, 0, *, or #.
wildcard?	A question mark following any wildcard or bracket expression matches zero or more occurrences of any digit that matches the previous wildcard. For example, 9[12]? matches 9, 91, 92, 912, 9122, 92121, and many others.
wildcard+	A plus sign following any wildcard or bracket expression matches one or more occurrences of any digit that matches the previous wildcard. For example, 3[1-4]+ matches 31, 3141, 3333, and many others. Note that the simple digit string 3 would not match this pattern, because the + wildcard requires that at least one digit matching the previous wildcard be consumed.
X	The X wildcard is a convenience wildcard that matches one occurrence of any digit in the range 0 to 9. This wildcard is functionally equivalent to the range expression [0-9].
!	The ! wildcard is a convenience wildcard that matches one or more occurrences of any digit in the range 0 to 9. This wildcard is functionally equivalent to the range expression [0-9]+.
. and @	The section "Other Wildcards (@ and .)" discusses these wildcards.

Route Patterns and grep(1)

UNIX users might have noticed a strong similarity between route patterns and regular expressions. UNIX has a robust command line interface that offers many elegant text-processing tools. One tool, grep(1), uses regular expressions to fulfill a common need for those who regularly work with command line interfaces, searching through a text stream for the occurrence of a specified word.

For example, if you had a directory containing text files of letters and memos and you needed to find all files that related to your taxes, you might tell grep(1) to look for the word *tax*. However, because *tax* might start a sentence, a simple search for *tax* would fail to find occurrences of the capitalized *Tax*. Although you could do two different searches, combining the two searches and weeding out duplicate hits would be onerous, and furthermore, more complicated search criteria might vastly increase the number of individual searches that you would have to do. Using the regular expression [Tt]ax is one way you can find all instances of the word *tax*, both capitalized and lowercase.

To do the search, grep(1) looks through every individual line of every file looking for *specific* substrings that match the *general* pattern that the regular expression represents. Grep(1) prints *all* matching lines.

On the other hand, the call routing component does the opposite. It takes the *specific* sequence of digits dialed by the user and examines every *general* route pattern looking for the best *single* match.

Furthermore, although grep(1) concerns itself about what text strings currently match a regular expression, because users enter digits one by one, the call routing component must concern itself not only with which route patterns match the current sequence of dialed digits, but also with which route patterns might match if the user dials more digits. For example, the digit string 100 does not match the route pattern 1000; but if the user dials another 0, the route pattern matches perfectly. If CallManager were to take into account only the collected digits at a given moment in time, it would provide reorder tone to the user, because 100 does not match the route pattern 1000. Instead, CallManager realizes that if the user continues dialing, at some point in the future the collected digits might match a configured route pattern. Therefore, CallManager applies reorder tone only when the digits it has collected can never match a configured route pattern.

Dialing Behavior

The call routing component's behavior is sometimes counterintuitive, so a better understanding of the process it uses to select a destination can allow you to better troubleshoot problems.

In collecting a user's digits, the call routing component goes through the following steps:

Step 1   Compare the current sequence of dialed digits against the list of all route patterns and determine which route patterns currently match. Call the set of current matches *currentMatches*.

- If *currentMatche*s is empty, the user's dialed digit string does not currently correspond with a destination.

- If *currentMatches* contains one or more members, the call routing component determines the closest match. The *closest match* is the route pattern in currentMatches that matches the fewest number of route patterns. For example, the dialed digit string 2000 matches both route pattern 2XXX and 20XX. Although there are 1000 different dialed digit strings that match 2XXX, only 100 dialed digit strings match 20XX, and 20XX is therefore the closest match.

Step 2   Simultaneously, determine whether different route patterns might match if the user were to dial more digits. Call the condition of having potential matches for a dialed digit string *potentialMatches*.

- If *potentialMatches* holds true, the call routing component waits for the user to dial another digit. If the user dials another digit, the sequence of events restarts at step 1 using the new digit string.

- If *potentialMatches* no longer holds true or a dialing timeout has elapsed, the call routing component selects a destination.

- To select a destination, the call routing component looks at the closest match. The section "Example 2: Closest Match Routing" elaborates on closest match routing. If there is no closest match, the user's dialed digit string does not correspond with a destination. Furthermore, no more digits are forthcoming. CallManager rejects the call attempt.

- Otherwise, CallManager extends the call to the device associated with the closest match.

Examples can best explain this process. The following sections present three examples:

- "Example 1: Simple Call Routing" presents an example in which exactly one route pattern ultimately matches.

- "Example 2: Closest Match Routing" presents an example in which multiple route patterns match and CallManager uses the closest match routing algorithm to select a route pattern.

- "Example 3: Wildcards That Match Multiple Digits" presents an example that demonstrates the effect of wildcards that match multiple digits.

For purposes of the examples, assume that CallManager has been configured with the route patterns in Table 2-2.

Table 2-2   *Basic Dialing Behavior Example Route Patterns*

Route Pattern	Description
1100	Matches exactly the dialed digit string 1100
1200	Matches exactly the dialed digit string 1200
120X	Matches dialed digit strings in the range 1200–1209
130	Matches exactly the dialed digit string 130
1300	Matches exactly the dialed digit string 1300
13!	Matches all dialed digit strings of any length that begin with digit sequence 13 followed by at least one more digit in the range 0 through 9

Example 1: Simple Call Routing

In this example, a calling user goes off-hook and dials 1100. On collecting the final digit of the dialed digit string, CallManager selects exactly one route pattern and offers the call to the associated destination.

When the user goes off-hook, CallManager begins its routing process. The current set of dialed digits is empty. The set of current matches, *currentMatches*, is empty. Every route pattern in the table is a potential match at this point, so the condition of having potential matches, *potentialMatches*, is true. Table 2-3 shows the current set of potential matches. As long as *potentialMatches* holds true, CallManager must wait for more digits.

Table 2-3   *Patterns That Can Match, Example 1, No Dialed Digits*

Currently Dialed Digits: \<None\>
Current Matches
\<None\>
Patterns That Can Still Match
1100
1200
120X
130
1300
13!
Patterns That Can No Longer Match
\<None\>

When the user dials 1, the state of affairs does not change. No current match exists, and every route pattern in the table is a potential match.

Dialing another 1 eliminates many route patterns as possible matches. The patterns 1200, 120X, 130, 1300, and 13! are no longer potential matches for the dialed digit string. The only route pattern that remains in contention is 1100. However, *currentMatches* is still empty and *potentialMatches* still holds true. Even though 1100 is the only route pattern that the user could dial that might result in a match, CallManager must wait until the user does, in fact, dial the full string. Table 2-4 shows the current set of potential matches.

Table 2-4   *Patterns That Can Match, Example 1, Dialed Digits 11*

Currently Dialed Digits: 11
Current Matches
<None>
Patterns That Can Still Match
1100
Patterns That Can No Longer Match
~~1200~~
~~120X~~
~~130~~
~~1300~~
~~13!~~

The next 0 does not change the situation.

When the user dials the final 0, *currentMatches* contains route pattern 1100. Furthermore, as further digits would not result in a different route pattern matching, *potentialMatches* does not hold true. CallManager extends the call to the device associated with route pattern 1100. Table 2-5 shows the final set of potential matches.

Table 2-5   *Patterns That Can Match, Example 1, Dialed Digits 1100*

Currently Dialed Digits: 1100
Current Matches
1100
Patterns That Can Still Match
<None>
Patterns That Can No Longer Match
~~1200~~
~~120X~~
~~130~~
~~1300~~
~~13!~~

Example 2: Closest Match Routing

In this example, a calling user goes off-hook and dials 1200. On collecting the final digit of the dialed digit string, CallManager determines that two route patterns match the dialed digit string and uses the closest matching routing algorithm to select which route pattern is awarded the call.

The closest match for a dialed digit string is simply the route pattern that matches the fewest number of digit strings of equal length to the dialed digit string. For example, though the route pattern 1000 matches exactly one dialed digit string, the route pattern 1XXX, which matches any dialed digit string in the range 1000 to 1999, matches 1000 possible dialed digit strings. In any comparison between route patterns 1000 and 1XXX, the closest match routing algorithm gives route pattern 1000 precedence.

Closest Match Routing Versus Longest Match Routing

Cisco IOS gateways use a concept called *longest match routing*. Sometimes the term *longest match* is used to describe the type of pattern matching that CallManager does. But closest match routing and longest match routing are different.

With longest match routing, Cisco IOS gateways look at the number of initial digits that specifically match. For instance, given the dial peers 11.. and 1.11, Cisco IOS gateways prefer to match the former dial peer over the latter dial peer when the number 1111 is dialed, because the former dial peer begins with two specific digits and the latter begins with only one.

CallManager performs a calculation over the entire dial string. When comparing the dial string 1111 against patterns 11XX and 1X11, CallManager notes that, while 100 dial strings could match the first expression, only 10 could match the second, so CallManager matches the second.

In the end, unless you are doing wickedly creative things with your dial plan, it doesn't matter. Closest match and longest match routing work equivalently well in the field, because most dial plans use the initial digits of dial strings to disambiguate call routing.

The qualification "of equal length to the dialed digit string" in the preceding paragraph handles cases in which one or more of the route patterns being examined contains a wildcard that matches multiple dialed digits. For example, route pattern 1! matches any dialed digit string beginning with 1, and route pattern 13! matches any dialed digit string beginning with 13. The ! wildcard in these route patterns might match one, two, or more digits. As a result, the number of dialed digit strings that match either of these route patterns is infinite.

To decide among them, CallManager restricts the calculation of number of potentially matching dialed digit strings to only those of the same length as the dialed digit string itself. For instance, given the route patterns 1! and 13! and a dialed digit string of 13000, CallManager determines how many five-digit dialed digit strings could potentially match both route patterns. Thus, 13!, which matches 1000 five-digit strings, takes precedence over 1!, which matches 10,000 possible five-digit strings.

Returning to the example, when the user goes off-hook, CallManager begins its routing process. The current set of dialed digits is empty. The set of current matches, *currentMatches*, is empty. Every route pattern in the table is a potential match at this point, so the condition of having potential matches, *potentialMatches*, is true. As long as *potentialMatches* holds true, CallManager must wait for more digits. Table 2-6 shows the current set of potential matches.

Table 2-6   *Patterns That Can Match, Example 2, No Dialed Digits*

Currently Dialed Digits: <None>	
Current Matches	
	<None>
Patterns That Can Still Match	
	1100
	1200
	120X
	130
	1300
	13!
Patterns That Can No Longer Match	
	<None>

When the user dials 1, the situation does not change. No current match exists, and every route pattern in the table is a potential match.

Dialing 2 eliminates route patterns 1100, 130, 1300, and 13! as possible matches. The patterns 1200 and 120X are the only route patterns that can match. Table 2-7 shows the current set of potential matches.

Table 2-7   *Patterns That Can Match, Example 2, Dialed Digits 12*

Currently Dialed Digits: 12	
Current Matches	
	<None>
Patterns That Can Still Match	
	1200
	120X

Table 2-7   *Patterns That Can Match, Example 2, Dialed Digits 12 (Continued)*

Patterns That Can No Longer Match
~~1100~~
~~130~~
~~1300~~
~~13!~~

The next 0 does not change the situation.

When the user dials the final 0, *currentMatches* contains both route pattern 1200 and route pattern 120X. Furthermore, as further digits would not result in a different route pattern matching, *potentialMatches* does not hold true and CallManager must select a destination. Because 1200 is a closer match than 120X, CallManager extends the call to the device that owns route pattern 1200. Table 2-8 shows the final set of potential matches.

Table 2-8   *Patterns That Can Match, Example 2, Dialed Digits 1200*

Currently Dialed Digits: 1200	
Current Matches	
1200	Selected: Matches exactly one number
120X	Not selected: Matches 10 different numbers
Patterns That Can Still Match	
<None>	
Patterns That Can No Longer Match	
~~1100~~	
~~130~~	
~~1300~~	
~~13!~~	

Example 3: Wildcards That Match Multiple Digits

When a route pattern contains a wildcard that matches multiple digits, CallManager often must wait for an interdigit timeout to expire before it can route the call. This situation occurs because even if the route pattern containing the wildcard already matches, the user might intend to dial more digits. The most trivial example of this behavior is the route pattern !, which matches one or more occurrence of any number of digits. If a user dials 123 and matches the route pattern !, CallManager must continue to wait, because it has no assurances that the user is not planning to dial 1234. Routing the call prematurely might cause CallManager to send an incomplete dialed digit string to an adjacent network.

In the following example, a calling user goes off-hook and dials 1300. The route pattern 13! ensures that condition *potentialMatches* always holds true. Even if CallManager finds that route pattern 13! is the best match out of set *currentMatches*, CallManager must continue to wait, because it has no way of knowing if the user is really finished dialing.

In this example, when the user goes off-hook, CallManager begins its routing process. The current set of dialed digits is empty. The set of current matches, *currentMatches*, is empty. Every route pattern in the table is a potential match at this point, so the condition of having potential matches, *potentialMatches*, is true. As long as *potentialMatches* holds true, CallManager must wait for more digits. Table 2-9 shows the current set of potential matches.

Table 2-9   *Patterns That Can Match, Example 3, No Dialed Digits*

Currently Dialed Digits: <None>	
Current Matches	
	<None>
Patterns That Can Still Match	
	1100
	1200
	120X
	130
	1300
	13!
Patterns That Can No Longer Match	
	<None>

When the user dials 1, the situation does not change. No current match exists, and every route pattern in the table is a potential match.

Dialing 3 eliminates route patterns 1100, 1200, and 120X as possible matches; however, 130, 1300, and 13! are still possible matches. Table 2-10 shows the current set of potential matches.

Table 2-10   *Patterns That Can Match, Example 3, Dialed Digits 13*

Currently Dialed Digits: 13	
Current Matches	
	<None>
Patterns That Can Still Match	
	130

Table 2-10 *Patterns That Can Match, Example 3, Dialed Digits 13 (Continued)*

	1300
	13!
Patterns That Can No Longer Match	
	~~1100~~
	~~1200~~
	~~120X~~

The next 0 causes *currentMatches* to contain route patterns 130 and 13!. However, *potentialMatches* holds true, because the user's next digit might allow the same (13!) or a different (1300) route pattern to match. Table 2-11 shows the current set of potential matches.

Table 2-11 *Patterns That Can Match, Example 3, Dialed Digits 130*

Currently Dialed Digits: 130	
Current Matches	
	130
	13!
Patterns That Can Still Match	
	1300
	13!
Patterns That Can No Longer Match	
	~~1100~~
	~~1200~~
	~~120X~~

The fact that route pattern 13! shows up in both the list of current matches and the list of potential matches needs explaining. When a route pattern ends with a multiple match wildcard (!, range expressions ending with ? such as [1-5]?, or range expressions ending with + such as [1-5]+), CallManager recognizes that even though the current dialed number matches the route pattern, the user might intend to dial more digits.

The final 0 eliminates route pattern 130 as a possible match. *CurrentMatches* contains route patterns 1300 and 13!. CallManager cannot attempt a closest match routing determination, however, because route pattern 13! not only matches the current digit string (1300), but also matches a longer digit string (13000). The ! wildcard at the end of a route pattern means that condition *potentialMatches* always holds true. Table 2-12 shows the current set of potential matches.

Table 2-12   *Patterns That Can Match, Example 3, Dialed Digits 1300*

Currently Dialed Digits: 1300	
Current Matches	
	1300
	13!
Patterns That Can Still Match	
	13!
Patterns That Can No Longer Match	
	~~1100~~
	~~1200~~
	~~120X~~
	~~130~~

In such a case, the only event that allows CallManager to select a destination is an interdigit timeout. On receiving an interdigit timeout, CallManager knows that no more digits are forthcoming and can make a routing selection. In this example, after the timeout, CallManager selects route pattern 1300 using closest match routing rules. Table 2-13 shows the final list of potential matches.

Table 2-13   *Patterns That Can Match, Example 3, Dialed Digits 1300 with Timeout*

Currently Dialed Digits: 1300		
Current Matches		
	1300	Selected: Matches exactly one number
	13!	Not selected: Matches 100 different four-digit numbers
Patterns That Can Still Match		
	<None>	Interdigit timeout means no further digits are forthcoming
Patterns That Can No Longer Match		
	~~1100~~	
	~~1200~~	
	~~120X~~	
	~~130~~	

CallManager uses two timers to manage the system interdigit timeout as described in the following paragraphs.

Because users who go off-hook might need to spend extra time to locate the address they want to dial (on a crowded directory lookup web page or in a printed directory), CallManager uses one timer to dictate how long it waits for users to dial an initial digit upon going off-hook. The service parameter Off-hook to First Digit Timer (msec) defines the duration of the initial digit timer in milliseconds. The default for this timer is 15,000 milliseconds.

Subsequent digits are controlled with the CallManager service parameter T302 Timer (msec). T302 Timer (msec) defines the duration of the interdigit timer in milliseconds. The default for this timer is also 15,000 milliseconds.

One feature of CallManager that can be surprising to administrators familiar with other call agents is that CallManager does not assign special significance to the * or # characters. CallManager treats these characters just as any other digit. On other systems, # is sometimes used as an explicit cancellation of the interdigit timeout.

For instance, when users are dialing international numbers, call agents typically cannot detect when the user has fully composed the dialed number, because doing so would require that the call agent have full understanding of every national dial plan in the entire world. When users of these systems (and CallManager) dial the international access code for the country they're in (011 for the United States, 00 in many European countries), the system generally must rely on an interdigit timer to expire before routing the call.

Some systems treat the # key specifically as an indication from the user that the system should immediately route the call based on the digits the user has already provided.

In contrast, CallManager treats the # just like any other digit. On one hand, doing this permits you to use it at the beginning of dial patterns, to represent special abbreviated dialing sequences or access codes. On the other hand, it means that to replicate the use of # as an interdigit timer you might have to configure additional patterns.

The pattern 9.011! is a very typical pattern that a North American administrator would use to direct international calls to a PSTN gateway. This pattern matches digit strings beginning with 9011 and followed by at least one more digit 0 to 9. Because of the digit analysis rules described in section "Dialing Behavior," CallManager routes the call only after the interdigit timer expires. CallManager must refresh the timer after each digit, because CallManager doesn't know whether the user intends to continue dialing.

If the user dials #, according to the dialing rules, CallManager must apply reorder, because the ! wildcard specifically excludes the * and # digits from its list of matched digits. This behavior is similar to the treatment you receive if you define a pattern such as 12[1-4] (which matches the digit strings 121, 122, 123, and 124) and instead dial 125. 125 is not a digit string that is encompassed by 12[1-4], so CallManager rejects the call.

So, if you want to support the ability to use # as an interdigit timer, what can you do? Simply, you take advantage of CallManager's standard dialing behavior, which treats # just like any other digit. If, in addition to 9011!, you define the pattern 9011!#, you can support not only cases where the user dials 9011+*international number* and waits for timeout but also cases in which the user terminates the dialed digit string with #.

This works because as long as the user is dialing digits after 9011, both provisioned patterns consist as potential matches. For instance, if the dialed digit string is 9 011 33 12 34 56 78 90, CallManager considers that pattern 9011! matches the currently provided digits but that it must also keep waiting because the user might dial another digit. On the other hand, while pattern 9011!# is not a current match, if the user were to provide another digit, this pattern might match.

If the user provides no further digits before the interdigit timer expires, CallManager routes the call based on pattern 9011!. Instead, if the user dials 9 011 33 12 34 56 78 90 #, the digits the user provides cease to match pattern 9011! (because ! doesn't include the # character among its matching characters), but pattern 9011!# does match. Furthermore, because all other potential matches are removed from contention and because the final character of the pattern does not leave open the possibility that the user might provide more digits, CallManager routes the call immediately, which is exactly the behavior you desired when you added pattern 9011!#.

Overlapped Sending and Non-North American Numbering Plans

The previous section demonstrates that when you end a route pattern with a wildcard that matches multiple digits (! or range expressions ending in + or ?), CallManager must wait for the system interdigit timeout to expire before it can route the call. So why would you ever end a route pattern with a wildcard that matches multiple digits?

Many countries have variable-length national dialing plans. Unlike North America, in which the length of a public telephone number is fixed at 10 digits, countries with variable-length dial plans require users to dial a varying number of digits to identify a number in the PSTN. For instance, in Finland, a numbering area equivalent to a North American area code is called a telealue (TLA). Some TLAs are a single digit (2, 3, 5, 6, 9), while other TLAs are two digits (13, 14, 15, 16, 17, 18, 19). Within a TLA, different carriers own different number blocks, which range from three to five digits long. For instance, one carrier controls block 422 in TLA 19, while another carrier controls block 4251 in TLA 19. In other words, one carrier handles calls made from within Finland that begin with the six digits 019422; the other handles calls from within Finland that begin with the seven digits 0194251. (Users within Finland dial 0 before dialing the TLA.) Finally, subscriber numbers range from three to five digits long. As a result, the number of a Finnish resident is of an indeterminate length (in practice, eight or nine digits, but this value does not reflect mobile numbers or service numbers).

Because the number of digits in countries with variable-length numbering plans is so dependent on the particular digits dialed, such countries rely on *overlapped sending* in the PSTN to figure out how many digits to collect and where to route the call.

Overlapped sending is kind of like a bucket brigade. Figure 2-4 shows the principle under which overlapped sending works. Figure 2-4 depicts a network of four nodes (A, B, C, and D) and three users (1, 2, and 3). User 1 wants to call User 3, whose number is 0123333, composed of a one-digit region identifier (0), a three-digit node identifier (123), and a three-digit subscriber number (333). User 2's number is 01244444, composed of a one-digit region identifier (0), a three-digit node identifier (124), and a four-digit subscriber number (4444).

In Figure 2-4, no single node in the network understands the complete dialing plan. Node A understands that when a user attached to node A dials 0, it should send the call to node B. When node B receives the call, it recognizes that it needs more digits to determine the final destination and asks node A to pass on any digits that node A receives from User 1.

Node B understands that it must collect three digits before it can route the call further. If the digits are 123, it routes the call to node C. If the digits are 124, it routes the call to node D.

Nodes C and D, in turn, manage their portions of the numbering plan. Node C understands that it must collect three digits to select a subscriber, while node D requires four digits to select a subscriber. When User 1 dials 0123, node B offers the call to node C.

Node C performs the same steps that node B does when it receives a call. Node C recognizes that it requires three digits to make a routing selection and asks node B to pass on any digits that node B receives from node A (which, in turn, receives them from User 1). When node C receives the last three digits, it routes the call to User 3. Thus, in the manner that water buckets pass from hand to hand in a bucket brigade until they reach the fire, digits pass from node to node until they reach the spot that needs them.

Figure 2-4 *Overlapped Sending in a Simple Network*

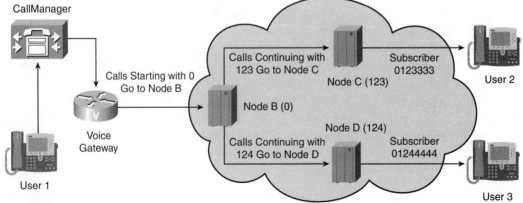

Versions of CallManager before release 3.1 do not support overlapped sending, but rather require that you provision knowledge of your entire network's numbering plan as route patterns. This requirement is acceptable for numbers within your network and for public numbers in a fixed numbering plan (because, for example, you can just configure a pattern like 9.XXXXXXXXXX to handle all patterns in the North American numbering plan). But variable-length numbering plans require the configuration of large numbers of such patterns just to provide network access.

Hence, in CallManager releases 3.0 and earlier, if you were an administrator in a country with variable-length numbering plans, you had three options.

■ Configure very specific route patterns on your trunk interfaces, in effect encoding the national network's knowledge of the national numbering plan into the database. This option requires a significant knowledge of your country's numbering plan, the patience to enter all of the route patterns, and constant monitoring of changes to the national numbering plan so that you can update your route patterns.

■ Replace CallManager's knowledge of the North American numbering plan with your country's numbering plan. Like the first option, this option requires extensive knowledge of your country's numbering plan, but it is a better solution because it means you can use the @ wildcard to represent your country's numbering plan. (For more information about the @ wildcard, see the section "Other Wildcards [@ and .].") However, the Cisco Technical Assistance Center (TAC) will not support any unofficial changes you make to the way the system uses the "@" route pattern, under CallManager version 3.0 and earlier.

■ Configure gateways with steering codes followed with the ! wildcard (which matches multiple digits). For example, imagine that in the sample network depicted in Figure 2-4, Node A was CallManager, the remaining nodes were the PSTN, and you associated the route pattern 0! with the gateway to node B. When User 1 dials 0, CallManager continues collecting digits from User 1 until the interdigit timeout expires, whereupon CallManager offers the complete number to the PSTN.

At the time of this writing, most administrators choose the third option, but also configure a few specific route patterns to handle numbers that their users often dial, relying on closest match routing to eliminate the interdigit timeout. Users strongly dislike long interdigit timeouts, because while CallManager is waiting for the timeout to expire, users think that something is wrong with the system. One approach to eliminate interdigit timeout is to use # as an interdigit timeout character. For example, assume that your external access code to a variable-length dialing plan is 0. If you configure 0!, when users dial any digit sequence beginning with 0, CallManager waits for interdigit timeout and then ships all dialed digits to the PSTN.

However, if you also configure 0!#, users who have been trained to terminate all external dialed number sequences with # can avoid the interdigit timeout. Because the ! wildcard matches only the digits 0 through 9, dialing # removes the 0! route pattern from contention, leaving only 0!#.

Because 0!# is not terminated with a wildcard that matches multiple dialed digits, condition *potentialMatches* ceases holding true and CallManager can route the call immediately. Pressing # is analogous to pressing the **SEND** button on a call made from a cell phone.

The good news is that CallManager release 3.1 and later supports overlapped dialing, rendering much of the advice in this section obsolete. If your PSTN supports overlapped sending, simply configure your route patterns with the *steering code* alone (without the trailing ! wildcard); when CallManager offers the call to the associated gateway or route list, the PSTN prompts CallManager to pass any further digits along.

The bad news is that CallManager supports overlapped dialing only for gateways with digital interfaces that use the Media Gateway Control Protocol (MGCP) protocol. If your network uses Cisco H.323 gateways for access to the PSTN, and your country uses a variable-length numbering plan, you must still choose from one of the three options this section presents.

Overlapped sending is built in to CallManager, but you must specifically indicate which patterns are candidates for overlapped sending. The route pattern setting Allow Overlap Sending tells CallManager whether it should consider the pattern as overlap-sending-capable.

Pre-4.0 versions of CallManager simply assumed that all patterns were overlap-sending-capable, but, as it turns out, this caused several problems. So long as digits arrived one at a time, it didn't really matter, because when CallManager matched the locally-configured pattern, it would simply offer the call to the destination gateway. If the destination gateway required more digits, it would simply request them. In the meantime, CallManager would queue up any dialed digits.

But problems arose with creative dial plans. For instance, examine the patterns 1234, as associated with an IP phone and the pattern 1XXXXXX, as associated with a gateway that could support overlapped signaling.

Before CallManager 3.1, if you provided the dial string 1234567 to the call routing component of CallManager, CallManager would match pattern 1XXXXXX instead of pattern 1234, because too many digits had been provided to match 1234.

When CallManager implemented automatic overlap sending, it had to start queuing up any additional digits—just in case the destination happened to ask for more. So, after this automatic overlap sending behavior was implemented, dial plans started to break. When 1234567 was dialed, CallManager would assume that the digits 1234 more closely matched the IP phone and digits 567 should be queued up.

In practice, an IP phone would never ask for more digits to be sent to it for routing purposes. As a result, a series of fixes was phased in over releases to first exclude IP phones from participating in overlapped dialing and, then, because the problem could manifest across different gateways, to require you to specifically configure which gateways might ask for more digits and which ones will never ask for more digits.

Dialing Behavior Refinements

The section "Dialing Behavior," for purposes of clarity, describes a simplified version of CallManager's call routing logic. The actual process is more involved. This section discusses six refinements to the basic dialing procedure:

- "Urgent Route Patterns" describes route pattern urgency, which can interrupt interdigit timing when CallManager must route a call immediately.

- "Outside Dial Tone" describes the logic that determines when CallManager applies outside dial tone.

- "Call Classification" talks about categorization of calls as either being OnNet or OffNet.

- "The Route/Block Flag" describes a specific option on route and translation patterns that permits you to block as well as route calls.

- "MLPP Precedence" defines the use of route patterns to classify calls according to call priority.

- "Forced Authorization Codes and Client Matter Codes" describes a feature that can cause callers to enter a second phase of dialing in which they must enter a password or account code in order to proceed with a call.

Urgent Route Patterns

As the preceding section mentions, when CallManager receives digits from the user, it waits to route the call until it is sure that it needs no more digits. A case in point is route patterns that end in a wildcard that matches multiple digits. CallManager must wait for the interdigit timeout to expire before it offers the call to the selected destination.

But if you need a call to route the very moment that a user provides sufficient dialed digits, you can use the Urgent Priority check box on the Route Pattern Configuration page to short-circuit the dialing procedure.

An urgent route pattern only has an observable effect if your dial plan contains overlapping route patterns. Your call routing plan contains overlapping route patterns if it is possible to dial a sequence of digits so that the call routing component can select a current match but must continue to wait for more digits because there are also potential matches. For example, if you assign directory number 99110 to a phone and also configure a gateway with route pattern 9.911 (for emergency services in North America), you create a dial plan with overlapping route patterns.

When a user in an emergency situation dials 9911, CallManager waits for the interdigit timeout to expire before routing the call, because CallManager does not know whether the user intends to dial 0 to complete a call to the station instead of the emergency response center.

You can use the Urgent Priority check box to protect yourself from this sort of configuration. By marking the 9.911 route pattern as urgent, you tell CallManager to route the call to the emergency center the instant that a user dials 9911. (Note, however, that in the example provided, marking the 9.911 route pattern as urgent has the side effect of preventing any user from dialing the phone with directory number 99110.)

Another common usage of the Urgent Priority check box comes into play for administrators in countries with variable-length numbering plans. The simplest configuration for countries with variable-length numbering plans is to configure a gateway with an outside access code (for example, 0) followed by the ! wildcard. However, this configuration introduces interdigit timeout into all external numbers that users dial. By configuring specific route patterns for numbers that their users commonly dial, administrators can eliminate the interdigit timeout for the commonly dialed patterns. Table 2-14 provides a sample configuration and explanation of a U.K. dialing plan.

Table 2-14 *Sample U.K. Dialing Plan*

Route Pattern	Priority	Description
9.00!	Normal	International calls.
9.0[1-57-9]XXXXXXX 9.0[1-57-9]XXXXXXXX 9.0[1-57-9]XXXXXXXXX	Normal	National calls, which can be 9, 10, or 11 digits (not counting the external access code), depending on the specific digits dialed after the 0[1-57-9] portion of the route pattern. This kind of overlapping route pattern configuration means that users who dial a national number requiring a lesser number of digits (9 in this example) must wait for the interdigit timer to expire before CallManager routes the call, because CallManager cannot be certain that the user does not intend to dial further digits.
9.037[0485]XXXXXX 9.08[56]0XXXXXXX 9.0802XXXXXXX	Urgent	More specific numbers in the national network. Marking these as urgent means that when CallManager selects these as the best match, it stops the interdigit timer. For instance, the first of these route patterns, 9.037[0485]XXXXXX, is a 10-digit number (not counting the external access code). The national route pattern 9.0[1-57-9]XXXXXXXX would normally match this route pattern, but the longer route pattern 9.0[1-57-9]XXXXXXXXX causes CallManager to keep the interdigit timer running. Marking 9.037[0485]XXXXXX as urgent causes CallManager to route the more specific route pattern immediately when a user dials it.

Two points about urgent route patterns to note especially:

- First, an urgent route pattern only takes effect if it is the best match at the time. If you define an urgent route pattern XXXX, a normal route pattern 8XXX, and a normal route pattern 80000, when users dial 8000, CallManager continues to wait for more digits, because the normal route pattern 8XXX is the best match.

- Second, defining an urgent route pattern limits the total number of route patterns you can usefully assign. If you define the route pattern 999 as an urgent route pattern, users can never dial longer digit sequences that begin with 999, because the urgent route pattern always takes priority.

Outside Dial Tone

Another subject that the call routing procedure described in section "Dialing Behavior" omits is providing outside dial tone. Outside dial tone is an indication that users expect when CallManager routes their calls off of the local network. To apply outside dial tone, check the Provide Outside Dial Tone check box on the Route Pattern or Translation Pattern Configuration pages for each route pattern that you consider to be off-network. For dialed digit strings that can match those patterns, the call routing component then applies outside dial tone at some point during the dial sequence.

> **NOTE** Outside dial tone is normally a different cadence from the tone provided when a user goes off-hook. However, by setting the service parameter Always Use Inside Dial Tone to True, you can cause the secondary tone played to sound exactly like the initial dial tone the user hears. This parameter does not otherwise affect CallManager's application of dial tone; CallManager still applies a secondary tone when its route configuration indicates that only patterns that require outside dial tone are candidate matches.

You cannot explicitly configure the point in the dialing sequence when CallManager applies outside dial tone. In addition, the decision to apply outside dial tone is completely independent of whether or where the route pattern contains a "." wildcard (described in the section ". Wildcard"). Rather, the call routing component applies outside dial tone at the point when all potential matches for a dialed digit string have had their Provide Outside Dial Tone box checked.

For example, consider the route patterns 9000 and 91XXXXXXX. 91XXXXXXX belongs to a trunk device and has had its Provide Outside Dial Tone box checked. Table 2-15 shows these route patterns.

Table 2-15   *Outside Dial Tone Example 1, Configured Route Patterns*

Configured Route Patterns	Provide Outside Dial Tone Check Box
9000	Do not apply outside dial tone
91XXXXXXX	Apply outside dial tone

When a user goes off-hook, CallManager applies inside dial tone. Table 2-16 depicts the current dialing state.

Table 2-16   *Outside Dial Tone Example 1, Dialed Digits <None>*

Currently Dialed Digits: <None>	
Current Matches	
<None>	
Patterns That Can Still Match	
9000	Do not apply outside dial tone
91XXXXXXX	Apply outside dial tone
Patterns That Can No Longer Match	
<None>	
Actions Taken: Apply inside dial tone	

The user dials 9 and CallManager turns off inside dial tone. At this point, CallManager cannot tell whether the user intends to dial the on-network number 9000 or the off-network number 91XXXXXXX, so it waits for the next digit. Table 2-17 depicts the current dialing state.

Table 2-17   *Outside Dial Tone Example 1, Dialed Digits 9*

Currently Dialed Digits: 9	
Current Matches	
<None>	
Patterns That Can Still Match	
9000	Do not apply outside dial tone
91XXXXXXX	Apply outside dial tone
Patterns That Can No Longer Match	
<None>	
Actions Taken: Turn off inside dial tone	

If the user then dials 1, CallManager eliminates the route pattern 9000 from its list of potential matches. At this point, all remaining candidates have had their Provide Outside Dial Tone box checked, and the call routing component chooses this moment to apply outside dial tone (see Table 2-18).

Table 2-18   *Outside Dial Tone Example 1, Dialed Digits 91*

Currently Dialed Digits: 91	
Current Matches	
<None>	
Patterns That Can Still Match	
91XXXXXXX	Apply outside dial tone
Patterns That Can No Longer Match	
9000	Do not apply outside dial tone
Actions Taken: All route patterns require outside dial tone. Apply outside dial tone.	

Now assume that an additional route pattern, 9124, has been configured. This route pattern could be a station device, call park, or Meet-Me conference code. Table 2-19 depicts this configuration.

Table 2-19   *Outside Dial Tone Example 2, Configured Route Patterns*

Configured Route Patterns	Provide Outside Dial Tone Check Box
9000	Do not apply outside dial tone
9124	Do not apply outside dial tone
91XXXXXXX	Apply outside dial tone

The steps that CallManager takes when the user goes off-hook and dials 9 are identical to those in Example 1. However, Table 2-20 shows that when the user dials the subsequent 1, CallManager waits, because at least one of the route patterns that can still match does not require outside dial tone.

Table 2-20   *Outside Dial Tone Example 2, Dialed Digits 91*

Currently Dialed Digits: 91	
Current Matches	
<None>	
Patterns That Can Still Match	
9124	Do not apply outside dial tone
91XXXXXXX	Apply outside dial tone
Patterns That Can No Longer Match	
9000	Do not apply outside dial tone
Actions Taken: <None>	

As long as what the user dials keeps the route pattern 9124 in contention as a possible match, CallManager defers applying outside dial tone. For example, if the user continues by dialing 2 (yielding currently dialed digits of 912), CallManager continues to defer application of outside dial tone. However, if instead of dialing 2, the user dials 7 (yielding currently dialed digits of 917), the route pattern 9124 can no longer match, and CallManager applies outside dial tone, because all potentially matching route patterns have had their Provide Outside Dial Tone box checked.

If your system plays outside dial tone later in a dial string than you expect, be sure to look for route patterns that overlap with the route patterns for which you are expecting to hear outside dial tone, but for which you have not checked the Provide Outside Dial Tone box. These conflicting route patterns might be Meet-Me conference or call park ranges, in which case you need to change these ranges so that they do not conflict with the off-network route pattern in question.

On the other hand, if you receive outside dial tone sooner than expected (usually because you want to use access codes that are longer than a single digit), introduce a new route pattern that is identical to your access code, but do not check the Provide Outside Dial Tone box. (You can assign this route pattern to the same gateway or route list to which the full route pattern connects.) CallManager suppresses outside dial tone until the user dials the last digit of the access code. Table 2-21 presents an example in which the access code for external numbers is 999.

Table 2-21   *Outside Dial Tone Example 3, Configured Route Patterns*

Configured Route Patterns	Provide Outside Dial Tone Check Box
999	Do not apply outside dial tone
999.1XXXXXXX	Apply outside dial tone

Just as in the previous examples, CallManager applies inside dial tone when the user goes off-hook and turns off inside dial tone after the user dials 9. Table 2-22 depicts the dialing state when the user dials 99.

Table 2-22   *Outside Dial Tone Example 3, Dialed Digits 99*

Currently Dialed Digits: 99	
Current Matches	
<None>	
Patterns That Can Still Match	
999	Do not apply outside dial tone
999.1XXXXXXX	Apply outside dial tone
Patterns That Can No Longer Match	
<None>	
Actions Taken: <None>	

CallManager continues suppressing outside dial tone because route pattern 999 might still match the user's dialed digits. Table 2-23 presents the dialing state when the user dials another 9 (yielding dialed digits of 999).

Table 2-23   *Outside Dial Tone Example 3, Dialed Digits 999*

Currently Dialed Digits: 999	
Current Matches	
999	
Patterns That Can Still Match	
999.1XXXXXXX	Apply outside dial tone
Patterns That Can No Longer Match	
<None>	
Actions Taken: All potential matches require outside dial tone. Apply outside dial tone.	

Adding the route pattern 999 thus suppresses outside dial tone until the moment that you want it applied.

Call Classification

While the Provide Outside Dial Tone check box dictates whether a caller hears outside dial tone at some point during dialing, it doesn't necessarily mean the call is an outside call. To actually classify a call as an outside call, use the Call Classification list box on the Route Pattern Configuration page. OffNet indicates that a given call is leaving your network (and may generate a charge); OnNet indicates that a given call is staying on your network.

The Call Classification list box also exists on CallManager gateway pages as well. It indicates how CallManager should classify calls arriving through the gateway, and it takes on the values OffNet, OnNet, or Use System Default. The Use System Default setting tells CallManager to classify calls according to the service parameter Call Classification.

Call classification works in conjunction with two service parameters (Block OffNet To OffNet Transfer and Drop Ad Hoc Conference) that attempt to control toll fraud. Toll fraud can occur, for instance, if someone within your organization places a call to an international destination, places the answering party on hold, calls another international party, and then transfers the parties together. Voilà! Free international calling—at least for the called parties; unfortunately, you're paying the bill. A similar scenario is possible using the conference feature.

When you set Block OffNet To OffNet Transfer to False, CallManager permits all transfers. When you set Block OffNet To OffNet Transfer to True, CallManager looks at the call classification of the parties being transferred together before allowing the user to complete the transfer.

Call classification isn't really call classification; it's party classification. When a party *places* a call, he is classified according to the type of device from which he is calling. For instance, Cisco IP Phones are always considered OnNet devices (by the CallManager cluster to which they are registered). On the other hand, some gateways might attach to purely internal destinations (such as a legacy PBX in your network), while others may represent connections to the PSTN. CallManager has no way to tell the difference, so it relies on you to set the Call Classification box to define calls arriving through the gateway as OnNet or OffNet.

The party that *receives* a call is classified according to the call classification associated with his pattern or directory number. As with placed calls, the directory numbers associated with Cisco IP Phones are automatically classified as OnNet. Calls to gateway destinations must route through a route pattern, and they take their classification from the call classification you specify on the Route Pattern Configuration page.

So when an IP phone calls an IP phone, the calling party is classified as OnNet by virtue of her IP phone's implicit device setting and the called party is classified as OnNet by virtue of his IP phone's implicit directory number setting. When an IP phone calls out a gateway, the calling party is classified as OnNet by virtue of her IP phone's implicit device setting and the called party is classified according to what you've set on the Route Pattern Configuration page. For instance, even if the call goes to the PSTN, you might want to classify numbers that terminate within your local calling region as OnNet anyway. When a gateway calls an IP phone, the calling gateway is classified according to what you've set on the gateway configuration page and the called party is OnNet by virtue of being an IP phone.

When deciding whether to complete a transfer, the transfer feature looks at the classification of the parties on the call. If both are OffNet and the service parameter Block OffNet to OffNet Transfer is set to True, CallManager denies the transfer attempt and displays a message to the transferring party.

The conference setting works similarly, but instead of preventing the conference, it dictates under what conditions the conference should survive. The Drop Ad Hoc Conference setting takes the following values:

- **Never** allows the conference to persist until all parties have dropped out.

- **When Conference Creator Drops Out** causes the conference to end when the person who created the conference leaves it. This value setting can be inconvenient if the creator accidentally hangs up on a conference call.

- **When No OnNet Parties Remain in the Conference** relies on call classification. If only OffNet parties remain in the conference, CallManager clears the conference if this value is set.

MLPP Precedence

Multilevel Priority and Preemption (MLPP) is a feature primarily used by military installations that want to provide a way for important personnel to be able to preempt lower-priority calls on a given phone.

MLPP relies on a standard form of addressing in which the precedence level of a call is indicated by an initial set of digits (01 to 04) on a dialed digit string. CallManager does not include such hard-coded rules in its call routing component; rather, it simply allows you to associate a precedence level with any matching string. For instance, digit strings beginning with 01 typically denote calls of priority flash override; by defining pattern 01XXXX and associating the Precedence Level Flash Override to it, you can conform to the military specifications. However, this approach also leaves you free to define number formats of your own if, for example, you want to have a number to break into your coworkers' calls at lunchtime to arrange vital details such as at which local restaurant to eat.Precedence level follows the call, and, if the call encounters an MLPP-enabled phone or gateway, the precedence level affects the how the call is treated. In the case of phones, it prompts the user and requires him to hang up on any lower-priority calls; in the case of gateways, it can force calls to clear if all circuits on the gateway are in use. Appendix A, "Feature List," provides additional information about MLPP.

The Route Pattern Configuration page and Translation Pattern Configuration page simply allow you to associate priority values with a call when the associated pattern matches. CallManager supports the following values, listed in order from lowest to highest priority:

1. Default

2. Routine

3. Priority

4. Immediate

5. Flash

6. Flash Override

7. Executive Override

Unlike the other settings, the Default setting simply indicates that CallManager should not modify the precedence of a call when the associated route or translation pattern is selected. For instance, a call might arrive from another system prioritized as Immediate. If the provided digits match a local pattern with a Precedence Level of Default, the call remains Immediate. Setting any other value causes the selected value to overwrite whatever value the call already had.

TIP Although it might seem a natural fit, Cisco recommends that you *not* use MLPP as a way to provide emergency calls higher priority than normal calls but rather recommends that you set aside dedicated trunks to the PSTN to be used for emergency calls.

This recommendation exists for a few good reasons. One issue is that emergency response centers often have limited trunk capacity. Certain emergencies might generate a high call volume, and, although using preemption might guarantee that each emergency call routes off your enterprise network, it doesn't guarantee (past the first few calls) that the emergency response center will receive all these calls. At some point, all the preemption logic accomplishes is the disruption of valid nonemergency calls without allowing redundant emergency callers to reach the emergency response center.

Among the nominally nonemergency calls that might be preempted are calls that, while nominally nonemergency, actually are part of your enterprise's emergency policies. Even worse, some of these nominally nonemergency calls might be calls from the emergency response center back into your enterprise. Some laws regarding 911 compliance require that the emergency response center be provided a caller ID that can be used by the emergency response center to dial back into the enterprise should an emergency caller somehow be disconnected.

Thus, by simply reserving some facilities specifically for 911 calls, you ensure that enough capacity exists for emergency callers to reach the emergency response center without running the risk of preempting equally vital calls that happen not to be specifically to 911.

The Route/Block Flag

When a given pattern matches, the default behavior that applies is to route the associated call. However, CallManager specifically permits to you block calls when a given pattern is matched. The Route Option field on the Translation Pattern Configuration and Route Pattern Configuration pages permits you to block a call: When you specify **Block this pattern**, CallManager rejects the call if the blocked pattern happens to be the best match for the dialed string. The rejection of the call is done with the cause value you select from the following list:

- No Error

- Unallocated Number

- Call Rejected

- Number Changed

- Invalid Number Format

- Precedence Level Exceeded

If the call came from a different system, through an ISDN or H.323 trunk, the cause value is returned as the Cause Information Element (IE) in Q.931 signaling. The system where the call originated can then apply different outcomes for the call, based on the cause that is returned. For instance, if you choose "unallocated number" as the cause for a blocked pattern, the calling system will be able to abort any further attempts to reroute the call through a different network, avoiding trying another path to reach a destination that is nonexistent. The section "Miscellaneous Solutions" later in the chapter provides some examples of the use of the Route Option field.

Forced Authorization Codes and Client Matter Codes

Forced Authorization Codes and Client Matter Codes provide a twist to CallManager's digit collection process or, to be more precise, a postscript. Both of these features kick in after CallManager finds the closest match for a set of dialed digits. They can be thought of as a second phase of digit collection.

You create forced authorization codes (FAC) and client matter codes (CMC) from the Feature menu in CallManager Administration. Forced authorization codes and client matter codes can consist of any string of numeric digits up to 16 digits long. Forced account codes also have an associated authorization level that takes values from 1 to 255. Higher numeric values correspond to higher authorization levels.

The purpose of forced authorization codes is to require users who place calls to certain destinations—most often long distance or international calls—to enter an authorization code to prove to CallManager that it should route the call.

When CallManager matches a pattern for which the Required Forced Authorization Code check box has been checked, instead of immediately routing the call, it plays a tone to the caller. The caller must enter a valid authorization code. Entry of digits is terminated either when the caller dials # or when the interdigit timer expires.

Upon collecting a forced authorization code, CallManager compares the authorization level configured with the code against the authorization level configured on the Route Pattern Configuration page. If the level of the code equals or exceeds the level on the pattern, CallManager proceeds with the call.

The purpose of client matter codes is to require users to enter an account number upon placing a call that CallManager logs into the call detail records (CDR) upon call completion. A reporting tool can later extract the account codes from the CDR database and properly bill clients for the time spent by the caller on the account.

Client matter codes operate nearly identically to forced authorization codes. When CallManager selects as closest match a route pattern with the Require Client Matter Code check box checked, it plays a tone to the caller and requires him to enter digits. Digit entry expires when either the caller presses the # key or the interdigit timer expires.

Route patterns support the simultaneous support of both forced authorization and client matter codes. When both are configured, CallManager first prompts for the forced authorization code and then prompts for the client matter code.

Forced authorization codes and client matter codes are not compatible with the Allow Overlap Sending flag. When either the Require Client Matter Code or Require Forced Authorization Code check boxes are checked, CallManager Administration disables the Allow Overlap Sending check box. Similarly, when the Allow Overlap Sending check box is checked, CallManager Administrator disables the Forced Authorization Code and Client Matter Code fields.

Other Wildcards (@ and .)

The section "Route Patterns and Route Filters" deliberately glosses over some of the most common wildcards you use: the @ and . wildcards.

@ Wildcard

Unlike the convenient wildcards X and ! and the range-matching notations, the @ wildcard does not represent any particular set of matching characters. The @ wildcard causes CallManager to add the set of national route patterns for the numbering plan that you specify in the Numbering Plan drop-down list on the Route Pattern or Translation Pattern Configuration pages. One way to think of the @ pattern is that it matches any number that you can dial from a residential phone in the country associated with the selected numbering plan. For example, specifying the @ pattern along with the North American numbering plan allows users to dial 911 and 555 1212 and 1 800 555 1212 and 011 33 12 34 56 78 90.

The @ pattern is a macro. When you configure it, CallManager looks up a list of route patterns associated with the dialing plan you have specified and adds them individually. This might cause CallManager to appear to violate closest match routing rules.

For instance, different individual route patterns in the North American numbering plan match the four dialing strings 911 and 555 1212 and 1 800 555 1212 and 011 33 12 34 56 78 90. Table 2-24 shows some sample route patterns.

Table 2-24   *Sample Route Patterns in the North American Numbering Plan*

Dialing String	Matching Route Pattern	Description
911	[2-9]11	Services (311, 411, 611, 911)
555 1212	[2-9]XX XXXX	Seven-digit dialing
1 800 555 1212	1 [2-9]XX [2-9]XX XXXX	11-digit dialing
011 33 12 34 56 78 90	011 3[0-469] !	International calls to the valid two-digit country codes in the range 30–39

Assume that you associate the route pattern @ with a gateway that you want to use for all of your outbound calls. You have another gateway that you prefer to use for seven-digit local calls, so you configure the route pattern XXX XXXX on it. But when you dial 555 1212, your calls route out the first gateway. What is happening?

From your point of view, you configured the route patterns in Table 2-25.

Table 2-25   *Closest Matching and the @ Wildcard, User-Configured Patterns*

Route Pattern	Selected Destination
@	Gateway 1
XXX XXXX	Gateway 2

The specific route pattern XXX XXXX definitely appears to match fewer route patterns than the @ pattern. However, CallManager interprets @ as a macro expansion and actually treats your configuration as shown in Table 2-26.

Table 2-26   *Closest Matching and the @ Wildcard, CallManager-Expanded Patterns*

Route Pattern	Selected Destination
[2-9]11	Gateway 1
[2-9]XX XXXX	Gateway 1
1 [2-9]XX [2-9]XX XXXX	Gateway 1
011 3[0-469] !	Gateway 1
XXX XXXX	Gateway 2

When a user dials 555 1212, both [2-9]XX XXXX and XXX XXXX match. [2-9]XX XXXX is the more specific, and thus the call routes to gateway 1.

To avoid this situation, when you configure route patterns that you want to take precedence over the @ pattern, either be as specific as possible in describing your route patterns, or preferably, use route filters (described in the section "Route Filters").

. Wildcard

The . wildcard is unlike other wildcards in that it does not match digits at all. Rather, the call routing component uses the . wildcard to fulfill its secondary responsibility of address translation.

The . wildcard functions solely as a delimiter. When it appears in a route pattern, it divides the dial string into PreDot and PostDot sections. This has no effect on what digit strings the route pattern matches. Rather, you use the . wildcard in conjunction with *digit discarding instructions*.

Digit discarding instructions are one way to tell the call routing component which dialed digits should be kept before the call is offered to the selected device. Most digit discarding instructions can be used only in conjunction with route patterns that contain the @ wildcard. However, some digit discarding instructions rely on the PreDot section that the . wildcard defines. Further details about digit discarding instructions (and other transformations) are in the section "Digit Discarding Instructions."

Route Filters

As described, the @ wildcard is an all-or-nothing affair. When present, it matches all of the valid numbers for the national numbering plan specified, even those you would prefer your users did not dial.

Route filters are the mechanism by which you can cause CallManager to add only a subset of the route patterns for a given numbering plan. For example, using route filters, you can cause an @ pattern to match only the national emergency numbers. You can also use route filters to distinguish local calls from long distance calls or to limit access to toll services.

Route filters are a test that CallManager applies to individual route patterns in a numbering plan included by the @ wildcard. CallManager examines each valid route pattern in the numbering plan and applies the test. If a particular route pattern passes the test, CallManager adds it into its routing tables, and users are able to dial numbers that match the route pattern. If a particular route pattern fails the test, CallManager skips over it, and users are unable to dial numbers that match the route pattern. Route filters work by allowing CallManager to add only the subset of a numbering plan whose *tags* fulfill the constraints that *operators* impose.

Route Filter Length Limitation

The maximum length of the route filter, written out as a textual expression and not including any tags with values of NOT-SELECTED, must not exceed 1024 characters. If you need a more complicated route filter, you can usually split the route filter across several route patterns. For instance, suppose you need to define the route pattern 9.@ and apply a route filter that includes emergency calls, calls to information services, international calls, and calls to a variety of specific area codes. The total length of the filter required, however, exceeds the 1024-character limit.

Route filters of this length consist of several clauses connected by the OR operator. To resolve this problem, break the route filter up into several route filters where different clauses of the long route filter are joined by the OR operator. Then associate the smaller route filters with the duplicate copies of the route pattern.

For instance, the example filter describes emergency calls *or* calls to information services *or* international calls *or* calls to a variety of specific area codes. You can break up the lengthy clause by defining one 9.@ with a route filter for emergency calls, another 9.@ with a route filter for information services, another 9.@ with a route filter for international calls, and other 9.@ route patterns with route filters for the specific area codes. Because each route filter selects a different subset of the numbering plan, it is perfectly fine to reuse the same route pattern multiple times.

Tags

Tags are named substrings of individual route patterns for a given national numbering plan.

For instance, the route pattern 1 [2-9]XX [2-9]XX XXXX exists in the North American numbering plan. It is composed of four sections. The first section, 1, denotes the call as a toll call. The second section matches an area code. The office code and the subscriber follow. The numbering plan file for the North American numbering plan encodes this knowledge as the tags LONG-DISTANCE-DIRECT-DIAL, AREA-CODE, OFFICE-CODE, and SUBSCRIBER. In contrast, the route pattern [2-9]XX XXXX contains only the OFFICE-CODE and SUBSCRIBER tags.

Table 2-27 shows the tags that the North American numbering plan contains, and it provides representative digit strings for each tag. Bold type in Table 2-27 indicates the section of the example number that corresponds to the listed tag.

Table 2-27   *Tags in the North American Numbering Plan*

Tag Name	Example Number	Description
AREA-CODE	1 **214** 555 1212	The area code in an 11-digit long distance call
COUNTRY-CODE	01 1 **33** 1234567890 #	The country code in an international call
END-OF-DIALING	01 1 33 1234567890 **#**	The #, which ends interdigit timeout in international calls
INTERNATIONAL-ACCESS	**01** 1 33 1234567890 #	The initial 01 of an international call
INTERNATIONAL-OPERATOR	01 **0**	The digit that denotes the operator component of an international call
LOCAL-AREA-CODE	**214** 555 1212	The area code in a 10-digit local call
LOCAL-DIRECT-DIAL	**1** 555 1212	The initial 1 some seven-digit calls require
LOCAL-OPERATOR	**0** 555 1212	The initial 0 some operator-assisted seven-digit calls require

Table 2-27 *Tags in the North American Numbering Plan (Continued)*

Tag Name	Example Number	Description
LONG-DISTANCE-DIRECT-DIAL	**1** 214 555 1212	The initial 1 required for long distance direct-dial calls
LONG-DISTANCE-OPERATOR	**0** 214 555 1212	The initial 0 required for operator-assisted long distance calls
NATIONAL-NUMBER	01 1 33 **1234567890** #	The national number component of an international call
OFFICE-CODE	1 214 **555** 1212	The office or exchange code of a North American call
SATELLITE-SERVICE	01 1 881 **4** 1234 #	A specific value associated with calls to the satellite country code
SERVICE	1 **411**	Access to local telephony provider services
SUBSCRIBER	1 214 555 **1212**	A particular extension a given exchange serves
TRANSIT-NETWORK-ESCAPE	**101** 0321 1 214 555 1212	Long distance carrier code
TRANSIT-NETWORK	101 **0321** 1 214 555 1212	The escape sequence used for entering a long distance carrier code

Operators

Operators are the functions that determine whether a given route pattern passes the tests you specify.

There are four operators:

- <tag> EXISTS, whose test is passed if the route pattern under inspection contains the specified tag.

- <tag> DOES-NOT-EXIST, whose test is passed if the route pattern under inspection does not contain the specified tag.

- <tag> == <value>, whose test is met if 1) the route pattern under inspection contains the tag and 2) a nonempty intersection exists for the set of route patterns that the pattern expression in <value> matches and the set of route patterns that the pattern expression associated with tag matches.

- <tag> NOT-SELECTED, whose test is passed under all conditions. The NOT-SELECTED operator is a value that exists only in CallManager Administration to represent that you have not selected an operator for a particular tag. It simply means "none of the above."

An example might help clarify the tortured description of the == operator. One route pattern defined in the North American numbering plan is [2-9]XX XXXX (see Figure 2-5). This pattern consists of an office code and a subscriber. The first section of the route pattern, [2-9]XX, corresponds to the tag OFFICE-CODE.

Figure 2-5 *Pattern [2-9]XX XXXX in the North American Numbering Plan*

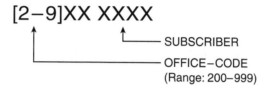

Assume that you specify OFFICE-CODE == [1-3]XX in a route filter. When determining whether to add the pattern [2-9]XX XXXX into the routing tables, CallManager intersects the route pattern [2-9]XX from the numbering plan with the route pattern [1-3]XX in the route filter. [2-9]XX matches all dialed digit strings in the range 200–999, while route pattern [1-3]XX matches all dialed digit strings in the range 100–399. The intersection of these sets is all dialed digit strings in the range 200–399. As a result, CallManager determines that the route pattern under inspection matches the filter's test. It inserts into the internal routing tables the route pattern that represents the intersection of the value you specified and the entry in the numbering plan, namely, [23]XX XXXX. Figure 2-6 depicts the application of the route filter.

You can string operators together with the Boolean operators AND and OR. When you string operators together with OR, CallManager includes a route pattern under inspection if either of the specified conditions exist. When you string operators together with AND, CallManager includes a route pattern under inspection only if both of the specified conditions exist.

For example, the route filter AREA-CODE EXISTS OR SERVICE EXISTS causes CallManager to include both the route pattern [2-9]11, which matches information and emergency services in the North American numbering plan, and the route pattern 1 [2-9]XX [2-9]XX XXXX, which matches long distance toll calls in the North American numbering plan. [2-9]11 contains the SERVICE tag, and 1 [2-9]XX [2-9]XX XXXX contains the AREA-CODE tag.

However, the route filter AREA-CODE EXISTS AND SERVICE EXISTS causes CallManager to include absolutely no route patterns, because no number in the North American numbering plan has both an area code and a service number.

Figure 2-6 *Intersection of Two Pattern Ranges Because of a Route Filter*

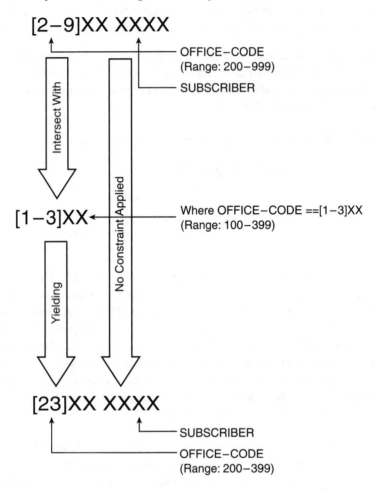

Route Filter Operation

When an @ pattern has an associated filter, the filter affects the macro expansion that takes place. Before adding an individual route pattern from the numbering plan to the system, CallManager checks to see whether that particular route pattern passes the tests specified in the route filter. If the route pattern does not qualify, CallManager will not add it, which means that users cannot dial it.

It is important to note that route filters in themselves do not explicitly block calls. They tell CallManager not which patterns to exclude but which patterns to include. A route filter that specifies AREA-CODE == 900 does not eliminate calls to area code 900 (reserved for toll services in the United States); rather, it tells CallManager to include only those route patterns in the North American numbering plan where the area code is 900. In other words, it configures the system so that toll-number calls are the only destination users can dial. (You can block these numbers. See the section "Routing by Class of Calling User" for details.)

The best way to see how route filters operate is to look at some examples. For instructive purposes, these examples use the North American numbering plan and assume that the @ pattern expands only to the route patterns in Table 2-28.

Table 2-28 *Route Patterns Used for Route Filter Example*

Route Pattern	Description	Tags
[2-9]11	311, 411, 611, 911	SERVICE
[2-9]XX XXXX	Seven-digit dialing	OFFICE-CODE SUBSCRIBER
[2-9]XX [2-9]XX XXXX	10-digit dialing	LOCAL-AREA-CODE OFFICE-CODE SUBSCRIBER
1 [2-9]XX [2-9]XX XXXX	11-digit dialing	LONG-DISTANCE-DIRECT-DIAL AREA-CODE OFFICE-CODE SUBSCRIBER
01 1 3[0-469] !	International dialing to valid two-digit country codes in the range 30–39	INTERNATIONAL-ACCESS INTERNATIONAL-DIRECT-DIAL COUNTRY-CODE NATIONAL-NUMBER

If you specify the route pattern 9.@ with no route filter, CallManager indiscriminately adds each route pattern in Table 2-28, preceded by 9. Thus, users can dial 9 911 and 9 555 1212, as well as 9 1 900 555 1212. Table 2-29 lists the route patterns that CallManager adds.

Table 2-29 *Route Patterns Added When No Route Filter Is Specified*

Added Route Patterns	Tags in the Route Pattern
9 [2-9]11	SERVICE
9 [2-9]XX XXXX	OFFICE-CODE, SUBSCRIBER
9 [2-9]XX [2-9]XX XXXX	LOCAL-AREA-CODE, OFFICE-CODE, SUBSCRIBER

Table 2-29   *Route Patterns Added When No Route Filter Is Specified (Continued)*

Added Route Patterns	Tags in the Route Pattern
9 1 [2-9]XX [2-9]XX XXXX	LONG-DISTANCE-DIRECT-DIAL, AREA-CODE, OFFICE-CODE, SUBSCRIBER
9 011 3[0-469] !	INTERNATIONAL-ACCESS, INTERNATIONAL-DIRECT-DIAL, COUNTRY-CODE, NATIONAL-NUMBER

If instead, you add the same route pattern but use a route filter that specifies SERVICE EXISTS, CallManager adds only those route patterns that contain the SERVICE tag. (In North America, the SERVICE tag matches numbers such as 411 for directory information and 911 for emergency services.) Your users can access network services but no other numbers. Table 2-30 lists the added route patterns.

Table 2-30   *Route Patterns Added for the Route Filter SERVICE EXISTS*

Accepted Route Patterns (Contain SERVICE Tag)	Tags in the Route Pattern
9 [2-9]11	SERVICE
Rejected Route Patterns	**Tags in the Route Pattern**
9 [2-9]XX XXXX	OFFICE-CODE, SUBSCRIBER
9 [2-9]XX [2-9]XX XXXX	LOCAL-AREA-CODE, OFFICE-CODE, SUBSCRIBER
9 1 [2-9]XX [2-9]XX XXXX	LONG-DISTANCE-DIRECT-DIAL, AREA-CODE, OFFICE-CODE, SUBSCRIBER
9 011 3[0-469] !	INTERNATIONAL-ACCESS, INTERNATIONAL-DIRECT-DIAL, COUNTRY-CODE, NATIONAL-NUMBER

The route filter COUNTRY-CODE DOES-NOT-EXIST eliminates the international dialing route pattern. Users can access network services and local and long distance numbers. Table 2-31 lists the added route patterns.

Table 2-31   *Route Patterns Added for the Route Filter COUNTRY-CODE DOES-NOT-EXIST*

Accepted Route Patterns (Lack COUNTRY-CODE Tag)	Tags in the Route Pattern
9 [2-9]11	SERVICE
9 [2-9]XX XXXX	OFFICE-CODE, SUBSCRIBER
9 [2-9]XX [2-9]XX XXXX	LOCAL-AREA-CODE, OFFICE-CODE, SUBSCRIBER
9 1 [2-9]XX [2-9]XX XXXX	LONG-DISTANCE-DIRECT-DIAL, AREA-CODE, OFFICE-CODE, SUBSCRIBER

Table 2-31 *Route Patterns Added for the Route Filter COUNTRY-CODE DOES-NOT-EXIST (Continued)*

Rejected Route Patterns	Tags in the Route Pattern
9 011 3[0-469] !	INTERNATIONAL-ACCESS, INTERNATIONAL-DIRECT-DIAL, COUNTRY-CODE, NATIONAL-NUMBER

The route filter AREA-CODE == [89]00 OR AREA-CODE == 888 OR AREA-CODE == 877 demonstrates the way in which the equal operator can constrain a route pattern. This filter allows users to dial 11-digit numbers to the toll-free ranges 800, 877, or 888 and to the toll-range 900. Table 2-32 lists the added route patterns.

Table 2-32 *Route Patterns Added for the Route Filter AREA-CODE == [89]00 OR AREA-CODE == 888 OR AREA-CODE == 877*

Added Route Patterns (Contain AREA-CODE Tag, Constrained to Specified Ranges)	Tags in the Route Pattern
9 1 **[89]00** [2-9]XX XXXX	LONG-DISTANCE-DIRECT-DIAL, AREA-CODE, OFFICE-CODE, SUBSCRIBER
9 1 **888** [2-9]XX XXXX	LONG-DISTANCE-DIRECT-DIAL, AREA-CODE, OFFICE-CODE, SUBSCRIBER
9 1 **877** [2-9]XX XXXX	LONG-DISTANCE-DIRECT-DIAL, AREA-CODE, OFFICE-CODE, SUBSCRIBER
Filtered Route Patterns (Lack AREA-CODE Tag)	**Tags in the Route Pattern**
9 [2-9]11	SERVICE
9 [2-9]XX XXXX	OFFICE-CODE, SUBSCRIBER
9 [2-9]XX [2-9]XX XXXX	LOCAL-AREA-CODE, OFFICE-CODE, SUBSCRIBER
9 011 3[0-469] !	INTERNATIONAL-ACCESS, INTERNATIONAL-DIRECT-DIAL, COUNTRY-CODE, NATIONAL-NUMBER

The bold type in the above table shows that the values specified on the equals operator have constrained the area code substring of the North American numbering plan to a particular range. In each case, the generalized substring [2-9]XX, which matches any digit string between 200 and 999, has been modified so that it matches only the intersection between the substring and value specified in the route filter.

Useful Route Filters for the North American Numbering Plan

This section presents some route filter configurations for the North American numbering plan that you might find useful.

It describes how to use route filters to do the following:

■ Block calls where the user has selected a long distance carrier

■ Block international calls

■ Route just local numbers

■ Route just toll-free numbers

■ Eliminate interdigit timing between 7-digit and 10-digit route patterns

■ Block 900 numbers

Block Calls Where the User Has Selected a Long Distance Carrier

In North America, users can select a long distance carrier by dialing at the beginning of their number the digits 101 followed by a four-digit carrier code. CallManager digit discarding instructions (see the section "Digit Discarding Instructions") call this type of dialing 10-10-Dialing.

On the North American numbering plan Route Filter page, the tag TRANSIT-NETWORK-ESCAPE filters numbers in which the user has included the 101 carrier selection digits. Configuring a route filter with the value TRANSIT-NETWORK-ESCAPE DOES-NOT-EXIST blocks calls that include the carrier selection code.

The difference between configuring a route filter to block long distance carrier selection and using the digit discarding instructions **10-10-Dialing** is that the route filter blocks a user's call attempt if the user dials the carrier selection code, while the digit discarding instructions permit the call to go through but silently strip out the carrier selection portion of the dialed number.

Block International Calls

You can block international calls with the route filter INTERNATIONAL-ACCESS DOES-NOT-EXIST. In the North American numbering plan file, the tag INTERNATIONAL-ACCESS corresponds to the initial 01 of international dialed calls. By specifying a route filter that prevents CallManager from including route patterns beginning with this tag, you prevent CallManager from matching any numbers beginning with 01. You block international calls by never adding them in the first place.

Route Just Local Numbers

Routing just local numbers typically requires stringing together several route filter clauses joined by OR.

Local calls can vary dramatically by geographical region. Some regions have 7-digit local calls, some metropolitan regions have a mixture of 7- and 10-digit local calls, and other regions have 10-digit local calls.

Seven-Digit Dialing

If your region has seven-digit dialing and you want to permit users to dial *only* seven-digit numbers, defining the route filter SERVICE DOES-NOT-EXIST AND LOCAL-AREA-CODE DOES-NOT-EXIST AND AREA-CODE DOES-NOT-EXIST AND INTERNATIONAL-ACCESS DOES-NOT-EXIST should suffice. Filtering against SERVICE DOES-NOT-EXIST blocks calls to information and emergency services, LOCAL-AREA-CODE blocks 10-digit calls, AREA-CODE DOES-NOT-EXIST blocks 11-digit long distance calls, and INTERNATIONAL-ACCESS blocks international calls.

If you want to, say, permit calls to services, long distance calls, or international calls, you simply exclude the appropriate operator expression from the proposed route filter.

The LOCAL-AREA-CODE section of the defined route filter deserves some more explanation. You might have noticed that in some cases, a proposed route filter uses the tag AREA-CODE and in other cases it uses the tag LOCAL-AREA-CODE. The tag LOCAL-AREA-CODE represents the area code as it appears in 10-digit numbers.

Some metropolitan regions of North America require users to dial 10 digits for all of their local calls. This means that CallManager must include both 7-digit patterns and 10-digit patterns in its expansion of the North American numbering plan, because you can deploy CallManager in different geographic regions. Because of CallManager's analysis process, however, unless you explicitly exclude the 10-digit pattern when you are in a 7-digit dialing region, CallManager will wait for the interdigit timer to expire before offering your 7-digit calls to the PSTN.

On the other hand, the AREA-CODE tag represents the area code as it appears in 11-digit numbers (typically direct-dial and calling-card long distance calls) in the North American numbering plan. Using two different tag names for essentially the same subsection of a North American number assists those administrators in 10-digit dialing regions who want to permit 10-digit local calls while blocking 11-digit toll calls. By specifying the filter AREA-CODE DOES-NOT-EXIST, such administrators can screen out all of the toll calls while leaving the 10-digit calls untouched. The section "Eliminate Interdigit Timing Between 7-Digit and 10-Digit Patterns" expands on this wrinkle of CallManager's North American numbering plan.

Metro Dialing

Some geographical regions have metro dialing. In metro dialing, a user in a home area code needs to dial only 7 digits, but a few neighboring area codes, also local calls, require the user to dial 10 digits. Metro dialing is typically the most problematic, because some 11-digit calls might actually be local calls, while some 10-digit calls might be toll calls. In such cases, you might need to specify criteria down to the office code level to provide full local access. (Another approach is to define an @ pattern to perform general filtering and to define separate specific patterns, such as 972 813 XXXX, to handle the exceptional cases.)

If your region has metro dialing, define a route filter in which one clause specifies seven-digit dialing and subsequent clauses define the nontoll area codes on an area-code-by-area-code basis. For instance, in the Dallas-Fort Worth area in 1995, the following route filter would provide general metro dialing access from the point of view of a user in the 972 area code:

> LOCAL-AREA-CODE DOES-NOT-EXIST AND AREA-CODE DOES-NOT-EXIST AND INTERNATIONAL-ACCESS DOES-NOT-EXIST
>
> OR
>
> LOCAL-AREA-CODE == 214
>
> OR
>
> LOCAL-AREA-CODE == 817

Because the user in the 972 area code dials seven digits to call other numbers in the 972 area code, the first part of this route filter handles any seven-digit calls that the user in the 972 area code dials. The second part of this route filter handles 10-digit calls starting with 214 that the user dials, and the third part of this route filter handles 10-digit calls starting with 817 that the user dials.

You can add exceptional cases as additional clauses or as separate route patterns.

Note especially the use of the tag LOCAL-AREA-CODE. The LOCAL-AREA-CODE tag represents an area code as dialed as part of a 10-digit North American number (for example, 214 555 1212). The same area code in an 11-digit North American number (0 214 555 1212 and 1 214 555 1212) corresponds to the tag AREA-CODE.

10-Digit Dialing

A 10-digit dialing route filter is like a metro dialing routing filter, but you need not include the route filter for 7-digit dialing. For instance, in the Dallas-Fort Worth area in 2000, the following route filter provides general 10-digit dialing access:

> LOCAL-AREA-CODE == 214
>
> OR
>
> LOCAL-AREA-CODE == 817

OR

LOCAL-AREA-CODE == 972

OR

LOCAL-AREA-CODE == 940

Again, you can add exceptional cases (11-digit local calls) as additional clauses or as separate route patterns.

Route Toll-Free Numbers

In the North American numbering plan, area codes 800, 866, 877, and 888 are dedicated to toll-free numbers. The following route filter provides access to only these services:

AREA-CODE == 800

OR

AREA-CODE == 877

OR

AREA-CODE == 888

Eliminate Interdigit Timing Between 7-Digit and 10-Digit Patterns

Because some geographical regions use 7-digit dialing and others use 10-digit dialing, the North American numbering plan shipped with CallManager must accommodate both types of dialing. Furthermore, because the IP network permits stations homed to a particular CallManager to be in different geographical locations, CallManager must be able to support both types of dialing simultaneously.

As a result, the North American numbering plan shipped with CallManager includes both route patterns [2-9]XX XXXX and [2-9]XX [2-9]XX XXXX. The problem that occurs is with the 10-digit route pattern in place, users of the 7-digit pattern must wait for the interdigit timeout to expire before CallManager routes their 7-digit calls.

Eliminating the interdigit timeout means configuring CallManager to eliminate the 10-digit route pattern for users of 7-digit dialing. Configure the route filter LOCAL-AREA-CODE DOES-NOT-EXIST to eliminate the [2-9]XX [2-9]XX XXXX pattern from the list of patterns in the North American numbering plan and associate it with your @ pattern.

> **NOTE** Actually, the route pattern set that CallManager uses to implement 7- and 10-digit patterns in the North American numbering plan is rather more complex. CallManager represents 7- and 10- digit patterns using 4 patterns:
>
> - [2-9][02-9]X XXXX
>
> - [2-9]X[02-9] XXXX
>
> - [2-9][02-9]X [2-9]XX XXXX
>
> - [2-9]X[0-29] [2-9]XX XXXX
>
> The patterns are constructed in this matter in order not to create overlap between service patterns such as [2-9]11. A digit string such as 911 doesn't match patterns 1 or 3, because the second wildcard in these patterns doesn't match the second 1 in the digit string, and 911 doesn't match patterns 2 or 4 because the third wildcard in these patterns doesn't match the third 1 in the digit string.
>
> But the simpler patterns [2-9]XX XXXX and [2-9]XX XXX XXXX demonstrate the principles that this section is communicating without complicating the issue with the addition of more confusing patterns.
>
> You can discover exactly what patterns CallManager loads for any given dial plan by inspecting the files stored in the dialPlans subdirectory of the CallManager installation directory.

Block 900 Numbers

The previous route filters in this section operate by using inclusion. That is, the clauses provided define a subset of the North American numbering plan that includes only those patterns that you want to be routed and excludes those patterns you want to block.

As long as the restrictions placed use the EXISTS or DOES-NOT-EXIST operators, you can use one route filter to define which patterns should be routed. EXISTS specifies that CallManager should route all valid number ranges for a particular tag, while DOES-NOT-EXIST specifies that CallManager should route no valid number ranges for a particular tag.

When you need to specify only *some* of the valid number ranges for a particular tag, use the == operator. However, CallManager does not support a != (not-equals) operator. As a result, although you can specify a route filter such as AREA-CODE == 900, rather than blocking 900 numbers, this filter routes 900 numbers and blocks all other types of calls.

However, you can still block 900 numbers with the use of two route patterns. First, configure an @-pattern with the route filter AREA-CODE == 900. On the route pattern, however, click the radio button Block This Pattern. This configuration specifies that CallManager should block all external calls with area code 900.

To make all non-900-numbers route, configure another @-pattern with no route filter at all. Using closest match routing rules (see the section "Example 2: Closest Match Routing"), if a user dials a dialed digit string containing an area code of 900, the route pattern with the route filter AREA-CODE == 900 matches, which causes CallManager to block the call. Because an external call to another area code matches only the unfiltered pattern, CallManager routes the call.

An example can best illustrate the process that occurs. Table 2-33 shows a representative sample of route patterns that CallManager adds when you specify the route pattern 9.@.

Table 2-33 *Sample Route Patterns Added By 9.@*

Route Pattern	Description
9 [2-9]11	Services (311, 411, 611, 911)
9 [2-9]XX XXXX	Seven-digit dialing
9 1 [2-9]XX [2-9]XX XXXX	11-digit dialing
9 011 3[0-469] !	International calls to the valid two-digit country codes in the range 30–39

When you specify the route filter, AREA-CODE == 900, CallManager includes only those route patterns that have an area code tag. Furthermore, CallManager constrains the route pattern so that the tag can match the number 900 (see Table 2-34).

Table 2-34 *Route Pattern Added by 9.@ Where AREA-CODE == 900*

Route Pattern	Description
9 1 900 [2-9]XX XXXX	11-digit dialing to the 900 area code

When you add both route patterns and specify that CallManager should route calls to 9.@ but block calls to 9.@ where AREA-CODE == 900, the routing tables appear as displayed in Table 2-35.

Table 2-35 *Combined Routing Tables*

Route Pattern	Treatment
9 [2-9]11	Route this pattern
9 [2-9]XX XXXX	Route this pattern
9 1 [2-9]XX [2-9]XX XXXX	Route this pattern
9 011 3[0-469] !	Route this pattern
9 1 900 [2-9]XX XXXX	Block this pattern

If a user dials 911 or a seven-digit number, it is evident that CallManager routes the call. When a user dials an 11-digit number, however, closest match routing rules ensure that the user's call is handled properly. Table 2-36 shows that when a user dials 9 1 214 555 1212, CallManager finds a unique match for the 9.@ route pattern and routes the call.

Table 2-36   *Routing Treatment for Number 9 1 214 555 1212*

Currently Dialed Digits: 9 1 214 555 1212	
Current Matches	
9 1 [2-9]XX [2-9]XX XXXX	Route this pattern
Patterns That Can Still Match	
<None>	
Patterns That Can No Longer Match	
9 [2-9]11	
9 [2-9]XX XXXX	
9 011 3[0-469].!	
9 1 900 [2-9]XX XXXX	
Actions Taken: <None>	

When a user dials 9 1 900 555 1212, on the other hand, CallManager finds two matching route patterns in the routing tables, uses closest match routing rules to select between them, and then applies the appropriate treatment. Table 2-37 shows CallManager selecting the blocked route pattern 9.@ where AREA-CODE == 900 over the more generic route pattern 9.@. As a result, CallManager rejects calls to 900 numbers.

Table 2-37   *Routing Treatment for Number 9 1 900 555 1212*

Currently Dialed Digits: 9 1 900 555 1212	
Current Matches	
9 1 900 [2-9]XX XXXX	Block this pattern Selected: Matches 8,000,000 numbers
9 1 [2-9]XX [2-9]XX XXXX	Route this pattern Not selected: Matches 6,400,000,000 numbers
Patterns That Can Still Match	
<None>	
Patterns That Can No Longer Match	
9 [2-9]11	
9 [2-9]XX XXXX	
9 011 3[0-469].!	
Actions Taken: <None>	

This strategy of configuring a general route pattern to allow most calls through, but then configuring specific route patterns with blocking treatment to screen a very specific small set of calls, recurs often in enterprise deployments.

Dialing Transformations

Dialing transformations allow the call routing component to modify either the calling number or the dialed digits of a call. Transformations that modify the calling number are calling party transformations, while those that modify the dialed digits are called party transformations.

Translation Patterns Versus Dialing Transformations

CallManager also uses a concept called *translation patterns* (described in section "Translation Patterns"), and indeed, translation patterns rely heavily on dialing transformations to operate. But translation patterns and dialing transformations are separate concepts. Dialing transformations is a generic concept that refers to any setting in CallManager that can change the calling number or dialed digits. Dialing transformations appear not only on the Translation Pattern Configuration page, but also on the Route Pattern Configuration page, numerous gateway configuration pages, and in service parameters.

Calling party transformations affect the calling number but not the calling name of a call. For example, when one Cisco IP Phone calls another, normally the called phone sees two pieces of information: the directory number of the calling phone and the any display name that you have entered on the Directory Number Configuration page for the calling phone. Figure 2-7 depicts the display of a Cisco IP Phone that is receiving a call.

The Display (Internal Caller ID) field in the Directory Number Configuration page has limited scope. When a user places a call, CallManager provides this name to all ringing devices for station-to-station calls within the cluster. While all stations are ringing, CallManager displays the contents of the Alerting Name field on the caller's station, but when a ringing device answers, CallManager ensures that this name is displayed on the caller's IP phone.

When a call leaves the private network, there is often no provision in the network protocol to provide calling party name information to the PSTN or alerting and connected name information from the PSTN to the caller. Some protocols, notably QSIG and DMS versions of Primary Rate Interface (PRI), however, do provide for transmission of the calling number, the connected number, the calling name, the alerting name, and the connected name, and CallManager transmits this information whenever the protocol permits.

Figure 2-7 *Calling Number and Name During Call Presentation*

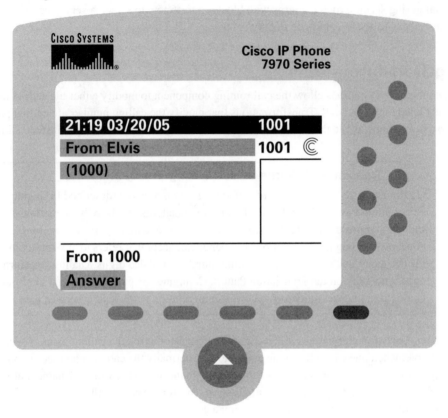

You usually need calling party transformations only for display purposes. For instance, enterprises very commonly require that the central switchboard number for an organization be provided as the calling number for all external calls. Even when you want to actually transmit the calling party's *direct inward dial* (DID) number, however, you still must configure some sort of calling party transformation. The PSTN usually wants to see the number of the calling user's address *from the PSTN's point of view* rather than the internal directory number you have assigned your user; unless the internal directory numbers are fully qualified PSTN numbers, a transformation is needed to adapt to the PSTN's expected numbering scheme. Calling party transformations are not limited to calls to the PSTN, though. If you so choose, you can apply them to calls between your users.

Called party transformations modify the digits the calling user actually dials. Strictly speaking, they do not affect which destination CallManager selects because the selection is based on the digits that the calling user dials, not the transformed called number; however, the transformed called number is often reanalyzed by translation patterns or by other systems to subsequently route the call.

The transformation just modifies those digits before CallManager sends them to a selected device. However, if the selected device looks at the dialed digits to further route the call, the transformation can indeed affect which device ultimately receives the call. This sort of steering occurs most often when CallManager offers a call with a modified called number to a gateway connected to an adjacent network.

This section discusses the transformations permitted at different stages of the transformation process. It covers the following topics:

- "When CallManager Can Apply Dialing Transformations" discusses five opportunities during the call routing process that CallManager has to apply dialing transformations.

- "About Device Types That CallManager Supports" provides an overview of the types of station and trunk devices that CallManager supports, because routing settings are often particular to only certain types of devices.

- "About Masks" discusses masking, an operation that commonly occurs during many stages of the call routing process.

- "About Name and Line Presentation" discusses the options CallManager provides for keeping the names and numbers of callers and called parties private from each other.

- "Dialing Transformation-Related Service Parameters" discusses some CallManager service parameters that relate to calling and called party transformations. The transformations these settings provide are somewhat inconsistent. Some apply to inbound calls, while others apply to outbound calls. Most settings take effect for only some of the devices that CallManager supports.

- "Transformations on the Originating Device" discusses the first opportunity that CallManager has to transform calling and called numbers, at the point where CallManager first receives a call. These transformations are highly device-dependent.

- "Transformations in Translation Patterns, Route Patterns, and Route Lists" discusses the second, third, and fourth opportunities where CallManager can transform calling and called numbers. These transformations are very regular, and thus, this section can discuss them as a group.

- "Transformations on the Terminating Device" discusses the fifth and final opportunity where CallManager can transform calling and called numbers, just before CallManager offers the call to the destination. Just like the transformation on the originating device, transformations on the terminating device are highly device-dependent.

When CallManager Can Apply Dialing Transformations

Calling and called party transformations can occur in five stages during CallManager's routing process. These stages occur in order, although not all of them need to occur. For instance, if the number that the user dials does not correspond to a translation pattern or route list, no translation-pattern-based or route-list-based transformations occur. The five stages, in order, are as follows:

1. At the originating device

2. As part of translation pattern

3. As part a route pattern

4. As part of a route list's operation

5. At the terminating device

A Detour to Discuss the Stages of Call Routing

To fully understand the stages of call routing means understanding a little of what goes on in the internal logic of CallManager. CallManager consists of a large number of independent logical components that interact in a complex manner. Each logical component has very limited responsibilities to reduce the complexity of any individual component. For example, to each Cisco IP Phone, CallManager assigns one component whose responsibility is to serve as a control point for actions (going off-hook, pressing buttons, and so on) that a user performs. But when a Cisco IP Phone places a call, CallManager dynamically creates a component that understands how to perform the functions of a call. Other components handle the high-level concepts of "call transfer" or "two-party call" or "route pattern lookup." To process a simple station-to-station call, CallManager passes messages among at least 40 components.

When this section talks about a transformation occurring at the originating device, it does not mean that the physical device itself or even the software embedded within it is applying a dialing transformation. Rather, it means that the logical component in CallManager that represents the originating device is applying a dialing transformation.

This is not to say that devices themselves never have call routing capabilities of their own. Cisco IOS gateways, in particular, have very robust dialing transformation capabilities, but those capabilities are outside the scope of this book.

First, CallManager settings for the originating device can modify the dialed digits before control of the call passes the digits to the call routing component. This process happens, for instance, when a call from the PSTN comes into CallManager. Depending on what digits the PSTN sends, you might find it necessary to convert the address from a PSTN address to a local directory number.

Second, if the destination selected is a translation pattern, CallManager applies the calling and called party transformations associated with the translation pattern to change the calling and called numbers. After CallManager applies the dialing transformation, digit analysis uses the resulting called number to select another destination. Sometimes, the transformed digits cause CallManager to match a new translation pattern. In such a case, CallManager applies the calling and called party transformations of the newly selected translation pattern to select a new destination. CallManager breaks such chains of translation patterns after ten iterations to prevent infinite routing loops. The section "Translation Patterns" contains further information about translation patterns.

The third opportunity that the call routing component has to apply dialing transformations is when the dialed digits match a route pattern or directory number. When the dialed digits select a route pattern, CallManager applies the calling and called party transformations configured on the Route Pattern Configuration page.

Fourth, after any translation patterns have been analyzed, if the destination is a route list (described in the section "Call Hunting Constructs"), CallManager applies any calling and called party transformations specified on the route between the route list and individual route groups within the route list. Unlike other transformations in this sequence, transformations on a route list *override* the ones that the route pattern or translation pattern applies. In all other cases, the changes that CallManager applies are cumulative. For instance, if CallManager prepends the digit 9 to a dialed number of 1000 at the originating device, and the terminating device subsequently prepends an 8, the resulting called number is 891000. On the other hand, if a called party transformation on the route pattern prepends the digit 9 to the dialed number 1000, but a called party transformation on the route between the route list and an individual route group prepends an 8, the resulting called number is 81000, not 981000. The settings on the route list's route group details undo the transformations that the route pattern applies. This behavior allows you to define transformations on a route pattern that are correct for most cases, but that you want to supersede for calls out particular route groups.

When you add calling and called party transformations to a route pattern or translation pattern, CallManager logs the transformed numbers in the CDRs and renders the transformed numbers on the display of the calling phone. CallManager does not insert transformations specified on the route list's route group details (or applied by an individual egress gateway) in the CDRs or render them on the calling device.

Fifth, CallManager can modify the calling and called parties just before handing the call to the associated device (such transformations exist exclusively on trunk devices).

Figure 2-8 shows a picture of the transformation process. A Cisco IP Phone places a call. When CallManager passes the call request to call control, CallManager modifies the digits according to any dialing transformations configured for the phone. If the digits provided match a translation pattern, CallManager applies the dialing transformations configured for the translation pattern. At some point, CallManager selects a destination and applies any dialing transformations configured for the route pattern or directory number selected. If a route list is the target of the call, CallManager applies any dialing transformations on specific routes selected. Finally, CallManager applies any dialing transformations configured on the terminating device. All of these opportunities to transform the calling number and called number means that they can differ quite dramatically by the time CallManager has routed a call.

Figure 2-8 *Locations Where Transformations Occur*

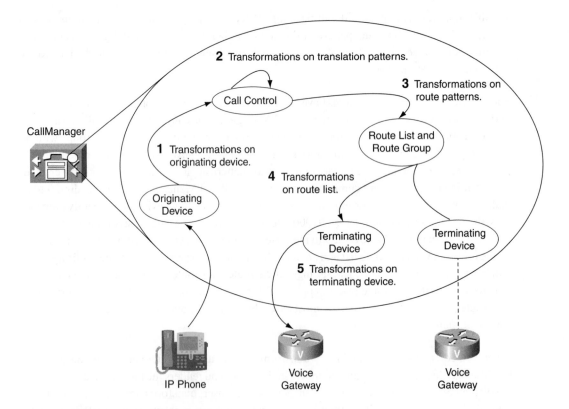

About Device Types That CallManager Supports

Although CallManager can transform the calling and called numbers at the originating and terminating devices, the dialing transformations available are often quite protocol-dependent. For instance, the dialing transformations that you can configure for an analog phone connected to the Cisco VG200, which uses the MGCP, are not the same as those that you can configure for the Cisco 2600 router, which uses the H.323 protocol.

Chapter 4, "Trunk Devices," and Chapter 3, "Station Devices," go into great detail about the specific gateway and station devices that CallManager supports.

About Masks

CallManager uses a common operation called *masking* throughout the transformation process, so it is worthwhile to discuss it before continuing.

Mask operations allow you to suppress leading digits, to change existing digits while leaving others unmodified, and to insert leading digits. A mask operation requires two pieces of information, the number to be masked and the mask itself.

In the mask operator, the number is overlaid by the mask, aligned so that the last character of the mask overlays the last digit of the number. Where the mask contains a digit, the mask's digit supersedes the number's digit. Where the mask contains an X, the corresponding digit of the number is used. And if the number is longer than the mask, the mask obscures the extra digits, as if the stencil were opaque at that point. Figure 2-9 shows some examples.

Figure 2-9   *Transformation Mask Operation*

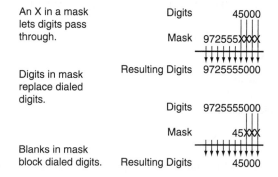

About Name and Line Presentation

Grouped among the calling and called party transformation settings are *presentation settings*. Strictly speaking, presentation settings do not modify the calling or called names or numbers but instead dictate whether the users involved in a call are permitted to view the calling or called name or number. Calling line ID presentation settings control whether the called party can view the caller's number or name and whether the destination party can view the forwarded party's numbers or names in call diversions. Connected line ID presentation settings control whether the calling party can view the number or name of the called party while the called party's phone is ringing or after it has answered.

Calling line ID presentation settings exist not only on route and translation patterns, but also on all trunk devices (including intercluster trunks, H.323 trunks, and SIP trunks), QSIG gateways, and MGCP gateways containing PRI trunks. H.323 gateways include the similar field Calling

Party Presentation. Valid values for the Calling line ID, Calling name ID, Connected line ID, and Connected name ID fields are Default, Allowed, and Restricted.

Name and line presentation is cumulative—the last node to apply a presentation setting to a call takes precedence. The settings Allowed and Restricted (whether on translation patterns, route patterns or directly on the gateways themselves) overwrite whatever presentation setting comes in; however, Default simply carries forward the current setting in the call. By default, calls from Cisco IP Phones allow presentation of calling name, calling line ID, connected name, and connected line ID, and the Default setting on a translation or route pattern carries these permissions forward unless you specifically override them (with a Restricted value on a route or translation pattern).

For instance, assume you have three CallManager clusters. A set of IP phones in the numbering range 1000 to 1999 is hosted by cluster 3, and route patterns are set up to route calls from other phones in cluster 1 through cluster 2 to cluster 3.

CallManager cluster 1 sets the following settings for route pattern 1XXX, which directs calls to cluster 3 via cluster 2:

- Calling name: Allowed

- Calling line: Allowed

- Connected name: Restricted

- Connected line: Restricted

CallManager cluster 2 sets the following settings in route pattern 1XXX, which directs inbound calls from cluster 1 to cluster 3:

- Calling name: Default

- Calling line: Default

- Connected name: Default

- Connected line: Default

CallManager cluster 3 sets the following settings for translation pattern 1XXX, which directs calls to directory numbers in cluster 3 in the range 1000 to 1999:

- Calling name: Restricted

- Calling line: Restricted

- Connected name: Allowed

- Connected line: Allowed

The number of the caller is presented to the called party in the initial call offering. As a result, the last calling presentation setting to take effect on the call is the setting in cluster 3. Thus, the caller's name and number are not presented to any phones in cluster 3 because the calling name and line presentation in cluster 3 is set to Restricted.

The number of the called party is presented to the caller in the initial ringing message and presented again when the called party answers. These messages start from the called party and head towards the caller. As a result, the last connected presentation setting to take effect on the call is the setting in cluster 1. Thus, the connected party's name and line are not presented to any phones in cluster 1, because the connected name and line presentation in cluster 1 is set to Restricted for calls the caller places in the 1000 to 1999 range.

On the Phone Configuration page, Cisco IP Phones also present a check box called Ignore Presentation Restriction (internal calls only). When checked, Cisco IP Phones always display the name and line, when they are available, of any party they're conversing with, even if the party has requested that the name or number be restricted. This setting is appropriate for authorized users such as hotel receptionists, because it allows you to otherwise configure calls between rooms as private calls while permitting the receptionist to see the identity of a calling room.

NOTE   The presentation restriction example in this section uses a multiple-cluster scenario because it most clearly illustrates the way that presentation indicators override each other. However, you can still use presentation indicators within a cluster through the use of translation patterns in conjunction with calling search spaces and partitions.

For example, assume that you're running a hotel and want prevent the name and number from being displayed on room-to-room calls. Assume that your room numbers consist of four-digit numbers in the range 1000 to 1999.

First, you would assign all room IP phones to a partition such as RoomPhones. In a traditional environment, each phone would include this partition in its own calling search space in order to permit direct calls between phones. However, in this case, you instead want room to room calls to first route through a translation pattern that forces the calling and connected names and line IDs to be restricted.

Therefore, you define pattern 1XXX in partition RoomToRoom and ensure that partition RoomToRoom is in the calling search space of all the room phones. On this translation pattern, you set the presentation indicators to Restricted and specify a calling search space that includes partition RoomPhones. When a room phone dials a number like 1010, CallManager matches the translation pattern 1XXX, marks the call with restriction indicators, and then re-offers the call to the phones in partition RoomPhones. Using the Ignore Presentation Restriction (internal calls only) flag, you could even permit certain phones in the RoomPhones partition to see the name and number of another calling phone, despite the restrictions that the translation pattern applies.

If this seems like gobbledygook, it is probably because this chapter has not yet discussed the calling search spaces and partitions concepts. See the section "Calling Search Spaces and Partitions" for more information.

Dialing Transformation-Related Service Parameters

Numerous CallManager settings related to call routing exist as service parameters.

When service parameters take effect for a particular gateway type, the settings apply to all gateways that your CallManager controls and not individual gateways. For instance, if you configure the Strip # Sign from Called Party Number service parameter, all gateways modify the dialed digits in accordance with the Strip # Sign from Called Party Number service parameter. The service parameter does not permit you to use the Strip # Sign from Called Party Number option for one particular gateway connected to CallManager while other gateways connected to CallManager ignore the service parameter.

Furthermore, CallManager service parameters related to routing do not always apply to all gateway protocols. The section "About Device Types That CallManager Supports" describes the device types that CallManager supports.

Service parameters are a vestige of the call routing settings that existed in the *scm.ini* file before release 3.0. Although CallManager 3.1 and later provides alternative ways to achieve the functions that most of these settings provide, these settings still are effective. Table 2-38 shows the list of routing-related service parameters and a checklist of which protocols for which the settings take effect.

Table 2-38   *Supported Service Parameter Dialing Transformations by Device Type*

Service Parameter Dialing Transformation	SCCP Station Devices	MGCP Station Devices	H.323 Station Devices	SCCP Trunk Devices	MGCP Trunk Devices	H.323 and SIP Trunk Devices
Calling Party Number Screening Indicator				✓		
Matching Calling Party Number With Attendant Flag				✓[2]	✓[2]	
Overlap Receiving Flag For PRI					✓[1]	
Strip # From Called Party Number				✓	✓	✓
Unknown Caller ID				✓	✓	✓
Unknown Caller ID Flag				✓	✓	✓
Unknown Caller ID Text				✓	✓	✓
Numbering Plan Info					✓[1]	
National Number Prefix					✓[1]	
International Number Prefix					✓[1]	
Subscriber Number Prefix					✓[1]	
Unknown Number Prefix					✓[1]	

[1]T1-PRI and E1-PRI interfaces only

[2]FXO interfaces only

Calling Party Number Screening Indicator

Calling Party Number Screening Indicator affects calls that CallManager routes out MGCP digital gateways. The setting allows you to specify the value of the screening indicator field in the calling party number information element of the Integrated Services Digital Network (ISDN) protocol. This element indicates to the attached ISDN network whether CallManager scrutinized the calling number it provides. Note that CallManager never actually screens the number. When calls are placed from Cisco IP Phones, CallManager always provides the calling number configured for the phone. When calls arrive at CallManager via trunk interfaces, these interfaces might provide a calling number. Setting the Calling Party Number Screening Indicator service parameter does not actually cause CallManager to compare such calling numbers against any of CallManager's configured destinations, but rather simply allows CallManager to spoof an appropriate setting for an attached network that might otherwise have a problem with an unscreened number.

Table 2-39 shows the values the setting takes, along with a description of the meaning that the ISDN protocol assigns to these settings.

Table 2-39 *Values of Calling Party Number Screening Indicator*

Value	Description
Calling number not screened	User provided, not screened: The user device provides the value in the calling number. The setting indicates that CallManager did not scrutinize it.
Calling number screened and passed	User provided, verified, and passed: The user device provides the value in the calling number. The setting indicates that CallManager has checked it against a list of acceptable numbers and declared it acceptable, although CallManager performs no such screening.
Calling number screened and failed	User provided, verified, and failed: The calling user device provides the value in the calling number. The setting indicates that CallManager has checked it against a list of acceptable numbers and that it is not valid. Again, CallManager doesn't actually perform screening; this setting simply affects what CallManager reports to the attached network.
CallManager provides calling number	Network provided: CallManager provides the calling number.
Default setting	Default: CallManager sets up its default value for the screening indicator—user provided, not screened.

Only change this setting if the attached ISDN network rejects your outbound calls because it finds the value of the screening indicator unacceptable. (Determining this fact requires detailed debugging of the trace file.) However, the value you set has no effect on the tasks CallManager actually performs in relation to the calling number. In other words, CallManager performs no actual screening and verification of the calling number. Rather, it simply changes the value of the ISDN field it provides to the ISDN network to provide flexibility in interworking with different varieties of ISDN.

Matching Calling Party Number With Attendant Flag

This setting provides a simple way to emulate the functionality of a small PBX or key system. Small PBXs typically associate inbound analog trunks on a one-for-one basis with user stations. The PBX offers incoming calls over an analog trunk to the corresponding station, and conversely, outbound calls from the station select the corresponding analog trunk. This allows a small business to provide internal users with unique external directory numbers but still to use low-cost analog loop start trunks.

An analog loop start trunk is just like the analog phone line that most people have at home. Analog loop start trunks have limited ability to communicate calling and called party information. When a user places a call from a private network to the PSTN, no way exists for the private network to indicate to the PSTN the public phone number of the calling user. Rather, the PSTN uses the number assigned to the loop start trunk as the calling number. Similarly, when the PSTN offers the call to the private network, the PSTN has no way to provide the actual digits the calling user dialed; rather, it assumes that the inbound call directly terminates on the appropriate phone.

This setting works with analog gateways running the Skinny Gateway Control Protocol and with Cisco MGCP gateways. The gateway setting Attendant DN described in the section "Attendant DN" automatically routes incoming calls from an analog trunk to the specified directory number. This behavior is exactly what is required to handle the trunk-to-station behavior of a small PBX.

The setting Matching Calling Party Number With Attendant Flag handles the station-to-trunk calls. When this value is set to True, CallManager makes sure that the trunk selected for a station's outbound call is the same as that it uses to handle the station's inbound calls. To perform this function, it routes the outbound call out the trunk whose Attendant DN is the directory number of the calling station.

This setting works best if you have a single gateway for external calls, because you can assign a single route pattern such as 9.@ to the gateway and ensure that CallManager presents all users' external calls to this gateway. If you have several gateways, to ensure that CallManager presents a given user's external call to the associated gateway, you need either to place all of your gateways in a route list (see the section "Call Hunting Constructs" for more information) or to use calling search spaces and partitions to route the calling user to the appropriate gateway (see the section "Calling Search Spaces and Partitions").

Overlap Receiving Flag for PRI

This value enables *overlapped receiving*. Many countries implement national numbering plans that use variable-length subscriber numbers. Complicated tables of area codes or city codes determine the actual length of a subscriber. Unless a telephone system intimately understands the country's numbering plan, efficiently giving calls to and receiving calls from such networks requires providing or receiving digits one at a time. Receiving digits one at a time from the network is called overlapped receiving. By default, overlapped receiving is enabled and the sending complete indicator is disabled.

If your route plan contains route patterns that begin with similar digit strings (for instance, 9XXX and 9XXXX), leaving overlapped receiving enabled can cause routing delays when CallManager receives calls over trunks that use these settings. Disable this capability by changing the Overlap Receiving Flag For PRI to False.

Strip # from Called Party Number

Administrators who manage call routing for countries with variable-length numbering plans for which CallManager support does not yet exist must configure route patterns such as 0! to get CallManager to provide the proper number of digits to the PSTN. Because route patterns ending in the ! wildcard introduce interdigit timing on all calls, such administrators often also configure equivalent route patterns (in this case, 0!#) so that knowledgeable users who terminate their outbound calls with a # need not wait for the interdigit timeout to expire.

Before such calls enter the PSTN, the dialed # must be stripped. This setting is enabled by default. When set to True, CallManager strips the final # (if it exists) of a dialed digit string before CallManager routes the call out the gateway.

Unknown Caller ID, UnknownCallerIDFlag, and UnknownCallerIDText

Unknown Caller ID, Unknown Caller ID Flag, and Unknown Caller ID Text affect calls that originate from a gateway. When calls arrive from the PSTN, often caller ID is not available. Setting the Unknown Caller ID Flag to True tells CallManager to provide a calling number and name for inbound calls that do not contain such information. The contents of Unknown Caller ID Text become the calling name, and the contents of Unknown Caller ID become the calling number.

Numbering Plan Info

Calls to ISDN and H.323 networks include information that attempts to classify the number dialed. The section "Called Party IE Number Type" discusses this information in more detail.

This information, however, tends to be rather troublesome in practice, because many networks are particular about the manner in which the information is encoded. The Numbering Plan Info service parameter provides a way to tweak this information if your system is having difficulty communicating with a connected system. The Numbering Plan Info service parameter takes the following values:

- 0 disables the setting, which causes CallManager to format the numbering plan information according to the call routing component's best judgment and the settings on the terminating device.

- 1 causes CallManager to encode the numbering plan field of the called party information element to Unknown, if the type of number field of the called party information element, as determined by CallManager, is also Unknown.

- 2 causes CallManager to encode the numbering plan field of the called party information element as Private, and the type of number field of the called party information element as Unknown.

If the system you have connected CallManager to is complaining about the encoding of the called number—a fact you can determine only through detailed analysis of the call rejection messages the connected system returns—changing this setting might resolve the problem.

Transformations on the Originating Device

This section describes the first opportunity CallManager has to transform the calling or called numbers—when the component that controls the caller's device offers the call to the call control component. These dialing transformations vary from device type to device type. The section "About Device Types That CallManager Supports" describes the device types that CallManager supports.

Table 2-40 provides an overview of the different kinds of originating device dialing transformations, along with a checklist of which protocols support which transformations.

External Phone Number Mask

All station devices use the Directory Number Configuration page. This page contains a field that is important in transformations, the External Phone Number Mask. Although the external phone number mask does not, in itself, effect any transformations, it allows you to configure a line's number from the PSTN's point of view—the line's external number. When you configure a value in this field, the value also shows up in the top line of the Cisco IP Phones 7905, 7912, 7940, 7941, 7960, 7961, 7970, and 7971 as the phone's external phone number.

For station-to-station calls, the calling line's directory number shows up as the calling number. However, for station-to-trunk calls, you can configure the destination route pattern so that it instead uses the line's external number as the calling number.

The external phone number mask is truly a mask (see the section "About Masks"). If you are fortunate enough to be able to map the final digits of a phone's external number directly to its internal extension, and if you are using auto-registration, you can use a mask value in this field instead of an individual number, and it saves you some data entry. (For information about auto-registration, see Chapter 3.)

Table 2-40   *Supported Originating Device Dialing Transformation by Device Type*

Originating Device Dialing Transformation	SCCP Station Devices	MGCP Station Devices	H.323 Station Devices	SCCP Trunk Devices	MGCP Trunk Devices	H.323 and SIP Trunk Devices
External Phone Number Mask	✓	✓	✓			
Prefix Digits		✓[1]			✓[2]	✓[1]
Num Digits		✓			✓[5]	✓[5]
Expected Digits		✓			✓[5]	✓[5]
Attendant DN					✓[4]	
Significant Digits					✓[3]	✓
Redirecting Number IE Delivery—Inbound					✓[3]	✓

[1] Called Prefix DN

[2] On T1-PRI and E1-PRI interfaces, it is called Prefix DN; on T1-CAS, Prefix Digits; not supported on other interfaces

[3] On T1-PRI and E1-PRI interfaces only

[4] On FXO interfaces only

[5] On T1-CAS only

For example, assume your system uses four-digit directory numbers. Furthermore, your site does not require overlapping dial plans (as might be required for multiple tenants) and it is small enough that it is served by a single area code and office code (say, 214 and 555, respectively). When you specify the mask 214555XXXX under the Auto-registration Information section on the Cisco CallManager Configuration page, when a new device registers, CallManager automatically assigns it the external phone number mask 214555XXXX. When it receives its directory number (say, 1212), this configuration tells CallManager that the newly registered line's external phone number is 2145551212. If you also check the Use External Phone Number Mask check box for the route pattern that routes calls to the PSTN, CallManager presents your users' full external numbers to the PSTN when they place calls.

The external phone number mask also provides you with a means by which you can hide the external phone number of your users when they place external phone calls. If you set a phone's external phone number mask to your switchboard number and then check the Use External Phone Number Mask check box on the route pattern you use for routing external calls, CallManager presents the switchboard number as the calling phone's calling number.

Prefix Digits

These fields crop up under slightly different names in many of the devices. You can usually find these fields by clicking specific ports in the gateway configuration page.

Prefix Digits can contain a sequence of digits (*, #, 0 through 9). CallManager Administration also calls this field Prefix DN. Prefix Digits can contain a sequence of digits (*, #, 0 through 9). When a gateway configured with prefix digits receives a call from an associated gateway, CallManager modifies the dialed digits by prepending the digits you specify to the dialed number. For example, if a gateway provides the dialed digits 1000 and you specify prefix digits of 3, CallManager modifies the dialed digits to 31000.

Some subtleties exist about how prefix digits operate with different types of gateways. When CallManager connects to a gateway using a digital telephony protocol such as H.323 or ISDN, inbound calls from these gateways usually provide all the digits the calling user dialed in the call setup attempt. This type of dialing is called *enbloc dialing*.

When CallManager connects to a gateway using an analog protocol or by a digital protocol such as MGCP, particularly when a POTS phone is connected to the gateway, the digits the user dials arrive from the gateway one by one. This type of digit collection is called *overlapped dialing*. When you configure prefix digits in conjunction with a gateway controlling a POTS station, CallManager immediately attempts to route the call based on the configured prefix digits. In the usual case, the prefix digits you specify are not sufficient for CallManager to select a destination, and CallManager waits for more digits from the calling user.

However, you can implement a hotline or Private Line Automatic Ringdown (PLAR) function with POTS phones by relying on CallManager's treatment of Prefix Digits. PLAR is a feature whereby CallManager can ring a specified extension the moment that a user places a call from a particular station.

PLAR works when the Prefix Digits you specify are sufficient to permit CallManager to immediately select a destination. In this case, CallManager immediately offers the call to the specified destination. For instance, if your enterprise has a security desk with number 61111, by configuring prefix digits of 61111 for an analog gateway with an attached analog phone, you cause CallManager to immediately ring the security desk when a user picks up the POTS phone.

> **TIP** The section "Hotline Functionality" describes a different way that you can configure PLAR, one that works with all devices but which requires a slightly more complicated configuration.

Expected Digits and Num Digits

The gateway settings Expected Digits and Num Digits work in tandem. Expected Digits tells CallManager how many digits you expect the calling user to be dialing. Num Digits tells CallManager how many of those digits are significant to selecting a destination.

Num Digits is the easier of these settings to explain. Its heritage is the trunk interfaces, where you can often predict which digits a connected network sends. On a trunk interface, these settings tell CallManager to expect to receive n digits, the last m of which are significant for routing purposes. For instance, the central office might provide seven digits as the called number, but because the first three digits are always the office code, you just want to use the last four digits to route the call. Configuring 7 for Expected Digits and 4 for Num Digits causes CallManager to ignore the first three digits sent by the central office. If your dial plan is reasonably simple, as is often the case if your enterprise is smaller than 1000 users, using Num Digits provides you a simple way to maintain a four- or five-digit dial plan for your internal phones. (If your enterprise needs to support a large number of users whose external numbers are connected to a large number of telephone exchanges, Num Digits is often not powerful enough to handle the routing of your inbound calls. The section "Extension Mapping from the Public to the Private Network" describes how you can use translation patterns to route your inbound calls.)

Although the Num Digits setting tells CallManager how many digits you want to keep, the Expected Digits setting tells CallManager how many digits the PSTN is going to send. When the gateway to which CallManager is connected uses enbloc dialing, the Expected Digits setting is superfluous; because the call setup attempt contains all of the digits the calling user dialed, CallManager can immediately use the Num Digits setting to extract the digits that you want to route with. Expected Digits is a setting applicable to gateways connected to CallManager by protocols that use overlapped dialing. In such instances, CallManager needs to know how many digits to collect before using the Num Digits setting to extract the digits you want to route with.

When you configure these settings for a station device, they behave identically to this setting on a trunk device. CallManager ignores the first few digits that the user dials and uses subsequent digits to route the call.

Attendant DN

Analog trunks are just like the analog phone lines that run into most people's houses. On an analog phone line, when a user goes off-hook, the phone closes the circuit from the central office to permit current to flow, and the central office prepares to place a call. In the case of tone dialing, the central office connects your line to a tone detector, which listens to the stream of tones that emanate as you dial your phone and converts them to dialed digits.

When you configure an analog gateway as an FXO analog port, CallManager plays the part of the central office. As a result, when CallManager detects that the trunk has been taken off-hook, it must dial a preconfigured number. This number is the Attendant DN. Attendant DN is a setting that is much like Prefix Digits, which is described in the section "Prefix Digits"; when a call comes in over the gateway, CallManager automatically provides the specified digits to the call routing component. If you do not provide such a number, Cisco IOS gateways play a dial tone for the caller so that the user can provide digits.

Significant Digits

Digital trunk devices support variants of the ISDN signaling protocol. ISDN differs from analog protocols in that ISDN endpoints interpret the voltage levels on the trunk as either on or off values. This interpretation allows CallManager to assign meanings to particular patterns of on and off values and receive information, such as the calling and called party, directly in the call attempt. Unlike the analog gateways, which must dial a preconfigured number, digital gateways receive called party information directly in the call setup message. CallManager can transform this information by using settings on the Gateway Configuration page for circuit-switched gateways and the Trunk Configuration page for IP trunk interfaces.

PRIs have no setting that corresponds to the Expected Digits settings because the call setup request usually encodes all the digits of the called number.

For PRI interfaces, the Num Digits setting (see the section "Expected Digits and Num Digits" earlier in the chapter) is actually configured using the Significant Digits field. The Significant Digits field presents you with options to select any number from 0 to 32 as well as the setting All. If you select All, CallManager processes all digits of the called number. However, if you specify any other setting, the number in the Significant Digits setting indicates how many of the final digits of the dialed number that CallManager should use to route the call. For example, if the Significant Digits is set to 4, when CallManager receives a call for 9725551212, CallManager truncates all but the last four digits and routes using the digits 1212.

When used in conjunction with overlapped receiving (see the section "SendingCompleteIndicator and OverlapReceivingForPriFlag"), the Significant Digits field might not operate as you expect. The Significant Digits setting operates only on the first batch of digits the calling gateway provides to CallManager. In overlapped receiving, the gateway does not provide all of the digits at once. In fact, the first message that the gateway sends to CallManager often contains no digits at all. As a result, CallManager probably will not suppress any of the digits coming in from the gateway.

For example, assume you have set Significant Digits to 4 and the gateway provides the digits 9725551212 one digit at a time. The first digit (9) arrives and CallManager applies the Significant Digits setting to it. Because the Significant Digits setting specifies to keep four of the initial digits, CallManager keeps the first digit. Then CallManager passes through all of the subsequent digits without complaint. Had all of the digits arrived in the call setup, CallManager would have truncated 9725551212 to 1212. When using overlapped receiving, unless you know that the initial setup that the gateway sends to CallManager contains more digits than the Significant Digits setting, do not use the Significant Digits setting.

Transformations in Translation Patterns, Route Patterns, and Route Lists

This section describes the second through fourth opportunities during which CallManager can apply transformations as part of the routing process. The second opportunity occurs if the dialed digits match a translation pattern, the third occurs when a route pattern is ultimately selected, and the fourth occurs if the selected destination is a route list.

The section "Translation Patterns" describes translation patterns, and the section "Call Hunting Constructs" describes route lists. However, it is worth noting here that the transformations associated with a route list *override* those that the route pattern applies. That is, although other dialing transformations you apply have a cumulative effect, the transformations you specify on a route between a route list and a route group undo any transformations that the Route Pattern Configuration page applies. This capability allows you to define default dialing transformations on the route pattern, which you selectively override if a call goes out a particular set of gateways. For instance, in North America, long distance carriers expect to receive ten digits for calls to the PSTN. However, local carriers expect the digit 1 to precede long distance calls. Typically, to save costs, enterprises prefer their long distance calls to route directly to a long distance carrier. However, if all gateways to the long distance carrier are busy, by using a route list, you can route the call to a gateway connected to a local carrier as an alternate choice. In such a case, you could define dialing transformations on the route pattern to throw away the access code and long distance 1 that the user dials so that calls to the long distance carrier consist only of 10 digits. If the route list determines that all gateways to the long distance carrier are busy, however, by setting different dialing transformations on the route group containing gateways to the local carrier, you can cause CallManager to discard only the access code and keep the initial 1 on the long distance call.

To prevent a particular route group from overriding the transformations you associate with a route pattern, leave the transformation mask fields of the route group empty and be sure to select <None> rather than NoDigits for digit discarding instructions.

Called Party Transformations

Three types of called party transformations can be configured in the call routing component and on route lists. They are as follows:

- Digit discarding instructions, which you use primarily with the @ wildcard and allow you to discard meaningful subsections of numbers in the national network. They are critical for implementing toll-bypass solutions, where the long distance number that the calling user has dialed must be converted into a local number from which CallManager passes the digits to the PSTN.

- Called party transformation mask, which allows you to suppress leading digits, change existing digits while leaving others unmodified, and insert leading digits.

- Prefix digits, which allow you to prepend one or more digits to the called number.

CallManager applies the transformations in the order listed.

Digit Discarding Instructions

Digit discarding instructions allow you perform conversions of a dialed number specific to a national numbering plan. For the North American numbering plan, you can strip access codes, suppress long distance carrier selection, convert numbers to achieve toll-bypass operations, and strip trailing # from international number sequences. Because digit discarding instructions are dial-plan specific, this section describes only those digit discarding instructions that apply to the North American numbering plan.

In general, digit discarding instructions apply only to route patterns that contain the @ wildcard. However, you can use the digit discarding instruction PreDot with route patterns that use the . wildcard even if they do not contain the @ wildcard.

Digit discarding instructions consist of one or more of the following identifiers grouped into three sections. The access code section lets you remove initial digits from a dialed string. The toll-bypass section allows you to turn dial strings that represent long distance calls into dial strings that represent local calls. Finally, the trailing-# instruction lets you strip a dialed end-of-dialing terminator from international calls to prevent it from going to an adjacent network (which might have trouble processing it).

Digit discarding instruction identifiers are additive, so the digit discarding instruction PreDot 10-10-Dialing combines the effects of each individual identifier. If you do not want to discard any digits, select NoDigits.

Table 2-41 describes the groups and identifiers and provides sample dialed digit strings. Substrings in bold denote which digits CallManager discards.

Table 2-41   *Digit Discarding Instructions Groups and Identifiers*

Instructions	Discarded Digits (for Route Pattern 9.8@)	Used For
Access Code		
PreDot	**98** 1 214 555 1212	Stripping access codes
PreAt	**98**1 214 555 1212	Stripping access codes
Toll Bypass		
11/10D->7D	98 **1010321 1 214** 555 1212	Toll bypass to a seven-digit dialing region
11D->10D	98 **1010321 1** 214 555 1212	Toll bypass to a 10-digit dialing region
IntlAccess IntlDirect Dial	98 **011** 33 0123456789 #	Removal of international access codes for routing by globally significant number
IntlTollBypass	98 **011 33** 0123456789 #	Toll bypass from country to country
10-10-Dialing	98 **1010321** 1 214 555 1212	Long distance carrier code suppression
Trailing-#		
Trailing-#	98 011 33 0123456789 **#**	Suppression of end-of-dialing character

Called Party Transformation Mask

Values in this field can truncate or expand the dialed digit string and change individual digits before CallManager sends the digits to a connected network or device. The section "About Masks" discusses mask operation.

Prefix Digits

This field can contain *, #, or digits 0 through 9. CallManager prepends this field to the called number before it is sent to the next stage of the routing process.

Calling Party Transformations

Three types of calling party transformations can be configured in the call routing component and on route lists:

- Use External Phone Number Mask check box, which instructs the call routing component to use a calling station's external phone number rather than its directory number as the calling number

- Calling party transformation mask, which allows you to suppress leading digits, change existing digits, leave other digits unmodified, and insert leading digits

- Prefix digits, which allow you to prepend the specified digits to the calling number

CallManager applies the transformations in the order listed.

Use External Phone Number Mask Check Box

Setting this flag sets the calling number to the external phone number mask configured on the calling line, rather than the directory number of a calling line. See the section "About Masks" for details about the ways that masks work and the section "External Phone Number Mask" for more details about the external phone number mask.

If no external phone number mask is configured on the calling line, or if the call originates from a device that does not have an external phone number mask setting, the call routing component uses the directory number (in the case of calling user devices) or the provided calling number (in the case of calling trunk devices) instead.

Calling Party Transformation Mask

Values in this field can truncate or expand the calling number and change individual digits before CallManager sends the calling number to a connected switch or device. The section "About Masks" discusses mask operation.

The section "External Phone Number Mask" describes one method by which you can cause PSTN users to see your company switchboard's number as the calling number, rather than the direct number of your users when they place calls to the PSTN. Calling party transformation masks provide another method. By specifying your switchboard's number as a calling party transformation mask in the Route Pattern Configuration page, you cause CallManager to replace the calling user's calling number with that of the company switchboard. Alternatively, providing a mask value such as 972813XXXX can permit you to present a fully qualified national number (such as 9728131000) to the PSTN when a directory number (such as 1000) places a call.

Prefix Digits

This field can contain *, #, or digits 0 through 9. CallManager prepends this field to the calling number before sending it to the next stage of the routing process. Prepending digits can permit you to fully qualify the calling numbers CallManager presents to the PSTN or add access codes to calls you present to connected PBXs.

Transformations on the Terminating Device

Trunk devices have settings that relate to the calling and called numbers. The settings described in this section correspond to the fifth and final place in CallManager where transformations can occur in the call routing process. Table 2-42 describes the dialing transformations and provides a checklist of which settings affect which gateways.

Table 2-42 *Supported Terminating Device Dialing Transformations by Device Type*

Terminating Device Dialing Transformation	SCCP Station Devices	MGCP Station Devices	H.323 Station Devices	SCCP Trunk Devices	MGCP Trunk Devices	H.323 Trunk Devices
Caller ID DN					✓[1]	✓
Calling Party Selection					✓[1]	✓
Calling Line ID Presentation					✓[1]	✓
Called Party IE Number Type					✓[1]	✓
Calling Party IE Number Type					✓[1]	✓
Called Numbering Plan					✓[1]	✓
Calling Numbering Plan					✓[1]	✓
Number of Digits to Strip					✓[1]	
Display IE Delivery					✓[1]	✓
Redirecting Number IE Delivery – Outbound					✓[1]	✓
Send Calling Name in Facility IE					✓[2]	
Connected Line ID Presentation					✓[1]	

[1]T1-PRI and E1-PRI interfaces only
[2]T1-PRI interfaces only

Caller ID DN

Caller ID DN provides a mechanism to set the calling number of calls that CallManager extends to a gateway. It is a mask value (see the section "About Masks"). Values set in this field operate on the calling number that previous transformation steps generate.

Calling Party Selection

Calling Party Selection has one of three values:

- Originator

- First Redirect Number

- Last Redirect Number

This setting determines what number is presented as the calling number when call forwarding occurs.

If no forwarding at all has occurred, all three values contain the calling number of the originator. If CallManager has forwarded the call once, both the first redirect number and last redirect number are the calling number of the forwarding phone, while the originator is the calling number of the originator. If CallManager has forwarded the call twice, the originator is the calling number of the calling user, the first redirect number is the calling number of the first forwarding phone, and the last redirect number is the calling number of the last forwarding phone. If the call forwards more than once, the last redirect number reflects the calling number of the last device to forward the call.

Why would you set this field? If the system that the gateway is connected to is in charge of maintaining the billing records for calls from CallManager, you might want to bill not the actual originator of a call, but the party that caused the call to forward out the gateway. If the adjacent system uses the calling number to determine who to bill, this setting effectively allows you to control the billing.

Calling Line ID Presentation

This setting has values of None, Allowed, and Restricted. If set to None or Allowed (either value has the same effect), this setting indicates to the attached network that the called party is allowed to see the calling number. If this field is set to Restricted, the called party is prohibited from seeing the calling number.

Called Party IE Number Type

This setting has values of Cisco CallManager, Unknown, National, International, and Subscriber. The setting dictates how CallManager represents the called number to the network to which the gateway provides access.

Calls to ISDN networks include not only the dialed digits but also an indication of what the calling system believes the numbers represent. The Type of number field indicates to the system that receives the call whether the digits provided represent a national number, an international number, or whether the calling system even knows what the nature of the dialed number is. Although this setting was a nice idea on the part of the architects of ISDN, in practice, it (and its brethren, Calling Party IE Number Type, Called Party Numbering Plan, and Calling Party Numbering Plan) usually just causes problems. For example, one setting that the ISDN messages permit is Private, which represents to the called system that the calling system believes the provided digits are a number on a privately owned network. PSTN systems may decide that they do not want to route calls tagged with the type of number Private, even if the actual digits contained in the call setup represent an actual PSTN number. Conversely, if the PSTN is providing you with a Centrex service (in which the PSTN operates as a PBX so that you can network remote offices), the PSTN might require the type of number be encoded as Private for an interoffice call, even if the provided digits are sufficient to allow the PSTN to route the call to a remote office. In summary, even if the digits you provide are correct, the system to which you offer the call might reject the call if the Type of number field is not what it expects. Therefore, CallManager provides settings to permit you to control the Type of number and Numbering plan fields in case the network to which you connect your gateway is particular about the encoding of these fields.

By default, this value is set to Cisco CallManager, which means CallManager fills in this number as best it can. This setting usually works fine. If the pattern the calling user dials matches an @ pattern, CallManager fills in the number as national or international based on the numbering plan (see the section "The North American Numbering Plan"). For non-@ patterns, CallManager punts and encodes the number as **Unknown**.

If an attached network has problems with the number type that CallManager encodes, changing this setting may resolve the problem. Particularly if you live in a country that does not use the North American numbering plan and you have configured specific route patterns to route calls out gateways, you might find that the PSTN balks at CallManager's encoding of the number type as Unknown. Changing this setting to National can resolve the problem.

Calling Party IE Number Type

This setting has values of Cisco CallManager, Unknown, National, International, and Subscriber. The setting dictates how CallManager represents the calling number to the network to which the gateway provides access.

By default, CallManager encodes the number as Unknown, and this setting works in most cases. If an attached network has problems with the number type that CallManager encodes, changing this setting may resolve the problem.

Called Numbering Plan

ISDN networks expect telephone systems to provide not only the number type of a called number, but also the numbering plan it believes the number applies. This setting has values of Cisco CallManager, ISDN, National Standard, Private, and Unknown.

By default, CallManager encodes the number as ISDN. If an attached network has problems with the default numbering plan that CallManager encodes, changing this setting can resolve the problem.

Calling Numbering Plan

This setting has values of Cisco CallManager, ISDN, National Standard, Private, and Unknown.

By default, CallManager encodes the number as ISDN. If an attached network has problems with the default numbering plan that CallManager encodes, changing this setting can resolve the problem.

Number of Digits to Strip

Setting this value instructs CallManager to strip the specified number of digits from the beginning of all called numbers before passing the call to an adjacent network. If you administer a network in a country with a variable-length dialing plan, you might find this setting useful, because the discarding mechanisms that digit discarding instructions (see the section "Digit Discarding Instructions") provide are not available, and because called party transform masks enable you only to truncate a number to a fixed number of final digits.

Display IE Delivery

This setting controls the delivery of the display information element (IE). The display information element permits a telephone system to ask another system to display the contained information. Many telephone systems use it to communicate the display name of the calling user. When you enable this option for a particular gateway, CallManager places the contents of the **Display** field (on the Directory Number Configuration page) into the display information element before CallManager extends a call to the attached gateway.

Redirecting Number IE Delivery

This setting controls the delivery of the redirecting number information element. Suppose that a phone on a telephone system calls another phone on the same telephone system, and the call forwards to different telephone system that manages the voice messaging system for the enterprise. The new telephone system needs to know what directory number the caller originally dialed so that the voice messaging system can deliver the caller's voice message to the correct voice messaging box number. The redirecting number information element permits one telephone system to communicate this information to another. Enabling this flag permits CallManager to communicate the original dialed number to the connected network.

Translation Patterns

Translation patterns are a mechanism that allows you to introduce a level of routing indirection into the call routing process. They allow you to define aliases for the endpoints in your network.

Why do you need to define such aliases? This section discusses a few reasons:

- Security desk and operator functionality

- Hotline functionality

- Extension mapping from the public to your private network

- Insertion of access codes in the Received Calls and Missed Calls menus of Cisco IP Phones

- Multiple-tenant applications

You configure translation patterns almost exactly like route patterns. They have the same calling and called party transformations, and they use the same wildcard notation.

Unlike route patterns, translation patterns do not correspond to a physical or logical destination. Instead, a translation pattern relies on the calling and called party transformations to perform its function. Although route patterns use transformations simply a way to change the presentation of the calling or called parties, translation patterns use the results of called party transformations as a set of digits for a new analysis attempt. CallManager then uses the results of the second analysis attempt to determine which destination to ring.

The second analysis attempt might itself match a translation pattern. In this case, CallManager applies the calling and called party transformations of the matching translation pattern and uses the results as the input for another analysis attempt. To prevent routing loops, CallManager breaks chains of translation patterns after ten iterations.

An example might help to explain. Imagine that you have the translation patterns and route patterns listed in Table 2-43.

Table 2-43   *Translation Pattern Example*

Configured Translation and Route Patterns
Translation Pattern: 1XXX Called Party Transformation Mask: 2XXX
Translation Pattern: 2XXX Prefix Digits: 8
Route pattern: 8.XXXX Gateway: Gateway A

When a user dials the number 1000, this configuration causes CallManager to offer the user's call to Gateway A with a called number of 82000. This process consists of the following steps:

Step 1   The dialed digits 1000 match the translation pattern 1XXX. CallManager applies the called party transformation mask 2XXX to the dialed digits 1000, yielding 2000.

Step 2   CallManager uses the resulting number, 2000, as the input for another analysis attempt. This attempt matches the translation pattern 2XXX. CallManager applies the prefix digit 8 to the digits 2000, yielding 82000.

Step 3   CallManager uses the resulting number, 82000, as the input for another analysis attempt. This attempt matches the route pattern 8.XXXX. CallManager offers the call to Gateway A, the gateway associated with the route pattern.

One configuration field that appears for translation patterns, but which does not appear for route patterns, is **calling search space**. When the new analysis is attempted, the analysis is attempted using the calling search space configured for the translation pattern, rather than the calling search space of the originating device. This behavior can allow a user to call a number in a partition that the user's calling search space would not normally permit the user to dial. The section "Calling Search Spaces and Partitions" describes calling search spaces and partitions.

Translation patterns, therefore, differ from route patterns; when route patterns match, CallManager always extends the call to the destination associated with the route pattern. The dialing transformations that CallManager applies have a purely cosmetic effect in that they change the calling number and called number, but do not cause CallManager to select a different destination. (However, if the destination to which CallManager offers the call is a gateway or other CallManager cluster, the gateway or CallManager cluster can use the transformed called number to decide where to route the call.)

On the other hand, translation patterns have no associated destination. The called party number transformations that CallManager applies do directly affect which destination CallManager selects, because CallManager uses the results of the transformation to select a new destination. The new analysis attempt might match a route pattern or directory number, or the attempt may match another translation pattern, in which case CallManager attempts another analysis. Figure 2-10 presents a flowchart of this process.

Figure 2-10   *Translation Pattern Flowchart*

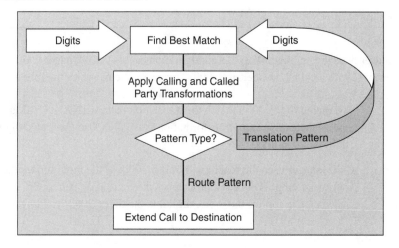

The rest of this section describes different translation pattern configurations:

- "Security Desk and Operator Functionality" discusses a mechanism by which you can associate an easily remembered directory number with an emergency service, while maintaining a fixed-length directory number plan.

- "Hotline Functionality" discusses a mechanism by which you can automatically ring a particular extension when a phone goes off-hook.

- "Extension Mapping from the Public to the Private Network" describes how you can map the discontinuous number ranges that the telephone company might assign you to a contiguous range for internal extensions.

- "Insertion of Access Codes in the Received Calls and Missed Calls Menus of Cisco IP Phones" describes how you can use translation patterns to insert outside access codes for calls that your users receive. Inserting the access codes allows your users to use the Dial softkey on the Received Calls and Missed Calls menus of their IP Phones. Normally, users must use the EditDial softkey to modify the number of a received or missed call in order to return a received or missed call.

- "Multiple-Tenant Applications" discusses a few strategies that use translation patterns to deal with the problems that arise when different organizations with independent dial plans share a single CallManager.

Security Desk and Operator Functionality

The operator or security desk is often just a phone in your network with a standard four- or five-digit extension. However, for the desk to be useful with the least amount of hassle for your users, it is desirable to be able to assign these special extensions a directory number that is out of the ordinary (such as 0) and thus easier for your users to remember in an emergency.

One way to accomplish this task is, of course, to assign unusual directory numbers directly to these stations. However, having unusual directory numbers in a particular number block makes configuration of inbound routing more complex. Inbound calls often route based on the last four or five digits of an externally published number. If you want these special stations to receive inbound calls for other networks, you have to configure special routing to convert very specific extension numbers to your unusual numbers.

Translation patterns allow you to give numbers that are compatible with the rest of your numbering plan to these special stations, but to assign them aliases in the cluster. This allows your users to have easy-to-remember emergency numbers without the pain of configuring all ingresses to the cluster with special routing instructions.

To configure a dialing alias, specify the alias as a translation pattern and make sure that calling users include the partition that contains the translation pattern in their calling search spaces. In the called party transformation mask, enter the extension that you want to be called. In the translation calling search space, enter a calling search space that contains the partition associated with the destination extension. Figure 2-11 shows a security desk example.

Figure 2-11 *Security Desk Example*

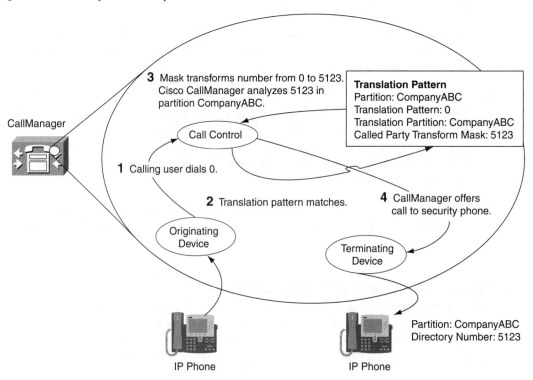

The example relies on the provision of the translation and route patterns in Table 2-44.

Table 2-44   *Security Desk Example Patterns*

Configured Route and Translation Patterns	Comments
Partition: CompanyABC Translation pattern: 0 Translation calling search space: CompanyABC Called party transformation mask: 5123	Translation calling search space CompanyABC contains partition CompanyABC.
Partition: CompanyABC Route pattern: 5123	5123 is a phone with directory number 5123. CallManager considers directory numbers as route patterns, and these can be the destination that a translation pattern selects.

When the calling user dials 0, CallManager performs the following steps:

Step 1   The dialed digit 0 matches the translation pattern 0. CallManager applies the called party transformation mask 5123 to convert the called number to 5123.

Step 2   CallManager uses the resulting number, 5123, as the input for another analysis attempt. This attempt matches the security phone's directory number. CallManager offers the call to the security phone with dialed digits of 5123.

Hotline Functionality

A hotline or private line automatic ringdown (PLAR) configuration causes a specified destination to ring immediately when the hotline extension goes off-hook. It is simply a special case of an operator configuration.

In an operator configuration, translation patterns cause the operator extension to ring when a single digit is dialed. In a hotline configuration, the specified destination rings before a user dials any digits. By specifying a translation pattern containing no digits, you can cause the transformation and reanalysis to occur immediately after the user takes the phone off-hook.

The only wrinkle is that of interdigit timing. Translation patterns always have urgent priority, which means that as soon as the user enters a digit sequence for which a translation pattern is the best match, the call routing component applies the translation immediately, even if subsequent digits would cause a different route pattern to match. This behavior means that if you configure a hotline translation pattern and group it in the same route partition as all of your other route patterns and directory numbers, whenever any device goes off-hook for any reason, the hotline extension rings. Users never have the opportunity to dial any digits.

To prevent this behavior from occurring, you must put the hotline translation pattern in its own partition and configure the hotline extension's calling search space so that it looks in the hotline partition to resolve its analysis requests. The section "Calling Search Spaces and Partitions" discusses calling search spaces and partitions. Figure 2-12 shows an example of hotline configuration.

Figure 2-12 *Hotline Configuration*

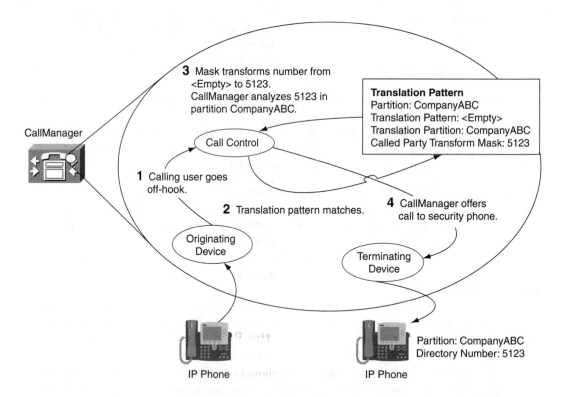

The example relies on the provision of the translation and route patterns in Table 2-45.

Table 2-45   *Hotline Configuration Example Route Patterns*

Configured Route and Translation Patterns	Comments
Partition: Hotline Translation pattern: <Empty> Translation calling search space: CompanyABC Called party transformation mask: 5123	Translation calling search space CompanyABC contains partition CompanyABC.
Partition: CompanyABC Route pattern: 5123	5123 is a phone with directory number 5123. CallManager considers directory numbers as route patterns, and these can be the destination that a translation pattern selects.

When the calling user whose calling search space includes the Hotline partition goes off-hook, CallManager performs the following steps:

Step 1   When the user goes off-hook, this provides CallManager with an empty set of dialed digits, which match the translation pattern <Empty> in the Hotline partition. CallManager applies the called party transformation mask 5123 to convert the called number to 5123.

Step 2   CallManager uses the resulting number, 5123, as the input for another analysis attempt. The calling search space that CallManager uses for the analysis attempt is the calling search space of the translation pattern, CompanyABC. This attempt matches the hotline's directory number. CallManager offers the call to the hotline phone with dialed digits of 5123.

Extension Mapping from the Public to the Private Network

If your campus grows past 1000 users, you might need to use translation patterns to preserve your internal extension numbering scheme. Local phone carriers often sell numbers in blocks of 1000. For example, if a single exchange serves your campus, the phone company might lease you the block of 1000 numbers from 813 5000 to 813 5999.

So long as you do not exceed 1000 users, it is possible to use gateway settings to map the block of 1000 users that the phone company assigns you to your internal numbering scheme. For example, if you prefer your users to be in the numbering range 8000 to 8999, when the PSTN provides 813 5XXX as the called number, you can use dialing transformations on the Gateway Configuration page to strip all but the final three digits and prepend an 8 (see the section "Transformations on the Originating Device").

However, if your network grows past 1000 users, there is no guarantee that the next block of 1000 numbers that the phone company assigns you will be contiguous with your previous range. In fact, even if the same central office serves you, the phone company might assign you a different exchange number. At this point, performing a transformation in the gateway does not work.

For instance, suppose that the phone company has given you two ranges, 555 5XXX and 555 9XXX. You can no longer just keep the last three digits and prepend 8 in the Gateway Configuration page, because a call to 555 5000 and a call to 555 9000 both get transformed to the directory number 8000.

However, if you choose to keep the final four instead of the final three digits, the discontinuity of the numbering range affects your internal numbering plan. A call to 555 5000 is transformed to 5000, while a call to 828 9000 is transformed to 9000. Setting aside for a moment that your existing users (who were in the range 8000 to 8999) can no longer receive calls until you renumber them to the 5000 range, the split numbering range at the central office is now visible to your internal network. If you have previously set up an initial steering digit of 5 for features such as call park or for intercluster calls, the split numbering range might force you to reorganize your numbering plan, probably to the frustration of your users.

On the other hand, anticipating that your campus might grow to beyond 1000 users, if you keep the 7000 to 7999 range open (or better yet, assign users five-digit directory numbers), by using translation patterns, you can map inbound calls in the 555 5XXX range to the internal 8XXX range while directing inbound calls in the 555 9XXX range to the internal 7XXX range.

To configure this setup, perform no transformations at the inbound gateway. Instead, set up two translation patterns in a partition visible only to your inbound gateways (see the section "Calling Search Spaces and Partitions"). Set one translation pattern to 555 5XXX with a called party transformation mask of 8XXX, and set the other translation pattern to 555 9XXX with a called party transformation mask of 7XXX.

When an inbound call arrives in the 555 5XXX range, the corresponding translation pattern matches, and CallManager transforms the called number to 8XXX. Then, because translation patterns cause reanalysis to occur, CallManager uses the transformed digits to select the actual destination to ring. Figure 2-13 shows the behavior that occurs when a call comes in for 555XXXX.

The example relies on the provision of the translation and route patterns in Table 2-46.

Table 2-46   *Patterns for Transforming Inbound Calls to Deal with a Discontinuous Numbering Range*

Configured Route and Translation Patterns	Comments
Partition: InboundTranslations Translation pattern: 5555XXX Translation calling search space: CompanyABC Called party transformation mask: 8XXX	Translation calling search space CompanyABC contains partition CompanyABC.
Partition: CompanyABC Route pattern: 8123	8123 is a phone with directory number 8123. CallManager considers directory numbers as route patterns, and these can be the destination that a translation pattern selects.

Figure 2-13   *Transforming Inbound Calls to Deal with a Discontinuous Numbering Range*

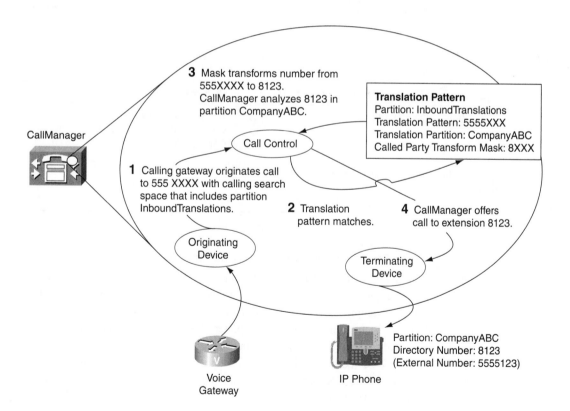

When the PSTN sends a call through the gateway to 5558123, CallManager performs the following steps:

Step 1 The gateway provides CallManager with the digits 5558123, which matches the translation pattern 8135XXX in the InboundTranslations partition. CallManager applies the called party transformation mask 8XXX to convert the called number to 8123.

Step 2 CallManager uses the resulting number, 8123, as the input for another analysis attempt. The calling search space that CallManager uses for the analysis attempt is the calling search space of the translation pattern, CompanyABC. This attempt matches the phone with directory number 8123. CallManager offers the call to the phone with dialed digits of 8123.

The preceding translation patterns suffice for a company of up to 1000 users. If your network grows past 1000 users and the phone company gives you numbers in the 828 9XXX range, by adding the following translation patterns, you can map the 9XXX range (which probably overlaps with your outside access code) to 7XXX. Table 2-47 shows the translation pattern that maps the new range.

Table 2-47 *Translation Pattern for Transforming Inbound Calls to Deal with a Discontinuous Numbering Range*

Configured Route and Translation Patterns	Comments
Partition: InboundTranslations Translation pattern: 5559XXX Translation calling search space: CompanyABC Called party transformation mask: 7XXX	Translation calling search space CompanyABC contains partition CompanyABC.

Directory Number Lengths and CallManager

CallManager has no particular reliance on four-digit directory numbers. You can use any number of digits for your internal extensions and adjust the translation tables appropriately. For example, if the example network this section presented used 5-digit extensions in the range 50000 to 51999, changing the translation pattern 5555XXX to use a called party transformation of 50XXX maps inbound calls in the 5XXX of the 813 exchange to number ranges 50000–50999. Similarly, changing the translation pattern 5559XXX to use a called party transformation of 51XXX maps inbound calls in the 9XXX range of the 555 exchange to number ranges 51000 to 51999.

Insertion of Access Codes in the Received Calls and Missed Calls Menus of Cisco IP Phones

Cisco IP Phones 7905, 7912, 7920, 7940, 7941, 7960, 7961, 7970, and 7971 provide users a **directories** button with several menu items, among them Missed Calls and Received Calls. When a user receives a call, the phone places the calling number in the Missed Calls menu if the user does not answer the call, and the Received Calls menu if the user does answer the call.

These menus also provide two softkeys: Dial and EditDial. Figure 2-14 shows a representation of the Missed Calls menu.

Pressing the **Dial** softkey causes the phone to place a new call by dialing the digits of the selected missed call entry. Unfortunately, in many cases, CallManager rejects calls placed using the **Dial** softkey, because a user's calling number is not always the same set of digits that a user must dial to return the call.

Figure 2-14   *Missed Calls Menu of Cisco IP Phone*

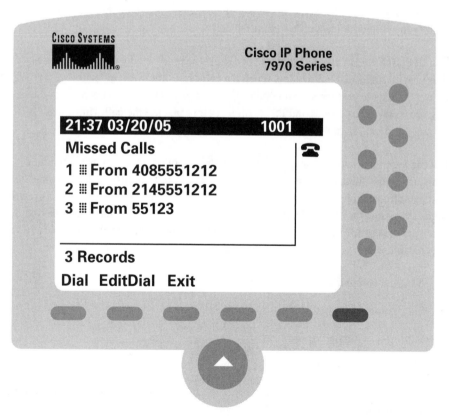

For instance, if a phone in the PSTN with number 408 555 1212 calls a phone controlled by CallManager in the Dallas area, the calling number that the Dallas phone receives is 408 555 1212, and thus the Dallas phone records 408 555 1212 in its Missed Calls or Received Calls menu. However, practically every enterprise requires an external access code such as 9 to provide access to an external line. Furthermore, in this example, the Dallas's phone return call is a long distance call, which the North American PSTN requires also to start with a 1. So although the phone receives 408 555 1212 as the calling number, to return the call, the Dallas phone must dial 9 1 408 555 1212.

This situation is complicated by the fact that for other types of calls, the return number needs to have just the access code without the 1. For instance, if phone connected to the Dallas PSTN with number 214 555 1212 calls a Dallas phone controlled by CallManager, to return the call, the Dallas phone must use an access code but omit the 1: 9 214 555 1212.

Finally some calls need neither an access code nor PSTN digits added. For instance, if phone 55123 in the Dallas enterprise calls phone 55004 in the Dallas enterprise, 55123 shows up as the calling number in the Missed Calls or Received Calls menu, and phone 55004 does not need to modify the stored digits at all to return the call.

The IP Phone has no way to predict which digits need to be added for which types of calls, and thus provides an **EditDial** softkey. When a user presses the **EditDial** softkey, the Cisco IP Phone allows the user to edit the stored number before it places the call. This permits the user to insert any necessary access codes and PSTN digits before placing the call. Unfortunately, it requires several additional button presses, which users find quite cumbersome.

CallManager provides two ways to deal with this problem. One way is via inbound transformations that always prepend a specific set of prefix digits (such as 91) and a set of outbound translations that strip these digits on a context-sensitive basis (such as rewriting these digits as 9 when the area code of the caller does not require an initial 1, but leaving both 9 and 1 when the area code of the caller must be dialed with a preceding 1). Another, clearly superior way if you can use it is via the following service parameters:

- National Number Prefix

- International Number Prefix

- Subscriber Number Prefix

- Unknown Number Prefix

These service parameters rely on the *Type of Number* field in the Calling Party Number information element supported by the PRI protocol. Service providers, particularly in Europe, might carefully classify the calling numbers of calls they offer to your enterprise. The following list summarizes the types of numbers:

■   National numbers reflect addresses available in the host country's numbering plan.

■   International numbers reflect addresses available in other countries' numbering plans.

■   Subscriber numbers, in a called number, can represent other extensions served by the same exchange as your enterprise, but might also be used by service providers to indicate calls offered by branch offices connected via tie lines if you've subscribed to a Centrex service.

■   Unknown numbers are otherwise unclassified numbers.

The service parameters specified in the preceding list enable you to define type-of-number-specific transformations of a calling party number. For instance, you could define International Number Prefix as 9011 and National Number Prefix as 91, in order to automatically prepend a 9011 to calls from outside of North America and 01 to calls from within the North American numbering plan. Because long distance direct dial digits are sometimes needed and sometimes not and because 10- versus 7-digit dialing can vary from North American city to North American city, this approach might not completely solve the problem, but for the variable-length numbering plans used by many European countries, this approach works fine.

Unfortunately, the only real good way to find out how your service provider is classifying calling numbers is to look at decoded traces. CallManager's CCM trace prints out decoded ISDN messages.

If your service provider isn't consistently classifying calling party numbers, your only recourse for permitting the one-touch redials from the Missed and Received Calls directory is to use a less optimal approach. Translation patterns can allow you to permit one-touch redials from the Missed and Received Calls directory because they give you an opportunity to modify the calling number before CallManager presents a call to an IP Phone. By modifying the calling number, you can insert the appropriate access codes and PSTN digits for calls to IP Phones in your enterprise.

Modifying the calling number does have consequences, though. Modifying the calling number means that when an IP Phone receives an external call, the displayed calling number will contain any access codes and PSTN digits. This solution permits you either to display the pure calling number and require the user to press the **EditDial** softkey for many calls, or to display a modified calling number and allow the user to press the **Dial** softkey for calls. Currently, you cannot have it both ways.

Configuring translations on inbound calls requires two separate steps.

First, you must modify the calling number for calls from the PSTN to CallManager, which causes CallManager to insert the appropriate access codes and PSTN digits.

Second, you must modify the called number for calls from CallManager to the PSTN. This step properly handles the insertion of PSTN digits. In the example above, calls from the PSTN come from both 408 555 1212 and 214 555 1212. The PSTN expects that calls dialed to the 408 area require a leading 1, while calls to the 214 area code require no leading digits at all. CallManager requires a leading 9 to distinguish calls to internal destinations from calls to external destinations. Therefore, for calls to the 408 area code, CallManager needs to prefix 91 for the IP Phone to return the call, and for calls to the 214 area code, CallManager needs to prefix just 9 for the IP Phone to return the call. However, both calls come in over the same gateway, and CallManager cannot look at the calling number to decide which digits to prefix. If CallManager prefixes just 9, the return call to 9 1 408 555 1212 fails because of lack of a required PSTN digit. If CallManager prefixes 91, the return call to 9 214 555 1212 fails because of an excess PSTN digit.

Configuring a translation for calls from CallManager to the PSTN permits you to indiscriminately prefix 91 for calls to CallManager. Then, for calls to the PSTN, you can eliminate the extraneous digits when needed for calls that do not require them.

The following example describes this procedure. Figure 2-15 shows the network that this section has already described, with two phones connected to a CallManager in Dallas, one phone connected to the Dallas PSTN, and one phone connected to the San Jose PSTN.

Figure 2-15   *Sample Network for Access Code Insertion*

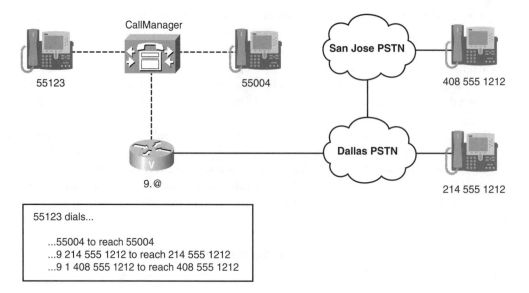

Handling the translations for calls to a Dallas phone relies on the provision of the translation and route patterns in Table 2-48.

Table 2-48 *Patterns for Inserting Access Codes for Calls to a CallManager Phone*

Configured Route and Translation Patterns	Comments
Partition: InboundTranslations Translation pattern: 55XXX Translation calling search space: CompanyABC Calling party prefix digits: 91	CallManager inserts 91 before the calling number of calls from the PSTN. The translation calling search space CompanyABC contains the partition CompanyABC.
Partition: CompanyABC Route pattern: 55004	55004 is a phone with directory number 55004. This phone has a calling search space that contains partitions CompanyABC, OutboundTranslations, and PSTNGateways.
Partition: CompanyABC Route pattern: 55123	55123 is a phone with directory number 55123. This phone has a calling search space that contains partitions CompanyABC, OutboundTranslations, and PSTNGateways.
Partition: PSTNGateways Route pattern: 9.@	The gateway to the PSTN is in its own partition, to which phones do not have direct access. The gateway's calling search space contains the partition InboundTranslations. Assume for simplicity that the gateway throws away all but the final 5 digits of the called number that the PSTN provides for calls to CallManager.

When IP Phone 55004 dials 55123, CallManager performs the following step:

Step 1   The digits 55123 match the directory number 55123 in the CompanyABC partition. CallManager delivers the call directly to IP Phone 55123 with 55004 as the calling number.

When San Jose phone 408 555 1212 dials 214 555 5123, CallManager performs the following steps:

Step 1   The PSTN gateway throws away all but the last five digits of the number the San Jose user dialed, yielding 55123. The calling number that the PSTN provides is 408 555 1212.

Step 2   CallManager uses the calling search space of the gateway to analyze the dialed digits. The digits 55123 match the route pattern 55XXX in the InboundTranslations partition. CallManager applies the calling party prefix digits of 91 to convert the calling number from 408 555 1212 to 9 1 408 555 1212. CallManager does not change the called number at all, because no called party transformations are configured for the translation pattern.

Step 3 CallManager uses the unchanged called number, 55123, for another analysis attempt. This time CallManager uses the calling search space of the translation pattern—CompanyABC—to perform the analysis. The digits 55123 match the directory number 55123 in the CompanyABC partition. CallManager delivers the call to IP Phone 55123 with 9 1 408 555 1212 as the calling number.

When Dallas phone 214 555 1212 dials 214 555 5123, CallManager performs the following steps:

Step 1 The PSTN gateway throws away all but the last five digits of the number that the San Jose user dialed, yielding 55123. The calling number that the PSTN provides is 214 555 1212.

Step 2 CallManager uses the calling search space of the gateway to analyze the dialed digits. The digits 55123 match the route pattern 55XXX in the InboundTranslations partition. CallManager applies the calling party prefix digits of 91 to convert the calling number from 214 555 1212 to 9 1 214 555 1212. CallManager does not change the called number at all, because no called party transformations are configured for the translation pattern.

Step 3 CallManager uses the unchanged called number, 55123, for another analysis attempt. This time, CallManager uses the calling search space of the translation pattern—CompanyABC—to perform the analysis. The digits 55123 match the directory number 55123 in the CompanyABC partition. CallManager delivers the call to IP Phone 55123 with 9 1 214 555 1212 as the calling number.

Using the preceding approach to translate outbound calls also enables you to use a hybrid approach for managing the Missed and Received Calls menus. This approach uses the numbering-plan-specific service parameters to translate the calling numbers of inbound calls but uses translation patterns to translate outbound calls. For instance, you could prepend **9011** to international calls and **91** to national calls, even if the return call might not necessarily require the long digit direct dial digit. Configuring outbound translations as in Table 2-49 could permit you to strip the superfluous digit while saving you from having to configure the inbound translations.

Figure 2-16 shows the Missed Calls menu that results from IP Phone 55123 receiving the three calls just described.

Figure 2-16 *Missed Calls Menu Showing Transformed Numbers*

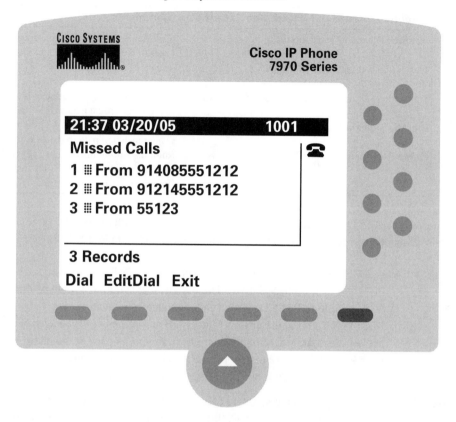

Note that the call from IP Phone 55004 has no prefix digits added, although both of the calls from the PSTN have access code 9 and PSTN digit 1 added. In the case of the call from San Jose, the modified number is identical to the number that the user dials to call the San Jose phone. But in the case of the call from Dallas, the modified number includes PSTN digit 1. If the user dials the number as shown, the Dallas PSTN rejects the call because of the extra digits. Configuring an outbound translation eliminates this problem. Table 2-49 shows the translation pattern required to strip the excess PSTN digit from the local call.

When IP Phone 55123 presses the **Dial** softkey for the call with digits 9 1 408 555 1212, CallManager uses the calling search space of the IP Phone to analyze the dialed digits 9 1 408 555 1212. These digits match the route pattern 9.@ in partition PSTNGateways. CallManager delivers the call to the PSTN gateway with called number 9 1 408 555 1212.

Table 2-49   *Translation Patterns Used to Remove Excess PSTN Digits for Calls to the PSTN*

Configured Route and Translation Patterns	Comments
Partition: OutboundTranslations Translation pattern: 91.214XXXXXXX	CallManager strips the preceding 91 for calls to the 214 area code and then uses the access code 9.
Translation calling search space: PSTNGateways DigitDiscardingInstructions: PreDot Called Party Prefix Digits: 9	Another way to configure this translation pattern uses route pattern 9.@ and a route filter with clause AREA-CODE == 214. The translation pattern then specifies the digit discarding instruction 11D->10D, which throws away the PSTN digit 1 while retaining the access code 9.

However, when IP Phone presses the **Dial** softkey for the call with digits 9 1 214 555 1212, CallManager performs the following steps, which remove the extra PSTN digit:

Step 1   CallManager uses the calling search space of the IP Phone to analyze the dialed digits 9 1 214 555 1212. These digits match both the route pattern 9.@ in partition PSTNGateways and the translation pattern 91.214XXXXXXX in partition OutboundTranslations. CallManager applies the digit discarding instructions of PreDot to convert the number from 9 1 214 555 1212 to 214 555 1212, and then CallManager applies the called party prefix digit of 9, yielding 9 214 555 1212.

Step 2   CallManager uses the modified called number, 9 214 555 1212, for another analysis attempt. This time, CallManager uses the calling search space of the translation pattern—PSTNGateways—to perform the analysis. The digits 9 214 555 1212 match route pattern 9.@ in the PSTNGateways partition. CallManager delivers the call to the PSTN gateway with called number 9 214 555 1212.

Multiple-Tenant Applications

In a multiple-tenant environment, one CallManager or CallManager cluster serves two or more independent organizations, each with its own numbering plan. The scope of responsibility of the person or organization managing the CallManager cluster can vary dramatically. At the small end of the scale is the landlord who provides the phone service for the tenants in the building (either commercial or residential). This type of deployment is termed *multitenant*. At the large end of the scale is the Internet service provider (ISP) or telephone service provider that manages a network of CallManagers and resells phone services to many companies with separate facilities, who may or may not have PBXs of their own. This type of deployment is called *IP Centrex*. The difference from a routing point of view is simply in amount of configuration; the basic call routing mechanisms used for both types of deployments are essentially the same. This book uses the term *multitenant* rather than *IP Centrex* when describing such deployments, and *service provider* when referring to the person or organization that provides multitenant services.

In a multitenant deployment, the numbering ranges for each organization might be completely isolated from each other, or they might have numbers in common, such as a security desk. Particularly because gateways are simply resources for placing calls to and receiving calls from other networks, two tenants can share gateways.

Extension Mapping for Multiple Tenants

Everything that applies to extension mapping for a single tenant applies for multiple tenants. If an inbound call arrives over a gateway, you must map the full externally published number to the proper internal extension number. Setting a calling search space on the translation pattern is extremely important here, because identical directory numbers that different tenants own must be treated as separate extensions instead of as a shared line appearance.

For example, assume there is a multiple-tenant environment in which a service provider uses one CallManager to route calls for company ABC and XYZ. Company ABC has an appearance of line 1000 registered in partition ABC, and company XYZ has an appearance of line 1000 in partition XYZ.

Company ABC's line 1000 is reachable from the PSTN as 828 8000, while company XYZ's line 1000 is reachable from the PSTN as 813 5000. The similar configuration to the one described in the previous section allows inbound calls to reach the appropriate station, though the calling search space must be set appropriately.

For example, assume that company ABC's external numbers are all in the 828 8XXX range, while company XYZ's are all in the 813 5XXX range. By eschewing any transformations in the gateways themselves, you can configure two translation patterns in a partition that only the gateway can see.

The first route pattern, 828 8XXX, uses a called party transformation mask of 1XXX. Furthermore, the translation calling search space for the translation pattern must be set to a calling search space that contains partition ABC but not XYZ.

The second route pattern, 813 5XXX, has an associated called party transformation mask of 1XXX. Its translation calling search space is set to a calling search space that contains partition XYZ but not partition ABC.

Figure 2-17 shows this configuration.

Figure 2-17 *Extension Mapping for a Multitenant Configuration*

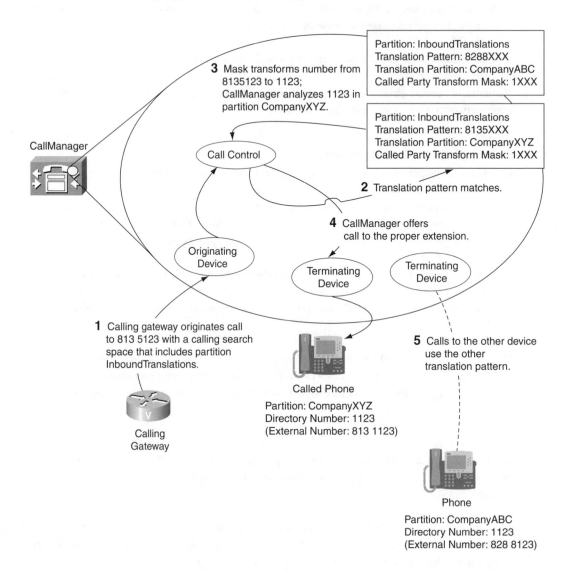

Calls Between Tenants

A wrinkle of multitenant configurations that is not present for single-tenant configurations is that of calling between tenants. Independent tenants do not call each other using their internal directory numbers. To each tenant, the other tenant should be indistinguishable from a company that the PSTN serves.

This requirement means that not only the called party must be transformed for intertenant calls, but also the calling party must be transformed. Suppose user A at extension 1000 in company ABC calls user B extension 2000 in company XYZ. If the called party's missed calls display shows the call as coming from calling number 1000, when user B tries to call user A back by dialing 1000, user B instead reaches extension 1000 in user B's own company.

One way to handle this issue is not to handle it at all. When user A dials user B, user A dials user B's external number. If user A is allowed to make outbound calls, this call routes out a gateway to the PSTN, which in turn routes the call right back into the CallManager cluster as an external call. If you have configured extension mapping, user B's display reflects the correct information.

Unfortunately, this configuration wastes gateway resources. Furthermore, the PSTN charges you for a call that the CallManager cluster can connect on its own.

Translation patterns can resolve this problem. For calls among tenants of a cluster, one can define for each tenant translation patterns that transform the calling and called numbers appropriately and extend the call directly to the called party.

For example, assume user B's external phone number is 828 2000. User A probably dials this number after first dialing an access code, such as 9. The following steps allow user A's calls to route directly to user B:

Step 1   Define the translation pattern 9 828 2XXX in a partition that is in user A's calling search space.

Step 2   Set the called party transform mask to 2XXX.

Step 3   Set the translation pattern calling search space to a calling search space containing partition XYZ but not ABC.

Step 4   If you have defined external phone number masks for all of your station devices, check the Use External Phone Number Mask check box for the translation pattern; otherwise, set a calling party transformation mask of 813 XXXX.

When user A dials user B's external number, the dialed number gets transformed to user B's extension in company XYZ's partition. CallManager uses the results of this transformation for the reanalysis and extends the call directly to user B. The calling party transformation ensures that user B's display reflects user A's external rather than internal number.

User B should have a corresponding translation pattern for calls to company ABC. Figure 2-18 shows this configuration.

Figure 2-18 *Calls Between Tenants*

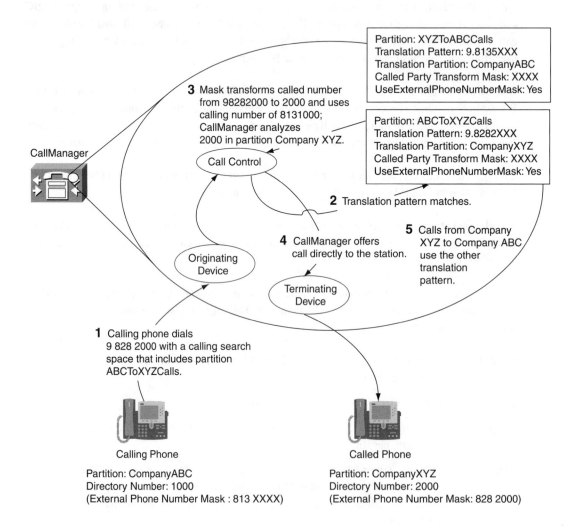

Partition: XYZToABCCalls
Translation Pattern: 9.8135XXX
Translation Partition: CompanyABC
Called Party Transform Mask: XXXX
UseExternalPhoneNumberMask: Yes

3 Mask transforms called number
from 98282000 to 2000 and uses
calling number of 8131000;
CallManager analyzes
2000 in partition Company XYZ.

Partition: ABCToXYZCalls
Translation Pattern: 9.8282XXX
Translation Partition: CompanyXYZ
Called Party Transform Mask: XXXX
UseExternalPhoneNumberMask: Yes

CallManager

Call Control

2 Translation pattern matches.

5 Calls from Company
XYZ to Company ABC
use the other
translation
pattern.

4 CallManager offers
call directly to the station.

Originating
Device

Terminating
Device

1 Calling phone dials
9 828 2000 with a calling search
space that includes partition
ABCToXYZCalls.

Calling Phone

Partition: CompanyABC
Directory Number: 1000
(External Phone Number Mask : 813 XXXX)

Called Phone

Partition: CompanyXYZ
Directory Number: 2000
(External Phone Number Mask: 828 2000)

Call Hunting Constructs

Call hunting constructs is a somewhat awkward name that attempts to indicate that the function
of these constructs is to serially or simultaneously offer calls not to a single device but to a set of
devices. CallManager supports two integrated call hunting constructs.

Hunt lists allow you to serially offer calls to groups of IP phones placed in line groups. Line
groups, in turn, permit you to simultaneously or serially offer calls to lines that they contain. Hunt
lists and line groups provide you a fairly rich toolset for disposing of calls; in addition to

provisioning different hunt algorithms, you can instruct CallManager how to treat calls when an endpoint in a line group doesn't answer or is busy. The section "Hunt Lists and Line Groups" covers hunt lists.

Route lists allow you to serially offer calls to groups of gateways or IP trunks placed in route groups. Route lists provide a couple of search algorithms and support number transformation capabilities. The section "Route Lists and Route Groups" covers route lists.

Hunt Lists and Line Groups

Although the capability to offer a call directly from one user to another is a beautiful thing, often users are closely tied together into groups. For instance, you might have a group of receptionists who handle inbound calls to a particular department or even a particular store, whose job it is to route callers to an appropriate person to answer their questions. Or you might have a phone at a main desk that should accept all inbound calls but which you would like to ring in a back room after a short delay if the front desk cannot take the call because the receptionist had to step away for a moment.

Hunt lists and line groups provide you a way to associate a group identity with a set of phones, and they allow you to set up some fairly complex criteria for the routing of inbound calls.

Hunt lists and line groups work together to handle an inbound call, and they provide slightly different algorithms for treating a call. The basic workflow for setting up call hunting is as follows:

Step 1   Identify sets of closely related directory numbers to which you desire calls to be offered.

Step 2   Assign the directory numbers into line groups. If you'd like all the phones in the set to ring simultaneously, then these phones *must* be in the same line group. When CallManager offers a call to a given line group, it offers the call to the phones in the group according to the distribution algorithm you specify on the group.

Step 3   Construct a hunt list by placing one or more line groups in order. When CallManager offers a call to a given hunt list, it offers calls in top-down order to each line group that the list contains.

Step 4   Associate one or more addresses called *hunt pilots* to your hunt list. The hunt pilot is the number that callers dial to start the call distribution and its number is distinct from that of any of the directory numbers in the line groups that the hunt list contains. Hunt pilots provide ways to dispose of the call if the call is not accepted by any of the line groups in the hunt list.

Put simply, a hunt pilot is an address that points to a hunt list. A hunt list contains a list of line groups. Line groups contain a list of directory numbers. When a caller dials digits that match the hunt pilot, the routing algorithms on the hunt list and line groups determine the order in which CallManager offers the call to destinations. Figure 2-19 illustrates the relationships between hunt pilots, hunt lists, and line groups.

Figure 2-19   *Hunt List Composition*

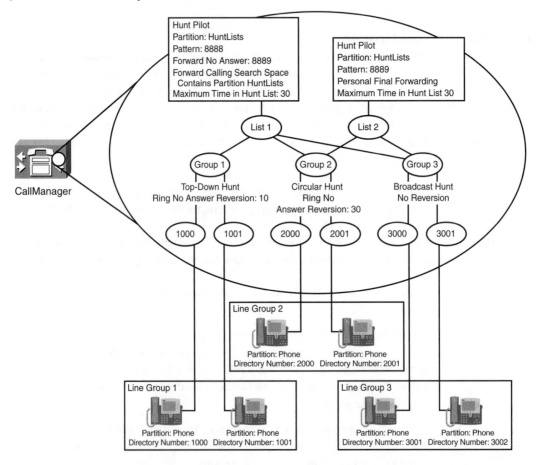

Figure 2-19 depicts three pairs of phones. Each pair belongs to a single line group. Each line group uses a different hunting algorithm. Line group 1 searches in a top-down order, line group 2 searches in a circular order, and line group 3 uses a broadcast search. (The section "Line Groups" provides specific information about the line group distribution algorithms.)

Each line group is contained in either one or two hunt lists. Hunt list 1 contains line groups 1, 2, and 3. Hunt list 2 contains line groups 2 and 3. Hunt lists always distribute calls in top-down order to the line groups that they contain.

Each hunt list is assigned its own hunt pilot. (You can assign multiple pilots to a single hunt list.) Hunt pilot 8888 points to hunt list 1, and the final disposition for hunt list 1, if no one in the hunt answers the call is to forward to hunt pilot 8889. Hunt pilot 8889 points to hunt list 2, and its final disposition is to forward the call according to personal call coverage settings. (The section "Hunt Pilots" discusses hunt pilot specific settings in more detail.)

Each line group in the hunt list contains the default Hunt Option Try next member; then try next group in hunt list for the No Answer, Busy, and Not Available conditions. Other options permit the following:

- To continue searching within the line group but not to proceed to the next line group within the list

- To immediately skip to the next line group within the list

- To stop hunting entirely

When a caller dials 8888, CallManager performs the following steps:

Step 1   Hunt pilot 8888 offers the call to hunt list 1.

Step 2   Hunt list 1 offers the call to the first group in its list, line group 1.

Step 3   Line group 1 offers the call to the phones in its group using a top-down algorithm.

Step 4   If no device in line group 1 accepts the call, hunt list 1 offers the call to the second group in its list, line group 2.

Step 5   Line group 2 offers the call to the phones in its group using a circular algorithm.

Step 6   If no device in line group 2 accepts the call, hunt list 1 offers the call to the third group in its list, line group 3.

Step 7   Line group 3 rings all phones in its group simultaneously.

Step 8   If no device in line group 3 accepts the call, hunt list 1 follows its final disposition rules, which, in this case, sends the call to hunt list 2.

Step 9   Hunt list 2 offers the call to the first group in its list, line group 2.

Step 10   Line group 2 offers the call to the phones in its group using a circular algorithm.

Step 11   If no device in line group 2 accepts the call, hunt list 2 offers the call to the second group in its list, line group 3.

Step 12   Line group 3 rings all phones in its group simultaneously.

Step 13   If no device in line group 3 accepts the call, hunt list 1 follows its final disposition rules, which, in this case, sends the call to the personal final destination.

The following sections discuss the options for line groups, hunt lists, and hunt pilots in more detail.

Line Groups

Line groups permit you to set the following options:

- A distribution algorithm, which allows you to dictate the order in which CallManager rings the phones in the line group. Line groups support the following four distribution algorithms:

  - **Top Down**, which causes CallManager to always ring available phones within the groups in strict list order, starting with the first directory number contained in the line group and ending with the last directory number contained in the line group.

  - **Circular**, which causes CallManager to, on successive calls to the line group, start the hunt with successive lines within the group. For instance, in a line group with the circular distribution algorithm, the *first* call handled by the line group begins by ringing the first directory number within the line group and ending with the last directory number contained in the line group. The *next* call handled by the line group begins by ringing the second directory number within the line group and proceeding to the last number in the line group, whereupon the hunting returns to the first directory number in the line group and continues hunting until all available lines have been offered the call.

  - **Longest Idle**, which causes CallManager to monitor the status of directory numbers within the group and order them based on how recently they were active on a call. CallManager offers calls to available lines within the group starting with the least recently used directory numbers and proceeding to the most recently used.

  - **Broadcast**, which causes CallManager to offer the call simultaneously to all available directory numbers within the line group.

- Hunt options, which work along with the RNA (Ring no answer) Reversion Timeout. Hunt options allow you to specify the treatment of calls when CallManager offers the call to a directory number within the group but that directory number does not answer, is busy, or is unavailable (possibly unregistered).

The following list describes these conditions in more detail:

— The Not Available condition describes how the line group should treat the call when it encounters an endpoint that is not in service or whose status is unknown. The Not Available setting takes effect only when the distribution algorithm you've selected is Circular or Top Down. If you select the Longest Idle or Broadcast algorithms, the line group always uses the hunt option associated with the No Answer condition to treat the call.

— The Busy condition describes how the line group should treat the call when it encounters an endpoint that is actively engaged in another call. The Busy setting takes effect only when the distribution algorithm you've selected is Circular or Top Down. If you select the Longest Idle or Broadcast algorithms, the line group always uses the hunt option associated with the No Answer condition to treat the call.

— The No Answer condition describes how the line group should treat the call when it encounters an endpoint that does not answer the call. The line group rings a non-responsive phone until either the T301 service parameter (which defines the maximum call alerting time) for the system expires or until the RNA Reversion Timeout on the line group expires. The No Answer setting takes effect for all distribution algorithms.

The preceding list describes the conditions for which a hunt list option can be set. The following list describes the available options:

— **Try next member; then, try next group in Hunt List** is the standard distribution command. When the hunt list encounters the appropriate condition on one of its members, it simply proceeds to the next member within the group. If all members within the group have been offered the call, then the hunt continues to the next line group within the hunt list. When the Broadcast algorithm is selected, the line group has no next member to select, so setting this value tells the hunt list to simply proceed to the next line group in the hunt list.

— **Try next member, but do not go to next group** causes the line group to proceed to the next member within the group. However, if all members within the group have been offered the call, then the hunt list ceases hunting and disposes of the call as if the hunt list were exhausted. When the Broadcast algorithm is selected, the line group has no next member to select, so setting this value tells the hunt list to simply provide a busy signal to the caller.

— **Skip remaining members, and go directly to next group causes** the hunt to immediately proceed to the next line group in the hunt list, even if the current line group has not offered the calls to all of its members. When the Broadcast algorithm is selected, the line group has no next member to select, so setting this value tells the hunt list simply to proceed to the next line group in the hunt list. Why would you use this option? Because the line group can respond to multiple conditions. For instance, you might want to fully search through a group when a given directory number is busy. But if one or more group members are away from the phone, you might not want a caller to have to wait for the RNA Reversion Timeout to expire for each member in the group. By setting the Skip remaining members, and go directly to next group for the No Answer condition, you can direct the caller to a voice mail system using the forwarding options on the hunt list.

— **Stop hunting** causes CallManager immediately to stop hunting. When set on the busy condition, CallManager disposes of the call as if the hunt list had been exhausted; when set on the not available option, the caller hears the reorder signaling; and when set on the no answer condition, the call rings on the selected directory number (or directory numbers in the case of the Broadcast distribution algorithm) until the T301 service parameter expires.

In addition to the call treatment options, line groups allow you to temporarily bring members in and out of service by administratively moving them from the Selected DN/Route Partition list box to the Removed DN/Route Partition list box, and vice versa.

Hunt Lists

Hunt lists themselves offer no meaningful call distribution algorithms. Hunt lists always offer calls to line groups in sequential order, starting from the first line group listed in the Selected Groups list box and proceeding to the final line group listed.

You can administratively move line groups in and out of service *within the displayed hunt list* by moving them from the Selected Groups list box to the Removed Groups list box, and vice versa.

Furthermore, you can temporarily enable or disable an entire hunt list by using the Enable this Hunt List check box.

Hunt Pilots

Hunt pilots are really just fancy route patterns (and you thought they couldn't get any fancier!) As such, they exhibit most of the same characteristics of route patterns. For instance, they

- Belong in partitions

- Support pattern notation

- Support route filters

- Belong in numbering plans

- Allow the setting of MLPP precedence

- Support routing or blocking or calls

- Can provide outside dial tone to the caller

- Can bypass the interdigit timer (by setting the Urgent Priority flag)

- Support transformations of the calling and called parties

- Support presentation settings for the calling and called parties

Hunt pilots differ from route patterns in that they support forwarding options, which enable you to specify a final disposition for a call handled by a hunt list. You can also use this disposition to route calls to other hunt lists, phones, gateways, and so on—basically anywhere you could forward a call.

Hunt pilots support the following forwarding options:

- The Forward Hunt Busy option enables you to specify where the call should route when all endpoints within the line groups that the associated hunt list contains were unable to take the call because they were busy.

- The Forward Hunt No Answer option enables you to specify where the call should route when at least one endpoint within the line groups that the associated hunt list contains was offered the call. Forward Hunt No Answer triggers either when the associated hunt list is completely exhausted or when the Maximum Hunt Timer, which you configure on the hunt list, expires without one of the endpoints in the hunt list having answered the call.

Hunt lists allow you to set up two types of forwarding options.

- You can forward calls that exhaust the list to a fixed destination by setting a specific Destination and Calling Search Space in the appropriate field.

- You can forward the list to a destination associated with the previous target of the call who has forwarded the call to the hunt list by checking the Use Personal Preferences check box.

When you select the Use Personal Preferences check box, CallManager treats the call based on the Forward No Coverage settings that you configure on the *original destination* for the call.

For instance, hunt lists can be provisioned to provide some "backup" for an individual user. Suppose that you are a member of a particular highly regarded team. If a caller attempts to reach you, you could set your forwarding options to send the call to voice mail—but this approach means that a caller, who might have had an urgent question or one that could be quickly answered by your team, must wait for you to check your voice messages before receiving help. By setting the forward no answer on your phone and creating a hunt list that contains the other members of your group, you can direct the caller to your group.

The possibility exists, however, that none of your group is currently available to take your call. In this case, you'd like to be able to direct the call to voice mail or perhaps to your personal cell phone. Simply using the static Destination in the hunt list doesn't quite suffice. If all members of your team wanted to treat calls the same way, you'd have to set up one hunt list per team member, which would be administratively painful. By specifying a Forward No Coverage destination on your phone and selecting the Use Personal Preferences check box, when the hunt list is exhausted it forwards to your personally selected destination, not to a general, fixed destination.

A personal destination takes effect only if the call was originally placed to a destination (currently, an IP phone) that has a Forward No Coverage setting. If the call is directly to a hunt list with Use Personal Preferences set, the caller hears reorder—for such hunt lists, a static destination generally suffices.

For a different example, assume phone 2000 has Call Forward All set to hunt pilot 8000, and that hunt pilot 8000 has none of its optional forwarding fields set. When another phone (say, phone 1000) dials 2000, CallManager immediately forwards the call to hunt pilot 8000, and a hunt begins. If no hunt parties answer, then a reorder tone will be played to the caller because no other final disposition was configured.

Now assume hunt pilot 8000 has its Forward Hunt No Answer destination set to 9 1 303 499 7111. Repeating the call this time results in a final disposition. When hunting exhausts, the forward settings on the hunt list apply and CallManager redirects the call OffNet to 9 1 303 499 7111, in this case, the atomic time at the National Institute of Standards and Technology (NIST).

Finally, assume that, in addition to having a Forward Hunt No Answer setting, hunt pilot 8000 has its Forward Hunt No Answer Use Personal Preference check box checked. Even though the destination field is still set to 9 1 303 499 7111, the user preference check box now takes priority.

Direct calls to the hunt pilot still result in the call being forwarded to NIST, but callers who first dial another number that is forwarded to the hunt pilot receive call treatment based on the settings of the forwarded phone.

If the forwarded phone has no Forward No Coverage fields set, then the caller hears reorder. If the caller is classified as an external caller and the Forward No Coverage External field on the forwarding party is set, then when the hunt list associated with the pilot is exhausted, CallManager redirects the call to the Forward No Coverage External destination. If, instead, the caller is classified as an internal caller and the Forward No Coverage Internal field on the forwarding party is set, then when the hunt list is exhausted, CallManager redirects the call to the Forward No Coverage Internal destination.

Route Lists and Route Groups

Life is sweet when you have only one gateway for calls to the PSTN. You configure the gateway with the route pattern you want to use for external calls, and as long as the gateway has an available trunk, it can route calls to the PSTN. But when your network grows beyond the capacity of a single gateway, you are posed with a problem: How do you configure CallManager so external calls can use both gateways, and how can you make CallManager choose the correct gateway when only one gateway has trunks available?

Route lists and route groups are the answer. This section contains the following subsections:

- "Route List and Group Operation" provides an overview of the process that route lists and route groups use to route calls.

- "Assigning Gateways to Route Groups and Route Groups to Route Lists" discusses the details of assigning gateways and trunks to route groups.

- "Route-Based Calling and Called Party Transformations" discusses how calling and called party transformations on a route list can override the calling and called party transformations you have specified on a route pattern.

Route List and Group Operation

The behavior of route lists and route groups is straightforward.

A route group represents several individual trunks and gateways to CallManager as a single high-capacity gateway. A route group is little more than a list. When a route group receives a call, it offers the call to the devices in its list according to its distribution algorithm. Route groups support both Top Down and Circular distribution algorithms; these algorithms work as described in the section "Hunt Lists and Line Groups."

If the device can accept the call, the route group's job is done. If the device rejects the call (because it is being fully utilized or is out of service), however, the route group then offers the call to the next device in its list. Only when all devices have rejected the call does the route group reject the call.

Route lists take the abstraction that route groups provide one step further. Although a route group is an ordered list of gateways, a route list is an ordered list of route groups. Where a route group sequentially offers calls to devices in its list, a route list sequentially offers calls to route groups in its list. A route list rejects an outgoing call only when no route groups in its list can accept a call.

Together, route lists and route groups allow you to control which gateways route outgoing calls. They also allow you to order your gateways so that you can route calls over gateways connected to less-expensive service providers before routing calls over gateways to more expensive service providers.

Finally, route lists provide you with additional routing control. The calling and called party transformations on route lists allow you to override, on a route-by-route basis, the calling and called party transformations that you assigned to the route pattern that selected the route list. You might need to override transformations on a particular route basis to properly format a number for the gateway that receives a call. Figure 2-20 demonstrates these features of a route list.

Figure 2-20 *Route List and Route Group Operation*

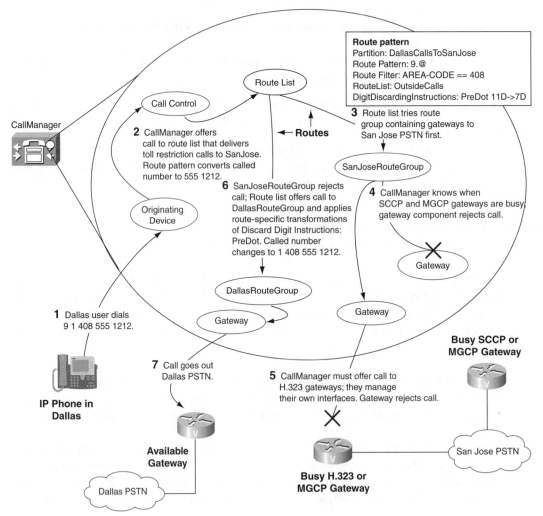

Figure 2-20 depicts a CallManager that controls two gateways in San Jose and a gateway in Dallas. For routing purposes, the two gateways in San Jose are equivalent—that is, it does not matter which gateway handles a particular call—and they belong to the same route group. The gateway in Dallas belongs in a separate route group.

Both route groups belong to a route list that handles calls from Dallas to San Jose. The route list attempts to provide toll restriction by trying to route the call to the San Jose gateways before the Dallas gateway. The route pattern 9.@ with route filter AREA-CODE == 408 is associated with the route list so that it handles calls to the 408 area code. Furthermore, dialing transformations on the route list convert the 12-digit number that the user dials into a 7-digit number for routing on the San Jose PSTN.

When a user in Dallas dials 9 1 408 555 1212, the route list performs the following steps:

Step 1   First, it attempts to offer the call to the first gateway listed in the San Jose gateways route group. This gateway is an MGCP gateway connected to the San Jose PSTN. Because CallManager manages the state of the trunk interfaces of MGCP gateways, the gateway component can immediately reject the call attempt.

Step 2   Second, it attempts to offer the call to the second gateway listed in the San Jose gateways route group. This gateway is an H.323 gateway, which manages the state of its own trunk interfaces. CallManager offers the call to the gateway, but the gateway rejects the call.

Step 3   The San Jose route group rejects the call that the DallasToSanJose route list extended, so the DallasToSanJose attempts to route the call over the PSTN. It extends the call to the Dallas gateways route group. The transformations that the route pattern applied to the called number to convert it to 555 1212, however, would prevent the call from routing from Dallas, so dialing transformations on the route override the called party transformations the route pattern applied. The route converts the number to 1 408 555 1212 and then offers the call to the Dallas gateway.

Step 4   The Dallas gateway is available and routes the call over the PSTN.

Assigning Gateways to Route Groups and Route Groups to Route Lists

Route lists are composed of route groups, which, in turn, are composed of gateways. This section describes the process of building the route group and route list structure. It consists of two subsections:

- "Assigning Gateways to Route Groups" defines the criteria by which you determine which gateways should share a route group.

- "Assigning Route Groups to Route Lists" discusses briefly some of the ways that you might choose to place route groups in route lists.

- "QSIG and non-QSIG Route Lists" describes restrictions on the types of gateways that can coexist in a route list.

The order of these sections is representative of the way in which you should build your route list structure. First, you start by configuring gateways, which you then place into route groups. When the route groups are organized, you place them in route lists. Finally, you control routing to these route lists by assigning route patterns.

Assigning Gateways to Route Groups

Each gateway endpoint a CallManager can route to can exist in, at most, one route group. The term *gateway endpoint* is deliberately a bit vague. For purposes of discussing route groups, a gateway endpoint is not necessarily a gateway, nor is it a particular span or channel on the gateway. Rather, an endpoint differs based on the type of gateway.

For example, CallManager has no control over which interface an H.323 gateway, such as the Cisco 2600, routes outbound calls; the H.323 protocol contains no provision for specific interface selection on an H.323 gateway. Rather, the configuration of the Cisco 2600 router determines which interface routes the call. As a result, even if an H.323 gateway contains several individual spans, these spans cannot be added on a span-by-span basis to different route groups. The finest routing granularity that CallManager has for H.323 gateways is the gateway level.

In contrast, CallManager can select individual spans on MGCP gateways with analog interfaces, and as a result, you can place individual spans in different route groups.

Channels of an ISDN or T1 span differ. T1s and E1s are single digital spans that are divided into 23 or 30 logical channels. Although CallManager can route calls to particular channels, it cannot include individual channels in different route groups. You must assign digital interfaces to route groups on a span-by-span basis.

Table 2-50 presents the level of routing granularity CallManager has for each general type of gateway. See Chapter 4 for more information about gateway types.

Table 2-50   *Routing Granularity by Gateway Type*

Gateway Type	Granularity
MGCP gateway analog interfaces	Span
MGCP gateway digital interfaces	Span (but not channel, except for T1-CAS)
H.323 gateways	Gateway

How should you assign interfaces to route groups? The most flexible way is to assign one interface per route group; however, even though the External Route Plan Wizard takes this approach, it is by far the most unwieldy. As a guideline, assuming you do not need to reserve certain interfaces for privileged users, you should place all interfaces that route to the same type of carrier in the same routing area in the same route group.

For instance, assume you have three gateways. Gateway 1 provides access to a PBX. Gateway 2 is hooked up to a local carrier in the PSTN. Gateway 3 is hooked directly to a long distance carrier.

Gateway 1 probably provides access to extensions that the PBX manages. Even if it provides outside access (through trunk interfaces that the PBX manages), it cannot share route group membership with either Gateway 2 or Gateway 3. Because neither Gateway 2 nor Gateway 3 provides access to the PBX extensions, they are not equivalent for routing purposes.

Gateway 2 and Gateway 3 also probably should not share route groups, even though they nominally provide access to the same place.

One reason is that calls to a long distance carrier require only ten digits for long distance calls; long distance carriers that see the initial long distance direct-dial digit reject the call.

In addition, Gateway 3 provides you with less-expensive access for long distance calls, while Gateway 2 provides you with inexpensive local calls. This situation means that you prefer local calls to route first out Gateway 2 and then out Gateway 3 as a last resort, while long distance calls route out Gateway 3 and then Gateway 2 as a last resort. As a route group can list its gateways in only one order, the gateways must be in different route groups to provide you with the behavior you want.

As a result, Gateway 2 and Gateway 3 are not equivalent for routing purposes, and each must be in its own route group.

If you add a Gateway 4, connected to the PBX, add it to the same route group as Gateway 1, because the gateways are completely equivalent from a routing standpoint.

Assigning Route Groups to Route Lists

Route lists are ordered lists of route groups. Although a given gateway endpoint can exist in at most one route group, a route group can exist in any number of route lists. Figure 2-21 presents a logical view of route lists, route groups, and gateways.

Figure 2-21 *Route Lists, Route Groups, and Gateways*

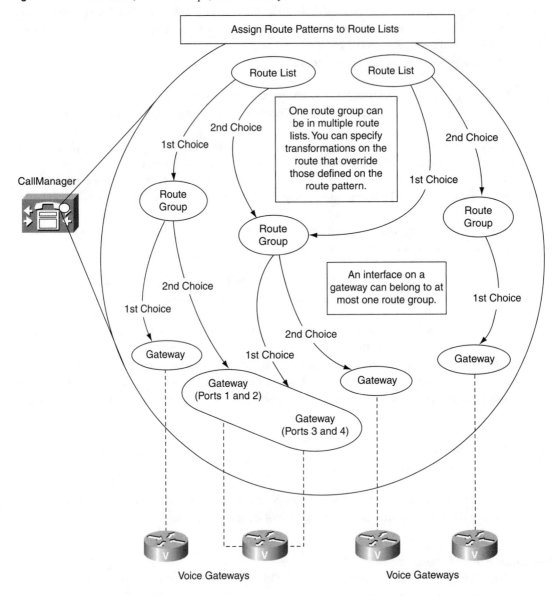

A route list is simply a gateway search pattern. For every unique order in which you want to attempt to route calls to gateways, you need one route list.

The purpose of a route list is wholly determined by the route pattern you assign to it and the route groups it contains. The External Route Plan Wizard relies heavily on route lists to provide a fine granularity of permission levels for external dialing, and to implement a variety of fallback strategies when gateways are busy or not available. The section "Routing by Geographic Location (or What the External Route Plan Wizard Builds)" describes in detail the way that the External Route Plan Wizard uses route lists for this task.

Figure 2-22 *Route Lists Used for Carrier Selection*

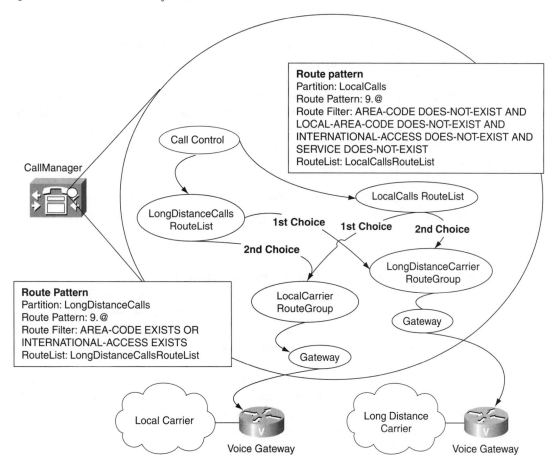

However, you can use route lists for purposes other than routing based on geographical location. You can use route lists to select outbound gateways based on anticipated cost. For instance, if you have one route group for gateways connected directly to a long distance carrier and another route group for gateways connected to a local carrier, you can define two route lists to route outbound calls accordingly. Figure 2-22 demonstrates such a configuration.

On the first route list, you define a route pattern and route filter that routes local calls. Although the way in which one dials local calls varies among geographical regions in North America, the route pattern 9.@ with route filter AREA-CODE DOES-NOT-EXIST AND LOCAL-AREA-CODE DOES-NOT-EXIST AND INTERNATIONAL-ACCESS DOES-NOT-EXIST AND SERVICE DOES-NOT-EXIST selects all seven-digit calls that a user dials.

For this first route list, you assign as the higher-priority route group the one that contains gateways connected to the local carrier. The lower-priority route group is the one that contains gateways connected to the long distance carrier.

When users dial a number that matches a seven-digit route pattern, CallManager offers the call to the local carrier gateways before trying the long distance carrier gateways.

On the second route list, you define a route pattern and route filter that routes long distance calls, such as 9.@ with route filter AREA-CODE EXISTS OR INTERNATIONAL-ACCESS EXISTS. For this route list, you assign as the higher-priority route group the one that contains gateways connected to the long distance carrier. The lower-priority route group is the one that contains gateways connected to the local carrier.

When users dial a dialed digit string that includes an area code or international access code, CallManager offers the call to the long distance carrier gateways before trying the local carrier gateways.

Route-Based Calling and Called Party Transformations

The association between a route list and one of its route groups is called a *route*. The example in the section "Assigning Route Groups to Route Lists" glosses over a detail about the dialed digits when offering a call to a local carrier versus a long distance carrier. Elaborating on this detail can demonstrate the way that called party transformations work with routes.

When CallManager offers a long distance call to a local carrier in North America, often the area code must be preceded with a 0 for operator access for a 1 for a direct-dialed call. This is usually not a problem, because users expect to dial these extra digits. On the other hand, when CallManager offers a call to a long distance carrier, any leading 0 or 1 causes the long distance carrier to reject the call.

Also, when CallManager offers a local call to a local carrier, the call is likely to route properly, but when offering a call to a long distance carrier, CallManager must explicitly include the area code as part of the dialed number. In geographical regions with seven-digit dialing, the caller does not dial any area code for calls to local numbers.

When route lists contain route groups that have different requirements for the dialed digits, the calling and called party transformations on the route pattern do not suffice. Instead, CallManager must transform the calling and called parties on a route-by-route basis. When you select a route group from the Route List Configuration page, CallManager Administration opens the Route Details Configuration page, where you can customize the dialing transformations that CallManager applies when it offers a call to the selected route group *from the current route list*.

Each route contains the same calling and called party transformations that exist on the route pattern itself. The calling party transformations are the Prefix Digits, Calling Party Transformation Mask, and the Use External Phone Number Mask check box. The called party transformations are the Digit Discarding Instructions, Called Party Transformation Mask, and Prefix Digits.

If all the calling party transformations in the route group details for a specific route group are assigned the default values, the calling party transformations of the route pattern take effect. However, if one of the calling party transformations on the route is set, the calling party transformations on the route group details take effect, instead of the ones on the route pattern.

Similarly, if all the called party transformations for the route group details for a specific route group are assigned the default values, the route pattern's transformations apply. But if any of the called party transformations are specified on the route group details, these settings take effect instead. To prevent digit discarding instructions from taking effect, the value on the route must be <None>, not NoDigits, which causes the full dialing string to be restored.

Note that when you specify transformations on a translation pattern or route pattern, these transformations manifest both on the display of the calling IP phone and in the CDRs. Transformations in the route group details, however, do not reflect themselves on the caller's phone or in the CDRs.

Therefore, completing the example begun in the section "Assigning Route Groups to Route Lists" requires specifying, on a route-by-route basis, the called party transformations to apply to the dialed digits.

When a user dials a local call, the user provides a seven-digit number. For the route from the route list to the route group containing gateways to the local carrier, the only transformation that CallManager needs to apply is to discard the PreDot section of the dialed number. However, for the route from the route list to the route group containing long distance gateways, CallManager must not only discard the PreDot section of the dialed number, but also prepend the local area code (for example, 972). (If different calling users can make local calls from different area codes, you must use several route lists.)

When a user dials a long distance call, the user provides an 11-digit number. For the route from the route list to the route group containing gateways to the local carrier, CallManager needs only to discard the PreDot section of the dialed number. However, for the route from the route list to the route group containing long distance gateways, CallManager must discard any leading 0 or 1, as well as the PreDot section of the dialed number. The digit discarding instruction PreDot 11D->10D accomplishes this task. Figure 2-23 presents this configuration.

Figure 2-23 *Local and Long Distance Route Lists*

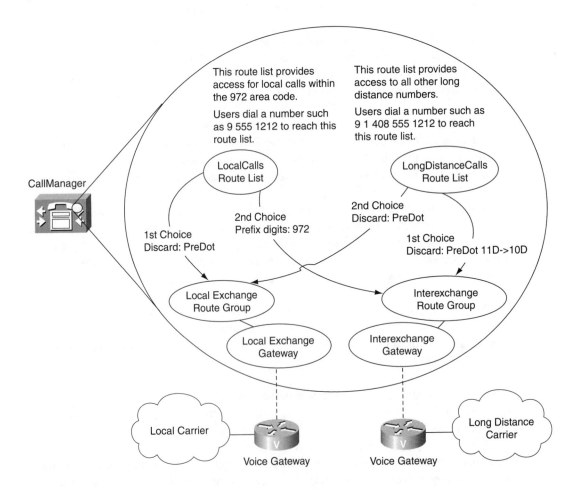

QSIG and Non-QSIG Route Lists

Since the release of CallManager 3.3, CallManager has been incorporating the QSIG protocol to foster feature interoperability with other PBXs and clusters. QSIG, described more thoroughly in Chapter 4, is a framework that allows PBXs to send feature-related messages to each other, as opposed to the traditional basic call protocols that existed prior to QSIG.

Prior to CallManager 4.0, route lists could be composed of any combination of gateway protocols. However, the QSIG protocol imposes some requirements that have made the rules for intermixing gateways in route lists more complicated.

When a feature in one PBX issues a feature message such as "invoke call transfer" to another, QSIG takes into account that the message might encounter non-QSIG trunks along the signaling path. Because non-QSIG trunks don't have the capability to carry the feature message, if the receiving PBX were to try to force the message to cross the non-QSIG span, the feature request would be lost, which would leave the issuing PBX hanging, waiting for a response.

Therefore, QSIG permits a method of operation that allows a PBX to act as a "gateway" PBX. Essentially, the receiving PBX acts as a proxy for the true recipient of the message, which is isolated behind a non-QSIG trunk.

Sometimes, important QSIG messages take place over an actual call SETUP message. SETUP messages contain the digits that enable PBXs to locate a final destination. PBXs are expected to look at the target of the SETUP and determine whether the SETUP is targeted at something local, such as a phone, or if the SETUP is supposed to transit to another PBX. If the SETUP needs to transit, the action of the receiving PBX depends on whether the transit link is QSIG or non-QSIG. If the transit link is QSIG, the PBX simply forwards the QSIG message, but if the transit link is non-QSIG, the PBX needs to operate in "gateway" mode.

Route lists pose a problem for this QSIG behavior. The function of a route list is to find an available gateway, but route lists do this by actually offering the call to the gateway. This puts CallManager in a Catch-22. If the gateway that is to be selected turns out to not be QSIG-capable, CallManager should have operated in gateway mode, but, because the call has been offered, it's too late to do so. If, instead, CallManager arbitrarily decides to operate in gateway mode, some feature transparency will be lost any time a SETUP ends up selecting a route list.

Because this limitation was fairly severe, the CallManager team worked hard to figure out a way to relax the restriction. Some complex internal code permits CallManager to mix certain types of QSIG and non-QSIG gateways—namely, QSIG gateways can be freely intermingled with non-QSIG SCCP and MGCP gateways. However, QSIG gateways cannot be intermingled with H.323 gateways.

With MGCP and SCCP gateways, CallManager understands much more clearly what the state of the calls are on those gateways. As a result, when receiving a QSIG message in a SETUP, CallManager can scout ahead to determine whether a QSIG or a non-QSIG span will actually select the call. Using this information, CallManager can decide whether to act as a gateway PBX for the message. Unfortunately, H.323 gateways are more self-contained—CallManager cannot even see what circuit-switched interfaces are hooked up to them, much less whether any resources are left on those gateways. Therefore, when deploying QSIG in your network, limiting your gateway deployments to MGCP or SCCP gateways can help ensure that you get the routing flexibility of route lists and the feature transparency of QSIG.

Calling Search Spaces and Partitions

This section discusses calling search spaces and partitions, a powerful but complex pair of mechanisms by which you can customize dialing restrictions for individual users. Calling search spaces and partitions allow you to administer such policies as routing by geographic location, routing for multiple tenants, and routing by security level of calling user.

The need to configure routing by geographic location occurs because of the nature of VoIP telephony. In an IP network, the location of the endpoints is largely irrelevant. A computer in a cubicle in the United States can connect to a computer in the United Kingdom as easily as it can connect to the computer in the neighboring cubicle. Furthermore, large enterprises can and do interconnect all of their geographically distributed sites so that everyone can access the same data applications. As a result, CallManager must take into account the fact that two phones controlled by one CallManager may reside in different locations. When one user dials an emergency number, the emergency call may need to route to a different gateway than when a different user dials the same emergency number. In addition, having IP connectivity among all of your enterprise's sites permits you to take advantage of *toll restriction*. Toll restriction is a process by which your enterprise can save money by avoiding routing calls over the PSTN when the endpoints involved in the call are connected by your private data network.

The need to configure routing by organization occurs because you can control devices owned by different companies or departments within a single company using a single CallManager. Perhaps you are an engineer, and your neighbor is in marketing. Because an engineer is likely to require complex computer software packages on the computer, and a marketer is more likely to run standard software, different IS departments might maintain your computers. Customizing call routing by the organization to which a user belongs allows you to set up a common help desk number that users can call when they encounter computer difficulties, but to route those calls to different departments. Taken to an extreme, one CallManager could serve members of completely different companies with completely independent route plans, a configuration termed multitenant or IP Centrex.

The need to configure routing by security level of calling user occurs because you need to prevent unauthorized users from placing calls that cost your enterprise money. For example, executives within your enterprise might need to make international calls, while office personnel within your enterprise need to be limited to only national numbers, and lobby phones need to be limited to emergency services and internal extensions.

This section contains the following subsections:

- "Calling Search Space and Partitions Analogy" presents an analogy that might clarify how calling search spaces and partitions work.

- "Calling Search Space and Partition Operation" describes the way in which calling search spaces and partitions work. It also presents a simple example and then discusses some unusual aspects of calling search spaces and partitions.

Calling Search Space and Partitions Analogy

Calling search spaces and partitions allow you to configure individualized call routing, because they restrict the route patterns that CallManager can access on behalf of a calling user. When seeking a match for a calling user's dialed number, CallManager restricts its search to only those route patterns that reside in the partitions that are listed in the calling user's calling search space. The following example serves as an analogy that might help explain calling search spaces and partitions.

Figure 2-24 depicts two people, Rita and Dave. Rita wants to call Dave.

For Dave to be called, he must have a phone number. Furthermore, if he wants people to call him, he needs to list his number in a directory. Assume Dave lists his number in the local white pages. (Although in real life, Dave could list his number in multiple directories, for purposes of this analogy, he can choose only one directory in which to list his number.) To call Dave, Rita needs to know his number. Rita looks for Dave's number by searching through any directories to which she has access.

If she owns the local yellow pages, her little black book, and a copy of the local white pages, when she looks for Dave's number, she finds it in the local white pages. Knowing it, she can dial it, and Dave's phone rings. Lacking the white pages, however, she is unable to call Dave, because none of the directories she owns lists his number.

The directory in which Dave lists his number is equivalent to the partition in which you list a route pattern, while the list of directories that Rita looks through to find Dave's number is equivalent to the calling search space you assign to calling devices.

Using calling search spaces and partitions allows you to give each device in your network a different picture of the routing landscape. As a result, you can configure your network so that when different users dial the same digit string, CallManager selects different destinations. This ability allows you to solve problems when your users are geographically dispersed, have different calling privileges, and belong to different organizations with independent dial plans. The section "Case Studies" discusses some complex configurations that use calling search spaces and partitions, but first, the section "Calling Search Space and Partition Operation" describes the basics.

Figure 2-24 *Calling Search Space and Partition Analogy*

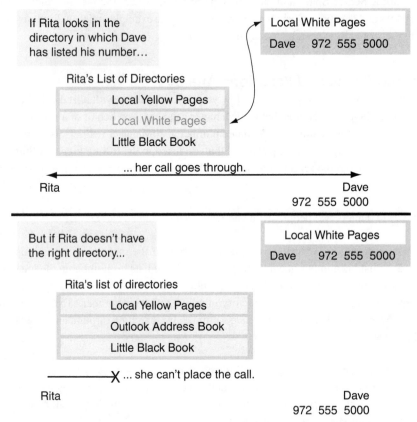

Calling Search Space and Partition Operation

Partitions divide the set of all route patterns into subsets of equally reachable destinations. *Equally reachable* means that a user who can call any single member of the subset can call all members of the subset.

A partition is simply a name you choose to identify a subset. For example, if you need a subset to contain the directory numbers of all user devices in your company (for example, Company ABC), you can create a partition named after your company ("ABC") and then assign the partition to all directory numbers in your system. Any user who can call one of the stations in partition "ABC" can call any of the stations in partition "ABC."

Devices to which you do not assign a partition belong to the <None> or *null* partition. Assigning a route pattern to the null partition makes its address visible to every device in the system.

A partition is an attribute of an address. It belongs to called entities; it has no bearing on who a device can call. Membership in a partition does not automatically mean that a device can call other devices in the partition. The list of partitions in a device's calling search space is the sole dictator of who it can call.

Partition assignment exists virtually everywhere in CallManager where you assign an address: route patterns, translation patterns, directory numbers, in addition to Meet-Me conference numbers, call park numbers, and so on.

Assigning partitions to addresses is not sufficient in itself to allow you to impose dialing restrictions. Partitions merely divide the global address space into meaningful subsets. After assigning partitions, you must assign calling search spaces to your calling users.

A calling search space is nothing more than an ordered list of partitions. A device's calling search space determines the partitions in which it is allowed to look when resolving dialed digit strings to called destinations. Calling search spaces implicitly include the null partition as the last (and thus lowest priority) partition in the list.

Calling search spaces belong to *calling* entities. Naturally, this includes stations and gateways. However, it also includes the CTI interface, which can redirect incoming calls, and call forward, which originates new calls on behalf of a called destination.

Calling search spaces are ordered. However, when analyzing a dialed digit string, the call routing component looks through every partition in the calling search space (including the null partition). Even if the call routing component finds a match in the middle of the routing analysis, closest match routing rules (see the section "Example 2—Closest Match Routing") apply. CallManager seeks the closest match among all the partitions listed, even if the closest match exists in the last partition in a calling search space.

For example, assume that route pattern 1XXX exists in partition A, and the route pattern 1000 exists in partition B. A device with a calling search space that starts with partition A and ends with partition B dials 1000. CallManager extends the call to the device with route pattern 1000, even though 1XXX both matches the dialed number and precedes partition B in the device's calling search space.

Calling search space order comes into play only if two or more partitions contain addresses that match equally closely. In such a case, the call routing component selects the destination from the first partition among the partitions containing a match for the dialed digit string. To put it another way, CallManager uses the order of partitions in a calling search space only to break ties.

The rest of this subsection covers the following topics:

- "Calling Search Space and Partitions Example" provides a simple example to show how to use calling search spaces and partitions.

- "Calling Search Spaces on Line and on Station" explains why both line and station have calling search space fields.

- "Call Forwarding Calling Search Spaces" describes how the different calling search spaces associated with call forwarding operate.

- "Message Waiting Indicator" describes how CallManager uses calling search spaces and partitions to set voice message waiting indicators.

- "Time-of-Day Routing" describes the use of partitions to implement time-of-day call routing.

- "QSIG Calling Search Spaces" describes how CallManager uses calling search spaces to handle the QSIG features of path replacement, call completion, and call forward by rerouting.

Calling Search Space and Partitions Example

A multiple-tenant installation provides the clearest illustration of how calling search spaces and partitions work. In a multiple-tenant environment, one CallManager or CallManager cluster that a single service provider administers serves two independent organizations, each with its own numbering plan. The numbering ranges for each organization may be completely isolated from each other.

Figure 2-25 presents a simple multiple-tenant configuration that demonstrates two calls, one that succeeds and one that fails. Company ABC has a station with directory number 1000 and a station with directory number 2000. Company XYZ has a station with directory number 1000 and a station with directory number 3000. Users in Company ABC can call each other but not the users in Company XYZ and vice versa.

In CallManager, no address is complete unless it consists of both a route pattern and a partition. (Keep in mind that all destinations—directory numbers, call park numbers, Meet-Me conference numbers—are route patterns.) The previous paragraph, therefore, commits an egregious error in omitting that the partition is associated with the directory numbers. If the partition is equivalent to the directory in which one lists a number, it seems reasonable to list Company ABC's directory numbers in partition ABC and Company XYZ's directory numbers in partition XYZ. Above all, the stations with directory number 1000 must be listed in different partitions. If you list them in the same directory, they represent a shared line appearance.

Figure 2-25 *Multiple-Tenant Example*

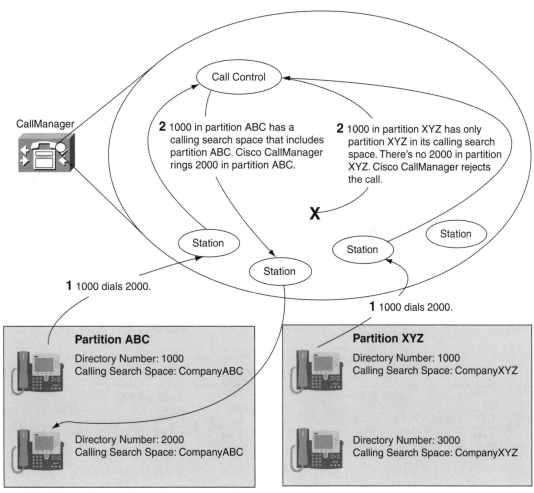

Simply setting up the partitions is not enough to complete the routing setup. You must assign each station a calling search space. Because the stations in Company ABC must be able to call other stations in Company ABC, assign them a calling search space that includes partition ABC but not partition XYZ. Assign stations in Company XYZ a calling search space that includes partition XYZ but not ABC.

When the user at directory number 2000 dials 1000, the call routing component looks through the partitions listed in the calling search space to find a match. Because directory number 2000's calling search space contains only partition ABC, the call routing component finds the directory number 1000 in Company ABC. If, on the other hand, the user dials 3000, the call routing component does not find it, and the caller hears reorder tone.

Figure 2-26 presents a modification of the multiple-tenant example. Once again, it shows two calls. In this example, users in Company ABC can call not only other Company ABC users, but also Company XYZ users. Users in Company XYZ can still call only Company XYZ users.

Figure 2-26 *Revised Multiple-Tenant Example*

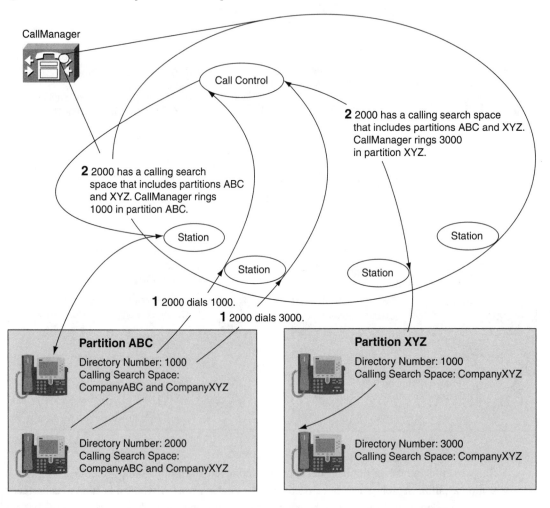

To accomplish this task, the calling search space that users in Company ABC use includes both partition ABC and XYZ. Assume partition ABC is first in the calling search space.

Now, when the user at directory number 2000 dials 1000, the call routing component finds matching route patterns in both partition ABC and XYZ. Because the matches are equal, CallManager still routes the call to the user at directory number 1000 in Company ABC. However, if the user at directory number 2000 dials 3000, the call routing component finds the matching route pattern in partition XYZ and offers a call to the associated destination.

Figure 2-27 revises the example yet again to illustrate closest match routing. Again, the example shows two calls. Assume that the route pattern 3XXX provides Company ABC users access to a PBX through a voice gateway. Because only Company ABC users can dial to the PBX, the route pattern 3XXX is listed in partition ABC.

Figure 2-27   *Revised Multiple-Tenant Example*

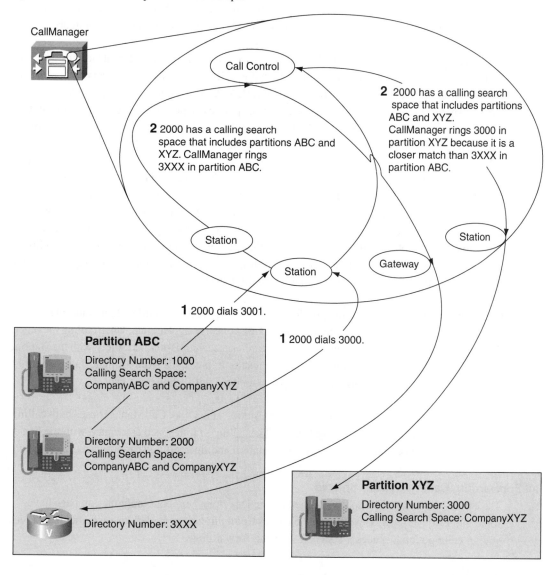

CallManager

Call Control

2 2000 has a calling search space that includes partitions ABC and XYZ. CallManager rings 3000 in partition XYZ because it is a closer match than 3XXX in partition ABC.

2 2000 has a calling search space that includes partitions ABC and XYZ. CallManager rings 3XXX in partition ABC.

Station

Station

Station

Gateway

1 2000 dials 3001.

1 2000 dials 3000.

Partition ABC

Directory Number: 1000
Calling Search Space:
CompanyABC and CompanyXYZ

Directory Number: 2000
Calling Search Space:
CompanyABC and CompanyXYZ

Directory Number: 3XXX

Partition XYZ

Directory Number: 3000
Calling Search Space: CompanyXYZ

When the user dials directory number 3001, CallManager extends the call to the voice gateway. However, when the user at directory number 2000 dials 3000, the call routes to the user in Company XYZ instead of routing to the PBX, even though the caller's calling search space lists partition ABC before partition XYZ. This behavior occurs because CallManager searches through every listed partition when analyzing dialed digits. Regardless of the order of the partitions in a calling search space, CallManager always delivers a call to the device with the closest matching route pattern.

Calling Search Spaces on Line and on Station

A common question is "Why does a calling search space exist on both the Directory Number Configuration page and the Phone Configuration page, and which one should I configure?"

A calling search space exists on the Phone Configuration page so that different stations with the same line appearance can route differently. Because CallManager servers can serve stations that are in different Local Access and Transport Areas (LATA), CallManager must provide a mechanism for routing each station's calls differently. For example, emergency calls from a station in San Jose must route to the San Jose PSTN, even if the San Jose station shares a line appearance with a Dallas station (whose emergency calls must route to the Dallas PSTN).

A calling search space exists on the Directory Number Configuration page so that different line appearances on a station can route differently. The justification for this configuration is a little more strained. One application is for a security guard desk in a multiple-tenant installation. Because different tenants might have phones with identical directory numbers, the security desk needs to be able to place calls to any tenant. As the example in the section "Calling Search Space and Partitions Example" illustrates, calling search space order causes the call routing component to choose from among equal matches to a dialed digit string.

One approach for dealing with the problem is to give the security guard's phone multiple line appearances. When calling one tenant, the guard uses one line appearance; when calling the other, the guard uses the other. If the guard's calling search space was associated solely with the station, such a configuration still would not work. As a result, to have calls from a single station route differently, calling search spaces must also be associated with a line appearance.

If you configure calling search spaces for both a station and a line, CallManager uses both calling search spaces to analyze a dialed digit string. The calling search space associated with the line takes priority when equal matches exist in the station and line calling search spaces.

Call Forwarding Calling Search Spaces

The call forwarding search spaces defined on the Directory Number Configuration page have some interesting effects. The Directory Number Configuration page defines seven fields that let you set calling search spaces associated with call forwarding:

- Call Forward All Calling Search Space

- Call Forward Busy Calling Search Space (internal and external)

- Call Forward No Answer Calling Search Space (internal and external)

- Call Forward No Coverage Calling Search Space (internal and external)

Using these fields, you can forward a user's calls to destinations the user could not normally call directly. Conversely, you can prevent the user from forwarding calls to certain destinations, even if the user could normally dial such destinations directly. For instance, using call forwarding search spaces, you can prevent a user from forwarding a phone to long distance or international destinations. This sort of configuration prevents a toll-fraud scenario, by which a user call forwards a phone to an international destination and then calls the office phone from home to make a free (to the user but not to your enterprise) long distance call.

The call forward busy and call forward no answer calling search spaces you define always take effect. In particular, when you set the call forward busy or call forward no answer calling search space to <None>, CallManager grants the forwarding phone access to only the null partition. The call forward all calling search space operates differently.

If you define a call forward all calling search space other than <None>, it always takes effect. However, if you leave the call forward all calling search space set to <None>, when the user forwards the phone from the phone itself or from the user configuration pages, the calling search space that CallManager uses for the call forward is the calling search space that the user uses when placing direct calls.

This behavior allows a user who shares line appearances in different geographical locations (perhaps because the user travels regularly from one location to the other) to forward the phone according to the appropriate geographic location.

While the calling search spaces associated with the seven different call forwarding settings define which partitions CallManager should use to resolve the forward destination, you can specify the actual forward destination in one of two fields:

- The Coverage/Destination field is the more straightforward. If you enter digit strings in these fields and do not check the associated Voice Mail check box, CallManager resolves these digits against the corresponding call forward calling search space to determine which destination to route the call to.

- CallManager, however, also allows you to specifically forward the call to voice mail by checking the Voice Mail check box for a particular forwarding type. The following section, which discusses CallManager's treatment of voice mail, provides more information about this setting.

Calling Search Spaces Interaction with Unified Messaging Systems

Unified messaging systems provide a place where you can centralize your enterprise's data communications. At a minimum, such systems handle the integration of voice mail, e-mail, and fax information. CallManager's direct interaction with such systems is in the voice mail domain. CallManager interacts with unified messaging systems using the following types of interfaces:

- **SCCP**—Used by unified messaging systems such as Cisco Unity

- **Analog gateways managed through a Simple Message Desk Interface (SMDI)**—Used by most legacy voice mail systems

- **QSIG**—Used by PBXs or other CallManagers that host a voice mail system and that connect to CallManager over a QSIG digital interface

- **JTAPI**—Used by voice mail systems that connect to CallManager using an application interface

All types of unified messaging systems interact with CallManager in essentially the same manner. That is, the nature of the communication between the systems can be boiled down to the following dialog:

- When CallManager offers a call to a unified messaging system, the unified messaging system needs to know to which voice mailbox to redirect the call.

- When a caller has left a message in a voice mailbox, or when a voice mail user deletes all pending messages, CallManager needs to receive a notification from the unified messaging system about which device to notify about the status of pending messages.

The lingua franca of this communication is through directory numbers (from CallManager's point of view) or mailbox numbers (from the unified messaging system's point of view). That is, CallManager delivers a call to a unified messaging system, CallManager provides a mailbox number, and when the unified messaging system delivers a voice mail notification message, the unified messaging system delivers the directory number of the device that should be notified of pending messages. Whether you call it a directory number or a mailbox number, the information the two systems share is simply a number.

CallManager, however, does not deal in bare numbers. Every route pattern and directory number in CallManager's configuration resides in a partition (even if that partition is set to <None>), and when routing calls, CallManager uses the calling search space of the calling device.

Unified messaging systems do not understand calling search spaces and partitions, so CallManager must maintain a calling search space on behalf of the unified messaging system to properly route the message waiting indication. Furthermore, when CallManager has overlapping extensions, as in the case of multitenant installations, it is sometimes necessary to perform number translation to ensure both that messages from two different users do not end up in the same voice mailbox, and that CallManager delivers message waiting notifications to the correct users.

This section covers the following topics:

- "About Cisco Messaging Interface (CMI)" discusses one method that CallManager uses to integrate with voice messaging systems.

- "About Non-SMDI-Based Unified Messaging Systems" discusses another method that CallManager uses to integrate with voice messaging systems.

- "Delivering the Correct Mailbox Number to Unified Messaging" discusses CallManager settings that inform a voice messaging system about which voice messaging box should receive a voice message.

- "Message Waiting Indicator" discusses the CallManager settings that permit a voice messaging system to set message waiting indicators for IP Phones.

About Cisco Messaging Interface (CMI)

Many traditional unified messaging systems connect to CallManager by SMDI. SMDI is a standard protocol specifically designed to permit different telephone systems to integrate with voice mail systems. It uses an RS-232 interface between a telephone system and a voice mail system to communicate information between the systems.

SMDI provides three types of messages:

- Messages about calls from the telephone system to the voice mail system. These messages include the voice messaging box number, whether the call is direct or forwarded, and trunk interface over which the telephone system presents the call.

- Message waiting indications from the voice mail system to the telephone system.

- Error messages between the systems.

CallManager connects to voice messaging systems with the help of the CMI service. The CMI service observes calls from CallManager to a voice mail system and manages the RS-232 SMDI interface between CallManager and the legacy voice mail system.

Figure 2-28 presents a typical connection between CMI and CallManager. When CallManager offers a call to the gateway to the voice mail system, CMI sends an SMDI message to the voice mail system that tells the voice mail system to associate the incoming call with a particular voice messaging box. When the calling user leaves a voice message, the voice mail system, in turn, sends an SMDI message to CMI, which tells CallManager to set the message waiting indicator on the appropriate phone.

Figure 2-28 *SMDI Interaction Between CallManager and a Legacy Voice Mail System*

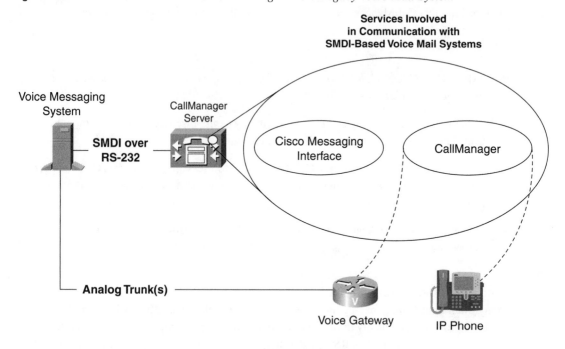

CMI has several service parameters that must be set properly in order to function. CallManager user documentation describes these parameters, but Table 2-51 summarizes the ones that are inextricably intertwined with CallManager call routing settings.

Table 2-51 *CMI Service Parameters Related to CallManager Routing Settings*

CMI Service Parameter	Description
Message Waiting Indicator Calling Search Space	The calling search space that CMI should use when telling CallManager to set a phone's message waiting indicator
Voice Mail DN	The directory number (or route pattern) associated with the voice mail system
Voice Mail Partition	The partition associated with the voice mail system

About Non-SMDI-Based Unified Messaging Systems

Unified messaging systems that use SCCP or H.323 interact directly with CallManager. They do not rely on the CMI service or an RS-232 connection. Rather, when CallManager offers a call to these systems, the call setup message directly provides them with the information that they need to deliver the voice message.

When non-RS-232-based voice messaging systems need to set a message waiting indicator for a particular phone, they do it in a rather unusual manner. CallManager includes a message waiting feature that unified message systems can access by dialing numbers you configure in CallManager Administration (**Feature > Voice Mail > Message Waiting**).

When a voice messaging system needs to set a message waiting indicator, it calls either the message waiting on or message waiting off directory number and provides the directory number of the phone whose message waiting indicator should change as the calling number.

Message waiting numbers are patterns like other dialable addresses and thus belong in partitions. When configuring a message waiting number, the calling search space of the calling voice mail system needs to contain the partition of the message waiting on or message waiting off number.

Message waiting numbers have their own search spaces. CallManager uses the calling search space that you associate with the message waiting numbers to locate the Cisco IP Phones for which you want to leave a message waiting indicator; therefore, the calling search space for the message waiting number should contain the partition of your IP Phones (or of a translation pattern that selects your IP Phones—see the section "Message Waiting Indicator").

CallManager service parameters control several settings related to voice messaging. Table 2-52 lists these settings.

Table 2-52   *CallManager Service Parameters Related to Voice Messaging*

CallManager Service Parameter	Description
Multiple Tenant MWI Modes	When set to True, this setting permits you to use translation patterns to convert voice messaging box numbers back into directory numbers when a voice mail system issues a command to set a message waiting indicator. It defaults to False. The section "Message waiting Indicator" explains this function in more detail.

Mix and Match

You can mix and match the communication methods between CallManager and your unified messaging system.

For instance, you can run CMI for purposes of delivering the voice message box to the unified messaging system, but have the unified messaging system call CallManager's message waiting numbers to set a phone's message waiting indicator. Or you can have CallManager deliver the voice message box directly over SCCP or H.323 while delivering the message waiting indicator through SMDI and CMI.

Although in normal cases you would not mix these methods of integration with voice mail, depending on your unified messaging system, mixing these methods might be the only way you can both leave messages in the appropriate mailboxes and receive message waiting indications.

Delivering the Correct Mailbox Number to Unified Messaging

In CallManager 4.1, you configure voice mail information for an endpoint by building a voice mail profile (Feature > Voice Mail > Voice Mail Profile) and associating it with the endpoint on the Directory Number Configuration page.

Voice mail profiles consist of several pieces of information:

- A voice mail pilot describes the primary address to which you have associated voice mail. Voice mail pilots contain two primary pieces of information, a voice mail pilot number and a calling search space. The voice mail pilot number represents the pattern that you have assigned to the voice mail system, and the calling search space includes the partition that you have assigned to the pattern that includes the voice mail system.

  The voice mail pilot can represent a variety of destinations. For instance, with QSIG-based voice mail, the pilot number can represent but a single gateway. With SCCP-based voice mail systems such as Cisco Unity, this pilot number can represent a hunt list containing the individual Unity voice mail ports. With legacy voice mail systems connected via Cisco MGCP gateways, this pilot number can point to a route list that selects one or more MGCP gateways that connect to the voice mail system.

  When you configure a voice mail pilot, you are not actually defining the routing construct needed to route the call to the actual voice mail system. For example, if you have Cisco Unity voice mail, you must still configure a hunt list containing individual voice mail ports.

  Instead, consider the voice mail pilot as a call forwarding destination; when CallManager determines that the call must go to voice mail, it directs the call to the number you configure using the associated calling search space. For the call to be processed properly, you must configure the destination (a hunt pilot or route pattern) that will handle the call.

  In fact, the voice mail pilot is very much like a forwarding destination. When you check the Voice Mail check box by the Forward All, Forward No Answer Internal, Forward No Answer External, Forward Busy Internal, Forward Busy External, Forward No Coverage Internal, and Forward No Coverage External settings, the destination to which CallManager forwards the call and the calling search space that CallManager uses to forward the call is not that on the Directory Number Configuration page. Instead, the destination is the voice mail pilot and voice mail calling search space you configure in the voice mail profile assigned to the line.

CallManager also uses the voice mail pilot as the target called when IP Phone users press their **messages** button.

Voice Mail Check Box

You can always manually configure the forwarding calling search spaces and specify the actual address of the voice mail system directly on the Directory Number Configuration page, but using the voice mail profile is better, especially if you have multiple voice mail systems connected to CallManager.

When you check this check box, the check box setting supersedes any specific digit string you have configured in the Coverage/Destination field. Instead, CallManager uses as the call forward destination the voice mail pilot that you have configured in the voice mail profile associated with the forwarded directory number. Instead of using the call forwarding calling search spaces you configure on the Directory Number Configuration page, CallManager uses the calling search space you've associated with the selected voice mail pilot.

So why not just manually configure the voice mail pilot number directly on the Directory Number Configuration page? If you have but a single voice mail system attached to CallManager, this option is a viable one. However, CallManager can simultaneously support more than a single voice mail system. When more than one voice mail system is in use, it might happen that the voice mail boxes of the IP Phones connected to CallManager are hosted on one system, while other IP Phones have their voice mailboxes on another system.

It might also happen that an IP Phone associated with one voice mail system sets its call forward all setting to an IP phone whose mailbox resides on another system.

When you check the Voice Mail check box on the Directory Number Configuration page, you inform CallManager that the configured forward destination is intended to be voice mail. Because the caller presumably wants to leave voice mail for the party that she dialed instead of the call forwarding target, CallManager strives to communicate to voice mail systems the identity and voice mailbox of the originally called party. If the forward target diverts the call to its voice mail pilot and CallManager communicates the voice mailbox of the original target of the call, at best, the voice mail system will be unable to find the voice mailbox of the original target and, at worst, the caller will leave a voice message in the voice mailbox of a completely unrelated party. By checking the Voice Mail check box, you allow CallManager instead to divert the call to the voice mail system associated with the original target of the call. When CallManager then communicates the voice mailbox number of the original target, the voice mail system that receives the call can store the recorded message for the proper party.

- A voice mailbox mask, which CallManager combines with the directory number with which you have associated the voice mail profile. For instance, if you configure a voice mailbox mask of 972813XXXX in a profile, when you associate the voice mail profile with directory number 5123, CallManager provides the voice mailbox number 9728135123 to the voice mail system. If you do not specify a voice mailbox mask, CallManager simply provides the directory number as the voice mailbox number.

Not all unified messaging systems handle the voice message box number. The following list describes how CallManager manages the voice message box for different types of unified messaging systems:

- **SCCP**—Cisco Unity connects to CallManager using the Skinny Client Control Protocol (SCCP). When CallManager delivers a call to Cisco Unity, it provides both the directory number and voice message box of the phone that received the call. Currently, Cisco Unity determines in which voice message box to leave the caller's message based on the directory number that CallManager provides.

- **H.323**—H.323 provides information about the destination into which a unified messaging system should leave voice mail using the redirecting number information element.

  Incidentally, CallManager sets up the redirecting number information element for calls across digital gateways using the same logic. If you connect CallManager to another telephone system with a digital interface, and the other system manages the unified messaging for your enterprise, this behavior can affect the voice message box that the unified messaging receives.

  For instance, if phone 1000 calls phone 2000 controlled by CallManager, and CallManager subsequently forwards the call to the unified messaging system on the other telephone system, the redirecting number information element tells the other system that the call has previously been forwarded so that the voice messaging system can deliver any voice message to the correct voice message box. For the redirecting number, CallManager uses the voice messaging box you have configured for phone 2000, or 2000 if you have not configured a voice message box.

- **Analog gateways connected with CMI and SMDI**—CMI always uses the masked voice mailbox you configure when informing a voice messaging system about a call.

- **Voice mail systems hosted by other PBXs that support QSIG interfaces**—CallManager, as part of call forwarding or call transfers, communicates any configured voice mailbox to an attached PBX using application protocol data units (APDU) when forwarding takes effect. If you have not configured any voice mailbox for the forwarded phone, CallManager instead communicates the directory number of the forwarded phone.

Voice mail profiles allow you to deal with multiple-tenant configurations, because voice messaging systems do not understand calling search spaces or partitions. Without the voice message box information, CallManager can provide only the directory number of a called phone to a voice messaging system.

In a multiple-tenant configuration, two users may have the same directory number. CallManager does not provide partition information to voice messaging systems, so how can these systems decide which voice message box to deliver the voice mail message to?

They cannot. Therefore, by providing voice mail profiles, CallManager permits you to map duplicate directory numbers to unique ones (for example, the external numbers by which users in the PSTN call your enterprise).

Message Waiting Indicator

When a message is left for a user in a voice messaging system, the system tells CallManager to turn on the message waiting indicator for the user by one of the following methods:

- The voice messaging system sends an SMDI command to CMI containing the voice message box that received a voice message to CMI.

- The voice messaging system calls CallManager's message waiting on and off numbers and provides as the calling number the voice message box of the phone whose message waiting indicator must be changed.

- The voice messaging system, hosted on another PBX or CallManager, delivers a message waiting indicator to the attached PBX or CallManager, which forwards a QSIG mwActivate APDU to the CallManager node that actually hosts the phone whose indicator must be lit.

CallManager uses the number that the voice message box provides and the calling search space parameter associated with the voice mail system to locate the phone whose message waiting indicator must be changed.

For the message waiting on and off numbers, configuration requires two steps. On the voice mail port that you have configured to handle the message waiting indicator command from the voice mail system, you must configure a calling search space that contains the partition that contains the Message Waiting On and Message Waiting Off numbers. The calling search space CallManager uses for this lookup is the calling search space you configure on the voice mail port or, for CMI, the CMI service parameter Message Waiting Indicator Calling Search Space.

Upon receiving the command to light or extinguish the message waiting lamp, the Message Waiting feature needs to locate the directory number whose lamp needs to be lit or extinguished. The calling search space CallManager uses for this lookup is the calling search space you configure under the Message Waiting Configuration page.

Figure 2-29 *Transforming Voice Messaging Box Numbers to Set Message Waiting Indicators*

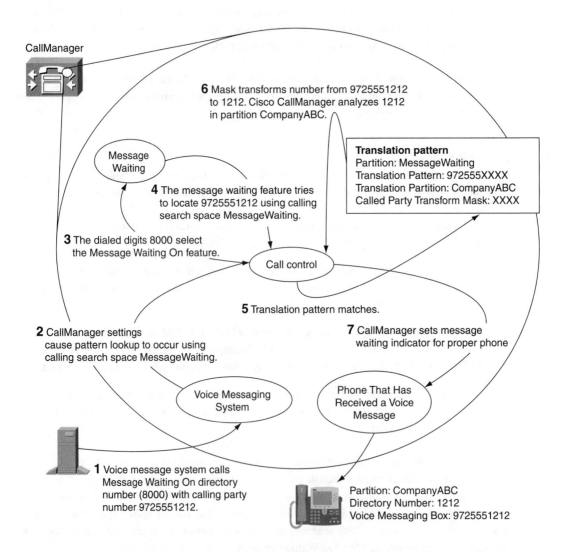

CallManager

6 Mask transforms number from 9725551212 to 1212. Cisco CallManager analyzes 1212 in partition CompanyABC.

Message Waiting

Translation pattern
Partition: MessageWaiting
Translation Pattern: 972555XXXX
Translation Partition: CompanyABC
Called Party Transform Mask: XXXX

4 The message waiting feature tries to locate 9725551212 using calling search space MessageWaiting.

3 The dialed digits 8000 select the Message Waiting On feature.

Call control

5 Translation pattern matches.

2 CallManager settings cause pattern lookup to occur using calling search space MessageWaiting.

7 CallManager sets message waiting indicator for proper phone

Voice Messaging System

Phone That Has Received a Voice Message

1 Voice message system calls Message Waiting On directory number (8000) with calling party number 9725551212.

Partition: CompanyABC
Directory Number: 1212
Voice Messaging Box: 9725551212

When the voice message box and directory number are the same, this lookup locates the number of the appropriate phone. But when the voice message boxes and the directory numbers of your phones differ, as is usually the case in multitenant installations, you must use translation patterns to direct the message waiting indicator to the correct phone. Using translation patterns for this purpose requires that you set the CallManager service parameter Multiple Tenant MWI Modes to True. Figure 2-29 shows the behavior that occurs when a voice messaging system attempts to set the message waiting indicator for the phone with voice message box 9725551212. It depicts a scenario that uses the message waiting on number. The same configuration works for the SMDI method of setting the message waiting indicator.

The example relies on the provision of the route and translation patterns in Table 2-53.

Table 2-53   *Patterns for Transforming Voice Messaging Box Numbers to Set Message Waiting Indicators*

Configured Route and Translation Patterns	Comments
Partition: MessageWaiting Translation pattern: 972813XXXX Translation calling search space: CompanyABC Called party transformation mask: XXXX	Translation calling search space CompanyABC contains partition CompanyABC.
Partition: CompanyABC Route pattern: 1212	1212 is a phone with directory number 1212.

When a voice messaging system calls the message waiting on number, CallManager performs the following steps:

Step 1   The voice messaging system calls CallManager's message waiting on directory number (8000) and specifies as the calling number 9725551212: the voice message box of the phone whose message waiting indicator CallManager must set.

Step 2   The message waiting feature takes the information about the calling device (the calling search space and calling party number) and asks the call routing component of CallManager to look up the device. You can think of this process as the message waiting feature placing a special message-waiting-indicator call in which the calling party information that the voice messaging system provides becomes the called party information for setting the message waiting indicator.

Step 3   The lookup matches the translation pattern 972555XXXX, because the calling party number—9725551212—becomes the called party number for the message-waiting-indicator call. CallManager applies the called party transformation mask XXXX to the number 972555XXXX to convert the called number to 1212.

Step 4   CallManager uses the resulting number, 1212, as the input for another analysis attempt. The calling search space CallManager uses for the analysis attempt is the calling search space of the translation pattern, CompanyABC. This attempt matches the phone with directory number 1212. CallManager sets the message waiting indicator of the phone with dialed digits of 1212.

Time-of-Day Routing

CallManager 4.1 allows you to associate schedules with partitions. These schedules describe when a partition is active. Patterns that you place in active partitions can be routed to by CallManager, but when a partition becomes inactive, the patterns in that partition become "invisible," and calls no longer route to those partitions.

Setting up time-of-day routing is a three-step process:

Step 1   Define a set of time periods. A time period is simply a persistent or recurring time duration. You configure time periods in the Time Period Configuration page (**Route Plan > Class Of Control > Time Period**).

Time periods consist of three fields: a start time, an end time, and a repetition indicator that allows you either to specify a ranges of days of the week (such as Monday to Friday) or a specific date (such as June 25).

Step 2   Arrange time periods into a time schedule. A time schedule is a more complex arrangement of time periods. For instance you might arrange a time schedule that includes the following:

- Every Monday through Friday from 08:00 to 17:00

- December 25, all day (which you specify by indicating No Office Hours for the start and end times on that day)

- January 1, all day

You configure time schedules in the Time Schedule Configuration page (**Route Plan > Class Of Control > Time Schedule**).

Step 3   Associate a time schedule with a partition (**Route Plan > Class Of Control > Partition**). When you assign a time schedule, you have two options:

- Allow CallManager to apply the time schedule according to the time zone of the calling device. For instance, if a given partition is active from 08:00 to 17:00 and the caller is in New York, New York callers can only reach patterns defined in the partition from 08:00 to 17:00 eastern time

(GMT –05:00). However at 18:00 eastern time, the same partition would be available to callers in San Jose (GMT –08:00). You configure the time zone of the calling device in its device pool.

You should use the time zone of the caller to control time-of-day routing when you don't want a caller to place calls to certain destinations outside of certain specific time periods. For instance, you might not want New York callers to place calls outside of office hours.

- Allow CallManager to apply the time schedule according to a fixed time zone. You should use a fixed time zone when you don't want patterns to receive calls outside of certain specific time periods. For instance, if you don't want New York phones to receive calls after office hours, you can associate a weekly time schedule of 08:00 to 17:00 and place it in the fixed time zone of GMT –05:00.

When a partition becomes unavailable due to a time zone transition, the call routing component of CallManager routes the call as if the patterns in the partition didn't even exist. This means that unless you configure some alternate route, callers hear reorder.

Sometimes, instead of blocking the call, you might want to route the call differently. For instance, you might want to explicitly permit all outside calls during the hours of 08:00 to 17:00, but prompt users for a forced authorization code after normal working hours.

In this case, you must configure two patterns, in different partitions, with different time schedules attached. For instance, to prompt for a forced account code after normal working hours, you configure the following:

- One time period called Workdays defining Mondays through Fridays, 08:00 to 17:00.

- One time schedule called WorkHours containing time period Workdays.

- One time period called BeforeHours defining Mondays through Fridays, 00:00 to 08:00.

- One time period called AfterHours defining Mondays through Fridays 17:00 to 24:00.

- One time period called Weekends defining Saturdays and Sundays, all day.

- One time schedule called NonWorkHours containing time periods BeforeHours, AfterHours, and Weekends.

- One partition called DuringHoursOutsideCalls containing the patterns that your enterprise uses to reach PSTN gateways. With this partition, you associate the caller-based time schedule WorkHours.

- Another partition called NotDuringHoursOutsideCalls containing copies of the patterns that your enterprise uses to reach PSTN gateways. Unlike the standard route patterns, however, check the Requires Forced Authorization Code check box. (See "Forced Authorization Codes and Client Matter Codes" for more information about configuring Forced Authorization Codes.)

During work hours, partition DuringHoursOutsideCalls will be active. If a caller were to dial an outside number such as 9 1 214 555 1212, it would find its match in partition DuringHoursOutsideCalls and route to your enterprise's PSTN gateways.

At 17:00 based on the caller's time zone, partition DuringHoursOutsideCalls becomes inactive, but, simultaneously, partition NotDuringHoursOutsideCalls becomes active. Now number 9 1 214 555 1212 matches the pattern in the latter partition, and CallManager prompts for an account code.

QSIG Calling Search Spaces

QSIG is a protocol designed to foster feature transparency between PBXs. Chapter 4 discusses QSIG in more detail, but certain QSIG features have call routing implications.

Traditional telephony features operate via the progressive extension of call legs. For instance, if a phone on PBX 1 calls a forwarded phone on PBX 2, PBX 2 traditionally affects the call forward by simply further extending the call in the forward direction. If, say, the forward destination is an extension on PBX 1, this approach creates a hairpin. Traditional call forwarding generates one call leg from PBX 1 to PBX 2 for the original call, which turns around and heads back to PBX 1 to reach the call forwarding target.

QSIG changes this dynamic by allowing PBX 2 to issue a command to PBX 1 to cause the call forwarding to be effected from PBX 1's point of view. This approach eliminates the hairpin, but it has call routing effects—CallManager's call routing constructs are always concerned about routing calls forward. How do backward routing messages such as QSIG impact it?

The following subsections discuss QSIG features that perform routing-related activities.

- "Call Forward by Rerouting" discusses the QSIG forward by rerouting feature, which allows you to prevent signaling hairpins from occurring when calls forward from one PBX to another.

- "Path Replacement" discusses the QSIG path replacement feature, which allows you to remove hairpins after they develop.

Call Forward by Rerouting

Call forward by rerouting is a QSIG feature that allows you to optimize the call signaling path when a call from CallManager to a PBX forwards to some other destination or when a call from a PBX to CallManager forwards somewhere, as long as CallManager and the PBX are connected via a QSIG gateway.

By default, CallManager operates according to the QSIG forward switch model. The QSIG forward switch model is nothing other than just a traditional telephony call forwarding model where the forwarding PBX extends new call legs toward the call forward destination. The QSIG forward switch model defines QSIG messages that can allow the caller to see the identity of the new ringing destination and the called party to see that the call has been forwarded.

The forward switch model is reliable and trustworthy, but it has the drawback of creating nonoptimized signaling paths. This can most easily be seen when considering the case where a call from one PBX crosses a circuit to another PBX, which forwards the callback to the first PBX. This model creates a signaling hairpin and consumes two circuits between the PBX, even though the final call between caller and forward target need not use any circuits at all. (When the connection between the PBX and CallManager is via an IP trunk, the consequences of call hairpinning are much less, because only the call signaling hairpins—VoIP media is always directly from calling endpoint to called endpoint.)

The forward by rerouting model changes the operation of the call forwarding feature so that rather than the forwarding PBX extending a call in the forward direction, call forward sends a message along the original circuit to the calling PBX and asks it just to call the call forward target directly.

In uniform enterprise numbering plans, this doesn't cause a problem. If you are using route codes to get from PBX to PBX, however, forwarded calls might fail. This failure can occur when the number that the forward target uses to reach the forward destination differs from the number that the caller uses to reach the forward destination.

An example that can demonstrate this problem follows. Alice is at 1000 and is served by PBX 1. Bob is at 2000 and is served by PBX 2. Carol is at 3000 also is at PBX 2. Assume that the enterprise route plan is set up so that when PBX 1 calls PBX 2, users at PBX 1 must prefix the called extension number with 888.

When Bob forwards his phone to Carol, Bob naturally enters the number that he would use to dial Carol—3000. However, if QSIG forward by rerouting triggers, then when Bob's phone forwards, the numbering plan that the forward destination (3000) is resolved against isn't that of PBX 2. It's that of PBX 1, because the forward by rerouting feature is requesting PBX 1 to dial the destination. PBX 1 doesn't have access to the numbering plan of PBX 2.

However, PBX 1 can't reach Carol's phone using the digits 3000—PBX 1 reaches Carol's phone using the digits 8883000. A call that would route via forward switch is dropped when forwarding by rerouting.

The previous example, although a good demonstration of the core problem, doesn't specifically affect CallManager. Before CallManager requests a calling PBX to attempt call forward by rerouting, it screens the forward destination that is configured. If CallManager decides that the forward destination is managed locally, CallManager uses the switch model for call forwarding, because any reroute request wouldn't optimize the path anyway—it would just route back to CallManager.

Although CallManager is safe from the preceding example, it's not hard to construct cases where CallManager would not be able to detect, much less prevent, the problem. The core problem occurs any time the forwarding party points to a destination that the calling party would reach with a different dial string.

This chapter has stated several times that CallManager can't process dialed digits without having a calling search space against which to resolve the digits. When call forward by rerouting occurs, what calling search space does CallManager use?

CallManager's standard call forwarding uses the specific calling search space that is associated with the forwarding settings for the forwarded phone. Associating a specific call forwarding search space allows you to configure phones to permit a caller to directly dial outside destinations (using the line's and/or the device's calling search spaces) but not to forward calls to outside destinations (because of restrictions built in to the call forwarding calling search space). This configuration can prevent a toll-fraud scenario where users forward their phones to international destinations and then call their phones from home to get free (for them) international calling.

When different users in your organization have different permissions, call forwarding by rerouting can encounter problems. For instance, assume a lobby phone served by PBX 1 only has permissions to dial internal destinations. Your phone on PBX 2 has permissions to call internal and external destinations and, furthermore, can forward to external destinations. You step away from your desk and forward incoming calls to your cell phone.

If a client attempts to reach your desk phone from the lobby, normally CallManager uses your phone's calling search space to resolve the address and forwards the call to your cell phone. However, the QSIG protocol provides no way for PBX 2 to indicate calling search space information to PBX 1 and, furthermore, even if such a field existed, the calling search spaces of PBX 2 probably wouldn't make any sense to PBX 1. In short, when the user in PBX 2 forwarded the call, he implicitly did so under the assumption that the routing rules of PBX 2 applied. When rerouting occurs, the call operates using PBX 1's dial plan, which is clearly not the intent of the user served by PBX 2.

When CallManager receives a request to reroute a call, rather than use any of the permissions associated with the forwarded phone, CallManager simply uses the basic calling search space of the caller to resolve the forward target. In a dial plan with unified dialing and a standard permissions structure, using the basic calling search space of the caller can work; if your enterprise call routing plan is tricky, however, it's probably best to ensure that the service parameter Forward By Reroute Enabled is False (which, by default, it is).

Path Replacement

While call forward by rerouting is a feature that operates specifically for the call forwarding and that prevents hairpins from forming, path replacement is a feature that operates for call forwarding and transfer and that repairs signaling hairpins after they have already formed.

Path replacement allows you to specify a time delay using the service parameters Start Path Replacement Minimum Delay Time (sec) and Start Path Replacement Maximum Delay Time (sec). After either call forwarding or call transfer is invoked and completed and if QSIG path replacement is enabled (via the Path Replacement Enabled service parameter), CallManager waits for the minimum delay time to expire and then attempts to optimize the signaling path. If one of the endpoints involved in the transfer or call forward is served by a different PBX connected to CallManager by a QSIG trunk, this request can result in a call rerouting message being sent to that PBX (or CallManager, if QSIG tunneling over H.323 is being used).

Similarly, a transfer or call forwarding attempt on a different PBX connected via a QSIG trunk might result in CallManager receiving a path replacement request from the PBX.

The same issues that plague call forwarding by rerouting when the numbering plan isn't transparent also pose a problem for path replacement.

Path replacement takes a different tack on the problem. Because path replacement is just attempting to optimize the path from node to node after a connection has already been established, CallManager's implementation of path replacement requires that you assign each CallManager cluster its own unique identifier (configured using the Path Replacement PINX Id service parameter). When providing another system with a number to reroute to in order to replace the path, rather than provide the address of one of the endpoints, which could be subject to dial-plan transparency issues, CallManager provides the Path Replacement PINX Id instead. When issuing the replacement call, an attached PBX will puts, as the called address, the Path Replacement PINX Id.

In turn, however, you have to make sure that the PINX Id is a valid routable number, which might require you to provision some route patterns. For instance, imagine a configuration where CallManager cluster 1 is connected to CallManager cluster 2 over a QSIG gateway and where CallManager cluster 2 is connected to a PBX over a QSIG gateway. A call exists from CallManager cluster 1 to the PBX and the PBX asks for path replacement.

In response to the request, CallManager cluster 2 must provide a routable number to the PBX. For this purpose, CallManager uses the Path Replacement PINX Id. In CallManager cluster 2, by virtue of configuring the service parameter, you define the pattern, but it's possible that the replacement call will also route through Call Manager cluster 1. Unless you configure a specific route pattern on the cluster 1-to-cluster 2 link, the replacement call won't be able to reach cluster 1.

Typically, the worst thing that can happen when the routing for path replacement isn't completely configured is simply that the path won't be replaced. The endpoints will still converse via the unoptimized path and the call won't drop.

Case Studies

This section of the document describes how all the components described in this chapter—route patterns, route filters, calling and called party transformations, translation patterns, calling search spaces, and partitions—work together to allow you to configure complex routing.

This section covers the following topics:

- "Routing by Class of Calling User" discusses routing by class of calling user. This section shows you how to define three different degrees of external access so that your most trusted users can place all classes of calls, your average users can place a more restrictive class of calls, and your untrusted users can place only the most restrictive calls.

- "Routing by Geographic Location (or What the External Route Plan Wizard Builds)" discusses routing by geographic location in a geographically distributed area. It describes both toll restriction and scenarios where toll-restriction calls must fall back to the PSTN because of fully utilized or nonfunctional gateways.

Routing by Class of Calling User

A common requirement in telephone networks is to be able to restrict the types of calls that users can make. For example, a company executive might have unrestricted dialing privileges: emergency, local, long distance, and international calls are equally accessible. On the other hand, a phone in a lobby might be able to call only internal extensions and emergency numbers. In between these extremes are those phones that you want to prevent from accessing Caribbean area codes and toll services (such as 900 services).

Configuring calling user restrictions uses several of the concepts this chapter introduces:

- Naturally, user restrictions require route patterns.

- Typically, the numbers that you want to restrict are those in the PSTN. This requirement means that the call routing component must be able to distinguish between types of calls to the PSTN, which, in turn, indicates the use of route filters.

■ If you want to apply different restrictions to different users, you must use calling search spaces and partitions.

Figure 2-30 provides a representative example that you can refer to when configuring your dial plan to deny certain types of calls to certain users. It concerns itself solely with calls to the PSTN.

Figure 2-30 *User Restrictions*

Lobby Phone
Can call other internal extensions and emergency numbers.

Office Personnel Phone
Can call internal extensions, emergency numbers, and long distance numbers, but not international or 900 numbers.

Executive Phone
Can call internal extensions, emergency numbers, and long distance numbers, including international and 900 numbers.

Voice Gateway
Provides access to the public network.

Company ABC requires three levels of outside calling privileges. Executives have no restrictions on calls they can place. Office personnel can place calls to emergency numbers, local numbers, and long distance numbers, but they cannot place international calls or calls to 900 numbers. Lobby phones can place calls only to emergency numbers.

Company ABC also has a single gateway, which employees of all levels use for outside calls. This gateway is not in a route list. The access code for calls to the PSTN is 9, and CallManager strips this access code before offering the call to the PSTN.

User-Restriction Configuration Process

The first step in configuring the user restrictions is to define route pattern and filter combinations for the different levels of PSTN access.

Executives have the simplest route pattern configuration, because they can call all PSTN numbers. The route pattern is 9.@ (which matches 9 followed by any valid number in the North American numbering plan). You must strip the initial 9 before CallManager offers the call to the gateway, so associate digit discarding instructions of PreDot with the route pattern. Assign this route pattern to partition Executives. Table 2-54 shows the route pattern configuration information for an executive's PSTN access.

Table 2-54 *Executive Access Route Pattern Information*

Field	Value
Partition	Executives
Route pattern	9.@
Route filter	<None>
Digit discarding instructions	PreDot
Route This Pattern	

Office personnel have a more complex route pattern configuration. Office personnel can call some but not all PSTN numbers. This restriction requires the use of route filters.

Office personnel cannot dial two types of numbers. The first type, international numbers, is easy to deal with. Defining the route filter NonInternationalCalls with value INTERNATIONAL-ACCESS DOES-NOT-EXIST and associating it with route pattern 9.@ instructs CallManager to route all PSTN calls that do not contain the North American international access code of 011. This route pattern is assigned to partition OfficePersonnel.

Preventing office personnel from dialing numbers with the area code 900 is trickier. Defining a route filter with value AREA-CODE == 900 does the exact opposite of what is intended: Users can dial only those PSTN numbers where the area code is 900. But there is no not-equals operator, so how does one block 900 numbers?

The solution lies in closest match routing. Rather than attempting to configure a single route pattern and filter that accomplishes all of the restrictions, you can define an additional route pattern and route filter to give restricted numbers special treatment. In this case, if you define the route filter 900Numbers with value AREA-CODE == 9XX, associate it with route pattern 9.@ in partition OfficePersonnel, and then check the **Block This Pattern** check box, when an office member dials a number with an area code of 900, closest match routing will cause the restrictive route pattern (9.@ where AREA-CODE == 900) to match in preference to the more general route pattern (which does not constrain AREA-CODE at all). As a result, CallManager applies the blocked treatment. Calls to other area codes, however, do not match the restrictive route pattern at all, so those calls go through just fine. Table 2-55 shows the route pattern configuration information for an office member's PSTN access.

Table 2-55   *Office Personnel Access Route Pattern Information*

Field	Value
Partition	OfficePersonnel
Route pattern	9.@
Route filter	InternationalCalls (INTERNATIONAL-ACCESS DOES-NOT-EXIST)
Digit discarding instructions	PreDot
Route This Pattern	
Partition	OfficePersonnel
Route pattern	9.@
Route filter	900Numbers (AREA-CODE == 900)
Digit discarding instructions	PreDot
Block This Pattern	

Lobby phones have the most restrictive routing restrictions of all; they can call only 911. Defining the route filter 911Calls with value SERVICE == 911 and associating it with route pattern 9.@ instructs CallManager to route all PSTN calls that are specifically intended for 911. You must strip the initial 9 before CallManager offers the call to the gateway, so associate digit discarding instructions of PreDot with the route pattern. Assign the route pattern to partition LobbyPhones. Table 2-56 shows the route pattern configuration information for a lobby phone's public access.

Table 2-56   *Lobby Phone Access Route Pattern Information*

Field	Value
Partition	LobbyPhones
Route pattern	9.@
Route filter	911Calls (SERVICE == 911)
Digit discarding instructions	PreDot
Route This Pattern	

The configuration is not completed. Although the route patterns on the gateway have been configured properly, the calling users have not. You must define calling search spaces for the calling users. Furthermore, it is a good idea to put your phones' extensions within their own partition. For this purpose, define partition ABC for the phones within the enterprise. Table 2-57 lists all defined partitions and a short description of the types of route patterns each contains.

Table 2-57 *Partitions for User-Restriction Example*

Partition Name	Description
ABC	Contains all phones within the enterprise
LobbyPhones	Contains gateway route patterns that provide access solely to emergency services
OfficePersonnel	Contains gateway route patterns that provide access to noninternational and non-900-number calls
Executive	Contains gateway route patterns that provide access to all external numbers

To complete the configuration, you must define the calling search spaces defined in Table 2-58.

Table 2-58 *Calling Search Spaces for User-Restriction Example*

Calling Search Space	Partitions Contained Within
Executives	ABC, Executives
OfficePersonnel	ABC, OfficePersonnel
LobbyPhones	ABC, LobbyPhones
Gateway	ABC

Calling search space Executives contains partitions ABC and Executives, which permit executive phones to call internal extensions and all PSTN numbers; calling search space OfficePersonnel contains partitions ABC and OfficePersonnel, which permits access to internal extensions and noninternational, nontoll PSTN numbers; calling search space LobbyPhones contains partitions ABC and LobbyPhones, which permits access to internal extensions and emergency PSTN numbers. Finally, it is important not to forget the gateway, which needs to be able to offer PSTN calls to the users. Calling search space Gateway provides access to internal extensions. Assigning the appropriate partition and calling search space to each phone and to the gateway completes the configuration and provides each user with the appropriate level of PSTN access. Figure 2-31 presents a representation of the final configuration.

For explanatory purposes, this section uses a naming convention for the gateway partitions designed to indicate which users can call which route patterns. The section "Routing by Geographic Location (or What the External Route Plan Wizard Builds)" presents a different naming convention that indicates type of call permitted that is more flexible in the long run.

Figure 2-31   *User Restriction Configuration Diagram*

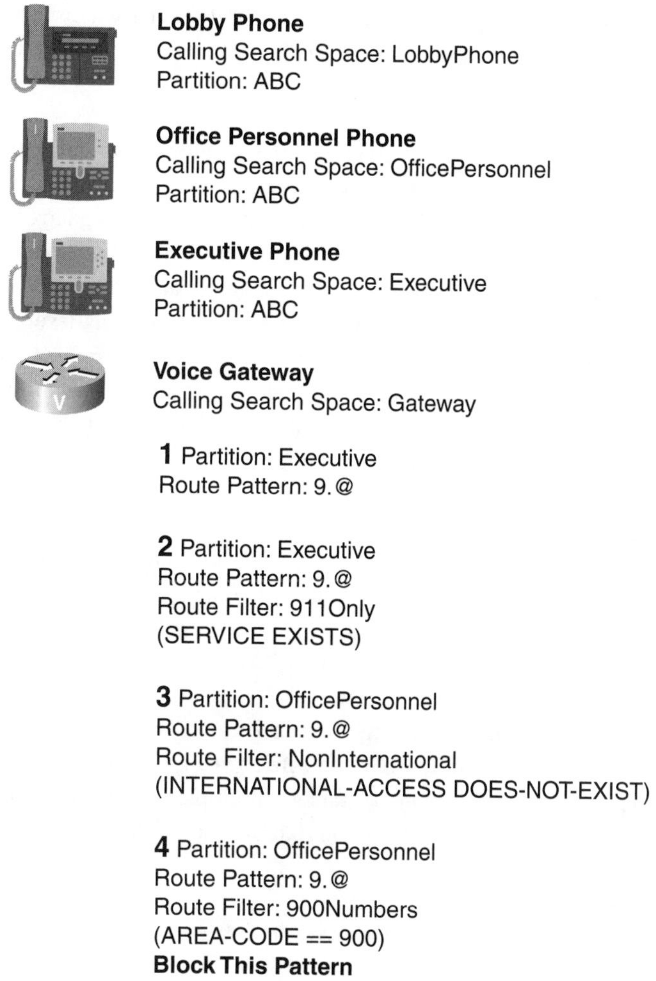

Lobby Phone
Calling Search Space: LobbyPhone
Partition: ABC

Office Personnel Phone
Calling Search Space: OfficePersonnel
Partition: ABC

Executive Phone
Calling Search Space: Executive
Partition: ABC

Voice Gateway
Calling Search Space: Gateway

1 Partition: Executive
Route Pattern: 9.@

2 Partition: Executive
Route Pattern: 9.@
Route Filter: 911Only
(SERVICE EXISTS)

3 Partition: OfficePersonnel
Route Pattern: 9.@
Route Filter: NonInternational
(INTERNATIONAL-ACCESS DOES-NOT-EXIST)

4 Partition: OfficePersonnel
Route Pattern: 9.@
Route Filter: 900Numbers
(AREA-CODE == 900)
Block This Pattern

Routing by Geographic Location (or What the External Route Plan Wizard Builds)

A major advantage of routing voice over an IP network is that it allows users served by one Local Access and Transport Area (LATA) to access gateways in a different LATA without actually having to make a call through the PSTN. This can allow you to manage the costs of your telephone network by bypassing the PSTN when possible.

The External Route Plan Wizard is an automated tool that allows you to set up a toll-bypass configuration in North America more easily. It is ideal if you have a distributed enterprise connected by a very high bandwidth, very redundant data network with gateways in different call routing areas.

The External Route Plan Wizard asks you about the locations in which your gateways reside and asks you to describe what area codes are local to each gateway. It also asks you general questions about how you want calls to be routed. Given this information, it organizes your gateways into route groups and puts the route groups into many different route lists. With each route list, the External Route Plan Wizard associates a narrow range of calls, for instance, emergency calls or international calls. Then, the External Route Plan Wizard sets up six levels of user access per routing area in your enterprise: emergency calls only; emergency and internal calls only; emergency, internal, and local calls only; emergency, internal, local and toll-bypass calls only; emergency, internal, local, and long distance calls only; all calls, including international. Once the External Route Plan Wizard finishes, you can browse to each phone in your enterprise, assign the appropriate calling search space, and expect calls from your phones to route appropriately.

The chief drawback of the External Route Plan Wizard is that it generates immense amounts of data. Each gateway in your organization gets its own route group, each location generates six route lists, and each location generates seven partitions and six calling search spaces.

This section simply describes what the External Route Plan Wizard does to set up a toll-bypass configuration. If you are unable to use the External Route Plan Wizard because you run a non-North American site, if you simply want to create a leaner, meaner version of a geographically aware routing plan, if you run a site that manages multiple tenants, or if you simply want an explanation of the prodigious output that the External Route Plan Wizard generates, then keep reading.

A toll-bypass configuration draws on almost every one of the components described in this chapter:

- Naturally, a toll-bypass configuration requires route patterns.

- A toll-bypass configuration requires the dial plan to be able to distinguish types of outside calling. For instance, emergency calls must route out only those gateways local to the calling user. Local calls should preferentially route out gateways local to the calling user. On the other hand, calls to other LATAs where you manage gateways need to route preferentially to those remote gateways. Finally, long distance and international calls can route out any gateway in the network. The need to distinguish between types of PSTN call requires the use of route filters.

- When a user dials a long distance number that routes to a remote gateway, usually the number the user dialed is not a valid number when dialed from the remote gateway itself. From the user's point of view, the number is a long distance number, so CallManager should accommodate a long distance numbering format. For instance, North American users typically dial 11 digits when dialing another geographic region. But the same destination as dialed by a user in the remote location is either seven or ten digits. Allowing the call to route properly once it reaches a remote location requires using called party transformations.

- Calling number is also an issue when a call crosses LATA boundaries. If a user in Boston places a toll-bypass call through a gateway in Orlando, how should CallManager represent the calling number? If it presents a Boston calling number, the Orlando central office may complain, because it does not recognize the number of the caller. It is often necessary either to transform the calling number to an attendant number in the remote location or to alias the calling number to a number that is valid in the remote location. These modifications require the use of calling party transformations.

- If locations contain more than one gateway, route lists provide a way to maximize gateway usage.

- Users in different locations need to reach different locations, even if they dial the same digit strings. For instance, a user in Dallas who dials 911 needs to reach Dallas emergency services, while a Boston user needs to reach Boston emergency services. Giving different users different views of the same network requires the use of calling search spaces and partitions.

Geographical Routing Problem Description

Figure 2-32 provides a representative example that you can refer to when configuring your dial plan to handle geographical routing configurations.

Company ABC has two locations, one in Dallas and one in San Jose. A high-bandwidth, highly redundant IP network connects the sites. Each site runs CallManager. CallManagers are clustered. Where the devices register is not relevant for routing purposes; a San Jose phone registered to the Dallas CallManager still physically resides in San Jose and routes as a San Jose phone.

There are three levels of PSTN access. Lobby phones can dial only internal extensions and emergency numbers. Office personnel can dial local and long distance calls, in addition to internal extensions and emergency numbers. Executives can dial all of the aforementioned types of calls, plus international calls.

The San Jose site has many phones, but this example concentrates on just four phones. 30000 is the attendant (who has office member access privileges), 31000 is a lobby phone, 31100 is a office member phone, and 31200 is an executive phone. One gateway in San Jose provides access to the PSTN. The gateway is connected to the 555 exchange in the 408 area code. The PSTN has assigned a range of 5000 to 5999 to the San Jose site. For purposes of this example, users in San Jose dial seven digits to make local calls.

Figure 2-32 *Geographical Routing Example*

San Jose Devices

30000 and 31100
Office personnel phones that can call internal extensions and non-toll, non-international PSTN numbers.

31000
Lobby phone that can call only extensions and emergency numbers.

31200
Executive phone that can call internal extensions and all PSTN numbers.

Gateway to San Jose PSTN
San Jose users use this gateway for their emergency calls and local calls. CallManager prefers to route their long distance and international calls out this gateway.

Dallas users use this gateway for calls to the San Jose public network. They use this gateway as a backup for their long distance and international calls.

Dallas Devices

40000 and 41150
Office personnel phones that can call internal extensions and non-toll, non-international PSTN numbers.

41050
Lobby phone that can call only extensions and emergency numbers.

41250
Executive phone that can call internal extensions and all PSTN numbers.

Gateway to Dallas PSTN
Dallas users use this gateway for their emergency calls and local calls. CallManager prefers to route their long distance and international calls out this gateway.

San Jose users use this gateway for calls to the Dallas public network. They use this gateway as a backup for their long distance and international calls.

The Dallas site also has many phones, but this example only needs to describe four of them. 40000 is the attendant (who has office personnel access privileges), 41050 is a lobby phone, 41150 is an office member's phone, and 41250 is an executive phone. A gateway in Dallas provides access to the PSTN. The gateway is connected to the 555 exchange in the 972 area code. The PSTN has assigned a range of 2000 to 2999 to the Dallas site. Users in Dallas dial 10 digits to make local calls.

Outbound calls route according to Table 2-59.

Table 2-59   *Routing Preferences for Geographical Routing Example*

Calls from San Jose...	
...to a San Jose extension...	...route directly to the extension
...to a Dallas extension...	...route directly to the extension
...to emergency numbers...	...route out the San Jose gateway only
...to local numbers...	...route out the San Jose gateway only
...to Dallas local numbers...	...route out the Dallas gateway, but fall back to the San Jose gateway as a long distance call if the Dallas gateway is busy or not available
...to long distance numbers...	...route out the San Jose gateway, but fall back to the Dallas gateway if the San Jose gateway is busy or not available
...to international numbers...	...route out the San Jose gateway, but fall back to the Dallas gateway if the San Jose gateway is busy or not available
Calls from Dallas...	
...to a San Jose extension...	...route directly to the extension
...to a Dallas extension...	...route directly to the extension
...to emergency numbers...	...route out the Dallas gateway only
...to local numbers...	...route out the Dallas gateway only
...to San Jose local numbers...	...route out the San Jose gateway, but fall back to the Dallas gateway as a long distance call if the San Jose gateway is busy or not available
Calls from Dallas...	
...to long distance numbers...	...route out the Dallas gateway, but fall back to the San Jose gateway if the Dallas gateway is busy or not available
...to international numbers...	...route out the Dallas gateway, but fall back to the San Jose gateway if the Dallas gateway is busy or not available

Building a toll-bypass configuration occurs in two phases:

- The section "Outbound Dialing" describes how to build the route groups and route lists for external access, how to create route filters for different levels of user access and routing by geographical region, how to transform the calling and called parties, and how to assign calling search spaces.

- The section "Inbound Dialing" describes how to build translation patterns to map external phone numbers to internal extensions and how to assign calling search spaces to control the destinations inbound gateway calls can reach.

Outbound dialing

Configuring outbound dialing consists of the following steps:

- "Route Group and Route List Creation" describes how to assign the gateways to route groups and how to build route lists to provide varied access to the route groups.

- "Route Filter Creation and Route Pattern Assignment" describes the route patterns and filters you must assign to the route lists to ensure that a calling user's call routes out the proper gateways.

- "Applying Calling and Called Party Transformations" describes the transformations you must apply to the calling and called numbers for the PSTN to properly process your calls.

- "Calling Search Space Creation, Calling Search Space Assignment, and Phone Configuration" describes how to assign calling search spaces to each user so that each user has the proper level of external access.

Route Group and Route List Creation

This subsection describes the first step in creating a toll-bypass network: creation of the route groups and route lists that the toll-bypass network uses.

Defining the route groups is simple. One gateway provides access to the San Jose PSTN; the other provides access to the Dallas PSTN. Each needs its own route group. Assign the San Jose gateway to route group SanJoseGateways and the Dallas gateway to route group DallasGateways.

Before defining the route lists, a concept introduced in Table 2-59 must be discussed. Table 2-59 introduces a concept that the External Route Plan Wizard uses, fallback. Fallback is the process of offering a call to a less desirable gateway after all desirable gateways have been exhausted.

The External Route Plan Wizard uses three types of fallback:

- Local call fallback is the strangest of the bunch. The External Route Plan Wizard prefers to route local calls from a given location only out gateways that reside in that location. If local call fallback is enabled, after all local gateways have been tried, CallManager routes local calls to gateways in different geographic locations. This process transforms a local call into a long distance call, potentially an expensive proposition.

- *Toll-bypass fallback* is more straightforward. If a caller makes a call to a remote geographic location and CallManager can determine that a gateway in the IP network resides in that location, CallManager prefers to route calls over the IP network to the remote gateway, rather than routing calls to a local gateway that must route them through the PSTN. This process is called *toll bypass*, and it requires turning a long distance call into a local call. But if all remote gateways are busy or not available, toll-bypass fallback tells CallManager to go ahead and route the call out a local gateway.

- *Long distance and international fallback* extends the External Route Plan Wizard's default option for routing long distance and international calls. The External Route Plan Wizard prefers to route long distance and international calls out a gateway that is local to the calling user. Long distance and international fallback allows CallManager to try gateways in remote locations if the local gateways are busy or not available.

Table 2-59 describes toll-bypass fallback and long distance and international fallback, but not local fallback. Some calls fall back from Dallas gateways to San Jose gateways, while others fall back from San Jose gateways to Dallas gateways. Other types of calls do not fall back at all.

Each type of fallback selects route groups somewhat differently. Every time that route group selection order must vary, one must create a route list. If different routes need different transformations, more route lists may be required. Table 2-60 shows which route lists need to be created as a result of the fallback strategy.

Table 2-60 *Route List Requirements*

Calls from San Jose...	Description
...to emergency numbers route out the San Jose route group only	These calls require no route-specific transformations.
...to local numbers route out the San Jose route group only	**Action:** Create route list SanJoseLocal, which contains only the San Jose route group.
...to Dallas local numbers route out the Dallas route group, but fall back to the San Jose route group as a long distance call if the Dallas route group is busy or not available	This call requires route-specific transformations. When a user dials an 11-digit Dallas number, the call must be converted to a local call before it routes out the Dallas gateway, but if it falls back to the San Jose gateway, all 11 digits must be sent. In addition, if a toll bypass call from a San Jose calling number routes out a Dallas gateway, it is sometimes necessary to provide a Dallas calling number so that the local carrier does not reject the call. The Dallas attendant number can serve this purpose. **Action:** Create route list TollBypassToDallas, which contains the Dallas route group followed by the San Jose route group.

continues

Table 2-60 *Route List Requirements (Continued)*

Calls from San Jose...	Description
...to long distance numbers route out the San Jose route group, but fall back to the Dallas route group if the San Jose route group is busy or not available ...to international numbers route out the San Jose route group, but fall back to the Dallas route group if the San Jose route group is busy or not available	These calls require route-specific transformations. If a long distance call from a San Jose calling number routes out a Dallas gateway, it is sometimes necessary to provide a Dallas calling number so that the local carrier does not reject the call. The Dallas attendant number can serve this purpose. **Action:** Create route list SanJoseLongDistance, which contains the San Jose route group followed by the Dallas route group.

Calls from Dallas...	Description
...to emergency numbers route out the Dallas route group only ...to local numbers route out the Dallas route group only	These calls require no route-specific transformations. **Action:** Create route list DallasLocal, which contains only the Dallas route group.
...to San Jose local numbers route out the San Jose route group, but fall back to the Dallas route group as a long distance call if the San Jose route group is busy or not available	This call requires route-specific transformations. When a user dials a seven-digit San Jose number, the call must be converted to a local call before it routes out the San Jose gateway, but if it falls back to the Dallas gateway, CallManager must convert the dialed number to 11 digits to route the call across the PSTN. In addition, if a toll bypass call from a Dallas calling number routes out a San Jose gateway, it is sometimes necessary to provide a San Jose calling number so that the local carrier does not reject the call. The San Jose attendant number can serve this purpose. **Action:** Create route list TollBypassToSanJose, which contains the San Jose route group followed by the Dallas route group.
...to long distance numbers route out the Dallas route group, but fall back to the San Jose route group if the Dallas route group is busy or not available ...to international numbers route out the Dallas route group, but fall back to the San Jose route group if the Dallas route group is busy or not available	These calls require route-specific transformations. If a long distance call from a Dallas calling number routes out a San Jose gateway, it is sometimes necessary to provide a San Jose calling number so that the San Jose local carrier does not reject the call. The San Jose attendant number can serve this purpose. **Action:** Create route list DallasLongDistance, which contains the Dallas route group followed by the San Jose route group.

Route Filter Creation and Route Pattern Assignment

The enterprise rules listed in Table 2-59 describe seven types of calls:

- **Emergency calls**—These are the same whether dialed from San Jose or Dallas.

- **Local calls in San Jose**—These consist of seven-digit calls to the San Jose PSTN.

- **Local calls in Dallas**—These consist of 10-digit calls to the Dallas PSTN.

- **Toll-bypass calls to Dallas**—These consist of 11-digit calls from San Jose to the Dallas area codes.

- **Toll-bypass calls to San Jose**—These consist of 11-digit calls from Dallas to the San Jose area code.

- **Long distance calls**—These are the same whether dialed from San Jose or Dallas.

- **International calls**—These are the same whether dialed from San Jose or Dallas.

Table 2-61 presents the list of route filters to create, their values, and a description of their purposes.

Table 2-61   *Route Filters for Geographical Routing Example*

Route Filter	Value	Description
Emergency	SERVICE EXISTS	Network services such as information (411) and emergency services (911)
SanJoseLocal	OFFICE-CODE EXISTS AND LOCAL-AREA-CODE-DOES-NOT-EXIST AND AREA-CODE DOES-NOT-EXIST	Seven-digit calls, which represent local calls in the San Jose area
DallasLocal	LOCAL-AREA-CODE == 972 OR LOCAL-AREA-CODE == 214	10-digit calls to area codes 214 and 972, which are local calls in the Dallas area
TollBypassToDallas	AREA-CODE == 972 OR AREA-CODE == 214	Long distance calls to area codes 214 and 972
TollBypassToSanJose	AREA-CODE == 408	Long distance calls to area code 408
LongDistance	AREA-CODE EXISTS	Long distance calls to area codes that no gateways in the enterprise network serve
International	INTERNATIONAL-ACCESS EXISTS	Calls to international destinations

In all cases, the route pattern is 9.@. The enterprise rules define two locations and three levels of outside calling. This argues for six different partitions for outside dialing. An additional partition can handle calls between extensions. Create the following partitions in Table 2-62.

Table 2-62 *Partitions for Geographical Routing Example*

Partition	Description
ABC	This partition contains the directory numbers of internal extensions.
SanJoseEmergency	This partition contains the route pattern that San Jose users access for their emergency calls.
SanJoseLocalAndLongDistance	This partition contains the route patterns that San Jose users access for local, toll-bypass, and long distance calls.
SanJoseInternational	This partition contains the route patterns that San Jose users access for international calls.
DallasEmergency	This partition contains the route pattern that Dallas users access for their emergency calls.
DallasLocalAndLongDistance	This partition contains the route patterns that Dallas users access for local, toll-bypass, and long distance calls.
DallasInternational	This partition contains the route patterns that Dallas users access for international calls.

Having created the route filters and partitions, assign the partitions, route patterns, and filters according to Table 2-63. Remember that the route lists control the gateway access order. For example, route list SanJoseLocal selects only those gateways connected directly to the San Jose PSTN, while route list DallasInternational first selects gateways connected to the Dallas PSTN, but then uses gateways connected to the San Jose PSTN if the Dallas gateways are busy or unavailable.

Table 2-63 *Route Pattern and Filter to Route Lists for Geographical Routing Example*

Partition	Pattern	Filter	Route List
SanJoseEmergency	9.@	Emergency	SanJoseLocal
SanJoseLocalAndLongDistance	9.@	SanJoseLocal	SanJoseLocal
SanJoseLocalAndLongDistance	9.@	TollBypassToDallas	TollBypassToDallas
SanJoseLocalAndLongDistance	9.@	LongDistance	SanJoseLongDistance
SanJoseInternational	9.@	International	SanJoseInternational
DallasEmergency	9.@	Emergency	DallasLocal
DallasLocalAndLongDistance	9.@	DallasLocal	DallasLocal
DallasLocalAndLongDistance	9.@	TollBypassToSanJose	TollBypassToSanJose
DallasLocalAndLongDistance	9.@	LongDistance	DallasLongDistance
DallasInternational	9.@	International	DallasInternational

Applying Calling and Called Party Transformations

Having defined the route lists and assigned the route patterns and filters, you must handle route-specific and non-route-specific transformations. Table 2-60 describes which routes require route-specific transformations.

Assign non-route-specific digit discarding instructions according to Table 2-64. Non-route-specific digit discarding instructions belong directly on the route pattern.

Table 2-64   *Non-Route-Specific Transformations*

Partition	Route Pattern	Route Filter	Digit Discarding Instruction
SanJoseEmergency	9.@	SERVICE EXISTS	PreDot
SanJoseLocal	9.@	OFFICE-CODE EXISTS AND LOCAL-AREA-CODE-DOES-NOT-EXIST AND AREA-CODE DOES-NOT-EXIST	PreDot
DallasEmergency	9.@	SERVICE EXISTS	PreDot
DallasLocal	9.@	AREA-CODE == 972 OR AREA-CODE ==214	PreDot

Assign route-specific called party transformations according to Table 2-65. To assign route-specific called party transformations, click specific route groups within the context of a given route list.

Table 2-65   *Route-Specific Transformations*

Route List	Route Group	Digit Discarding Instructions	Calling Party Transform Mask	Use External Phone Number Mask
TollBypassToDallas	DallasGateways	PreDot 11D->10D	972 555 0000	No
TollBypassToDallas	SanJoseGateways	PreDot		Yes
TollBypassToSanJose	SanJoseGateways	PreDot 11D->7D	408 555 0000	No
TollBypassToSanJose	DallasGateways	PreDot		Yes
SanJoseLongDistance	SanJoseGateways	PreDot		Yes
SanJoseLongDistance	DallasGateways	PreDot	972 555 0000	No
DallasLongDistance	DallasGateways	PreDot		Yes
DallasLongDistance	SanJoseGateways	PreDot	408 555 0000	No

Calling Search Space Creation, Calling Search Space Assignment, and Phone Configuration

This final stage is simple. You must create the calling search spaces and then assign them to the calling devices. With two locations and three levels of external access, you require six calling search spaces. Create calling search spaces according to Table 2-66.

Table 2-66 *Outbound Calling Search Spaces for Geographical Routing Example*

Calling Search Space	Contains Partitions	Description
SanJoseLobbyPhone	ABC, SanJoseEmergency	Provides access to internal extensions and PSTN services only
SanJoseOfficePersonnel	ABC, SanJoseEmergency, SanJoseLocalAndLongDistance	Provides access to internal extensions, PSTN services, and local, toll-bypass, and long distance calls
SanJoseManager	ABC, SanJoseEmergency, SanJoseLocalAndLongDistance, SanJoseInternational	Provides access to internal extensions and all PSTN numbers
DallasLobbyPhone	ABC, DallasEmergency	Provides access to internal extensions and PSTN services only
DallasOfficePersonnel	ABC, DallasEmergency, DallasLocalAndLongDistance	Provides access to internal extensions, PSTN services, and local, toll-bypass, and long distance calls
DallasManager	ABC, DallasEmergency, DallasLocalAndLongDistance, DallasInternational	Provides access to internal extensions and all PSTN numbers

After defining the calling search spaces, assign them according to Table 2-67. External phone number masks result from the exchange number and phone number range the phone company has assigned Company ABC in San Jose and Dallas. Finally, assign directory numbers for all phones to partition ABC.

Table 2-67 *Assignment of Calling Search Spaces*

Extension	Calling Search Space	External Phone Number Mask
San Jose Phones		
30000	SanJoseOfficePersonnel	408 555 5XXX
31000	SanJoseLobbyPhone	408 555 5XXX
31100	SanJoseOfficePersonnel	408 555 5XXX
31200	SanJoseManager	408 555 5XXX

Table 2-67   *Assignment of Calling Search Spaces (Continued)*

Extension	Calling Search Space	External Phone Number Mask
Dallas Phones		
40000	DallasOfficePersonnel	972 555 2XXX
41050	DallasLobbyPhone	972 555 2XXX
41150	DallasOfficePersonnel	972 555 2XXX
41250	DallasManager	972 555 2XXX

Inbound Dialing

For inbound dialing in a toll-bypass scenario, it is theoretically possible to have a phone be reachable by inbound dialing from any gateway in any geographical location. Such a configuration means that every internal number would have several external phone numbers. For example, if station 41050 were dialable from the San Jose gateway, in addition to 41050's Dallas address of 972 555 2050, 41050 would also have a San Jose external address of 408 555 5050. This type of configuration would very quickly consume any spare numbers you bought from the PSTN, and would be rather cumbersome to implement.

As a result, this example concerns itself with making Dallas extensions available from Dallas gateways and San Jose extensions available from San Jose gateways. This problem is therefore not truly related to a toll-bypass configuration, but it does provide some guidance for inbound dialing.

Inbound dialing configuration consists of performing the tasks in the following sections:

■   "Define Translation Patterns" recaps how to use translation patterns to map external phone numbers to internal extensions.

■   "Define and Assign Inbound Calling Search Spaces" describes how to assign calling search spaces to control the destination's inbound calls through gateways can reach.

Define Translation Patterns

Although this example permits the use of gateway called party transformations to convert an inbound phone number to an extension number, configuring the map using translation patterns saves some reconfiguration effort if you ever purchase another phone number range from the phone company.

San Jose gateways and Dallas gateways need individualized translation patterns. Define the translation patterns defined in Table 2-68.

Table 2-68 *Translation Patterns*

Partition	Translation Pattern	Translation Partition	Called Party Transformation Mask
SanJoseTranslations	408 555 5XXX	ABC	31XXX
DallasTranslations	972 555 2XXX	ABC	41XXX

Define and Assign Inbound Calling Search Spaces

After defining the translation patterns, you must create calling search spaces and assign them to the gateways. Create the calling search spaces Table 2-69.

Table 2-69 *Inbound Calling Search Spaces for Geographical Routing Example*

Calling Search Space	Contains Partitions	Description
SanJoseTranslations	SanJoseTranslations	Provides access to the extension mapping tables when the PSTN offers calls to CallManager over San Jose gateways
DallasTranslations	DallasTranslations	Provides access to the extension mapping tables when the PSTN offers calls to CallManager over Dallas gateways

Assign calling search space SanJoseTranslations to the San Jose gateway and calling search space DallasTranslations to the Dallas gateway.

Note that calling search spaces and partitions, when assigned this way, prevent tandem calls from one gateway to another. However, users can transfer or forward (unless you are also using call forward calling search spaces) inbound calls out gateways.

Geographical Routing Summary

Although configuring CallManager for geographical routing requires a complex configuration, the complexity stems from the fact that the call routing tasks CallManager must perform are themselves complex.

Configuring geographical routing requires the following steps:

Step 1   Think about the users in your network and how you want CallManager to treat their calls. What types of calls are permitted? Do you want toll restriction? What types of fallback routing do you want to permit?

Step 2   Configure your outbound dialing:

- Provision your gateways.

- Define route groups to contain gateways that connect to the same network.

- Create one route list for each unique route group search pattern that your network needs. Assign route groups to each route list appropriately.

- Define route filters that properly describe the levels of external access you want to permit. Provide outside access by narrowly tailoring these route lists to permit just one class of external call. For instance, if your network provides two levels of outside access, national numbers and unlimited access, define one route filter that defines access to national numbers only and another that defines access to international numbers only. By providing your most privileged users access to route patterns with both route filters, you give them unlimited access.

- Define partitions for each unique level of external access you want to provide. Define a partition for internal extensions.

- Assign partitions, route patterns, and route filters with the appropriate route lists.

- Set up the appropriate dialing transformations. This means using a combination of dialing transformations on the route pattern and dialing transformations on the routes themselves, when fallback or toll restriction means that certain route groups must receive a specific set of called digits.

- Build calling search spaces for each level of external access and assign them to the phones in your enterprise.

Step 3   Configure your inbound dialing:

- Define translation patterns that map the external number ranges that the PSTN assigns you to the internal ranges that your network requires.

- Define calling search spaces for the gateways in each of your geographic locations and assign them to the gateways in these locations.

Miscellaneous Solutions

This section contains some miscellaneous solutions that did not fit well in any other section of this chapter. The solutions discussed here are as follows:

- "Insertion of Access Codes in the Placed Calls menu of Cisco IP Phones" describes how to keep a user's dialed digit string intact so that the user can use the **Dial** softkey to redial previously placed calls.

- "Automatic Rerouting of Calls when Call Admission Control Fails: describes the use of Automated Alternate Routing (AAR) to direct a caller to a different destination when there's no bandwidth available to place a call to a branch office served by a Centralized CallManager deployment model.

- "One-to-One Station-to-Trunk Mapping" describes a common small PBX requirement, mapping calling users to specific outbound analog trunks, and vice versa.

- "Fallback Routing to Another PBX" describes a way to ease migration of users from an existing phone system to CallManager.

- "Multiple Call Appearances" describes how you can emulate a traditional PBX feature in which the same directory number appears on multiple lines.

- "Enhanced 911 Support" describes considerations for providing the proper calling number for emergency services in North America.

Insertion of Access Codes in the Placed Calls Menu of Cisco IP Phones

The Placed Calls menu of Cisco IP Phones such as 7905, 7912, 7920, 7940, 7941, 7960, 7961, 7970, and 7971 permits a user to quickly redial numbers that the user has previously dialed from the phone. However, the number that the phone stores is not always exactly the number that the user has dialed, because the phone stores the number after the call routing component has applied dialing transformations.

Typically, this means that the numbers in the Placed Calls menu lack any enterprise outside access code that you have provisioned, because the called party transformations on the route pattern usually strip off outside access codes.

Users who employ the Placed Calls menu can use the **Edit Dial** softkey to edit the stored number before placing the call, but users find this process cumbersome.

You can retain the access code for placed calls, however, by deferring your application of called party transformations until later in the call routing process. Instead of applying called party transformations in the Route Pattern Configuration page, assign your outbound gateways to a route group and perform the called party transformations there. This configuration hides the called party transformations from the calling phone and ensures that the **Placed Calls** menu contains the untransformed number. (Note, however, that the CDRs that CallManager logs will contain the access code, as well.)

Automatic Rerouting of Calls when Call Admission Control Fails

The centralized CallManager deployment model offers administrators significant benefits in that it allows them to administer branch offices of an enterprise from a single IP-PBX. This model relies on hosting all CallManagers in a central campus site and hosting only phones and local access gateways in the branch office. Through IP, the remote devices receive the call signaling and media control they need from the centralized CallManagers. Cisco Survivable Remote Site Telephony (SRST) can take control of the phones should the IP WAN fail.

Often, branch offices don't have extraordinarily high-speed links to the main campus. As a result, the IP WAN is sometimes able to accommodate only a limited number of calls. When this is the case, the use of CallManager locations-based call admission control can ensure that you don't oversaturate the bandwidth and degrade the voice quality of all calls traversing the link.

However, when call admission control denies a call, it's a shame to give the caller a reorder signal when the call could potentially reach the called party via the gateway in the branch office. The Automated Alternate Routing (AAR) feature solves this problem.

AAR essentially does what a normal user might try to do upon getting a reorder signal from a call to a branch office. If a user were to hear reorder from dialing an internal directory number, the user might instead try to dial the full external number for the extension in the branch office, thus routing the call though a PSTN gateway near the caller, through the PSTN, and into a PSTN gateway near the called party. This manual dialing bypasses the network congestion.

While a user probably knows what to dial if the call to the directory number is denied—the user can look up the remote number in a directory for instance—CallManager doesn't know unless you tell it. Therefore, the AAR feature allows you to configure a set of transformation rules that convert the internal extension number into a full E.164 number.

Configuring AAR relies upon four steps:

Step 1   Configuring the external phone number mask for phones in your enterprise. The external phone number mask essentially defines the raw public network number for a phone. For instance, in North America, a phone might have the number 214 555 1212 on the public network.

Step 2   Enterprises most often rely on external access codes to route calls to the PSTN (for example, 9 is used to route a call throughout the PSTN in most North American PBXs). As a result, prefix digits often need to be added to route the caller's automated redial attempt out to the public network. Therefore, you must define AAR groups to define these transformation rules.

AAR groups operate as a matrix. When a reroute is required, CallManager looks at the AAR group associated with the caller and the AAR group associated with the called party. For each unique ordered pair of groups, you define which digits must be prepended for CallManager to modify the number to something that routes to the public network. For instance, in a country with a completely uniform numbering plan, you might put all your phones and gateways in a single AAR group with the single prefix digit 9, to allow the redial call to prepend your PSTN access digit. All phones are deemed to be part of the same dialing domain when they all are addressed with the same structure on the PSTN (for example, NPA NXX XXXX in North America).

> **NOTE**   The combination of the external phone number mask with the AAR group normalizes all AAR calls within North America to a structure of 9 1 NPA NXX XXXX, and relies on the locally significant AAR calling search spaces to adapt the string in cases where the destination is reachable using a 7-digit or 10-digit local dialing pattern. Local variations can be accommodated by the AAR calling search space of the calling device. For instance, a New York number may be called by dialing 9 1 212 555 1234 from California (in fact, from probably anywhere in North America except New York), but if the same destination is called from a phone within the same seven-digit local calling area in New York, only 9 555 1234 is required. The solution is to insert a translation pattern in the AAR calling search space of all phones within the same local seven-digit calling area: The translation pattern would need to be 91212.555XXXX, and would strip digits PreDot, followed by the prepending of 9.

If phones are situated in different dialing domains, you must configure different AAR groups. For instance, if an enterprise has phones from the same cluster in both North America and England, a New York number might be reachable from another North American site by prepending 91 to the number contained in the external phone number mask (212 555 1234), but you might need 001 prepended to call this same number from the site in England. AAR groups allow you to define unique prepending rules for each pair of source-destination dialing domains.

Step 3   After you've configured the AAR group matrix under **Route Plan > AAR Group**, assign the AAR groups to the appropriate devices. Assignment of AAR groups is always on the respective device page.

Step 4   Because the AAR calling search space is invoked only when a call to an on-net destination has been denied by call admission control, it is okay to include toll-call route patterns even if the regular calling search space of the calling phone is not allowed toll calls. Remember that the AAR calling search space is invoked only if the original call is to an OnNet destination and that destination is part of the calling phone's permitted destinations. A very permissive AAR calling search space does not allow for calls to unauthorized destinations resulting in toll fraud.

One-to-One Station-to-Trunk Mapping

Small PBXs associate calling stations to specific analog trunks, and vice versa. The service parameter Matching Calling Party With Attendant Flag (see the section "Dialing Transformations") provides a quick way to ensure that a given calling station's external calls route over a specific analog trunk.

However, if you have several analog gateways, to ensure that the calling user's call is presented to the correct gateway, you must put all of your analog gateways in a route list to successfully use the Matching Calling Party With Attendant Flag. If you have more than a few gateways, this configuration is not efficient, because CallManager attempts to offer external calls to each analog interface one at a time until CallManager finds the analog interface with an Attendant DN that matches the calling number.

Calling search spaces and partitions offer a solution, if a cumbersome one. For inbound calls, you can use the same field as the gateways with analog interfaces do: configure the associated phone's directory number as the Attendant DN setting for the analog port.

For external dialing, however, provision each external trunk with its own @ pattern (or other external dialing pattern) and then assign each route pattern a unique partition. A calling user includes one of the unique partitions in the calling search space, which causes the calling user's outbound calls always to route to one specific trunk.

For example, assume you have two users, Alice, with directory number 1000, and Bill, with directory number 2000. In addition, you have an MGCP gateway with two loop start trunks. Inbound calls from the first trunk route to Alice, and Alice's outbound calls route out the first trunk. Inbound calls from the second trunk route to Bill, and Bill's outbound calls route out the second trunk.

To route the inbound calls correctly, you must simply assign Alice's directory number (1000) as the Attendant DN of the first port and Bill's directory number (2000) as the Attendant DN of the second port.

Routing outbound calls requires that you use calling search spaces and partitions. Create two partitions, CallsFromAlice and CallsFromBill. Create the route pattern 9.@ in partition CallsFromAlice and associate it with the first trunk. Then create the route pattern 9.@ in partition CallsFromBill and associate it with the second trunk. Finally, assign Alice a calling search space that includes partition CallsFromAlice and assign Bill a calling search space that includes partition CallsFromBill.

When Alice dials an external number such as 9 1 408 555 1212, her dialed digit string matches the 9.@ pattern associated with the first trunk, because her analysis request can only see the route patterns defined in partition CallsFromAlice. On the other hand, when Bill dials an external number, his dialed digit string matches the 9.@ pattern associated with the second trunk. Figure 2-33 presents this behavior.

Figure 2-33 *One-to-One Trunk-to-Station Mapping*

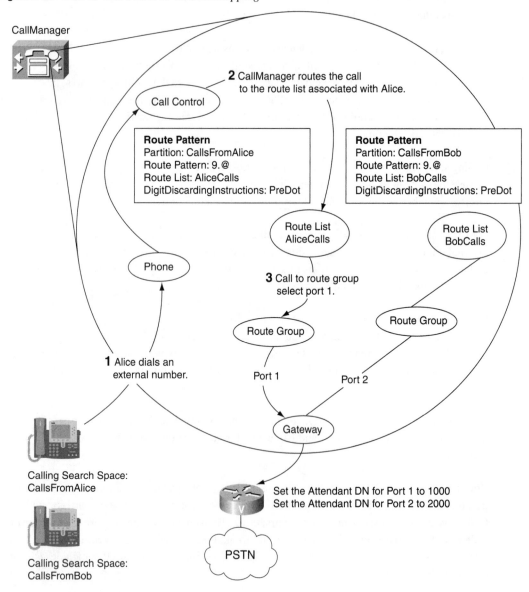

Fallback Routing to Another PBX

If you migrate users from another telephone system to CallManager, which is connected to the other telephone system by a gateway, you might want to maintain the directory numbers of those users who have moved.

When you migrate users from one system to another, directory numbers within a directory number range are often spread between both systems. For example, if your directory number range is 8000 to 8999, CallManager might serve directory numbers 8101, 8301, and 8425, while the other telephone system serves all other extensions in the range.

Maintaining the routing between the two systems would be a very difficult task if you had to enter all of the extensions that the other phone system manages into the CallManager database one by one.

Using closest match routing, you can define a pattern, such as 8XXX, on the gateway to the other system. When a user that CallManager serves dials an extension that CallManager also serves, closest match routing causes specific pattern to match; however, if a user dials a number that CallManager does not control, route pattern XXXX sends the call to the other system.

For example, assume CallManager serves directory numbers 8101, 8301, and 8425. Route pattern XXXX corresponds to the gateway to the other phone system. If a user dials 8101, CallManager offers the call to the phone it controls, but if a user dials 8500, CallManager routes the call to the gateway to the other phone system.

If that was all there was to it, this configuration would not deserve its own section. However, what if the other phone system does not control any phone with directory number 8500? If the other phone system is configured to route unknown directory numbers to CallManager, the two systems will play table tennis with the call. The call forwards from system to system until it consumes all trunk resources between the systems. The call clears at that point, but the situation ties up all of the trunks temporarily. If the systems are connected by nonphysical resources such as intercluster trunks, CallManager bounces the calls between the systems indefinitely.

Calling search spaces and partitions allow you to break the routing loop. If you put the fallback pattern XXXX in a partition that is not included in the gateway's calling search space, when the other telephone system routes the outgoing call to 8500 back into CallManager, CallManager does not find any matches for the dialed number and rejects the call before the routing loop consumes all the gateway resources.

Multiple Call Appearances

Traditional PBX phones provide users with a one- or two-line display and rows of buttons next to LEDs. The limited user interface means that providing complex user features is quite a challenge.

Users of PBX phones, especially administrative assistants, require the ability to take numerous calls at a single number. In addition, users need to be able to transfer individual calls to other destinations, no matter how many calls currently terminate on the line. Traditional PBX phones accomplish this by permitting multiple appearances of the same directory number to appear on a single phone. These multiple appearances are termed *call appearances*. As new calls arrive at a phone with multiple call appearances, traditional PBXs offer them to unoccupied call appearances. By selecting different call appearances, a user at a phone can move from call to call and transfer individual users.

CallManager does not support multiple call appearances. If you assign a particular directory number to a line on a particular IP phone, CallManager Administration will not allow you to assign it to another line on that phone. However, using calling search spaces and partitions, you can emulate traditional call appearances very closely. Figure 2-34 shows an IP phone configured with multiple call appearances.

Figure 2-34 *Multiple Call Appearances on an IP Phone*

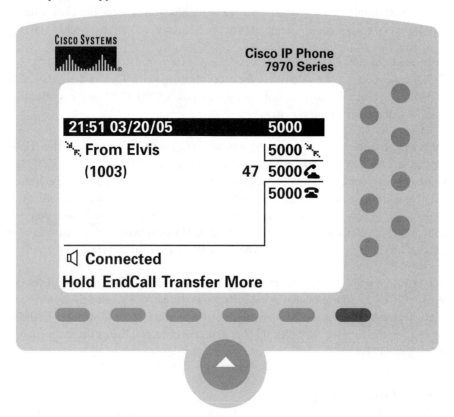

This functionality relies on the fact that, to CallManager, identical directory numbers in different partitions are different destinations. Because partition names do not show up on IP phone displays, to the user at 5000, it appears that there are three call appearances of directory number 5000.

Assume that you want to configure a phone with directory number 5000 with three line appearances. Create the partitions in Table 2-70.

Table 2-70   *Partitions for Multiple Call Appearances*

Partition	Description
Standard	Assigned to the first call appearance of the IP phone, this partition represents the partition to which you normally assign your phone users
Line2	Assigned to the second call appearance of the IP phone
Line3	Assigned to the third call appearance of the IP phone

When a call arrives for directory number 5000, if the first call appearance is busy, you want CallManager to forward the call to the second call appearance; likewise, if the second call appearance is busy, you want CallManager to forward the call to the third line appearance. Finally, if the third call appearance is busy, CallManager forwards the call to voice mail. Assume that the voice mail pilot number is 5050.

If the user is not present at the phone, CallManager rings the phone until the call forward no answer timer expires. Whether the call is ringing at the first, second, or third call appearance, if the user does not answer, CallManager should forward the call to voice mail.

Making the call forward from line appearance to line appearance means using some call forward calling search spaces. Configure the calling search spaces in Table 2-71.

Table 2-71   *Calling Search Spaces for Multiple Call Appearances*

Calling Search Spaces	Partitions	Description
Standard	Varies	This calling search space includes whatever partitions the users need to place their day-to-day calls. At the very least, this calling search space typically includes the ability to call other internal extensions, emergency services, and voice mail.
Line2	Line2	This calling search space permits a user to call any call appearance assigned to the Line2 partition.
Line3	Line3	This calling search space permits a user to call any call appearance assigned to the Line3 partition.

Given these calling search spaces and partitions, you can configure phone 5000 according to Table 2-72.

Table 2-72 *Directory Number Configuration Pages for Multiple Call Appearances*

First Call Appearance			
Setting	**Value**		**Description**
Directory Number	5000		
Partition	Line1		
Calling Search Space	Standard		Provides access to all numbers the user is permitted to dial
Call Forward Busy	Destination	Calling Search Space	Forwards the call to line 2 when line 1 is busy
	5000	Line2	
Call Forward No Answer	Destination	Calling Search Space	Forwards the call to voice mail when line 1 does not answer
	5050	**Standard**	
Second Call Appearance			
Setting	**Value**		**Description**
Directory Number	5000		
Partition	Line2		
Calling Search Space	Standard		Provides access to all numbers the user is permitted to dial
Call Forward Busy	Destination	Calling Search Space	Forwards the call to line 3 when line 2 is busy
	5000	Line3	
Call Forward No Answer	Destination	Calling Search Space	Forwards the call to voice mail when line 2 does not answer
	5050	**Standard**	
Third Call Appearance			
Setting	**Value**		**Description**
Directory Number	5000		
Partition	**Line3**		

Table 2-72   *Directory Number Configuration Pages for Multiple Call Appearances (Continued)*

Third Call Appearance			
Setting	**Value**		**Description**
Calling Search Space	Standard		Provides access to all numbers the user is permitted to dial
Call Forward Busy	Destination	Calling Search Space	Forwards the call to voice mail when line 3 is busy
	5050	Standard	
Call Forward No Answer	Destination	Calling Search Space	Forwards the call to voice mail when line 3 does not answer
	5050	Standard	

Enhanced 911 Support

This section describes some aspects of emergency call handling in North America, but it is by no means a complete treatise on the subject. Rather, it informs you of some of the issues you may need to consider when configuring emergency call routing for your enterprise. Furthermore, legal requirements for emergency calls differ from state to state, so the information and example configuration that this section presents may not be valid in your enterprise's locale. At the time of this writing, at least seven states have legal requirements relating to emergency calls: Kentucky, Illinois, Mississippi, Tennessee, Texas, Vermont, and Washington.

In North America, the number for emergency services is 911. Local carriers route 911 calls to Public Safety Answering Points (PSAP). PSAPs are staffed with trained personnel and equipment that can properly handle emergency calls.

The North American PSTN treats calls to 911 very specially. Unlike other calls to the PSTN, after a call reaches the switches owned by the local carrier, calls to 911 usually route over an independent telephone network. Unlike a traditional call, the PSTN routes 911 calls based on the number of the caller, not the dialed digits. Note that different trunk interfaces deliver the calling number in different ways, and some trunk interfaces cannot deliver a calling number at all. For these latter trunk interfaces, the PSTN manages the calling number.

Users directly connected to the PSTN who dial 911 cause the local carrier to perform several database lookups when it handles the call. The piece of information that starts the lookups is the calling number of the user. Using this calling number, the local carrier looks in several databases to find the emergency service number (ESN), which indicates which PSAP needs to handle the call, and the automatic location identification (ALI), which provides a street address associated with the calling user. The PSAP informs the authorities of this address when dispatching medical, police, or fire-safety personnel to aid the caller.

Clearly, it is important to ensure that this address enables officials to actually locate the person in trouble. If your enterprise serves more than a few users, you should take special pains to ensure that the calling number you provide allows the local carrier to return an ALI that locates the caller's position accurately; one approach is to reserve some enterprise numbers specifically for the purpose of providing a calling number for 911 calls that can identify a caller's area to within a few thousand square feet, including building and floor number. (Having such a number is essential for extensions in your enterprise, such as lobby phones, that may not have external phone numbers.) Customizing the ALI database entry for a particular calling number typically requires that you contact the local carrier and public safety authorities.

Complicating the problem is that if the local carrier routes an emergency call to the incorrect PSAP because of incorrect calling number information, the PSAP is usually unable to redirect the call to the appropriate PSAP, because the tandem trunk networks over which 911 calls typically do not directly connect one PSAP to another.

CallManager supports basically two approaches to handling emergency calls:

- First, you can route emergency calls to a dedicated attendant station, along with the extension number of the calling user. In turn, the attendant contacts emergency personnel, usually remaining conferenced in on the call to assist if necessary.

- Second, you can route emergency calls directly to the local carrier by routing the call to a gateway connected to the local carrier and providing the digits 911. You must provide the appropriate calling number to the local carrier so that the carrier can route the call to the correct PSAP and provide the required ALI.

Figure 2-35 presents a small example network that demonstrates a 911 configuration. It depicts a distributed enterprise. One CallManager serves users in Dallas and in Richardson (a Dallas suburb). The enterprise has gateways connected to both the Dallas and the Richardson PSTN. Both the Dallas and the Richardson offices have an attendant whose directory number provides a good calling number to present to the PSTN for 911 calls; the attendant's location is reasonably close to the locations of users in the branch office.

Figure 2-35   *Example Network for 911 Routing*

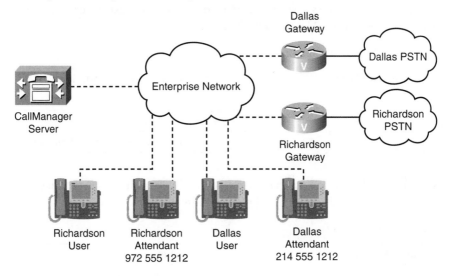

The configuration supports three types of calls to the PSTN:

■ 911 calls from Richardson users route to the gateway connected to the Richardson PSTN with the calling number of the Richardson attendant.

■ 911 calls from Dallas users route to the gateway connected to the Dallas PSTN with the calling number of the Dallas attendant.

■ All other calls route to the Dallas gateway first and to the Richardson gateway if the Dallas gateway is unavailable. (Note that despite this example to the contrary, it is an excellent idea to reserve a gateway or at least an interface on a gateway specifically for 911 calls. This way, you can guarantee that a caller in trouble can reach the PSTN.)

The configuration defines three different gateway access methods, which calls for the use of a route list. Assuming that you have already provisioned the gateways, you need to create the route groups in Table 2-73.

Table 2-73   *Route Groups for 911 Routing*

Route Group Name	Gateways Contained
DallasGateways	DallasGateway
RichardsonGateways	RichardsonGateway

You have three different search algorithms. The first, used for 911 calls from Richardson, selects just the gateways connected to the Richardson PSTN. The second, used for 911 calls from Dallas, selects just the gateways connected to the Dallas PSTN. The last, used for all other external calls, selects the Dallas gateways first and the Richardson gateways next. Three search algorithms require three route lists, which Table 2-74 lists.

Table 2-74 *Route Lists for 911 Routing*

Route List Name	Route Groups Contained
Richardson911Calls	RichardsonGateways
Dallas911Calls	DallasGateways
PSTNCalls	DallasGateways, RichardsonGateways

Distinguishing 911 calls from other calls requires using a route filter. The route filter that Table 2-75 lists selects only 911 calls from the North American numbering plan.

Table 2-75 *Route Filter for 911 Routing*

Route Filter Name	Value
911Calls	SERVICE == 911

The sample configuration requires individualized routing. CallManager routes calls from Dallas users who dial 911 differently from calls from Richardson users who dial 911. Individualized routing requires the creation of partitions and calling search spaces. Table 2-76 contains the partitions that this example requires, and Table 2-77 contains the calling search spaces that this example requires.

Table 2-76 *Partitions for 911 Routing*

Partition Name	Description
PSTNCalls	Contains route patterns that grant PSTN access to all enterprise users
Dallas911	Contains the route pattern that grants 911 access to Dallas users
Richardson911	Contains the route pattern that grants 911 access to Richardson users

Table 2-77 *Calling Search Spaces for 911 Routing*

Calling Search Space	Contains Partitions	Description
DallasUsers	Dallas911, PSTNCalls	Provides customized PSTN access for Dallas users
RichardsonUsers	Richardson911, PSTNCalls	Provides customized PSTN access for Richardson users

Then, assign route patterns to the route lists. Table 2-78 lists the route patterns to define.

Table 2-78   *Route Patterns for 911 Routing*

Route Pattern	Description
Partition: PSTNCalls Route Pattern: 9.@ Route List: PSTNCalls Use External Phone Number Mask: Yes Digit Discarding Instructions: PreDot	Provides general access to the PSTN. CallManager strips the 9 from the called number before extending the call to the PSTN. CallManager uses the external phone number mask that you configure on the calling user's Directory Number Configuration page as the calling number.
Partition: PSTNCalls Route Pattern: 9.@ Route Filter: 911Calls Route List: Richardson911Calls Use External Phone Number Mask: No Calling Party Transformation Mask: 9725551212 Digit Discarding Instructions: PreDot	Contains the route pattern that grants 911 access to Richardson users. Closest match routing rules ensure CallManager selects this route pattern when a Richardson user dials 911. CallManager strips the 9 from the called number and substitutes the Richardson attendant's number for that of the caller.
Partition: PSTNCalls Route Pattern: 9.@ Route Filter: 911Calls Route List: Dallas911Calls Use External Phone Number Mask: No Calling Party Transformation Mask: 2145551212 Digit Discarding Instructions: PreDot	Contains the route pattern that grants 911 access to Dallas users. Closest match routing rules ensure CallManager selects this route pattern when a Dallas user dials 911. CallManager strips the 9 from the called number and substitutes the Dallas attendant's number for that of the caller.

Finally, make sure that you assign the calling search space DallasUsers to phones in Dallas and RichardsonUsers to phones in Richardson, and set up the external phone number mask for each phone.

International Numbering Plans

The call routing component of CallManager is extensible. In previous sections, the @ wildcard has always been described in the context of the North American numbering plan. As described in the section "@ Wildcard," the @ wildcard is a macro that, based on the numbering plan you select, adds many route patterns on your behalf. By default, CallManager Administration permits you to select only North American Numbering Plan from the Numbering Plan drop-down list.

The list of route patterns that CallManager adds is available in an administrator-accessible file. In the installation directory of CallManager is a subdirectory called dialPlan. (The CallManager service parameter DialPlanPath tells CallManager where to look for the numbering plan file.) When CallManager initializes, it looks in this subdirectory for information about the supported numbering plans. When you configure an @ pattern from the Route Pattern Configuration or Translation Pattern Configuration pages, you are instructing CallManager to expand the @ wildcard according to one of the files in this subdirectory.

You can modify how CallManager interprets the @ pattern by modifying the dial plan file; however, Cisco TAC does not support such modifications of the dial plan file. Furthermore, while changing the file does affect how CallManager expands the @ pattern, it does not affect how CallManager Administration presents other dial plan-related settings, such as digit discarding instructions or route filters. Rather, the administration pages derive this information from tables that exist in the CallManager database schema. Nevertheless, examining the files in the dialPlans subdirectory, you can see exactly how CallManager interprets the @ pattern on a dial-plan-by-dial-plan basis.

File Format

The file is a little more complex than just a list of route patterns, however, because for CallManager to correctly apply digit discarding instructions and route filters, you need to tell it what substrings of a given number are meaningful for routing purposes. For example, the seven-digit North American numbering plan route pattern [2-9]XX XXXX contains two meaningful substrings, an office code and a subscriber.

As described in the section "Tags," these meaningful substrings are called *tags*. The tags defined for a given numbering plan dictate which tags are available on the Route Filter Configuration page and which parts of a dialed number can be discarded using digit discarding instructions.

The following is a short excerpt from the NANP file, which defines the North American numbering plan, that describes a long distance number preceded by a request for a particular long distance carrier:

```
# 101 XXXX 1 [2-9]XX [2-9]XX [2-9]XX
P: 101       TRANSIT-NETWORK-ESCAPE
P: XXXX      TRANSIT-NETWORK
P: 1         LONG-DISTANCE-DIRECT-DIAL
P: [2-9]XX   AREA-CODE
P: [2-9]XX   OFFICE-CODE
P: XXXX      SUBSCRIBER
T: N
```

Each route pattern in a numbering plan is represented as several lines of text followed by a blank line. The first character on each line of text defines one of five types of records:

- **#**—A line beginning with # is treated as a comment line. The call routing component ignores these lines when expanding an @ wildcard.

- **P**—This type of line is by far the most important. In this line, you describe a substring for a particular route pattern. This type of line has one mandatory argument and an optional argument. The first argument is a description of the substring itself, in pattern notation (see the section "Route Patterns and Route Filters"). The second argument, if present, describes the tag name you want to associate with this substring. The tag name can be anything you want, though it can contain only alphabetic characters and hyphens. Most route patterns consist of several P lines that together define the entire route pattern.

- **T**—A line beginning with T: specifies whether the type of number represents an international number or a national number. When followed by an N, the route pattern is considered national; when followed by an I, it is considered international. Digital signaling interfaces such as PRI require CallManager to characterize a dialed number when it offers a call to the PSTN for the call to route correctly. When you set the Called Party IE Number Type option to Cisco CallManager on any digital gateway configuration page, you tell CallManager to set up the called number based on this value in the numbering plan file.

- **U**—A line beginning with U: specifies that a route pattern is urgent. When a route pattern is urgent, if the user dials a string that matches the route pattern, all interdigit timing is circumvented. When followed by a Y (for yes), the route pattern is considered urgent; when followed by an N or if the line is not present at all, it is considered normal. The NANP file characterizes the information and emergency services as urgent route patterns so that you do not accidentally hamper access to emergency services by creating an extension such as 9110.

- **W**—A line beginning with W: specifies associated information. This line is not currently used, but it should be used for setup of the network-specific facilities information element in ISDN. CallManager associates any information following the tag with the route pattern, and the destination device can use this information to make decisions. In the case of the current NANP file, operator calls are followed with a W: line that specifies OP or OP/P so that PRI code can configure the outbound called number information as an operator call. CallManager currently ignores this line.

International Dial Plans

Cisco makes dial plans for other countries available at Cisco.com (http://www.cisco.com/pcgi-bin/tablebuild.pl/IDP). Users with a Cisco Service Agreement can access these dial plans and install them on CallManager. Following the link grants you access to a tool from which you can download an installer (.exe) for currently supported dial plan files.

Currently, Cisco provides dial plans for Japan, Netherlands, Portugal, Singapore, Australia, Russia, New Zealand, Great Britain, Belgium, and Greece.

Troubleshooting

This section describes the Cisco CallManager Dialed Number Analyzer tool, which can help you debug problems with your dial plan, and covers some common problems relating to call routing in CallManager.

Cisco CallManager Dialed Number Analyzer

Cisco CallManager Dialed Number Analyzer is a CallManager add-in that enables you to enter in calling and called numbers and receive a report that describes the following:

- How CallManager intends to route the call

- How CallManager changes the calling party number

- How CallManager changes the called party number

The Dialed Number Analyzer allows you either to originate the call as if from a configured CallManager device (such as an IP phone or trunk) or simply to provide a set of dialed digits along with a calling search space that the Dialed Number Analyzer should use to resolve the dialed digits. Dialed Number Analyzer also supports time-of-day routing and permits you to simulate how the call would route depending on the time of day it was placed.

Figure 2-36 presents the output generated from a sample CallManager system, in which the provided called number was 9 1 800 555 1212. The figure displays the initial result set that Dialed Number Analyzer provides.

At the top level, among other information, the tool reports on the digits that were dialed (Dialed Digits), whether the call routes or is blocked, the transformed called party number (Called Party Number), and the top-level device that CallManager offers the call to (CCM-RTP-01_Cluster). The figure also has expanded the Outside Dial Tone item and the Matched Pattern Information item to indicate exactly which pattern CallManager matched and at what point in the dial string that CallManager would play outside dial tone.

Other menu items reveal more information. For example, expanding the Call Flow menu item displays a more detailed picture of how CallManager routes the call. Figure 2-37 displays these details.

Figure 2-36 *CallManager Dialed Number Analyzer Summary Results*

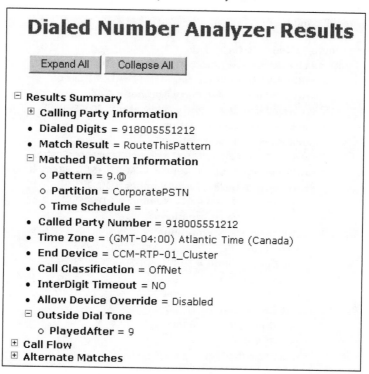

Figure 2-37 indicates that CCM-RTP-01_Cluster corresponded to a route list. This route list contained route group CCM-RTP-01 Cluster (an intercluster trunk) and route group CCM-RTP-01 Cluster PRI (a Catalyst 6000 gateway with a T1 network module). The device information for the network module has been expanded to expose some relevant routing fields.

Also of interest, but not expanded in Figure 2-37, is the Route Pattern item, which demonstrates exactly how the call routing component of CallManager parses the number, and the Alternate Matches item, which upon expansion reveals the full set of candidate patterns that CallManager considered. Looking at the details for this latter item can reveal configured overlapping patterns that may have crept into your configuration.

Figure 2-37 *CallManager Dialed Number Analyzer Summary Results*

```
⊞ Results Summary
⊟ Call Flow
    ⊞ Route Pattern :Pattern= 9.@
    ⊟ Route List :Route List Name= CCM-RTP-01_Cluster
        ⊟ RouteGroup :RouteGroup Name= CCM-RTP-01 Cluster
            • PreTransform Calling Party Number = 1000
            • PreTransform Called Party Number = 918005551212
            ⊞ Calling Party Transformations
            ⊞ Called Party Transformations
            ⊞ Device :Type= InterClusterTrunk-NonGatekeeperControlled
        ⊟ RouteGroup :RouteGroup Name= CCM-RTP-01 Cluster PRI
            • PreTransform Calling Party Number = 1000
            • PreTransform Called Party Number = 918005551212
            ⊞ Calling Party Transformations
            ⊞ Called Party Transformations
            ⊟ Device :Type= CiscoCatalyst6000T1PriGateway
                ○ End Device Name = S0/DS1-0@SDA00D09738641F
                ○ PortNumber = 0
                ○ Device Status = Registered
                ○ AAR Group Name =
                ○ AAR Calling Search Space =
                ○ AAR Prefix Digits =
                ○ Call Classification = OffNet
                ○ Calling Party Selection = Originator
                ○ CallingLinePresentation = Default
                ○ ConnectedLinePresentation = Default
                ○ Number Of Strip Digits = 0
                ○ CallerID DN =
⊞ Alternate Matches
```

Note that the Dialed Number Analyzer has some limitations:

■ It operates by analyzing a copy of the CallManager database's routing configuration. You must specifically import your current routing configuration into the Dialed Number Analyzer before performing any analysis. If you add or remove patterns or directory numbers from CallManager Administration, you must re-import the routing information.

■ It provides information only about how the call routes through a single CallManager cluster. Other CallManager servers (via intercluster trunks) or Cisco IOS gateways (which have their own powerful routing capabilities) or PBXs might take the routing information that CallManager provides and use it as input into their own routing logic.

Nevertheless, CallManager Dialed Number Analyzer can be a powerful tool for detecting and discovering the root cause of routing problems.

CallManager Applies Outside Dial Tone Too Late

This problem always occurs because a pattern exists that overlaps with the route pattern to which you want CallManager to apply outside dial tone. Usually, through inspection, you can discover another route pattern, directory number, translation pattern, or feature-related number that begins with the same sequence of digits as the route pattern in question.

Check all other route patterns in the system to see whether any of them begin with the same digit sequence as the pattern for which you expect outside dial tone. CallManager only applies outside dial tone when all possible matching route patterns have had their Provide Outside Dial Tone box checked. Patterns such as directory numbers and features cause the suppression of outside dial tone when their range overlaps with that of a route pattern. See the section "Outside Dial Tone" for more details.

CallManager Applies Outside Dial Tone Too Early

This problem occurs when you are using outside access codes that are longer than a single digit. Because of the way that CallManager's outside dial tone logic works, you must configure a separate route pattern that specifically suppresses outside dial tone until the digit that you want. Note particularly that the location of the . wildcard in a route pattern has no effect on when CallManager applies outside dial tone.

To delay the application of outside dial tone, add a route pattern that represents just your outside access code, but leave the Provide Outside Dial Tone check box unchecked. This configuration will cause CallManager to suppress outside dial tone until all digits of the access code have been dialed, because the access code itself, for which outside dial tone is not applied, suppresses the application of outside dial tone. See the section "Outside Dial Tone" for details about outside dial tone.

Seven-Digit Calls to the North American PSTN Wait 10 Seconds Before Routing

Because some geographical regions use 7-digit dialing and others use 10-digit dialing, the North American numbering plan that ships with CallManager must accommodate both types of dialing. Furthermore, because the IP network allows stations in different geographical locations to register with the same CallManager, CallManager must support both types of dialing simultaneously.

Defining a route filter of LOCAL-AREA-CODE DOES-NOT-EXIST and associating this route filter with your @ pattern prevents CallManager from adding the numbering plan record in the North American numbering plan that routes 10-digit local calls.

Phone A Can Call Phone B, but Not Vice Versa

This problem usually, but not always, is related to calling search spaces and partitions. In the most common scenario, the partition in which station B is listed is in station A's calling search space, but not vice versa. You might be encountering this problem if CallManager applies reorder while phone B is dialing phone A, or if CallManager applies reorder immediately on collecting all the digits of phone A.

See the section "Calling Search Spaces and Partitions" for more information about calling search spaces and partitions.

Route Pattern 9 XXX XXXX and Route Pattern 9.@ Are Defined, but CallManager Never Selects Route Pattern 9 XXX XXXX

The @ pattern causes CallManager to add many specific patterns, some of which may match a dialed digit string more closely than the ones you configure.

You can either more narrowly tailor the route pattern you add or use route filters on the @ pattern to eliminate the more closely matching route pattern. See the section "@ Wildcard" for more information about how closest match routing and the @ wildcard interact.

Digit Discarding Instructions on a Route Pattern Are Defined, but the Digit Discarding Instructions Are Not Taking Effect

There are two common causes of this problem.

The first main cause is that digit discarding instructions generally apply only to @ patterns. It is particularly tempting for users who configure patterns such as 0!# to attempt to configure the digit discarding instruction trailing-#. Unfortunately, this digit discarding instruction simply removes the END-OF-DIALING terminator as specified in the North American numbering plan. To discard trailing-# from a non-@ pattern, configure the Strip # Sign From Called Party Number service parameter.

The second main cause occurs when route lists are in operation. If you configure the digit discarding instructions NoDigits instead of <None> on a particular route, you instruct CallManager to ignore the digit discarding instructions defined on the route pattern and instead apply the ones defined on the route. In this case, the digit discarding instruction NoDigits tells CallManager to restore the original dialed digit string.

CPU Usage on a CallManager Server Rises to 100 Percent, Memory Usage Escalates, and Ultimately CallManager Restarts

If you can trace this problem to a particular phone call that a user makes, it might be due to a call routing loop. A convenient configuration pattern is to direct all calls to unknown extensions out a trunk to another system. For example, you might configure pattern XXXX to route all unknown four-digit extension numbers to an adjacent PBX.

If the other system also has such a generic route pattern, when CallManager routes the call to it, the other system does not find any phone to which to extend the call. As a result, its logic sends the callback to CallManager, which again forwards the call to the other system. The call loops indefinitely, consuming CPU and memory until CallManager cannot cope anymore. (In traditional circuit-switched systems, this problem can occur but is less serious, because at some point, all of the circuits between the systems are exhausted and the call tears down.)

Eliminating this problem means making sure that when a call arrives from another system, CallManager cannot immediately forward that call out another gateway connection. To accomplish this task, give the gateway from the other system a calling search space that does not include the partition in which the gateway itself resides. See the section "Calling Search Spaces and Partitions" for more information.

Summary

This chapter has covered all aspects of call routing in CallManager. It has discussed route patterns and route filters, CallManager's fundamental call routing concept.

From discussing route patterns, it moved on to dialing transformations, the means by which you effect the calling and called numbers that CallManager presents as part of offering calls.

Translation patterns provide a way to alias other route patterns. This powerful tool provides you with the opportunity to modify the calling and called numbers and select new destinations based on the resulting digits.

Route lists and route groups allow you to set up search patterns across your enterprise's gateways to ensure that you fully utilize the most cost-efficient gateways in your enterprise.

The sections about calling search spaces and partitions discussed a mechanism by which you can customize routing on a user-by-user basis. Using calling search spaces and partitions, you can route calls by the type or geographic location of the calling user.

Several case studies and miscellaneous examples described how all of the call routing fundamental concepts work together to solve complex problems. Although none of the case studies represents a complete solution to the most complex enterprises, by studying the approaches these examples described, you can apply the proposed solutions to your enterprise's specific problems.

One section of this chapter discussed CallManager's treatment of the North American numbering plan and described how you can replace it if you so choose, although this task is not for the meek.

Finally, a troubleshooting section summarized common problems that administrators encounter with CallManager's call routing capabilities and proposed solutions.

CHAPTER **3**

Station Devices

This chapter describes the interaction between CallManager and station devices, including station functionality and the protocols they use to communicate with Cisco CallManager. The station protocol is part of the Protocol/Aggregation Layer within CallManager. CallManager contains several signaling layers, each of which has distinct functions. For example, the Call Control Layer handles all of the call signaling that controls call setup, teardown, and call routing; and the Protocol/Aggregation Layer handles all protocol-specific signaling required for specific devices.

This chapter discusses the following topics:

- **Definition of Station Devices**—Introduces the station device in the context of CallManager

- **Overview of Station Devices Supported by CallManager**—Differentiates users from stations and categorizes the station devices by protocol

- **Station Device Features**—Introduces the feature content offered to users of the station devices

- **SCCP Station Devices**—Describes the functionality of the devices that support the Skinny Client Control Protocol (SCCP) and provides an overview of the protocol that supports the devices

- **Cisco VT Advantage**—Describes the functionality of the PC-based Cisco VT Advantage that provides video functionality for Cisco IP Phones

- **Computer Telephony Interface (CTI) Devices**—Describes the interface support for devices that connect to CallManager through CTI, including CTI route points, CTI ports, and CTI-monitored/controlled IP phones

- **IP Phone Registration and Security**—Provide descriptions of how station devices use TFTP and ways to secure IP phones

- **H.323 Endpoint Devices**—Describes the H.323 endpoints and provides an overview of CallManager's H.323 protocol support

Appendix C, "Protocol Details," provides detailed information for signaling protocols such as SCCP, and application protocols like JTAPI and XML. After reviewing this chapter, refer to Appendix C for additional, related information.

Figure 3-1 shows the block structure of CallManager. The darker shading in Figure 3-1 highlights the software layers and blocks within CallManager that this chapter describes in detail. Other blocks are highlighted with lighter shading. They are part of the station signaling path, but are given lighter coverage.

Figure 3-1 *CallManager Block Structure Diagram*

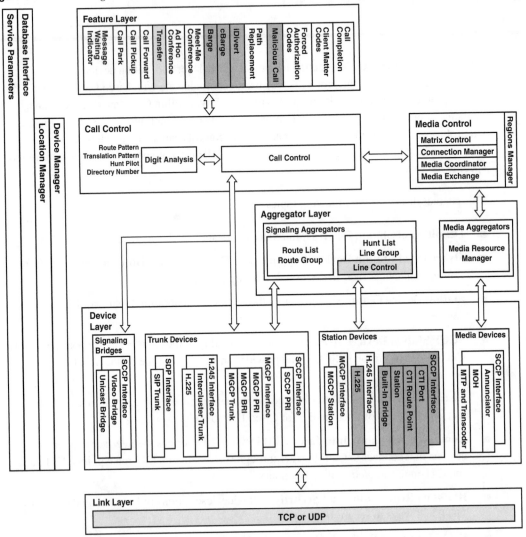

The software in the Media Control Layer handles all media connections CallManager makes between devices. Whereas the Call Control Layer sets up all of the signaling connections between call endpoints and CallManager, the Media Control Layer directs the devices to establish streaming connections. The Media Control Layer can insert other media processing devices into a call and create appropriate streaming connections to those devices without the Call Control Layer knowing about them.

The blocks in the Protocol/Aggregation Layer control the media processing devices. They provide the device interface and handle all communication between the devices and CallManager.

Definition of Station Devices

A *station device*, as opposed to a gateway device, is any device that is characterized as a terminal endpoint. A *terminal endpoint* is a device or software application that provides real-time, two-way communication for a single user. The remainder of this chapter often refers to a station device simply as a *station*.

Software applications that act as station devices include the following:

- Cisco applications

- Third-party applications

- Cisco Interactive Voice Response (IVR)

- Auto attendant

- Voice mail/unified messaging

A station device and a gateway device provide similar yet contrasting functionality. A *gateway* provides real-time, two-way communication between the packet-based network and other stations on either another packet-based network or a circuit-switched network. A gateway provides service for multiple users or provides access connections for simultaneous use by multiple users. A gateway can provide protocol support to terminate multiple stations attached to the gateway device or it can be used to interconnect CallManager with other packet network systems. Gateways can also be used to terminate trunks attached to the Public Switched Telephone Network (PSTN) or to a corporate switch, such as a Private Branch Exchange (PBX).

In contrast, a station usually supports a single user at a time, although one station can support multiple users who log in and out of the station at different times. Although a station can consist of multiple lines and might have the capability of terminating multiple connections, stations typically have only a single connection active at a time and provide only a single media stream to a user. Figure 3-2 shows examples of various stations and a sample gateway device.

Figure 3-2 *Station Devices*

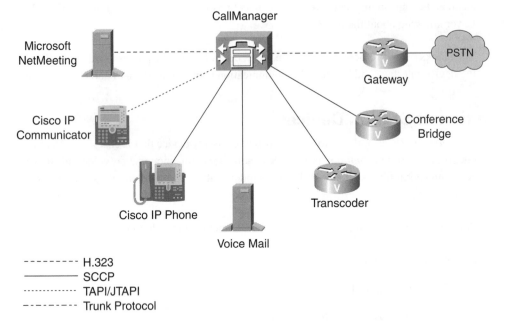

CallManager

Microsoft
NetMeeting

PSTN

Gateway

Cisco IP
Communicator

Conference
Bridge

Transcoder

Cisco IP Phone

Voice Mail

- - - - - - - - H.323
———————— SCCP
·············· TAPI/JTAPI
- - - - - - - - Trunk Protocol

Overview of Station Device Features Supported by CallManager

CallManager supports numerous station device features, which are discussed by feature category.
You'll also learn about the architectural capabilities required to provide the feature functionality.

User/Station Distinction

A *user* is a person or software application that uses a station to communicate with another user.
For the purposes of this chapter, a user has a station with one or more directory numbers that can
be dialed to communicate with the other user.

You assign each user a directory number, or more simply, a phone number, which users or software
applications dial when they want to call each other or route calls to users. All stations have at least
one directory number. A station can also have multiple directory numbers, one directory number
per line.

Users communicate over a media path, typically audio, that is established between two stations
during a call. CallManager allows devices with dissimilar signaling protocols to establish a
connection and communicate. The protocol of the caller might be SCCP, for example, whereas the
protocol of the destination might be H.323.

Line Appearance Model

The line appearance model of the station devices applies to all station devices and encompasses the concept of *multiple line appearances* and *shared line appearances*. Each station device has one or more lines, and each line is associated with a specific directory number. A user dials a directory number to place a call. Each station has at least one line and associated directory number, but can also have multiple lines, each with a separate and unique directory number. The term *multiple line appearances* refers to when a single station has multiple directory numbers.

You can associate one directory number with one or more stations. The term *shared line appearances* refers to when the same directory number appears on multiple devices. With a *shared line appearance*, users can have stations in multiple places (main office, remote office, or home) with the same line appearance and can receive calls at any of these locations. When a user dials a directory number, CallManager rings all stations that have an appearance of that directory number. When a user dials a directory number, CallManager rings all stations that have an appearance of that directory number. The call can then be answered at any station with that line appearance.

Figure 3-3 shows three stations. Each station has a unique directory number. In addition, Station 3 has a second directory number that is a shared line with Station 2. This allows the station to answer calls directed to either Station 2 or Station 3 (directory number 1002 or 1003). When a caller dials directory number 1002, both Stations 2 and 3 indicate an incoming call, and the call can be answered at either station.

Every station feature that is call related involves one or more calls in progress. Each call is associated with a particular line on a specific station device, referred to as a *line appearance*. A line appearance on a station is where incoming calls arrive or outgoing calls originate. A line appearance can support an active call as well as calls that are on *hold*. An active call can be an arriving call, a call being initiated, or a call that has been connected and at least two parties in the call are exchanging media (voice media in the case of a voice call). When you invoke a feature on the currently connected call that causes the media to the far end of the connection to be suspended, the far end connection is placed on *hold*. This can be done by invoking the *hold* feature explicitly via the **Hold** softkey or indirectly by accepting a new incoming call or by initiating a transfer or conference, for example. An active call on a shared line appearance is active on one station and classified as remote-in-use on other stations with a shared line appearance. Remote-in-use shows you that the call is currently active on another phone with the same line appearance.

Figure 3-3 *Station Devices and Directory Numbers*

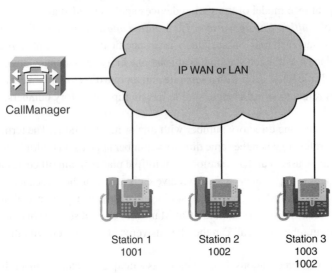

As of CallManager release 4.0, a line appearance on a station can support an active call and many calls that are on hold. The configuration for a line appearance includes two settings:

- **Maximum Number of Calls**—Enables you to control how many call instances can be present on the line appearance, including active, held, and remote-in-use

- **Busy Trigger**—Enables you to control when an incoming call will be rejected, triggering the call to be sent to the call forward busy destination, if configured

These two settings control the point at which no new incoming calls are allowed as well as the upper limit on the total calls for the line. Some station devices can handle more calls than other devices. The configuration of these fields establishes maximum settings, but the station may do less if it is not configured to support the maximum that is configured on another device. Because the configuration fields are set per line appearance, you can allow some phones to accept more calls than other phones in a shared line appearance. As more calls come into a directory number that is a shared line appearance, some stations might ring whereas others do not because some of the stations reach the configured busy trigger and do not accept new incoming calls.

Multiple stations can share a common line, meaning that there is a line with the same directory number on each of these stations. Stations that share a line can also have other lines that are present on the station independent of the shared line. The other lines each have a directory number that might be present on other stations. This means that a station can share one line with a particular group of stations and share other lines on the station with other groups of stations. For example, Station A shares line 1 (DN 1000) with Station B and Station C. Station C shares line 2 (DN 2000) with Station A and Station D. Station C also has a third line, DN 3000, which is not shared with any other station. You set up the directory numbers that appear on each station to meet the particular needs of the user for the particular station. The lines on a station that are shared lines provide some unique functionality to the stations that share the line. When a user places a call from a shared line on one particular station, the other stations that share the line see that a call is in progress. When the user receives an incoming call on the shared line, the call is presented to every station that has a line appearance with that directory number, and any of the stations can answer the incoming call. All calls, including active, held, and remote-in-use calls, are visible at the station with the shared line appearance unless the call initiator or receiver blocked the information with the privacy feature or the station has already exceeded the maximum number of configured calls. After the user places a call on hold, any station with the shared line appearance can retrieve the held call and resume the conversation. A new call can be initiated on a shared appearance line as long as the maximum number of calls configured for the directory number of the shared line has not been reached. The maximum number of calls that can be in progress for the shared line appearance applies to the combined total for the line, regardless of which station or stations have active calls in progress or which station put a particular call on hold.

Use up/down navigation control on the station or the **Select** softkey to select a particular a call on a line. In the case of shared line, the calls that you can select are the calls that are not active or locked by another device. A call is locked by another device when it is currently in the middle of a feature such as transfer or conference or if it is selected on another station. You select a particular call to take a particular action on the call, such as joining the selected call to another call.

Shared Line Examples

Sharing the same line on multiple phones enables a group of users to spread the call volume when there are more calls than one person can handle. The calls ring on multiple stations. The following sections examine a few examples of the value of shared lines.

Shared Line for Small Support Group

Shared lines can prove valuable for small teams that handle numerous incoming calls, such as a customer product group. Because the group typically takes an initial call requesting assistance, the shared line can deliver the call to all the phones in the small group that provides the needed support. Although not practical for a large support organization, which would be better handled by a call center application, the shared line can be leveraged in small teams that want all calls to ring at all available stations.

Consider a small support team of five people that provides technical assistance for a particular product in your organization. The support calls are not frequent, and there are seldom more active calls than the team can handle. Each member of the small team is trained to handle general product questions so it's not important who takes the initial call. If there are detailed questions in a particular area, one member of the team has more detailed knowledge about the hardware, another has detailed knowledge about the software, and a third has specialized knowledge of the database. If you configure a shared line appearance on each phone of the support team, any available member of the support team will be able to take an incoming support call. If the call is for a general support question, the assistance will be provided by the initial support team member and requires no other action. If one team member takes a call and discovers that the caller needs another of the team members with a particular special knowledge, you can put the call on hold and ask the team member with that expertise to pick up the call. When you make the request, you indicate which call is to be retrieved by the call number assigned to the call when it arrived. When a call arrives and receives a call number, the call number does not change as other calls arrive and terminate on the line.

As shown in Figure 3-4, if the call is call number five, and while the call is on hold, calls three and four hang up, the calls are not renumbered, and call number five stays call number five. New calls will arrive and replace calls three and four that were terminated. As long as call five stays on the original line, even if it is held and retrieved repeatedly, it will stay call number five.

Figure 3-4 *Caller Number Assignments*

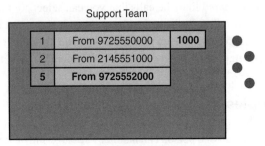

Call number, once assigned, does not change as
new calls arrive and other calls are terminated.

Shared Line for Executive Support

Shared line appearances can also add value for an executive assistant. If an executive needs support at all times, there might be a need for more than one assistant to be able to handle the calls. If the first assistant is currently busy on a call, the backup assistant will be able to see that the call needs to be answered and can take the call. Multiple assistants can have a line appearance of several executives on their phone and provide backup support for the other assistants. Shared lines make it possible to have one or more backup assistants and handle temporary overload situations and still be able to provide adequate coverage for the executive.

To provide backup coverage for multiple executives with a group of executive assistants, you can configure a shared line appearance of each of the executives on all of the phones of the assistants. As an example, assume that five executives each have their own assistant. Backup coverage by the other assistants if one particular assistant was on a call would provide improved coverage for each executive and allow the assistants to provide backup coverage for each other. As shown in Figure 3-5, the primary line for each assistant would be the number assigned to the assistant. The second line would be a shared line appearance of the executive that the assistant supported. The other four lines on the assistant phones would be shared lines of the other four executives. With this configuration, each assistant has access to incoming calls to any of the five executives.

Figure 3-5   *Executive Assistant Coverage*

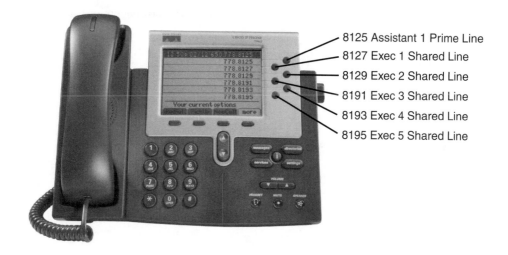

8125 Assistant 1 Prime Line
8127 Exec 1 Shared Line
8129 Exec 2 Shared Line
8191 Exec 3 Shared Line
8193 Exec 4 Shared Line
8195 Exec 5 Shared Line

Station Features

Several key station features were introduced in CallManager releases 3.1 through 4.1. The sections that follow cover each of these features in more detail.

Distinctive Ring per Line

Stations can have more than one line configured, which also means that there is more than one directory numbered configured on the station. A visual indication is provided by default for incoming calls on the line on which the incoming call is ringing, but there is no audible difference to indicate which line is ringing unless the station is configured with a different ring for each line. The distinctive ring feature allows end users to configure the ring type for each line, if desired. If each line has a distinctive ring, the ring itself, in addition to the visual line indication, helps identify the line on which the incoming call is ringing. The option to change the ring settings for each line is provided in the settings menu on the phone (press the **settings** button).

Change Ring Settings

When an incoming call arrives at a station, the station device notifies you of the incoming call audibly and visually by default. Audible and visual notification of incoming calls is configurable based on whether the station is currently in use or currently idle. If the phone is in use (for example, active on a call), you might or might not want the phone to audibly ring when another call arrives at your station. As shown in Figure 3-6 later in this chapter, the option to **Change the Ring Settings for your phone** in the Cisco CallManager User Options web page (CCMUser) allows users to set the ring behavior of the phone when it is idle and when it is in use; each condition can employ a different notification behavior. The following options are available when the phone is idle:

- Ring normally

- Ring once

- Flash only

- Do nothing

The following options are available when the phone is in use:

- Ring normally

- Ring once

- Flash only

- Beep only

- Do nothing

Each line on a phone can have a different ring setting depending on whether the phone is idle or in use. Users can configure their own preferences via CCMUser if you have enabled the enterprise parameter Show Ring Settings (**System > Enterprise Parameters**). The parameter is disabled by default.

Block Calling ID on a Per-Call Basis

Sometimes you want to control whether your calling line identification is sent to the far-end device when you make an external call. In fact, in some states and countries, the ability to block calling information is required by law. Be sure to check local requirements to ensure you are providing this capability when needed.

When a call is placed from a station, the directory number of the line that was used to make the call is sent to the far-end device that is receiving the call. Transmission of this information is Calling Line Identification Presentation (CLIP). For some calls, users might want or need the ability to block CLIP from being transmitted. The ability to restrict the calling line identification presentation for a particular call is possible through Call Line Identification Restrictions (CLIR).

You set up the CLIR for either a gateway or for a route or translation pattern. By configuring CLIR for a gateway, the CLIR feature is enabled for all external calls that are made through that gateway. To control the CLIR on a call-by-call basis, you configure a particular route pattern or translation pattern that will apply CLIR for all calls that use the route pattern or translation pattern. For example, a route pattern of *679.@ could be defined with CLIR set for the route pattern. Using this route pattern, users can dial *679 and the destination number. Doing so would block transmission of the calling line identification to the far end (destination) of the call. For those calls that users don't mind having CLIP sent, the normal 9.@ pattern can be used. Additional route patterns blocking CLIP for OnNet calls can also be configured, allowing users to block the calling information for both internal (OnNet) and external (OffNet) calls.

Malicious Call Identification

The Malicious Call Identification (MCID) feature enables users to mark the active call as malicious. When a call is flagged as malicious, several events occur:

- An alarm record is generated and you can configure a text message to be delivered to you detailing the date, time, and physical identifier of the device in use by the victim of the malicious call

- The call detail record (CDR) for the active call is flagged with a Malicious Call Trace (MCT) indication

- For OffNet calls via ISDN PRI circuits on MGCP gateways, the OffNet PSTN is notified of the malicious call. This notification allows the OffNet system to take appropriate action, such as notifying legal authorities

The user can invoke MCT from any SCCP-based phone or SCCP-based gateway such as the VG248 and ATA-186. Chapter 4, "Trunk Devices," offers more details on the OffNet PSTN notification of malicious calls. Chapter 7, "Call Detail Records," addresses the CDR details for malicious calls.

To extend malicious call trace functionality to users, you must configure the **MCID** softkey on the softkey template. The user presses the **MCID** softkey during an offending call. An audible tone confirms that the call was registered as malicious and, for phones with a display, a visual indication of the calling line ID and caller's name displays. After invoking MCID, the user can either continue with the call or hang up.

Barge/cBarge/Privacy

The *barge* and *cBarge* features allow you to add yourself to (that is, barge into) a call that is active on another station on a line that you share with a remote station. *Privacy* controls whether other users who share a line with you can see call information and have the ability to barge or cBarge into a call on your station. Barge utilizes the conferencing capability of the station device, whereas cBarge uses a conference bridge resource. Because the conferencing capability of the station device is more limited than the conference resource device, cBarge offers additional functionality than barge. Privacy controls the ability of others sharing the line to see the call or to barge into the call.

Privacy

Privacy allows you to control the visibility of call information displayed at other stations that have a shared line appearance of a line on your station. It also controls the ability of someone at another station to be able to barge or cBarge into your conversation. You can configure a **Privacy** button and whether a tone plays to all parties when a user barges into the call. The privacy feature is configured at the device level via the Privacy field on the Phone Configuration page in Cisco CallManager Administration (**Device > Phone**) and at the system level via the clusterwide CallManager service parameter Privacy Setting. The Privacy Setting parameter is enabled by default, so if you want to disable privacy for certain stations, you can do so in the Phone Configuration page only for those stations that you do not want to have access to the privacy feature. The CallManager service parameter Party Entrance Tone controls whether a tone plays when a user barges into a call; it is enabled by default (**Service > Service Parameters >** *select a server* **> Cisco CallManager**). You must configure the **Privacy** button on a button template and assign that template to all phones you want to have the **Privacy** button.

The **Privacy** button enables you to toggle the privacy setting on or off and control the privacy treatment of all new calls to or from your station and any existing active call at your station. If you currently have an active call, press the **Privacy** button to invoke privacy so that no one will be able to barge into the call and the information about your calls will be removed from the display at all stations that have a shared line appearance with you. The privacy setting remains active until you press the **Privacy** button again. Even after the call has ended, privacy will apply to new calls until you toggle privacy off. The **Privacy** button has an icon to indicate on/off status. The status is maintained through phone reset as well as CallManager reset; however, in the case of a CallManager reset and the Publisher being down at the same time, the Privacy setting that was stored in the database prior to the Publisher crash is what will be reflected on the phone when the Publisher is restored. If the user changed the Privacy status during the Publisher and CallManager outage, the new setting will not be maintained when the Publisher and CallManager connection gets restored.

Barge

The barge feature enables you to add yourself into an active call on a shared line appearance, forming a three-party conference utilizing the barged station's conference capability. To define terminology, the following parties are involved in a barged call:

- The *barger* or *barging station* is the party pressing the **Barge** softkey to be added to a call that is active on one of the phone's shared line appearances.

- The *barged station* is the phone that has an active call on a shared line appearance.

- The *third party* is in an active call with the barged station. The third party can be a station or a device external to the system if the call is connected through a gateway or it can be a conference bridge if the barged station is currently in a conference call.

As described in the previous section, if you are in an active call on a line that also appears on other stations, you control whether others who share the line appearance can barge into the call. If you do not want others to be able to barge into the call, you can use the **Privacy** button to prevent others from seeing the call information or barging into the call.

To barge into a call that is in progress on a shared line, you must first press the line button of the call you want to barge into and then use the navigation control to scroll to the specific call. After the active call is highlighted, press the **Barge** softkey to be added to the call in progress. If the Party Entrance Tone service parameter is enabled, a barge tone plays to the active participants in the call to alert them that someone has barged into the call. After you have been added to the call and a tone has announced your arrival, you should begin talking and announce your presence.

The **Barge** softkey adds you to the current call by using the conference capability of the station device. The station device is capable of supporting a three-way conference, so adding a third party to the existing conversation does not interrupt the active voice communication. If another user attempts to barge into the call, that barge attempt will not succeed and the barging party receives the message "Exceed Maximum Parties." The cBarge function, described in the following section, is similar to barge, but it uses a separate conference bridge resource rather than the limited station conference capability. Because of this, more than three parties can be added to the conference. Although the station's conference capability is limited, the advantage of barge over cBarge is that no additional conferencing resources are required and there is no momentary break in the conversation while the parties are moved to the conference device. Barge has some limitations:

- Supported on Cisco IP Phone models 7940, 7941, 7960, 7961, 7970, and 7971 only.

- G.711 is the only supported codec.

- Both stations involved in the barge operation must support the barge feature.

- The barged station must have the built-in bridge enabled.

The cBarge feature eliminates many of these limitations. See the following section, "cBarge," for more information.

After you barge into an existing call, in addition to a barge tone (if configured) announcing your presence, the station line display updates to reflect the current call status. Only your display for the active call updates to reflect the barge; the active call display of the other two parties in the call does not change.

If you are the first party to hang up from the barged call, the other two parties are still connected to each other and hear no break in the voice stream. A "beep beep" tone announces your departure. If you barge into a call and the barged station disconnects, a momentary break in the voice stream occurs and then you and the remaining person in the call (the third party) will be connected and you can continue the conversation. Your line display updates to reflect the call as a call between you and the third party. If the barged station terminates the call, the call disconnects and all three parties are released.

After you barge into a call, the person at the barged station can initiate a feature such as hold, transfer, conference, or call park, that causes the barged call to be put on hold. In this case, you, the barging party, are disconnected from the call and the barged party's feature request (for hold, and so on) proceeds normally. However, if the third party in the call initiates a feature that results in a hold, both you and the barged station remain in the call and the feature proceeds normally. Likewise, if you barge into a call and initiate a feature that results in a hold operation, both the barged station and the third party remain in the call and the feature proceeds normally. When a hold results in two parties remaining in the call while a feature is being initiated, no music is sent to the held parties, and they are still connected and can continue a conversation.

cBarge

The conference barge (cBarge) feature allows you to add yourself to an active call on a shared line appearance, forming a multiple-party conversation utilizing a conference bridge shared resource device. As described in the previous section, if you are in an active call on a line that also appears on other stations, you control whether others that share the line appearance can barge into the call. If you do not want others to be able to barge into your calls, press the **Privacy** button.

To cBarge into an active call that is in progress on a shared line, press the line button of the call you want to cBarge into and then press the **cBarge** softkey to be added to the call in progress, forming a multiple-party conference. The active participants in the call hear a barge tone to signify that someone has been added to the call. After you have been added to the call and a tone has announced your arrival, you should begin talking and announce your presence.

Pressing the **cBarge** softkey adds you to the current call by using the conference resources that are defined for the system. The conference resource devices are capable of multiple-party conferences, up to the maximum number of participants that you configured for the conference resource device. Barging into the existing conversation causes a momentary interruption in the active voice communication while the call moves to the conference bridge. Other bargers who have the same shared line and try to barge into the same call will succeed in their cBarge attempt so long as there are available conference bridge resources and the total number of participants has not exceeded the maximum number allowed by the conference bridge device configuration. If the cBarge attempt does not succeed, the barger receives notification that the cBarge operation did not complete.

The same terminology used to describe the barge feature also describes the following cBarge scenarios. After you press the **cBarge** softkey to barge into an existing call, a barge tone announces your presence and the station line display updates to reflect the current call status. Your display and the display of the barged station updates to "To Conference" to reflect the cBarge operation. If possible, the third party's display also reflects the cBarge operation (if the third party is OnNet using a Cisco IP Phone).

If you are the first party in the cBarged call to disconnect, the other two parties are removed from the conference bridge and reconnected as a direct connection between the formerly barged station and the third party. A momentary break in the voice stream occurs while the connection is changed. A "beep beep" tone announces your departure, and the displays of the barged station and the third party change to reflect the direct connection between the two devices. If you cBarged into a call and the barged station disconnects, a momentary break in the voice stream occurs, after which you and the remaining person in the call are connected directly and you can continue the conversation. Your line display updates to reflect the call as a call between you and the other party. If the third party in the call disconnects, a momentary break in the voice stream occurs, and then you and the barged station are connected and you can continue the conversation. Your line display and the barged station's line display updates to reflect the call as a call between you and the barged station.

After you barged into a call via cBarge, either the person at the barged station or the third party can initiate a feature such as hold, transfer, conference, or call park. In this case, both you and the remaining party, either the barged station or the third party, remain in the call and the feature proceeds normally. Likewise, if you initiate a feature that results in a hold operation, both the barged station and the third party remain in the call, and the feature proceeds normally. When a hold results in two parties remaining in the call while a feature is being initiated, no music is sent to the held parties, and they are still connected and may continue a conversation.

Join

The *join* feature allows you to select a number of calls in the same line appearance and join together with these calls in a conference. You will be a participant in the conference. Alternatively, the direct transfer feature offers the ability to connect two selected calls but not participate in the call, as described later in the "Direct Transfer" section. Both join and direct transfer are limited to calls that are in the same line appearance and cannot be used for calls on different lines.

Join makes it easy to form a conference between you and other calls that already appear on the same line appearance on your station. First, select the calls in progress at your station that you want to conference. To select the calls, use the phone's navigation control to highlight the calls that you want to join, and then press the **Select** softkey for each call that you want to select. A check mark appears next to the selected call to indicate that it has been selected. You can select your currently active call and any other held calls that are not marked remote in use, meaning that they are active calls on another station. Second, press the **Join** softkey to connect you with the selected calls in a conference.

> **TIP**   To save keystrokes when selecting calls, if no calls have been selected via the **Select** softkey, the currently active call and the currently highlighted call are the default selected calls for the feature. If you just want to join the currently active call and a single held call, for example, you just highlight the held call and press **Join** during an active call.

You can join individual calls as well as one existing conference call if you are the controller of the existing conference call. If you select two conference calls to be joined, the join operation will not succeed.

> **NOTE**   A CallManager service parameter, Drop Ad Hoc Conference, determines how conferences such as those created with the join feature are terminated. See the section "Dropping Conference Participants" for more information.

Direct Transfer

Direct transfer enables you to join two calls from the same line appearance together into a single call. You will not be included in the call. If you want to form a conference in which you do participate, use the join feature described in the preceding section.

Direct transfer is an easy way to form a new call between two calls that already appear on your line appearance. First, use the navigation control on your phone to select the calls at your station that you want to connect together directly. Next, press the **DirTrfr** softkey to connect the selected calls together. The two parties will be connected to each other in a new call and will no longer be present on your station.

Generally, one of the two calls you plan to connect with another call is your currently active call. If that is the case, simply use the navigation control to highlight the other call and then press the **DirTrfr** softkey. You do not have to be in an active call to use direct transfer. You can scroll to any two held calls (so long as they are not marked remote in use, meaning that they are active at another station), select each one by highlighting the call, press the **Select** softkey, and then press the **DirTrfr** softkey to directly connect the two selected calls.

You can use direct transfer for individual calls as well as one existing conference call if you are the controller of the existing conference. In the case of a conference call, the individual call that you select will be added to the existing conference when you press the **DirTrfr** softkey and you will no longer be a part of the conference. If you select two conference calls to be directly transferred, the direct transfer will not succeed.

> **NOTE** A CallManager service parameter, Block OffNet To OffNet Transfer, determines whether transfers between external (OffNet) parties are blocked (not allowed). Allowing external transfers could result in toll fraud issues.

iDivert

The immediate divert (*iDivert*) feature enables you to divert a call to voice mail. You must have a voice mailbox configured for the iDivert feature to work. The following types of calls can be used with the iDivert feature:

- **Incoming call that is currently ringing but not yet answered**—Press the **iDivert** softkey when you have an incoming call to immediately transfer the call to your voice mail.

- **Call on hold**—Highlight the held call and press the **iDivert** softkey to immediately transfer the held call to voice mail.

- **Active call**—Inform the caller that you are sending him or her to voice mail to leave a message, and then press the **iDivert** softkey to send the call to your voice mail.

- **Outbound call that you initiated**—After you are connected to the called party, you can request the information that you want to have in the form of a voice message, and then press the **iDivert** softkey to immediately transfer the person you called to your voice mailbox. If you make an outbound call, and are interrupted and have to put the person on hold, you may explain, prior to putting the person on hold, that you will either get back to the person right away or transfer the call to voice mail. If after you put the call on hold, you realize that you'll be detained and not be able to resume the call, you can highlight the held call and press the **iDivert** softkey to transfer the call to voice mail.

Service URLs/Speed Dials

The buttons along the right side of the station are considered line/feature buttons. Any line/feature buttons that are not configured for lines can be used for other functions, including speed dial numbers, or service URL buttons, which allow users to press a one-button shortcut to an XML service. You assign line/feature buttons via the phone button template assigned to users' phones (**Device > Device Settings > Phone Button Template**).

After you have assigned a button template with a combination of lines, speed dial buttons, and service URLs, advise users that they can assign speed dials and/or service URLs via the Cisco CallManager User Options web page, as shown in Figure 3-6.

Figure 3-6 *Cisco CallManager User Options Web Page*

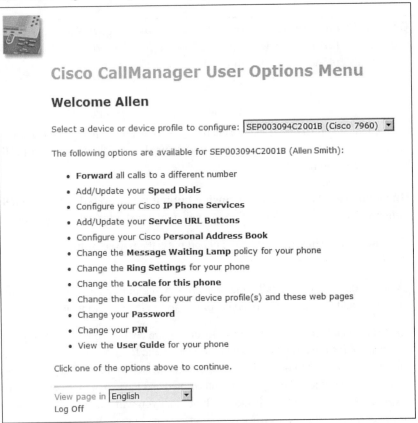

Cisco CallManager User Options Menu

Welcome Allen

Select a device or device profile to configure: SEP003094C2001B (Cisco 7960)

The following options are available for SEP003094C2001B (Allen Smith):

- **Forward** all calls to a different number
- Add/Update your **Speed Dials**
- Configure your Cisco **IP Phone Services**
- Add/Update your **Service URL Buttons**
- Configure your Cisco **Personal Address Book**
- Change the **Message Waiting Lamp** policy for your phone
- Change the **Ring Settings** for your phone
- Change the **Locale for this phone**
- Change the **Locale** for your device profile(s) and these web pages
- Change your **Password**
- Change your **PIN**
- View the **User Guide** for your phone

Click one of the options above to continue.

View page in English
Log Off

Configuring line/feature buttons for speed dial or service URLs provides users with access to the desired number or service with one quick button press. In addition to the line/feature buttons that you assign to the phone button template, the abbreviated dialing feature provides more speed dial buttons for a grand total of up to 99 speed dials, all configurable in the Cisco CallManager User Options web page. As shown in Figure 3-7, the speed dials are broken into two groups:

■ **Speed dial settings on the phone**—These speed dials refer to speed dial buttons you have configured on the phone button template.

■ **Speed dial settings not associated with a phone button**—These speed dials refer to speed dials associated with the abbreviated dialing feature (described in the section that follows).

Figure 3-7 *Configuring Speed Dial Numbers in Cisco CallManager User Options Web Page*

Abbreviated dialing is described in the following section.

Abbreviated Dialing (AbbrDial)

Abbreviated dialing allows you to dial a one- or two-digit index number that has been associated with a speed dial number. After you start dialing the index number, an **AbbrDial** softkey dynamically appears on the phone. Press the **AbbrDial** softkey to speed dial the number associated with the index number that was entered.

Users configure the speed dial numbers for abbreviated dialing in the Cisco CallManager User Options web page, as shown in Figure 3-7. The speed dials are numbered; the number is the index number that a user must dial prior to pressing the **AbbrDial** softkey. For example, using the speed dial settings shown in Figure 3-7, when Allen wants to order lunch at Joe's Pizza, he dials 8 and then presses the **AbbrDial** softkey. CallManager automatically dials 9, the access code Allen's company requires to call an OffNet destination, followed by the number: 214-555-1121.

To use abbreviated dialing, the phone must be on-hook. The **AbbrDial** softkey is not configurable on the softkey template. It appears dynamically when users begin entering a digit on the phone. However, the softkey only functions if the user has configured an associated speed dial number via the Cisco CallManager User Options web page.

> **TIP** Another way to access frequently called numbers is the IP phone service My Fast Dials. By using this service, you can create fast dials that you access through the **services** button or via a **services URL** button that has been configured on the phone button template. Because you can assign a specific IP phone service to a line/feature button that has been configured for service URL, you can access the My Fast Dials service with a single button press, and then select the fast dial of your choice by dialing a one- or two-digit index number for the entry that you want to call. Single-button access to a service is not limited to the My Fast Dials service, but this is probably one of the more frequently used service URLs that users will want to assign to a line button. You can learn more about My Fast Dials in the section "Cisco Personal Address Book" in Appendix A, "Feature List."

Dropping Conference Participants

You can drop conference participants from an Ad Hoc conference if you are the conference controller. An *Ad Hoc conference* is a type of conference in which a controlling station, the conference controller, manually adds conference participants one at a time. The conference controller can remove participants from a conference using two different Ad Hoc conference features:

- **Drop Last Party**—Enables you to drop the last party who joined the conference

- **Drop Any Party**—Enables you to drop a specific participant in the conference

A CallManager service parameter, Drop Ad Hoc Conference, determines how an Ad Hoc conference such as those created via the **Confrn**, **Barge**, and **Join** softkeys, terminates. The options are as follows:

- **Never**—The conference remains active a) after the conference controller hangs, and b) after all OnNet parties hang up. Choosing this option means that if OnNet parties conference in OffNet parties and then disconnect, the conference stays active between the OffNet parties, which could result in potential toll fraud.

- **When Conference Controller Leaves**—Terminate the conference when the conference controller hangs up or when the conference controller transfers, redirects, or parks the conference call and the retrieving party hangs up.

- **When No OnNet Parties Remain in the Conference**—Terminate the conference when there are no OnNet parties remaining in the conference.

You can learn more about Ad Hoc conferences in Chapter 5, "Media Processing," and in the section "Conference/Confrn" in Appendix A.

Drop Last Party

During an active or held Ad Hoc conference, the conference controller can press the **RmLstC** softkey to drop the last party who joined the conference. You must configure the **RmLstC** softkey on the softkey template and assign the template to phones for it to be available (**Device > Device Settings > Softkey Template**). Alternatively, the **ConfList** softkey enables the conference controller to view a list of conference participants and drop the selected station, as discussed in the following section.

Drop Any Party

During an active Ad Hoc conference, conference participants (including the conference controller) can press the **ConfList** softkey to view the list of conference participants. Pressing the **ConfList** softkey invokes an application that runs as a service on the station and provides a list of conference participants. The conference controller can drop a participant by using the phone's navigation control to scroll through the list to highlight a name/number and then pressing the **Remove** softkey to drop the highlighted participant from the conference. You can repeat this operation until all parties who you want to drop from the conference have been removed. The **ConfList** softkey is automatically available and requires no configuration.

Configurable Display of Forwarded Call Information

You can specify, on a per-line basis, the types of information that users see when calls are forwarded to their stations. Each line on a station can display different forwarded call information based on the settings configured in the Forwarded Call Information Display area on the Directory Number Configuration page in CallManager Administration (**Device > Phone >** *find and select a phone > click a line number*).

To better understand the display capabilities that can be configured for each line on a station, the following explanations help to clarify some common terms.

Each line on your station that can be used for calls has an associated directory number. If you originate a call, the line that you use to place the call, for display purposes, is referred to as the *calling line ID* (CLID) or simply calling party number. There is also a display name associated with that line on your station, and it is referred to as the *calling name ID* (CNID) or simply the calling party name.

When you make a call by dialing the directory number of the person you want to reach, the number that you dial is referred to as the *original dialed number* (ODN). Because calls might be forwarded one or more times, the original dialed number might not be the actual number of the line that is answered when the call is completed. The final directory number used to extend the call when the call is actually completed is referred to as the *redirected dialed number* (RDN).

The following check boxes are provided on the Directory Number Configuration page in CallManager Administration. All can be enabled or disabled by selecting/deselecting the check box. These check boxes control the display of information for calls that have been forwarded to the phone. By default, for forwarded calls that arrive at your phone, you will see the original dialed number and the calling party name.

- **Caller name (also known as calling name ID [CNID])**—Enabled by default

- **Caller number (also known as calling line ID [CLID])**—Disabled by default

- **Redirected number (also known as redirected dialed number [RDN])**—Disabled by default

- **Dialed number (also known as original dialed number [ODN])**—Enabled by default

Consider the following example: A call arrives at John's station on the line associated with directory number 4444. Delon Whetten originated the call on line 1111, and called Anne Smith at 2222. Anne had forwarded 2222 to Chris Pearce at 3333. Chris had forwarded 3333 to you at 4444. In this example, the calling party name is Delon, and the calling party number is 1111. The original dialed number is 2222. The redirected dialed number is 3333. When the phone arrives at John's station, the information that displays depends on the display options that you configured for John's station. Table 3-1 shows the information that displays for each of the display option combinations you can configure.

Table 3-1   *Call Info Display*

	Caller Number Enabled Caller Name Disabled	Caller Number Disabled Caller Name Enabled	Caller Number Enabled Caller Name Enabled	Caller Number Disabled Caller Name Disabled
Dialed Number Enabled **Redirected Number Disabled**	Forward 1111 For 2222	Forward Delon Whetten For Anne Smith	Forward Delon Whetten (1111) For Anne Smith (2222)	Forwarded For 2004
Dialed Number Enabled **Redirected Number Enabled**	Forward 1111 For 2222 By 3333	Forward Delon Whetten For Anne Smith By Chris Pearce	Forward Delon Whetten (1111) For Anne Smith (2222) By Chris Pearce (3333)	Forwarded For 2222 By 3333
Dialed Number Disabled **Redirected Number Enabled**	Forward 1111 By 3333	Forward Delon Whetten By Chris Pearce	Forward Delon Whetten (1111) By Chris Pearce (3333)	Forwarded By 3333
Dialed Number Disabled **Redirected Number Disabled**	Forward 1111	Forward Delon Whetten	Forward Delon Whetten (1111)	Forwarded

Configurable Text Label per Line

The Line Text Label field on the Directory Number Configuration page (**Device > Phone >** *find and select a phone > click a line*) enables you to configure a line with a text display rather than a directory number display.

For a station with only a few lines (perhaps a private line and a second line that is shared with another station), using the directory numbers for identification will probably suffice. For users who typically answer calls for multiple people and have numerous shared lines, however, the text display with names for each line is much more acceptable. If a line has an incoming call for John Alexander, a quick glance will let the user know that it is a call on John's line. It is then much easier to quickly answer with a greeting such as "Hello, John Alexander's office."

Alerting Name

The Alerting Name field enables you to configure the name that you want displayed on the calling station when a call is in the Alerting (ringing) state. For example, if you dial John Alexander at

214-555-1000, while the call is ringing at John's phone, the display on your phone shows "To John Alexander (2145551000)." The QSIG protocol uses this field as part of the Identification Services, but this field applies to all calls and is a part of the caller ID information that CallManager sends. The alerting name may differ from the name that displays when the call is connected. If you do not configure an alerting name, only the phone number or "Name Not Available" might display on the calling phone.

Auto Answer

Auto answer means that an incoming call is automatically answered at the station. A headset or speakerphone must be enabled and idle (not in use) for auto answer to occur. Two types of auto answer are available:

- **Auto answer with headset**—Provides hands-free operation with the use of a headset

- **Auto answer with speakerphone**—Provides a hands-free point-to-point intercom between two IP stations

These capabilities prove especially useful for users who receive many calls during the day and need hands-free operation. You can configure the auto answer functionality on the Directory Number Configuration page for any line on a station (**Device** > **Phone** > *find and select a phone* > *click a line*).

When auto answer with headset is enabled for a particular line on a station, the user hears a single beep (also called a *zip tone*) announcing the call, and then the call is automatically answered. If the user is currently in an active call, the new incoming call is not automatically answered. Auto answer with headset requires the use of a headset. The call is not automatically answered if the headset is not plugged into the back of the station and the **HEADSET** button enabled. Because the feature is designed so that calls will be answered automatically, auto answer with headset cannot be assigned to shared line appearances.

Auto answer with speakerphone provides a hands-free intercom between two stations. If a call is already active on the station when another incoming call arrives, auto answer will not occur and the call continues as a normal incoming call.

To allow a station to use intercom functionality to reach another station, you configure auto answer with speakerphone on a dedicated line on a station. The dedicated line has a directory number associated with it, for example 1111. Any user who dials 1111 is immediately connected to the station via the speaker. You should probably limit the number of people who could dial the intercom number, and you can achieve that limitation by defining a partition for 1111 and restricting the stations that have access to the 1111 partition in their calling search space. To provide single-button intercom capability, assign a speed dial to the line button on the stations that can access the intercom number, and the stations will be able to use the intercom line by simply pressing the speed dial button.

Media Termination at Route Points

The *media termination route points* enable an application to answer a call, determine the appropriate action to take for the call, and then route the call based on that determination. To allow you to direct calls to an application and allow the applications to process the calls, you can define a route point associated with a directory number as a virtual station capable of receiving calls and taking action on the calls. You can provision calls to be sent to route points based on the appropriate criteria that qualify the calls that need processing by a particular application. The route point will receive the calls and allow the application to do whatever processing is required for the call. The call answered by the application can later be redirected to a CTI port or a station. The route point can receive multiple simultaneous calls, and therefore the media and port for the each new call is provided by the route point. The following features are available for your use in the application:

- Answer

- Multiple active calls

- Redirect

- Hold

- Un-hold

- Drop

With these features available to applications to take action on calls that are sent to the application, you can develop very powerful applications for special call handling at a route point. In a simple call distribution example, your application would do the following:

1. Answer a call answered at the route point.

2. Play an announcement that the call will be directed to the next available agent.

3. Place the call on hold.

4. Monitor the available agents and when one becomes available redirect the call to the available agent.

The route point provides a place to hang on to the call and direct the activities of the call to get it to the right destination.

Overview of Station Devices Supported by CallManager

Station devices that CallManager supports, as shown in Figure 3-8, include H.323 stations, voice mail/unified messaging, IP phones, Unicast conference devices, transcoders, and voice applications such as Cisco IP Communicator. Chapter 5 discusses conference devices and transcoders in detail. In addition to explaining the supported devices, this section differentiates a user from a station and categorizes station devices by protocol and then subdivides them by device capabilities.

Figure 3-8 *System Station Devices*

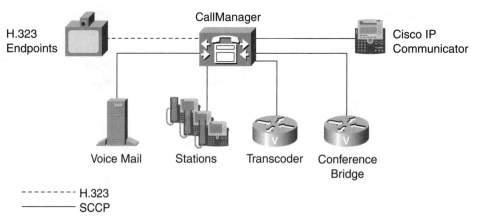

The three basic protocols CallManager uses to communicate with station devices are as follows:

- Skinny Client Control Protocol (SCCP)

- H.323

- Computer Telephony Integration (CTI)

The CTI interface provides Telephony Application Programming Interface (TAPI) and Java TAPI (JTAPI) application layer support. Although stations can reside on the other side of a gateway, the stations discussed in this chapter are limited to those that communicate directly with CallManager. Refer to Chapter 4 for gateway communication and protocols such as Media Gateway Control Protocol (MGCP).

Role of CallManager for Stations

CallManager provides call control on behalf of stations or gateways. In the case of stations, stations indicate requests for service to CallManager, and CallManager acts on the requests for service. The requests for service include such tasks as device initialization, device configuration information, call origination, call acceptance, call termination, call information, media statistics, and feature activation. CallManager provides the call control engine for the devices that are configured in the CallManager database via CallManager Administration.

The signaling from CallManager to the station is the call signaling path. The media path for the exchange of media between stations does not pass through CallManager. The stations stream media directly between the stations or directly from a station to a media processing device, such as a Unicast conferencing device or a transcoder.

SCCP Overview

SCCP is a lightweight, simple, stimulus protocol. The signaling path is a TCP/IP connection that the station establishes to CallManager. The station interface message set encompasses three basic areas:

- Registration and station management

- Call control

- Media stream (audio) control

CallManager directs the establishment of the media connection, but the station and device to which the station is connected establish the media stream directly to each other. You can learn more about SCCP in Appendix C.

Computer Telephony Integration (CTI) Overview

CTI provides a communication interface into CallManager. Both JTAPI and TAPI make use of CTI communication with CallManager. The CTI interface is specific to communication between the Cisco TAPI service provider and CallManager. The TAPI service provider is a layer external to CallManager that is used by TAPI applications to communicate with CallManager without requiring knowledge of the CTI interface.

Microsoft's TAPI for Windows simplifies telephony application development. The interface abstracts the telephony services from the actual hardware and software infrastructure of CallManager. Applications developed with TAPI are more portable and less subject to change when the CallManager infrastructure changes.

JTAPI is a Java-based interface that provides similar abstraction for Java-based development. JTAPI also abstracts the application development from the CallManager infrastructure. JTAPI extends application portability to include not only independence from CallManager infrastructure, but also independence from any particular operating system.

Figure 3-9 shows the role of the CTI protocol in the application infrastructure of CallManager. You can learn more about the CTI protocol in Appendix C.

Figure 3-9 *CTI Protocol*

H.323 Endpoint Overview

An *H.323 endpoint* is a device or software application that communicates with CallManager using the H.323 protocol specification. The Microsoft NetMeeting software application is an example of an H.323 endpoint.

The H.323 Recommendation from the International Telecommunication Union Telecommunication Standardization Sector (ITU-T) contains a set of very complex protocols that work together under the H.323 protocol umbrella. These protocols (for example, H.225.0 and H.245) manage the connection and the media for a communication session. The frame structure for the multiplex layer allows for a vast multitude of services. However, the complexity is more extensive than is required for simple voice communications. H.323 stations must maintain state information for a call and thus are relatively complex. By contrast, SCCP provides both features and services for relatively low-cost user stations that require no protocol state processing.

Figure 3-10 shows the relationship of the protocols under the H.323 umbrella specification. You can learn more about the H.323 protocol in Appendix C.

SCCP Station Devices

The family of Cisco IP Phones has evolved from the 79*xx* series IP Phones to the expanded 79*xx*G series IP Phones. The G stands for global and indicates a phone with icons on the buttons rather than words. The interface to the full family of Cisco IP Phones uses the same SCCP. As the Cisco IP Phone family evolved to include the 79*xx*G series, SCCP expanded, but the interface is backward compatible to support the earlier 79*xx* series IP Phones.

Figure 3-10 *H.323 Protocol Specification*

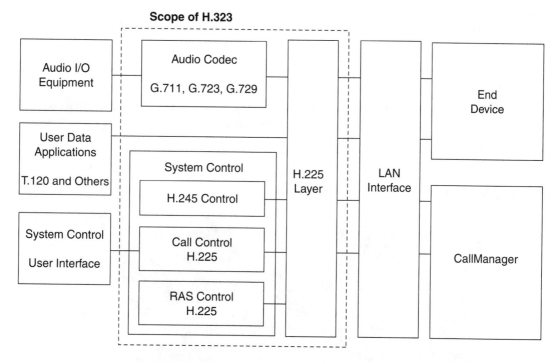

Cisco IP Phones

The Cisco IP Phone family includes the following models:

- Cisco IP Phone 7902G

- Cisco IP Phone 7905G

- Cisco IP Phone 7912G

- Cisco IP Phone 7940G

- Cisco IP Phone 7941G

- Cisco IP Phone 7960G

- Cisco IP Phone 7961G

- Cisco IP Phone 7970G

- Cisco IP Phone 7971G-GE

- Cisco IP Phone 7985G

In addition, the family of phone products includes the following:

■ Wireless IP Phone 7920

■ IP Phone Expansion Module 7914

■ IP Conference Station 7936

The product set also extends to include the Cisco IP Communicator, Cisco ATA 186 with 10BASE-T uplink, Cisco ATA 188 with 10/100BASE-T uplink, and the analog phone gateways Cisco VG248. Figure 3-11 shows the Cisco IP Phone family as well as the Cisco IP Communicator.

Figure 3-11 *Cisco IP Phone Family*

Cisco IP Phone 7902G

The Cisco IP Phone 7902G is an entry-level business set that is good to use in areas with low telephone traffic and no need for application support (because there is no display). The phone provides a single line with a single directory number. With no display, there are fixed feature keys rather than softkeys to support redial, transfer, conference, and messages.

The Cisco IP Phone 7902G supports inline power and offers a visual message waiting indicator to indicate voice messages and a hold button. There is a speaker for call monitoring, but no microphone.

Cisco IP Phone 7905G

The Cisco IP Phone 7905G is a single-line, inline-powered set that you would most likely use in common areas with low to medium telephone traffic, such as a hallway, manufacturing floor, reception area, or office cubicle. The phone provides a pixel-based display with five lines of display text, softkeys, and the standard date/time/menu title. Like the Cisco IP Phone 7902G, the phone provides a dedicated hold key and a visual message waiting indicator. The phone has speaker capability for call monitoring, but no microphone.

Cisco IP Phone 7912G

The Cisco IP Phone 7912G is single-line, inline-powered phone best suited for low to medium telephone traffic, such as an office cubicle. The Cisco IP Phone 7912G offers a five-line pixel-based display, softkeys, the date/time/menu title. The Cisco IP Phone 7912G includes a 10/100BASE-T, two-port Ethernet switch, a dedicated hold button, and visual message waiting indicator. The phone has speaker capability for call monitoring, but no microphone.

Cisco Wireless IP Phone 7920

The Cisco Wireless IP Phone 7920 is a wireless IEEE 802.11b IP Phone that supports up to six lines/speed dials. The pixel display provides feature access via the four-way navigation control and menu button, plus a hold and mute button and two softkeys for dynamically presented calling options. The voice encoding in the phone supports both G.711 and G.729A. Standard or extended Li-ion batteries are available.

Cisco IP Phones 7940G, 7941G, 7960G, 7961G, 7970G, and 7971G-GE

Cisco IP Phones 7940G, 7941G, 7960G, 7961G, 7970G, and 7971G-GE offer a large display pane, multiple softkeys, and allow web-based applications to be launched from the **services** button. The user interaction for making calls, phone setup and configuration, and use of features is enhanced by the use of the large display and user-friendly interface. The Cisco IP Phones 79410 and 7941G provide two line/feature buttons, the Cisco IP Phones 7960G and 7961G provide six line/feature buttons, and the Cisco IP Phones 7970G and 7971G-GE provide eight line/feature buttons.

The Cisco IP Phones 7940G, 7941G, 7960G, 7961G, and 7970G all include the following:

- Display area that provides visual information to the user based on the button selected.

- A **messages** button, which provides access to voice mail.

- A **?** or **i** button, which provides help functionality.

- A **services** button, which allows access to web-based applications to extend the capability of the phone.

- A **directories** button, which provides access to the directory capabilities of the phone, which include calls received, calls placed, and calls missed. Personal and corporate directories can also be added to the directory functionality.

- A **settings** button, which allows access to phone settings such as screen contrast, ring types, network phone configuration, and more.

- Softkey buttons (four on the Cisco IP Phones 7940G, 7941G, 7960G, and 7961G and five on the Cisco IP Phones 7970G and 7971G-GE) provide access to call processing-related features.

- Numeric keypad.

- Navigation control via the two- or four-way rocker control.

- Volume control.

- Programmable line/feature buttons (eight on the Cisco IP Phones 7970G and 7971G-GE, six on the Cisco IP Phones 7960G and 7961G, and two on the Cisco IP Phones 7940G and 7941G).

- **SPEAKERPHONE**, **MUTE**, and **HEADSET** buttons.

In addition to the capabilities in the preceding list, Cisco IP Phones 7961G and 7941G also provide a high resolution display (320 × 240), lighted line keys, IEEE standard 802.3af inline power, and support for Cisco legacy power. Cisco IP Phone 7971G-GE provides an internal 10/100/1000BASE-T two-port Ethernet switch with 802.1Q capability. Also, Cisco IP Phones 7970G and 7971G-GE include the following features:

- High-resolution, large graphical display (320 × 234), supporting 12-bit color depth

- Touch screen display

- LED line lamps

- Adjustable backlit display

The **?** or **i** button, **directories** button, and **services** button each have an associated URL. Each URL identifies for the phones the location of an XML service accessed by the phone when the appropriate button is pressed. A set of default URLs come pre-installed with CallManager and are accessible via the Enterprise Parameters Configuration page (**System > Enterprise Parameters**).

You can override the URL to allow the phone capabilities to be extended. The section "Cisco IP Phone Services" describes how you can use the **services** button to extend capabilities.

Cisco IP Phone 7914 Expansion Module

The Cisco IP Phone 7914 Expansion Module adds 14 illuminated buttons to Cisco IP Phone 7960, 7970, and 7971, or 28 additional buttons when two Cisco IP Phone 7914s are added. The Expansion Module has a large LCD display for directory numbers or speed dial names.

Cisco IP Phone Conference Station 7936

The Cisco IP Conference Station 7936 is an IP-based full-duplex hands-free conference station. In addition to basic calls, the conference set provides the following standard features:

- Hold

- Transfer

- Mute

- Call park

- Pickup

You get 360-degree room coverage provided by a digitally tuned speaker and three microphones. An external microphone kit includes two optional microphones for additional coverage in larger rooms. The conference station is configured as easily as any other station.

Cisco IP Phone 7985G

The Cisco IP Phone 7985G is a SCCP-based personal desktop audio/video phone that, in addition to standard audio calls, offers all the components necessary for video calls—camera with lens cap, large 8.4" LCD display, speakerphone with a headset jack, keypad, and handset—integrated into a single IP phone. The phone supports H.264, H.263+, H.263, and H.261 video standards, IEEE Power over Ethernet (PoE), automatic port configuration using Cisco Discovery Protocol (CDP), and includes a 2-port Ethernet switch for a co-located PC.

Video calls occur just like audio phone calls: the user simply dials the number and if the called party has a video-enabled endpoint, the call automatically proceeds as a video call. If the called party does not have video capabilities, the call occurs as an audio-only call. The Cisco IP Phone 7985G provides forward, conference, transfer, and hold capabilities on video calls, all through an intuitive and familiar Cisco IP Phone user interface.

Cisco IP Communicator

Cisco IP Communicator is a software-based IP phone application that runs on a PC. IP Communicator has VPN client support and acts as a supplemental telephone when traveling, a telecommuting device, or a primary desktop telephone. The functionality is very similar to a Cisco IP Phone 7970G, although for IP Communicator you use a mouse for touch screen functionality of the Cisco IP Phone 7970G phone.

Cisco IP Phone Registration

To function, IP phones must register with CallManager. The phones first determine a prioritized list of CallManager nodes with which to register. After a list of CallManager nodes is determined, the phone attempts to register with the first (primary) CallManager node. If registration succeeds, the primary CallManager node is responsible for handling the exchange of SCCP messages necessary for call control for the IP phone. The IP phone also establishes and maintains a connection to a secondary CallManager node, with which it registers in the event that the phone loses connectivity with the primary CallManager node.

The phone sends a KeepAlive message to the server with which it is currently registered. The interval between KeepAlive messages to the primary and secondary CallManager nodes is configurable via the Station KeepAlive Interval and Station and Backup Server KeepAlive Interval service parameters respectively (**Service > Service Parameters** > *select a server* > **Cisco CallManager**); the default interval is 30 seconds for the primary node and 60 seconds for the backup node. The phone detects connection problems with CallManager through KeepAlive or TCP/IP errors on call signaling traffic. If the phone cannot reestablish the connection to the primary CallManager node, the phone registers to the secondary CallManager (failover) and continues operation. The phone attempts to reconnect to the primary CallManager and if successful, the phone unregisters from the secondary CallManager and reregisters with the primary CallManager (fallback). This process is known as *failover* and *fallback*.

You can also configure a Cisco Survivable Remote Site Telephony (SRST) reference as the last device in the CallManager list. This proves especially useful in a remote site configuration where the phones and CallManager are connected over a WAN network. SRST provides users with fallback support for the IP phones that cannot access the primary, secondary, or tertiary CallManager in the CallManager because of CallManager failure or loss of connectivity across the WAN. For the remote sites attached to Cisco multiple-service routers across the WAN, SRST ensures that your remote users receive continuous (although minimal) service by providing call handling support directly from the SRST router.

SDL Message Queues in CallManager

CallManager has internal Signal Distribution Layer (SDL) message queues that determine the priority of SCCP messages such as KeepAlives, phone registration, call processing functions, and so on. The messages are divided into priority queues to help manage the load on CallManager nodes when the system is operating at capacity. The queues help ensure that higher-priority messages, such as KeepAlives, are processed by CallManager before lower-priority messages such as database updates. For example, when a CallManager system is newly installed, all phones in the system try to register. Such an influx of station registration messages can cause problems such as delayed dial tone if they are not properly prioritized. Because off-hook notifications are processed in a higher-priority queue than initial station registration requests, users who have phones that are already registered will not experience delayed dial tone when they go off-hook to place a call due to the pending station registration requests which are managed in a lower-priority queue. Users of phones that have not yet registered with any CallManager (and therefore are not even operational) will not likely notice the slightly longer delay for registration due to the registration messages being processed in the lower queue.

Five queues exist:

- **High**—This queue handles messages related to timeout events, internal CallManager KeepAlives, certain gatekeeper events, and internal process creation, among other events.

- **Normal**—This queue manages messages for call processing functions, key presses, on-hook and off-hook notifications, among other events.

- **Low**—This queue handles messages for station device registration (except the initial station registration request message), among other events.

- **Lowest**—This queue handles initial station registration request messages during device registration, among other events.

- **Database updates**—This queue, added in CallManager release 4.1(2), manages database messages, such as requests and updates.

Because phones register at the same time that calls are in progress on a CallManager node, registration messages are handled by CallManager in a lower-priority queue to give higher priority to the active calls and not delay call processing activity. Registrations proceed at the maximum rate that they can be processed, but they will not have an excessive impact on users' call activity. The priority of SDL messages such as device registration is statically configured in CallManager.

In the case of a fallback situation, phone registration can take a longer period of time to occur than during initial device registration or failover device registration. The service parameter Maximum Phone Fallback Queue Depth controls the number of messages allowed to queue for the CallManager node that is coming back online after a failover. You'll notice that although the range for this parameter is 1 to 500, the default value is 10. The value is kept low to preserve CallManager performance and make sure that phones that are successfully registered to a working CallManager do not sever that connection until they can be assured of registering to a new working node without excessive delay.

The phone can use Domain Name Server (DNS) or Dynamic Host Configuration Protocol (DHCP) and Trivial File Transfer Protocol (TFTP) to determine initially the IP address of the prioritized list of CallManager nodes to which the phone can register. Although each of these services can ease implementation, they are not all required.

DNS, for example, is not required if CallManager nodes use IP addresses as their names in the Cisco CallManager Configuration page (**System > Cisco CallManager**); for networks not running DHCP, you can use static IP addressing. Figure 3-12 shows the interaction of the phone with DNS, DHCP, TFTP, and CallManager during the initial registration.

Figure 3-12 *Cisco IP Phone Initialization*

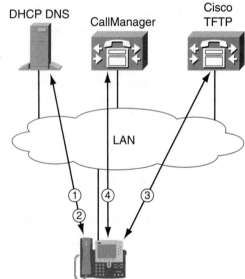

① Get IP address, mask, DNS.
  • Static or DHCP

② Get TFTP Server address (use any one of these; listed in the order of preference the phone uses to select the TFTP server address):
  • Static address
  • DNS resolution of CiscoCM1.domain.name
  • DHCP Option 150 or DHCP Option 66 with DNS name or dotted-decimal address

③ Get configuration from TFTP server.
  • XML file with list of up to three CallManager servers.
  • Verify firmware version. If version update is required, get the new firmware load.

④ Register with CallManager.

DHCP is a service provided with Microsoft Windows or the Cisco Network Registrar that automatically assigns IP addresses to devices on the network. Cisco IP Phones are DHCP-enabled by default. If DHCP is not in use, use the **settings** button on the phone to disable DHCP and manually configure the IP address of the phone and the TFTP server address. Disabling DHCP and manually configuring the IP addresses prevents mobility of the phone. Assuming DHCP, DNS, and

TFTP services are running, the phone goes through the following sequence of events to register initially with a CallManager node:

1. The phone requests an IP address from the DHCP service.

2. As part of the DHCP response, the DHCP server returns the TFTP server address to the phone.

   The TFTP address can include two TFTP servers for redundancy. If the phone encounters a TFTP timeout, it will try the other TFTP address. The phone supports redundancy through static configuration on the phone, through DHCP option 150, and through DNS resolution. IP phones have an order of preference that they use to select the address of the TFTP server. If the phone receives conflicting or confusing information from the DHCP server, the phone uses the following sequence to determine what information is valid:

   a. You can configure the phone with a TFTP server address through the phone configuration. This manually configured address overrides the TFTP address sent by the DHCP server.

   b. If a phone does not receive a TFTP server address from the DHCP server (either via Option 150 or Option 66), the phone will attempt to resolve the DNS name CiscoCM1. It is not necessary to name the TFTP server CiscoCM1, but you must enter a DNS name record to associate CiscoCM1 with the address or name of the TFTP server. This name can resolve to multiple addresses. The phone uses the first two addresses to populate the TFTP Server 1 and TFTP Server 2 fields.

   c. The phone uses the site-specific Option 150. This option is a list of 32-bit IP addresses. The phone uses the first two addresses to populate the TFTP Server 1 and TFTP Server 2 fields.

   d. The phone uses the value of Next-Server in the boot process. This DHCP configuration parameter has traditionally been used as the address of the TFTP server. When configuring BOOTP servers, this field is typically referred to as the address of the TFTP server. This information is returned in the siaddr field of the DHCP header.

   e. The phone also accepts the Optional Server Name parameter. This DHCP configuration parameter is the DNS name of a TFTP server. This Optional Server Name field can contain a DNS name or a dotted-decimal IP address. Additionally, this name can resolve to multiple addresses. The phone uses the first two addresses to populate the TFTP Server 1 and TFTP Server 2 fields.

   f. The phone accepts Option 066, which is the name of the boot server. Option 066 normally replaces the Optional Server Name field when option overloading occurs. This Optional Server Name field can contain a DNS name or a dotted-decimal IP address.

After the phone receives the TFTP address, the phone requests its configuration information from the TFTP server. The configuration information includes a prioritized list of up to three CallManager nodes. The configuration information is in the form of an Extensible Markup Language (XML) file. The XML file contains additional information, including the phone load version.

3. The phone establishes communication with the highest CallManager node in the prioritized list and sends a registration request. If the phone requested a configuration (.cnf) file and not an XML file, the phone also sends a version request and checks the phone load version. If the phone firmware version matches the current phone firmware version, the phone continues with the registration process. If the phone needs a new firmware version, the phone aborts the registration process and downloads a new version of the phone firmware from the TFTP server. After the phone loads the new firmware, the phone restarts the registration process. If the phone processed an XML file for the configuration information, the version has already been verified and is not requested from CallManager.

4. When the phone successfully registers, the DHCP and TFTP communications are not repeated unless the phone experiences a hard reset through a power off/on sequence or by a reset from CallManager Administration or experiences a TFTP timeout.

NOTE   If the phone encounters a TFTP timeout, the phone alternates between TFTP Server 1 and TFTP Server 2. The phone continues using the selected server as long as it is available. If the phone resets, the initial TFTP attempt is to TFTP Server 1.

Cisco IP Phone Security

Cisco IP Phone models 7940G, 7941G, 7960G, 7961G, 7970G, and 7971G-GE work in concert with CallManager to provide additional levels of security over and above the security provided by the network infrastructure. Phone security targets three areas:

■   Configuration

■   Device identity and configuration file security

■   Media privacy

The basic functionality to provide the additional level of security includes Transport Layer Security (TLS), secure Real-Time Transport Protocol (SRTP), and authenticated configuration files for the phones. TLS provides call signaling integrity and privacy between CallManager and IP phones. The SRTP adds encryption to the media stream between phones to provide integrity and privacy at the voice stream level. Authentication at the configuration file level adds certificates to provide device identity security.

Configuration

The following phone configuration options affect the degree of security enjoyed by IP phones:

■ Gratuitous ARP

■ PC Port

■ PC Voice VLAN Access

■ Settings Access

These fields appear on the Phone Configuration page in CallManager Administration (**Device > Phone >** *find and select a phone*). All are enabled by default.

> **TIP** To change these settings quickly for a number of devices, use BAT (**Configure > Phones > Update Phones > Use query >** *run a query for the phone models you want to update settings for*).

Gratuitous ARP Field

IP phones accept Gratuitous Address Resolution Packets (GARP). Because some devices announce their presence on the network with GARP, a false GARP message could be sent to the phone with a false claim to be the default router. To block this possibility, you can disable GARP via the Gratuitous ARP field.

PC Port Field

Many IP phones have a PC port to which a user can attach a PC device. In lobby or conference rooms, you might not want PC devices to be attached to the phones. You can disable this capability via the PC Port field.

PC Voice VLAN Access Field

For a phone that does need PC connectivity enabled, you can configure the phone to isolate the VLAN from a PC attached to the phone by disabling the PC Voice VLAN Access field. Packets from the network come to the phone and are also sent to the PC port. Some of the packets are destined for the phone and some are destined for the PC. You can configure the phone for special handling of packets that are tagged with the voice VLAN. If you disable the PC Voice VLAN Access field, any packets received from the switch and tagged as VLAN will not be sent to the PC port. Any packets received from the PC port that are tagged with voice VLAN will be dropped. This field allows you to disable access to the voice VLAN from the device attached to the PC port of the phone.

> **NOTE**   The PC Port and PC Voice VLAN Access fields are not available on
> Cisco IP Phone 7912 models.

Settings Access Field

You might want to control access from the phone to the phone's own network configuration
(**settings** button). You can restrict or disable access to network configuration at the phone by
choosing **Disabled** or **Restricted** in the Settings Access field. The Restricted option means that
only user preferences and volume settings can be changed; Disabled means that when the **settings**
button is pressed, no options display at all and no volume settings can be changed.

Device Identity and Configuration File Security

Device identity security enables you to ensure that all CallManager devices in the system are
legitimate devices and that the clients are connected to a legitimate CallManager node. If you have
a device on the network that is not a legitimate device, you could have calls being made that are
unauthorized or you could have excessive signal traffic directed at CallManager and interfering
with normal call traffic signaling. If a software entity on your network masquerades as
CallManager, some of your stations could be removed from the system without the knowledge of
the user at those stations. Authentication between CallManager and the end device is designed to
make hijacking of phone sessions significantly more difficult.

Phone models that support security request and receive a digitally signed Certificate Trust List (CTL)
file from the TFTP server. The CTL file provides public keys for all CallManager nodes and the
security tokens. The list provides the phone with the trusted list of CallManager servers. The phone
examines the signature and verifies it using the security token information from the CTL file. The
configuration files received by the phone from the TFTP server are signed and verified by the phone.

The phone establishes a TLS session with CallManager to begin the registration process.
CallManager has a certificate that is included in the CTL and is used by the phones during TLS
session establishment. The phone also has a certificate that it uses to authenticate the phone to
CallManager. With mutual authentication, the TLS handshake establishes a secure connection,
authenticating the certificates in CallManager and in the phone.

A number of factors contribute to the security mode you choose for your CallManager cluster,
such as the phone devices in the network, the level of security that those phones can support, and
the level of security required for your network. The Cluster Security Mode enterprise parameter
(**System > Enterprise Parameters**) determines the security mode for the cluster. Two choices exist:

- Nonsecure, which allows phones to register with no security

- Mixed security, which disables auto-registration and allows the registration of both secure
  devices and nonsecure devices

Device security is controlled at the device and system levels. The device level takes priority. If the Device Security Mode field on the Phone Configuration page is set to Use System Default, the value specified in the Device Security Mode enterprise parameter determines the device security. Three options exist:

- Authenticated (only device authentication and signaling authentication)

- Encrypted (device authentication, signaling authentication, and encryption)

- Nonsecure (no device authentication, signaling authentication, or encryption)

Media Privacy

If signaling authentication is established between CallManager and both endpoints and both endpoints are capable of media encryption, media privacy is possible for the call between the phones. To ensure privacy of the media (voice data), the phones encrypt the media they exchange. To have encrypted media, both ends of the connection must be authenticated and you must have SRTP-capable endpoints. Any intermediate connection that does not support SRTP, such as a transcoder, media termination point (MTP), monitoring bridge, or intercluster call, excludes the call from encryption eligibility. These devices are described in more detail in Chapter 5.

CallManager enables encryption by creating the media session encryption key and salt (see the following sidebar for more information) for each call that requires encryption, and securely delivering the key and salt to each of the endpoints. After these keys and salt are securely delivered to the phones, the phones use the key pairs for the SRTP media session to protect the media. The encryption is established for each direction of the call. For a single voice call, there are two independently encrypted streams, one in each direction, for your voice conversation.

What Is Salt?

One of the problems that occur in Cipher Block Chaining (CBC) mode symmetric encryption (which is used in CallManager for TLS) is that for the first block of data, you need to have something that already went through the cipher. The *salt* is simply a block of random information that acts as that first block. It is random so that it is more difficult to precompute crypto attacks based on known plain text. (For example, in e-mail, there is always a From and a To block at the first of the packets.) In the case of the media streams, the salt performs the same type of function in that it increases the difficulty of crypto analysis of the SRTP stream. It is not part of the actual key that the encryptor uses, but acts as additional data.

Call Signaling

SCCP is a simple stimulus interface between the Cisco IP Phone and CallManager. The communication takes place over a TCP/IP connection that the phone establishes to CallManager on port 2000. Once established, the connection remains as long as the phone is capable of initiating or accepting calls. SCCP provides a means of receiving stimulus events from the phone such as off-hook, on-hook, and button press events, which include keypad digits, fixed keys, softkeys, and line keys. SCCP also provides a means of sending control information to the phone to drive the specific behavior required for the phone to provide the user with the correct information as calls are made and features are handled. You can review the details of SCCP in Appendix C.

Cisco IP Phone Services

Cisco IP Phone models 7905, 7912, 7920, 7940, 7941, 7960, 7961, 7970, and 7971 are capable of deploying customized IP phone services. The services make use of the keypad, softkeys, and display to interact with the user. The services are deployed using the HTTP protocol, which is available on standard web servers such as Microsoft Internet Information Server (IIS). Users access IP phone services by pressing the **services** button. The enterprise parameter URL Services specifies the web page that gets called when the **services** button is pressed.

Overview of Cisco IP Phone Services

When the user presses the **services** button, the display provides a list of services that have been subscribed to the phone. The user can select a menu item by either scrolling to it and pressing a softkey or by pressing the number associated with the menu item.

You add IP phone services to CallManager in the Cisco IP Phone Services Configuration page (**Feature > Cisco IP Phone Services**). After the service is made available in CallManager, users subscribe and unsubscribe to the list of available IP phone services in the Cisco CallManager User Options web page. After subscribing to a phone service, the user can access it by pressing the **services** button or a line/feature button that has been configured for a service URL. (See the section "Service URLs/Speed Dials" in this chapter.)

When the user selects an IP phone service, the phone uses its HTTP client to send the HTTP request to the web server that the URL address specifies. The phone is not a web browser and cannot parse HTML. The response to the HTTP request is either plain text or packaged in specifically defined XML wrappers. The phone receives the object returned by the web server and interacts with the user as specified by the text or XML data type supported by the phone. For example, a simple IP phone service might be a weather lookup. The user subscribes to the Weather service, presses **services**, and selects the Weather service. Text on the phone display prompts the user to use the phone's keypad to enter a Zip code and press the **Submit** softkey. The phone's

HTTP client sends the HTTP request to the specified weather web server, which returns the requested information and the weather for the specified Zip code displays on the phone.

Phone-Supported XML Objects

When progressing through the data page returned by the web server, the phone simply processes the text or XML data objects to update the display and process user input as directed. Table 3-2 lists the extent to which the XML objects are supported across the Cisco IP Phone models.

Table 3-2 *XML Objects Supported by Cisco IP Phone Model*

Phone Model XML Object	7905/7912	7920	7940/7960	7941/7961/ 7970/7971/IP Communicator
CiscoIPPhoneText	X	X	X	X
CiscoIPPhoneMenu	X	X	X	X
CiscoIPPhoneIconMenu	Icons ignored	X	X	X
CiscoIPPhoneDirectory	X		X	X
CiscoIPPhoneInput	X		X	X
CiscoIPPhoneImage		X*	X	X
CiscoIPPhoneImageFile				X
CiscoIPPhoneGraphicMenu		X*	X	X
CiscoIPPhoneGraphicFileMenu				X
CiscoIPPhoneExecute	Forced to Priority 0 (execute immediately)	Forced to Priority 0 (execute immediately)	X	X
CiscoIPPhoneError	X	X	X	X
CiscoIPPhoneResponse	X	X	X	X

* The Cisco IP Phone 7920 has only a 128- $\times$ 59-pixel display and 2 grayscales. If an image with 4 grayscales is sent to the phone, the phone splits the image into 2 grayscales. (0–1 are treated as 0, and 2–3 get treated as 1.)

Each of the XML data types supported by the phone is described in Appendix C. Data types are the building blocks of IP phone services. You need to learn about data types if you are planning to write your own IP phone services. If you intend to write your own IP phone services, please see Appendix C.

> **TIP** Consult the following resources if you plan to write IP phone services and applications:
>
> - The Cisco Press book *Developing Cisco IP Phone Services*, ISBN: 1-58705-060-9, by Darrick Deel, Mark Nelson, and Anne Smith
>
> - "Cisco IP Phone Services Application Development Notes" white paper: http://www.cisco.com/univercd/cc/td/doc/product/voice/vpdd/cdd/
>
> - The Cisco IP Phone Services Software Development Kit available at the following link or search Cisco.com for "Cisco IP phone services": http://www.cisco.com/en/US/products/hw/phones/ps379/products_data_sheet09186a00800925a8.html
>
> - Hot Dispatch: http://www.hotdispatch.com/cisco-ip-telephony

Cisco VT Advantage

Cisco Video Telephony (VT) Advantage extends the capability of Cisco IP Phone models 7940, 7941, 7960, 7961, 7970, and 7971 to include video telephony functionality. Cisco VT Advantage is a desktop video application for the PC that is co-located with a supported Cisco IP Phone model. VT Advantage enables you to use your PC to display the video. As you interface normally with your IP phone, the application is notified and sends (if your PC is equipped with a Cisco VT Camera) and receives video if both you and the other party in the call are video-enabled. With Cisco VT Advantage, video is as easy as making a phone call. To be able to send video from Cisco VT Advantage on your PC, you need a Cisco VT Camera. For added security, Cisco IP Phones only communicate with Cisco VT Advantage running on a PC that is co-located and connected through the PC port on the phone. Figure 3-13 shows the Cisco VT Advantage.

Figure 3-13 *Cisco VT Advantage*

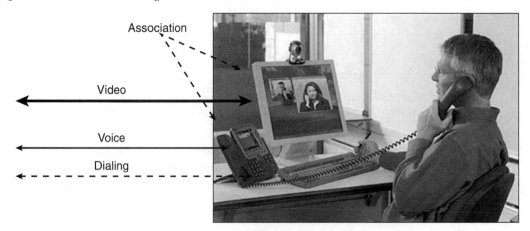

Cisco VT Advantage running on a PC,
associated with a Cisco IP Phone in CallManager

Cisco VT Advantage automatically establishes a video stream during a basic call to or from another video-enabled device, which could be another Cisco IP Phone with Cisco VT Advantage, an H.263-enabled endpoint, or an H.323 terminal, including most H.323 conferencing MCUs. VT Advantage is notified of the call activity and automatically establishes the video and pops up a window on your PC when video is established. The video stream is activated when the audio stream is active. If the audio stream is stopped while initiating a hold, transfer, or conference operation, the video stream stops as well. The video functionality mirrors the audio functionality. If you initiate a consultation transfer and the current call is placed on hold while you establish a call with the target of the transfer, if so equipped, a video connection is established during the consultation transfer, just like the audio. Bandwidth controls have been expanded to cover video, and Cisco VT Advantage is regulated by the bandwidth restrictions you configure. Cisco VT Advantage provides icons to give you visual state information to indicate Idle, Connected, Video Muted, or No IP Phone, and you can configure Cisco VT Advantage so that you are prompted before a video call connects.

Computer Telephony Interface (CTI) Devices

This section describes CallManager's application interface implementation and the underlying CTI. CTI is the internal interface to CallManager, on which the standard interfaces, such as TAPI and JTAPI, are supported. CTI communication from the application platform to CallManager is through TCP/IP.

CTI Application Architecture Overview

The CTI application architecture provides a means of controlling call behavior from external applications. CallManager provides already developed applications and a development infrastructure to allow third-party application development.

Figure 3-14 shows the CallManager infrastructure that supports the applications. The applications run on the application platform and make use of the application services. Applications provide a high-level functionality that is usually specific to a particular need, such as IP Contact Center, voice messaging/unified messaging, and so on. The applications might have media termination functionality or might simply control stations that actually terminate the media. The application platform and services provide the application programming interface (API), call control protocols, administration and serviceability functionality, and directory and database interfaces.

Figure 3-14 *CallManager Application Infrastructure*

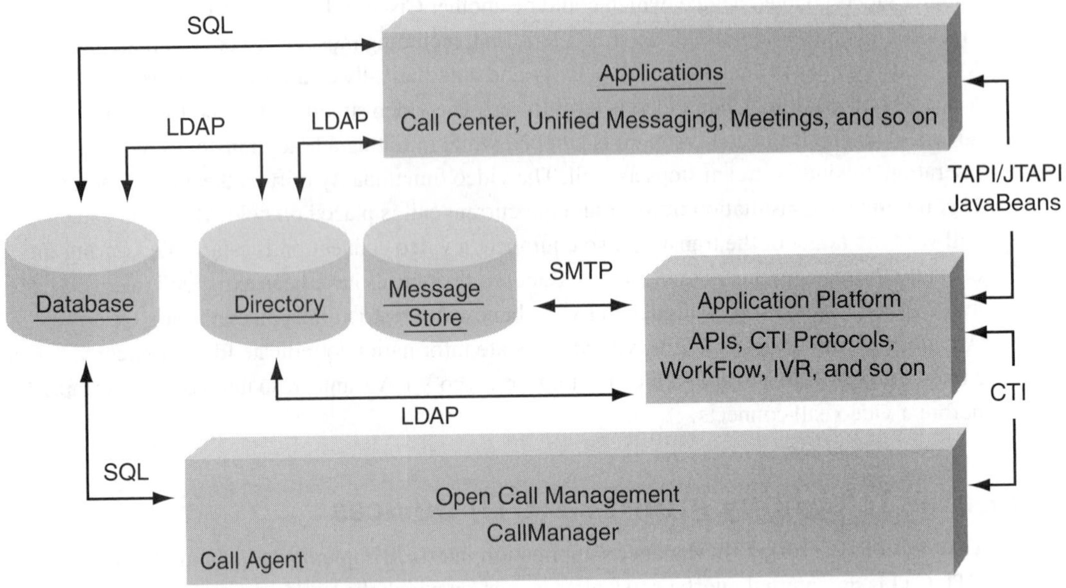

Application Layers External to CallManager

Application layers that are external to CallManager allow an application to interface to CallManager. The two primary application service APIs supported by CallManager are TAPI and JTAPI. These two APIs enable developers to extend the capabilities of CallManager to meet specific enterprise needs. The choice of TAPI or JTAPI is based on the particular needs and preferences of your organization.

The Cisco architecture for both TAPI and JTAPI, shown in Figure 3-15, supports a redundant connection to CTIManager so that if one CTIManager is down, the application can still communicate with the other CTIManager and continue functioning.

TAPI

Microsoft's TAPI for Windows was initially used for first-party device control for devices that were co-resident, such as controlling modems. The application would initiate a modem connection from the software running on the personal computer to a destination provided by the application. TAPI was extended to include a telephony server for third-party remote control, such as PBX devices. The TAPI framework abstracts the telephony services from the CallManager infrastructure. The applications are more portable and insulated from the effect of changes in new CallManager releases.

Figure 3-15 *Cisco CTIManager Redundancy*

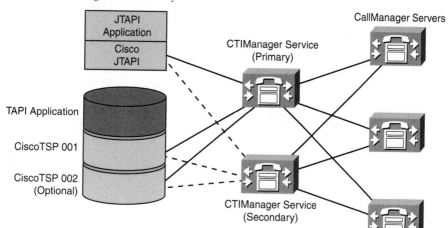

Figure 3-16 illustrates the components that make up the TAPI architecture and reside in the PC running the telephony application. The TAPI architecture is an abstraction layer between the TAPI applications and the underlying hardware and transport protocols of CallManager. The TAPI application accesses the device-specific controls for communications and call processing through a dynamic link library (DLL). Each TAPI application is a separate process that communicates using TAPI with Tapi32.dll or Tapi3.dll, provided by Microsoft. Tapi32.dll and Tapi3.dll communicate with the TAPISRV.EXE process using a private remote-procedure call (RPC) interface. TAPISRV.EXE is a Microsoft process that runs as a Windows service. TAPISRV.EXE communicates with the telephony service provider (TSP) using Telephony Service Provider Interface (TSPI). The Cisco TAPI Service Provider (Cisco TSP) is a DLL that runs under the TAPISRV.EXE process. The Cisco TSP communicates with CallManager through a TCP/IP interface known as CTIQBE. The Quick Buffer Encoding (QBE, pronounced "cube") format is based loosely on Microsoft's TAPI buffer format. QBE defines C-language structures that can be byte-copied directly to or from an input/output stream. The Cisco TSP allows developers to create customized IP telephony applications for CallManager.

The Cisco TSP supports first-party call control or third-party call control. In first-party call control, the application terminates the audio stream. With third-party call control, the application controls the audio stream of some other audio stream-terminating device. The device can be a particular station or a group of stations for which the application is responsible. CallManager for TAPI currently supports 2.0 and 2.1.

Figure 3-16   *Cisco TAPI Architecture*

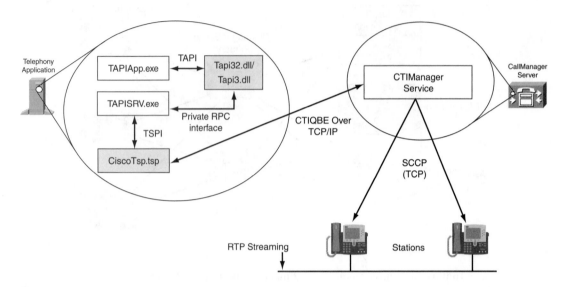

CallManager supports many CTI-controlled/monitored devices and the number depends on the CallManager server size. Depending on the server size, CallManager can scale up to 2500 CTI devices per CallManager server, up to 2500 CTI devices per "provider," and up to 10,000 CTI devices per CallManager cluster.

JTAPI

JTAPI provides similar functionality for Java-based applications development. JTAPI supports call control and primitive media support. Compared to TAPI, JTAPI is more operating system independent. CallManager for JTAPI currently supports JTAPI 1.2.

CallManager supports many CTI-controlled/monitored devices and the number depends on the CallManager server size. Depending on the server size, CallManager can scale up to 2500 CTI devices per CallManager server, up to 2500 CTI devices per "provider," and up to 10,000 CTI devices per CallManager cluster.

See Appendix C for specific details of the following JTAPI packages:

- Core Package

- Call Center Package

- Call Center Capabilities Package

- Call Center Events Package

- Call Control Package

- Call Control Capabilities Package

- Call Control Events Package

- Capabilities Package

- Events Package

- Media Package

- Media Capabilities Package

- Media Events Package

CallManager also provides the following RTP Termination extensions:

- Special CallManager device types (CTI ports) can be registered by applications.

- Devices must be preprovisioned (no programmatic creation).

- Codec and RTP parameters are selected by CallManager during call setup.

- An application must implement an RTP stack, although Java Media Framework (JMF/JavaSound) is allowed for client applications.

CTI Layer

The CTI layer within CallManager provides a generic interface to the application layer. The CTI layer is the means by which the CallManager-specific capabilities of the application layer are implemented.

Figure 3-17 shows the CTI functionality within CallManager. CTI communicates with the application platforms through the TCP/IP layer to provide the CTI functionality of CallManager. The CTI layer is an integral part of CallManager.

CTI interacts with the other CallManager components through the Signal Distribution Layer described in Chapter 1, "Cisco CallManager Architecture." CTI works together with the station module to provide the signals from a CTI device. If a station device such as a Cisco IP Phone is being controlled by an application, CTI interacts with the station module in CallManager responsible for the particular station being controlled.

Figure 3-17 *CallManager CTI Functionality*

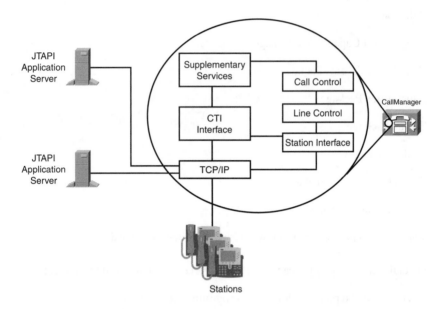

The application also needs information about activity at a selected station. CTI receives notification about station activity, known as *events*, from the station components for stations that the application is monitoring.

CTI also interacts with the supplementary services component to provide additional call control capabilities, such as transfer and conference. The CTI component can invoke supplementary services on behalf of stations being controlled or directly for CTI application devices. CTI also sends event notifications of supplementary service activity for selected stations being monitored by an application.

H.323 Endpoint Devices

An *H.323 endpoint* is a station device that communicates with CallManager using the H.323 protocol specification. The H.323v4 protocol in CallManager supports gateways and endpoints, as well as Registration, Admission, and Status (RAS) protocol for communication with a gatekeeper. The gatekeeper provides address translation and controls access to the network for H.323 devices based on bandwidth availability.

H.323 Protocol Support

Figure 3-18 shows the H.323 protocol components that CallManager supports.

Figure 3-18 *H.323 Protocol Components*

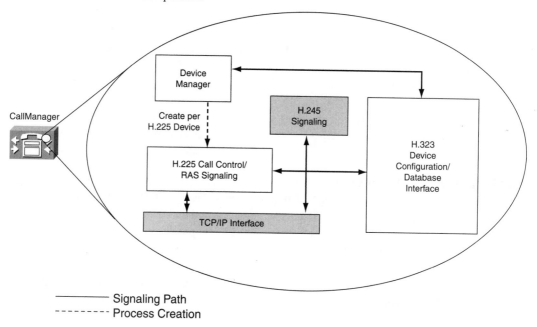

The audio compression components known to CallManager are as follows:

- Global System for Mobile Communications (GSM)

- G.711

- G.722

- G.723

- G.728

- G.729

CallManager supports the capabilities negotiation for these audio compression types. CallManager provides the system control components for H.245 for media setup, H.225 for call control, and H.225 RAS for gatekeeper communication, if a device is configured for gatekeeper control. CallManager provides support for video and data. The video protocols supported include H.261 and H.263. Data support includes data application capability H.224 and T.120.

The H.323 umbrella specification encompasses several additional specifications. The particular implementation in CallManager includes H.225 and H.245 signaling for proper operation of the H.323 endpoint. It provides for call control, capability exchange, signaling of commands and indications, and messages to open and fully describe the content of logical channels for media streams. CallManager terminates the H.225 signaling originated by any H.323 device defined in the database and directed to CallManager. The call can terminate at any endpoint, gateway, or cluster accessible by CallManager, regardless of the protocol of the terminating device. Likewise, CallManager extends, by H.225 signaling, a call to any H.323 device defined in the database from any endpoint, gateway, or cluster accessible by CallManager, regardless of the protocol of the originating device. The H.225 and H.245 signaling is always between CallManager and the H.323 endpoint. As with other station protocols, the media streaming uses RTP for the media, and the media streaming is done directly between the two devices and does not go through CallManager.

H.323 Device Configuration

Use CallManager Administration to configure all H.323 endpoint devices that communicate with CallManager. CallManager uses directory numbers for all endpoint access, including H.323 endpoints. You must also assign all configured H.323 endpoint devices a directory number. Other users use the directory number to extend a call to the H.323 endpoint. No advantage exists in having an H.323 endpoint under gatekeeper control as in the case of an H.323 gateway because these endpoints support a single call to or from a CallManager-controlled device. Refer to Chapter 4 for a detailed discussion of gatekeeper control for H.323 gateway devices.

Gatekeeper Functionality

H.323 endpoints can be configured as gatekeeper-controlled. If an endpoint is gatekeeper-controlled, the gatekeeper is identified as part of the H.323 device configuration. CallManager registers the H.323 endpoint with the gatekeeper when it initializes. The specified gatekeeper controls all calls made to or from the H.323 endpoint. The H.323 gatekeeper signaling is RAS, as defined in the H.323 protocol specification.

Summary

This chapter covered the concepts of endpoints, stations, and users. You learned about new features introduced in CallManager since release 3.1, such as multiple calls per line, shared lines, and barge/cBarge/privacy functionality. The enhanced IP phone services application development capability offers additional key development improvements. Of particular interest are the new phone models along with the new feature content, which provide additional opportunities for leveraging CallManager functionality.

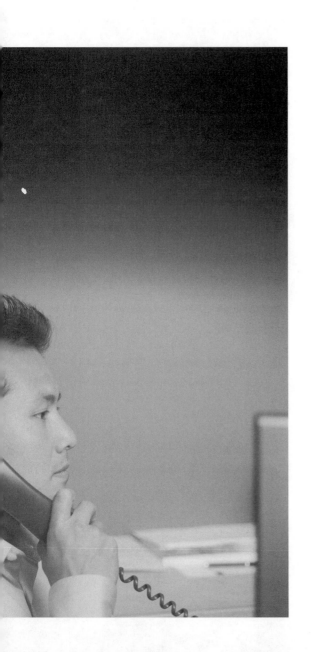

CHAPTER 4

Trunk Devices

This chapter discusses the gateway protocols that Cisco CallManager uses to communicate with Cisco gateway and trunk devices.

The primary purpose of station devices is to provide telephony services to individuals, and the primary purpose of gateway devices is to connect telephony networks to each other. CallManager uses gateway devices to allow IP telephony users to connect to non-IP-enabled telephony networks such as the Public Switched Telephone Network (PSTN) or on legacy circuit-switched Private Branch Exchanges (PBX).

CallManager also uses IP-to-IP trunking to connect members in one CallManager cluster to other voice over IP (VoIP) networks. In addition, IP trunking is used to connect one CallManager cluster to another CallManager cluster when an enterprise deploys multiple clusters for scalability, geographical, or administrative reasons.

Because CallManager supports a variety of circuit-switched and VoIP protocols, one function it can serve in your network is as a protocol translator, to connect gateways that support different call signaling protocols.

This chapter includes the following sections:

- "Architectural Overview of Trunk Devices" presents the general structure whereby CallManager supports voice gateways and IP trunks.

- "Overview of Circuit-Switched Interfaces" discusses the analog and digital protocols that traditional telephony networks use to communicate with gateways associated with CallManager. This section also discusses a variant of Q.931 called QSIG, which is designed to foster feature transparency between PBXs.

- "VoIP Gateway Security" briefly addresses the techniques you can use to provide for authenticated, authorized, and private communication from Cisco gateways.

- "H.323 Gateways" discusses CallManager's use of the H.323 ITU-T protocol for control of gateways. It describes the basic components of an H.323 network, the individual protocols that comprise H.323, and the use of CallManager intercluster trunks, which run a variant of

H.323, to connect CallManager clusters together, either directly or via an H.323 gatekeeper. This section also provides a detailed breakdown of the fields in H.323 messages that CallManager supports.

- "MGCP Gateways" discusses CallManager's use of MGCP for control of VoIP-to-circuit-switched gateways.

- "SIP" discusses CallManager's support for the Session Initiation Protocol (SIP), which currently permits CallManager to connect in a basic way to SIP networks.

Appendix C, "Protocol Details," provides detailed information for H.323, QSIG, and SIP signaling protocols. After reviewing this chapter, refer to Appendix C for additional, related information.

Architectural Overview of Trunk Devices

Figure 4-1 shows the block structure of CallManager. CallManager contains several signaling layers, each of which has distinct functions. For example, the Call Control Layer handles the call signaling that controls call setup, teardown, and call routing.

The software in the Media Control Layer coordinates all media connections that CallManager makes between devices. It can insert other media processing devices into a call and create appropriate streaming connections to those devices. As indicated in Chapter 1, "Cisco CallManager Architecture," in the Cisco VoIP solution, the actual media always streams directly between the end devices involved in a call. However, CallManager can also insert other media processing devices into a call, such as audio transcoding and conference bridge resources, depending on the media requirements needed for each call. Chapter 5, "Media Processing," contains more information about CallManager's handling of media devices.

The Protocol and Aggregator Layers handle all protocol-specific signaling required for specific devices. These blocks serve to translate protocol-specific signaling into the internal signaling used to communicate with the Call Control and Media Control Layers.

Figure 4-1 indicates with shading the software layers and blocks within CallManager that this chapter describes. In particular, CallManager implements logic in the Protocol Layer to communicate with gateways via native VoIP signaling protocols such as H.225, MGCP, and SIP and logic in the Media Control Layer to handle H.245 media.

Figure 4-2 shows how gateway devices enable communication between CallManager and circuit-switched networks such as the PSTN. From a control point of view, Cisco VoIP gateways act very much like IP phones. They are VoIP endpoints that happen to mediate between the packet- and circuit-switched worlds.

Figure 4-1 *CallManager Block Structure Diagram*

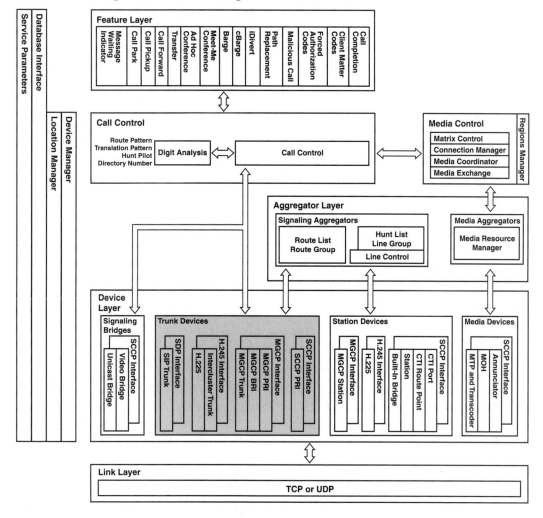

Like IP phones, CallManager controls Cisco VoIP gateways using signaling control protocols (which in an Alice-to-Bob call answers the question "Does Bob want to talk to Alice?") and media control protocols (which answers the question "How should Alice and Bob talk?").

In the case of IP phones, the endpoint always terminates both the signaling and the media protocols. On the other hand, VoIP gateways, although they always terminate the media control protocol, sometimes simply pass through the signaling control protocol used by the circuit-switched network. This process is called *backhauling*.

Figure 4-2 *Gateway Trunking Devices*

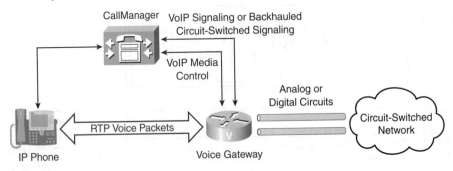

To understand how a particular gateway interacts with CallManager, therefore, you need to concentrate mainly in two areas:

- What protocol the gateway is using to connect to the circuit-switched network

- What protocol the gateway is using to connect to CallManager

For connectivity between the gateway and the circuit-switched network, Cisco voice gateways support a range of traditional analog and digital interfaces.

The following section, "Overview of Circuit-Switched Interfaces," discusses the analog and digital protocols that traditional telephony networks use to communicate with Cisco voice gateways.

For connectivity between CallManager and the VoIP gateway, CallManager supports four protocols:

- **Skinny Gateway Control Protocol (SGCP)**—The analogous protocol to Skinny Client Control Protocol (SCCP), which CallManager uses to provide signaling and media control functions for Cisco IP Phones. Cisco no longer sells any VoIP gateways that run SGCP, so this book doesn't discuss this protocol in detail.

- **H.323**—An ITU-T recommendation that uses the ITU-T recommendations H.225 for signaling; H.245 for media control; and the Registration, Admission, and Status (RAS) protocol for registration and call admission. The section "H.323 Gateways" goes into detail about this protocol.

- **Media Gateway Control Protocol (MGCP)**—An IETF standard protocol, defined in RFCs 2705 and 3435 among others, that uses a text-based protocol to permit a Media Gateway Controller (MGC)—a function that CallManager fulfills—to establish and tear down calls. MGCP messages provide good media control messages and some rudimentary signaling messages. The section "MGCP Gateways" describes this protocol.

■ **Session Initiation Protocol (SIP)** — An IETF standard related to Hypertext Transfer Protocol (HTTP) that uses a text-based protocol for both signaling and, via Session Description Protocol (SDP) bodies, media control. The section "SIP" describes this protocol.

Overview of Circuit-Switched Interfaces

Interfaces to the PSTN come in two flavors — analog and digital.

In analog interfaces, a microphone directly converts voice energy into electrical energy on a wire, while a speaker on the far end of the wire converts the electrical signal back into voice energy. The underlying voice technology does not differ significantly from that used since the beginning of the twentieth century.

In digital interfaces, voice energy from the speaker is sampled by the phone and converted into a sequence of binary numbers (a process called *analog-to-digital conversion* [ADC]). The bits in these binary numbers are then encoded on to the wire in sequence, with zeroes representing one voltage level and ones representing a different voltage level. A digital-to-analog converter (DAC) in the receiving device can then convert the numbers back into a close approximation of the original voice energy.

Because the voice information is first being encoded, digital systems can interleave nonvoice information in the information stream sent to the other end of the wire. This interleaving allows digital interfaces to support signaling protocols (which allow the phone system to deal with a wider variety of call scenarios than traditional analog techniques) and signaling information (such as reasons for call clearing, calling name and number, and called name and number).

Analog Trunks

Analog interfaces come in three flavors:

■ Foreign Exchange Station (FXS)

■ Foreign Exchange Office (FXO)

■ Ear and Mouth (E&M)

The sections that follow describe these interfaces in more detail.

FXS/FXO Trunks

FXS/FXO signaling is the most common type of signaling used by residential phones. FXS/FXO signaling can also be used for trunk connections between two PBXs or between a PBX and a central office switch. When connecting analog devices using these interfaces, always pair an FXO device on one end to an FXS device on the other end; two FXS or FXO devices cannot directly communicate. In a residence, the RJ-11 wall jack provides an FXO interface to the analog phone, and in the switching office (or concentrator), a corresponding FXS interface exists to connect the switch to the phone.

FXS/FXO signaling is carried over a pair of wires, twisted to permit the signal to carry over a longer distance. The pair of wires comprises a single circuit, which is always connected in the switch (which provides electricity to the circuit via a battery or electrical ground connection) and which is only connected in the phone when the phone is off-hook.

Signaling occurs via making and breaking the circuit. Two major signaling schemes exist: loop-start signaling and ground-start signaling.

In *loop-start signaling*, which is the kind most commonly used in residential service, when the phone goes off-hook, the circuit is closed, and the central office detects the change in current. The central office then inserts tone detectors to collect the digits, which are sent as tones on the wire. When offering calls, the switch applies ring voltage to the line and, when voltage changes when the user answers and completes the circuit, connects the user through to the caller.

All the preceding discussion talks about phones, even though this is the trunks chapter. What gives?

In a CallManager cluster, when you deploy gateways running loop-start FXO signaling, CallManager essentially emulates a standard home phone. So, when a user places a call to the PSTN from a Cisco 79xx series IP Phone, when the gateway receives the call, it simply takes the FXO interface off-hook. Similarly, when the IP Phone user hangs up, the analog gateway simply goes back on-hook.

In a residential environment, the central office always leaves its part of the loop-start circuit connected. Only the phone side of the circuit actually hangs up on a call by breaking the circuit; in effect, the central office has no way to hang up on the phone side. The loop-start signaling scheme, thus, relies on a user's physical presence at the phone to recognize that the far end has hung up (a valediction such as "goodbye," silence on the line, impatience, or other purely human reasons) and to disconnect the circuit. In other words, an FXO loop-start interface lacks *disconnect supervision*, because the FXS interface can't hang up (discounting more recent techniques such as power denial and battery reversal, which certain analog devices, by convention, can interpret as a disconnection by the far end).

As a result, when a machine, such as a packet- to circuit-switched gateway is playing the part of the user, scenarios arise in which the gateway doesn't realize that the far end has hung up and therefore leaves the call connected. In extreme cases, such as when an incoming FXO call is transferred back out another FXO gateway, the circuits can be taken permanently out of service (and potentially a large phone bill rung up).

Cisco gateways provide a variety of ways to deal with the lack of disconnect supervision on FXO loop-start trunks. The Cisco Press book *Troubleshooting Cisco IP Telephony* goes into more detail about the sorts of problems that can arise with the lack of disconnect supervision and possible solutions.

Unlike loop-start signaling, ground-start signaling does not suffer from the lack of disconnect supervision. In ground-start signaling, the gateway on the FXO interface can detect changes in the current, and the FXS side of the connection changes its behavior to indicate disconnection.

Table 4-1 indicates the Cisco gateways that offer FXS and FXO interfaces.

Table 4-1   *Cisco Gateways/VICs That Offer FXS/FXO Interfaces*

Gateway Model	Gateway Control Protocol
Cisco IOS Integrated Routers	
Cisco 1750	MGCP, H.323, SIP
Cisco 1751	MGCP,H.323, SIP
Cisco 1760	MGCP, H.323, SIP
Cisco 1800 series	MGCP, H.323, SIP
Cisco 2600 series	MGCP, H.323, SIP
Cisco 2800 series	MGCP, H.323, SIP
Cisco 3600 series	MGCP, H.323, SIP
Cisco 3700 series	MGCP, H.323, SIP
Cisco 3800 series	MGCP, H.323, SIP
Cisco Standalone Voice Gateways	
Cisco Voice Gateway 200 (VG200)	MGCP, H.323, SIP
Cisco Access Analog Trunk Gateway (AT-2, AT-4, AT-8)	Skinny Gateway Control Protocol
Cisco Access Analog Station Gateway (AS-2, AS-4, AS-8)	Skinny Gateway Control Protocol
Cisco VG224 Analog Phone Gateway	Skinny Client Control Protocol
Cisco VG248 Analog Phone Gateway	Skinny Client Control Protocol
Cisco IAD2420	MGCP
Cisco Catalyst Voice Gateway Modules	
Cisco Catalyst 4000 Access Gateway Module (WS-X4604-GWY)	MGCP, H.323, SIP
Cisco Catalyst 4224 Voice Gateway Switch	MGCP, H.323, SIP
Cisco Catalyst 6000 24-Port FXS Analog Interface Module (WS-X6624-FXS)	MGCP
Cisco Communication Media Module (WS-X6600-24FXS)	MGCP

E&M Trunks

E&M interfaces are most commonly used on PBXs. Unlike FXO/FXS interfaces, E&M trunks rely on a four-wire, six-wire, or eight-wire circuit.

In E&M signaling, two of these wires—E and M—are used to communicate signaling information. From a practical standpoint, this means that E&M trunks don't suffer from the disconnect supervision issues that can trouble FXS/FXO deployments and that a condition called glare can occur. *Glare* occurs when both sides of the wire simultaneously go off-hook on the interface. Glare avoidance allows one or the other side to back down gracefully.

Table 4-2 lists Cisco gateways/VICs that support E&M interfaces.

Table 4-2 *Cisco Gateways That Offer E&M Interfaces*

Gateway Model	Gateway Control Protocol
Cisco IOS Integrated Routers	
Cisco 1751	MGCP, H.323, SIP
Cisco 1760	MGCP, H.323, SIP
Cisco 1800 series	MGCP, H.323, SIP
Cisco 2600 series	MGCP, H.323, SIP
Cisco 3600 series	MGCP, H.323, SIP
Cisco 3700 series	MGCP, H.323, SIP
Cisco 3800 series	MGCP, H.323, SIP
Cisco Standalone Voice Gateways	
Cisco Voice Gateway 200 (VG200)	MGCP, H.323, SIP
Cisco Catalyst Voice Gateway Modules	
Cisco Catalyst 4000 Access Gateway Module (WS-X4604-GWY)	MGCP, H.323, SIP
Cisco Catalyst 4224 Voice Gateway Switch	MGCP, H.323, SIP

Digital Trunks

Digital interfaces come in three basic flavors:

- Channel Associated Signaling (CAS) trunks

- Basic Rate Interface (BRI) trunks

- Primary Rate Interface (PRI) trunks

In addition, PRI trunks can run a protocol called QSIG, which fosters feature interoperability between PBXs.

What is the common characteristic of these interfaces? They're based on the concepts of time-division multiplexing (TDM) and pulse code modulation (PCM).

Using analog technologies, if you want to support 24 simultaneous active calls, you must pull 24 sets of wires from your service provider into your enterprise.

Reducing the number of wires required to manage multiple conversations necessarily means that somehow these conversations need to be able to learn how to share the capacity of a single wire. In the 1960s, Bell System introduced the T-carrier system, which defines exactly how this task can be done. A different system, the E-carrier system, is used in Europe.

The T-carrier system depends on TDM. In TDM, the idea is each user of a particular facility must "take turns" communicating.

Figure 4-3 captures the essence of the stratagem.

Figure 4-3   *Time-Division Multiplexing*

Assume that Alice and Bob are conversing and Carol and Dave are conversing. Alice and Carol must share the same communications facility. They both want to encode a sentence to send to their respective partners.

If Alice were to say her entire sentence before Carol could start to say her sentence, the conversations would be full of long pauses. Instead of encoding full sentences, however, the communication could be broken into smaller bits; then Alice and Carol could communicate simultaneously. This process of breaking communications into a small piece is the process of *sampling*.

Assume that Alice and Carol, in the space of one second, say exactly a single word and that the system is breaking the communications into one-second samples. Each sample, therefore, contains a single word.

Also assume that the communications facility between the women and the men is capable of transmitting two samples every second.

To prevent Alice's and Carol's conversations from becoming hopelessly entangled, Alice and Carol can take turns putting their samples into the communication facility.

If by prior arrangement Alice places her samples into the communications facility in odd-numbered turns and Carol places her samples into the communications facility in even-numbered turns, all the information can be encoded into the same stream in the jumbled yet orderly fashion depicted.

Then, if also via the prior arrangement, Alice's partner Bob agrees to listen to the communications facility only on odd-numbered turns and Carol's partner Dave agrees to listen to the communications facility only on even-numbered turns, Bob and Dave can extract the original utterance.

In the encoding scheme listed in Figure 4-3, the single facility shared by Alice and Carol is effectively divided into two independent virtualized circuits or channels. Furthermore, in any given second, two samples of information are being communicated—Alice's during the first half-second and Carol's during the second half-second. When Alice and Carol have both taken a turn, the words they transmitted—one from Alice and one from Carol—are called a *frame*.

According to a theory called *Nyquist's theorem*, to accurately encode an analog audio signal into a digital system and then accurately resynthesize the analog version, the frequency with which you must sample the signal must be at least twice the highest frequency present in the original analog signal. The spoken voice's highest frequency is around 3500 cycles per second. Rounding to 4000 cycles per second for good measure (and friendly math) and then doubling the sample rate for digital encoding yields 8000 samples per second.

Chapter 1 introduced codecs, which are different encoding schemes for converting analog speech into digital information. One of these codecs, G.711, uses PCM encoding. For each sample in a block of 8000 samples, PCM converts the analog frequency to a value between 0 and 255—in binary, this is an 8-bit number in the range 00000000 to 11111111. Therefore, one second's worth of encoded audio contains 64,000 bits of information.

The original T-carrier system was therefore designed around units of 64,000 bits per second. The base unit, called a DS0, has a rate of transmission sufficient to carry a single PCM-encoded audio stream in real time; other interfaces are named in ascending order and correspondingly carry multiple DS0s worth of traffic. Table 4-3 presents the T-carrier classifications.

Table 4-3   *T-Carrier Rates*

T-Carrier Class	Number of DS0s
T1	24 DS0s
T2	96 DS0s
T3	672 DS0s

T-carrier classifications align with the DS classifications, so a T1 is also called a DS1.

E-carrier classifications don't line up directly with the DS system. Table 4-4 presents the number of DS0s provided by the different E-carrier classifications.

Table 4-4   *E-Carrier Rates*

E-Carrier Class	Number of DS0s
E1	32
E2	128
E3	512
E4	2048
E5	16,384

To recap, one second of speech encoded as PCM requires 64,000 bits of data, and each DS0 provides a transmission rate of 64,000 bits per second. The higher grade the interface, the more active channels it supports. So why exactly can one trunk interface support more channels than another?

Well, when a digital interface is transmitting a bit of information, what is really happening is that the interface is changing the voltage level on the line. This voltage change is transmitted down the line at light speed and detectors on the other side are monitoring the voltage changes. It's like a message being transmitted via Morse code, in which dots represent one voltage level (or levels) and dashes represent another voltage level. The faster the voltage levels change, the more sophisticated the equipment needs to be in order to make sure that no bits are "skipped."

The need to avoid "skipping bits" has another effect on the transmission of digital information. More information than just the sampled voice data is transmitted across the pipe. As mentioned in Figure 4-3, Bob and Dave can recover Alice's and Carol's conversation by agreeing, respectively, to listen to the first and second channels within a given frame. But by peeking at the wire, how is Bob to know which is the first frame and which is the second frame?

Bob drives his decision as to which channels are which by looking at his watch. In a perfect world, Alice is putting her sample on the communications facility during the first half of every second and Bob should be pulling his off in the first half of every second. But if Bob's watch is just a smidgen fast or slow, pretty soon he'll be pulling samples off of the communications facility at the end, not the beginning, of every second.

Therefore, digital trunks always reserve some of the bandwidth to encode framing bits, whose purpose is specifically to synchronize the clocks of the transmitter and receiver.

Finally, given that control information such as call signaling, caller ID, and called number information can also be encoded as a series of bits, digital trunks usually have a way of encoding information in addition to the voice samples being communicated.

So, to summarize, over a digital trunk

Step 1   Every 1/8000 of a second, Alice's, Carol's, and, on a T1, 22 of their friends' voices are sampled and encoded using PCM into an 8-bit number.

Step 2   Each sample is interleaved on the wire at a specific moment in times, a process called TDM.

Step 3   When all the samples have been transmitted, the system adds a framing bit, the purpose of which (among other things) is to eliminate clock slippage.

CAS Trunks

CAS is a digital protocol that can emulate loop-start, ground-start, or E&M trunks. In CAS signaling, call events are signaled directly in the same channels that the voice bearer data uses.

Figure 4-4 presents a sample T1 frame. T1 interfaces support 24 channels of information, each capable of carrying 8 bits of information at a time. Thus, each T1 frame can carry one 1/8000 second PCM sample for up to 24 speakers.

Adding a framing bit yields the following:

$$8 \times 24 + 1 = 193 \text{ bits per frame}$$

In order not to "fall behind" the sampler, each second, a T1 must be able to serialize 8000 samples for 24 speakers. In other words, a T1 can serialize 8000 193-bit frames per second. This capacity amounts to 1,544,000 bits per second for a T1, which is more commonly written as a rate of 1.544 kbps.

Figure 4-4 *T1 Frame*

Framing Bit
— Frame 1
Frame 24

CAS trunks group frames into yet larger groups called superframes. One framing strategy called *Superframe* (SF) formatting groups frames into groups of 12; a framing strategy called *Extended Superframe* (ESF) formatting groups frames into groups of 24.

Each frame in the superframe still has its framing bit. In SF formatting, this means that every superframe contains 12 bits of information that can be used to communicate information outside of the actual sampled audio, while in ESF formatting, every extended superframe contains 24 bits of information that can be used to communicate information outside of the sampled audio. At 8000 frames per second on T1, 666 SF superframes or 333 ESF superframes can be sent.

With 24 channels, signaling events might need to be communicated for any of 24 current calls. So CAS uses bits from the bearer channels to flag the system when a particular channel has a signaling event to communicate. Instead of using the eighth bit of any given sample to communicate actual audio information, the eighth bit of specific samples is used to communicate a signaling event.

In SF formatting, the low-order bits of each sample in the sixth frame is called the *A bit*, and the low-order bits of each sample in the twelfth frame is called the *B bit*. ESF formatting uses these bits as well as the low-order bits in the eighteenth frame (the C bit) and the low-order bits in the twenty-fourth frame (the D bit).

This robbed bit has little effect on an audio call. In any given 8-bit sample, the eighth bit is the least-significant bit. For example, if the 8-bit value 01010100 (decimal 40) were changed to 01010101 (decimal 41), the human ear would be unlikely to notice a difference. For circuit-switched data, however, even a difference of 1 bit could corrupt a file.

Therefore, when circuit-switched data is sent over T1 CAS interfaces, the eighth bit in a channel cannot be meaningfully used to carry information. As a result, T1-CAS supports at most a transfer rate of 56 kbps for circuit-switched data connections.

Table 4-5 presents the gateways/VICs that support CAS interfaces.

Table 4-5   *Cisco Gateways That Offer CAS Interfaces*

Gateway Model	Gateway Control Protocol
Cisco IOS Integrated Routers	
Cisco 1800 series	H.323, MGCP, SIP
Cisco 2600 series	MGCP, H.323, SIP
Cisco 2800 series	MGCP, H.323, SIP
Cisco 3600 series	MGCP, H.323, SIP
Cisco 3700 series	MGCP, H.323, SIP
Cisco 3800 series	MGCP, H.323, SIP
Cisco 7200	H.323
Cisco 7500	H.323
Cisco AS5300	H.323
Cisco AS5350	H.323
Cisco AS5400	H.323
Cisco AS5850	H.323
Cisco Standalone Voice Gateways	
Cisco Voice Gateway 200 (VG200)	MGCP, H.323, SIP
Cisco Access Digital Trunk Gateway DT-24+	MGCP
Cisco IAD2420	MGCP
Cisco Catalyst Voice Gateway Modules	
Cisco Catalyst 4000 Access Gateway Module (WS-X4604-GWY)	MGCP, H.323, SIP
Cisco Catalyst 4224 Voice Gateway Switch	MGCP, H.323, SIP
Cisco Catalyst 6000 8-Port Voice T1/E1 and Services Module (WS-X6608-T1)	MGCP
Cisco Communication Media Module (WS-X6600-6T1)	MGCP

BRI and PRI Trunks

Both BRI and PRI are digital protocols based on the ITU-T specifications Q.921 and Q.931, which form the basis for the Integrated Services Digital Network (ISDN). ISDN is an end-to-end digital network capable of supporting voice and data connections.

Strictly speaking, this end-to-end connection is rarely provided solely via BRI and PRI. BRI and PRI are interfaces that the specifications implicitly assume operate only at the edge of a carrier network. In other words, BRI and PRI simply handle the last mile of connectivity from your service provider to your equipment. Q.931 defines two roles, network and user, to participants in a Q.931 signaling exchange, and service providers invariably take on the role of the network. The user and network roles effectively correspond to the roles of client and server.

However, in enterprise telephony deployments, ISDN connections are often used to connect premise equipment not only to the PSTN but also to other equipment owned by the enterprise. In such cases, the enterprise must denote one side of the interface as the user side and the other as the network side, although in practice the relationship between the switches is usually more peer to peer in nature.

For any digital protocol to be successful, it is mandatory that signals encoded by one end of a signaling link be transmitted reliably to the other end of the link. In ISDN, Q.921 fulfills this role.

Q.931 is the protocol that fulfills the requirements of both the signaling and media control phases of a call. That is, in a call from Alice to Bob, it answers the questions "Does Bob want to talk to Alice?" and "How should Bob talk to Alice?"

Unlike analog protocols, digital protocols foster the exchange of out-of-band information about a particular communication session. For example, in traditional analog caller ID, to get the identity of the caller to display on a residential phone, the information isn't sent directly within the FXO signaling itself, which is really only capable of managing off-hook and on-hook events. Rather, traditional caller ID is sent by the PSTN in between the first and the second rings of the phone using a modem signal. That is, caller ID-capable phones incorporate a special-purpose modem to decode the provided name and number and display it.

Inherently digital interfaces such as BRI and PRI don't need to go to such lengths. Rather, ISDN encodes information such as calling number, calling name, codec type, clearing causes, and tone information directly in the Q.931 signaling.

Figure 4-5 depicts the Q.931 signaling sent when a user (with directory number 1000) connected to a switch via an ISDN connection dials 2000, a number associated with another user connected via an ISDN to a different switch. (The protocol used to connect the switches to each other.)

Figure 4-5 *ISDN Call*

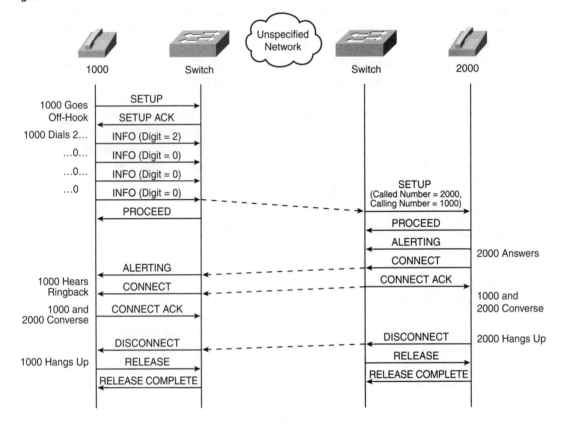

Unlike CAS, BRI and PRI use Common Channel Signaling (CCS). With CCS, one of the 24 channels (or, for E1-PRI, 32 channels) is reserved specifically for signaling.

Each ISDN span supports different combination of channels. D channels have a rate of 64 kbps (16 kbps for BRI) and carry the signaling required to set up calls (Q.921 and Q.931). B channels have a rate of 64 kbps and carry the actual circuit-switched voice or data.

BRI is designed for residential users and supports two B and one D channels. The flow depicted in Figure 4-5 is consistent with a BRI connection, because it demonstrates the caller's switch collecting dialed digits one at a time from the caller.

PRI, on the other hand, is enterprise oriented. It's less about connecting individual user devices to a network and more about connecting switches to each other. PRI comes in two main formats, T1 and E1.

In North America, PRI is deployed over T1 trunks and supports 23 B and 1 D channels; however, in Europe, PRI is deployed over E1 trunks and supports 30 B and 1 D channel (sometimes with a backup D channel).

> **NOTE** Using a technique called *non-facility associated signaling* (NFAS), multiple digital circuits can be grouped so that all share the D channel of one member of the group. This technique frees up the D channels of the trunks in the other groups for voice traffic. Cisco gateways support this technique when running H.323 or SIP, but CallManager does not yet support it for MGCP.

For the most part, BRI and PRI provide a signaling interface that is sufficient to handle basic calls. The Q.932 standard adds extensions that permit ISDN switches to provide PBX features to the digital phones they serve. However, although Q.932 permits an ISDN user to invoke features, Q.932 doesn't ensure that the feature operates transparently when the users involved in the feature are served by different switches. For instance, if Alice calls Bob, and Bob transfers Alice to Charlie, in many cases, Alice's display won't reflect that she is now talking with Charlie.

A PRI variant called QSIG provides a sophisticated infrastructure that allows features to interoperate transparently. CallManager supports the QSIG protocol both across MGCP gateways and from cluster to cluster using H.323 tunneling of QSIG. The section "QSIG" later in the chapter provides more details.

Table 4-6 lists the Cisco gateways that support PRI interfaces.

Table 4-6 *Cisco Gateways That Offer BRI and PRI*

Gateway Model	Gateway Control Protocol
Cisco IOS Integrated Routers	
Cisco 1760	MGCP, H.323, SIP
Cisco 2600 series	MGCP, H.323, SIP
Cisco 2800 series	MGCP, H.323, SIP
Cisco 3600 series	MGCP, H.323, SIP
Cisco 3700 series	MGCP, H.323, SIP
Cisco 3800 series	MGCP,H.323, SIP
Cisco 7200	H.323
Cisco 7500	H.323
Cisco AS5300	H.323
Cisco AS5350	H.323
Cisco AS5400	H.323

Table 4-6   *Cisco Gateways That Offer BRI and PRI (Continued)*

Gateway Model	Gateway Control Protocol
Cisco AS5850	H.323
Cisco Standalone Voice Gateways	
Cisco Voice Gateway 200 (VG200)	MGCP, H.323, SIP
Cisco Access Digital Trunk Gateway DE-30+	MGCP
Cisco Access Digital Trunk Gateway DT-24+	MGCP
Cisco Catalyst Voice Gateway Modules	
Cisco Catalyst 4000 Access Gateway Module (WS-X4604-GWY)	MGCP, H.323, SIP
Cisco Catalyst 4224 Voice Gateway Switch	MGCP, H.323, SIP
Cisco Catalyst 6000 8-Port Voice T1/E1 and Services Module (WS-X6608-T1) (WS-X6608-E1)	MGCP
Cisco Communication Media Module (WS-X6600-6T1) (WS-X6600-6E1)	MGCP

ISDN Timers

Layer 3 timers permit CallManager to recover from errors in the Q.931 interface. This section describes the ISDN Q.931 timers that CallManager uses. In MGCP gateways, CallManager terminates the Layer 3 signaling; however, H.323 gateways terminate the Layer 3 signaling from the attached circuit-switched network, so these timers have no effect there. Instead, H.323 gateways use H.225 timers to achieve the same results, because H.323 emulates Q.931 messages over the H.225 protocol.

Table 4-7 shows the configurable timers that CallManager uses for gateway Layer 3 Q.931 processing. The table provides default values for each parameter, but parameters are user-configurable.

Table 4-7   *Layer 3 Timers*

Parameter	Default Time (in Seconds)	Timer Description
TimerT301	180	Starts when CallManager receives a ringing indication from a terminal (or network) to which it has offered a call; stops when it receives an answer indication.

Table 4-7   *Layer 3 Timers (Continued)*

Parameter	Default Time (in Seconds)	Timer Description
TimerT302	10	Starts when CallManager receives a dialed digit (INFO) from a calling terminal; stops when CallManager has collected enough digits to route the call.
TimerT303	10	Starts when CallManager sends a call setup request (SETUP) to a terminal; stops when it receives any message in response (PROCEED, ALERTING, PROGRESS, CONNECT).
TimerT304	20	Starts when CallManager forwards digits from a caller to another network in an overlap dialing scenario (INFO); stops when CallManager receives an indication that the attached network has received enough digits to route (PROCEED).
TimerT305	30	Starts when CallManager initiates clearing to a terminal with DISCONNECT; stops when it receives a clearing acknowledgement (RELEASE).
TimerT306	30	Starts when CallManager initiates clearing to a terminal with a DISCONNECT containing a progress indicator; stops when it receives a clearing acknowledgement (RELEASE).
TimerT308	4	Starts when CallManager issues a release message to a terminal (RELEASE); stops when it receives a final clearing acknowledgement (RELEASE CONFIRM).
TimerT309	90	Starts when CallManager detects a problem with the data link; stops when the data link recovers.
TimerT310	20	Starts when CallManager receives an indication that an attached network can route the provided digits (PROCEED); stops when the called device rings or answers (ALERTING, PROGRESS, or CONNECT).
TimerT313	4	Starts when CallManager answers a call (CONNECT); stops when the interface acknowledges the connection (CONNECT ACK).
TimerT316	120	Starts when CallManager issues a RESTART on an ISDN facility; stops upon receiving an acknowledgement (RESTART ACK).
TimerT317	300	Starts when CallManager receives a RESTART; stops when associated interface has been purged.
TimerT321	30	Starts when CallManager detects a link issue; stops upon restoration of the link.
TimerT322	4	Starts when CallManager issues a STATUS ENQUIRY to discover the state of the connected channel; stops upon receipt of a response (STATUS).

QSIG

QSIG is an ISDN-based protocol that has its roots in standards originally defined by the European Computer Manufacturing Association (ECMA). ECMA submitted the drafts for QSIG to the International Standards Organization (ISO) for standardization.

QSIG defines a framework by which different vendor call agents (called a *PINX* [Private Integrated Services Network Exchange] in QSIG) can provide feature transparency among each other in a privately owned network (called a *PISN* [Private Integrated Services Network] in QSIG).

What is *feature transparency*? Basically, it comes down to the ability, from a feature point of view, to make multiple call agents appear as a single call agent. So if a transfer is performed on one PINX in the PISN, the newly connected party information shows up on the display of the transferred party, even if the transferred party is served by a different PINX in the PISN. Feature transparency also allows PINXs to remove hairpins from transferred and forwarded calls and to monitor the state of endpoints served by different PINXs in the PISN.

But QSIG isn't really just a collection of definitions of feature flows that vendors agree to adhere to for interoperability. Okay, it *is* that, but it's also a framework for providing the transparency.

Digital protocols such as PRI and BRI are based on Q.931. Although Q.931 is an excellent protocol for establishing basic calls, it isn't designed for end-to-end feature operation. Its purpose is the establishment of end-to-end connections.

Early versions of Q.931 did try to put actual support for features in the protocol. For instance, early versions of Q.931 supported a TRANSFER message, and Q.932 provides messages for HOLD and RETRIEVE and a method of passing feature button presses to the serving switch. But it quickly became clear that, although it was possible for vendors to agree on ways that basic calls should be processed, every vendor's feature set was quite different and quite extensive and having to revisit and extend the definition of the protocol that was simply designed to manage placing basic calls would ultimately be unworkable. For example, should Q.931 have implemented a CALLBACK message? A CALL PICKUP message? A GROUP CALL PICKUP message?

QSIG, therefore, although it defines a specific basic call message flow, is notable in that its basic call messaging provides for information to be passed in basic call messages that the protocol logic is meant to be specifically ignorant of.

QSIG relies on some of the same principles underlying the IP infrastructure that makes up the Internet. Figure 4-6 demonstrates a simple IP network.

In the world of IP communications, the function of the network is to permit applications to talk to each other. To oversimplify dramatically, the world can be divided into applications and routers. Both applications and routers are assigned IP addresses, but the only IP addresses of consequence are the IP addresses associated with the applications. The router's IP addresses are simply the glue that connects application to application.

Figure 4-6 *Simplified IP Infrastructure*

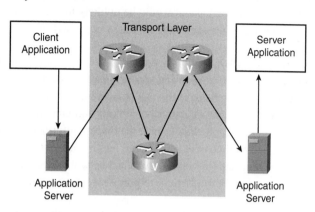

In the world of IP, applications must often communicate data across a long distance, perhaps as a part of a client/server relationship. The Internet works because it provides a framework by which the applications don't really care how that data gets from the client to the server and by which the routers don't care what data is actually communicated from end to end.

IP does this by providing a system for encapsulating opaque data. Application data is broken into chunks and then "stuffed" into "envelopes" on which the address of the terminating address is "written." When delivering a packet thus addressed, the routers simply look at the address on the packet without having to decode any of the information it contains. The packet contents are strictly for the applications themselves to understand.

The feature model in a QSIG network is very much like a client/server model for applications in an IP network. Before the creation of the QSIG feature framework, features were self-contained within a particular PBX. For instance, Figure 4-7 demonstrates a traditional call forward operation in a non-QSIG framework.

Figure 4-7 *Forwarding in a Non-QSIG Network*

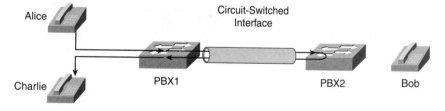

In Figure 4-7, if Alice on PBX 1 were to call Bob on PBX 2 and Bob were to forward his call to Charlie on PBX 1, the feature operation would typically occur wholly within PBX 2—PBX 2

would simply extend a new call back to PBX 1. PBX 1 would be unlikely to realize that Alice's outbound call had been forwarded, and it would be unlikely to realize that the inbound leg from PBX 2 to Charlie was actually the same call as Alice's outbound call.

Even though, before QSIG, PBX vendors needed to solve the problem of "How should Charlie's phone display that the call is from Alice and was originally to Bob?" these solutions typically involved adding vendor-specific fields to the Q.931 signaling. That is, features were transparent if all the vendor equipment was identical, but, when mixing equipment, phone displays didn't update after feature invocations. And, note that, even if the display information could be communicated from PBX 1 to PBX 2, the method of extending call legs in the forward direction to effect features means that the call signaling and (in a circuit-switched network) media hairpins. Thus two circuits are used in a call that ultimately would have required no circuits at all.

QSIG changes this feature model considerably. QSIG looks at the problem of communicating information between switches as the problem of communication information between actual applications that happen to be running on the call agent. For instance, in a message waiting scenario in which a voice mail system attached to one call agent needs to light a lamp on a phone connected to another call agent, QSIG wonders "What if there were a message waiting client feature on the switch that is hosting the voice mail whose job is, when asked by the voice mail system, to issue a message waiting application message to a message waiting server feature on another call agent, which, in turn, could actually light the lamp on the phone?" Figure 4-8 illustrates this model.

Figure 4-8 *MWI in a QSIG Network*

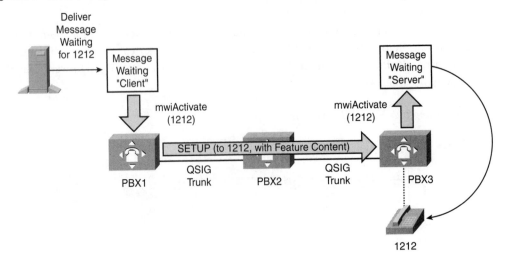

Figure 4-8 depicts a PISN of PBXs. It depicts two message waiting indicator (MWI) features, a client and a server. Although the picture illustrates these features as outside of the PBXs, in practice PBXs contain these features. When the message waiting feature client receives a lamp-on command from the voice mail system for extension 1212, it wants to communicate this command to the MWI feature "server" in the node in the PISN that actually controls extension 1212.

To accomplish this, the MWI client encodes the command to activate the message waiting indicator and then asks the call control component—the part of the call processing software that handles basic call setup, typically using an ISDN protocol such as Q.931—to wrap the MWI activation command in an envelope and deliver it to the PINX that serves extension 1212.

Then, using the same call routing logic that would operate when routing a basic call to the node controlling 1212, the call agent network layer routes the call containing the application payload. When the node controlling 1212 is reached, the Call Control Layer in that node detects that a payload exists (but not the full nature of the payload) and routes the payload to the MWI "server" within that node.

Hence, in a fundamental way, feature-to-feature communication in a QSIG network parallels client-to-server communication in an IP network. In both systems, an application wants to communicate information to another application. In both systems, the applications have network addresses—IP addresses in the case of data networks, numeric directory numbers in the case of QSIG. In both systems, applications stuff their information into envelopes on which the network address of the peer application is written. And in both networks, the underlying network layer in each network looks at the destination address specified and routes the information independent of the payload. As in the data network depicted in Figure 4-6, the applications don't care how information gets from end to end, and the routers don't care what application information is in the envelope. In Figure 4-8, the PINXs hosting the MWI client and server don't really care how the information gets through the PISN, and the PINX in the middle doesn't really care what application information the message contains. While in an IP network there are many pure applications that don't perform routing functions, in QSIG the PINXs typically have both application and routing roles, although these roles can be thought of as distinct. Figure 4-9 shows an abstraction of a TCP packet and a QSIG "packet."

Although there's a philosophical similarity between IP networks and QSIG networks, there are also several significant differences. In an IP network, connection establishment is normally done as a completely independent step. After the connection has been established, peer applications can exchange information.

Figure 4-9 *Comparison Between TCP and QSIG "Packets"*

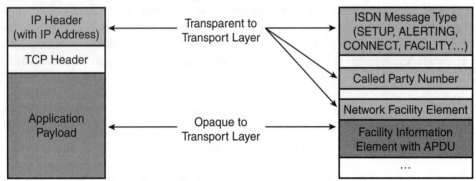

In QSIG, many features occur while the connection itself is being established. For instance, in a forwarded call, the recipient of the call wants to know the caller information and the original destination of the call while the call is being offered, not when the call is answered. As a result, application information is typically not present in an IP network on the messages that establish an end-to-end data connection (via TCP, for instance). In QSIG, however, application information, or application protocol data units (APDU), can be present on the Q.931 messages that establish (SETUP) and tear down (DISCONNECT) connections, as well as many that happen in between (ALERTING, CONNECT).

When QSIG needs to communicate information on an already existing connection, it uses a specially defined message called FACILITY, whose sole purpose is for the communication of application-to-application information.

In an IP network, the predominant models for application interactions are client/server or peer to peer. In QSIG, there tends to be at least one feature agent per participant in a feature interaction. So, while message waiting features are client/server, a call transfer relates a transferee, a transferor, and a transfer destination. Therefore, the QSIG flow involves communication between three agents, each of which represents one participant in a call.

In an IP network, most connections are purely data related.

In QSIG, most connections occur for the purpose of voice communications between the endpoints involved. For example, when a transfer completes, users have the expectation not only that they can see who they are talking to (the data information of the call) but also that they can converse over media channels reserved as part of call establishment.

Therefore, QSIG supports a few models for delivery of APDUs:

- **Connectionless**—Sort of the QSIG analog to UDP, this method uses the FACILITY message to deliver information from one PINX to another PINX without actually establishing a connection. APDUs delivery is not guaranteed end to end. Almost no QSIG features use this type of delivery mechanism.

- **Connection-oriented, call independent**—The method used by the MWI example earlier— after all, the voice mail system doesn't actually want to stream information to a listener. This method doesn't actually set up any media channels between the sending and receiving PINX. Rather, the connection that exists between the PINXs is signaling-only, and communication is over the D channel between the PINXs.

- **Connection-oriented, call dependent**—The method used by the majority of PINX features, this method provides for delivery of both data relating to a call while setting up the media channels for the conversation.

QSIG Rerouting Features

Because QSIG relies on feature agents to accomplish feature operations, it permits a feature model that the traditional method of effecting features does not.

Figure 4-7 illustrated a traditional call forwarding scenario across an inter-PINX trunk. In the scenario, a call from a user on one PINX to a second user on another PINX that forwards to a third user on the first PINX causes a signaling and media hairpin.

With QSIG, it's possible for a feature agent on the redirecting node (either the transferor or forwarder) to instead of extending a new leg in the forward direction to ask the feature agent that represents the redirected call (either the transferee or forwarded caller) to place the call to the destination directly. This pattern of redirection allows the redirected call to be established according to the most efficient path. For some features, QSIG offers one variant that relies on redirection to remove hairpins and refresh phone displays and another variant that simply guarantees display refreshes but does not perform the more complex hairpin removal. For instance, the call forwarding rerouting variant removes circuit hairpins, but the call forwarding switch variant does not.

In a circuit-switched network, it minimizes the number of circuits that must be used to handle redirected calls. In a packet-switched network, media tends to flow directly from end to end. However, even VoIP call agents sometimes introduce devices that intercept and forward media (for example, MTPs, which Chapter 5 describes). QSIG features that use rerouting can eliminate redundant MTPs from the media path.

This rerouting pattern introduces routing complexity. For instance, in Figure 4-7, if Bob is used to dialing Charlie's number differently from the way Alice does, when Alice's PINX is asked to reroute the call, the call might misroute. Chapter 2 covers such routing scenarios in more detail.

QSIG and CallManager

CallManager supports the QSIG protocol (both the ISO and ECMA 2 variants) over gateways that run MGCP. In addition, CallManager supports QSIG between CallManager clusters using a technology called *QSIG tunneling*, which H.323 defines in Annex M1.

Table 4-8 lists the QSIG features that CallManager supports, the type of QSIG connections used (connectionless, connection-oriented call dependent, connection-oriented call independent), and whether the feature incorporates rerouting.

Table 4-8 *Supported QSIG Features*

Feature	Connection Type	Reroute?	Function
Path replacement	COCD	Yes	Eliminate signaling and media hairpins after a call forward (switch variant) or call transfer occurs.
Call transfer	COCD	No	Communicate new connected party information after a call transfer occurs.
Call forward (switch variant)	COCD	No	Communicate new connected party information after a call forward occurs.
Call forward (rerouting variant)	COCD	Yes	Effect a call forward by asking the originating PINX to place a call to the destination on behalf of the forwarded party. This feature only kicks in if CallManager determines that the destination party is on another node and if you enable the service parameter Forward By Reroute.
Message waiting indicator	CICD	No	Allows voice mail systems to deliver message waiting for indications to devices connected to different PINXs from the voice mail system. CallManager allows systems to activate or deactivate the message waiting indicator but not to query the existing setting (a feature called *interrogation*).
Call completion on busy Call completion on no reply	CICD and COCD	Yes	Allows a user on one PINX who receives a busy signal or no answer from a user on another PINX to monitor the status of the called user and get prompted to place a call to the called user when he or she becomes available.

Table 4-8   *Supported QSIG Features (Continued)*

Feature	Connection Type	Reroute?	Function
Calling line presentation and restriction	COCD	No	Present the name and number of the caller and ringing/connected party, while honoring privacy settings on the caller and called party.
Calling name presentation and restriction			
Alerting name presentation and restriction			
Connected line presentation and restriction			
Connected name presentation and restriction			

Appendix C provides detailed information about the APDUs for each feature.

VoIP Gateway Security

Speaking in the most general terms, securing your VoIP traffic consists of setting up policies that ensure that the endpoints involved in communication are authenticated and authorized and that the information streams are kept private.

Authentication is the process whereby one network component (for instance, CallManager) validates the identity of another, such as a gateway or IP phone. Authentication can simply be one-way, in which case one component can trust the identity of the other but not vice versa. Authentication can also be two-way, in which case both components can be confident as to the identities of each other.

Authentication is quite important because it prevents issues that can arise when a network interloper impersonates an otherwise valid user. For instance, if Cisco IP Phones don't authenticate CallManager or other network services, it is possible that they could be provided with the IP addresses of an interloper's hacked CallManager. Calls from valid users could be routed via the compromised CallManager and maliciously redirected, or information relating to the numbers that valid users dial could be logged. On the other hand, if CallManager doesn't authenticate the devices, an interloper could introduce his own device on to the network and steal phone service or, worse, impersonate a valid user and wreak mischief in the valid user's name.

Authorization is the process whereby a network component defines what types of services that an authenticated component can access. For example, you can configure CallManager routing to provide long distance calls for certain valid users but not for other valid users.

Privacy is the process whereby communications between network components is secured from the scrutiny of unauthorized intruders. It prevents intruders from eavesdropping on conversations or capturing information such as dialed numbers from call attempts.

A secure network requires that authentication, authorization, and privacy be implemented at many layers in the network. Although Cisco IP Phones and gateways are IP devices that support various voice and video protocols, they are also fundamentally network devices. Therefore, in addition to the authentication, authorization, and privacy techniques that ensure that these devices are valid, authorized VoIP devices, for full security you must also implement security policies that allow you to secure the link layer of your network. Therefore, techniques such as 802.1x authentication allow you to ensure you admit only valid Ethernet devices to your Ethernet network, and techniques such as LEAP or 802.11i ensure that you admit only valid wireless devices to your 802.11 wireless LAN. This book, however, describes security only insofar as it relates to a device's characteristics as a VoIP device, and, furthermore, it simply provides an overview of the techniques— implementing a secure network is a topic that can easily merit a book of its own.

As Chapter 1 indicates, any VoIP session consists of three phases. The call signaling and media control phases allow a caller to initiate a call with a called party and for both parties in the communication to exchange the information (IP address, IP ports, and media capabilities, among others). The media exchange phase consists of the actual exchange of encoded voice or video packets using Real-Time Transport Protocol (RTP). In a Cisco IP Communications network, CallManager manages the call signaling and media control connections from devices in the network, but media exchange is directly from device to device.

Authentication, Authorization, and Privacy of Signaling Connections Between CallManager and Cisco Gateways

For connections to Cisco gateways, CallManager relies on IPSec, regardless of the VoIP protocol (H.323, MGCP, SIP) that CallManager uses to communicate with the gateway. IPSec is a set of protocols developed by the IETF to support the secure exchange of IP packets. IPSec both allows CallManager and the Cisco gateway to mutually authenticate each other and to ensure the privacy of the signaling stream via Data Encryption Standard (DES). You can find detailed instructions on how to configure IPSec between CallManager and Cisco Voice Gateways at the following link or search Cisco.com for "Configuring IPSec between a server and device":

http://www.cisco.com/warp/customer/707/2000.html

CallManager provides authorization primarily through the policies that you administer in CallManager Administration. When CallManager can establish the identity of a device, it can associate the device with the network policies that you have specified for that device. For instance, calling search spaces enable you to define a routing policy on a device-by-device basis.

Authentication, Authorization, and Privacy of Media Connections Between Cisco VoIP Endpoints

VoIP endpoints send media to each other using RTP as defined in IETF RFC 1889. The IETF standard RFC 3711 defines a set of extensions to this protocol that provides for sender authentication and media privacy.

CallManager 4.1 can help negotiate SRTP sessions only for some of its devices. Of the IP phones that CallManager 4.1 supports as of September 2005, only Cisco IP Phones 7940, 7941, 7960, 7961, 7970, and 7971 support the sending and reception of SRTP streams. Of the gateway devices, CallManager can help negotiate the SRTP stream only for gateways running MGCP. The IOS command **mgcp package-capability srtp-package** enables you to enable SRTP on a supported MGCP gateway.

SRTP currently works with CallManager 4.1 and gateways running Cisco IOS Software Release 12.3.11. The supported IOS gateways are as follows:

- Cisco 2600XM

- Cisco 2691

- Cisco 2800

- Cisco 3640A

- Cisco 3660

- Cisco 3700

- Cisco 3800

- Cisco VG224

Cisco network modules supported are as follows:

- NM-HDV2

- NM-HD-1V

- NM-HD-2V

- NM-HD-2VE

- EVM-HD

- PVDM2

SRTP provides for privacy because it encrypts the payload using the Advanced Encryption Standard Counter Mode (AES-CM) encryption algorithm and signs the payload using the secure hash algorithm HMAC-SHA1.

H.323 Gateways

The *H.323 recommendation* from the International Telecommunication Union Telecommunication Standardization Sector (ITU-T) is an umbrella specification that defines how terminals, gateways, and gatekeepers provide communication services over packet-based networks. The specification is called an *umbrella specification* because it references other specifications for the call control, media control, and media coding and decoding specifications.

The protocols of interest in this chapter are as follows:

- RAS

- H.225

- H.245

- Audio codecs G.711, G.722, G.723, G.728, G.729a, and GSM

- Video codecs H.261, H.263, and H.264

The call signaling phase of an H.323 call uses RAS and H.225. The function of the call signaling phase is to coordinate the offering and answering of a call between two parties. In addition to its functions related to call signaling, RAS provides messages to allow H.323 endpoints to associate themselves with network elements that can help with call routing and call admission control (which can prevent VoIP calls from overutilizing network bandwidth and degrading the voice quality of all calls). H.225 handles the basic call setup and teardown.

The media control phase of an H.323 call uses H.245. The function of the media control phase is to provide the endpoints with the information they need to send and receive properly encoded media streams to and from each other.

The media exchange phase of an H.323 call allows the speakers on either end of a call to exchange information. G.711, G.723, G.729a, and GSM are codecs that encode audio information, while H.263 allows an endpoint to encode and decode video information.

CallManager and the H.323 Control Model

H.323 defines several network elements and several models for controlling calls. The most important of the network elements are *endpoints* and *gatekeepers*.

H.323 endpoints are the entities that place and receive calls, and the protocols are therefore designed for the establishment of sessions in between these endpoints. However, endpoints need not necessarily be user devices, but instead can serve as gateways from one type of network to another or even as just a protocol suite to another protocol suite.

H.323 gatekeepers are centralized points that fulfill an administrative role. They can aggregate endpoint registrations, provide a centralized call routing function for endpoints, and manage network resources to ensure that network bandwidth is not oversubscribed.

Figure 4-10 demonstrates three main control models for H.323 calls.

> **NOTE**   This chapter doesn't discuss two other models—one in which a direct-mode gatekeeper handles RAS but routes media through a proxy, and one in which the gatekeeper routes H.225, H.245, and the media through a proxy. Neither of these are common CallManager deployment models.

The peer-to-peer model includes no gatekeeper at all. Endpoints communicate directly with each other, first via H.225 to coordinate the establishment of a call and then with H.245 to establish the media flow between the two endpoints. The other models include a gatekeeper. Using a gatekeeper necessitates the use of RAS, which permits endpoints to locate gatekeepers to serve them, register with those gatekeepers, and, when calls are placed, to ask for permission to admit calls into the network. In the direct signaling model, endpoints communicate with the gatekeeper using only RAS for call admissions and, when it admits calls, the gatekeeper provides enough information to the endpoints for them to negotiate H.225 call signaling and H.245 media control signaling with each other. In the gatekeeper-routed call, endpoints communicate not only RAS but also H.225 and H.245 signaling to the gatekeeper. Certain gatekeepers may also route the actual media flow through themselves by controlling the H.245 addresses.

Figure 4-10   *H.323 Call Models*

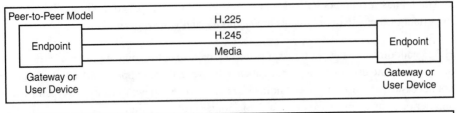

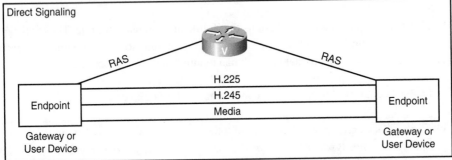

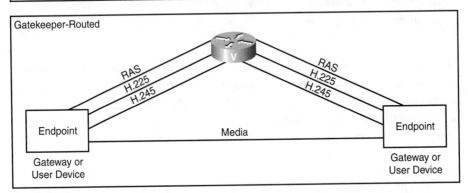

CallManager fits into the H.323 model as follows:

■ **CallManager acts as an H.323 endpoint**—As previously mentioned, H.323 endpoints need not simply be user devices. Cisco IOS H.323 gateways, for instance, operate using VoIP protocols on their network interfaces and translate this signaling to activity on a circuit. Similarly, CallManager acts as an IP-to-IP call signaling and media control gateway to permit H.323 devices to communicate with non-H.323 devices such as SCCP endpoints. (Unlike Cisco IOS H.323 gateways, however, CallManager doesn't terminate the media path.) Figure 4-11 shows the similar roles that Cisco IOS H.323 gateways and CallManager have.

In H.323, in many respects, H.323 endpoints are completely autonomous entities. For example, if one endpoint in a call is supporting a variety of circuit-switched interfaces, the other endpoint doesn't see those interfaces. To it, the other endpoint acts as a black box.

From a configuration standpoint, this means that H.323 endpoints that act as gateways are call agents in their own right. In practice, this means that if you deploy Cisco IOS H.323 or other H.323 gateways, you must often configure call routing settings directly on both CallManager and the H.323 gateways that connect to it.

■ **CallManager acts according to the peer-to-peer and direct signaling models**—In H.323, endpoints either signal each other directly or, via an H.323 gatekeeper, indirectly. Using CallManager Administration, you can configure static associations between CallManager H.323 trunks and other CallManagers and H.323 gateways—the peer-to-peer model—or you can configure CallManager H.323 trunks to allow a gatekeeper to provide routing and call admission control via RAS—the direct signaling model.

When the other end of an H.323 trunk is CallManager or a set of CallManagers, the connection is given the special term *intercluster trunk*. But, in fact, except for a few wrinkles in the media negotiation when CallManagers are connected via H.323 trunk, CallManager relates to other CallManagers as if they were H.323 gateways. (In the peer-to-peer model, you provision CallManager-to-CallManager trunks explicitly, so CallManager adjusts for the slightly different media signaling. In the gatekeeper models, CallManager automatically detects whether the other side is a CallManager and adjusts its signaling accordingly.)

One other distinction between intercluster trunks and IP trunks to gateways is that CallManager supports H.323 Annex M, which permits the tunneling of the QSIG protocol over H.323 connections. CallManager uses QSIG tunneling to provide better feature transparency between clusters. The subsection "QSIG" goes into more detail about QSIG.

Figure 4-11 and Figure 4-12 show CallManager using the peer-to-peer and direct signaling models to access both H.323 gateways and other CallManagers.

Figure 4-11   *CallManager's Role as H.323 Endpoint*

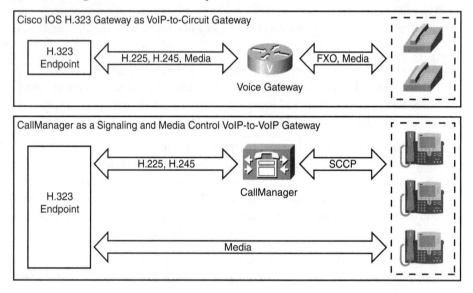

H.323 Call Signaling Details

This section goes into more detail about the actual signaling exchanges that occur in RAS, H.225, and H.245, and describes the ways in which CallManager uses these protocols.

RAS

H.323 endpoints use the Registration, Admission, and Status (RAS) protocol to interact with H.323 gatekeepers. RAS provides the following functions for endpoints:

- Gatekeeper location, provided via the GRQ, GCF, and GRJ messages

- Endpoint registration and KeepAlive, provided via the IRQ, IRR, RAI, RAC, RRQ, RCF, RRJ, URQ, UCF, and URJ messages

- Call routing, call admissions, and call clearing, provided with the ARQ, ACF, ARJ, DRQ, DCF, DRJ, LRQ, and LCF messages

- Mid-call bandwidth adjustments, provided via the BRQ, BCF, and BRJ messages

Figure 4-12 *CallManager's Support for H.323 Call Models*

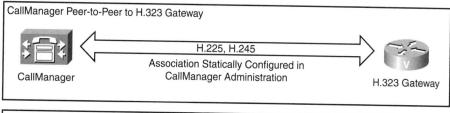

CallManager Peer-to-Peer to H.323 Gateway

CallManager

H.225, H.245
Association Statically Configured in
CallManager Administration

H.323 Gateway

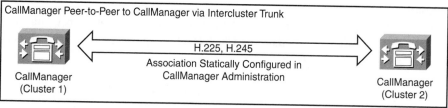

CallManager Peer-to-Peer to CallManager via Intercluster Trunk

CallManager
(Cluster 1)

H.225, H.245
Association Statically Configured in
CallManager Administration

CallManager
(Cluster 2)

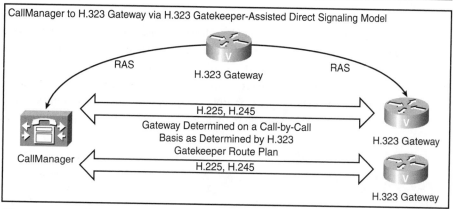

CallManager to H.323 Gateway via H.323 Gatekeeper-Assisted Direct Signaling Model

RAS

H.323 Gateway

RAS

CallManager

H.225, H.245
Gateway Determined on a Call-by-Call
Basis as Determined by H.323
Gatekeeper Route Plan
H.225, H.245

H.323 Gateway

H.323 Gateway

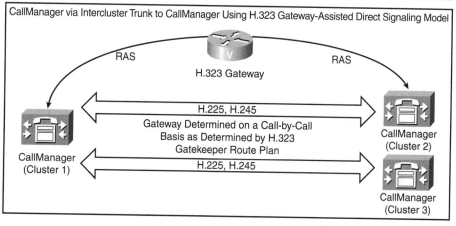

CallManager via Intercluster Trunk to CallManager Using H.323 Gateway-Assisted Direct Signaling Model

RAS

H.323 Gateway

RAS

CallManager
(Cluster 1)

H.225, H.245
Gateway Determined on a Call-by-Call
Basis as Determined by H.323
Gatekeeper Route Plan
H.225, H.245

CallManager
(Cluster 2)

CallManager
(Cluster 3)

The sections that follow describe each of these functions in more detail. Each section first describes the standards-supported methods and then describes how these standards are implemented in CallManager.

At the end of this section, "RAS Messaging Details" provides a detailed breakout of the RAS messages CallManager sends and receives.

Finding a Gatekeeper

Endpoints that need to be controlled via H.323 must first locate a gatekeeper with which to register. H.323 provides two methods by which H.323 endpoints can find a gatekeeper: manual discovery and automatic discovery.

In manual discovery, the H.323 is statically configured with the address of the gatekeeper that serves it.

In automatic discovery, an H.323 endpoint broadcasts the GRQ (Gatekeeper Request) message on multicast address 224.0.1.41. Gatekeepers in the network listening for such requests examine the specified address of the requestor (which can be either an alphanumeric alias or an E.164) and decide whether they want to serve the requesting endpoint. Gatekeepers that do want to be considered return a GCF (Gatekeeper Confirm) message; those that do not return a GRJ (Gatekeeper Reject) message or send no reply at all. Figure 4-13 depicts this procedure.

Figure 4-13 *Automatic Gatekeeper Discovery*

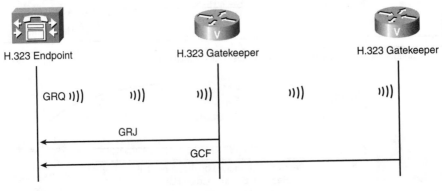

CallManager does not support automatic gatekeeper discovery. Instead, when you add a gatekeeper-controlled H.323 gateway or gatekeeper-controlled intercluster trunk, CallManager Administration allows you to specify the address of a primary gatekeeper that CallManager's H.323 interface should register with.

Registering with a Gatekeeper

When a gatekeeper-controlled H.323 endpoint learns which gatekeepers are available to control it, it chooses to register with one of them.

To register, an H.323 endpoint issues an RRQ (Register Request) message, which the gatekeeper responds to with an RCF (Register Confirm) message if it wants to accept the registration and an RRJ (Register Reject) message if it wants to deny the registration. The RRQ contains information that the gatekeeper uses to authorize inbound and outbound calls to and from the endpoint. For instance, a registration contains the IP and port information that callers should use when they attempt to establish an H.225 session with the registering endpoint.

RAS is a protocol that operates over UDP. Unlike TCP, UDP does not establish and maintain connections. As a result, it is possible for an endpoint to register with a gatekeeper and then disappear from the network. The gatekeeper needs some way of knowing when this event occurs.

When you configure CallManager with the address of your gatekeeper, you specify a few values. One of these values is a gatekeeper refresh timeout, which defaults to 60 seconds (Registration Request Time To Live field on the Gatekeeper Configuration page). To keep the gatekeeper informed that CallManager is still operating, CallManager periodically sends a lightweight RRQ as a registration keepalive. If the H.323 gatekeeper doesn't receive a periodic refresh of the registration, it expires the registration of the endpoint.

Several other fields configured on the Trunk Configuration page in CallManager Administration come into play during registration:

- Zone settings

- Technology prefix settings

- Device pool settings

Zones

The *zone* setting helps gatekeepers determine which H.323 endpoints they control. Cisco IOS gatekeepers only accept registrations for endpoints that register with zone information that the gatekeeper's configuration has defined as local to it. If you are using a gatekeeper, you should assign each CallManager cluster in your enterprise its own unique zone.

Technology Prefix

The *technology prefix* is a routing-related setting that allows a gatekeeper to differentiate between groups of endpoints in the same zone. When an endpoint registers, it communicates both its zone information and its technology prefix, and the gatekeeper associates these values. The section

"Admitting Calls" describes how zones and technology prefixes relate when a gatekeeper admits calls on to the network.

Device Pool

Like other CallManager devices, you assign device pools to H.323 trunk devices. *Device pools*, which contain CallManager group lists, normally control which CallManager nodes a physical device such as an IP phone attempt to connect to during registration. But CallManager's H.323 trunks are built directly in to the software and therefore cannot possibly lose their connection to CallManager. What's going on?

Like with physical IP devices, the CallManager list for H.323 trunks relates to redundancy. If, when you created an H.323 trunk, you created it only a single CallManager and statically associated it with either a gateway or a single CallManager in another cluster, calls between endpoints in your enterprise connected via the H.323 trunk will fail if a particular CallManager crashes. For example, in Figure 4-14, if either CallManager 1B or 2E fails, IP phones in cluster 1 cannot call IP phones in cluster 2.

Figure 4-14 *Nonredundant H.323 Trunk*

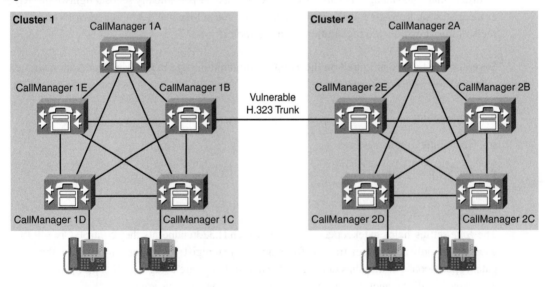

Therefore, when a CallManager cluster comes online, each CallManager starts one instance of the H.323 trunk on each configured H.323 trunk that includes the CallManager in its device pool. This behavior provides redundancy, but in a different way depending on whether the trunk is peer to peer or gatekeeper controlled.

When the trunk is peer to peer, in addition to configuring a device pool, you also configure a specific list of up to three IP addresses to which the H.323 trunk should connect. Because CallManager creates one H.323 trunk instance per CallManager in the CallManager list and the trunk is configured with up to three IP addresses to connect to in another cluster, this creates a 3×3 meshed connection between the clusters, as depicted in Figure 4-15.

Figure 4-15 *Redundant Peer-to-Peer H.323 Trunk*

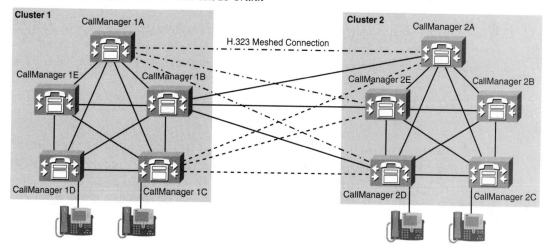

When a user in one cluster calls a user in the other cluster over a peer-to-peer H.323 trunk, two load-sharing strategies occur.

The first load-sharing algorithm relates to which internal trunk device the CallManager cluster selects for placing the outbound call to the other cluster.

When CallManager attempts to place a call on behalf of a user, CallManager may create the call on any node in the cluster (although it typically creates the call on the same node as the caller). If CallManager detects that an H.323 trunk to the caller's destination trunk exists on the same node as the call, CallManager uses that local instance. If no such local instance exists, CallManager chooses randomly from the H.323 trunk instances selected by the call. Assuming callers are evenly distributed around the active nodes in a cluster, this strategy can provide an even load across the H.323 trunk instances that the CallManager nodes create.

After a given H.323 trunk instance has been given the opportunity to extend the call to the other cluster, a round-robin approach takes over. For each subsequent call, the H.323 trunk instance selects the next IP address in its list of remote CallManager nodes. This process tends to spread out the burden of incoming peer-to-peer H.323 calls. It's important that H.323 trunks in the receiving cluster be configured on the appropriate CallManagers to ensure the outbound call is accepted.

When an H.323 trunk is configured as gatekeeper controlled, the device pool provides a similar load-sharing mechanism via a different method.

When, in a given CallManager, an H.323 gatekeeper-controlled trunk comes online, it looks to see whether the other H.323 trunks in its device list have come online. When registering with the H.323 gatekeeper, CallManager specifies each other online H.323 trunk in its device pool as an alternate endpoint.

When resolving a dialed address, the H.323 gatekeeper, instead of specifying just a single H.323 call signaling address in the admission response, specifies all addresses sent in the original registration, including the alternate endpoints. In conjunction with the load-sharing mechanism whereby CallManager selects either a local or a random outbound trunk, this allows an H.323 trunk to attempt to route a call to alternate destinations if the attempt to contact the primary CallManager fails.

With gatekeeper-controlled H.323 trunks, the gatekeeper is also a component that is subject to failure. Therefore, just as endpoints can specify alternate endpoints when registering (via RRQ), when an endpoint registers, an H.323 gatekeeper can specify alternate gatekeepers when accepting a registration (via RCF). If, when an H.323 trunk attempts to place an outbound call, it cannot contact its gatekeeper, it can contact one of the alternate gatekeepers provided on the original registration.

When confirming the registration and providing a list of such alternate gatekeepers, the H.323 gatekeeper can specify the requiresRegistration field. When this field is set, an H.323 trunk issuing a call must actually register with one of the alternate gatekeepers before asking the alternate gatekeeper to admit the call.

Admitting Calls

When a gatekeeper-enabled endpoint wants to place or receive a call, it first asks for permission from the gatekeeper via the ARQ (Admissions Request) message. Although the ARQ includes information about the calling party and the called party, this information is only indirectly related to the actual call establishment. Rather, the sending of the ARQ is primarily related to policy enforcement.

When deploying an H.323 gatekeeper with CallManager, admissions requests hinge primarily on two factors. First, H.323 gatekeepers permit you to configure a multiple-cluster route plan in a centralized place. Without a gatekeeper, if your deployment exceeds two clusters, configuring a route plan to route calls in between clusters requires quite a bit of redundant configuration, because you must manually provision routes from cluster to cluster.

Figure 4-16 demonstrates the redundancy when you use the peer-to-peer model in a network requiring three or more clusters. In this figure, directory numbers are scattered around the enterprise with no use of number blocks to help algorithmically route the call. As a result, when a directory number is added to one cluster, specific routes must be provisioned in the other two clusters to route the call. Although it's certainly possible to manage such a deployment, the configuration isn't ideal.

Figure 4-16 *Redundant Routing Information in a Multiple-Cluster Peer-to-Peer H.323 Network*

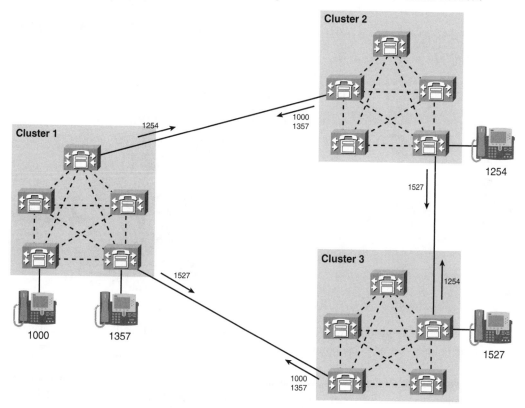

If you use a gatekeeper-routed model instead, you can configure routing so that all calls that a given cluster doesn't know how to route locally query the gatekeeper, which has a centralized configuration containing all routable addresses for the enterprise. This configuration scales much better because instead of having to configure a given address once in CallManager and once each in every other CallManager cluster, you just need to configure the address twice, no matter how many clusters you have. Figure 4-17 demonstrates this technique.

Figure 4-17 *Routing Information in a Multiple-Cluster Gatekeeper-Controlled H.323 Network*

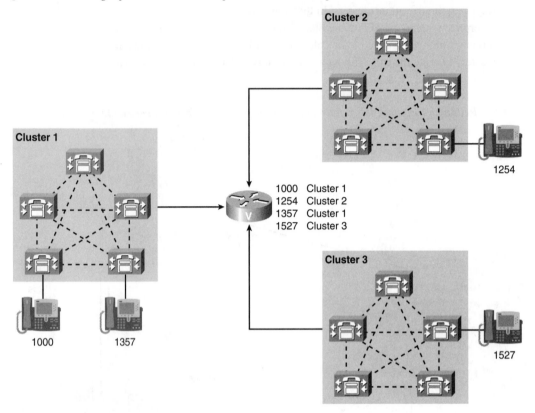

As the section "Registering with a Gatekeeper" mentioned, zones also allow H.323 gatekeepers to set up policies related to endpoints grouped in a zone.

In particular, with IOS gateways, you can associate a certain amount of bandwidth that is available for calls to and from the zone. When you use gatekeeper-based call admission control, the gatekeeper tracks all gatekeeper-assisted H.323 calls and deducts a codec-based amount of bandwidth for each call placed between zones. When the bandwidth is exhausted, the gatekeeper permits no calls into or out of the depleted zone until one of the calls in the zone releases.

When an endpoint places a call, it provides the dialed address to the gatekeeper. The Cisco IOS gatekeeper compares these digits to the DN ranges assigned to each zone. For instance, assume cluster A manages directory number range 40000 to 49999, and cluster B manages directory number range 50000 to 59999. The following gatekeeper configuration allows the gatekeeper to understand the different numbering ranges:

```
zone local cluster-A cisco.com
zone prefix cluster-A 4....
zone local cluster-B cisco.com
zone prefix cluster-B 5....
```

If a caller dials 45555, CallManager's gatekeeper-controlled H.323 trunk provides these digits to the gatekeeper. By comparing the dialed digits to the zone prefixes, the gatekeeper identifies the dialed address as being related to cluster A.

Upon identifying the zone, the Cisco gatekeeper looks for specifically registered endpoints in that zone. For instance, one could deploy a bunch of non-CallManager-controlled H.323 endpoints that specifically register their addresses with the Cisco gatekeeper.

When CallManager registers with a gatekeeper, it provides its zone information, but it does not provide any information related to specific endpoints; that is, CallManager does not register specific contacts for its SCCP phones, MGCP and H.323 gateways, route patterns, translation patterns, and so on. Instead, CallManager relies on a feature of the Cisco gatekeeper called the *default technology prefix*.

Normally, if the gatekeeper locates no specific registered contact, it rejects the call. But if you configure a default technology prefix with

```
gw-type-prefix 1# default-technology
```

then when no specific match is found, the Cisco gatekeeper looks for endpoints that have registered with the specified technology prefix (in this case, 1#) and chooses one of *these* endpoints to route the call to. In the example, the dialed digits 45555 would first bind to zone cluster A, then the gatekeeper would find no specifically registered alias, the gatekeeper would find its default technology prefix of 1#, and then the gatekeeper would offer the call to the H.323 trunks that registered in the cluster A zone with technology prefix 1#.

As a result, for intercluster routing, you'd configure the zone of cluster A's H.323 trunks as **cluster-A** and its technology prefix as **1#** and the zone of cluster B's H.323 trunks as **cluster-B** and its technology prefix as **1#**.

When users conversing over an admitted call finish their conversation, each H.323 endpoint notifies the gatekeeper of call termination via the DRQ (Disengage Request) message, which the gatekeeper accepts by sending a DCF (Disengage Confirm) message (and rejects by sending a DRJ [Disengage Reject] message, although it's hard to conceive of a case in which a gatekeeper would do this in practice).

Changing Bandwidth Mid-Call

When configuring a gatekeeper with zone information, you can specify a maximum amount of bandwidth available for calls to and from that zone. When an H.323 endpoint asks the gatekeeper to admit the call to the network, it provides an amount of bandwidth that it wants the gatekeeper to grant. If the zone has been provisioned with a bandwidth limit, the gatekeeper compares the highest-bandwidth codec in the list of capabilities against the bandwidth available for the zone. If enough bandwidth is available, the gatekeeper admits the call.

Sometimes during a call, the codecs used by endpoints in a conversation can change. RAS includes the BRQ (Bandwidth Request) message to handle this event. If the gatekeeper wants to approve the bandwidth request, it issues a BCF (Bandwidth Confirm) message; if not, it returns a BRJ (Bandwidth Reject) message. If the bandwidth request is not granted, CallManager clears the affected call.

If the required bandwidth for an H.323 call changes during the call—for instance, if a phone in one region places the call on hold, and a phone in a different region retrieves the call—CallManager notifies the gatekeeper of the new information so that the gatekeeper can properly track the amount of network bandwidth available. Because an attempt to change bandwidth might get rejected and cause calls to drop, you must specifically enable bandwidth adjustment using CallManager service parameters.

Gatekeepers can also request that endpoints adjust bandwidth. If CallManager receives a BRQ, it responds with a BRJ.

RAS Messaging Details

The RAS message support provided by CallManager is the H.225 version 2 protocol. Refer to Appendix C for detailed information about specific fields in H.225 RAS messages.

H.225

H.225 is the protocol used in H.323 to actually offer a call to a destination. Unlike RAS, which is always supported over UDP, H.225 can run over UDP or TCP. CallManager supports H.225 over TCP but not UDP.

The default port for H.225 call signaling is well-known port 1720, although CallManager allows you to configure this per each H.323 device.

If multiple H.323 devices are configured with the same port, it would seem logical that CallManager could not reconcile messages from different H.323 endpoints. However, when accepting inbound H.225 messages from a given IP address, CallManager examines the source IP address to determine to which inbound trunk the message is inbound. CallManager delivers the inbound H.225 message to the H.323 trunk you've configured that specifies the sender's IP address as its peer. However, this limitation does prevent you from specifying two different peer-to-peer H.323 trunks to the same IP address, which you might want to do if you want to take advantage of trunk-level policy settings such as calling search space or CallManager locations.

CallManager gatekeeper-controlled H.323 trunks act differently. When CallManager instantiates these trunks, it dynamically selects a port for receiving inbound messages and, when registering the trunk with the gatekeeper, provides the gatekeeper with this trunk value. As a result, with gatekeeper-controlled trunks, you can set up multiple H.323 trunks to apply different CallManager policy settings for different inbound calls. Similarly, when CallManager attempts to have a call admitted on to the network, one of the values that the gatekeeper specifies in the ACF message is the IP address and port to which CallManager should send the outbound call offering message.

When using gatekeeper-controlled trunks, you can specify one H.323 trunk that listens on port 1720. The service parameter Device Name of GK-controlled Trunk That Will Use Port 1720 enables you to specify the name of the gatekeeper-controlled H.323 trunk that listens on the well-known port. This can guarantee that H.323 endpoints on the other side of firewalls can still communicate with CallManager, because using dynamic ports might require that a firewall administrator unsecure more ports than are needed for processing H.323 calls.

Figure 4-18 presents the steps involved in call establishment via RAS and H.225.

Figure 4-18 *H.225 Call Establishment*

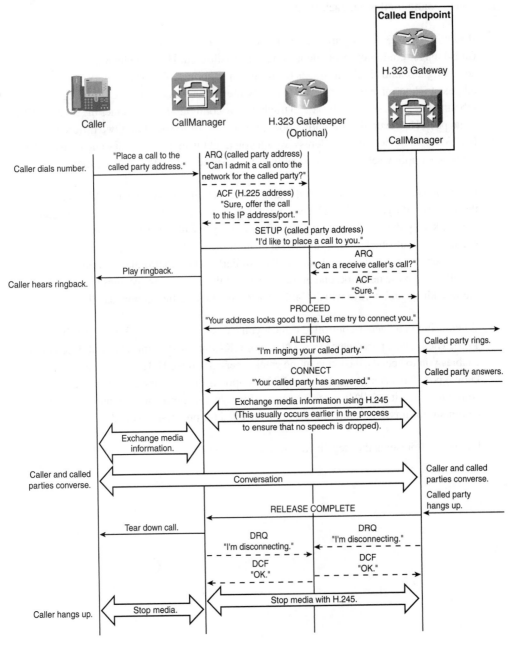

In Figure 4-18, a non-H.323 caller composes the address of a called party and provides the information to CallManager, whose routing tables indicate that the call should be offered out an H.323 trunk.

If the trunk is gatekeeper-enabled, CallManager first asks for permission from the gatekeeper to place the call. The gatekeeper examines the dialed address (possibly transformed by CallManager), possibly checks to see whether there is enough bandwidth to admit the call based on the caller's specified codec, and then admits the call, providing CallManager the IP address and port to which it must issue the call request.

After the gatekeeper (if one exists) grants permission, CallManager issues a call setup request to the selected gateway on the appropriate IP address and port. In some cases, this setup includes information about the media addresses of the caller, a process called *fast start*. H.245 describes the media processes related to fast start more extensively.

If the receiving H.323 gateway or CallManager is gatekeeper-controlled, it also queries the gatekeeper, this time to ask permission to receive a call. If such permission is granted, the receiving H.323 endpoint can present the caller to the called user. In the case of the trunk devices this chapter describes, the gateway is likely to issue a call setup request of its own to the connected network.

Assuming the receiving endpoint considers the address complete, it notifies CallManager with a PROCEED message. In many cases, this first backward message contains information about the receiving endpoint's media information to enable CallManager to begin setting up media channels for conversation. This approach, called *early media*, helps ensure that after the called party answers none of her speech is dropped or "clipped" because no end-to-end media path has yet been established.

When the terminating network offers the call to the called party, it sends some sort of alerting indication (which varies according to the nature of the terminating network) to the receiving endpoint, which sends an H.225 ALERTING message to CallManager. This message allows CallManager to instruct the related gateway to provide ringback to the caller.

When the called party answers, the terminating network sends some sort of answer indication (which varies according to the nature of the terminating network) to the receiving gateway, which sends an H.225 CONNECT message. If media is not yet established between the caller and called party, the CONNECT message causes CallManager to issue the H.245 control messages needed to establish media.

After all media information has been exchanged, the two parties can converse. When one hangs up—in this case, the called party—the receiving gateway receives disconnection information, and issues an H.225 RELEASE COMPLETE message to CallManager. If the receiving endpoint and CallManager are gatekeeper-controlled, they issue DRQ messages to the gatekeeper to notify it of call termination.

Upon receiving RELEASE COMPLETE, CallManager starts tearing down the media channels between caller and called party, and the call concludes.

H.225 Messaging Details

The call signaling protocol that is supported in the H.323 protocol umbrella is H.225. H.225 includes the call signaling messages and the RAS messages. This section covers the specific details of the call signaling messages.

H.225 messages follow the ITU-T Q.931. In H.225, the user-user information element (UUIE) conveys the H.225-related information. The H.323 user information protocol data unit (PDU) is ASN.1-encoded. The ASN.1 is encoded using the basic aligned variant of the packed encoding rules as specified in X.691. The ASN.1 structure begins with H323-UserInformation.

Tables in Appendix C list each H.225 message and provide the specific fields of the H.225 call signaling messages that CallManager exchanges with an H.323 gateway or CallManager H.323 trunk (GW in table). See Appendix C for more information.

H.245

H.245 is the protocol used in H.323 to allow endpoints to coordinate their media.

Originally, in H.323, H.225 controlled just the actual mechanics of call offer and answer, and then H.245 took over to permit the exchange of media information. This approach sometimes led to clipped speech, so a procedure called fast start was defined.

Before learning about fast start, you need to understand the purer H.245 flows.

Like H.225, H.245 signaling occurs over a TCP session. Four major types of events occur over an H.245 session:

- **Determination of which side of the H.245 is the master and which is the slave**—This assignment of roles allows the protocol to deal with glare conditions within the protocol and doesn't directly relate to the media session itself.

- **Exchange of capabilities**—This event permits the endpoints in the conversation to choose a media encoding method that they can be confident that the other side supports. Although CallManager can be configured to insert special devices called "transcoders" (discussed in Chapter 5) into a conversation between two parties that don't otherwise share a common codec, direct end-to-end media streams are preferable.

- **Exchange of streaming IP address and port**—This event tells the endpoints where to send their encoded media stream.

- **Mid-call button presses for interaction with connected services**—Connected services include services such as voice mail and interactive voice response (IVR) units.

One of the functions of RAS in the gatekeeper-controlled model was to provide to the calling H.323 endpoint the IP address and port with which it should attempt to establish the H.225 session (TCP or UDP).

Similarly, one of the functions of the H.225 session is to provide the endpoints, both calling and called, with the IP address and port to which the H.245 session (TCP) should be established. In H.225, the caller generally provides the address to which the called party should send H.245 control messages on the SETUP message; the called party provides the address to which the calling party should send H.245 control messages on one of the following backward messages:

- PROCEED

- ALERTING

- CONNECT (or PROGRESS)

In the backward direction, the earlier this information is communicated, the earlier the end-to-end media connection can be established.

Finally, one of the functions of the H.245 session is to provide the endpoints with the IP address and port to which the actual encoded media should be sent (Real-Time Transport Protocol [RTP] headers, wrapped in UDP packets).

Because CallManager wants to be involved in the signaling session and the media control session but not the exchange of media, CallManager constructs the messages so that the signaling and media transport addresses point to it but the actual media addresses are those of the endpoints. Figure 4-19 demonstrates this progression.

Figure 4-19 *Progressive Establishment of Call Sessions*

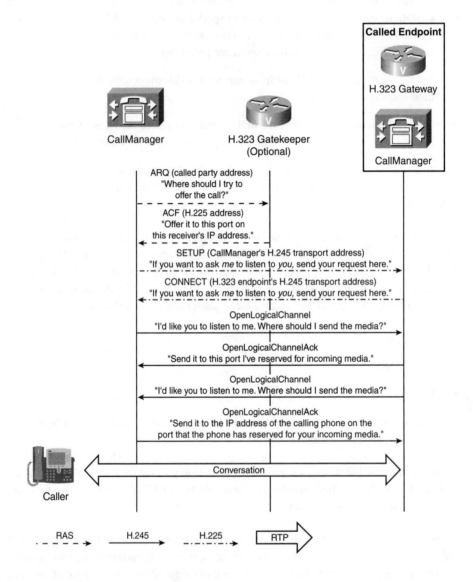

Figure 4-20 illustrates a full H.245 message exchange between two H.323 endpoints.

Use of H.245 to Provide Features

Because H.323 decouples the media control signaling from the call signaling, it provides a way for endpoints to change bandwidth mid-call, to add new channels of information to an existing call (such as video or application collaboration), or to renegotiate codecs mid-call.

Figure 4-20 *H.245 Message Exchange*

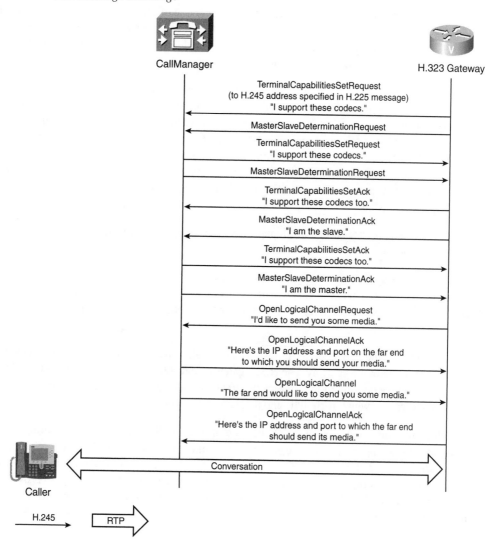

The ITU specification H.450 defines a framework by which H.323 endpoints can provide call-related features such as transfer, call completion, call forwarding, and others. CallManager does not support this standard. Nevertheless, H.323 endpoints can participate in features in three ways:

- CallManager supports the carriage of hookflash and dialed digits through the H.245 userInfoIndication field. This allows H.323 endpoints to interact with IVRs, voice mail systems, and so on.

■ Many CallManager features operate solely through the use of established calls. Although an H.323 endpoint cannot park a call, because the version of H.323 CallManager supports does not give CallManager a way to detect that the H.323 endpoint wants to invoke a feature, an H.323 endpoint can retrieve a parked call, because this operation requires only that an endpoint be able to offer a call containing the address of the park code.

■ H.323 endpoints can passively participate in features invoked via Cisco IP Phones via support for mid-call renegotiation of capabilities. H.323 requires that endpoints suspend sending media when they receive a mid-call request to select a new codec from an empty list of codecs. This capability is termed *empty capability set support*. What it means is that although an H.323 endpoint doesn't have a way to initiate a transfer or hold or other mid-call feature, if an IP phone that the H.323 gateway is talking with initiates such a feature, the gateway's media stream can be temporarily suspended while CallManager acts on the IP phone's feature request. CallManager uses this capability to effect features such as hold and transfer.

Figure 4-21 demonstrates how CallManager uses the empty capability set to effect a call park and call park retrieval.

In Figure 4-21, 2000 parks a call from an H.323 gateway. CallManager tells the gateway that 2000 supports no codecs, which the gateway interprets as a requirement to suspend sending media to 2000. (As part of the park operation, CallManager also tells 1000 to cease sending media to the gateway.)

When 1000 dials the park code to retrieve the call, CallManager begins another H.245 media control session with the gateway. The H.323 gateway and 1000 exchange codecs via CallManager and, as part of the coordination of the media streams, CallManager provides the gateway the IP address and port to which it should send media and vice versa.

Not all H.323 endpoints support the receipt of empty capability sets. When configuring CallManager to support one of these gateways, you must configure the H.323 trunk to use a *media termination point* (MTP). The MTP is a device that CallManager can insert into a call to insulate endpoints from incompatibilities between each other's media control processing, to provide dual-tone multifrequency (DTMF) relay, and to provide call progress tones. Chapter 5 goes into more details about MTPs.

H.245 Fast Connect

One charge levied against H.323 is that it can cause clipping—the loss of the first few seconds of a voice conversation (often the important first words "Hello?") because media negotiation occurs in a completely separate phase from the actual call establishment.

With the use of fast connect (also called *fast start*), H.323 allows endpoints to embed information about the IP address, port, and codecs that they want to use for a particular conversation in the H.225 messages actually used to place the call. CallManager can respond to and forward fast start requests that it receives.

Figure 4-21 *H.245 Feature-Related Message Exchange*

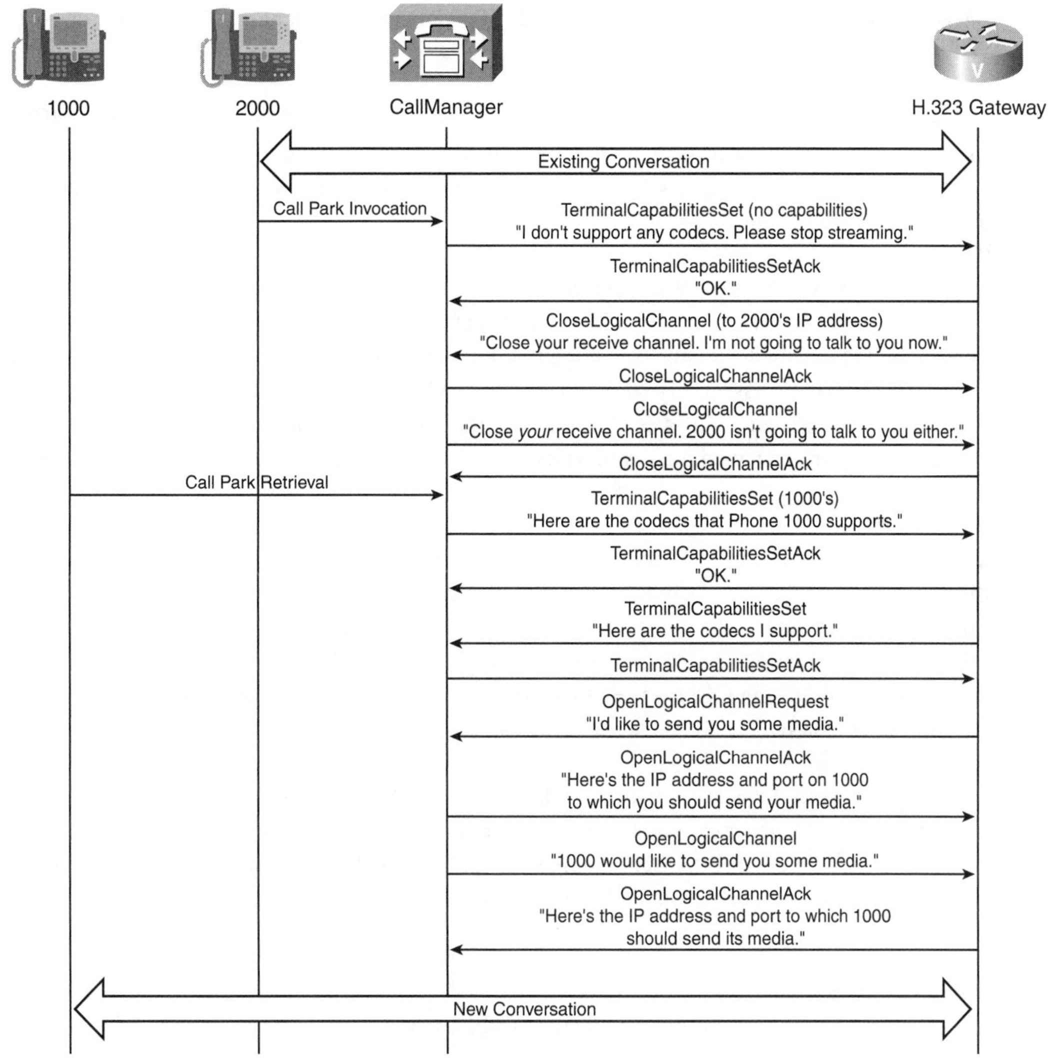

Fast start can speed the establishment of a conversation and avoid clipping. However, because mid-call feature invocations don't generate H.225 events, the full H.245 media renegotiation of necessity must occur. As a result, although the media channels related to initial call setup can occur quickly, media resumption can sometimes take longer when calls are transferred, retrieved from hold, retrieved from park, or the calls are the subject of other mid-call features. Normally, this isn't an issue. When receiving calls, users are conditioned to immediately answer with a "Hello," but users generally have fewer ingrained expectations when a mid-call feature is invoked.

MGCP Gateways

MGCP was defined by the IETF in RFC 2705. Many companies, including Cisco, have chosen to support the IETF draft and have interoperability among products.

MGCP is a text-based protocol, which means that, given the raw data used to encode an MGCP message, if your computer were asked to print it, you could read the message. In contrast, H.323 is binary-based, so printing raw Q.931 messages results in a string of gobbledy-gook punctuated with entertaining beeps.

Unlike H.323, which is a peer-to-peer protocol, MGCP is more like a client/server protocol. MGCP is based on the concept of a Media Gateway Controller (MGC). The MGC serves as the call signaling and media control signaling intelligence for gateway devices (termed "endpoints," as in H.323) that are essentially slaves to the MGC. Gateway devices terminate circuit-switched signaling interfaces and, via MGCP, provide a set of primitives whereby the MGC can establish, modify, and tear down media, as well as receive rudimentary call-related signaling and feature invocations.

Therefore, MGCP is quite different in philosophy from H.323. While H.323 defines a protocol by which quite intelligent, self-contained endpoints can communicate, MGCP provides a protocol that pushes many call-related decisions to the MGC. On one hand, this reduces the amount of duplicate configuration needed—with an MGCP gateway, CallManager provides the call routing intelligence, while with a Cisco H.323 gateway, you must configure dial peers to handle the routing of circuit-switched calls to the packet side and vice versa.

On the other hand, MGCP gateways are like every other VoIP device that CallManager controls. While each CallManager endpoint supports a variety of call signaling (SCCP, MGCP, H.225, SIP, SGCP) and media control (SCCP, MGCP, H.245, SDP, SGCP) protocols, when the call is finally established, endpoints encapsulate the media using RTP.

MGCP Messages

MGCP commands are the interface whereby CallManager receives basic signaling notifications from MGCP gateways and directs the gateway to establish, modify, and tear down media connections.

The gateway communicates these notifications and CallManager sends these commands using User Datagram Protocol (UDP).

Table 4-9 summarizes these commands, which fall into three classes:

■ Event triggers and notifications enable CallManager and the MGCP gateway to communicate call signaling events. The events communicated are sufficient to support such analog interfaces such as FXO and FXS, but not digital interfaces.

- Media establishment, modification, and teardown commands enable CallManager to manage connections on the gateway's IP interfaces to establish VoIP calls between the gateway and other VoIP devices.

- Restart- and failover-related messages enable CallManager to manage the gateway during registration and determine the state of existing calls when the gateway has lost its connection to a primary CallManager.

Table 4-9 *MGCP Command Summary*

Command Code	Command	Description
Event Triggers and Notifications		
RQNT request	Requests gateway to send notifications of specified events such as off-hook events and digit keypresses.	
NTFY	Notify	Allows a gateway to report the occurrence of the requested events.
Media Establishment, Modification, and Teardown Commands		
CRCX connection	Requests the gateway to create a connection to another endpoint.	
MDCX	Modify connection	Modifies the characteristic of an existing gateway connection.
DLCX	Delete connection	Deletes a gateway connection.
Restart- and Failover-Related Messages		
AUEP of an endpoint, including connection state, codecs, and so on.		
AUCX	Audit connection	Audits a connection to get the call ID.
EPCF	Endpoint configuration	Specifies the encoding of the signals an endpoint receives. For example, in certain international telephony configurations, some calls carry μ-law-encoded audio signals and others use A-law.
RSIP	Restart in progress	Allows a gateway to notify CallManager that a restart has occurred.

Q.931 Backhaul

MGCP is designed primarily for managing media. The word, after all, is part of the protocol's name. The signaling primitives aren't inherently powerful enough to communicate the information that circuit-oriented digital protocols such as Q.931 provide.

As a result, Cisco MGCP gateways running circuit-switched digital protocols such as PRI rely on a practice called *backhauling*. Although MGCP gateways that support digital interfaces do terminate the ITU-T Q.921 protocol (which ensures message integrity over the trunk itself), rather than terminate the call signaling protocol these gateways simply pass the Q.931 messages to CallManager for processing.

Figure 4-22 compares the practice of backhauling in MGCP versus the architecture of H.323. In H.323, the H.323 endpoint serves as a gateway for the media, for the media control signaling, and for the call signaling. In Cisco MGCP gateways, however, the gateway serves as a gateway for just the media (RTP on one side/circuit-switched media on the other) and the media control (MGCP on one side/Q.931 bearer negotiation on the other), but not for the call signaling, which is negotiated directly from the MGC to the circuit-switched network. (In contrast to the Layer 3 signaling, the gateway does terminate the Layer 2 signaling.)

Figure 4-23 demonstrates the signaling that occurs when CallManager receives a call from an MGCP FXS/FXO gateway. In this diagram, all messages are MGCP. All MGCP messages have acknowledgement messages. This message flow diagram eliminates acknowledgement messages in the interest of brevity, with the exception of one: the arrow labeled "200 c = IN IP4 10.83.129.8 m = audio 16396" indicates the successful receipt by the gateway of the CallManager's command to create a connection and provides the IP address and port to be used for the media.

Figure 4-22   *Signal Backhauling with MGCP*

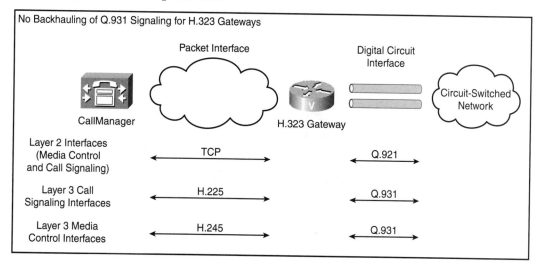

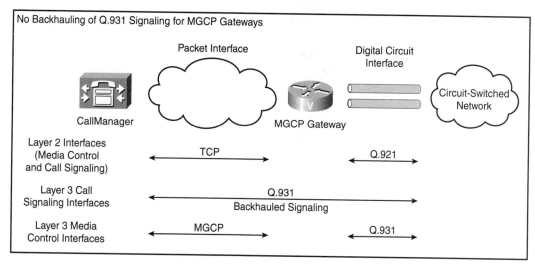

Figure 4-23 *Analog MGCP Call*

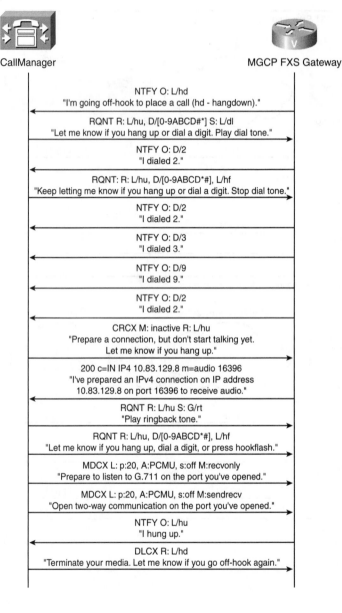

CallManager   MGCP FXS Gateway

NTFY O: L/hd
"I'm going off-hook to place a call (hd - hangdown)."

RQNT R: L/hu, D/[0-9ABCD#*] S: L/dl
"Let me know if you hang up or dial a digit. Play dial tone."

NTFY O: D/2
"I dialed 2."

RQNT: R: L/hu, D/[0-9ABCD*#], L/hf
"Keep letting me know if you hang up or dial a digit. Stop dial tone."

NTFY O: D/2
"I dialed 2."

NTFY O: D/3
"I dialed 3."

NTFY O: D/9
"I dialed 9."

NTFY O: D/2
"I dialed 2."

CRCX M: inactive R: L/hu
"Prepare a connection, but don't start talking yet.
Let me know if you hang up."

200 c=IN IP4 10.83.129.8 m=audio 16396
"I've prepared an IPv4 connection on IP address
10.83.129.8 on port 16396 to receive audio."

RQNT R: L/hu S: G/rt
"Play ringback tone."

RQNT R: L/hu, D/[0-9ABCD*#], L/hf
"Let me know if you hang up, dial a digit, or press hookflash."

MDCX L: p:20, A:PCMU, s:off M:recvonly
"Prepare to listen to G.711 on the port you've opened."

MDCX L: p:20, A:PCMU, s:off M:sendrecv
"Open two-way communication on the port you've opened."

NTFY O: L/hu
"I hung up."

DLCX R: L/hd
"Terminate your media. Let me know if you go off-hook again."

Figure 4-24 demonstrates the signaling that occurs when CallManager receives a call from an MGCP PRI gateway. This diagram contains a mixture of MGCP and PRI signaling and omits most MGCP acknowledgement messages. Backhauled signaling passes through the gateway either from or to the right side of the figure.

Figure 4-24 *Digital MGCP Call*

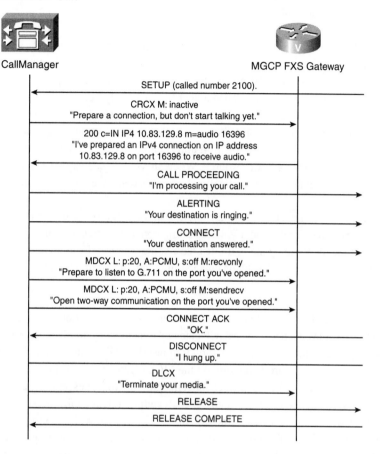

CallManager   MGCP FXS Gateway

SETUP (called number 2100).

CRCX M: inactive
"Prepare a connection, but don't start talking yet."

200 c=IN IP4 10.83.129.8 m=audio 16396
"I've prepared an IPv4 connection on IP address
10.83.129.8 on port 16396 to receive audio."

CALL PROCEEDING
"I'm processing your call."

ALERTING
"Your destination is ringing."

CONNECT
"Your destination answered."

MDCX L: p:20, A:PCMU, s:off M:recvonly
"Prepare to listen to G.711 on the port you've opened."

MDCX L: p:20, A:PCMU, s:off M:sendrecv
"Open two-way communication on the port you've opened."

CONNECT ACK
"OK."

DISCONNECT
"I hung up."

DLCX
"Terminate your media."

RELEASE

RELEASE COMPLETE

MGCP Gateway Failover

MGCP gateways register with CallManager based on their gateway configuration information. Once the gateway determines the IP address of CallManager, it establishes a TCP connection with CallManager for the purpose of sending backhauled Q.931 messages and sends a registration request.

If an MGCP gateway loses its connection to CallManager, there might be several calls in progress on the gateway. CallManager supports a feature called *call preservation*, which allows users on established calls to continue conversing. Though gateways and other endpoints must have connectivity to CallManager to establish calls, once the call has been answered, the signaling and media control channels are not actively used. By default, call preservation is available only for Cisco MGCP gateways, because the H.323 standards require existing calls to clear if the H.225 or

H.245 connection is lost. However, you can override this behavior in Cisco IOS gateways using the **no h225 timeout keepalive** command.

Cisco MGCP gateways backhaul their Q.931 signaling, but not their Q.921 signaling. As a result, if the connection from the gateway to CallManager drops, the circuit-switched side of the call need not be aware. Because, in VoIP, media streams directly from one endpoint to another, if an MGCP gateway loses its connection to CallManager for an already-active call, rather than clear the circuit-switched connection it can leave its connection up and continue to send and receive media on the IP side. When the circuit-switched side hangs up, or when the gateway begins receiving ICMP "destination unreachable" or "port unreachable" message on its IP media connection(s), the gateway can free up the circuit resource. When an MGCP gateway loses its connection to CallManager, the gateway automatically clears calls that have not yet reached an active state.

Until the gateway reregisters, unused channels on the gateway are unavailable to place or receive calls, because MGCP relies on a VoIP signaling connection to CallManager. Conversely, if the gateway immediately reregisters, it must have some way to inform its new CallManager which channels are in use; otherwise, CallManager might attempt to offer a new call to one of the circuits already in use.

So when an MGCP gateway loses its connection, it sends the Restart in Progress (RSIP) message to its backup CallManager. If the MGCP gateway is supporting an FXS/FXO or T1-CAS interface, CallManager responds with a Notification Request (RQNT), requesting to be notified of off-hook events from each configured endpoint on the MGCP gateway. CallManager then sends Audit Endpoint (AUEP) messages to each channel the gateway manages, and the gateway responds with the idle, busy, and out-of-service status of each endpoint. Once initialized, the MGCP gateway maintains existing calls and starts the initialization sequence with the tertiary CallManager node in the case of a failure of the secondary while simultaneously monitoring the connection to the primary CallManager so it can reregister should it become available again. After the gateway sends the registration to CallManager, CallManager creates a device process to handle the gateway communication and then informs the device manager process of the gateway registration. The device manager propagates the device registration information to all CallManager servers in the cluster so that the route list information is accurate for all CallManagers in the cluster. The gateway is available to place and receive calls again.

SIP

Session Initiation Protocol (SIP) is a text-based protocol used for multimedia communications over IP networks. SIP provides a framework for establishing voice and video point-to-point communications, conferencing, and text messaging. CallManager currently supports SIP to other call agents over its SIP IP trunk interface.

SIP is defined in IETF RFCs. RFC 3261 defines the basic set of rules that SIP entities must conform to. However, a host of other RFCs and drafts exist, and SIP entities generally implement some combination of the drafts listed in Table 4-10.

Table 4-10   *Partial List of SIP-Related Protocols*

RFC	Description
2327	Session Description Protocol
2543bis4	Original definition of SIP, superseded by RFC 3261
2833	RTP Payload for DTMF Digits, Telephony Tones, and Telephony Signals
3261	Session Initiation Protocol
3262	Reliable Provisional Responses
3264	Offer/Answer Model for the Session Description Protocol (SDP)
3265	SIP-specific event notification (SUBSCRIBE/NOTIFY)
3311	SIP UPDATE method
3515	SIP REFER method

SIP shares a familial resemblance to both Hypertext Transfer Protocol (HTTP) and Simple Mail Transfer Protocol (SMTP), which are both fundamental protocols used on the Internet—the former for World Wide Web communications and the latter for e-mail.

HTTP, SMTP, and SIP messages all consist of two major parts:

■ **A header section**—Contains many individual header fields that web servers, e-mail servers, and SIP entities use to fulfill the requirements of their respective protocols

■ **A body section**—Contains the payload information that HTTP, SMTP, and SIP endpoints actually attempt to render for the user

In the case of HTTP, the payload is most often HTML, the basis for web pages. In the case of SMTP, the payload is generally text-based e-mail, although graphical and audio content can also be provided via Multipurpose Internet Mail Extensions (MIME). In the case of SIP, the payload is generally Session Description Protocol (SDP), which, as should be familiar now, allows VoIP endpoints to negotiate IP addresses and ports for media communications using specific codecs.

SIP request and response messages are detailed in Appendix C.

Roles of SIP Elements

SIP divides the functions required for establishing sessions among several different types of elements. SIP strives to adhere to the end-to-end principle of the Internet, in which core elements serve the role in routing messages on behalf of smart elements at the edge of the network.

SIP defines the following entities:

- **User agents** (UA) are the edge elements that participate in sessions. IP phones, IP-to-circuit-switched gateways, and conferencing servers are all examples of SIP UAs.

    A SIP UA actually consists of two independent components—a user agent client (UAC) and a user agent server (UAS). Using SIP methods such as INVITE or SUBSCRIBE, UACs initiate sessions with SIP UASs, which issue responses to these messages. In the case of VoIP, because most devices both place and receive calls, VoIP endpoints provide both a UAS and UAC function.

- **Registrars** serve as repositories for SIP addresses and provide a lookup function that the SIP core can use to locate SIP UAs. SIP uses Internet-style Uniform Resource Identifier (URI) addressing, in which addresses can appear in the form *user@domain* or *user@IP address* (a sip: or sips: URI) or as a more traditional number (a tel: URI).

- **Redirect servers** are core elements that provide address translation services. When contacted by a UAC, redirect servers rewrite the address that the UAC is trying to contact and ask the UAC to contact this alternate destination (or destinations).

- **Proxy servers** are core elements that provide routing services. Although proxies can modify the SIP requests that they handle, they must do so according to rigorous rules defined in RFC 3261 (among others).

CallManager's SIP IP trunk serves as a signaling and media control interface to non-SIP–based devices such as SCCP IP phones, H.323 gateways, and MGCP gateways. As a result, CallManager is a SIP UA with both UAC and UAS functions.

Many call agents, CallManager included, can receive calls via one SIP interface and route calls out a different SIP interface. Unlike a SIP proxy, however, whose role primarily relies on transparent routing of SIP methods from endpoint to endpoint and whose function is to establish a single end-to-end session between the originator and its target, such call agents maintain two independent sessions, one from the originator to the call agent and one from the call agent to the target. This type of function is called a *back-to-back user agent* (B2BUA), and, when routing a call from one SIP interface to another, CallManager also fulfills this role.

SIP Call Flow

SIP is a transactional protocol. UACs issue certain methods that UASs issue responses to. Some responses are provisional and simply indicate that a given transaction is in the process of being handled. One provisional response is "180," for example, which simply indicates that the session target is being alerted. Other responses are final and terminate the transaction, typically either because the session was established (via a "200" message) or because the session could not be established.

SIP methods are not simply calls. For example, although an INVITE method might establish a voice call, it could also establish a data collaboration session. A SUBSCRIBE method doesn't establish a user-to-user communication session at all, but rather allows one UA to receive periodic notifications about the activities of another UA (or UAs). These notifications can relate to whether the target UA is establishing sessions of its own, whether the user of that UA is prepared to converse, or for several other purposes.

Table 4-11 indicates several different methods defined in SIP, the RFCs that define them, and a short description of their function.

Table 4-11   *SIP Methods*

Method	RFC	Description
INVITE	3261	Establishes a session (typically voice) between the UAC and UAS.
ACK	3261	Confirms establishment of a session between a UAC and UAS.
BYE	3261	Terminates an established session between a UAC and a UAS.
REGISTER	3261	Informs a registrar of a UA's contact addresses.
OPTIONS	3261	Allows a SIP element to find out the capabilities of another SIP element.
CANCEL	3261	When an INVITE is forking to multiple called parties (due to find-me-follow-me or shared line appearances) allows the UAC or intervening SIP proxy to "un-offer" the call.
PRACK	3262	Allows a UAC to confirm receipt of a provisional response.
SUBSCRIBE	3265	Allows a UAC to receive periodic state notification from a UAS.
NOTIFY	3265	Notifies a subscribed UAC of the state changes of a particular UA.
UPDATE	3311	Allows mid-session changes to the session's profile.
REFER	3515	Allows a UA in an established session to redirect the session to another UA, typically as part of a call transfer operation.

Currently CallManager supports only the following methods:

- INVITE

- BYE

- CANCEL

- ACK

- PRACK

- OPTIONS

- UPDATE

This list of methods permits CallManager to place basic calls but does not support call transfers initiated by SIP UAs contacted via the SIP trunk, to process MWI notifications delivered by SIP voice mail servers, or to process for general subscriptions (for presence or for call creation information) sent by SIP applications. Figure 4-25 illustrates a typical call flow between a UAC and a UAS.

In Figure 4-25, the caller issues an INVITE method to the target UAS. The INVITE method includes, in the body section of the message, a description of the type of session that the caller wants to establish, encoded in Session Description Protocol (SDP). The SDP indicates the IP address, IP port, and codecs that the caller wants to use for the destination. By specifying different SDPs, the caller can select different codec types (for voice or video or data collaboration), and by changing the body type to something entirely different, the caller can, in theory, establish a completely different type of session. The UAS of the SDP must accept at least one codec offered by the UAC, although it may also include additional codecs that it supports.

The target UAS receives the INVITE and wants to process it, so it first sends a "100 Trying" message, followed by a "180 Alerting" message when it rings the user and a "200 OK" message when the user answers. The "200 OK" doesn't actually map directly to an answer message like CONNECT in Q.931, but instead indicates that the target has decided to establish the session requested by the initial method, in this case an INVITE. The "200 OK" message contains the SDP for the target. Having exchanged media information, the UAC and UAS can begin sending media to each other.

The ACK method informs the UAS that its "200 OK" message was received, and conversation begins. At this point, and unlike other voice protocols, any proxy servers that have previously routed the call need not maintain any more state information. The transaction that was started with the INVITE method has completed.

Figure 4-25 *SIP Call Flow*

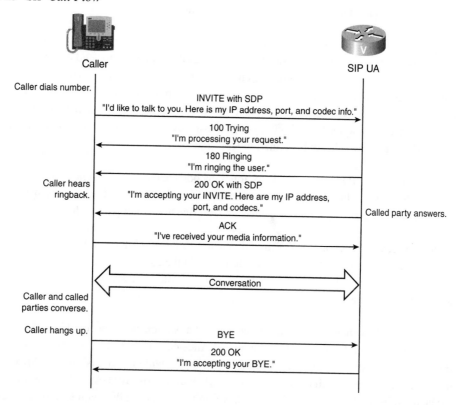

Caller

SIP UA

Caller dials number.

INVITE with SDP
"I'd like to talk to you. Here is my IP address, port, and codec info."

100 Trying
"I'm processing your request."

180 Ringing
"I'm ringing the user."

Caller hears
ringback.

200 OK with SDP
"I'm accepting your INVITE. Here are my IP address,
port, and codecs."

Called party answers.

ACK
"I've received your media information."

Conversation

Caller and called
parties converse.

Caller hangs up.

BYE

200 OK
"I'm accepting your BYE."

When the caller hangs up, the UAC purges the call by beginning another transaction. The BYE method allows a UAC to clear an existing session. The target UAS sends a "200 OK" message to confirm the session termination.

The call flow in Figure 4-25 represents a pure peer-to-peer SIP flow, but CallManager usually processes the call a little differently for three main reasons:

- Mid-call button presses

- Mid-call features

- Mid-call tones

Users often need to press keypad digits during a call to interact with telephony devices such as voice mail and IVRs. In the analog world, handling such events was reasonably straightforward. Terminal equipment converted the pressed button into a pair of pure tones that were simply played simultaneously directly into the voice channel. This encoding scheme is called *dual-tone multifrequency* (DTMF), and it is simply the tones that you might associate with touchpad dialing.

In the analog world, vendors placed tone detectors in the media path that listened for such tones and converted them into the appropriate menu selection.

In the digital world, things are more complicated. Several signaling paths exist that were not strictly available in the analog world. ISDN provides the capability for end equipment to place mid-call keypad presses in the signaling channel—thus bypassing the actual media channel entirely. H.323 provides a channel in the H.245 media control channel. Furthermore, with SIP, the encoding scheme comes almost full circle in that tones are encoded in the media channel—not as a traditional media payload itself, mind you, but as a special payload that communicates a signaled event. This encoding scheme is defined in RFC 2833.

Historically, Cisco IP Phones provide for tones encoded in the signaling channels but not via RTP. As a result, when CallManager needs to interwork Cisco IP Phones with SIP UAs that expect AVT tones, some conversion is required. However, CallManager is not part of the media path.

Furthermore, as the section "H.323" mentions, mid-call *media breaks* and *media makes* caused by features can be confusing to some VoIP endpoints. In the case of H.323, the introduction of an MTP allows endpoints that might not otherwise be capable of receiving an empty capability set to passively participate in features.

Finally, features such as transfer might require that a previously connected UA needs to revert to listening to some mid-call tone. For instance, if Alice calls Bob, Bob might choose to initiate a transfer. If Bob calls Charlie and completes the transfer while Charlie is ringing, Alice needs to hear ringback. After the call has been connected, however, most SIP UAs only allow you to change the characteristics of the media session. They don't necessarily allow you to suspend media and play some local tone. Therefore, if Charlie doesn't have the capability to play inband ringing, then Alice might listen to dead air until Charlie answers.

In all three cases, CallManager uses an MTP to work around the problem. CallManager allows you to configure a SIP trunk to use an MTP. As a result, a typical SIP call placed through CallManager looks as described by Figure 4-26.

In Figure 4-26, CallManager provides not the IP port and address of the originator, but instead provides the IP address and port of a selected MTP. The MTP performs the necessary interworking of the following:

■ Empty capability set for mid-call feature invocations by the Cisco IP Phone

■ DTMF for RFC 2833 to signaling-band tones

■ Call progress tones when a Cisco IP Phone invokes mid-call features

Figure 4-26 *CallManager SIP Call Flow*

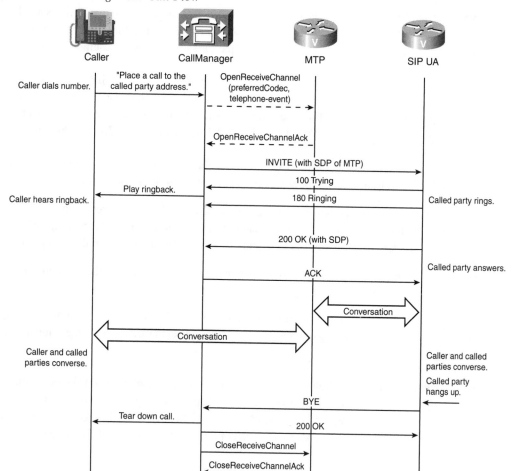

SIP UA-Initiated Features

Although the insertion of an MTP allows Cisco SCCP IP Phones to fully access all CallManager features, the limited set of methods supported by the SIP IP trunk prevents SIP UAs from invoking many features. However, such UAs can still access the following features:

- Hold and resume

- Call forwarding

- Presentation and restriction of calling line, calling name, connected line, and connected name

The sections that follow detail these features.

Hold and Resume

In SIP, the hold and resume features are media-level events. An endpoint that initiates a hold request asks the far end to suspend streaming media to it while suspending streaming media to the far end, and an endpoint that initiates a resume request asks the far end to resume streaming media.

SIP carries the media characteristics of the session in the body section of SIP messages, encoded in SDP. On an established session, a SIP UA that wants to initiate hold issues a new INVITE containing the dialog identifier for the existing session. The method of issuing a new INVITE on an existing session is termed a reINVITE. This reINVITE specifies one of three values in the SDP:

■   An a-line that indicates that the UA wants to set the mode of the conversation to inactive (while retaining the existing IP address and port information for the RTP).

■   An a-line that indicates that the UA wants to set the mode of the conversation to sendOnly while retaining the existing IP address and port information for the RTP. Setting the mode to sendOnly allows the holding UA to potentially stream music on hold to the held party.

■   A c-line that temporarily sets the IP address and port information for the communications session to 0.0.0.0.

The resume operation is a nearly identical operation, except that instead of changing the mode to inactive or sendOnly or zeroing out the IP address, the retrieving UA restores the original media information.

MTPs enable UAs to invoke hold and retrieve. (The MTP also insulates SIP UAs from hold and retrieve operations from Cisco SCCP IP Phones.) When processing hold from a SIP UA, CallManager suspends only the SIP UA-to-MTP stream while retaining the media stream between the held party and the MTP. CallManager does not introduce music on hold in these situations.

Call Forwarding

SIP UAs can provide call forwarding functionality via the 3xx series of provisional responses. When receiving an INVITE, if a SIP UA wants to divert the call, it can send a "302 Moved Temporarily" message. The originating UA is expected to issue INVITEs to the destination or destinations specified in the response.

CallManager's SIP trunk supports 302 and other 3xx messages. However, the processing for these messages occurs solely at the trunk itself—CallManager does not compare the redirection target against any provisioned phones, translation patterns, or route patterns. Instead, the SIP trunk consults DNS and issues the INVITE to the resulting IP address.

Presentation and Restriction of Calling Line, Calling Name, Connected Line, and Connected Name

For a fairly long, awkward feature name, this set of features is really quite straightforward. It's nothing more or less than caller ID and connected ID and your ability to decide whether the caller or called party gets to see the name, the number, neither, or both.

Calling and connected name describe the presentation of the name of the appropriate party, and calling and connected line relate to the phone number of the appropriate party.

SIP uses addresses in the form of *user@domain*, but just as in e-mail, the headers that contain this information provide you with the ability to indicate a display name. Therefore, if Alice is calling from 1000 in the cisco.com domain, the From: header of a SIP method might look like this:

```
From: "Alice" <1000@cisco.com>
```

SIP addresses can occur in any number of SIP header fields, but for line and name ID services with CallManager, only three are relevant:

■ The **From: header** indicates the originator of a SIP transaction. This field is a basic RFC 3261 header. All SIP UAs support it. When receiving a call, some UAs will render the information in this header as the caller ID.

■ The **To: header** indicates the target of a SIP transaction. This field is a basic RFC 3261 header. All SIP UAs support it. When receiving a call, some UAs will render the information in this header as the caller ID.

■ The **Remote-Party-Id header** is defined in an expired IETF draft that will never become a standard. This draft defines a new header whose purpose is specifically for calling and connected line and name ID. Unlike the From: and To: headers, this header takes into account the privacy of the caller and called parties by defining URI tags to indicate how the destination UA should or should not render the information. Although this header is not a formal standard, it is a de facto standard in the industry and no fully baked standardized approach to calling and called party ID services currently exists.

As Chapter 2 describes, call restriction settings exist on route patterns, translation patterns, and the device pages. The accepted values of these presentation fields are Allowed, Restricted, and Default. If the gateway setting is Allowed or Restricted, this value takes precedence. If set to Default, the gateway level uses the setting on the route or translation pattern. (If the value on the route or translation pattern is also Default, the resulting value is whatever the caller provided.)

When encoding a line number in for caller or connected ID purposes, CallManager places the number in the user portion of the *user@domain* URI. CallManager encodes name information in the accompanying text description section.

The Remote-Party-Id header provides URI tags that allow a UA to indicate whether the name or number privacy should be honored. When the name is restricted but not the number, CallManager sets the privacy tag to *name*; when the number is restricted but not the name, CallManager sets the privacy tag to *uri*; and when both are restricted, CallManager sets the privacy tag to *full*.

Because the From: header permits no such tags, when the name is restricted, CallManager encodes it as "Anonymous", and, when the number is restricted, CallManager doesn't encode a user part at all.

Table 4-12 illustrates the possible encoding values from the From: and Remote-Party-Id headers.

Table 4-12   *SIP Calling ID Restriction*

Restrictions	Header Encoding
Name allowed, number allowed	From: "Alice" <sip:1000@10.1.1.1> Remote-Party-Id: "Alice" <sip:1000@10.1.1.1>; party=calling;screening=none;privacy=none
Name allowed, number restricted	From: "Alice" <sip: 10.1.1.1> Remote-Party-Id: "Alice" <sip:1000@10.1.1.1>; party=calling;screening=none;privacy=none
Name restricted, number allowed	From: "Anonymous" <sip:1000@10.1.1.1> Remote-Party-Id: "Alice" <sip:1000@10.1.1.1>; party=calling;screening=none;privacy=name
Name and number restricted	From: "Anonymous" <sip: 10.1.1.1> Remote-Party-Id: "Alice" <sip:1000@10.1.1.1>; party=calling;screening=none;privacy=full

SIP Timers and Retry Counts

CallManager's SIP trunk operates over UDP, which is an inherently unreliable method of delivering IP messages. As a result, SIP incorporates timers and retries so that it can retransmit messages that have not been acknowledged under the assumption that those messages might have been lost.

CallManager enables you to configure the values for SIP timers and the number of retries in service parameters. Tables 4-13 and 4-14 present the service parameters, their default values, and a short description of the appropriate settings.

Table 4-13 *SIP Timer Service Parameters*

Parameter	Default	Description
SIP Trying Timer	500 ms	The amount of time CallManager should wait for a called UA to issue a 100 Trying after CallManager issues an INVITE.
SIP Connect Timer	500 ms	The amount of time CallManager should wait for a called UA to issue a 200 OK after CallManager issues an ACK.
SIP Disconnect Timer	500 ms	The amount of time CallManager should wait for a called UA to issue a 200 OK after CallManager issues a BYE.
SIP Expires Timer	180 s	The amount of time that CallManager can leave an unconfirmed INVITE outstanding; the call must be answered within this duration or CallManager clears the call.
SIP Rel1XX Timer	500 ms	The amount of time CallManager should wait before retransmitting a reliable 1XX response that has not been PRACKed.
SIP PRACK Timer	500 ms	The amount of time CallManager should wait for a called UA to issue a 200 OK after CallManager issues a PRACK.

Table 4-14 *SIP Retry Count Service Parameters*

Parameter	Default	Description
Retry Count for SIP BYE	10	When running UDP, the number of times CallManager should retransmit a BYE that has not received a 200 OK.
Retry Count for SIP CANCEL	10	When running UDP, the number of times CallManager should retransmit a CANCEL that has not received a 200 OK.
Retry Count for SIP INVITE	5	When running UDP, the number of times CallManager should retransmit an INVITE that has not received a 200 OK.
Retry Count for SIP PRACK	6	When running UDP, the number of times CallManager should retransmit a PRACK that has not received a 200 OK.
Retry Count for SIP Rel1XX	10	The maximum number of times CallManager retransmits an unacknowledged reliable 1XX response.
Retry Count for SIP Response	6	The maximum number of times CallManager retransmits an unacknowledged 1XX response.

Summary

This chapter examined the role of gateways in the CallManager architecture. Gateways bridge the gap between the packet-switched network and the circuit-switched network. This chapter described the circuit-switch technologies Cisco gateways support and the VoIP protocols H.323, MGCP, and SIP, which CallManager uses to talk to gateways and to other CallManagers. In addition, this chapter detailed the role of the gatekeeper and RAS, the H.323 gatekeeper communication protocol.

CHAPTER 5

Media Processing

This chapter attempts to cover everything you ever wanted to know about media processing resources and media connection processing, but were afraid to ask. It might not answer all the questions you have on the subject, but it should at least discuss the salient points and provide insight into how media streams are controlled and handled by Cisco CallManager.

Software applications such as Cisco MeetingPlace are not discussed in this chapter. Although MeetingPlace is a very powerful and useful system, has many useful functions and uses CallManager to connect calls to its conference bridges, it does not register with CallManager and cannot be controlled by CallManager directly. Because CallManager cannot allocate or control conference bridges or any other facilities provided by MeetingPlace, it is not discussed in this chapter; this chapter focuses on devices controlled directly by CallManager.

There are two signaling layers within CallManager. Each signaling layer has distinct functions. The Call Control Layer handles all the normal call signaling that controls call setup, teardown, and call routing. The second signaling layer is the Media Control Layer, which handles all media connection signaling required to connect the voice and video paths or media streams of the calls.

This chapter focuses on the Media Control Layer and is divided into two major sections:

- **Media Processing Overview**—Provides a general overview of media processing devices and how media connections are established between them. It also covers media resource allocation and control.

- **Architecture and Functionality of the Media Control Layer**—Offers more detailed information on the architecture and functionality of media processing and the related devices in CallManager. Each type of device is detailed and how it is connected and used by CallManager. Call preservation, which is the ability to maintain media connections (voice and video paths) in the event of failures, is also discussed.

> **NOTE** Chapter 3, "Station Devices," and Chapter 4, "Trunk Devices," cover call control signaling for both phones and gateways.

Figure 5-1 shows the block structure of CallManager.

Figure 5-1 *CallManager Block Structure Diagram*

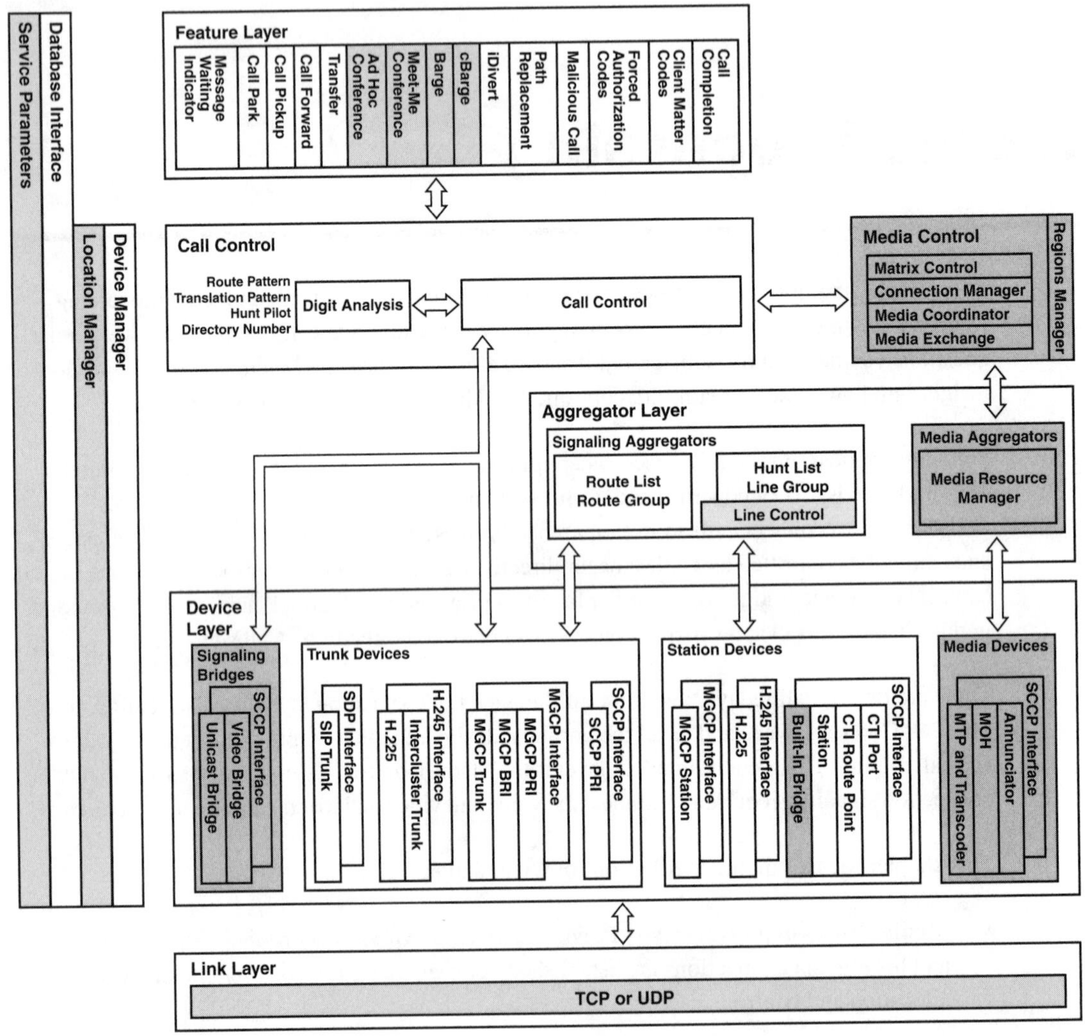

Figure 5-1 highlights the software layers and blocks within CallManager that are described in detail in this chapter. Other blocks are touched on lightly but are not highlighted because they are not covered in detail here.

The software in the Media Control Layer handles all media connections that are made between devices in CallManager. The Call Control Layer sets up and controls all the call signaling connections between call endpoints and CallManager. The Media Control Layer directs the devices to establish streaming connections among themselves. It can insert other necessary media processing devices into a call and create appropriate streaming connections to those devices without the Call Control Layer knowing about them.

The Media Control Layer becomes involved in a call when the Call Control Layer notifies the Media Control Layer that a call has been connected between two endpoints. The Media Control Layer then proceeds to establish the media streaming connections between the endpoints as required to set up the voice path for that call.

In some cases, the media streaming connections are established before the call is connected. CallManager connects the media streams early such as when a call is destined for the public switched telephone network (PSTN) through a gateway. The caller then hears the progress tones and announcements from the PSTN telling them what happened to the call such as ringback tone, busy tone, "The number you have called is not a working number", or "All circuits are busy now. Please hang up."

If the endpoints in the call report video capabilities, CallManager checks the locations bandwidth and if it allows video, it automatically attempts to open a video channel between the endpoints for the call. Whether or not video is actually sent on that channel depends on the video mute setting of the endpoint devices involved and whether sufficient bandwidth is available.

The blocks highlighted in the Protocol/Aggregation layers of Figure 5-1 are those that control the media processing devices. They provide the device interface and handle all communication between the devices and CallManager.

The *Media Resource Manager* (MRM) is a software component in CallManager that handles all resource allocation and de-allocation. When call processing or a supplementary service determines that a media processing resource of a particular type is needed, the request is sent to the MRM. The MRM finds an available resource of the requested type, allocates the resource, and returns the resource identification information to the requestor.

Media Processing Overview

CallManager controls the voice paths and other media connections such as video streams for all calls handled by CallManager. The *Media Control Layer* (MCL) is responsible for making all of these connections through the underlying network (LAN or WAN). The MCL is a signaling layer that signals between CallManager and the endpoint devices and instructs the devices on how to set up appropriate media streaming connections. The MCL itself does not process or handle the actual media streams. This is important because CallManager nodes do not get bogged down by processing all the streaming data from the thousands of calls being processed.

System administrators and, to a lesser extent, the users of the system are directly aware and have control over some endpoints. They are only indirectly aware or not aware at all of other endpoints that might be involved in a call. The user, for example, is directly aware of IP phones as endpoints in a call, indirectly aware of conference bridges and music on hold (MOH) servers, and not aware at all of transcoders, media termination points (MTP), gateways, and other such devices. In many cases, only the MCL is actually aware of all devices that are involved in a particular call and how the devices are connected. The connections between the devices create the voice and video paths for a call.

The major topics for this section are as follows:

- Definition of Common Terms and Concepts Used in Voice over IP (VoIP)

- Media Processing Resource Types

- Understanding Media Processing Resources

- Controlling the Allocation and Usage of Media Processing Resources

Definition of Common Terms and Concepts Used in Voice over IP

This definition section is not exhaustive, but it covers the most important concepts and terms relevant to this chapter.

Logical Channels

A *logical channel* is a streaming data connection between two endpoints. A logical channel, in effect, is a pipeline through the data network between two endpoints that carries streaming data.

As an analogy, a home contractor builds the water pipes in a home and constructs a pipeline between the home and the city water supply. After the pipeline connecting the city water supply and the new home has been completed, the contractor is finished. The city then supplies the water that flows through the pipeline to the new home.

In a similar fashion, CallManager directs the construction of the logical channel or "pipeline" through the data network, and the endpoints then control the data that flows through that logical channel. CallManager itself does not create the logical channels. Instead, it directs the construction of the logical channels by supplying the parameters and instructing the endpoints how to construct each logical channel and where to connect it.

When creating a logical channel, the creating entity specifies parameters that establish what kind of data is transported through that logical channel, in which direction it is transported, the size of the data stream, and so forth. All voice, video, fax, and other data streams are transported through these logical channels. Multiple logical channels can exist between any two endpoints.

The endpoints in a voice call, for example, are instructed to establish either one or two simplex (one-way) logical channels between them. One logical channel carries the voice data stream from the calling party to the called party, and the other carries the voice data stream from the called party back to the calling party. CallManager sometimes instructs an endpoint device, such as a Cisco IP

Phone, to create other logical channels such as video channels between themselves and other endpoints.

In another case, endpoint devices might be instructed to create one or more logical channels between themselves and a media processing resource, such as a conference bridge or a transcoder. This mechanism is used to create conferences and to provide MOH and other similar applications.

Voice Codecs

A *voice codec* is either a hardware or a software entity that converts an analog audio source into a digitized data stream, and vice versa. The codec packages the digitized data into a stream of data packets, each of which contains digitized voice data and is generated or sent at regular intervals. When silence suppression is enabled, variable numbers of bytes of data per interval can be generated, and it is possible that no packets of data are generated during silence. The interval at which codecs create and send data packets depends on the configuration of the packet sizes for each codec. You can set these configuration parameters through the Service Parameters page in Cisco CallManager Administration (**Service > Service Parameters >** *select a server >* **Cisco CallManager**). Table 5-1 defines the service parameters for controlling codec packet generation and their possible values in milliseconds.

Table 5-1   *Codec Packet Size*

Service Parameter	Set of Possible Values	Default Value
Preferred G711 Millisecond Packet Size	10 ms, 20 ms, 30 ms	20 ms
Preferred G729 Millisecond Packet Size	10 ms, 20 ms, 30 ms, 40 ms, 50 ms, 60 ms	20 ms
Preferred G723 Millisecond Packet Size	30 ms, 60 ms	30 ms
Preferred GSM EFR Bytes Packet Size	31 bytes, 32 bytes	31 bytes

NOTE   Changing the packet size that a codec generates can have both positive and negative effects on the system. In general, the smaller the packet size, the less latency you have in the voice stream, and the more bandwidth and processing power it takes to handle the increased packet load. The larger the packet size, the more latency you have in the voice stream, and the less bandwidth and processing power it takes to process the data stream.

In this chapter, all information about capacities for media processing devices, such as conference bridges bandwidth consumed in the network, is based on the default packet size for the codecs.

Codecs normally exist in endpoint devices such as IP phones, gateways, and media processing devices. The codec in a given IP phone converts the caller's voice from analog audio into a stream of data packets referred to as a *voice data stream* or a *media stream*. This stream of data packets is then routed to the other endpoint through a logical channel that has previously been established.

Different voice codecs are available and each codec follows a specific algorithm to convert analog voice into digital data. CallManager supports several different voice codec types, including the following:

- G.711

- G.722

- G.723

- G.726

- G.728

- G.729

- GSM

- Wideband

Each of these codecs produces a different set of digital data. G.723, G.729a, and GSM are classified as low-bandwidth codecs, and G.711 and wideband are considered high-bandwidth codecs. G.722 and G.728 are normally used in conjunction with video streams. Table 5-2 lists some common voice codecs used in the packet-switched world and describes the amount of bandwidth each consumes. G.722 and G.726 have multiple entries in Table 5-2 because these codec algorithms can be used at various bitrates. The bandwidths CallManager uses are listed in the table, and depending on the bandwidth in use, the codec will adapt.

Table 5-2 *Bandwidth Consumption by Voice Codec Type*

Type of Codec	Bandwidth Used for Data Packets Only	Bandwidth Used per Call (Including IP Headers) with 30 ms Data Packets	Bandwidth Used per Call (Including IP Headers) with 20 ms Data Packets
G.711	64 kbps	80 kbps	88 kbps
G.721	32 kbps	48 kbps	56 kbps
G.722	48 kbps	64 kbps	72 kbps
G.722	56 kbps	72 kbps	80 kbps
G.722	64 kbps	80 kbps	88 kbps

Table 5-2   *Bandwidth Consumption by Voice Codec Type (Continued)*

Type of Codec	Bandwidth Used for Data Packets Only	Bandwidth Used per Call (Including IP Headers) with 30 ms Data Packets	Bandwidth Used per Call (Including IP Headers) with 20 ms Data Packets
G.723	6.3 kbps	22.3 kbps	Not applicable
G.726	32 kbps	48 kbps	56 kbps
G.726	24 kbps	40 kbps	48 kbps
G.726	16 kbps	32 kbps	40 kbps
G.728	16 kbps	32 kbps	40 kbps
G.729a	8 kbps	24 kbps	32 kbps
GSM	13 kbps	29 kbps	37 kbps
Wideband*	256 kbps	272 kbps	280 kbps

*Wideband is not the same as G.722.

The most popular voice coding standards for telephony and packet voice include the following:

- **G.711 (A-law and μ-law)**—G.711 codecs encode the voice stream in the correct format for digital voice delivery in the PSTN. The processing requirements for encoding and decoding G.711 are very low, which makes it suitable for software-only implementations.

- **G.723.1**—G.723.1 is a low-bit-rate codec that provides good quality sound and has a stream rate of either 5.3 kbps or 6.3 kbps.

- **G.726**—A codec that provides high-quality voice, has varying stream rates that range from 16 kbps to 40 kbps, and is typically used in voice over packet gateways.

- **G.728**—A codec that is widely used for applications requiring very low algorithmic delay such as video and voice over DSL or voice over cable.

- **G.729a**—G.729a provides near toll-quality voice and provides a compressed stream bit rate of 8 kbps.

- **GSM**—GSM is a codec that is predominant in most of the world's cellular telephone systems. It provides a compressed stream rate of 13 kbps.

- **Wideband**—Wideband is a proprietary Cisco codec and is not the same as G.722. It produces a high-fidelity stream rate of 256 kbps. This codec is supported on Cisco IP Phones, software conference bridges, and MOH servers.

Video Codecs

A *video codec* is an entity that converts an analog video source into a digitized data stream, and vice versa. It is usually implemented on specialized hardware containing digital signal processors (DSP) and other support hardware. The codec packages the digitized data into a stream of data packets, each of which contains digitized video data and is generated or sent at regular intervals.

Video codecs normally exist in endpoint devices such as IP phones, H.323 video endpoints, conference servers, and other video-enabled devices. The codec in a given device converts the caller's video from analog video into a compressed stream of data packets of a specific format supported by that codec, and referred to generically as a *video data stream* or a *media stream*. This stream of data packets is then routed to the other endpoint through a logical channel that has previously been established.

Different video codecs exist, with each codec following a specific algorithm to convert video into digital data. CallManager supports video codec types H.261, H.263, and H.264. Each of these codecs implements a video standard and produces a different set of digital data. They are used for different purposes.

Video Standards

Some of the more popular video standards that CallManager supports and their usages are as follows:

- H.261 is a 1990 ITU video coding standard specifically designed for transmission over ISDN lines in that the data rates are multiples of 64 kbps. The standard supports Common Intermediate Format (CIF) and Quarter Common Intermediate Format (QCIF) video frames at resolutions of 352×288 and 176×144 respectively. The data rate of the coding algorithm was designed to be able to be set to between 40 kbps and 2 Mbps.

- H.263 is a video codec designed by the ITU-T as a low-bit-rate encoding solution for video conferencing. H.263 was first designed to be utilized in H.323-based systems, but now is finding use in streaming media via Real Time Streaming Protocol (RTSP) and Internet conferencing via SIP, too. H.263 is a suitable replacement for H.261.

- H.264 is a high-compression digital video codec standard written by the ITU-T Video Coding Experts Group (VCEG) together with the ISO/IEC Moving Picture Experts Group (MPEG) is the product of a collective effort known as the Joint Video Team (JVT). This standard is identical to ISO MPEG-4 part 10, also known as Advanced Video Coding (AVC). The final drafting work on the standard was completed in May 2003.

- T.120 is an ITU standard comprised of a suite of communication and application protocols. Using these protocols, developers can create compatible products and services for real-time, multipoint data connections and conferencing. With T.120-based programs, multiple users can participate in conferencing sessions over different types of networks and connections. You can collaborate using compatible data conferencing features such as program sharing, whiteboard conferencing, and file transfer.

- H.320 is an ITU umbrella standard that defines how real-time multimedia communications and conferencing are handled over switched or dedicated ISDN telecommunication links. The H.320 standard includes the following:

  — Audio: G.711, G.722, G.722.1, G.728

  — Video: H.264, H.263, H.261

  — Data: H.239, T.120

  — Control: H.221, H.231, H.242, H.243

- H.323 is an umbrella set of standards defining real-time multimedia communications and conferencing over packet switched networks. First adopted in 1996, H.323 borrowed many of the H.32x standards used by H.320, especially those for encoding/decoding the audio/video streams and the data sharing protocol (T.120), but it defined a new set for handling communication over the Internet.

Silence Suppression

Silence suppression is the capability to suppress or reduce the RTP packet flow on the network when silence is detected during a phone call. Silence suppression may also be called *voice activity detection* (VAD). When enabled, endpoints, such as Cisco IP Phones or gateways, detect periods of silence or pauses in voice activity and either stop sending normal RTP packets or reduce the number of packets sent during these pauses in a phone conversation. This reduces the number of RTP packets on the network and, thus, bandwidth consumed during the call.

To mask the silence suppression, the endpoint can play comfort noise. *Comfort noise* is also called white noise or background noise and is meant to make the user feel more comfortable that the call is still active while audio is being suppressed. Without comfort noise, the user might hear total silence. Some endpoints are capable of generating *pink noise*, which is background noise that resembles the background sounds from the current call.

Three service parameters control silence suppression, as shown in Table 5-3.

Table 5-3 *CallManager Service Parameters That Control Silence Suppression*

Service Parameter	Set of Possible Values	Default Value	Definition
Silence Suppression	True or False	True	Enables or disables silence suppression for all devices on a cluster wide basis.
Silence Suppression for Gateways	True or False	True	Enables or disables silence suppression for all gateways.
Strip G.729 Annex B (Silence Suppression) from Capabilities	True or False	True	If set to True, it removes silence suppression capability for G.729 codecs.

If users complain about the silence during a phone call or the comfort noise generated to replace it, you can disable silence suppression by setting the CallManager service parameters to False, and the calls will sound more natural. However, the calls will consume more bandwidth.

IP Phone

An IP phone in CallManager refers to a telephone device that contains, among other things, a digital signal processor (DSP), and another processor chip such as an ARM Risc processor. An IP phone can be plugged directly into an Ethernet port and looks like a standard network device to the network. An IP phone has an IP address, a Media Access Control (MAC) address, and is capable of using Dynamic Host Configuration Protocol (DHCP) and other standard network facilities.

During a call that is connected between two IP phones, each IP phone uses its codec (DSP) to create its own outgoing voice data stream. The voice data stream is sent through a logical channel to the other IP phone or other device to which it is connected. The IP phones also use their codecs (DSPs) to process the incoming voice data stream from the other IP phone or other endpoint device.

CallManager instructs each of the two IP phones to create a Transmit Logical Channel and a Receive Port between itself and the other IP phone in the call. The Transmit Logical Channel of one IP phone is connected to the Receive Port of the other IP phone.

Some IP phones can use their DSPs as a small conference bridge capable of supporting up to three participants. This capability is used by the barge feature.

If both endpoints in a call support video, CallManager can also instruct each of the two endpoints to create video channels between them.

Media Termination Point

A *media termination point* (MTP) is a software-based or hardware-based media processing resource that accepts two full-duplex stream connections. It bridges the media streams between the two connections and allows the streaming connections to be set up and torn down independently. An MTP might also be used to perform other processing on a media stream, such as digit detection and insertion (as defined in RFC 2833).

Transcode

To *transcode* is to convert a voice data stream from one codec type to another codec type. For example, transcoding G.729a to G.711 means to convert the G.729a data stream produced by one codec into a G.711 data stream consumed by another codec. Transcoding might also be used to change the sampling rate between two streams produced by the same type of codec.

Transcoder

A *transcoder* is a hardware-based device that takes the output stream of one codec and converts it in real time (transcodes it) into an input stream for a different codec type. In addition, a transcoder also provides the capabilities of an MTP and can be used to enable supplementary services for H.323 endpoints when required.

Call Leg

The term *call leg* is used when referring to a call signaling connection between two entities. In CallManager, the term refers to a call signaling connection between CallManager and an endpoint device. In a standard call (one that does not involve any media processing devices) between two IP phones, for example, there are two call legs: one between the originating IP phone and CallManager, and the other between CallManager and the destination IP phone.

This chapter does not discuss call legs because media connections are made point to point between two endpoints. They do not follow the call legs in that there are no media connections established between CallManager and the endpoints in a call. The MCL establishes all media connections, and it is not aware of the call signaling connections being processed in the Call Control Layer of CallManager.

Media Processing Resource Types

CallManager provides access to a variety of media resources. All media resources that are registered to any CallManager node in the cluster are made available to all CallManager nodes within the cluster.

A media processing resource is a software-based or hardware-based entity that performs some media processing function on the data streams that are connected to it. Media processing functions include mixing multiple streams to create one output stream, passing the stream from one connection to another, or transcoding the data stream from one codec type to another.

CallManager allocates and uses six types of media resources:

- Unicast conferencing resources
- MTP resources
- Transcoding resources
- MOH resources
- Annunciator resources
- Built-in bridge resources

This section discusses each of these resource types and explains their basic operation and purpose in the system.

Unicast Conferencing Resources

A *Unicast conference bridge* is a device that accepts multiple connections for a given conference. It can accept any number of connections for a given conference, up to the maximum number of participants allowed for a single conference on that device. There is a one-to-one correspondence between full-duplex media streams connected to a conference and participants connected to the conference. The conference bridge mixes the input streams together and creates a unique output stream for each connected party. The output stream for a given party is usually the composite of the input streams from all connected parties minus their own input stream. Some conference bridges mix only the three loudest talkers on the conference and distribute that composite stream to each participant (minus their own input stream if they were one of the talkers).

A Unicast conference server supports more than one conference bridge and is either hardware-based or software-based. CallManager allocates a conference bridge from a conference server that is registered with the cluster. Both hardware-based and software-based conference servers can be registered with CallManager at the same time, and CallManager can allocate and use conference bridges from both of them. Hardware-based and software-based conference servers have different capabilities. Some hardware-based conference servers can conference streams from different codecs together, although other hardware-based conference servers cannot. A software conference server is only able to conference streams from G.711 and wideband codecs.

Some station devices also have a DSP capable of supporting a small three-party G.711 conference. This conference bridge is allocated and used by the barge feature. CallManager knows about the station-based conference bridges, but it allocates the station-based bridge only when processing a barge request that is targeted for that station device. To use the station-based conference bridge in a barge operation, the **Barge** softkey must be used.

For features used to set up conferences such as Ad Hoc or Meet-Me conferences or Join, CallManager always allocates system-based conference resources. CallManager does not distinguish between the types of system-based conference bridges when a conference-allocation request is processed. CallManager cannot specifically allocate a hardware conference bridge or a software conference bridge or a videoconference bridge directly. It simply allocates a conference bridge from the pool of conference resources available to the device for which the conference bridge is being allocated.

You have control over the types of conference resources that are in the pool of resources available to a particular device. The section "Controlling the Allocation and Usage of Media Resources" covers this in detail. If you know that a particular endpoint, such as a gateway, normally needs a hardware conference bridge to take advantage of its mixed-stream conferencing capabilities, you could configure CallManager so that the gateway only has access to hardware conference resources. The same applies to video-capable endpoints or any particular group of devices that would normally need a particular resource type. You could also configure the device, or set of devices, so that it has access to software conference resources only after all hardware conference resources have been allocated, or any other arrangement that seems appropriate.

CallManager allocates a Unicast conference bridge when a user presses the **Confrn**, **MeetMe**, **Join**, or **cBarge** softkey on the phone. If no conference resources are available to that phone when the user presses the softkey, the request is ignored and no conference or barge is started. Unicast conference bridges can be used for both Ad Hoc and Meet-Me conferences.

Software-Based Unicast Conference Bridge

A *software Unicast bridge* is a standard conference mixer and is capable of mixing G.711 and wideband audio streams. Both G.711 A-law and G.711 μ-law streams can be connected to the same conference. The number of parties that can be supported on a given conference depends on the server where the conference bridge software is running and the configuration for that device. Because G.711 μ-law is the most common format in the United States, wideband and G.711 A-law streams are converted to G.711 μ-law before being sent to the mixer. The output streams from the mixer are returned to the endpoint as a μ-law stream, or converted back into G.711 A-law or wideband as required for a particular endpoint.

Hardware-Based Unicast Conference Bridge

A *hardware conference bridge* has all the capabilities of a software conference bridge. In addition, some hardware conference bridges can support multiple low-bit-rate stream types such as G.729a, GSM, or G.723. This allows some hardware conference bridges to handle mixed-mode conferences. In a mixed-mode conference, the hardware conference bridge transcodes G.729a, GSM, and G.723 streams into G.711 streams, mixes them, and then encodes the resulting stream into the appropriate stream type for transmission back to the user. Some hardware conference bridges support only G.711 conferences.

Hardware-Based Videoconference Bridge

A video conference bridge has all the capabilities of a hardware conference bridge. In addition, video bridges support H.261, H.263, H.320, or other video streams. A video conference bridge supports mixed conference types. A conference can be composed of all video endpoints, all audio endpoints, or a combination of video and audio endpoints.

Media Termination Points (MTP)

An *MTP* is an entity that accepts two full-duplex stream connections. The streaming data received from the input stream on one connection is passed to the output stream on the other connection, and vice versa. In addition, software-based MTPs transcode A-law to μ-law, and vice versa, and adjust packet sizes as required by the two connections. Hardware-based MTPs (transcoders) can also transcode data streams between two different codec types when needed. Some MTPs have the additional capability of supporting Dual-Tone Multi-Frequency (DTMF) detection and generation for SIP calls as specified in RFC 2833.

Figure 5-2 illustrates the connections to and usage of an MTP. MTPs are used to extend supplementary services to SIP endpoints and H.323 endpoints that do not support empty capability sets. When needed, an MTP is allocated and connected into a call on behalf of these endpoints. When the MTP is inserted, the media streams are connected between the MTP and the SIP or H.323 device and are not torn down for the duration of the call. The media streams connected to the other side of the MTP can be connected and torn down as needed to implement features such as hold, transfer, and so forth. There are both hardware- and software-based MTPs. Hardware MTPs are really transcoders being used as MTPs.

Figure 5-2   *MTP*

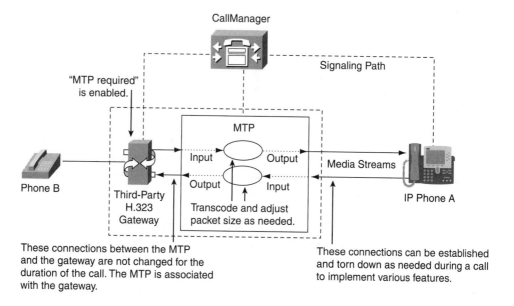

These connections between the MTP
and the gateway are not changed for the
duration of the call. The MTP is associated
with the gateway.

These connections can be established
and torn down as needed during a call
to implement various features.

Software-Based MTP

A *software-based MTP* is a device that is implemented by installing the Cisco IP Voice Media
Streaming App on a server. When the installed application is configured as an MTP application, it
registers with a CallManager node and tells CallManager how many MTP resources it supports.

A single software-based MTP device can handle many more calls than its hardware counterpart,
but it can only handle G.711 and wideband codecs. Software-based MTPs also support tone
detection and generation as specified in RFC 2833 for SIP endpoints. They also enable playing
tones as needed to endpoints in a call.

Hardware-Based MTP

A *hardware-based MTP* is a device that is implemented on a hardware blade that is plugged into
a hardware-switching platform, such as a Catalyst 6000 or a Catalyst 4000. Some Cisco IOS
platforms such as the 3700s, 2800s, and 3800s also support hardware MTPs. A hardware-based
MTP is really a transcoder being used as an MTP, because transcoders have MTP capabilities. The
device registers with a CallManager node as a transcoder and tells CallManager how many
resources it supports. Some hardware-based MTPs can also support transcoding operations
between connected endpoints. Transcoders when used as MTPs have the capability of handling

more codecs, such as G.729, G.723, and GSM. The codecs supported by a given hardware-based MTP vary depending on its transcoding capabilities.

Music on Hold (MOH) Resources

MOH resources are provided by software-based MOH servers that register with CallManager as MOH servers. MOH servers are configured through CallManager Administration, as are the other media processing devices.

Up to 51 different audio sources can be configured on the MOH servers. All MOH servers in the cluster have the same MOH source configuration. This allows CallManager to connect a held device to any MOH server in the cluster, and it receives the same audio source stream regardless of which server provides it.

A given IP phone can be connected to any available MOH output stream port, and the MOH server will connect the requested audio source to the output stream port where the IP phone is connected. The MOH server can have up to 50 different source files on its disk for each codec type that it supports, and when a particular source is requested, it streams the audio data from the source file through the designated output stream port. It is possible to connect all MOH output stream ports to the same audio source.

One fixed source is always identified as source 51. Source 51 is connected to a fixed source, usually a sound card, in the server. Any sound source that can be attached to the sound card can then provide the audio stream for source 51.

Each MOH server can supply up to 500 Unicast output audio streams or up to 204 Multicast audio streams. It can supply both stream types simultaneously, but the total stream count including both types cannot exceed the maximum. The number of streams that can be supported by a given server depends on such things as the speed of the server and which other services are running on that server. These maximum stream counts can only be achieved using high-end dedicated servers. In most cases, Cisco recommends configuring the servers with a smaller stream count. If the server has a security agent installed (even if it is deactivated) the maximum stream counts are normally about half the maximum values that would normally be supported by that server. You need to consider these factors along with server capabilities and the network infrastructure when configuring MOH servers.

When generating Multicast streams, each Multicast output stream requires a different audio source stream. Each audio source can supply an audio stream for each of the four different codecs that are supported. Thus, you can have up to 204 Multicast streams. If a single codec is used then a maximum of 51 Multicast sources can be used. The number 204 comes from 51 audio sources times 4 codecs each.

Annunciator Resources

Annunciator resources are provided by software-based servers that register with CallManager as annunciator servers. Annunciator servers are configured through CallManager Administration, as are the other media processing devices. Each annunciator can supply up to 400 simultaneous streams of either tones or announcements. Tones and announcements are considered the same as far as the annunciator is concerned.

All annunciators in the cluster have the same audio files. This allows CallManager to allocate an annunciator from any server that is available to play either a tone or an announcement. Annunciators can be connected to IP phones, gateways, MTPs, conference bridges, and other devices to inject either audio announcements or tones as required.

Announcements can be localized, allowing them to be used in different countries and locales. When a locale is installed on CallManager, the announcements and tones are associated with that locale. Two types of locales are installed on CallManager:

■ User locale

■ Network locale

Tones are installed as part of a network locale such as China or Taiwan, and announcements are installed as part of a user locale such as "Chinese (China)" or "Chinese (Taiwan)." Figure 5-3 illustrates a cluster of two CallManagers with media resources.

Figure 5-3 *A Cluster of Two CallManagers with Media Resources*

All resources are accessible by both CM1 and CM2

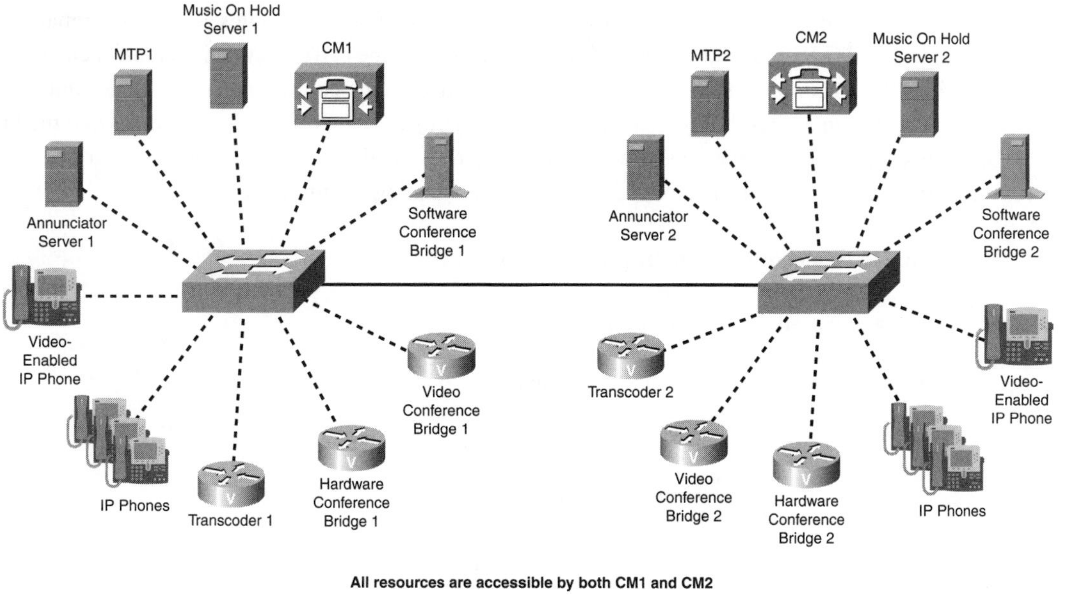

In Figure 5-3, a complement of media processing resources is registered with each of the CallManager nodes. Figure 5-3 illustrates that there can be both hardware-based media resources and software-based media resources in the same cluster and on the same CallManager node. All resources are available to both CallManager nodes, regardless of which one they are registered with.

Built-in Bridge Resources

Cisco IP Phones have an internal DSP that acts as a small conference bridge. This capability is referred to as a *built-in bridge*. The capability is used only to support the barge feature as described in Chapter 3. It can only support a maximum of three parties, including the phone itself as one of them. During barge operation (which is really a small three-party conference), this bridge supports only the G.711 codec. The built-in bridges are handled automatically by CallManager, and are not visible in the resource pools.

Understanding Media Processing Resources

To understand media processing resources, you must understand how voice, video, and other streaming data is generated and transported in VoIP networks. You also need to understand some of the basic system components, such as codecs, logical channels, and endpoints. This section assumes that you now have a general understanding of how the voice data streams are created and transported using these basic components. Chapter 1, "Cisco CallManager Architecture," explains the basics of VoIP.

Media processing devices in general do not support call signaling. Within the CallManager software, the device control process for a media processing device handles all the call signaling from the Call Control Layer for these devices, and none of the call signaling is actually sent to the devices. The media processing resources do understand media connection signaling. Media connection signaling is the signaling required to establish and control logical channels and media streams. The media processing resources are treated as standard devices as far as media connections are concerned, and media connection signaling is sent to the devices.

There are two categories of media processing resources:

■ Software-based media processing resources

■ Hardware-based media processing resources

Software-Based Media Processing Resources

A software-based media processing resource is typically a Microsoft Windows 2000 server that is running the Cisco IP Voice Media Streaming App. The Cisco IP Voice Media Streaming App can be configured to operate and register with CallManager as four different device types. Each type of device provides a specific function or set of functions to CallManager. The four device types are as follows:

- Software conference bridge

- MTP

- MOH server

- Annunciator

Each of these device types is discussed in detail in later sections. The physical location of the Cisco IP Voice Media Streaming server is not significant to CallManager, as long as the server is accessible to all the CallManager nodes in the cluster.

Hardware-Based Media Processing Resources

Hardware-based media processing resources are resources that either exist on hardware blades that plug into a network switching platform such as a Cisco Catalyst 6500 or another switching platform, or are DSP farms on various IOS gateways. Hardware-based resources have a complement of DSPs and other processors that give them additional capabilities, such as the capability to act as a transcoder or process video, that are not available on software-based resources. Hardware resources register with CallManager as a particular type of device. Each type of device provides a certain set of functions to CallManager. Three common types of hardware-based media processing devices are as follows:

- Hardware audioconference bridge

- Hardware videoconference bridge

- Transcoder

Each of these device types is discussed in greater detail in later sections.

Advantages and Disadvantages of Hardware and Software Media Processing Resources

Software-based resources generally provide fewer processing-intensive features than do their hardware counterparts. Table 5-4 shows you recommendations based on various goals.

Table 5-4   *Recommendations for Choosing Software-Based or Hardware-Based Media Processing Resources*

Goal	Recommendation	Reason
Reduced cost for processing G.711 streams	Software	Software-based media processing resources are less expensive per stream than their hardware-based counterparts.
No additional switching or routing platform requirements	Software	Software-based media processing resources generally require their own Windows 2000 server in all but very small installations, but they do not require that hardware be installed on a switching or routing platform.
Ability to process streams from multiple codecs	Hardware	Hardware-based media processing resources can handle G.711, G.729a, and G.723 voice data streams. Some devices can handle GSM streams. Wideband is not supported. For example, a hardware-based conference bridge is capable of running a mixed-mode conference (one with different stream types).
No additional server requirements	Hardware	Hardware-based media processing resources require hardware to be installed on either a switching or routing platform, but they do not require any network server support.
Video capability	Hardware	Video streams in general require hardware-based resources to process them.

Media Resource Registration

All media processing resources currently register and communicate with CallManager using the Skinny Client Control Protocol (SCCP). All Cisco IP Phones also use this protocol. Media processing resources do not use most of the protocol elements of SCCP. Media devices in general use some of the registration elements and the media control elements from this protocol.

Media Resource Device Registration Sequence

CallManager receives a registration request from a device. The registration request contains the device name and the device type. CallManager then attempts to look up the device in the database. If the lookup attempt is successful, all configuration information associated with this device is retrieved from the database, and the device is allowed to continue registering. Each device tells CallManager during the registration sequence how many full-duplex media streams it can support. CallManager creates appropriate resources to support that device based on its device type.

On the device side, each media resource is given a list of CallManager nodes in priority order to which it should attempt to register. The first CallManager in the list is its primary CallManager. If the primary CallManager fails or is not available for any reason, it attempts to register with the next available CallManager in its list. Each device can register with only one CallManager at a time. The device always registers with its primary CallManager if that node is available, and it reregisters with the primary CallManager when it becomes available again after a failure. CallManager can have multiple devices of the same type registered. Each of these devices might be configured to register to a different CallManager node or to the same CallManager node.

The Media Control Layer

The *Media Control Layer* (MCL) is a layer of software within CallManager that controls all media streaming connections between endpoints or devices in the CallManager system. The MCL directs the construction of the logical channels through the network for each call that is processed by CallManager.

This chapter does not discuss the elements that compose the underlying data network. It discusses only the logical connections made between the devices and endpoints that compose the CallManager system. All signaling and data streams are carried through an IP data network, and it is assumed for purposes of this discussion that the MCL can make all TCP/IP or UDP connections requested, and that the underlying network can carry all the voice, video, and other traffic as needed.

Users of the system are directly or indirectly aware of the endpoints in the call. For this discussion, consider the physical devices to be the endpoints in a call, and not the actual persons involved. Thus, if you pick up your phone and call another person, consider your phone as the originating endpoint of the call, and the called person's phone as the terminating endpoint of the call. Think of the voice and/or video streams as being created by your phone, traveling through the network, and being terminated by the called phone. You, a user, are aware of these two endpoints, because you directly used them by picking up one and dialing the other. The streaming data connections between endpoints might be for audio channels, video channels, or some combination. This section discusses audio and video connections and processing.

Audio Channel Processing in CallManager

Figure 5-4 depicts the signaling and streaming connections made between two audio endpoints (in this case, Cisco IP Phones and CallManager). MCL directs the phones to open two logical channels, one in each direction between the two phones.

Figure 5-4 *Calls Between Two Audio Endpoints*

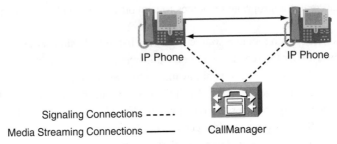

IP Phone   IP Phone

Signaling Connections - - - - -
Media Streaming Connections ———   CallManager

In some cases, it is not as simple as it seems at first glance. If the called party does not have an IP phone that is on the CallManager system directly, such as when you call home from your IP phone at the office, even though you can think of your voice traveling from your IP phone directly to the phone at home, in fact there are other endpoints or devices in the call as far as CallManager is concerned. In this case, the endpoints in the call are really your IP phone as the originating endpoint and a VoIP gateway as the terminating endpoint. The gateway connects directly to the Public Switched Telephone Network (PSTN), and the PSTN then carries the voice the remainder of the way. In this case, you are only indirectly aware of the endpoints. Figure 5-5 depicts that scenario.

Figure 5-5 depicts the signaling and streaming connections made between two endpoints (in this case, a Cisco IP Phone and an IP gateway). The MCL directs the IP phone and the IP gateway to open two logical channels, one each direction between the IP phone and the IP gateway.

All endpoints are not apparent to the users of the system. Sometimes the MCL inserts media processing entities into the voice data stream path without the user's knowledge. MTPs and transcoders are examples of these devices.

Figure 5-6 depicts the signaling and streaming connections made between three endpoints (in this case, two Cisco IP Phones and a transcoder). MCL instructs IP Phone A and Transcoder A to create two logical channels between themselves. It also instructs Transcoder A and IP Phone B to create two logical channels between themselves, making a total of four logical channels. The IP phones are not aware of the transcoder, and each phone believes that it has established a connection with another phone in the network. The two phones are logically connected, but the actual connections run through a transcoder.

Figure 5-5   *Call Between a Cisco IP Phone and a Non-IP Phone*

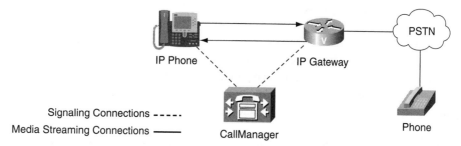

Some devices, such as conference bridges, are inserted at the user's request, and the user has indirect knowledge and control of their insertion. The control is indirect because the user cannot select the specific conference bridge to insert, but can indirectly select a conference bridge by pressing the **Confrn** softkey on the phone. No audio data travels between endpoints in the CallManager system without the MCL first instructing the endpoints involved in the call to establish media connections between them.

Figure 5-6   *Calls Between Two Cisco IP Phones Using a Transcoder*

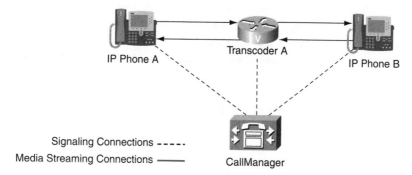

Video Channel Processing in CallManager

In contrast to audio channels, video channels are usually more directly controlled by the end users. A call can complete without video channels being established, but a call will never complete without audio channels. If you are using video, you are usually either directly or indirectly aware of video processing resources.

Video differs in many respects from audio. One of the differences is that the video streams created by and associated with a given call might not terminate on the same device as the voice streams. If the called party does not have a video phone that is on the CallManager system directly, but has a video-enabled endpoint such as Cisco VT Advantage, the voice streams are connected to the IP phone, and the video streams are connected to the associated PC.

On the other hand, if both endpoints are video endpoints, both the video and audio streams are connected directly to the endpoints. When you make a call from a video-enabled endpoint to an endpoint that does not support video, such as when you call home from your video-enabled IP phone at the office, your voice travels from your IP phone to a gateway that connects directly to the PSTN, and the PSTN then carries the voice the remainder of the way. In this case, the PSTN cannot carry video data, so the gateway is not video-enabled, and the call is connected without creating video channels.

Figure 5-7 depicts the signaling and streaming connections made between two video endpoints (in this case, two video-enabled IP Phones using Cisco VT Advantage). The MCL directs the IP Phone and the associated PCs to open two voice logical channels, one in each direction between the two IP Phones, and two video logical channels, one in each direction between the associated PCs. The respective cameras are connected to the video logical channels and pass video data directly between the PCs. The voice channels are connected normally, and voice data passes directly between the IP Phones.

Figure 5-7 *Call Between Video-Enabled Cisco IP Phones Using VT Advantage*

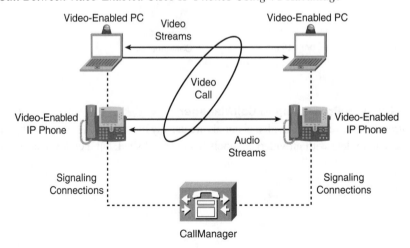

You do not do anything different when you make a video call than when you make a normal voice-only call. CallManager automatically understands when a video connection can be established, and automatically sets up the video and tears it down as appropriate. If you transfer a video call to a voice-only endpoint, the video is automatically terminated. Conversely if you call from your video-enabled IP Phone to a video endpoint and the video has been disabled, no video channels are established. If the called party then enables video, CallManager immediately attempts to establish a video connection between the endpoints.

Videoconferencing connections are similar to voice-conferencing connections in that the voice and video streams are directed through logical channels to a video conference bridge where the streams are mixed appropriately and mixed streams are generated for each endpoint in the conference and sent to their respective endpoints. As a user, you might be directly or indirectly aware of a conference bridge depending on the type of conference involved. Video conference bridges also support audio conferences and mixed audio and video conferences. In some cases, you might dial into a video bridge directly for a Meet-Me conference so you are directly aware of this bridge.

In some cases, such as Ad Hoc conferences, the conference bridge is inserted at the user's request, and users have indirect knowledge and control of their insertion in that you do not select the bridge directly. You indirectly select a conference bridge by pressing the **Confrn** softkey on the phone. If your phone is video-enabled, it can select a video bridge and connect a video conference if one is available.

No audio or video data travels between CallManager controlled endpoints in the CallManager system without the MCL first instructing the endpoints involved in the call to establish appropriate media connections between them. This enables the MCL to tear them down again at the end of the call or whenever it is appropriate.

Controlling the Allocation and Usage of Media Resources

You have great flexibility in controlling where resources register in the cluster and which endpoints can use the resource. You can organize the system based on geographical boundaries, on the structure of the underlying network infrastructure, or any other way you prefer. This section covers the following topics:

- Reasons to control the allocation of media resources

- Media resource default configuration

- How to control built-in bridge allocation

- How to control media resource allocation

Reasons to Control the Allocation of Media Resources

When allocating a media processing resource, it is important to be able to select which resource or set of resources can be used by a particular endpoint. If you have a geographically dispersed network, such as one that covers both Dallas and San Jose, and you have gateways in both Dallas and San Jose to handle local calls, it becomes very important where the media processing devices inserted into a call are physically located on the network. If CallManager inserts a media resource that is physically located in Dallas into a San Jose local call, the voice data for that call streams from the IP phone in San Jose to a media resource in Dallas and back to the gateway in San Jose, before going out over the PSTN for the local call. This is a very inefficient use of bandwidth and resources.

Because all media resources that are registered with CallManager are available to all CallManager nodes within the cluster, any CallManager node in the cluster can select and insert any available resource into a call, no matter where the device physically resides or the CallManager node to which it is registered. You have complete flexibility to configure the system any way you choose. You can associate media processing resources with endpoints so that if an endpoint requires a media resource such as a conference bridge, CallManager knows which set of conference bridge resources are available to that endpoint.

If CallManager is configured correctly, and you are making a local call from an IP phone in San Jose that requires a media resource, CallManager controlling the call selects a media resource from a pool of local resources in San Jose.

Media Resource Default Configuration

In the absence of any configuration defined in CallManager Administration, all media resource devices are available to any endpoint in the system. The resources are used in the order that they were read from the database, and no attempt is made to associate a media processing resource with any particular endpoint. This arrangement is usually fine for small installations in a single location. If the system is large or geographically dispersed, you will probably need to control media resource allocation.

How to Control Built-in Bridge Allocation

Built-in bridges are mini conference bridges within the IP Phones themselves, and appear as separate allocatable devices that are attached to or part of a specific IP Phone. You can enable the built-in bridge associated with a given IP Phone through CallManager Administration. Built-in bridges are currently used only by the barge feature. When a barge feature requests a conference bridge, it specifically requests the built-in bridge for a specified target device in the allocation request. If the built-in bridge for that device is enabled, the MRM allocates it and returns it as the conference bridge selected. If the built-in bridge requested is not available, the barge function will not work.

Allocation of the built-in bridge is not discussed in the remainder of this chapter because it applies only to the barge feature. A built-in bridge is allocated upon specific request for that particular device. It cannot be used as a general conference resource.

How to Control Media Resources Allocation

This section discusses media resource groups (MRG), media resource group lists (MRGL), and how they are used to control the allocation and usage of media processing resources. It also explains the algorithms used during the resource allocation process. The main topics are as follows:

- MRG definition

- MRGL definition

- The order of precedence for MRGL assignments

- Media resource allocation through Media Resource Manager (MRM)

- Organizing resource allocation using MRGs and MRGLs

Media Resource Group Definition

All media processing resources belong to at least one MRG. An MRG is essentially a list of media processing resources that are made available as a group. If a media processing resource is not explicitly assigned to an MRG, it belongs to the Null MRG.

The Null MRG is the default MRG that exists even when no MRGs have been explicitly created through CallManager Administration. When CallManager is first installed, the default configuration includes only the Null MRG and does not have any MRGLs defined. All media processing devices that register with a CallManager node are therefore assigned to the Null MRG by default. After MRGs have been created through CallManager Administration, media processing devices can be assigned to them. The Null MRG does not appear in CallManager Administration.

An MRG can contain one or more media processing resources of the same type. The same media processing resource can be a member of as many MRGs as are necessary to achieve the desired configuration. The types of media processing resources are as follows:

- Conference bridge

- MTP

- Transcoder

- MOH server

- Annunciator server

An MRG can contain one or more types of media processing resources. You can specify media processing resources of different types in any order, because their order is not a primary concern in the MRG.

Figure 5-8 illustrates the resources in the Null MRG. The grouping illustrated is a logical grouping and is not visible in CallManager Administration. When multiple resources of the same type are in an MRG, they are grouped together. This figure shows devices of each type and how they are grouped within the Null MRG. Notice that the MTP group includes both MTPs and transcoders. The conference resources contain hardware-based and software-based audio conference resources as well as video conference resources. These resources are allocated in the order that they appear in the list.

Figure 5-8 *Resources in the Null MRG*

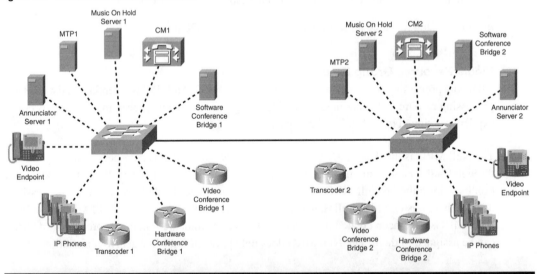

Null MRG				
MTP	**TRANSCODING**	**CONFERENCE**	**MOH**	**ANNUNCIATOR**
MTP1 MTP2 Transcoder 1 Transcoder 2	Transcoder 1 Transcoder 2	Software Conference Bridge 1 Hardware Conference Bridge 1 Video Conference Bridge 1 Software Conference Bridge 2 Hardware Conference Bridge 2 Video Conference Bridge 2	Music On Hold Server 1 Music On Hold Server 2	Annunciator Server 1 Annunciator Server 2

Resource allocation from the Null MRG on either CM1 or CM2 is as follows:

- **Conference allocation**—When a conference is needed by the phones on CM1, they get a software conference resource, or a hardware conference resource, or a video conference resource. This continues until there are no more conference resources.

- **MTP allocation**—Either a transcoder or an MTP is allocated when an MTP is requested.

- **Transcoder allocation**—Only transcoders are allocated when a transcoder is requested.

- **MOH allocation**—Both MOH servers are used, and the load is spread across both of them.

- **Annunciator**—Both annunciators are used and the load is spread across both of them.

Media Resource Group List Definition

After an MRG is created, you can add it to an MRGL. An MRGL is an ordered list of MRGs. An MRGL can have one or more MRGs in its list. When you create an MRGL, if it contains more than one MRG, specify the list in priority order. The list is searched from first to last when looking for an available media processing resource. When looking for a resource of a specific type, all resources of that type that are available in the first MRG from the list are allocated before any resources of that type are used from the second and subsequent MRGs in the list.

Figure 5-9 illustrates some characteristics of both MRGs and MRGLs. The same devices exist in more than one MRG, and the Music MRG exists in more than one MRGL. With this arrangement, the IP Phones on CM1 get media resources in a different order than the IP Phones on CM2. Video-enabled IP Phones get both a different set of resources and a different order than the IP Phones on either CallManager.

Resource allocation for IP Phones on CM1 (assigned to MRGL 2) is as follows:

- **Conference allocation**—The phones on CM1 get a software conference resource or a hardware conference resource or a video conference resource. All conference resources in the cluster are allocated as a single pool of resources, and no distinction is made between them.

- **MTP allocation**—All MTPs and transcoders in the cluster are allocated as a single pool of resources. There is no distinction made between them.

- **Transcoder allocation**—Only transcoders are allocated when a transcoder is requested.

- **MOH allocation**—Both MOH servers are used, and the load is spread across both of them.

- **Annunciator allocation**—Both annunciator servers are used, and the load is spread across both of them.

Figure 5-9 *Media Resource Group and List Structures*

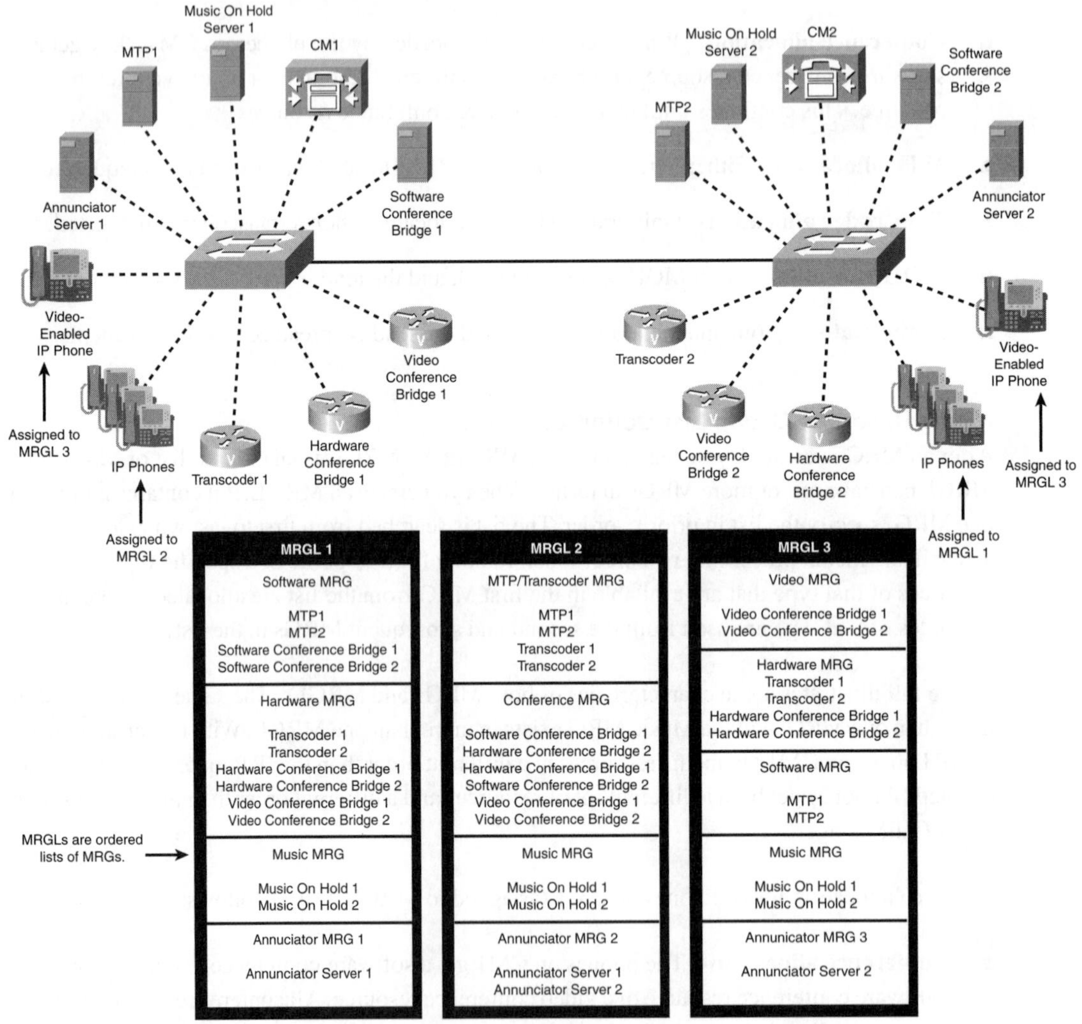

Resource allocation for IP Phones on CM2 (assigned to MRGL 1) is as follows:

■ **Conference allocation**—The phones on CM2 always get a software conference bridge until there are no more software conference resources in the cluster. Then they get hardware conference resources or video conferences resources until software resources are available again. Software resources always have priority over hardware conference resources and video conference resources. There is no priority given to hardware conference resources over video conference resources. Both hardware and video resources are allocated as a pool of resources.

- **MTP Allocation**—Software MTPs are allocated until there are no more software MTPs. Transcoders are allocated only when there are no software MTPs available. Software MTPs always have priority over transcoders.

- **Transcoder allocation**—Only transcoders are allocated when a transcoder is requested.

- **MOH allocation**—Both MOH servers are used, and the load is balanced across both of them.

- **Annunciator allocation**—All annunciators are allocated from annunciator server 1. Annunciator server 2 is not available to phones on CM2.

Resource allocation for video-enabled IP Phones on CM1 or CM2 is the same, and is as follows:

- **Conference allocation**—The video-enabled IP Phones on both CM1 and CM2 always allocate a video conference bridge if one is available. Then they get hardware conference resources until video conference resources are available again. Video resources always have priority over hardware conference resources.

- **MTP allocation**—When an MTP is requested, transcoders are allocated until there are no more transcoders available. Software MTPs are then allocated until a transcoder becomes available. Transcoders always have priority over software MTPs.

- **Transcoder allocation**—Only transcoders are allocated when a transcoder is requested.

- **MOH allocation**—Both MOH servers are used, and the load is balanced across both of them.

- **Annunciator allocation**—All annunciators are allocated from annunciator server 2. Annunciator server 1 is not available to video-enabled IP Phones.

The Order of Precedence for MRGL Assignments

Each endpoint device can have an MRGL associated with it. The two levels at which you can assign an MRGL are as follows:

- The device level

- The device pool level

When a CallManager needs a media resource for an endpoint during a call, CallManager requests a media resource of a specified type from the *Media Resource Manager* (MRM). The MRM finds the appropriate MRGL to use for that device by following the order of precedence, defined in Table 5-5.

Table 5-5   *MRGL Precedence Levels*

Order of Precedence Levels	Comments
MRGL assigned to a device	An MRGL assigned to a device applies only to that particular device. A media resource will be selected from the device's MRGL if one is assigned. If no resources of the requested type are available, it will then try to select a media resource from Null MRG.

Table 5-5 *MRGL Precedence Levels (Continued)*

Order of Precedence Levels	Comments
MRGL assigned to a device pool	The MRGL assigned to a device pool applies to all devices that are in that device pool. This is the most general level at which an MRGL can be assigned. It will be used when there is no MRGL assigned at the device level. If no resources of the requested type are available, it will then try to select a media resource from the Null MRG.
No MRGL assigned to the device pool or the device	If neither of these two entities have an MRGL assigned, CallManager uses the Null MRG for all media resource allocations required.

Media Resource Allocation Through Media Resource Manager

CallManager uses a simple two-step process to select a resource for a given allocation request once the MRGL is identified. Each step executes a simple algorithm. The interaction of these two algorithms makes control of the resource allocations very flexible.

The two-step allocation process is as follows:

Step 1   Get an MRG from the MRGL.

Step 2   Find a resource within that MRG, if one is available.

If the MRM finds an available resource of the specified type, it is returned to the requestor. If the selected MRG has no resources of the requested type, or the existing ones are not available, the MRM repeats this two-step sequence (perhaps multiple times) until either an available resource is found or all of the MRGs in the MRGL have been searched. Only if the MRM cannot find a resource of the specified type after searching all groups in the entire MRGL does it return an error indicating that no resources of that type are available.

Selecting an MRG from the MRGL

This algorithm selects and returns the next MRG from the list contained in the MRGL in priority order from top to bottom. The list is processed only once on each allocation request.

Selecting a Resource Within an MRG

Resources within an MRG are organized so that all resources of each given type are in a list together in the order presented in the MRG. In other words, it contains a set of lists, one for each type of resource that is present in that MRG.

This algorithm performs the following steps:

Step 1   Find the resource list for the type of resource requested.

Step 2   When the list is found, allocate the next available resource using a next-available algorithm on the list. The next-available allocation begins at the point in the list where the previous allocation request ended and looks for the next resource in the list that is available.

Step 3   If an available resource is found, allocate it and return it to the requestor. If one is not found, notify the MRM that one is not available in this MRG.

Figure 5-10 illustrates the allocation order within an MRG. All resources are contained in the MRG. For calls that require a transcoder, the allocation order is illustrated. Note that they are allocated in next-available fashion.

Figure 5-10   *Allocation Order Within an MRG for a Transcoder Request*

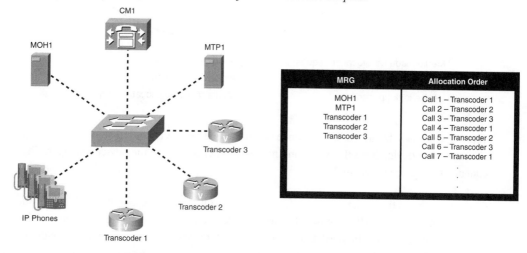

Allocating a resource is accomplished by finding a device in the list that appears to have resources available. The device control process maintains the resource status for each device, so the MRM sends an allocation request to the device control process and attempts to allocate a resource. If one is available and the device status is good, a resource is allocated and returned to the MRM. If one is not available or the device status is bad (not available), the MRM is notified that no resource is available on that device. Figures 5-11, 5-12, and 5-13 illustrate this.

Figure 5-11 shows the order of processing for resource allocation. The MRM gets a device name from the MRG and then sends a device look up request to the device manager. The device manager responds with the location of the device controller, whereupon the MRM sends an Allocation Request to the device controller. If the device controller has available resources, it responds with a Resource Allocation Response message, which is then returned to the requestor.

Figure 5-11 *Normal Resource Allocation Sequence*

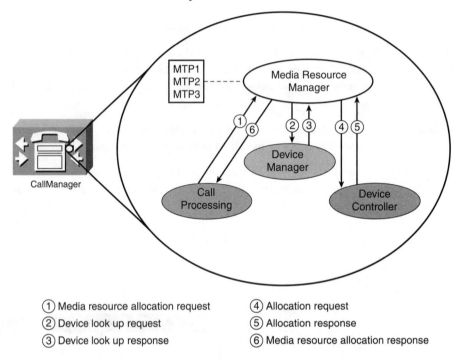

① Media resource allocation request   ④ Allocation request
② Device look up request   ⑤ Allocation response
③ Device look up response   ⑥ Media resource allocation response

Figure 5-12 shows the allocation sequence when the first device is not registered. The MRM selects another device from the MRG and makes another request to the device manager. The sequence then proceeds normally.

Figure 5-13 shows the sequence when the device controller has no resources available for the device. In this case, the MRM must select another device from the MRG, request the location of the device controller, and then ask that device controller whether it has a resource. The device controller responds with a Resource Allocation Response, and the Resource Allocation Response is returned to the requestor.

Figure 5-12 *Device Is Not Registered or Out of Service*

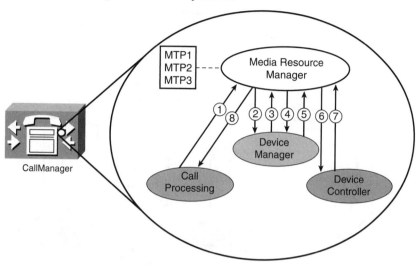

(1) Media resource allocation request   (5) Device look up response

(2) Device look up request   (6) Allocation request

(3) Device look up ERROR   (7) Allocation response

(4) Device look up request (next device from list)   (8) Media resource allocation response

When the MRM has exhausted the list of devices in the MRG and subsequently in the MRGL, it notifies the requestor that no resources of the requested type are available.

> **TIP** If you want the processing load for a given resource type spread across several media resource servers, put all media resource servers of a given type in the same MRG. Within a single MRG, a resource of a given type is allocated in a next-available fashion. This does not guarantee that it will spread the load evenly, but it will spread the load. If you want to force CallManager to allocate resources from the same server until no more resources are available on that server, you must put each resource server of the same type in a separate MRG, and organize the MRGs in the MRGL in the order that you want the resource servers used.

Figure 5-13 *Device Controller Has No Resources Available*

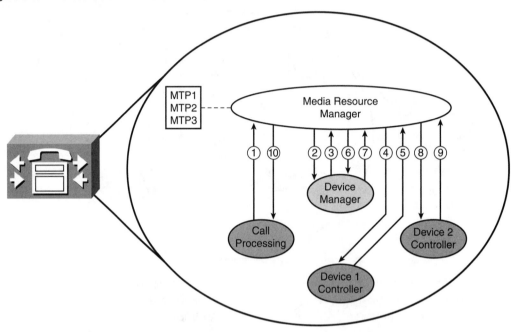

① Media resource allocation request ⑥ Device look up request (next device from list)
② Device look up request ⑦ Device look up response
③ Device look up response ⑧ Allocation request
④ Allocation request ⑨ Allocation response
⑤ Allocation ERROR no resources ⑩ Media resource allocation response

Organizing Resource Allocation Using MRGs and MRGLs

The resource allocation tools provided allow a great deal of flexibility in determining how CallManager allocates media processing resources. Several different arrangements are shown in this section. This is not an exhaustive set, but perhaps it is enough to spark some ideas and to help you understand how MRGs and MRGLs can be used effectively.

Figure 5-14 illustrates a possible arrangement of media resources within a CallManager cluster. In this example, different departments are homed on separate CallManager nodes. This arrangement forces phones in Sales to use resources from the Sales group, phones in Marketing to use resources in the Marketing group, and phones in Engineering to use resources in the Engineering group. In this case, the resources are registered with the same CallManager node as the phones and gateways. See Figure 5-15 for another possible arrangement.

Figure 5-14 *Media Resource Group Cluster Overview*

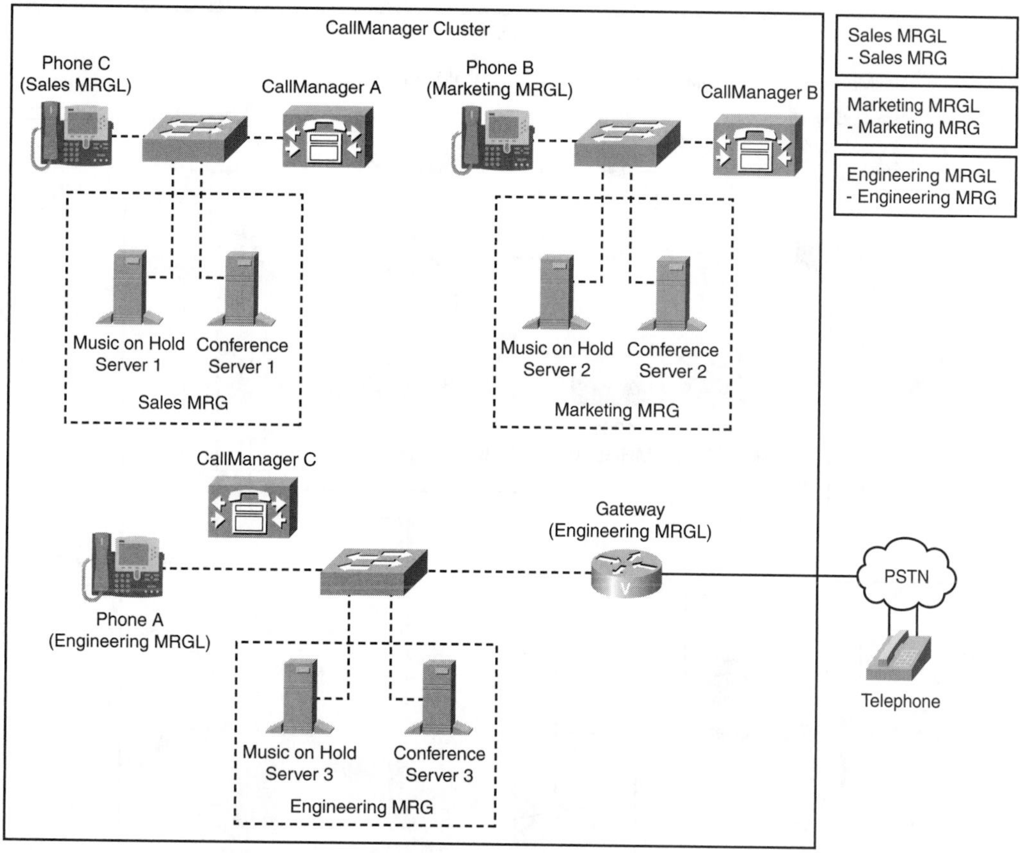

Figure 5-15 illustrates the fact that media resources are available throughout the cluster and do not have to be registered with the same CallManager from which they are used. All IP phones and the gateway in this figure have full access to media processing resources, even though in some instances the IP phones are registered to CallManager nodes that do not have any media processing resources registered to them. This arrangement still forces the IP phones on CallManagers A or B to use only resources from MRG1. The devices on CallManager C or D can use all resources, but they use the resources from MRG2 first. When those are exhausted, they can use the resources from MRG1.

Figure 5-15 *Media Resource Group System Overview*

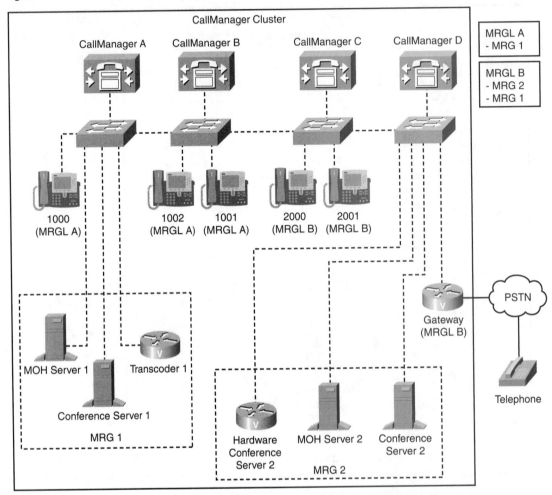

Figure 5-16 illustrates a possible arrangement for restricting access to media processing resources.

As shown, you can assign all resources to three groups (no resources are left in the default group). Create MRGL 1 and assign the three MRGs to it. Do not assign an MRGL at the device pool level. In the phone configuration, for the phones homed on CM1, do not assign an MRGL to them. These phones cannot use any media resources when they are configured this way because there are no resources available in the Null MRG and none available at the device pool level. Assign MRGL 1 to all the other IP phones. The other IP phones have access to all the resources.

Figure 5-16 *Using an MRGL to Restrict Access to Media Resources*

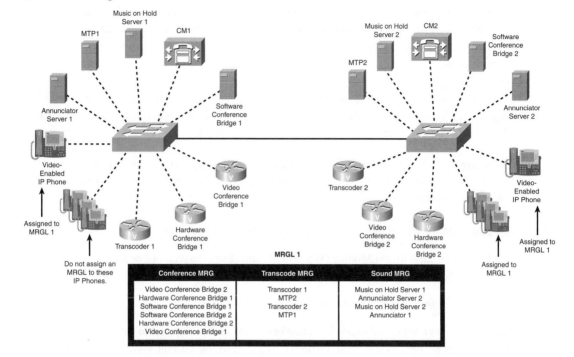

You can use the same concept to restrict any particular device or type of devices from groups of users. For example, if you want to restrict phones on CM1 from using any conference resources, create another MRGL, and add the two MRGs without the conference resources to it. Assign the MRGL without conference resources to the phones on CM1. Now they cannot access conference bridges.

Architecture and Functionality of the Media Control Layer

This section contains more detail on the devices and functions handled by the MCL. You can skip this section if you are not interested in such detail, or dive in if you really like this sort of thing. These are the major topics of discussion in this section:

- Conferencing and transcoding DSP resources

- Conference resource basic architecture

- Transcoding resource basic architecture

- MOH basic architecture

- Annunciator basic architecture

- Call preservation during system failures

Conferencing and Transcoding DSP Resources

The Communication Media Module (WS-SVC-CMM) with one or more conference and transcoding port adaptors (WS-SVC-CMM-ACT) is an example of a module that provides hardware conferencing and transcoding resources for CallManager. Videoconferencing resources are now available, too.

> **NOTE** A *transcoding session* is defined as one full-duplex codec translation between two different codecs. When a transcoder is used as an MTP, it also counts as one transcoding session.

The following is a partial list of gateways and switches that support transcoding resources. The currently supported devices might have changed, so you should search Cisco.com for the currently available transcoding resources.

- NM-HDV2 series of modules on the 26*xx*, 28*xx*, 37*xx*, 38*xx* gateways

- Communication Media Module (WS-SVC-CMM) line card with one or more conference and transcoding port adaptors (WS-SVC-CMM-ACT)

- Catalyst 6000 WS-X6608-T1 and Catalyst 6000 WS-X6608-E1 gateways

The following is a list of video conferencing bridges available. Again, the currently supported devices might change, so you should search Cisco.com for the currently available video bridges.

- Cisco IP/VC 3511 (video bridge)

- Cisco IP/VC 3520 (V.35/BRI H.323/H.320 gateway)

- Cisco IP/VC 3525 (PRI H.323/H.320 gateway)

- Cisco IP/VC 3540 (chassis-based bridge/gateway unit)

- Cisco VT Advantage

Limitations on Conferencing and Transcoding Resources

You might have several conferences running on the CallManager system using combinations of different codecs in them. For example, you might have one or more G.711 conferences running at the same time as one or more G.729a conferences. You might also have one or more conferences running where different endpoints in the conference use different codecs. Calls that use different codecs require different amounts of processing power from the DSPs on the conferencing resource. CallManager has no visibility into the allocation or usage of the DSP resources on media resource devices. The G.723 codec, for example, requires more DSP CPU cycles than does G.729a or G.711. The Catalyst 6500 CMM line card with conference and transcoding port adaptor modules register 128 resources per adaptor with CallManager, which would support 128 simultaneous calls using any available codec.

Conference Resource Basic Architecture

This section describes the architecture of all conferencing resources in CallManager and the components that form the basis of control and operation of the conferencing subsystem. This includes the Supplementary Services Layer, the Call Control Layer, the Protocol Layer, and the Media Control Layer.

Supplementary Services Layer

The Supplementary Services Layer in CallManager implements the feature operation as seen from a user perspective. It controls the operation of the feature and processes all softkey and button presses from the user after a feature has been activated. The Supplementary Services Layer in CallManager implements all features that exist in CallManager itself. For the conferencing features, it maintains all the conference information, such as which conferences are active and who the participants are for each one. This layer of processing is the one that processes all feature requests from the phones. When the conference supplementary services receives a conference request, it either processes the request or notifies the IP phone that there are no conference resources available. The Supplementary Services Layer interfaces directly with the Call Control Layer. It can communicate with the Protocol Layer only through call control.

Protocol Layer

The Protocol Layer receives and handles the device registration. It also handles all communication with the device. This layer also handles conference bridge device failures. Device failures and the subsequent handling of active conferences are both described in the section "Call Preservation During System Failures."

Creating and Managing Conference Bridge Resources

All conference bridge servers use SCCP to communicate with CallManager. This is true of both hardware-based conference servers and software-based servers. When a conference bridge server registers with CallManager, it provides several pieces of information needed by CallManager to communicate with the device and control conference allocation and usage on that device. The important ones for this discussion are as follows:

- Device name (conference bridge server name)

- Total number of resources (conference participants) that it can support (it takes one resource to support each conference participant)

- The number of resources that are currently active (normally set to 0)

- Number of resources (participants) that can be part of a single conference (this is an optional parameter)

- IP address of the device

- Device type

CallManager uses the device name provided at registration time to look up the device configuration information in the database. If the device is not configured in the database, the device is not allowed to register with CallManager. If the device is found in the database, it is allowed to complete registration, and CallManager creates a control process that communicates with the device and keeps track of the resources available for that device.

The device control process creates the number of conference bridge resources that the device can support using the total number of resources from the device registration message, and creates one conference bridge resource for every resource that the server supports. For instance, if a conference bridge supports 32 resources, CallManager creates 32 conference bridge resources to support this device. That means that from the CallManager perspective, it could create 32 separate conferences, each having 1 participant in it.

If the device provides the maximum number of resources that can be part of a single conference at registration time, CallManager uses that value to compute how many conference bridge resources to create. For example, if the device supports 6 conference resources or participants per conference and the device can support 24 resources total, CallManager creates 4 conference bridge resources. The control process registers the device with the Device Manager, which makes its resources available for allocation by the MRM.

> **NOTE** The number of conference bridge resources determines the number of conference bridges available on that device and, thus, the number of conferences that can be active simultaneously. Each conference bridge supports one active conference.
>
> Also, there is a one-to-one correspondence between the number of resources a device supports and the number of conference participants it supports.

Built-in Bridge Support for Barge Feature

Cisco IP Phone endpoints have a DSP inside the phone that can act as a small conference bridge. This capability is used only to support the barge feature, as described in Chapter 3. As far as the MCL is concerned, the barge feature activates a small conference, so resources are allocated as conference resources.

CallManager release 4.1 can take advantage of this small conference bridge during barge operations. This capability is either enabled or disabled, and depends on how the system is configured.

The advantage of using the built-in bridge in the phone is that no system conferencing resources are in use during barge feature operation. This makes conference bridge support essentially free for the barge feature because no additional hardware is needed.

The disadvantage is that the barge feature can use only the G.711 codec. Also, when the DSP in the phone is being used as a conference bridge, it is not available to process voice streams from low-bit-rate codecs such as G.729a or G.723.

Conference Resource Allocation and Control

The section describes in more detail how CallManager controls and allocates conferencing resources.

Allocating a Conference Bridge Resource

The conference supplementary service allocates one conference bridge resource for each conference that it starts. The conference bridge allocation is released when the conference is terminated. When the conference supplementary service needs a conference bridge for a new conference, it allocates a conference bridge using the MRM. The MRM does not attempt to distinguish between software-based audio conference bridges, hardware-based audio conference bridges, or video conference bridges when they are being allocated. It therefore allocates the next available conference bridge following the normal media resource allocation process. The allocated bridge can be either an audio hardware- or software-based conference bridge or a video conference bridge, depending on how conferencing resources are configured for that endpoint.

Mixed-Mode Audio Conference Support

CallManager supports mixed-mode conferences, which means that a single audio conference can consist of users with different codecs, such as G.729a, G.723, and G.711 codecs, in the same conference. This is supported directly by some hardware-based conference bridges. Some hardware-based audio conference bridges automatically provide any transcoding that is required, based on the codec type of the connected participant within the transcoding capabilities of that conference bridge device.

> **TIP** Hardware conference bridges do not all support the same set of codecs, so when you purchase hardware and configure the system, make sure that the conference bridge devices and transcoders in your system support the codecs that are required.
>
> Not all hardware conference bridges support mixed-mode conferences. If a conference bridge does not support mixed-mode conferences itself, CallManager allocates and inserts transcoders as required by the conference participants of a given conference. This is true for both software-based conference bridges and hardware-based conference bridges.

Mixed-Mode Conference Support for Catalyst 6000 Conference Bridges

Mixed-mode conferences on Catalyst 6000 WS-X6608-T1 and WS-X6608-E1 voice modules use DSPs to perform the transcoding operations for conferences. The conference mixers on the Catalyst 6000-based hardware conference bridges only mix G.711 streams and do not use a DSP for mixing. If a conference participant is using some other codec, such as a G.729a codec, the incoming stream is transcoded from G.729a to G.711 automatically before being sent to the mixer, and the output stream from the mixer is transcoded from G.711 to G.729a before being output to the conference participant. All such transcoding is handled transparently on the Catalyst 6000 voice modules.

When setting up a conference on this type of device, you are guaranteed the availability of a minimum of three conference resources. You cannot extend the conference unless additional resources are available on the device when you attempt to extend the conference.

Mixed-Mode Conference Support for Software Conference Bridges

Software conference bridges support G.711 A-law, G.711 μ-law, and wideband codecs. If a software conference bridge requires mixed-mode support for any other codecs, CallManager allocates and inserts transcoders as needed to handle the transcoding operations. Software conference bridges cannot transcode for any other codec type.

When setting up a conference on this type of device, you are guaranteed the availability of a minimum of three resources. You cannot extend the conference unless additional resources are available on the device when you attempt to extend the conference.

Mixed-Mode Conference Support for Gateway Supported Conference Bridges

The 26xx, 28xx, 36xx, and 38xx with voice processing modules do not directly support mixed-mode conferences. Their conference mixers only support G.711 A-law and μ-law. If mixed-mode conference support is needed when using these devices, CallManager allocates and inserts transcoders as needed.

Each conference on this device is mixed in a DSP. This limits the size of the conference to six or eight participants depending on which hardware is present, but has the advantage of guaranteeing that you can always have up to configured number of participants in each conference.

If CallManager knows that your conference is going to require more than three resources for features such as Join, where it is creating a conference from several current calls, it will request a conference bridge of sufficient size to accommodate the new conference.

If you know that a particular device is always used to set up large conferences and you want to use particular devices, such as Catalyst 6500 WS-SVC-CMM-ACT (up to 128 participants) or a software conference bridge (up to 48 conference participants), you could configure an MRGL for this device, and structure the MRGs with the appropriate devices in them in the order that you want them used. Such a setup would force the device to allocate from a resource pool that supports large conferences. (Conversely, you could construct another MRG and MRGL set with small conference resources in it and force another set of devices to use only those resources.)

> **TIP**   Software conference bridges can support much larger conferences if they are installed on a dedicated server. Cisco does not recommend or officially support larger configurations, but CallManager and the Cisco IP Voice Media Streaming App are both capable of supporting much larger configurations. Larger configurations might stress the limits of the underlying network; so if you want to experiment with them, you should consider the network implications also. Large conferences can also affect voice quality, so you should carefully test your intended configurations.

Video Conference Support

Video conference bridges are set up much like audio conference bridges. Calls are initiated using the **Confrn** softkey or the **MeetMe** softkey. The IP phone reports its capabilities to CallManager when it registers, so the call is handled appropriately based on the capabilities of the devices involved in the call. A video bridge is normally capable of supporting either video or audio conferences and mixed conferences containing both audio calls and video calls.

Whether a given endpoint gets an audio conference bridge or a video conference bridge when a conference is invoked is determined solely by the MRGL to which the device is assigned.

CallManager also supports the use of H.323 video bridges, but their resources cannot be invoked using the **Confrn** softkey on the IP phones themselves.

Extending Existing Conferences

CallManager does not guarantee that resources will be available to extend the conference on hardware-based or software-based conference resources. It is possible to allocate a conference bridge on a device that has plenty of additional resources available to extend the conference at the time it was allocated and still have those resources all used in other conferences by the time you attempt to extend your conference. It is also possible to allocate a conference on a device that only has sufficient resources available to establish the conference. In this case, the conference cannot be extended, even though it would normally be allowed to grow. Some devices, by their implementation, guarantee that at least six participants can join any conference.

Controlling the Usage of Conference Bridge Servers

CallManager provides flexible and powerful mechanisms to control the allocation of conference bridges and other media resources. Which conference server to use when allocating a conference bridge depends first on the system configuration relating to media resource allocation, and second on which device is controlling the conference. Conference servers can be included in an MRG. MRGs are assigned to one or more MRGLs. Each device in CallManager might have an MRGL assigned to it, either by default or explicitly when the device is configured through CallManager Administration.

> **NOTE**   Conference bridge servers are handled through MRGs and MRGLs the same as any other media processing resource. To understand how to configure and use MRGs and MRGLs to control conference bridge allocation, see the section "How to Control Media Resources Allocation."

> **NOTE**   CallManager allocates all conference resources based on the device and directory number the conference controller is using to set up the conference. The conference controller is the one who sets up the conference.

When CallManager determines that a conference bridge is needed, it allocates a conference bridge, using the MRGL assigned to the directory number that the conference controller is using on this call. If an MRGL is not assigned to the directory number explicitly, CallManager uses the MRGL assigned to the conference controller's device. Failing that, CallManager uses the MRGL assigned to the device pool. If there is no MRGL assigned to the device pool, CallManager uses the conference servers that are available in the Null MRG. This group contains all servers that are not explicitly assigned to at least one MRG. If no conference servers are in the Null MRG, conferencing is not available for this call.

Default Configuration for Conference Servers

The initial system configuration does not have any MRGs defined. This initial configuration causes all media resource servers registered with CallManager to be in the Null MRG. It also forces all devices to use the Null MRG for all media resources allocation requests. This is the simplest configuration and makes every conference server that registers with CallManager available to all devices that are registered to CallManager. This configuration is sufficient for small- or medium-sized installations, where there is no requirement to assign media processing resources to particular groups of devices.

Device Registration and Initialization

Each conference device has a list of CallManager nodes with which it is allowed to register. The list is in priority order. In general, each conference device attempts to register with its primary CallManager node, which is the first node in its list. If it cannot register with that CallManager node for some reason, it attempts to register with each of the other CallManager nodes in its list, from highest priority to lowest priority, until it successfully registers with one of them. Because conference devices use the SCCP, their failover and fallback characteristics are similar to other station type devices and are not covered in detail here.

> **NOTE**   The conference devices attempt to keep calls active in the event of failures. This along with their failover and fallback algorithms is covered in the section "Call Preservation During System Failures."

A Look at Device Registration from the Side of CallManager

You control device registration in the CallManager cluster. Every device that is allowed to register with the cluster must first be defined in the CallManager database through CallManager Administration. The only exception is when phones are configured to auto-register, which requires that you enable auto-registration. When you define media processing resources, those resources are given a name and device type. Depending on the device being defined, other parameters and information are required, such as the maximum resource count for that device. Specific configuration parameters for each device are covered in the device-specific section.

The media processing device registration sequence is as follows:

1. CallManager receives a registration request from a device, followed by a Station IP Port message that identifies the port that CallManager is to use when communicating with this device. The registration request contains the device name and the device type, among other things. CallManager then attempts to look up the device in the database using the device name. If the lookup attempt succeeds, all configuration information associated with this device is retrieved from the database, and the device is allowed to continue registering.

   See the section "Creating and Managing Conference Bridge Resources" for more details on what information is passed to CallManager on device registration.

2. CallManager sends a Register Ack message, followed by a Capabilities Request message.

3. The device sends a Capabilities Response message, followed by a KeepAlive message. The Capabilities Response message informs CallManager what codecs the device supports for incoming and outgoing media streams.

4. CallManager responds with a KeepAlive Ack, and the device registration is complete.

5. The device can send a StationMediaResourceNotificationMessage at any time following registration to inform CallManager of any changes in its resource processing capabilities, or to inform CallManager about its specific conference configuration. This message contains the following:

   - Maximum resources per conference

   - Number of resources in service

   - Number of resources out of service

6. CallManager uses the maximum number of resources per conference as the maximum size of conference participants this device supports in any one conference. The StationMediaResourceNotificationMessage is also used to decrease or increase the number of resources that the device can support at the current time (which can also change the number of resources that the device can support). This message is used whenever the device experiences an event that changes its processing capabilities, such as a nonrecoverable DSP failure, some of its resources have been allocated outside of CallManager control, the device has been reconfigured, and so forth.

After the device has been registered, all the CallManager nodes in the cluster have access to it and can allocate and use the media processing resources of that device.

Conferencing Limitations and Configuration Notes

CallManager in general has a "resource-centric" view of conferencing resources that are registered with it. This view is consistent with the implementation of both the software conference bridges and the Catalyst WS-6608-T1 and WS-6608-E1 hardware modules. When dealing with standard G.711 conferences, the view is accurate and complete. In these cases, CallManager creates one conference bridge resource for each resource that is registered by these devices. It requires at least three participants to set up an Ad Hoc conference. These devices support conference sizes ranging from three up to the maximum number of resources supported by the device. This means that CallManager has complete control over the resources registered and can establish any number of conferences of varying sizes, as long as the total number of resources used in the conferences does not exceed the number of resources registered by the device. The conference sizes are, of course, limited by the maximum sizes configured through CallManager Administration.

For example: The device registers 32 resources. It does not limit the maximum number of conference participants per conference at the device level, and the maximum participants for a conference at the system level is set at 32. In this case, CallManager creates 32 conference resources to support this device, which allows CallManager to set up a maximum of 32 simultaneous conferences on this device. The device can support from 1 to 32 simultaneous conferences using the 32 resources. Some of the possible configurations that CallManager could set up are as follows:

- A single conference with 32 participants

- Two conferences with 16 participants each

- Three conferences, one with 20 participants, one with 9 participants and the other with 3 participants

- Eight conferences with three participants each and two conferences with four participants each

- Ten conferences with three participants each

- Any other combination, so long as the total number of conference participants does not exceed 32

Some DSP farms used for conference bridges, such as those available on the 26*xx*, 28*xx*, 37*xx*, and 38*xx* series gateways, are not implemented in the same manner. These devices are more "DSP-centric" in that they implement each conference on a separate DSP. This means that a single conference is limited in size to the maximum number of resources that can be processed by one DSP. In this case, even though the device might register 24 resources, for example, the largest conference it can support is six participants, because each DSP can handle a maximum of six resources. When these devices register, they also supply the optional parameter Max Resources Per Conference, which informs CallManager about this configuration. When this parameter is provided, CallManager divides the registered resource count by this parameter to compute the number of conference resources to create for that device. If the device registers 24 resources and 6 resources maximum per conference, CallManager creates four conference resources for this device.

For example, one of these devices registers 24 resources and a maximum per-conference resource limit of six. The maximum participants for a conference set through CallManager Administration is six. CallManager creates four conference bridge resources for this device, which in turn allows CallManager to create four simultaneous conferences. CallManager could then use the 24 resources to set up conferences in the following configurations:

- Four conferences with six participants each

- Four conferences, each having between three and six participants each

- Four conferences with three participants each

- Any other combination, as long as the total number of conferences does not exceed four and the maximum participants per conference does not exceed six

> **TIP**   When using hardware that mixes conferences on the DSPs and the same device registration parameters as in the previous example, it is possible to use all the conference bridge resources and still have half of the resources unused, by setting up four conferences. This occurs when each conference has only three participants, which is the downside. The upside is that each conference has three more resources that are guaranteed to be available, and thus each conference can add three more participants, if desired.

Unicast Conference Bridge Application (Software)

The Cisco IP Voice Media Streaming App supports Unicast conferences and is a Cisco software application that installs on an MCS server during the CallManager installation process. In the installation, the component is called the Cisco IP Voice Media Streaming App and is common to the MTP, MOH, software Unicast conference bridge, and annunciator applications. The Cisco IP Voice Media Streaming App runs as a service under Microsoft Windows 2000.

Ad Hoc Conferencing

An Ad Hoc conference is established by using the **Confrn** softkey on the phone. The person who sets up the conference is referred to as the *conference controller*. As the conference controller, you add each participant to the conference and therefore have complete control over who joins the conference. You can also drop any participant from the conference that you choose based on the roster of conference participants provided. The conference participants can drop out of the conference any time they choose by hanging up the phone, thus terminating the call. As long as more than two participants remain in the conference, the conference bridge is still active, and the conference is maintained. When only two participants remain, they are connected directly, and the conference bridge is released.

Several variations exist as to the basic method of setting up a conference, but a conference controller always establishes an Ad Hoc conference. The conference controller sets up the conference by pressing the **Confrn** softkey during a call, calling a third person, and then pressing the **Confrn** softkey a second time. The first Confrn softkey press allocates the conference bridge for this conference. The second Confrn softkey press creates the conference and connects all three participants to it. The conference controller can continue to add additional participants to the conference until either the conference bridge being used is out of resources or the maximum number of participants as specified in system configuration is reached.

You can perform the same operation by using the **Join** softkey when the calls are already active. In this case, you select three or more calls and then press the **Join** softkey. CallManager allocates a bridge large enough to connect all the selected calls, and then connects each of the calls to the conference.

To add additional conference participants to the conference after it has been created, the conference controller presses the **Confrn** softkey on the phone. CallManager provides a dial tone to the controller; the conference controller then calls the person to be added, and presses the **Confrn** softkey again. The controller rejoins the conference, and the new participant is added to the conference.

Meet-Me Conferencing

A Meet-Me conference is established by using the **MeetMe** softkey on the phone. The person who sets up the conference is referred to as the *conference controller*. Unlike in an Ad Hoc conference, the conference controller does not have complete control over who joins the conference. The Meet-Me conference controller selects one of the Meet-Me conference numbers from the range specified for the CallManager node that is controlling the call. The conference controller then establishes the conference using that Meet-Me conference number. After the conference is established, anyone who calls that particular Meet-Me conference number is immediately connected to the conference.

Meet-Me Feature Operation

Two separate operations are involved in a Meet-Me conference call:

- A user must establish a Meet-Me conference by pressing the MeetMe softkey on the phone and then dialing a **Meet-Me** number from a range of numbers available for that particular CallManager node.

- After the conference has been established, each conference participant places a call to that particular Meet-Me conference number and is immediately connected into the conference.

> **TIP**   If more control is needed over who can participate in a Meet-Me conference, participants can be instructed to dial in to an operator or attendant who then transfers them to the conference number and announces their joining.

Conference Configuration

You enable Ad Hoc or Meet-Me conferencing in CallManager by completing the following steps:

Step 1   Install and configure one or more hardware conference bridges in the cluster. It is not important which CallManager the conference server registers with, so long as CallManager is in the cluster. All conference and other media resources are shared across the entire cluster.

or

Activate the Cisco IP Voice Media Streaming App (**Application > Cisco CallManager Serviceability > Tools > Service Activation**). When this service is activated, it creates the software conference bridge, MTP, MOH, and annunciator devices automatically in the CallManager database with default settings. You can then configure them as needed.

Step 2   Set the conference service parameters that control the size and operation of conferences. See Table 5-6.

Step 3   Configure the new conference devices.

The conferencing service parameters in Table 5-6 are clusterwide parameters. The service parameters that set the size of conferences are normally set to 4. You can configure a higher number if you choose. Some conference bridge devices are limited to six participants, some to eight participants. Some of the newer bridges can support up to 64 participants in an Ad Hoc conference and 128 in a Meet-Me conference.

Table 5-6 *CallManager Conferencing Service Parameters*

Service Parameter	Value	Description
Suppress MOH to Conference Bridge	Default: True Values: True or False	This parameter determines whether music on hold (MOH) plays to a conference when a conference participant places the conference on hold. Valid values specify True (CallManager does not play MOH to the conference when a conference participant presses the Hold button) or False (CallManager plays MOH to the conference when a conference participant presses the Hold button).
Maximum Ad Hoc Conference	Default value: 4 Range: 3–64	This parameter specifies the maximum number of participants that are allowed in a single Ad Hoc conference. The value of this field depends on the capabilities of the software/hardware conference bridge. Setting this value above the maximum capacity of the conference will result in failed entrance to a conference bridge if you try to add more ports than the specific conference bridge configuration allows. Warning: CTI applications and the Drop Any Party feature (accessed via the ConfList softkey) do not support more than 16 participants. Although an Ad Hoc conference can support more than 16 participants, the participant list used by CTI applications and the Drop Any Party feature will display only the 16 most recent conference participants
Maximum MeetMe Conference Unicast	Default: 4 Range: 1–128	This parameter specifies the maximum number of participants that are allowed in a single Unicast Meet-Me conference. The value of this field depends on the capabilities of the software/hardware conference bridge; for example, a software conference bridge conferences up to 128 participants. When a conference is created, CallManager automatically reserves a minimum of three streams, so specifying a value less than three allows a maximum of three participants.

What Happens When Conference Resources Are Not Available

If you attempt to create or extend an Ad Hoc conference or to create a Meet-Me conference when the necessary conference resources are not available, the conference will not be created or extended. The behavior that the conference controller or the potential participants sees will vary depending on what conference resource is not available, and when that was determined. The following behaviors might be observed.

Out of Resources When Creating a Conference

When you attempt to create a conference and a conference bridge is not available, CallManager does not respond to the **MeetMe** or **Confrn** softkey. In other words, the softkey/button presses are ignored. The user is notified of the failure condition. Possible reasons for this condition include the following:

- The conference bridge server has not registered with CallManager yet.

- The conference bridge server failed for some reason.

- All available conference bridges in the Null MRG are in use.

- No conference bridge servers are in the Null MRG.

- All available conference servers in the MRGL assigned to the conference controller are full.

- No conference servers are in the MRGL assigned to the conference controller.

Out of Resources When Extending an Ad Hoc Conference

When a conference is already active, the conference controller attempts to add another participant to the conference, but no more resources are available for this conference, the user is left on hold, and the conference controller is joined back into the conference.

Out of Resources When Extending a Meet-Me Conference

When a Meet-Me conference is active and no more resources are available, a user dialing the Meet-Me conference number will hear reorder tone (sometimes referred to as *fast busy*) and will not be connected to the conference.

Maximum Number of Participants in an Ad Hoc Conference Exceeded

When a conference already has the maximum number of participants allowed in an Ad Hoc conference and the conference controller attempts to add another participant to the conference, CallManager displays a message on the phone indicating that the conference has the maximum number of participants allowed, and the conference controller stays connected to the conference.

Maximum Number of Participants in a Meet-Me Conference Exceeded

When a Meet-Me conference is active and the maximum conference participant count has been reached, a user dialing the Meet-Me conference number will hear a reorder tone and will not be connected to the conference.

Maximum Number of Conference Bridges Supported

The maximum number of conference bridges supported by the device can differ from the number of conference resources created in CallManager. If the device does not provide the maximum number of participants that can attend a single conference, CallManager creates one resource for each resource registered. If the device supports 24 participants total and does not tell CallManager that it supports six participants per conference, for example, CallManager creates 24 conference bridge resources for that device, even though it can support only four conferences. Normally this should never happen. If it does, the device has a registration or configuration problem.

Unicast Conference Performance Statistics

Performance counters are available that monitor the usage of Unicast conference resources. All performance statistics are monitored through Microsoft Windows 2000 counters. You can monitor these counters in the Real-Time Monitoring Tool (RTMT) in Cisco CallManager Serviceability. CallManager provides three sets of counters that are maintained by each CallManager node:

- Unicast conference counters per CallManager node

- Counters per software conference server from a CallManager's perspective

- Counters per hardware conference server from a CallManager's perspective

Unicast Counters per CallManager

Each of the Unicast counters is for an individual CallManager node. They represent the total for all Unicast conference servers that are registered with that CallManager node, including both software and hardware counters. Table 5-7 lists the available counters and their meaning.

Table 5-7   *Unicast Conference Counters per CallManager Node*

Counter	Description
HWConferenceResourceTotal	This represents the total number of Unicast hardware conference resources provided by all hardware conference bridge devices that are currently registered with this CallManager.

Table 5-7   *Unicast Conference Counters per CallManager Node (Continued)*

Counter	Description
HWConferenceResourceActive	This represents the total number of Unicast conference resources that are in use on all hardware conference devices that are registered with this CallManager. Each conference resource represents the availability of three available full-duplex streams on this CallManager. A conference resource is considered active when it has been allocated. One resource is equal to one stream.
HWConferenceResourceAvailable	This represents the number of Unicast hardware conference resources that are not in use and are available to be allocated on all hardware conference devices that are registered with this CallManager. Each conference resource represents the availability of three available full-duplex streams on this CallManager. One resource is equal to one stream.
HWConferenceActive	This represents the number of active Unicast conferences on all hardware conference devices registered with this CallManager.
HWConferenceCompleted	This represents the total number of conferences that used a Unicast hardware conference bridge allocated from this CallManager and have been completed, which means that the conference bridge has been allocated and released. A conference is activated when the first call is connected to the bridge. The conference is completed when the last call disconnects from the bridge.
HWConferenceOutOfResources	This represents the total number of times CallManager attempted to allocate a Unicast hardware conference resource from those that are registered to this CallManager when none were available.
SWConferenceResourceTotal	This represents the total number of Unicast software conference resources provided by all software conference bridge devices that are currently registered with this CallManager.
SWConferenceResourceActive	This represents the total number of Unicast conference resources that are in use on all software conference devices registered with this CallManager. A conference resource is considered active when it has been allocated. One resource is equal to one stream.
SWConferenceActive	This represents the number of active conferences on all Unicast software conference devices registered with this CallManager.

continues

Table 5-7   *Unicast Conference Counters per CallManager Node (Continued)*

Counter	Description
SWConferenceCompleted	This represents the total number of conferences that used a Unicast software conference bridge allocated from this CallManager and have been completed, which means that the conference bridge has been allocated and released. A conference is activated when the first call is connected to the bridge. The conference is completed when the last call disconnects from the bridge.
SWConferenceResourceAvailable	This represents the number of new Unicast software-based conferences that can be started at this point in time for this CallManager. A minimum of three resources must be available for each new conference. One resource is equal to one stream.
SWConferenceOutOfResources	This represents the total number of times CallManager attempted to allocate a Unicast software conference resource from those that are registered to this CallManager when none were available either because they were all in use or none were registered. This counter includes failed attempts to add a new participant to an existing conference.

Counters per Software Conference Server from a CallManager's Perspective

Each software conference server registers with a CallManager independently, and CallManager maintains statistics about each software conference server that is registered. Table 5-8 lists the counters that are maintained for each registered software conference server.

Table 5-8   *Unicast Software Conference Counters per Software Conference Server*

Counter	Description
ResourceTotal	This represents the total number of conference resources provided by this software conference server. One resource is equal to one stream. This counter is equal to the sum of the counters ResourceAvailable and ResourceActive.
ResourceAvailable	This represents the total number of resources that are not active and are still available to be used at the current time for this software conference server. One resource is equal to one stream.
ResourceActive	This represents the number of resources that are currently in use (active) for this software conference server. One resource is equal to one stream.
OutOfResources	This represents the total number of times an attempt was made to allocate a conference resource from this software conference server and failed (for example, because all resources were already in use).

Table 5-8   *Unicast Software Conference Counters per Software Conference Server*

Counter	Description
SWConferenceCompleted	This represents the total number of conferences that have been allocated and released on this software conference server. A conference is started when the first call is connected to the bridge. The conference is completed when the last call disconnects from the bridge.
SWConferenceActive	This represents the number of software-based conferences that are currently active (in use) on this software conference bridge server.

Counters per Hardware Conference Server from a CallManager's Perspective

Each hardware conference server registers with a CallManager independently, and CallManager maintains statistics about each hardware conference server that is registered. Table 5-9 lists the counters that are maintained for each registered hardware conference server.

Table 5-9   *Unicast Hardware Conference Counters per Hardware Conference Server*

Counter	Description
ResourceTotal	This represents the total number of resources for this hardware conference bridge server. This counter is equal to the sum of the counters ResourceAvailable and ResourceActive. One resource is equal to one stream.
ResourceAvailable	This represents the total number of resources that are not active and are still available to be used at the current time for this hardware conference server. One resource is equal to one stream.
ResourceActive	This represents the number of resources that are currently in use (active) for this hardware conference server. One resource is equal to one stream.
OutOfResources	This represents the total number of times an attempt was made to allocate a conference resource from this hardware conference server and failed (for example, because all resources were already in use).
HWConferenceCompleted	This represents the total number of conferences that have been started and completed on this server. A conference is started when the first call is connected to the bridge. The conference is completed when the last call is disconnected from the bridge.
HWConferenceActive	This represents the number of conferences that are currently active (in use) on this hardware conference bridge server. One resource is equal to one stream.

MTP and Transcoding Resource Basic Architecture

This section describes the architecture of transcoding resources in CallManager, including a description of the Protocol Layer, the Media Control Layer, and device registration. Although the architecture is the same in many respects as conference resource architecture, there are important differences because transcoding resources are not signaling entities and are not known by the signaling layers.

Why to Use an MTP

An MTP is inserted on behalf of H.323 endpoints, such as third-party H.323 gateways that are involved in a call, to enable supplementary services to those endpoints. An MTP is only needed when an H.323 gateway does not support empty capability sets (ECS). Supplementary services include such features as hold, transfer, conference, park, and so forth. To implement these features, the logical channels to the endpoint must be closed and reopened again. Sometimes the logical channels are opened to another endpoint that differs from the first to implement a feature such as transfer.

An MTP is inserted on behalf of SIP endpoints to enable DTMF digit detection/generation as specified in RFC 2833. MTPs also supply ringback tone to SIP clients that are being transferred by an SCCP IP phone.

Figures 5-17, 5-18, and 5-19 illustrate the streaming connections created and torn down during a consultation transfer involving an H.323 endpoint.

Figure 5-17 shows the initial call from Phone B to IP Phone A. It goes through a third-party H.323 gateway that requires an MTP, so the MCL inserted an MTP into the media stream. It illustrates both the signaling and the media streaming connections.

Figure 5-17 *Call Transfer Initiation*

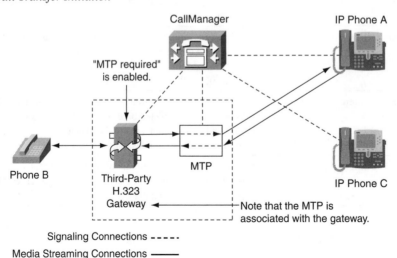

Signaling Connections - - - - -
Media Streaming Connections ———

Figure 5-18 illustrates the connections that exist after the user on IP Phone A pressed the **Transf...** softkey and called Phone C. Note that the media streams between the MTP and the H.323 gateway are still connected; so as far as the gateway knows, it is still connected to Phone A. The logical channels between the MTP and IP Phone A have been closed, and a new set of logical channels has been created between IP Phone A and IP Phone C. These two parties are talking to each other. After a short conversation, the user on IP Phone A presses the **Transf...** softkey again and completes the transfer.

Figure 5-18 *IP Phone A Transfers Phone B to Phone C*

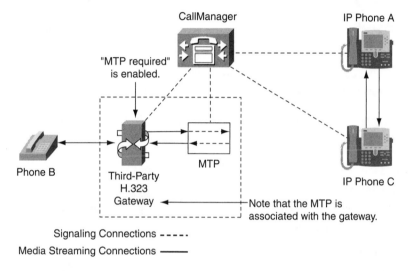

Figure 5-19 shows the final signaling and streaming connections that exist when the transfer has been completed. Logical channels have been connected between IP Phone C and the MTP. As far as call control signaling layers and the users involved know, IP Phone C is connected to Phone B. The use of the MTP is transparent to the users. If the MTP had not been inserted into the call when it was required, supplementary services would not have been available on that call.

Figure 5-19 *Transfer Completion*

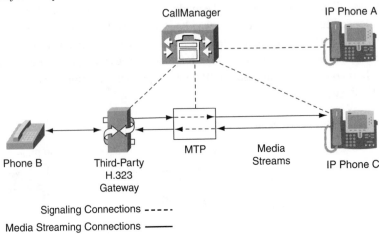

CallManager uses one of two basic methods to prevent the endpoint from tearing down the call when the media streams are closed, as follows:

■ Send the device a capability set with zero capabilities in it, and the device closes its media streaming connections

■ Insert an MTP into the media stream on behalf of the endpoint so that the media streams to the device are never closed

If the endpoint supports empty capability sets, when CallManager wants to close the media streams it sends the device a set of capabilities that has no capabilities in it. The device, on receiving that set of capabilities, closes all logical channels, but it does not tear down the call. CallManager can now establish a connection with another device. It sends the H.323 device another capability set with appropriate capabilities in it and then opens new logical channels to the new destination. H.323 v1 endpoints do not allow empty capability sets. If an endpoint does not support empty capability sets, it is not possible to extend any features to that endpoint directly. This is because the logical channels must be closed to implement any of the supplementary services such as those mentioned. As soon as the logical channels are closed, the H.323 endpoint tears down the call, even though it has not been instructed to do so through the signaling channels. In H.323 v2, the concept of empty capability sets was implemented. If the device is using H.323 v2 or a later protocol version, it allows CallManager, for example, to send a capability set to the H.323 device, which has no capabilities specified in it (an empty capability set). When the H.323 device receives these capabilities, it closes the logical channels and waits for a new capability set. All Cisco H.323 gateways support zero capability sets and thus do not require MTPs.

Figures 5-20 through 5-22 illustrate the connections and operation of an MTP in a SIP call where a SIP phone calls an IP phone extension 1005. 1005 answers the call and then blind transfers it to extension 1006.

Figure 5-20 shows the media connections that exist when the initial call is made from the SIP client to extension 1005 and the call was answered. Figure 5-21 illustrates the state of the call after a blind transfer has been initiated. The annunciator inserts a ringback tone toward the SIP client on command using an MTP. The tone plays until extension 1006 is answered or the call terminates.

Figure 5-20   *Initial Call from SIP Phone to Extension 1005*

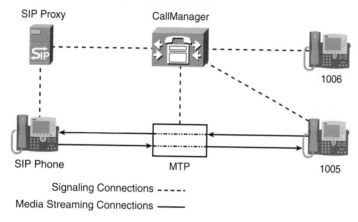

Figure 5-21   *Blind Transfer Initiated*

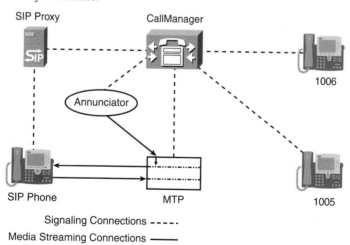

Figure 5-22 illustrates the final state of the call after extension 1006 has answered it.

Figure 5-22 *Blind Transfer Completed*

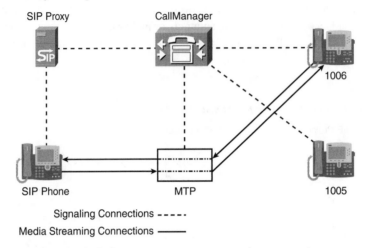

MTPs are also used to detect and generate DTMF tones from and to SIP clients respectively. Figure 5-23 illustrates DTMF detection between the SIP client and a MGCP gateway.

Figure 5-23 *DTMF Detection from SIP Phone*

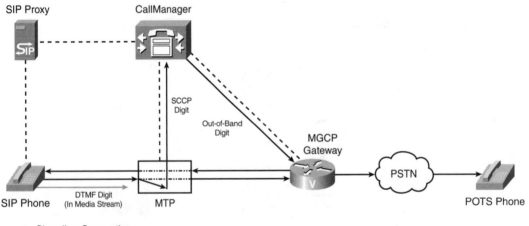

MTPs detect tones by looking for tone packets in the RTP stream. If found, the MTP captures the tone packet and forwards it to CallManager, where a digit notification is then sent to the gateway. Digits are inserted by an MTP when an out-of-band digit request is received by the MTP. It is inserted as a tone packet as specified by RFC 2833.

Figure 5-24 *MTP Allocation Flowchart*

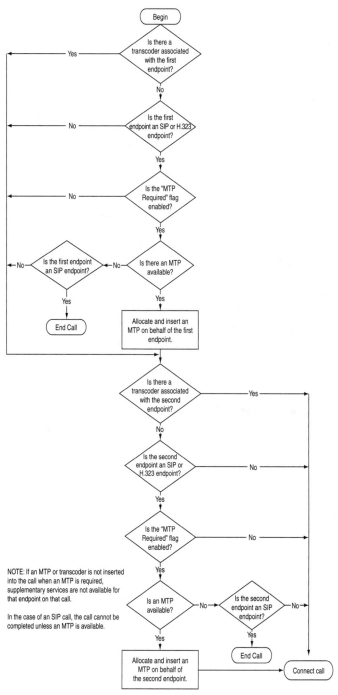

NOTE: If an MTP or transcoder is not inserted into the call when an MTP is required, supplementary services are not available for that endpoint on that call.

In the case of an SIP call, the call cannot be completed unless an MTP is available.

When an MTP Is Inserted

The MCL inserts an MTP on behalf of the following:

- SIP endpoints

- H.323 endpoints such as Microsoft NetMeeting clients

- H.323 gateways only if the MTP Required flag is enabled through CallManager Administration for that device

MTPs are used in support of SIP and H.323 endpoints and are not used for any other type of endpoint. The MCL follows the steps in Figure 5-24 to determine whether an MTP is required. Figure 5-24 illustrates the processing steps in the MCL to determine whether to insert an MTP. When the MCL determines that an MTP should be inserted, it allocates an MTP resource from the resource pool specified by the MRGL associated with that device. The MCL inserts the MTP resource into the call on behalf of a SIP or H.323 endpoint. The MTP resource use is not visible to either the users of the system or the endpoint on whose behalf it was inserted.

Why to Use a Transcoder

Transcoders are used to connect calls whose endpoints do not have a common codec. A transcoder can be used as an MTP if an endpoint in the call requires an MTP and none are available. Transcoders are allocated and inserted into a call automatically by the MCL. The use of a transcoder resource is not visible to either the users of the system or the endpoint on whose behalf the transcoder was inserted.

It is possible that the endpoint devices in the call have common codecs available, but they cannot use them because CallManager restricts their usage. Regions are commonly used to restrict the bandwidth between endpoints, which in turn limits the codecs that can be used by the two endpoints. If the region specifications require a low-bandwidth codec be used between the two endpoints, and the two endpoints do not have a common low-bandwidth codec, a transcoder will be inserted, if it is available. For example, if one endpoint supports only G.723 and the other supports only G.729a for low-bandwidth usage, a transcoder is required. Another example occurs when a call is transferred to voice mail and that voice mail system requires a G.711 input stream. If a low-bandwidth caller cannot use a G.711 codec (possibly because of region restrictions), a transcoder is inserted on behalf of the voice mail port to transcode the media stream from a low-bandwidth stream to a higher-bandwidth G.711 stream. Figure 5-25 illustrates an example of how the system is configured when transcoders are needed. Transcoders are invoked only if matching codecs do not exist at the endpoints of a call.

Figure 5-25 *The Insertion of a Transcoder into a Call*

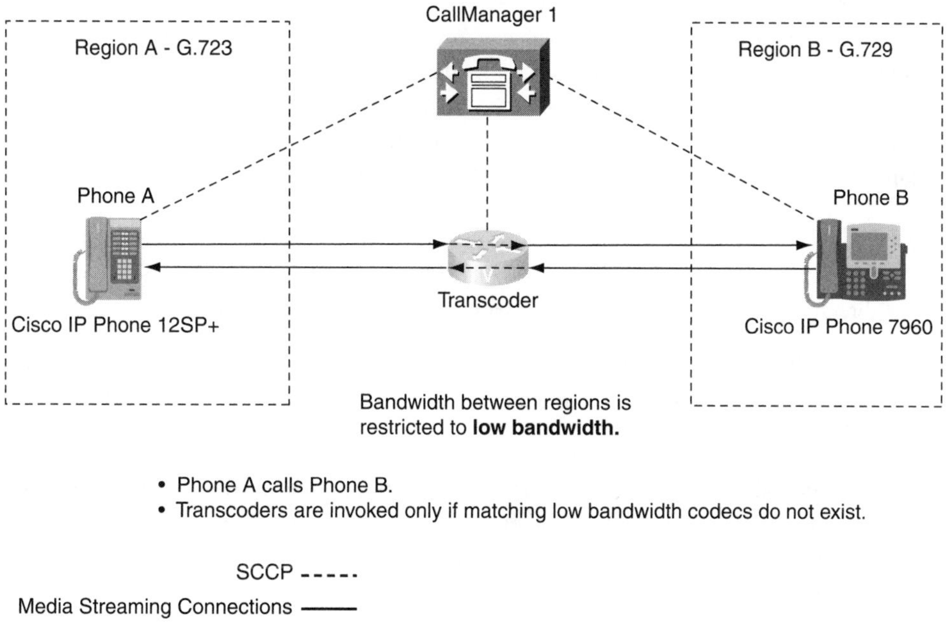

- Phone A calls Phone B.
- Transcoders are invoked only if matching low bandwidth codecs do not exist.

SCCP ‐ ‐ ‐ ‐
Media Streaming Connections ▬▬

Determining Which Device Needs the Transcoder

CallManager looks at the codecs for each endpoint in a call and, if a transcoder is required, allocates a transcoder using the MRGL assigned to the device that is using the highest-bit-rate codec in that call. If device A calls device B and device A is using a G.711 codec while device B requires a G.729a codec, the MCL in CallManager allocates a transcoder using the MRGL assigned to device A because G.711 codec produces a higher-bit-rate data stream.

On the other hand, assume that the same call were made between the same two devices but this time device A required the G.729a codec and device B was using its G.711 codec. The MCL in CallManager would allocate a transcoder using the MRGL assigned to device B because it is using the higher-bit-rate codec.

This general rule is always followed unless region specifications force allocations to occur in a different way. CallManager attempts to minimize the size of the data stream that is sent through the network. It makes the assumption that the transcoder is close to the device for which it is allocated. Therefore, if there is a low-bandwidth link between the two endpoints in a call, such as between a branch office and a main campus, the lower-bit-rate data stream crosses the low-bandwidth link between the two sites.

What Happens When Transcoders or MTPs Are Not Available When Needed

CallManager always attempts to connect calls whenever it can, and then provides supplementary services, if possible. Thus, if the choice is to connect the call without supplementary services or not to connect the call at all, CallManager by default chooses to connect the call, even with diminished capabilities. You can change this behavior by setting the CallManager service parameter Fail Call If MTP Allocation Fails to True, which will cause CallManager to fail the calls. With the default setting of False, CallManager follows these rules:

- If an MTP is required for an H.323 endpoint in a given call and neither an MTP nor a transcoder (to act as an MTP) is available at that point in time, CallManager connects the call directly, and supplementary services are not available on that call.

- If an MTP is required for a SIP endpoint in a given call and an MTP is not available at that point in time, CallManager terminates the call. All SIP calls through the SIP trunk require an MTP.

- If a transcoder is required, that means that the two endpoints do not have matching codecs and cannot communicate with each other directly. In this case, CallManager attempts to connect the call, which causes the call to terminate without ever establishing a media connection.

Rules for Inserting Transcoders and MTPs When They Are Available

As far as the MCL is concerned, a call is a connection between two parties. If the call is a conference call, for example, the MCL is not aware of the conference. To the MCL, a conference call is a series of individual calls. The fact that the second party in all of those individual calls is a conference bridge is of no particular interest to the MCL. The MCL simply makes connections between two parties as directed by call control. In the case of a conference call, the conference supplementary service is the only entity within CallManager that knows that there is a conference call being set up. In a conference call, each person connected to the conference bridge appears to the MCL as a separate call between the caller and the conference bridge. Because each party is individually connected to the conference bridge, the MCL inserts an MTP or transcoder only if one is required for that call. Thus, many MTPs or transcoders might be involved in a single conference, or none at all, depending on the requirements of each connection that is part of the conference.

The rules for inserting transcoders and MTPs apply to each individual call and can be quite complex in some instances. Provided first is a simple set of rules that will suffice for understanding how, in general, the selection is made. A more in-depth explanation follows for those interested in greater detail.

In any single call, MCL inserts a maximum of two MTPs. If a transcoder is required, normally only one transcoder is inserted in a call by a given CallManager cluster.

The MCL first obtains the capabilities of both endpoints involved in the call. The MCL does not attempt to make a connection until it has received the capabilities from both endpoints in the call.

Figure 5-26 shows the configuration where phones at a remote site call each other using G.711 both at the central office and at the remote office. The communication link between the remote site and the central campus is a low-bandwidth connection, so the calls over that link are restricted to G.723.

Figure 5-26 *Intercluster Calls with Restricted Bandwidth*

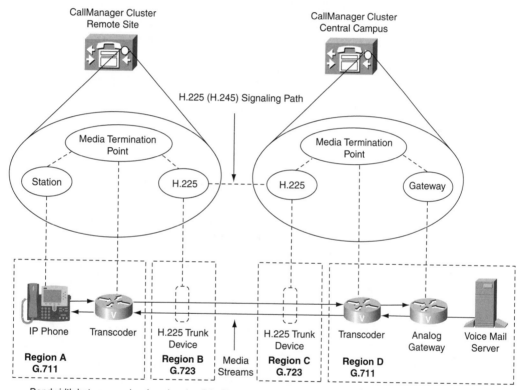

• H.225 trunk between CallManager clusters is used to connect all calls between clusters. In this configuration, transcoders are invoked because there is no common codec between the endpoint devices and the H.225 trunk due to region matrix specification.

NOTE: Because intercluster trunks are direct connections from CallManager to CallManager, no separate H.225 device physically resides on the LAN. Nevertheless, CallManager treats intercluster trunks as virtual gateways and routes call signaling and media control through them.

In this example, two transcoders are required because the region matrix forces a G.723 codec between the endpoints and the trunk devices. (The bandwidth between Region A and Region B is set to G.723, and the bandwidth between Regions C and D is set to G.723.) Within Regions A and D, the bandwidth is set to G.711. The CallManager node at the central campus inserts a transcoder between voice mail and the H.225 trunk, because the bandwidth between Region C and Region D is G.723 and voice mail does not support that codec. The CallManager node at the remote site inserts a transcoder between the phone and the H.225 trunk, because the Cisco IP Phone 7960 does not support the G.723 codec.

CallManager automatically inserts a transcoder when one is needed because of lack of a common codec between endpoints in a call. CallManager allocates a transcoder based on the capabilities of the endpoints involved in the call and the region matrix that is applicable to the respective endpoints. Table 5-10 describes MCL actions when determining whether to insert MTPs or transcoders.

Table 5-10   *Rules for Inserting MTPs and Transcoders Within a Single CallManager Cluster*

Current Resources Allocated in the Call	MCL Actions
No resources allocated	Match capabilities between two parties. If capabilities do not match, allocate a transcoder whose capabilities match at least one available codec on each endpoint. If both parties require an MTP, allocate an additional MTP for the other party.
No resources allocated	Match capabilities between two parties. If capabilities do not match and no transcoder is available whose capabilities match at least one available codec on each endpoint, terminate the call. (Not all transcoders support all capabilities of the endpoints.)
No resources allocated	Match capabilities between two parties. If capabilities match, check both parties to see whether they require an MTP. Allocate an MTP for each of the two parties that require one. If none are required, connect the call direct without any MTPs or transcoders.
One MTP	Match capabilities between MTP and the other party. If capabilities do not match, allocate a transcoder.
One MTP	Match capabilities between MTP and the other party. If capabilities match and MTP is required for other party, allocate another MTP.
One transcoder	If MTP is required for other party, allocate an MTP.
One transcoder and one MTP	No additional resource required.
Two MTPs	Match capabilities between the two MTPs. If capabilities do not match, allocate a transcoder.

H.323 devices usually do not require an MTP or transcoder, so the MCL does not allocate one unless the H.323 device has the MTP Required flag set. The Cisco H.323 gateways support all of the low-bandwidth codecs supported by Cisco IP Phones, so it usually comes down to configuring the right codec on the gateway to work with the phones. If this is not adequate because of various regions and third-party devices, you can explicitly invoke an MTP by enabling MTP Required for the gateway.

Device Control and Operation

The device control process maintains device status, resource availability, and other such information about the device. It is also responsible for device registration and all communication to and from the device. When the MRM is allocating resources, it always queries the device control process for available resources once a potential device is selected.

Device Registration and Initialization

Normally, when a device registers with a CallManager node, it has all its resources available. If the device was previously registered with a CallManager node that failed, and the MTP device had active calls at the time of the failure, the device still attempts to register with its backup CallManager node. Calls that are active on the server at the time it lost communication with its primary CallManager node are maintained in an active state. In other words, CallManager attempts to maintain all calls that are in an active state when a CallManager node fails. See the section "Call Preservation During System Failures" for more details on how calls are preserved.

MTP and Transcoder Configuration

You can enable MTPs and transcoders by completing the following steps:

Step 1   Install and configure one or more hardware transcoders in the cluster. It is not important which CallManager node the transcoder registers with, so long as the CallManager node is in the cluster. All transcoder and MTP resources are shared across the entire cluster.

or

Activate the Cisco IP Voice Media Streaming App. When you activate this service, it automatically creates an MTP device in the CallManager database with default settings. You can then configure it as needed.

Step 2   Configure the new transcoder devices or modify the MTP device configuration, if you choose.

MTP and Transcoder Performance Statistics

A number of performance counters are available to monitor the usage of MTPs and transcoders. All performance statistics are monitored through Microsoft Windows 2000 counters. You can monitor these counters using the Real-Time Monitoring Tool in CallManager Serviceability. CallManager provides three sets of counters that are maintained by each CallManager node:

- MTP and transcoder counters per CallManager Node

- Counters per MTP device from a CallManager's perspective

- Counters per transcoder device from a CallManager's perspective

MTP and Transcoder Counters per CallManager Node

Each of the counters described in Table 5-11 is for an individual CallManager. They represent the total for all MTP and transcoder servers that are registered with that CallManager node.

Table 5-11   *MTP and Transcoder Counters per CallManager Node*

Counter	Description
MTPResourceTotal	This represents the total number of media termination point (MTP) resources provided by all MTP devices that are currently registered with this CallManager.
MTPResourceActive	This represents the total number of MTP resources that are currently in use (active) on all MTP devices registered with this CallManager. Each MTP resource uses two streams. An MTP is in use when it has been allocated for use in a call.
MTPResourceAvailable	This represents the total number of MTP resources that are not in use and are available to be allocated on all MTP devices that are registered with this CallManager. Each MTP resource uses two streams.
MTPOutOfResources	This represents the number of times CallManager attempted to allocate an MTP resource from one of the MTP devices that is registered with this CallManager when none were available, either because they were all in use or none were registered. This also means that no transcoders were available to act as MTPs.
TranscoderResourceTotal	This represents the total number of transcoder resources provided by all transcoder devices that are currently registered with this CallManager.
TranscoderResourceActive	This represents the total number of transcoders that are in use on all transcoder devices registered with this CallManager. A transcoder is in use when it has been allocated for use in a call. Each transcoder resource uses two streams.

Table 5-11 *MTP and Transcoder Counters per CallManager Node (Continued)*

Counter	Description
TranscoderResourceAvailable	This represents the total number of transcoders that are not in use and are available to be allocated on all transcoder devices that registered with this CallManager. Each transcoder resource uses two streams.
TranscoderOutOfResources	This represents the number of times CallManager attempted to allocate a transcoder resource from one of the transcoder devices that is registered to this CallManager node when none were available, either because they were all in use or none were registered.

Counters per MTP Device from a CallManager's Perspective

Each MTP device registers with a CallManager independently, and CallManager maintains statistics about each MTP device that is registered. Table 5-12 contains the counters that are maintained for each registered MTP device.

Table 5-12 *Counters per Registered MTP Device*

Counter	Description
ResourceTotal	This represents the total number of MTP resources provided by this MTP device. This counter is equal to the sum of the counters ResourceAvailable and ResourceActive.
ResourceAvailable	This represents the total number of MTP resources that are not active and are still available to be used at the current time for the MTP device. Each MTP resource uses two streams.
ResourceActive	This represents the number of MTP resources that are currently in use (active) for this MTP device. Each MTP resource uses two streams. An MTP is in use when it has been allocated for use in a call.
OutOfResources	This represents the total number of times an attempt was made to allocate an MTP resource from this MTP device and failed (for example, because all resources were already in use).

Counters per Transcoder Device from a CallManager's Perspective

Each transcoder device registers with a CallManager independently, and CallManager maintains statistics about each transcoder device that is registered. Table 5-13 contains the counters that are maintained for each registered transcoder device.

Table 5-13 *Counters per Registered Transcoder Device*

Counter	Description
ResourceTotal	This represents the total number of transcoder resources provided by this transcoder device. This counter is equal to the sum of the counters ResourceAvailable and ResourceActive.
ResourceAvailable	This represents the total number of transcoder resources that are not active and are still available to be used at the current time for this transcoder device. Each transcoder resource uses two streams.
ResourceActive	This represents the number of transcoder resources that are currently in use (active) for this transcoder device. Each transcoder resource uses two streams.
OutOfResources	This represents the total number of times an attempt was made to allocate a transcoder resource from this transcoder device and failed (for example, because all resources were already in use).

Music on Hold (MOH)

For callers to hear MOH, an MOH server must be registered with the CallManager cluster. When the Cisco IP Voice Media Streaming App is activated, it creates an MOH device using default settings that support the basic MOH functionality. The MOH feature has two different aspects. The feature requires an MOH server to provide the MOH audio stream sources, and the feature also requires CallManager to be configured to use the MOH streams provided by the MOH server when a call is placed on hold. This section describes both aspects of the feature:

■ Configuring MOH servers

■ Configuring CallManager to use MOH

Configuring MOH Servers

An MOH server is a software application that runs on a Microsoft Windows 2000 server. It is installed as a service during CallManager installation and by default is deactivated. If an MOH server is needed, the Cisco IP Voice Media Streaming App service must be activated. If the MOH server is installed on a dedicated server, it can support up to a total of 500 MOH Unicast or Multicast streaming connections between all of its audio sources. All MOH servers in a cluster have the same audio source file configuration. This means that audio source 1 provides the same audio source on all MOH servers, audio source 2 provides the same audio source on all MOH servers, and so forth. One audio source on an MOH server can support from 1 to 500 MOH output streaming connections. In other words, the users connected to all 500 MOH output streams could be listening to the same music or audio source at the same time.

MOH servers support a total of 51 audio sources, 50 of which come from audio files on the disk. One audio source, source 51, is a fixed audio source connected to a sound card. An audio source file on disk can be encoded in one of several different formats for the supported codecs. Each of those 51 sources can support both Unicast and Multicast connections at the same time, and the source can be streamed for all supported codecs simultaneously. The MOH servers support G.711 (A-law and μ-law), G.729a, and wideband audio codecs.

The IP Voice Media Streaming App implements the MOH server. The IP Voice Media Streaming App is the same application software that implements software Unicast conference bridges and MTPs. Each source stream is essentially a nailed-up conference with a fixed identifier called an audio source ID. It has a single input stream that is streaming audio data from a data source, and one or more output streams that transport the streaming data to the devices that are connected to MOH. The source stream audio source IDs range from 1 to 51, with 51 being reserved for the single fixed data source that is usually from the sound card.

Figure 5-27 illustrates phones with particular source assignments and how the MOH server handles the connections. Figure 5-27 illustrates the basic architecture of the MOH subsystem. In this drawing, it is assumed that the MOH source assignment for each phone was already determined, and it is shown below the phone. A held device can be connected to any of the 500 possible MOH output streams and receive its specified audio source. When the logical channel is connected to the MOH server, the MOH server looks at the codec type being specified and the audio source ID supplied. It then connects the correct source to the port where that logical channel was connected.

Note that there is a source file on the disk for each of the codec types. This means that for source 1, which is Pop music, there are four files with the same music in them, but each of them is formatted for one of the different codecs. The MOH server selects the right source file to use based on the audio source ID supplied and the codec type specified in the logical channel connection. When the held device closes the logical channel to the MOH server, the MOH server stops the stream for that port as well.

Many logical channels can receive music from the same source file at the same time. As long as one logical channel is receiving music from a given source file, the MOH server continues streaming that source file. When there are no more connections to that source file, the MOH server stops streaming that source.

> **NOTE** The section "Configuring Cisco CallManager to Use MOH" explains in detail how to determine the source assignment for a particular call.

Figure 5-27 *MOH Stream Connections*

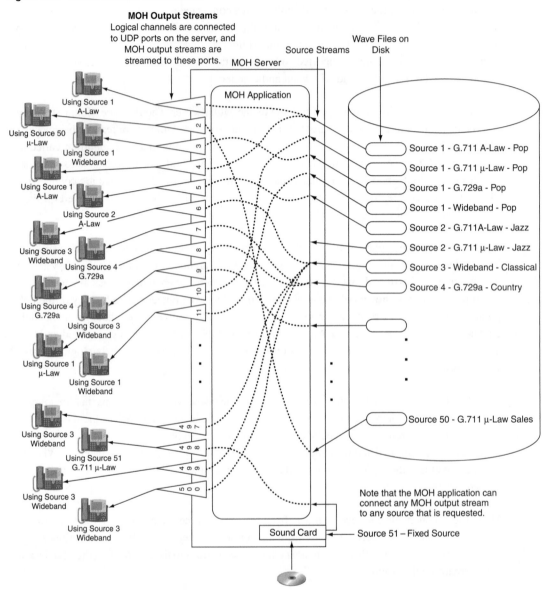

MOH Server Audio Source and Audio Source ID

An audio source can be either a file or a fixed audio source. The source files must be in either G.711 A-law or μ-law formats, recorded at a sampling rate of 8 kHz, G.729a, or wideband. These data sources are disk files containing audio data that has been transcoded or formatted for the particular codec type before being loaded onto the disk of the MOH server. There is a one-to-one correspondence between audio sources and audio source IDs.

The fixed data source is provided by the Windows audio input that is normally linked to the local sound card. This allows radios, CD players, or any other compatible sound source to be used. The stream from the fixed data source is transcoded in real time to support the codec that was configured through CallManager Administration. The fixed data source can be transcoded into G.711 A-law and μ-law, G.729a, and wideband. This is the only data source that is transcoded in real time. G.729 will consume about 5 to 7 percent of your total CPU time in this transcoding operation.

Using the MOH Audio Translator

When you want to add a new audio source or to update an existing one, the new audio source must be transcoded and converted to the proper format, and then copied to the proper location where the TFTP server can pick it up and send it to all MOH servers when requested. The MOH Audio Translator is used to accomplish this task.

To add a new audio source to the MOH servers, copy the source file into the Audio Source Input Directory as specified by the Cisco MOH Audio Translator service parameter MOH Source Directory. The default directory path for this directory is c:\Program Files\Cisco\MOH\ DropMOHAudioSourceFilesHere. Valid input files are most standard .wav and .mp3 files. It takes about 30 seconds to convert a 3-MB .mp3 file.

When the file is dropped into this directory, the Audio Translator service detects the file and automatically processes it, creating the audio source files needed for all supported codecs. The files are then moved to the output directory, along with all transcoded files that were created. The path for this directory is specified by the Cisco MOH Audio Translator service parameter Default TFTP MOH File Path. Whatever directory path is specified, \MOH will be appended to it. All transcoded files are stored in this MOH directory.

When you configure a particular audio source for a particular codec, CallManager Administration copies the files from the output MOH directory where they are stored to the TFTP file path directory. The path names used for these two directories can be changed by changing the values of the two Cisco MOH Audio Translator service parameters.

CAUTION   If Audio Translator is installed on the same server as CallManager and files are translated, CallManager might experience errors or slowdowns. This process consumes all available CPU cycles until it is done with the conversion. Cisco recommends that you do not install this service on a server where the CallManager service is activated and running.

Table 5-14 contains the service parameters used by the MOH servers and Audio Translator service.

Table 5-14 *Service Parameters for Audio Translator and MOH Server*

Service Parameter	Service It Applies To	Definition
MOHSourceDirectory	MOH Audio Translator	Defines the directory where new audio sources are dropped so that they will be transcoded for the supported codecs. This parameter applies servicewide.
DefaultTFTPMOHFilePath	MOH Audio Translator	Defines the directory path for the TFTP source directory. \MOH is appended to this path name to create the output directory. This parameter applies on a server-by-server basis.
DefaultTFTPMOHIPAddress	Media Streaming App	IP address or computer name of the server where the transcoded audio source files are located. This parameter applies on a server-by-server basis.
DefaultMOHCodec	Media Streaming App	Defines the codecs that are supported in this installation. The possible values are: G.711 μ-law, G.711 A-law, G.729, wideband. This parameter applies servicewide.

MOH Source Stream Play Mode

You configure the source play mode to one of two settings:

■ Continuous

■ One shot

CallManager is not aware of the play mode.

Continuous Play Mode

Continuous play mode causes the MOH server to stream the data from the audio source file in a loop. This means that as soon as it has streamed the file from start to finish, it immediately begins streaming from the start again. This continues for as long as this audio source is being streamed.

The MOH server keeps track of how many MOH output streams are connected to each audio source, and when the count reaches zero, the audio source streaming is stopped. The fixed audio source is always played continuously and is not stopped. If Multicast support is selected for this audio source, the audio source is played continuously, because the MOH server does not know when held devices are listening at a Multicast point.

One Shot Play Mode

One shot play mode, as it is currently implemented, is designed to support one connection at a time. It works as long as only one user is connected to a given audio source. The connected user always hears the complete audio clip from the beginning exactly one time. When the clip ends, the user hears silence until being retrieved from hold.

If any other users are connected to that audio source while the first user is still connected, they hear the clip starting wherever it was at the time the user was connected. If the clip is finished, they hear silence, just like the first caller. For example, if the first user already listened to half of the one shot audio clip when the second user was connected to the same audio source, the second user would only hear the second half of the clip, starting wherever the clip was in its playback when the user was connected. When all users are disconnected from the one shot audio source, the cycle starts again for the next user that is connected to the one shot source.

Handling MOH Stream Connections Errors

Table 5-15 shows what happens when the audio streams are not configured correctly in the system, and what will happen to the MOH stream connection if that error occurs.

Table 5-15   *Stream Connection Errors*

Error	Actions Taken
Audio source is not configured	If an audio source is selected that is not connected to an audio source file, the held devices will hear silence.
Connection to CallManager is lost	The MOH server terminates all current output stream connections. This is done because CallManager cannot disconnect the streams because it cannot talk to the MOH server. The callers that were hearing MOH will now hear silence.

MOH Server Initialization

When an MOH server is initialized, it checks the date and timestamp for its audio source files against the values stored in the CallManager database. If they differ, the new files are obtained from the default TFTP client as specified by the Cisco IP Voice Media Streaming App service parameter Default TFTP MOH IP Address. After the transfer is completed, the date and times on the MOH server are updated for each file that was transferred.

The same process is followed when the MOH server receives a change notification for the selected audio source. If the audio source is currently being streamed and a change is noted, the new audio source is retrieved and used when the current audio source is no longer active.

Summary of MOH Server Capabilities

The following are the current capabilities of the MOH servers:

- Supports a total of 500 one-way Unicast or Multicast audio output streams at the same time. All the output connections can be connected to one source stream or any combination of source streams. Note that a Multicast connection does not take any extra stream resources from the MOH server.

- Fifty audio source IDs, each of which is assigned to an audio source, can be specified.

- One fixed audio source (from sound card) can be used (audio source ID 51).

- An audio source can be configured to play in a continuous loop or one shot. If a source stream has the Multicast option selected, the data source is automatically played in a continuous loop, because the MOH server does not know when devices are connected to the Multicast points. The MOH server makes the assumption that someone is always connected to the MOH Multicast point. If the Multicast option is not selected, but the source stream is configured to play in a continuous loop, the music source is only played when output streams are connected to the audio source stream.

- G.711 A-law, G.711 μ-law, G729a, and wideband audio codecs are supported.

- Unicast and Multicast output is supported for each audio source.

> **TIP** The possibility exists for the MOH server to support up to 500 output streams simultaneously. As new server hardware becomes available with faster processors, this stream count will likely increase. These are the current limits.

MOH Multicast Configuration

CallManager Administration configures each MOH server with a Multicast base address and port, and it specifies whether the port or the IP address is to be incremented to create a range of Multicast IP addresses as required. Each MOH server must be configured with a different range of Multicast addresses. This prevents multiple servers from streaming audio to the same Multicast address.

It is not necessary for all MOH servers to support Multicast streams. One server can provide all 51 streams to 51 different Multicast addresses for each enabled codec. If all codecs are enabled, you must have 204 different Multicast addresses.

> **TIP**   It might be useful to configure two or more servers for Multicast so that if one server fails, Multicast is still available.

The MOH servers can provide each audio source as a Unicast stream and a Multicast stream. If Multicast output is desired, the Multicast check box for that source must be checked in the audio source configuration, and the MOH server must be configured for Multicast, as well.

Configuring CallManager to Use MOH

MOH is configured through CallManager Administration. After an MOH server has been configured in the database, it can be added to one or more MRGs. An MOH server is a standard media processing resource. Its usage can be controlled and configured the same as any other media processing resource by using MRGs and MRGLs.

Hold Types in CallManager

There are two different types of hold, as follows:

- User hold

- Network hold

User hold is invoked when a user directly places a call on hold by pressing the **Hold** softkey on a Cisco IP Phone. Network hold is invoked when a caller is placed on hold by some other feature, such as a transfer. The user presses the **Transf...** softkey on a Cisco IP Phone, and as a result, CallManager places the user on network hold until the transfer is completed.

How a Stream Source Is Selected When a User Is Placed on Hold

The stream source that a given held call hears depends on how both the device that originated the hold and the device being held are configured. The device that originated the hold determines which audio source is played to the user being held, and the device that is being held determines which MOH server will be used to supply the source audio stream. Figure 5-28 illustrates these connections.

Figure 5-28 illustrates a possible configuration of a cluster with two CallManager nodes in one location and a PSTN connection. The following examples use this configuration.

Figure 5-28 *How MOH Streams Are Selected*

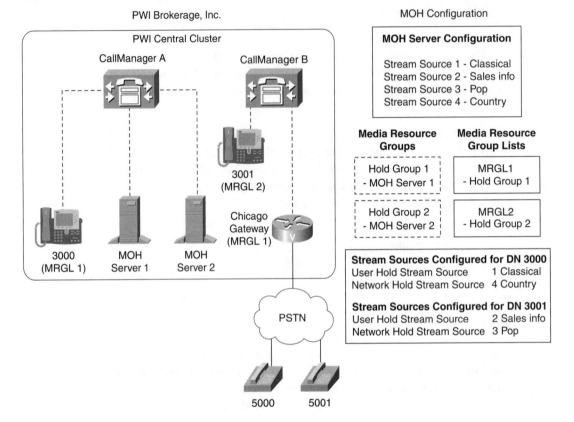

PWI Brokerage, Inc.

MOH Configuration

PWI Central Cluster

CallManager A

CallManager B

3001
(MRGL 2)

Chicago
Gateway
(MRGL 1)

3000
(MRGL 1)

MOH
Server 1

MOH
Server 2

PSTN

5000   5001

MOH Server Configuration

Stream Source 1 - Classical
Stream Source 2 - Sales info
Stream Source 3 - Pop
Stream Source 4 - Country

Media Resource Groups

Hold Group 1
- MOH Server 1

Hold Group 2
- MOH Server 2

Media Resource Group Lists

MRGL1
- Hold Group 1

MRGL2
- Hold Group 2

Stream Sources Configured for DN 3000
User Hold Stream Source   1 Classical
Network Hold Stream Source   4 Country

Stream Sources Configured for DN 3001
User Hold Stream Source   2 Sales info
Network Hold Stream Source   3 Pop

Example 1: Caller on 5000 Is Placed on Hold

Scenario: PSTN phone 5000 calls 3001 at PWI Brokerage Inc., and 3001 answers the call. 3001 places 5000 on hold.

In this example, 5000 is connected to MOH server MOH 1 because the gateway is assigned to MRGL1. MRGL1 has Hold Group 1 in its list. The caller is listening to the stream source 2 because the user hold stream for 3001 is set to stream source 2, which just happens to be a sales infomercial about new account types and services. The user on phone 5000 listens to a great sales pitch.

Example 2: Caller on 5001 Is Placed on Network Hold and then on User Hold

Scenario: PSTN phone 5001 calls 3000 at PWI Brokerage Inc. A stockbroker at 3000 answers and finds out that the caller wants to set up a new account. The stockbroker then transfers the caller to 3001 in new accounts.

When the stockbroker presses the **Transf...** softkey on the phone, the caller is placed on network hold. The caller then hears stream source 4, which is playing country music because the Network Hold Stream Source for 3000 is set to stream source 4, Country. The music is delivered from server MOH 1 because the gateway is assigned to MRGL1.

After a minute or two, the new account representative answers on 3001, but is extremely busy and puts the caller on 3001 on hold. Now the caller hears a nice sales pitch on all of the new accounts and services being offered. This occurs because the User Hold Stream Source for 3001 is set to stream source 2, Sales Info. The Sales Info stream is provided from MOH 1 because the gateway is assigned to MRGL1. Finally, the new account representative retrieves the call from hold and sets up the new account.

MOH and Conferences

Conference is a special case for MOH. With default settings, MOH is never played directly into a conference. If a conference participant places the conference on hold, CallManager recognizes this as a special case and does not connect that held call to MOH. The conference hears silence from that participant until he or she resumes the conference call. You can change this behavior by setting the CallManager service parameter Suppress MOH to Conference Bridge to False. This causes MOH to be played into a conference when the conference is placed on hold.

Configuring MOH in CallManager

Configuring and using MOH in CallManager can be very simple or very complex, depending on the requirements for your installation.

Initial MOH Configuration

MOH is disabled when CallManager is installed and the Cisco IP Voice Media Streaming App is not activated. In this configuration, CallManager plays Tone on Hold when a caller is placed on hold for any reason, if the endpoint device associated with that user is capable of generating Tone on Hold. If not, the caller hears silence.

Simplest MOH Configuration

The MOH server is installed when the Cisco IP Voice Media Streaming App is installed during the CallManager installation process. When the IP Voice Media Streaming App service is activated, it automatically installs a default sound source file, and it creates and configures an MOH device in the database. After MOH has been activated, all devices have access to MOH as soon as the MOH server registers with a CallManager node. By default, all callers hear audio source 1 from the MOH server anytime a call is placed on hold.

In this case, all devices are getting their MOH server through the Null MRG where the MOH server is declared by default because it is not part of any MRG. The Hold Stream Source defaults at the system level are set to audio source 1. This continues until you change the configuration by putting the MOH server into an MRG.

More Complex MOH Configurations

If a more complex configuration is needed, creating MRGs and MRGLs and assigning MRGLs to various devices in the system can achieve it. When you configure an MRG with an MOH server in it, you must also configure the Multicast/Unicast flag for that MRG.

The MOH User Hold Stream Source and the MOH Network Stream Source can be set to any MOH stream source that is configured on the MOH servers. If either User Hold Stream Source or Network Hold Stream Source is set to an audio source that has not yet been configured on the MOH servers, the callers will hear silence when connected to MOH.

A Multicast flag is in the MRG. If the Multicast box is not checked, Unicast streams are used for all MOH connections. If the Multicast box is checked, MOH allocation attempts try to allocate and use a Multicast stream connection. If Multicast MOH streams are not available, the held calls hear Tone on Hold, if their endpoint device supports it. Otherwise, they hear silence.

Order of Precedence of MOH Music Stream Source Assignments

MOH stream source assignments follow a defined order of precedence. When CallManager processes a hold request, it decides which MOH audio source stream to use based on the MOH stream source assignments in order of precedence, with 1 being the highest precedence. Table 5-16 defines the MOH source assignment order of precedence for both user hold and network hold.

Table 5-16 *MOH Stream Source Assignment Precedence*

MOH Source Assignment Order of Precedence	Comments
1. Assigned at the directory number level	The MOH stream source assigned at the directory number level applies only to that particular directory number and has precedence over all other MOH source assignments, if any, that are on the device level or device pool level.
2. Assigned at the device level	An MOH stream source assigned at the device level applies only to that particular device. The device level MOH stream source assignment has precedence over the MOH source assigned at the device pool level.
3. Assigned at the device pool level	The MOH stream source assigned at the device pool level applies to all entities that are assigned to that device pool. It has precedence over the system defaults.

Table 5-16 *MOH Stream Source Assignment Precedence (Continued)*

MOH Source Assignment Order of Precedence	Comments
4. Default system assignments	This is the most general level at which MOH stream sources can be assigned, and it applies when CallManager cannot find any other MOH stream source assignment that applies for a particular call based on the device and directory number used.

CallManager MOH Usage and Performance Monitoring

All performance monitoring provided by CallManager occurs through the use of Cisco-provided objects and counters. Each Cisco object contains one or more counters. You can monitor these counters in the RTMT in CallManager Serviceability. CallManager provides two sets of counters that are maintained by each CallManager node:

- MOH counters per CallManager

- Counters per MOH server from a CallManager's perspective

Counters per CallManager Node

Each of the following counters is for an individual CallManager node. They represent the total for all MOH servers that are registered with that CallManager node (see Table 5-17).

Table 5-17 *MOH Counters per CallManager Node*

Counter	Description
MOHMulticastResourceActive	This represents the total number of Multicast MOH resources that are currently in use (active) on all MOH servers registered with this CallManager.
MOHMulticastResourceAvailable	This represents the total number of Multicast MOH connections that are not being used on all MOH servers that are registered with this CallManager.
MOHTotalMulticastResources	This represents the total number of Multicast MOH resources or connections provided by all MOH servers that are currently registered with this CallManager.
MOHUnicastResourceActive	This represents the total number of Unicast MOH resources that are currently in use (active) on all MOH servers that are registered with this CallManager. Each MOH Unicast resource uses one stream.
MOHUnicastResourceAvailable	This represents the total number of Unicast MOH resources that are currently available on all MOH servers registered with this CallManager. Each MOH Unicast resource uses one stream.

continues

Table 5-17   *MOH Counters per CallManager Node (Continued)*

Counter	Description
MOHTotalUnicastResources	This represents the total number of Unicast MOH resources or streams provided by all MOH servers that are currently registered with this CallManager. Each MOH Unicast resource uses one stream.
MOHOutOfResources	This represents the total number of times that the Media Resource Manager attempted to allocate an MOH resource when all available resources on all MOH servers registered with this CallManager were already active, or none were registered.

Counters per MOH Server from a CallManager's Perspective

Each MOH server registers with a CallManager node independently, and CallManager maintains statistics about each MOH server that is registered. Table 5-18 lists and describes the counters that are maintained for each registered MOH server.

Table 5-18   *Counters per Registered MOH Server*

Counters	Description
MOHMulticastResourceActive	This represents the number of currently active Multicast connections to Multicast addresses served by this MOH server.
MOHMulticastResourceAvailable	This represents the number of MOH Multicast connections to Multicast addresses served by this MOH server that are not active and are still available to be used at the current time.
MOHTotalMulticastResources	This represents the total number of Multicast MOH connections allowed to Multicast addresses served by this MOH server.
MOHUnicastResourceActive	This represents the number of active Unicast MOH connections to this MOH server. Each MOH Unicast resource uses one stream.
MOHUnicastResourceAvailable	This represents the number of Unicast MOH connections that are not active and are still available to be used at the current time for this MOH server. Each MOH Unicast resource uses one stream.
MOHTotalUnicastResources	This represents the total number of Unicast MOH connections allowed by this MOH server. Each MOH Unicast resource uses one stream.

Table 5-18   *Counters per Registered MOH Server (Continued)*

Counters	Description
MOHOutOfResources	This represents the total number of times that the Media Resource Manager attempted to allocate an MOH resource when all available resources on all MOH servers registered with this CallManager were already active.
MOHHighestActiveResources	Indicates the largest number of simultaneously active MOH connections on this MOH server, including both Multicast and Unicast connections.

Video Call Processing Architecture

CallManager supports video as a normal part of call processing. If video is supported on a particular endpoint, then making a video call can be as simple as making a voice call. In fact, you do not have to do anything different when placing a video call. Locations and regions are used to control the bandwidth for video calls. Bandwidth is controlled separately for video and audio so that you can set limits on each of them independently.

When a call is attempted from an endpoint that supports video to another endpoint that also supports video, CallManager always attempts to set up both audio and video channels for the call. If CallManager cannot get the bandwidth required for the video call, it automatically retries the call as audio only. Video calls are supported for SCCP endpoints and H.323 endpoints.

CallManager Video Usage and Performance Monitoring

All performance monitoring provided by CallManager occurs through the use of Cisco-provided objects and counters. Each Cisco object contains one or more counters. You can monitor these counters in the RTMT in CallManager Serviceability. CallManager provides three sets of counters that are maintained by each CallManager node:

- Video counters per CallManager node

- Video conference server counters per CallManager node

- Counters per video conference server from a CallManager's perspective

Counters per CallManager Node

Table 5-19 documents a set of counters for an individual CallManager node. They represent the total for all video calls processed by that CallManager node.

Table 5-19 *Video Call Counters per CallManager Node*

Counters	Description
VideoCallsActive	This represents the number of active video calls with active video streaming connections on this CallManager.
VideoCallsCompleted	This represents the number of video calls that were actually connected with video streams and then released.
VideoOutOfResources	This represents the total number of times CallManager attempted to setup video channels when there was not sufficient bandwidth over the desired network link for the video channels, or the configured video bandwidth limit would have been exceeded.

Table 5-20 documents the set of video conference counters for each CallManager node. The counters represent the total for all video conferences on all video conference servers that are registered with that particular CallManager node.

Table 5-20 *Video Conference Server Counters per CallManager Node*

Counters	Description
VCBConferencesActive	This represents the number of active video calls with active video streaming connections on all video conference bridge devices registered with this CallManager.
VCBConferencesAvailable	This represents the total number of new video conferences that can be started on all video conference bridge devices registered with this CallManager.
VCBConferencesCompleted	This represents the total number of video conferences that used a video conference bridge allocated from this CallManager and have been completed, which means that the conference bridge has been allocated and released. A conference is activated when the first call is connected to the bridge. The conference completes when the last call disconnects from the bridge that was connected and released.
VCBConferencesTotal	This represents the total number of video conferences supported on all video conference bridge devices registered with this CallManager.
VCBOutOfConferences	This represents the total number of failed new video conference requests. A conference request can fail because (for example, the configured number of conferences are already in use).
VCBOutOfResources	This represents the total number of times that CallManager attempted to allocate a video conference resource from those that are registered to this CallManager when none were available.
VCBResourceActive	This represents the total number of video conference resources that are currently in use on all video conference devices that are registered with this CallManager.

Table 5-20   *Video Conference Server Counters per CallManager Node (Continued)*

Counters	Description
VCBResourceAvailable	This represents the total number of video conference resources that are not active and are currently available.
VCBResourceTotal	This represents the total number of video conference resources provided by all video conference bridge devices that are currently registered with this CallManager.

Counters per Video Conference Server from a CallManager's Perspective

Each Video Conference server registers with a CallManager independently, and CallManager maintains statistics about each Video Conference server that is registered. Table 5-21 lists and describes the counters that are maintained for each registered Video Conference server.

Table 5-21   *Counters per Registered Video Conference Server*

Counters	Description
ResourceTotal	This represents the total number of resources configured on this video conference server device. One resource is used per participant.
ResourceAvailable	This represents the total number of resources that are not active and are still available on this device to handle additional participants for this video conference server device.
ResourceActive	This represents the total number of resources that are currently active (in use) on this video conference server device. One resource is used per participant.
OutOfResources	This represents the total number of times an attempt was made to allocate a conference resource from this video conference server and failed (for example, because all resources were already in use).
ConferencesTotal	This represents the total number of video conferences configured for this video conference server.
ConferencesAvailable	This represents the number of video conferences that are not active and are still available on this video conference server.
ConferencesCompleted	This represents the total number of video conferences that have been allocated and released on this video conference server. A conference is started when the first call is connected to the bridge. The conference completes when the last call disconnects from the bridge.
ConferencesActive	This represents the total number of video conferences that are currently active (in use) on this video conference server. A conference is active when the first call is connected to the bridge.
OutOfConferences	This represents the total number of times an attempt was made to initiate a video conference from this video conference server and failed because this server already had the maximum number of active conferences allowed.

Annunciator/Tone Plant Processing Architecture

The annunciator architecture is very similar to the MOH architecture. These devices are known by both the call signaling layers and the MCL. Annunciators are used in CallManager to play various pre-recorded announcements and tones to a single party, a conference, or an MTP.

When CallManager is required to play a tone such as ringback, busy, or reorder, and is unable to have this performed by the end device, the annunciator can be used to perform this function. Announcements or tones are played by connecting a one-way stream from the annunciator to the device and then directing the annunciator to play the specific tone or announcement. This scenario is encountered, for example, on some H.323 devices where the endpoint is being transferred or forwarded.

In CallManager, annunciators are used to play both tones and announcements because they are all audio files as far as the annunciator is concerned. Each announcement or tone file has a particular identifier, and the system identifies the item it wants to play by that identifier. When CallManager connects a device to the annunciator, it specifies a network locale, a user locale, and the announcement or tone identifier. This enables the annunciator to play the appropriate localized tone or announcement.

Annunciators provide specific functions for features, including the following:

- To play a ringback tone to a SIP client when the SIP client is being transferred from an IP phone.

- To play Vacant Code Announcement (VCA). "Your call cannot be completed as dialed. Please consult your directory and call again or ask your operator for assistance. This is a recording."

- To play Isolated Code Announcement (ICA). "A service disruption has prevented the completion of your call. In case of emergency call your operator. This is a recording."

- To play ringback and other tones for transfers on H.323 intercluster trunks.

- To play a busy tone based on an error generated by CTI for H.323-related calls.

- To play beginning and ending tones for monitoring sessions.

- To play audible tones at the beginning and end of recording sessions.

- To play Blocked Precedence Announcements for the MLPP feature.

- To play announcements for MLPP calls being released abnormally.

- To play ringback tone to an Ad Hoc conference when a participant is added to the conference until the participant answers the call.

To an annunciator, a tone and any other announcement is the same thing. They are all recorded audio files stored on the disk of the annunciator server. Annunciators can play an announcement only once, or play it repeatedly until CallManager tells it to stop. An annunciator can notify CallManager when an announcement has finished playing if requested to do so.

After the annunciator device has registered, CallManager allocates resources from the annunciator device as needed, and connects them, as one-way streams, to devices such as IP phones, gateways, MTPs, and conferences. When the connection is established, CallManager starts an announcement by sending a StartTone SCCP message to the annunciator. The annunciator then starts playing the specified announcement file. If requested by CallManager, the annunciator device signals CallManager when the announcement has finished. The annunciator sends this signal only when CallManager indicates that an end-of-play notification is required. If the announcement is configured as repeating and CallManager requested an end-of-play notification, the annunciator notifies CallManager each time the announcement file has been played once, and continues until the playback is stopped.

CallManager stops playback of an announcement by sending a StopTone SCCP message to the annunciator. The annunciator automatically stops playback when the streaming connection between the annunciator and the listening device terminates.

The following tones are supported for the U.S. locale:

- **Line busy tone**—400–450 Hz tone for 0.5 second duration with 0.5 second silent period between tones

- **Alerting tone**—400–450 Hz tone for 0.67 to 1.5 second duration with 3- to 5-second silent period between tones

Annunciator devices support localization, so all tones and announcements can be localized as needed. The tones are network tones and are associated with the country that CallManager serves, as defined in the network locale. Having several different locales within the same country is possible. This structure allows for multiple languages within a given country.

You can specify both the network locale and the user locale for a device. The user locale specified for a device sets the language that will be played, and the network locale sets the tones that will be played. CallManager allows you to edit the announcements as needed.

Device Control and Operation

The Cisco IP Voice Media Streaming App implements the annunciator server. The IP Voice Media Streaming App is the same application software that implements software Unicast conference bridges, MTPs, and the MOH servers. It registers with CallManager in the same way as an MOH server.

When the annunciator device registers with CallManager, CallManager creates a control process that maintains device status, resource availability, and other such information about the device. It is also responsible for device registration and all communication to and from the device. When the

MRM is allocating resources, it always queries the device control process for available resources once a potential device is selected.

Configuring Annunciator Servers

You can enable annunciators in the system by activating the Cisco IP Voice Media Streaming App. When the IP Voice Media Streaming App is activated, an annunciator device is automatically created in the CallManager database with default settings.

Upon registration, the device informs CallManager how many resources it can support. Unlike conferencing and MTP resources, annunciator devices do not preserve any stream connections in progress when any a failure occurs. All tones or announcements in progress are interrupted at the time of the failure.

If you install the annunciator device on a dedicated server, it supports up to a total of 400 simultaneous streams. Each stream plays one announcement; thus, the annunciator device can play up to 400 simultaneous announcements. All annunciator servers in a cluster have the same audio source file configuration. This means that the tone or announcement file can be obtained from any available annunciator server. The same tone or announcement can be played on all active output streams simultaneously, or any mix of announcements or tones can be played as needed.

There is a separate audio source file for each tone or announcement for each of the four supported codecs. Thus each announcement has four audio files associated with it on the annunciator server.

The annunciator servers support the same audio codecs as MTPs and MOH servers, as follows:

- G.711 A-law

- G.711 μ-law

- G.729a

- Wideband

Annunciator Server Initialization

When an annunciator server initializes, it checks the date and timestamp for its audio source files against the values stored in the CallManager database. If the date and timestamps differ from the CallManager database values, the new audio source files will be loaded on the annunciator server. After the transfer is completed, the date and times on the annunciator server are updated for each file that was transferred.

CallManager follows the same process when the annunciator server receives a change notification for the selected audio source. If the audio source is currently being streamed and a change is noted, the new audio source is retrieved and used when the current audio source is no longer active.

> **NOTE**   CallManager supplies U.S. English tone and announcement audio source files with the system when it is installed. You can install additional locales on the system; when you do, additional announcement files are installed on CallManager as needed to support the new locale.

Annunciator Performance Statistics

A number of performance counters are available to monitor the usage of annunciators. All performance statistics are monitored through Microsoft Windows 2000 counters. You can monitor these counters in the RTMT in Cisco CallManager Serviceability. CallManager provides two sets of counters that are maintained by each CallManager node:

- Annunciator counters per CallManager node

- Counters per annunciator server from a CallManager's perspective

Counters per CallManager Node

Each of the counters listed and described in Table 5-22 is for an individual CallManager node. The counters represent the total for all annunciator servers that are registered with that CallManager node.

Table 5-22   *Annunciator Counters per CallManager Node*

Counter	Description
AnnunciatorResourceTotal	This represents the total number of annunciator resources provided by all annunciator devices that are currently registered with this CallManager.
AnnunciatorResourceActive	This represents the total number of annunciator resources that are currently in use on all annunciator devices registered with this CallManager.
AnnunciatorResourceAvailable	This represents the total number of annunciator resources that are not active and are currently available.
AnnunciatorOutOfResources	This represents the total number of times that CallManager attempted to allocate an annunciator resource from those that are registered to this CallManager when none were available.

Counters per Annunciator Server from a CallManager's Perspective

Each annunciator server registers with a CallManager node independently, and CallManager maintains statistics about each annunciator server that is registered. Table 5-23 lists and describes the counters that are maintained for each registered annunciator server.

Table 5-23 *Counters per Registered Annunciator Server*

Counter	Description
ResourceTotal	This represents the total number of annunciator resources configured for this annunciator device.
ResourceActive	This represents the total number of annunciator resources that are currently active (in use) for this annunciator device.
ResourceAvailable	This represents the total number of resources that are not active and are still available to be used at the current time for the annunciator device.
OutOfResources	This represents the total number of times an attempt was made to allocate an annunciator resource from this annunciator device and failed (for example, because all resources were already in use).

Call Preservation During System Failures

Call preservation refers to the capability of the CallManager node to maintain call connections during failure conditions on either the underlying network or the components within CallManager. This section describes the processing involved in call preservation and covers failure conditions for all major components. Call preservation is included in the media processing section because when a failure occurs, it is the media streaming that must be maintained to keep the call connected.

General Overview of Call Preservation

CallManager consists of a cluster of CallManager nodes, Cisco IP Phones, gateways that provide connections to the PSTN, and various media processing resources such as conference bridges, transcoders, MTPs, and annunciators. It can also support numerous other voice applications, such as call centers and *interactive voice response* (IVR) systems. Any of these entities can be involved in a call being processed by CallManager.

CallManager nodes provide call processing services and call connection control for all calls processed by a device. After a device has created media streaming connections to other devices under the direction of CallManager, the devices themselves control all aspects of the media streams and connections until directed to terminate the media streaming connections.

Each CallManager node maintains primary call state information for all calls that it controls. If a CallManager node is not involved in a given call, it has no knowledge of that call. If a CallManager node does not control a call but controls devices that are involved in the call, that CallManager node maintains only call state information relating to the devices registered to itself that are part of that call, and not the call itself. Because the various endpoint devices and media processing resources can be registered with different CallManager nodes in the cluster, the entities involved in a given call can be, and usually are, controlled by more than one CallManager node.

> **NOTE**   Normally without call preservation, each call that is controlled by a CallManager node that fails, or any call that involves a device that is controlled by a node that fails, would terminate immediately on the failure of any node or device involved in the call. This happens either because the other node or nodes involved in the call recognize the node or device failure and disconnect their end of the call (which ends media streaming), or because the devices themselves recognize that the CallManager node to which they are registered has failed. In that case, the device normally closes its media streaming connections and reregisters with another CallManager node.

With the enhanced call preservation, users are generally able to continue their conversations without call processing support. This means that while the call is still active, no supplementary services are available, and the call configuration cannot be changed for the duration of the call. Hanging up will clear the call.

Call preservation involves complex processing in both CallManager and the devices that register with CallManager. Many communication links of various types are involved in calls being processed. This creates complex recovery scenarios, because any one signaling path or any combination of paths might be broken.

The failure of any given device or CallManager node creates some interesting and complex failure and recovery scenarios. This section explores some of the failure possibilities and identifies recovery algorithms used by CallManager and the devices. The following topics are covered:

■   Failure and recovery objectives

■   Handling system and device failures

■   Device recovery and call preservation algorithms

■   Call preservation during device failure and recovery

Failure and Recovery Objectives

In several failure cases, the signaling path for call processing is interrupted, but the media streaming connections are not necessarily affected. When a CallManager node fails, for example, the media streams between devices are not affected. It is also possible that when communication between a CallManager node and a device fails, the streaming connections between devices are not affected. In this case, a CallManager node involved in the call might have communication with other devices that are in the call. It becomes the responsibility of all CallManager nodes involved in the call to clear down the signaling paths that are related to the failure, without instructing the devices with which they still have communication to clear the call as they would in normal circumstances when the signaling path is cleared.

CallManager does not know whether the streaming connections between the devices have been interrupted. In failure conditions, it becomes the responsibility of the devices involved in a call to maintain the streaming connections that are already established. This is true even when the signaling path between the device and its CallManager node has failed.

If communication between a device and its CallManager node did not fail, it is the device's responsibility to inform its CallManager node when the streaming connections have been closed in the same manner as they do in normal call processing.

When handling failure scenarios, CallManager attempts to accomplish the following objectives:

- Maintain all active streaming connections that existed at the time of the failure so that no active call is interrupted

- Clear all calls that are in the call setup phase at the time of the failure and were affected by the failure

- Maintain communication with all devices that are still accessible after the failure

- Recover all devices that were registered to a failed CallManager node

- Minimize downtime for CallManager nodes and devices involved in or affected by a failure

- Maintain normal system operation as much as possible during the failure

Handling System and Device Failures

Endpoint and media processing devices have responsibility for and control over media connections and media streams, after the streams have been established under the direction of CallManager. Maintaining them in a failure condition is primarily the devices' responsibility, but it also requires close cooperation with CallManager. Failures present unique and sometimes difficult situations that must be handled correctly to maintain active calls through the system.

The recognized failure cases are as follows:

- CallManager node failure

- Media processing device failure

- Endpoint device failure

- CallManager-to-device communication failure

- Node-to-node communication failure within a cluster

- Device-to-device communication failure

The main causes for each of these failure cases are defined and some of the failure scenarios are discussed in this section.

CallManager Node Failure

CallManager node failures can be caused by a CallManager software error, by a server failure, or by a network failure. If the failure is caused by a software error or a server failure, the failure causes call processing functions on that node to stop, and all communication with that node is lost.

When this failure occurs, all devices registered to that CallManager node recognize that their current CallManager node has failed. Similarly, the other CallManager nodes in the cluster detect the failure of that node. When a node failure occurs, all remaining CallManager nodes immediately execute a call preservation teardown of all calls that they are processing that involve the failed node. A call preservation teardown is the same as a normal teardown, except that all devices involved in the call are not notified that the call has been torn down, and the device control processes in CallManager for each of the devices involved in the call maintain low-level state information about the call so that they know the device is involved in a call without call signaling support. No new calls are extended to devices that are in a call preservation mode. The affected devices involved in a call maintain all active calls until the end user hangs up or the devices can determine that the media connection has been closed. No call processing features can be invoked on the preserved calls.

If the failure is caused by a network failure, call processing functions are still intact, but communications between that CallManager node and some or all of the devices registered with that node, as well as communication with other nodes in the cluster, might be lost. When communication with a node or device is lost, that device or node is treated as though it has failed.

A CallManager node recognizes that another node has failed when the TCP/IP link to the other CallManager node returns an error that indicates a link failure. If the communication link fails, the other node is considered to have failed.

A CallManager node recognizes that a device has failed in one of two ways: Either the TCP/IP link to the device returns an error that indicates the link has failed, or no KeepAlive request has been received from the device within its prescribed KeepAlive interval. Whether the device actually failed or just the link failed is not significant, because either case is treated the same.

Similarly, a device recognizes that its CallManager node has failed when CallManager fails to respond to its KeepAlive requests within the prescribed time. If the communication link has failed, the device recognizes the error when it receives an error from its TCP/IP stack that indicates the link has failed. Whether the CallManager node actually failed or only the communication link failed is not significant, because either case is treated the same.

Media Processing Device Failure

Typical media processing devices are audio conference bridges, video conference bridges, MTPs, transcoders, annunciators, and MOH servers. CallManager recognizes device failures when a KeepAlive timeout for that device occurs. The failure can be caused by a device software error, a server failure, or a network failure; to CallManager, however, it makes no difference. When a device fails for any reason, the result is a loss of communication with the device. Because all communication is lost, the device must execute its own failure and recovery algorithms. CallManager's responsibility in this case is to release its own call processing resources as appropriate without terminating the call or calls being handled by the device.

If the device truly failed, call streaming through the device also stops, and other devices involved in the call must detect the streaming failure and clear the call. The device's active CallManager node recognizes the device failure and clears call processing entities within CallManager that are associated with calls in the failed device.

If the device loses communication with CallManager while media streaming connections are active, the device assumes all responsibility for and control over all active connections and media streams. It must also find another CallManager node with which it can register. The device itself decides when and if it will register with CallManager while it has streaming connections active.

Endpoint Device Failure

Typical endpoint devices are Cisco IP Phones, other IP phones, gateways, video IP phones, and other similar devices. Device failures and loss of communication with a device are considered the same failure.

CallManager-to-Device Communication Failure

A communication failure to a device, regardless of the cause of the failure, is treated as a device failure. CallManager recognizes a device failure when a KeepAlive timeout occurs. CallManager also recognizes a device failure when the TCP/IP socket connection to the device is broken. When a device fails, all call processing resources associated with that device are released, and call signaling is cleared.

Node-to-Node Communication Failure Within a Cluster

A CallManager cluster is fully meshed between all CallManager nodes in the cluster, which means that there is a TCP/IP connection from each CallManager node to every other CallManager node in the cluster. If, for any reason, the TCP/IP link from any given CallManager node to any other CallManager node fails, the other node to which it is connected is considered to have failed. An appropriate call preservation teardown will occur for all calls associated with the failed node.

Device-to-Device Communication Failure

Device-to-device communications are usually in the form of logical channels or, in other words, media streaming connections that are carrying audio or video streaming data. When the communication path breaks, the error is detected as a media streaming error, and the CallManager node to which the device is registered is notified. Device-to-device call preservation is implemented completely in the devices, and the CallManager nodes involved in the call have little or no ability to help or influence the processing, other than making sure that CallManager does not clear the call. This allows the devices to handle processing in the best way they can and to report to CallManager when the call clears, if they are still registered.

Call Preservation Examples

The following two examples illustrate some of the complexities that exist even in these relatively simple configurations.

Example 1: Call Between Two Phones, Each Registered to a Different Node

Figure 5-29 shows a single node failure when two CallManager nodes are involved in a call.

Figure 5-29 *Single Node Failure When Two CallManager Nodes Are Involved in a Call*

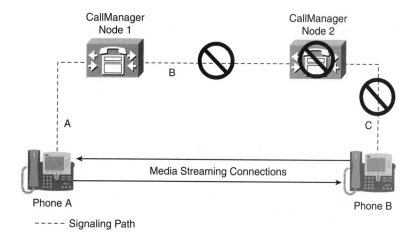

Note that Phone A is registered to CallManager node 1 and Phone B is registered to CallManager node 2. Phone A calls Phone B, and the call is connected successfully. If CallManager node 2 fails, CallManager node 1 recognizes that signaling path B has failed, and it does a call preservation call teardown for Phone A. Signaling path C also fails, and that failure is recognized by Phone B. This leaves only signaling path A and the media streaming connections still active. No call processing support is available for the remainder of this call, but the devices can continue streaming data to each other indefinitely. The phones tear down the media streaming connections when they are placed on-hook, thus terminating the call. Phone A reports the on-hook to CallManager node 1. Phone B will then register with its backup CallManager node. If CallManager node 1 fails, the same process occurs, with the actions on the two phones being reversed.

If the signaling path B fails, each CallManager node does a call preservation teardown for its respective phone. No call processing support is available for the remainder of the call. When either phone goes on-hook, the call is terminated. Both phones report the termination to their respective CallManager nodes, and each CallManager node will release all remaining low-level resources associated with the call.

Example 2: A Conference Call

Figure 5-30 illustrates the connections that are present for a conference call that was set up by Phone A. This example explains what happens to the call in call preservation situations caused by failures of various devices and communication links. Not all of the possibilities are discussed, but enough are discussed to illustrate how call preservation works.

Phone A sets up a conference, which includes A, B, and C. Several different scenarios could occur because of failures on this conference call. If CallManager 1 fails, signaling paths A, C, and F fail, and call processing for Phone A, who is the conference controller, is lost. The conference continues, but it cannot be extended to any other parties. When Phone A is placed on-hook, it terminates its media streaming connections to the conference bridge and registers with another CallManager node. The other participants in the conference terminate the conference normally. They are unaffected by the failure.

If CallManager 2 fails, signal paths A, B, D, and E fail, and call processing for the conference bridge and Phone B is lost. The conference can continue only if the conference bridge allows the media connections to remain active even though it cannot communicate with CallManager. No call processing functions are available on this conference call. Even though the conference controller is still active, the conference cannot be extended, because there is no communication between CallManager and the conference bridge. When Phone B is placed on-hook, it terminates its media streaming connections to the conference bridge and registers with another CallManager node. As soon as either Phone A or C hangs up, the conference terminates and the conference bridge registers with another CallManager node.

Figure 5-30 *Call Preservation for Conference Call*

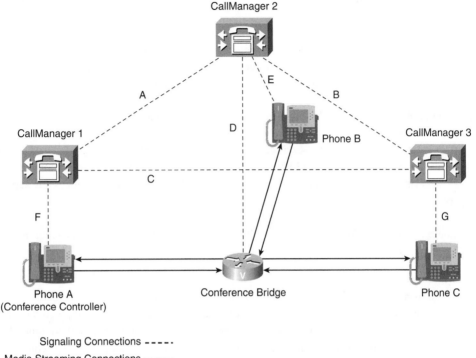

Signaling Connections - - - - -
Media Streaming Connections ———

If CallManager 3 fails, signaling paths B, C, and G fail. The conference can continue, but Phone C has no call processing functions available. The conference can also be extended because the conference controller and the conference bridge are unaffected by the failure. When Phone C is placed on-hook, it terminates its media streaming connections to the conference bridge and registers with another CallManager node.

If Phone A's network connection fails, signaling path F and the media streaming connections to Phone A are lost. This causes a normal call teardown for Phone A. The conference bridge recognizes the failure of the media streams and closes the media connections, leaving Phone B and Phone C in the conference. The conference cannot be extended because the conference controller is lost. Phone A registers with CallManager again when its network connection is restored.

If Phone B's or Phone C's network connection fails, signaling path E or G, respectively, and the media streaming connections to Phone B or Phone C are lost. This causes a normal call teardown for the affected phone. The conference bridge recognizes the failure of the media streams and closes the media connections to the lost phone, leaving Phone A and either Phone B or Phone C in the conference. Phone A can extend the conference, if desired, because the rest of the conference is not affected. The lost phone registers with CallManager again when its network connection is restored.

If signaling path A fails, it causes a call preservation teardown for all phones, because CallManager 1 was controlling the conference and each of the calls. Because CallManager 1 cannot talk to the conference bridge because of the signaling path failure, the entire conference goes into call preservation mode. The conference can continue without call processing support.

If signaling path B fails, it has no effect on the conference call.

If signaling path C fails, it causes a call preservation teardown for Phone C, because CallManager 1 was controlling the call from Phone C to the conference bridge, and the communication link to Phone C is lost. The conference continues, but Phone C does not have call processing support. The conference can be extended, if desired.

Combinations of failures can occur, resulting in even more complex recovery scenarios.

Recovering Devices After a Failure

CallManager is a multinode system, which provides redundancy for CallManager nodes that handle all call processing. All devices are not redundant, meaning, for example, if a Cisco IP Phone fails, there is no backup phone to take over. In the case of gateways, there might be redundancy, depending on the implementation of CallManager. Call processing redundancy is implemented in CallManager by creating a cluster of CallManager nodes, some of which serve as backups for other CallManager nodes in the event of a node failure.

All devices are intelligent endpoints and are responsible for finding a CallManager node with which to register. Redundant call processing support for devices is implemented by assigning each device an ordered list of CallManager nodes with which it is to register. The list is in priority order from first to last and is referred to as the *CallManager list*. The device registers with the first CallManager node that is in its list and currently available. The first CallManager in its list is often referred to as its *primary CallManager*. During failure conditions, a device registers with the CallManager node that is highest on its list and available when its primary CallManager fails. The process of unregistering with one CallManager node and registering with a CallManager node that is lower on the list is referred to as *failover*. Devices reregister with a CallManager node that is higher on their list during recovery from the failure. A failure recovery occurs when the primary CallManager node or another node higher on the list returns to service, or node-to-device communications are restored. The process of unregistering with one CallManager node and registering with a CallManager node that is higher on the list is known as *fallback*.

Devices and Applications That Support Call Preservation

The following list of devices and applications are known to support call preservation:

- Cisco IP Phones

- Software conference bridge (service)

- MTP (service)

- Cisco hardware conference bridges

- Cisco Transcoders

- Cisco non-IOS gateways using MGCP PRI backhaul

- IOS MGCP gateways

- SRST-enabled H.323 gateways

- CallManager Attendant Console

- CTI applications (depending on the endpoint devices involved)

- VG248 gateways

Devices and Applications That Do Not Support Call Preservation

The following devices and applications do not support call preservation:

- Non-SRST-enabled H.323 devices

- Annunciators

- MOH

Call Preservation Algorithms

The next sections describe the failover and fallback algorithms used by devices that are involved in active calls at the time of a failure. These algorithms do not specify how the device should decide to failover or fallback, but rather the actions that must take place once the device has made the decision to failover or fallback.

Failover Algorithms

Two algorithms are used by devices to determine when to fail over to a CallManager node that is lower on their list. Each device that is capable of maintaining calls in failure situations is required to implement either one or both of the algorithms. If the device implements both of the algorithms, you configure the device to use the one you prefer.

Graceful Failover

This algorithm allows the device to delay failover to another CallManager node until the device stops all active streaming connections. The device determines when to terminate the streaming connections based on the disconnect supervision options supported by that device. A Cisco IP Phone, for example, terminates its streams when the user hangs up the phone, or when it detects an error in transmission to the other endpoint in the call.

If no CallManager is lower in its list and is available when the device initiates a failover attempt, the device can reregister with the primary CallManager node if it is available, or another CallManager node that is higher in its list.

If no CallManager node is available when the device initiates a failover, the device terminates the active streaming connections after attempting to locate an available CallManager node for a reasonable amount of time. It continues looking for an available CallManager node to which it can register.

Immediate Failover

This algorithm allows the device to failover immediately to a CallManager that is lower in its list. When this device registers with the new CallManager node, it tells CallManager during registration how many connections it supports and how many of them are active at the time of registration. Thereafter, the device informs CallManager each time one of the active streams is closed.

When a device initiates a failover attempt, it is possible that no backup or lower-order CallManager node is available. In this case, the device can choose to reregister with the original primary or other CallManager higher in its list. This is exactly the same as a failover with a subsequent fallback.

If no CallManager node is available when the device initiates a failover, the device terminates the active streaming connections after attempting to locate an available CallManager node for a reasonable amount of time. It continues looking for an available CallManager node to which it can register.

Fallback Algorithms

Each device implements one or more of the following fallback algorithms. If the device supports more than one fallback algorithm, you configure which algorithm it uses. Only one configuration is active at any given time. A fallback does not occur because of an error condition directly. It is a recovery operation when some or all of the failure conditions have cleared. The device, therefore, has the opportunity to choose when it will fallback to its primary CallManager. Table 5-24 documents all allowed fallback algorithms.

Table 5-24 *Fallback Algorithms*

Fallback Algorithms	Description
Graceful algorithm	The device delays registering with a CallManager node that is higher in its list until all of its active streaming connections are stopped. This prevents any disruption to existing calls.
Immediate algorithm	The device immediately registers with a CallManager node that is higher in its list as soon as communications with that node are established. The registering device communicates the status of all active connections to the selected CallManager. It also notifies CallManager when each of the active connections is closed as the calls are cleared. When using this algorithm, all calls in progress at the time go into call preservation mode and do not have access to call processing services for the duration of the call.
Schedule-Time algorithm	In this case, you set a configurable timer. The timer must be set to expire within 24 hours from when it is set. On timer expiration, the Immediate algorithm is then invoked. This algorithm allows you to schedule a time when the device will fallback. If it is a phone, for example, it might be scheduled to fallback at 2 a.m., when it is not likely to be used.
Uptime-Delay algorithm	On detection that a CallManager node that is higher in its list is available, a user-configurable timer is set. On timer expiration, the Immediate algorithm is invoked. Basically the same as Schedule-Time algorithm, except that the user has control of the timer.
Graceful with guard timer	A guard timer is set. This guard timer can be statically implemented in the device or user-configurable. The Graceful algorithm is invoked. If the guard timer expires before fallback has been initiated per the Graceful algorithm, the Immediate algorithm is invoked. This basically says to wait until all calls are finished and the device is idle before executing a fallback. If this does not occur within a prescribed time, it forces a fallback. (Some devices might never go idle.)

TIP The Immediate option leaves the active maintained calls connected but without call processing support for remainder of their calls. The users cannot change the configuration of their calls and do not have access to features such as hold, transfer, conference, and so forth. This option also drops any calls that are in the process of being established. Only the calls that are already connected at the time of fallback are maintained. Because there is no CallManager node failure or communication failure condition in this case, the Immediate option is the least desirable of all the algorithms, because it affects active calls and is visible to the user.

Call Attempts During Failover and Fallback

It is possible that a new call setup is initiated from the device during the failover or the fallback time frame. The call attempt is handled in the following manner.

During the process of failover or fallback, when the device is not registered with a CallManager node, any new call setup request initiated from the device is ignored until the device has completed its registration with the CallManager node.

If the configured fallback algorithm is other than Immediate, registration with a CallManager node that is higher in its list can be delayed. During this time, the current CallManager node is still the active node and is capable of processing calls.

During any fallback delay introduced by a fallback option, the device processes new call setup attempts normally until the delay condition is satisfied and fallback can be initiated.

Cisco IP Phone Unregistration Sequence Requirements

Unregister requests from Cisco IP Phones are used when the phone is registered to a CallManager node lower in its list and a CallManager node that is higher in its list returns to service. When CallManager receives an unregister request, it checks for pending calls or connections to that phone, such as held calls, transfers in progress, call park in progress, and so forth. These calls can exist in CallManager without the Cisco IP Phone having an active media connection for that call. If CallManager determines that there are pending calls for the device, CallManager returns an unregister acknowledgement with a NAK, indicating that the device is not permitted to unregister at that time.

If CallManager determines that there are no pending calls for the device, it returns an unregister acknowledgement with an ACK, indicating that the Cisco IP Phone is free to register with the higher CallManager node.

Active Connection Management in Device Modules on Device Registration

Some devices can register with a CallManager node while involved in active connections. The following sections detail requirements that CallManager must satisfy to restore active connections and manage their release during call tear down.

Hardware Conference Bridge and Transcoders

When a hardware conference bridge or transcoder registers with CallManager, it reports the number of resources that it supports and the number of resources that are currently active on that device. CallManager notes the number of active resources, and it does not make these resources available for allocation until the device notifies CallManager that the resource is no longer active. The resource is then added to the available pool.

MGCP Gateway Device Modules

On MGCP gateway registration, the CallManager node sends the Audit Endpoint message to each endpoint of each PSTN interface of the registering gateway. When the endpoint returns a connection identifier in the Audit Endpoint Response, the device control process in CallManager marks the device endpoint active. This allows the gateway to control when the resource is released and ready for use.

For each connection identifier returned in the Audit Endpoint Response, the device module that is managing the gateway interfaces in the CallManager node marks the endpoints active to allow the endpoint to control release sequence.

For interfaces that use MGCP call control signaling and support either end-user or media streaming failure disconnect supervision, CallManager sends a Request Notify command to the gateway to have the gateway report call termination events to the CallManager node. As the calls are terminated, the endpoints are made available for use again.

There are specific requirements for MGCP gateways using MGCP call control signaling. MGCP call control signaling is supported for the following interfaces and platforms:

- FXO/FXS on IOS gateways

- T1-CAS on IOS gateways

There are specific requirements for MGCP gateways using PRI-backhaul call control signaling. PRI-backhaul signaling is supported for the following interfaces and platforms:

- T1-PRI on non-IOS (Catalyst 6000 WS-X6608-T1 and DT24+ gateways) and on IOS gateways

- E1-PRI on non-IOS (Catalyst 6000 WS-X6608-E1 and DE30+ gateways) and on IOS gateways

- FXS/FXO on non-IOS gateways

- T1-CAS on Catalyst 6000 WS-C6608-T1 and Catalyst 6000 WS-C6608-E1 gateways

For each of the active connections, the device control process that is managing the gateway ports in the CallManager node sets the ports in an active call state. When working with the PRI protocol, the device control process needs the Q.931 call reference value.

During normal call setup, the CallManager node includes the Q.931 call reference value in the Call ID parameter of the Create Connection command for each connection associated with the PRI interface. The MGCP protocol provides the audit connection sequence to relay active connection information from the gateway to the CallManager node.

Media Streaming Failure Disconnect Supervision Handling

Devices that support media streaming failure disconnect supervision report media failure signals to the CallManager node on detection of the failure. If the associated call is in a preserved state, it should be cleared (from a call control perspective) toward the device. Otherwise, it is assumed that the call will be cleared through normal means.

Summary

This chapter presented basic VoIP concepts and terms and explained their relationship to media processing devices. Six basic types of media processing resources are available to CallManager:

- Audio conferencing resources

- Video conferencing resources

- MTPs

- Transcoders

- MOH resources

- Annunciator resources

All media resources are shared across the entire cluster regardless of where the device is registered. This sharing allows for efficient use of media processing resources In addition, these resources can be associated with endpoint devices on a geographical basis or on any other grouping that seems appropriate. Resource sharing also provides the capability of restricting the use of media processing resources so that certain endpoints or groups of endpoints do not have access to one or more types of resources. Their usage can be organized such that the load is distributed across all resources of a given type, or it can be ordered such that either the hardware or software resources are used before the other type of resource is used. The grouping and ordering of the resources is very flexible and gives you a great deal of control over how media processing resources are registered and used within the cluster. This chapter also discussed the differences between hardware- and software-based resources, and the advantages and disadvantages of each.

CallManager supports a rich set of media processing capabilities, including audio and video processing. Conferencing is supported both by hardware- and software-based conferencing resources. Videoconferencing resources are not directly allocated but are included in the set of resources that you control by configuring their allocation and usage in MRGs and MRGLs.

Annunciators were added to CallManager to support MLPP and other specific announcements. Annunciators also play tones and are used as a tone plant when required. Tones and announcements are stored as .wav files on the annunciator's disk. The annunciator makes no distinction between them and simply plays specified .wav files over specified connections.

The Cisco IP Voice Media Streaming App can be installed and configured to support several software-based media processing capabilities, including the MOH server, software conference bridge server, MTP server, and the annunciator server.

This chapter introduced and explained call preservation. Call preservation attempts to maintain call connections that are active during failure conditions. In most instances, a call connection can be maintained so long as the endpoint devices involved in the call did not fail. When CallManager fails with calls active, the calls are maintained, but they have no call processing support. This means that they cannot place the call on hold or activate any other feature for the duration of that call. CDR billing information for these calls is not recorded. The algorithms used to recover failed devices were also explained.

After reading this chapter, you should understand the media processing resources that are available and the configuration options that are available through CallManager Administration. You should have a good comprehension of MRGs and MRGLs and the power they give you in configuring the media resources in your system. You should also have an understanding of the basic architecture and support for all media type devices, and the counters available to monitor the usage and state of these devices.

CHAPTER 6

Manageability and Monitoring

Cisco provides tools that can make managing your Cisco CallManager system simpler and faster. The Bulk Administration Tool (BAT) helps you perform add, update, export, and delete operations on a large number of users or devices through a single transaction. The CDR Analysis and Reporting (CAR) tool helps you manage billing records, among many other tasks. In addition to these manageability tools, there are several monitoring tools. Monitoring your system with the tools described in this chapter can help you make sure your system is running efficiently and pinpoint the cause of problems when they arise. They can also be used to help you plan for expansion and ensure quality of service (QoS). The following products are discussed in this chapter:

- Bulk Administration Tool (BAT)

- CDR Analysis and Reporting (CAR)

- Cisco CallManager Serviceability

- Real-Time Monitoring Tool (RTMT)

- Microsoft Performance

- Trace Collection Tool (TCT)

- Event Viewer

- Terminal Services Client

- Virtual Network Computing (VNC) Viewer

- CiscoWorks IP Telephony Environment Monitor (ITEM)

- Simple Network Management Protocol (SNMP) Management Information Bases (MIB)

- Cisco Discovery Protocol (CDP)

- Voice Log Translator (VLT)

The shaded blocks in Figure 6-1 illustrate the software layers and blocks within CallManager that contain manageability- and monitoring-related functionality. Unlike the other block diagrams in this book, Figure 6-1 is completely shaded. Because virtually every component in CallManager logs alarms, constructs CDR information, receives provisioning information through BAT, logs trace information, or sets CallManager performance counters, not a single CallManager layer or block escapes manageability and monitoring.

Figure 6-1 *CallManager Block Structure Diagram*

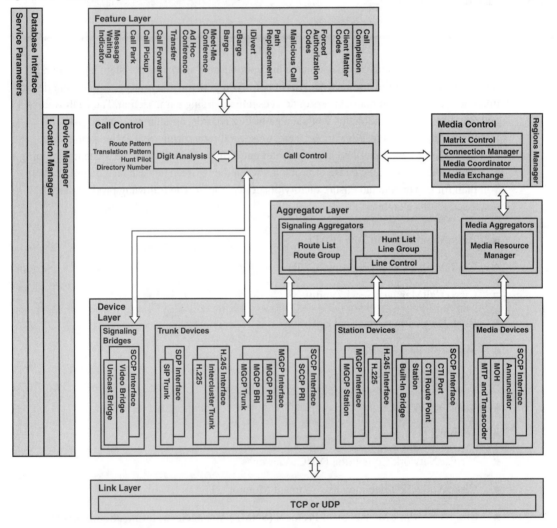

Manageability Tools

Manageability tools ease the burden of managing a large system. BAT and CAR are discussed in this section. Using these tools, you can perform bulk transactions, where a large number of users or devices are added, updated, or deleted from the CallManager database. In addition, you can run reports on the system to generate information about billing, traffic, gateways, and QoS statistics.

Bulk Administration Tool (BAT)

BAT lets you perform bulk add, update, and delete operations on the CallManager database. This means that for large systems, you can configure or update your CallManager database faster and with less manual entry. Different versions of BAT provide different features. This discussion focuses on BAT release 5.1, which is included with CallManager release 4.1.

With BAT release 5.1, you can perform the following bulk operations on the CallManager database:

- Add, update, and delete Cisco IP Phones, VG248 ports, computer telephony interface (CTI) ports, and H.323 clients

- Add, update, and delete users

- Add, update, and delete user device profiles

- Add, update, and delete Cisco IP Manager Assistant (IPMA) managers and assistants

- Add, update, and delete ports on a Cisco Catalyst 6000 FXS Analog Interface Module (WS-X6624)

- Add and delete Cisco VG200 analog gateways and ports

- Add, update, and delete forced authorization codes (FAC)

- Add, update, and delete client matter codes (CMC)

- Add, update, and delete pickup groups

- Export IP phones, users, and user device profiles

- Create reports on IP phones, users, IPMA managers and assistants, user device profiles, and VG200 gateways

Using BAT templates in combination with comma-separated value (CSV) files that you create, you can effect basic database changes that previously required labor-intensive manual entries in CallManager Administration. With BAT, instead of adding 100 phones one at a time in

CallManager Administration, you can create a BAT template and a CSV file (both of which are reusable for future bulk add transactions) and add the same 100 phones in one transaction. BAT includes an Excel template spreadsheet where you can enter data and create the CSV files automatically using macros in the spreadsheet. You should always use this Excel template, which is validated by BAT, for generating the CSV files to ensure they are properly formatted.

To help ensure against performance degradation on CallManager, BAT provides a formula to compute roughly how long it takes to complete a bulk transaction. This is useful information to know before you perform the transaction, because you can determine whether system performance will be impacted. If performance is an issue, perform the bulk transaction when the system is not heavily used.

BAT is available as a plugin application to CallManager Administration (**Application > Install Plugins**), and you must install it after installing CallManager. New versions of CallManager do not automatically upgrade BAT, so you should always run the BAT plugin installer after any CallManager upgrade.

> **NOTE**   Depending on the number of records you are adding, updating, or deleting to the CallManager database during the bulk transaction, BAT can consume a great deal of system resources. Therefore, Cisco recommends that BAT be used only during off-peak hours to minimize the impact on CallManager performance.

Reasons to Use BAT

BAT's goal is to save you time by reducing repetitive labor-intensive manual data entry tasks. This goal remains the same whether you are installing a new CallManager system or already have an existing system. BAT also combines tasks by allowing you to add users and devices (phones, gateways, or CTI ports) and associate users with their devices, all in one bulk transaction. BAT can also be very useful for adding or deleting FACs, CMCs, or setting up IPMA users.

Setting Up a New System or Installing New Devices

BAT is most useful when you are first setting up a system. The information you provide in the BAT template and CSV file (described in the section "CSV Files") can be as specific or generic as you want. If the information is generic, you can always update the device or user information in CallManager Administration later.

A common problem with new systems is misconfiguration. This problem can result because of incomplete understanding of how a feature works; often it is simply a data-entry mistake. With BAT, if you add devices, for example, and then realize after doing so that there is an error in the device configuration, you can simply modify the same CSV file to correct the error. You can then use it and the same BAT template to update the same set of devices. In this example, you would have to delete the misconfigured devices first before you could add them again, but you can do that using BAT, as well.

You might find that you want to restrict long distance dialing on certain phones in your company, such as lobby phones, conference room phones, or other phones that are located in common areas. You can use BAT to add or update that set of phones with a calling search space that blocks long distance dialing.

Working with an Existing System

BAT also proves useful when you have an established system for which you need to add a new block of users or devices or make the same update to many devices or users. For example, if you plan to delete a device pool, all phones currently using that device pool must be updated with a new device pool before the old one can be deleted from CallManager Administration. You can quickly update all phones using the existing device pool with the new one by running a bulk update on all phones using the old device pool.

Perhaps you want to change the voice mail access number, add a new voice mail access number, or add a speed dial to the Human Resources department for all phones. BAT lets you update all phones that have a common characteristic, such as device pool, location, or calling search space.

In another example, you could set up all the phones used by salespeople in your company with a special set of Cisco IP Phone services. Phone services are Extensible Markup Language (XML) services that you can configure using the Cisco IP Phone Productivity Services Software Development Kit (see Appendix A, "Feature List," and Appendix B, "Cisco Integrated Solutions," for more information). Perhaps you have services that tie in directly to a database showing current sales goals or a list of reference account contacts. Although this information is critical to salespeople, it might not be of much interest to anyone else in your company. You can add a specific set of phone services to phones belonging to the sales staff so that only their phones provide this service when the **services** button on a Cisco IP Phone is pressed. Likewise, if you have a common service that you want to appear on all phones in your company, such as your company's stock quote or a calendar showing paid holidays, you can specify this when adding the phones in BAT. As of mid-2005, BAT cannot be used to bulk add XML services that require parameters such as username and password. This means that services such as Personal Address Book (PAB) and the Fast Dial service cannot be added in bulk using BAT.

Figure 6-2 shows the Phone Options screen (**Configure > Phones / Users**) where you can perform various functions such as insert, update, and delete phones; export phones; add and update lines; reset phones; insert phones with users; generate phone reports; and perform bulk CAPF operations.

Figure 6-2 *Bulk Administration Tool*

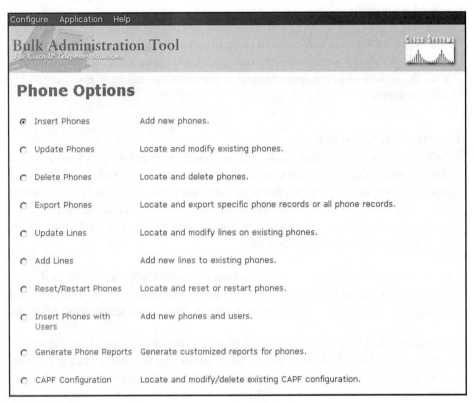

CSV Files

BAT's strength lies in its ability to allow you to make large device or user changes to the database without compromising customization of the devices or users. Using the CSV file, you can specify as much detail as you like about the devices you plan to add. For example, for phones you can supply directory numbers, Media Access Control (MAC) addresses, call forward no answer directory number, and more. After you have entered all the data in the CSV file and have created a BAT template, you can insert the data from CSV files and BAT templates into CallManager Administration. When the phones are plugged into the network, they register with CallManager and find their device settings based on the information inserted into the database from the CSV file.

You can use the sample Microsoft Excel spreadsheet template (available on the Publisher at C:\CiscoWebs\BAT\ExcelTemplate) to create the CSV file for each type of bulk transaction. A different tab is provided for users and each type of device: phones, gateways, gateways ports, and so on. When you first open the Excel spreadsheet, select the kind of device you want to create (phone, CTI port, H.323 client, and so on). For some operations you then click the **Create File Title** or **Create File Format** button, which prompts you to select the device and line fields you want to insert. Previous versions of BAT were not as flexible and required you to have all the available fields as columns in your spreadsheet.

After you have entered the data in the spreadsheet, click the **Export To BAT Format** button in the spreadsheet. A dialog box displays the default filename and location to which the file will be saved. The default filename is *Filetype#timestamp*.txt (e.g., PhonesUsers#06272005093545.txt). The filename indicates that this file was created on June 27, 2005 at 9:35:45 a.m. You can overwrite the default name with something more memorable, such as *June_new_hires.txt*. You should save CSV files in the appropriate subdirectory of the C:\BatFiles directory on the Publisher where BAT is installed. A subdirectory exists for each type of BAT import operation. For example, there is a subdirectory named C:\BatFiles\PhonesUsers where you store CSV files for phone and user import operations.

In the CSV file, you can specify individual MAC addresses for each phone or use a dummy MAC address. If the dummy MAC address option is used, the address can be updated later using the Tool for Auto-Registered Phone Support (TAPS).

Tool for Auto-Registered Phone Support (TAPS)

TAPS is an optional component of BAT that requires Cisco IP Interactive Voice Response (IP IVR) on a Cisco Customer Response Applications Server. You can also install TAPS on a CallManager server with Cisco Extended Services installed. You must enable auto-registration in CallManager for the TAPS feature to work. With TAPS, you can leave the MAC address blank in the CSV file and import this data using BAT with the **Create Dummy MAC Address** option selected. Later, when a Cisco IP Phone is plugged in, the user can retrieve device information for the new phone simply by dialing a TAPS directory number and entering his or her phone number. This is particularly useful when you want to configure devices for a group of users where a physical phone has not yet been assigned to the user. TAPS also proves useful when an existing user replaces his or her phone because of damage or defect. When users receive the new phone (same model), they can simply dial the TAPS directory number and then their current directory number, and TAPS downloads device information configured for the previous phone to the new phone.

Updating Phone Certificates

Another important function of BAT is the capability to bulk update Locally Significant Certificates (LSC) installed on your IP phones. These certificates are necessary if you are using the device authentication or media encryption features introduced in CallManager release 4.0.

Without BAT, you would have to go to each phone in CallManager Administration and set the Certificate Authority Proxy Function (CAPF) configuration to update the certificate on the phone. With BAT, you can tell the CAPF service to issue new certificates to all phones of a particular model (for example, all Cisco IP Phones 7960). This is especially useful for phones that do not come from the factory with a Manufacturing Issued Certificate (MIC) and therefore require an LSC before device authentication and encryption can be used.

Learn More About BAT

Detailed information about BAT is available at the following location:

http://www.cisco.com/univercd/cc/td/doc/product/voice/c_callmg/admin/bulk_adm/index.htm

CDR Analysis and Reporting (CAR)

CAR, a web-based application, provides reports about QoS, gateway usage, traffic details, user call details, and more. CallManager stores information about each call in call detail records (CDR) and call management records (CMR), collectively known as *CDR data*. This CDR data serves as the basic information source for CAR. This discussion focuses on CAR release 4.1, which is included with CallManager release 4.1.

CAR is available as a plug-in application to CallManager Administration (**Application > Install Plugins**). Once installed, you can access CAR from CallManager Serviceability under **Tools > CDR Analysis and Reporting**.

Reasons to Use CAR

CAR helps you obtain system capacity and QoS statistics by generating reports that give information about call activity and voice quality. CAR generates reports on the performance of the gateways and is also useful to associate calls to users and reconcile phone billing with usage. CAR can also be used for troubleshooting. For example, if several users report busy signals when dialing in to retrieve voice mail messages, you can run a voice mail utilization report in CAR to see whether all ports on the voice mail server are busy during peak usage hours. The information in this report can help you determine whether to add more ports to your voice mail server.

CAR provides reporting features for three levels of users:

- CAR administrators
- Managers
- Individual users

CAR administrators can use all of the features of CAR. Managers can monitor call details for the various groups and individuals in the company. Individual users can view details about their calls. Numerous reports are available in either detail or summary format.

CAR administrators can use CAR to monitor QoS. For example, reports generated in CAR help you detect QoS problems in the system and, to some extent, diagnose and isolate QoS problems. Note that QoS statistics are available only from devices that support sending CMRs to CallManager. At this time, only Cisco IP Phones and MGCP gateways have this functionality.

Other reports provide metrics on traffic, system overview, gateways, voice mail utilization, conference bridge utilization, Cisco IP Phone services, and more. Managers can use CAR to generate reports about usage for their department or select users to view top usage by cost, call duration, or number of calls. These reports can be useful to keep watch over expenses or to determine ongoing budgeting for departmental phone usage. Managers can also run detailed reports that help determine whether any unauthorized calls have been made by their department or select users. Individuals can use CAR to generate summary or detail reports for calls they made, which can prove useful for tracking phone numbers and call duration and for billing purposes.

> **NOTE** Users must be given the URL for CAR before they can access the system. Authentication is handled by the user ID established in the Global Directory in CallManager Administration. See the CAR documentation for more information.

Figure 6-3 shows the QOS Summary screen in CAR (**System Reports > QoS > Summary**). In this screen, you can specify the types of calls to include in the summary report and the timeframe that the report examines.

You can also view monthly summary reports by selecting the report in the **Available Reports** list box (shown in Figure 6-3). Available Reports are reports automatically generated periodically according to the CAR configuration. Figure 6-4 shows an example of a QoS monthly summary.

> **NOTE** CAR consumes a great deal of system resources when generating reports. Therefore, Cisco recommends that CAR be used to generate reports only during off-peak hours to minimize the impact on CallManager performance. By default, report generation is configured to run during the night, when system utilization is typically low.

Figure 6-3 *User-Configured QoS Summary Report*

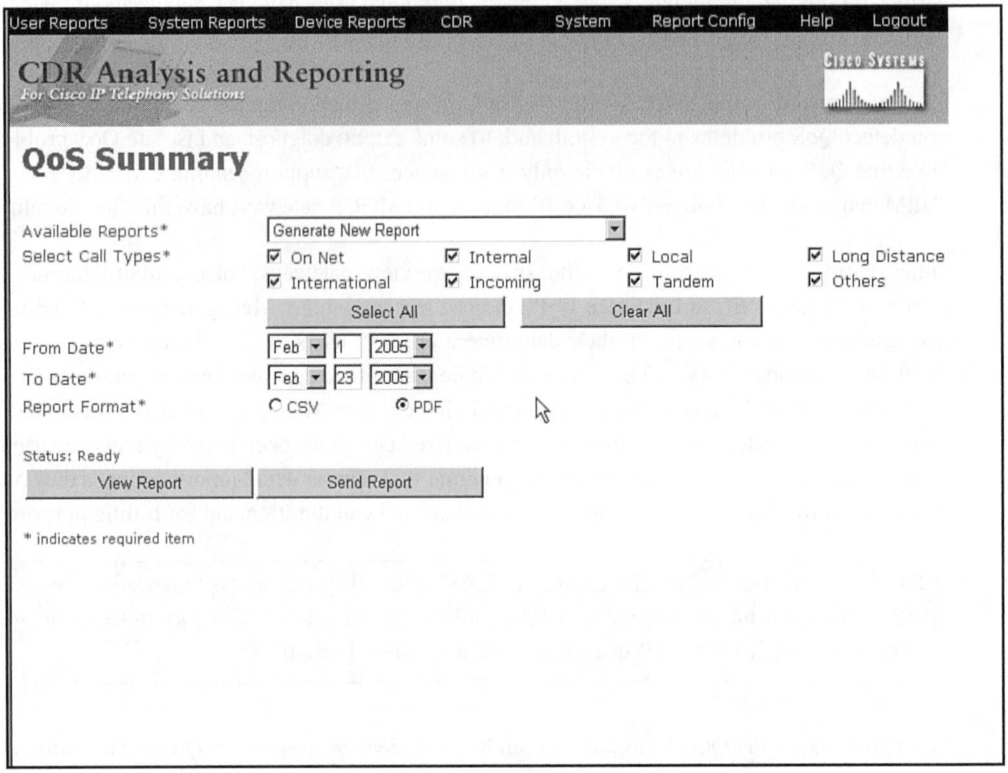

CAR Features

CAR provides all the reports already discussed plus access for the three levels of users. CAR enables you to schedule automatic generation of reports, the time that CDR data is loaded into the system, and CAR database maintenance. You can also set up alerts to notify you when certain conditions occur. The following sections describe the CAR features:

■ Loading CDR Data

■ Automatic Report Generation

■ Reports

■ CAR Database Maintenance

■ Alerts

Descriptions of these features follow.

Figure 6-4 *QoS Monthly Summary Report*

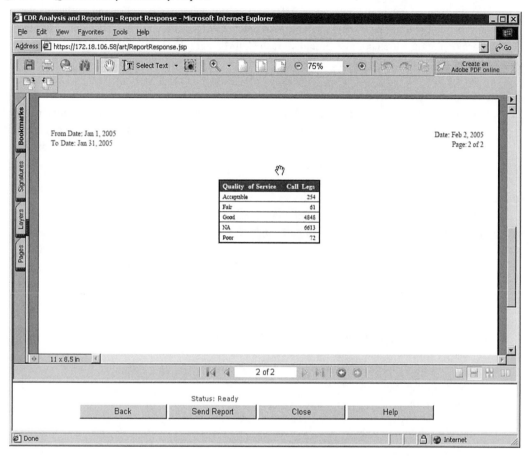

Loading CDR Data

CAR enables you to specify when CDR data (CDRs and CMRs) is loaded into the CAR database. You can schedule the loading of data at the nonpeak hours of CallManager. CAR uses data in the CAR database to generate reports, so data in CAR will be current only up to the last time CDR data was loaded into the CAR database.

CAR only loads CMRs for records that have an associated CDR. To get complete CDR data, ensure that both the **CDR Enabled Flag** and **Call Diagnostics Enabled** service parameters (**Service > Service Parameters >** *select a server* **> Cisco CallManager**) are set to True. CAR only purges CMRs if they are associated with CDRs, which means that if you set the **CDR Enabled Flag** service parameter to False and the **Call Diagnostics Enabled** service parameter to True, CallManager will continue writing CMRs to the hard drive until all available disk space has been depleted.

If you are using third-party software that reads CDR data from the CallManager database, ensure that it either deletes both CDRs and CMRs or does not delete CDRs, allowing CallManager to automatically purge the CDR data. Failure to delete CMRs associated to CDRs will result in disk space depletion which could eventually crash CallManager. Future versions of CallManager will prevent this condition from occurring.

Automatic Report Generation

CAR allows reports to be generated automatically at a user-specified time, which results in reports being automatically generated and stored for future use. You can view these reports quicker than reports that are generated on demand. Automatically generated reports can also be e-mailed to administrators after being generated.

Reports

CAR reports can be scheduled to run automatically or to be used on demand to track incoming or outgoing call quality, overall system performance, individual or group call usage (such as cost or duration of all calls), and gateway usage details, among many other functions. CAR reports display in either PDF form (using Acrobat Reader) or CSV format. Reports generated by CAR include the following:

- Individual/department bill reports
- Top N calls (by cost, duration or number) reports
- Cisco IPMA usage reports
- CTI application user reports
- Cisco IP Phone services reports
- Traffic summary reports
- CDR error reports
- Gateway reports
- Route plan reports
- Conference bridge reports
- Voice messaging reports
- QoS reports
- System overview reports
- FAC/CMC reports
- Malicious call detail reports
- Precedence call summary reports
- CDR search reports

Reports can be generated for viewing, printing, or e-mail distribution to interested parties by clicking the Send Report button in CAR.

Individual/Department Bill Reports

Individual/department bill reports (**User Reports > Bills**) provide information to enable users and managers to monitor their own or their department's calling records. Reports about user calls can be sent to relevant personnel (managers, high-usage users, and so on) to inform them of possible anomalies in their usage patterns.

Administrators can generate a report detailing the users who have a CTI port enabled (**User Reports > CTI Application User**). They can also generate reports for Cisco IP Manager Assistant (IPMA) usage (**User Reports > Cisco IPMA**).

Cisco IP Phone Services Reports

The Cisco IP Phone Services report (**User Reports > Cisco IP Phone Services**) enables administrators to view the number of users subscribed and the percentage of all users who are subscribed to each IP Phone service configured on the system. The report does not show how many times each IP Phone service is actually used.

Top N Calls Reports

Top N (where N represents "number of") reports (**User Reports > Top N**) are used to analyze the calls based on destinations, users, and calls. Call reports can be generated by charge, duration, or number of calls. The various call reports are as follows:

- Top N users in the organization or group who have incurred maximum charge or have used the phone for the maximum duration

- Top N destinations to which the organization or group has incurred maximum charge or spent maximum time

- Top N calls from the organization or group that incurred maximum charge or were for the maximum duration

CAR administrators or managers can generate these call reports.

Traffic Summary Reports

The traffic summary report (**System Reports > Traffic > Summary/Summary by Extension**) displays network usage patterns on an hourly and daily basis. This report helps you determine whether too much or too little equipment is deployed on the network. Only the system administrator can generate these reports.

Gateway Reports

Gateway reports (**Device Reports > Gateway**) provide gateway traffic details to help system administrators analyze the performance of gateways. The following information describes some of the available gateway reports:

- **Gateway detail**—Shows the performance of the various gateways in the enterprise and provides the date, origination time, termination time, duration, origination number, destination number, origination codec, destination codec, origination IP, and QoS of calls that used the gateway. It can be generated on demand by specifying the call classification, QoS grades, gateways, and date range. The report provides a list of calls that used the specified gateways. Gateways can be specified by type or by only those gateways that use a particular route pattern.

- **Gateway summary**—Shows a summary of the performance of the various gateways. It presents a matrix of the number of calls of various call classifications and QoS through a gateway. It also gives the total number of calls and the duration under each of the categories. The report is scheduled for generation every month but can also be generated on demand by specifying the call classification and date range.

- **Gateway utilization**—Provides an estimate of the utilization percentage of the gateways. You can examine the usage based on each hour of a day or by days of the week or month. Reports generate for each selected gateway. This report is most useful for capacity planning.

Route Plan Reports

CAR offers a variety of route plan reports (**Device Reports > Route Plan**). The following route plan reports are available:

- Route and line group utilization

- Route and hunt list utilization

- Route pattern and hunt pilot utilization

Each of these reports provides an estimate of the utilization percentage of the route plan component. As with the gateway reports, the utilization can be displayed on an hour-of-day, day-of-week, or day-of-month basis.

Conference Bridge Reports

Two reports are available for conference bridge resources (**Device Reports > Conference Bridge**).

- **Conference bridge utilization**—Enable you to do capacity planning for your conference bridge resources by showing the utilization of each of your conference bridge resources by time-of-day, day-of-week, or day-of-month.

- **Conference call details**—Shows information about all conference calls created during the report period. This report is available as a summary report or detailed report. The detailed report includes a listing of each participant and call detail information of each conference call, but the summary report does not.

Voice Messaging Reports

The voice message report (**Device Reports > Voice Messaging**) enables you to determine the estimated usage of your voice mail ports, which proves useful for capacity planning to determine whether you have enough voice mail ports to meet expected demand.

QoS Reports

You can use CAR to gather information on voice quality and manage CallManager QoS statistics and system capacity (**System Reports > QoS**). Calls are categorized into a voice quality category based on the information in the CMRs and the QoS parameters you provide. QoS reports provide information about the quality of calls for all phones in the network, which helps you determine whether any possible issues exist in the network. Reports include codec type, packets lost, jitter, and latency (although latency is not calculated by any endpoints at this time and will therefore always show zero). The administrator can specify the criteria to classify the QoS as Good, Acceptable, Fair, and Poor based on the reported statistics from an IP phone or gateway.

The QoS reports available are as follows:

- **QoS summary**—Helps managers and administrators analyze CallManager performance. The report can be scheduled for automatic generation every month or run on demand for a specified date range. It provides a pie chart that shows the distribution of the QoS grades that are achieved for the specified call classifications and periods and also provides a table that summarizes the calls for each QoS rating.

- **QoS detail**—Provides analysis of the voice quality grades achieved for calls. Use this report to analyze CallManager performance for a particular user or a group of users. The report provides the origination time, termination time, duration, origination number, destination number, call classification, origination codec, destination codec, origination IP address, origination span, and QoS. You can generate a report on demand by specifying the call classification, QoS grades, date range, and user(s).

System Overview Reports

The system overview report (**System Reports > System Overview**) provides a composite report consisting of some of the reports. This report gives a broad picture of the overall system performance, and it can be scheduled for automatic generation every month or generated on demand for any selected date range.

FAC/CMC Reports

Three reports (**System Reports > FAC/CMC**) are associated with the forced authorization codes (FAC) and client matter codes (CMC) features. These features help you manage call access and accounting. FAC regulates the types of calls that certain users can place, and CMC assists with call accounting and billing for calls that relate to billable client matters. The three reports are as follows:

- **Authorization code name**—Provides the originating and destination numbers, date and time that the call originated, call duration in seconds, call classification, and authorization level for calls that relate to each chosen authorization code name

- **Authorization level**—Provides the same information as the authorization code name report for each chosen authorization level

- **Client matter code**—Provides the originating and destination numbers, date and time that the call originated, call duration in seconds, call classification, and the client matter code for each chosen client matter code

Malicious Call Detail Reports

The malicious call detail report (**System Reports > Malicious Call Details**) lists all calls marked as malicious calls by the Malicious Call Identification (MCID) feature. This report is blank if the MCID feature has not been enabled or if no malicious calls have been flagged by end users.

Precedence Call Summary Reports

The precedence call summary report (**System Reports > Precedence Call Summary**) displays a call summary for all precedence calls made when using the Multilevel Precedence and Preemption (MLPP) feature. The call summary is presented as a stacked bar chart showing the number of calls for each precedence level. The report also provides an overall percentage distribution for each precedence level.

CDR Search

CDR search enables you to view CDR data from the CallManager database based on a specified date, gateway, extension number, user, cause for termination, precedence level, or malicious call designation. The results display the CDR data fields for records that match the selection criteria. You can also use CAR to export the raw CDR data to a CSV file for processing by an external application.

CAR Database Maintenance

You can configure CAR to notify you when the CAR or CDR database is reaching capacity (**System > Database >** *select the alert for CAR or CDR*). You can then manually purge the selected database (**System > Database > Database Purge**). You can also schedule automatic purging of records older than a specified number of days in the CAR database. You should periodically purge old database records to ensure you do not run out of hard drive space. Also note that after performing a purge, you could perform a system backup using the Backup and Restore System (BARS) utility to ensure the database transaction logs are also truncated.

Alerts

You can configure CAR to alert you when any of the following conditions occur:

- CAR or the CDR database size exceeds a limit you specify.

- The percentage of good calls drops below a specified range or the percentage of poor calls exceeds a specified limit.

- A user exceeds the daily charge limit.

Alerts are sent to the e-mail ID you specify when configuring the alert.

Learn More About CAR

Detailed information about CAR is available through the online help documentation contained within the CAR application or at the following location (Cisco.com login required):

http://www.cisco.com/en/US/customer/products/sw/voicesw/ps556/
products_administration_guide_chapter09186a00802df08f.html

Monitoring Tools

This section describes the tools that you can use to monitor CallManager and your network:

- Cisco CallManager Serviceability

- Real-Time Monitoring Tool (RTMT)

- Microsoft Performance

- Trace Collection Tool (TCT)

- Event Viewer

- Terminal Services Client

- Virtual Network Computing (VNC) Viewer

- CiscoWorks IP Telephony Environment Monitor

- SNMP MIBs

- Cisco Discovery Protocol (CDP)

- Voice Log Translator (VLT)

Cisco CallManager Serviceability

CallManager Serviceability provides alarms, traces, component version information, service activation and control, Quality Reporting Tool reports, and performance reports of Cisco IP Telephony components in a CallManager cluster. CallManager Serviceability is a web-based application installed with CallManager and accessible from CallManager Administration by clicking **Application > Cisco CallManager Serviceability**. You can access CallManager Serviceability by browsing to the CallManager server by IP address or Domain Name System (DNS) host name, if applicable.

CallManager Serviceability, shown in Figure 6-5, provides the following features:

- Alarm configuration and detailed alarm definitions

- Trace configuration, analysis, and collection

- Component version information

- Service Activation for adding and removing services

- Control center for starting and stopping services

- QRT Viewer for viewing IP phone problem reports

- Serviceability Reports Archive for viewing archived serviceability data

Figure 6-5 *Example of a Screen in CallManager Serviceability*

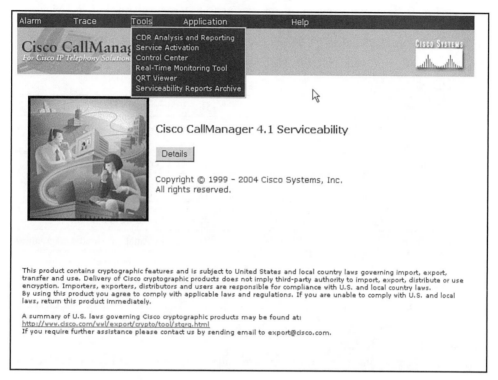

Alarm Configuration

The CallManager system generates alarms to notify you of various events. The alarms are categorized into different levels, as described in Table 6-1. As of CallManager release 4.1, only error levels Debug and Error trigger alarms. You can configure the system to have alarms forwarded to selected monitors, and for each monitor, you can also choose to capture alarms of certain levels. These settings are configured in the Alarm Configuration screen in CallManager Serviceability for each service (such as Cisco CallManager, Cisco TFTP, and so on). Alarm Configuration also enables you to apply a given configuration to all nodes in the CallManager cluster. The monitors to which alarms can be forwarded include the following:

■ **SDI trace log (also known as CCM trace)**—Display the alarms in the CCM/SDI trace files.

■ **SDL trace log (Cisco CallManager alarms only)**—Display the alarms in the SDL trace files.

- **Event Viewer**—View the alarms in Event Viewer; see the section "Event Viewer" later in this chapter for more information about viewing CallManager alarms in Event Viewer.

- **Syslog**—Specify the IP address of a syslog server to receive the messages.

Table 6-1   *Alarm Event Levels*

Level	Description
Emergency	The system is unusable.
Alert	Indicates a condition that warrants immediate action.
Critical	Indicates a critical condition.
Error	Indicates an error such as an unregistered device or a CallManager failure.
Warning	Indicates a warning condition.
Notice	Indicates a normal but significant condition.
Informational	Provides information messages only.
Debug	Provides detailed messages for use in debugging by Cisco engineers.

Alarm Definitions

You can view detailed alarm descriptions in CallManager Serviceability. Click **Alarm > Definitions** to view these definitions. A simple search dialog box is provided that allows you to search for and view alarms, their descriptions, and recommended actions. After a search has returned a list of alarms, you can click any part of the alarm description to see detailed information about that alarm. The detailed information also includes an explanation of any reason codes that are given as part of the alarm. For example, an alarm generated by a transient device will have a reason code that explains why the device is considered a transient device, which can help in diagnosing and solving problems in the CallManager system.

Figure 6-6 shows the Alarm Detail screen after a specific alarm (in this case, SDLLinkOOS) has been clicked from the Alarm Message Definitions screen. You can view detailed alarm information for any alarm by clicking it from the Alarm Message Definitions screen.

Figure 6-6 *Alarm Details Window*

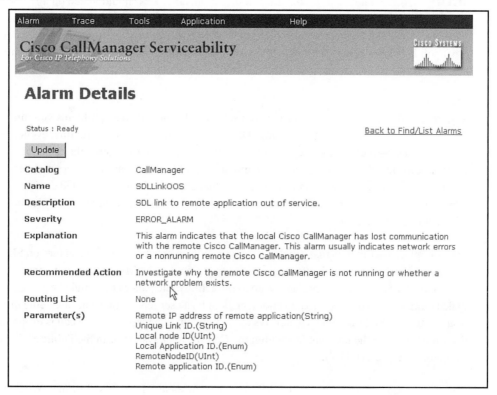

Tracing

Traces are diagnostic tools that can help you determine the cause of a problem. Running a trace can generate information you might need to identify or isolate the source or symptoms of a problem. The path to problem resolution becomes much simpler after you can point to the cause of the problem.

There are two kinds of traces:

■ SDI trace, which is more commonly known as CCM trace

■ SDL trace

> **NOTE** To generate good, usable trace information, all clocks should match on all CallManager-related devices. CallManager automatically installs the Network Time Protocol Daemon (xNTPD) for time synchronization. xNTPD provides a consistent time for all devices that poll it. This results in trace data that accurately reflects a single time across the system.

SDI Traces

SDI traces (also known as CCM traces) are useful for diagnosing most problems you might encounter with the CallManager system. SDI traces log different types of runtime events related to CallManager—including device names, their IP addresses, alarms, and other general information—to help you determine the origin of the problem. You can specify a set of devices for tracing so that the trace log contains only events that originate from the selected devices. The Cluster ID and nodeID appear in the trace files to help you determine which trace files belong to which node of the cluster.

For example, a user reports that a dialed number results in reorder tone. You can turn on SDI trace and trace only the phone and gateway involved to learn why CallManager cannot connect the user's call. This could show a problem with a conflicting route pattern that might be preventing the dialed number from being routed. In another example, a user reports that calls are being dropped. You can turn on SDI trace on the gateways to help identify the reason that the call is dropping and determine whether the problem lies within the CallManager system or in the Public Switched Telephone Network (PSTN).

You can choose to log SDI traces in XML format or in standard text-based format. When XML trace formatting is selected, the resulting trace logs can be used with Trace Analysis feature; however, Cisco recommends leaving trace levels set to text-based format for readability reasons.

> **NOTE** SDI tracing is enabled by default; however, the default logging level is Error, which provides limited debugging information beyond critical system failures.

SDI Trace Output

SDI traces generate files (for example, ccm000000000.txt) that contain traces of CallManager activities. These traces provide information about the CallManager initialization process, registration process, call flow, digit analysis, and related devices, such as Cisco IP Phones, gateways, gatekeepers, and more. This information can help you isolate problems when troubleshooting CallManager.

The trace files are stored in the following default location:

C:\Program Files\Cisco\Trace

> **NOTE**   Cisco recommends changing the default file location for trace files to the F: drive on dual-processor CallManager servers equipped with extra hard drives for trace collection.

If a trace is enabled, a new trace file is started each time CallManager restarts or when the designated number of lines or minutes has been reached. Although SDI traces do consume some system resources, leaving SDI traces enabled during routine system operation does not typically impact performance unless the system is heavily loaded.

SDL Traces

The Cisco Technical Assistance Center (TAC) and Cisco engineers use SDL traces to diagnose difficult problems. The only time you should change the SDL trace configuration is when directed to do so by TAC. SDL trace logs state transitions only for CallManager and Cisco CTI Manager. Cisco engineers use SDL traces to find the cause of an error. You are not expected to understand the information contained in an SDL trace. However, while working with TAC, you might be asked to change the SDL trace configuration and provide the resulting trace files to TAC.

> **NOTE**   Before gathering any SDL traces in CallManager Serviceability, you must enable SDL tracing in CallManager Administration. The Cisco TAC representative requesting the trace can advise you on how to enable SDL tracing.

Trace Configuration

Trace configuration allows you to specify the criteria for SDI tracing. Click **Trace > Configuration** to select the server you want to trace, and then select the service on that server, such as Cisco CallManager, the Database Layer, CTI Manager, and so on. Figure 6-7 shows the Trace Configuration screen with the default values selected. You can custom configure the trace by selecting the level of trace, the trace fields, and device names (if applicable). Table 6-2 provides a list of the debug trace level settings.

Table 6-2 *Debug Trace Levels*

Level	Description
Error	Use this level for all traces generated in abnormal paths, such as coding errors or other errors that normally should not occur.
Special	Use this level for all informational, nonrepetitive messages, such as process startup messages, registration messages, and so on. All system and device initialization traces are at this level.
State Transition	Use this level to trace call processing events or normal events traced for the subsystem (traces for signaling layers).
Significant	Use this level to trace media layer events.
Arbitrary	Use this level to generate low-level debug traces. This level is best suited for a testing setup or for debugging difficult problems in a subsystem.
Detailed	This level is used for detailed debug information or highly repetitive messages that are primarily used for debugging, including KeepAlives and responses.

CallManager Serviceability provides the option of device-based filtering, which proves useful when a certain problem is known to be occurring on a specific device and you want to only view trace information related to that device. You select device name-based tracing in the Trace Configuration screen. Selecting the devices and then running the trace returns results for any events involving the selected devices.

By default, trace results are saved in a file. You can choose to save traces in TXT format, where up to 10,000 lines can be saved and the file can be viewed in any text editor, or you can choose to save the results in XML format; however, XML-formatted trace files are limited to fewer than 2000 lines.

After a trace starts, it continues until you turn it off. When tracing reaches its limit in the trace files, it begins to overwrite trace data, starting with the earliest trace files/lines. To view an XML trace, you can use Trace Analysis (see the following section, "Trace Analysis"). To view a text-based trace, open the trace in a text editor. Figure 6-7 shows the SDI trace configuration page in CallManager Serviceability.

Figure 6-7   *SDI Trace Configuration Page*

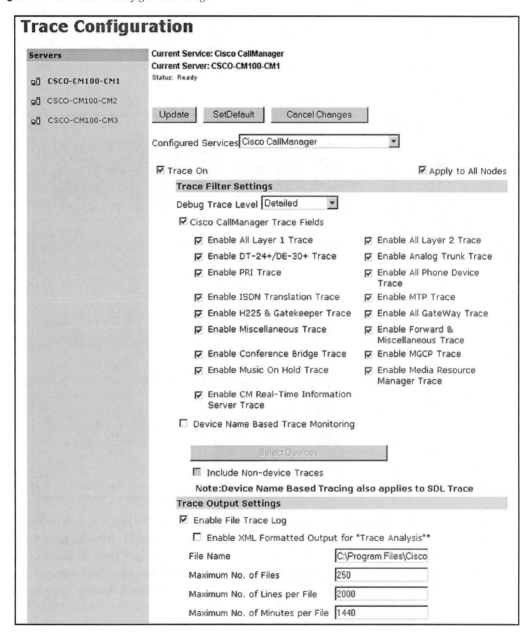

Troubleshooting Trace Settings

The Troubleshooting Trace Settings page enables you to easily configure trace settings for troubleshooting most services without having to configure each service one at a time. The Troubleshooting Trace Settings page uses trace levels based on Cisco TAC recommendations. Figure 6-8 shows the Troubleshooting Trace Settings page in CallManager Serviceability.

Figure 6-8 *Troubleshooting Trace Settings Page*

Services	Select all Nodes for a Service	172.18.106.58	172.18.106.59
Check all Services for a Node	☐	☐	☐
Cisco Certificate Authority Proxy Function	☐	☐	N/A
Cisco CTL Provider	☐	☐	☐
Cisco Extended Functions	☐	☐	☐
Cisco CDR Insert	☐	☐	☐
Cisco Database Layer Monitor	☐	☐	☐
Cisco RIS Data Collector	☐	☐	☐
Cisco MOH Audio Translator	☐	☐	N/A
Cisco Telephony Call Dispatcher	☐	☐	☐
Cisco CTIManager	☑	☑	☑
Cisco IP Voice Media Streaming App	☐	☐	☐
Cisco Messaging Interface	☐	☐	N/A
Cisco Tftp	☐	☐	☐
Cisco CallManager	☑	☑	☑
Cisco Extension Mobility	☐	☐	N/A
Cisco IP Manager Assistant	☐	☐	N/A
Cisco WebDialer	☐	☐	N/A

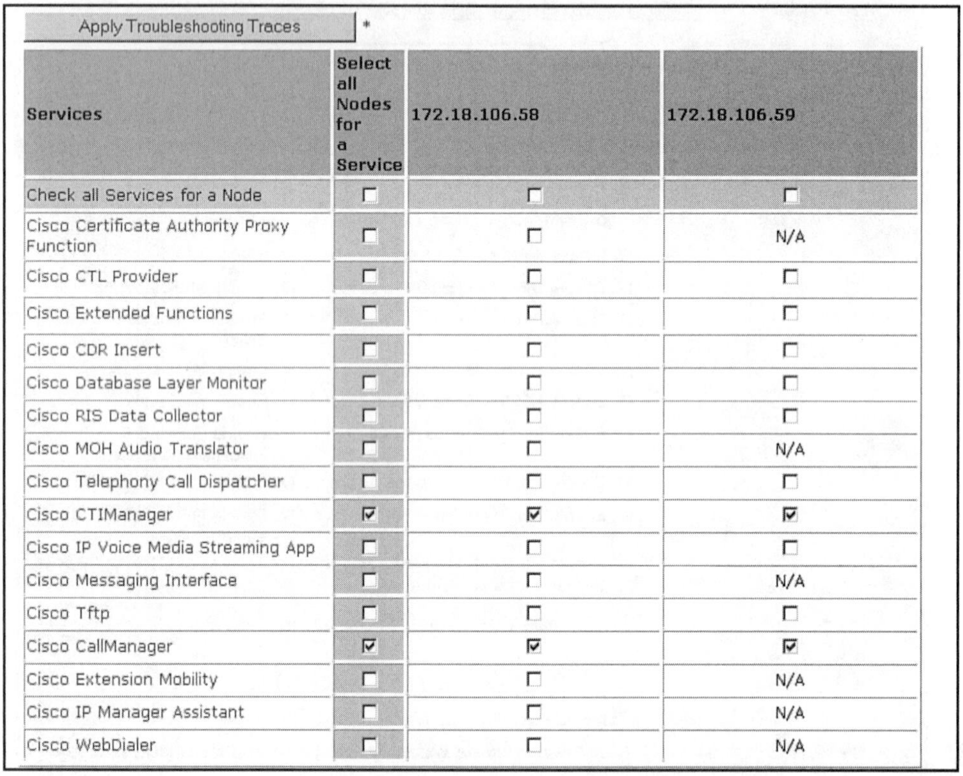

(Apply Troubleshooting Traces)

To apply the TAC-recommended trace settings for a service, select the check box corresponding to the service for which you want to enable traces. You can choose **Select all Nodes for a Service** to enable traces for a particular service on all nodes in the cluster or use **Check all Services for a Node** to select all the services on a particular node. When Troubleshooting Trace Settings are enabled, you cannot manually change trace settings until you disable Troubleshooting Trace Settings.

Trace Analysis

Trace Analysis allows you to perform post-filtering on an XML trace file so that only the relevant information displays. Because trace files can be large and encompass so much information, the ability to reduce and sort that information can be useful. You must know which trace file you want to analyze to use Trace Analysis. Click **Trace > Analysis** to choose a trace file and specify the selection criteria and the fields you want displayed in the Trace Analysis results.

With Trace Analysis, you can specify collection criteria such as the following:

- Cisco CallManager host

- Device name

- IP address

- Trace type

- MGCP endpoint

You can filter the trace so that only the pertinent information displays. The following information can be displayed or filtered out of the trace:

- Cluster

- Date and time

- CallManager node

- Trace type

- IP address

- Correlation tag

- Application name

- Information

- Device name

In practice, administrators who are proficient in reading CallManager trace files find that reading and filtering through a raw text-based trace file is much quicker and easier than using Trace Analysis. Also, Trace Analysis is very slow for large amounts of trace data. Future CallManager releases might see XML tracing and the Trace Analysis features removed.

Performance Impact

Trace Analysis runs as a low-priority task so that it does not disrupt higher-priority CallManager functions. However, you should us it judiciously because it can be resource-intensive. Memory impact on the CallManager system is minimal, as long as only a few concurrent users run analysis at any given time. If possible, run Trace Analysis only when the CallManager system is not busy. Because traces are being collected and merged into an output file, the tool continuously accesses the disk. Also, be certain the CallManager system has enough disk space for the temporary output files. Currently, no user interface is available to clean up these temporary files, but the tool does automatically recycle them.

Service Activation

Before a service can be used on a CallManager node in a cluster, it must be activated, which you can do on the Service Activation page in CallManager Serviceability (**Tools > Service Activation**). Activating or deactivating a service notifies members of a cluster that the service state has changed by adding a record into the database, and also modifies the startup type of the Windows service from Disabled to Automatic or vice versa.

> **CAUTION**   You should never change the service startup type for any Cisco service directly from the Windows Services Administrative Tool. Always use Service Activation to change the startup type.

Control Center

CallManager Serviceability enables you to start and stop services by clicking **Tools > Control Center**. The Control Center also indicates whether the services on the CallManager nodes are currently running or stopped.

QRT Viewer

The Quality Reporting Tool (QRT) service enables you to add a softkey that allows end users to report problems with their IP phone. To view reports submitted by QRT, you must use the QRT Viewer in CallManager Serviceability (**Tools > QRT Viewer**).

QRT Viewer enables you to select a server in the cluster and a date/time range. After clicking **Get Logs**, a page showing all QRT reports submitted during that timeframe displays, including details such as the date and time of the report, the problem being reported, the device from which the report was submitted, and voice quality statistics (packet loss, jitter, and so on) if the problem was reported during a call.

Figure 6-9 shows a sample QRT report indicating that a user was unable to place a call and received a fast busy (reorder) tone. The report shows the date and time the problem occurred, device name, phone number, and IP address.

Figure 6-9 *QRT Report*

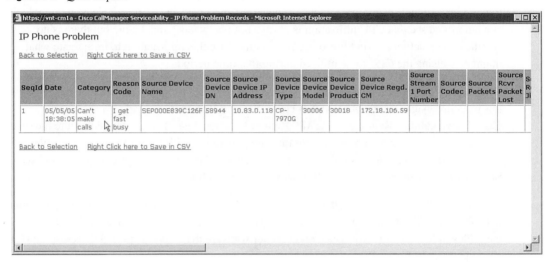

Serviceability Reports Archive

CallManager Serviceability monitors various aspects of a CallManager cluster and generates nightly reports in PDF format. You can access these reports from the Serviceability Reports Archive in CallManager Serviceability (**Tools > Serviceability Reports Archive**).

Each day, five reports are generated:

- **Alert report**—Shows the number of alerts by severity, number of alerts per server in the cluster, and the top 10 alerts.

- **Call activities report**—Shows an hour-by-hour graph of calls attempted and calls completed for the day and a breakdown of calls per gateway type. This information is helpful for determining your peak traffic periods.

- **Device statistics report**—Provides hourly graphs showing the number of registered phones, gateways, and trunks.

- **Server statistics report**—Shows CPU, memory, and hard disk usage statistics in an hourly graph.

- **Service statistics report**—Shows the number of CTI devices registered and the number of TFTP requests and errors in an hourly graph.

The Serviceability Reports Archive data is presented in a graphical format that enables you to view trends or any sudden events that might have occurred on a given day. For example, you might look at a report and see that CPU utilization is always high between 3 and 4 a.m., but there is no significant call activity during this time. You can then use this information to investigate what might be causing the CPU to be utilized during that time period.

By default, the Serviceability Reports Archive stores the last seven days of data. You can increase this in CallManager Administration (**Service > Service Parameters** > *select a server* > **Cisco Serviceability Reporter > RTMT Report Deletion Age**). You can also configure the time that the reports are generated. By default they are generated at 12:30 a.m.; you can modify the time in CallManager Administration (**Service > Service Parameters** > *select a server* > **Cisco Serviceability Reporter > RTMT Report Generation Time**).

In addition to these PDF reports, the raw performance data used to generate the reports is available in C:\Program Files\Common Files\Cisco\Longs\RTMTLogger on the Publisher. You can open these files in Microsoft Performance or any other software that supports the CSV file format (for example, Microsoft Excel).

Component Version Information

You can check the versions of installed components by clicking **Help > Component Versions**. Version information proves useful when you are trying to verify whether you have the latest version of an installed component.

Learn More About Cisco CallManager Serviceability

Detailed information about CallManager Serviceability is available at the following location:

http://www.cisco.com/univercd/cc/td/doc/product/voice/c_callmg/4_1/service/serv412/index.htm

Real-Time Monitoring Tool (RTMT)

The Real-Time Monitoring Tool (RTMT) is a client plug in that enables you to view real-time serviceability information for a CallManager cluster from a remote PC. RTMT provides real-time clusterwide system monitoring, performance monitoring, and device monitoring. You can monitor CallManager and Windows 2000 performance objects and counters in chart view or table view using the **Performance** tab in RTMT. You can also set thresholds and generate alerts that can be sent to you as e-mail or pop-up messages. Alerts can be configured for CallManager on a per-node basis, or on phones, gateways, ports, Cisco TFTP, and much more.

RTMT includes several charts and tables that provide an overview of the CallManager cluster. Figure 6-10 shows the summary page in RTMT, which displays the memory utilization, CPU utilization, number of registered IP phones, calls in progress, and active gateway ports on a single screen. Note that each server in the cluster is represented by its own line on the chart.

Figure 6-10 *RTMT Summary Screen*

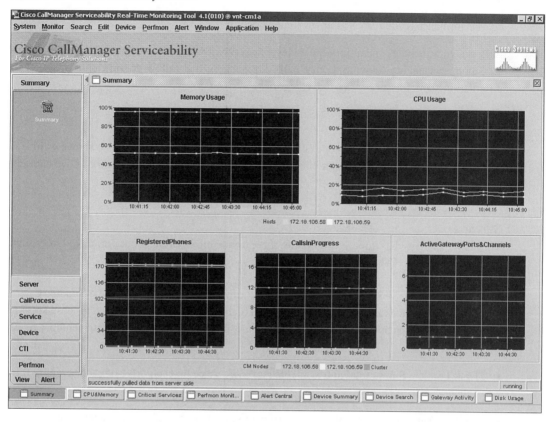

RTMT has two main tabs on the bottom left:

- **View**—Enables you to view real-time data

- **Alert**—Lists all configured alerts and their status

RTMT View Tab

The View tab has seven categories:

- Summary

- Server

- CallProcess

- Service

- Device

- CTI

- Performance (called "PerfMon" in some versions)

Each category includes one or more subcategories, each of which has graphs and tables similar to the Summary category shown in Figure 6-10. The sections that follow provide additional information about the seven View tab categories.

Summary

The Summary category only has one subcategory, also named Summary, which shows memory utilization, CPU utilization, number of registered IP phones, calls in progress, and active gateway ports and channels.

Server

The Server category has three subcategories that provide information about server resources such as CPU and memory. The three subcategories are as follows:

- **CPU&Memory**—Shows memory and CPU utilization graphs similar to the Summary category. Also lists all processes on each node of the CallManager cluster and process-specific information such as CPU utilization, private memory bytes in use, and virtual memory bytes in use.

- **Disk Usage**—Shows total and available hard disk space on each drive of each server in the cluster.

- **Critical Services**—Lists all services critical to the operation of CallManager for each node in the cluster along with a status of up (working), down (not working), or not activated. This table also shows how long each of the services has been up, enabling you to determine whether a service has restarted unexpectedly.

CallProcess

The CallProcess category has four subcategories that provide call processing statistics such as number of calls active on the system. The four subcategories are as follows:

- **Call Activity**—Shows the number of calls completed and calls attempted in the last sampling interval. Also shows the number of calls in progress.

- **Gateway Activity**—Allows you to view statistics for various gateway types: MGCP PRI, MGCP FXS, MGCP FXO, MGCP T1, and H.323. This page provides statistics such as Channels Active and Calls Completed for each gateway type.

- **Trunk Activity**—Shows the number of calls in progress and calls completed for H.323 and SIP trunks.

- **SDL Queue**—Displays the number of signals in each of the four SDL queues: High, Normal, Low, and Lowest. Also displays the number of signals processed during the last sampling interval. If signals are being processed at a rate slower than they are put into the queue, you will see the queue size increase. This can cause performance degradation on the CallManager system and is usually due to some kind of system resource limitation such as CPU, memory, or disk I/O.

Service

The Service category has three subcategories that provide information about TFTP and directory services as well as heartbeat information for various services. The three subcategories are as follows:

- **Cisco TFTP**—Monitors the operation of all TFTP services in the cluster by displaying the total number of TFTP requests, the number of requests where the file was not found, and the number of TFTP requests that were aborted.

- **Directory Server**—Shows the operational and replication status of the directory services on all nodes in the CallManager cluster.

- **Heartbeat**—The CallManager, TFTP, and Telephony Call Dispatcher (TCD) services all have a heartbeat counter that increments periodically to indicate the service is still processing calls. This page shows the heartbeat status for CallManager, TFTP, and TCD. If the heartbeat of a service stops, this category indicates that the service is in a state where it is unable to process calls.

Device

The Device category has two subcategories that provide information on registered devices and enable you to search for specific devices on the cluster. The two subcategories are as follows:

- **Device Summary**—Shows a graph of the number of registered phones, gateways, and media resources and provides a breakdown by gateway type and media resource type in table format.

- **Device Search**—Provides monitoring information about devices in the CallManager cluster, their IP addresses, their real-time status (such as whether they are successfully registered to CallManager and to which CallManager node), and other useful device information. For devices that support an HTTP server, such as phones and some gateways, you can right-click the specific device information to open an HTTP connection to the selected device. You can then browse information stored locally on the device, such as network configuration and statistics information. You can also launch related screens in CallManager Administration by right-clicking a device type (phone, gateway, voice mail, and so on).

CTI

The CTI category has two subcategories that provide information on CTI devices such as number of open devices and a CTI search similar to the device search on the Device category. The two subcategories are as follows:

- **CtiManager**—Shows the number open CTI devices, the number of open CTI lines, and the number of CTI connections to each node in the CallManager cluster.

- **CTI Search**—Enables you to search for CTI devices and applications registered to the CallManager cluster. This can prove useful for monitoring whether a CTI application is registered properly with CallManager. The CTI Search subcategory also tells you what user ID an application is using to authenticate with CallManager. If the login is failing, the CTI Search subcategory shows the reason for the failure.

Performance

The Performance category has only a single subcategory, called Performance. This category provides access to the same counters available in Microsoft Performance and enables you to configure alerts based on those counters.

Figure 6-11 shows various counters in table view in the RTMT window. RTMT provides the current, minimum, maximum, and average value for each counter. You can see descriptions of every counter by right-clicking the counter and selecting **Counter Description**.

With RTMT, you can select and monitor real-time performance counters that you specify in your CallManager cluster. You can configure multiple tabs under the Performance category. You can configure the view for each tab to be either graph or table format. The graph format provides 6 panes per category, accommodating up to 18 counters. You can add counters to the panes by double-clicking them from the list of counters. You can also drag and drop counters to layer up to three counters in a single pane. You can add new categories to monitor additional counters. For example, you might have eight T1 lines and are capacity-planning to determine whether to acquire additional T1 lines. You can monitor the counters associated with T1 gateways to determine when usage is approaching the limit. Another example is for load balancing. You can monitor the same counters from two different CallManager nodes in the cluster and put them on the same chart to see whether one CallManager is more heavily loaded than the other. You might decide to change the configuration to balance the load better.

Figure 6-11 *Monitoring Performance Counters in RTMT*

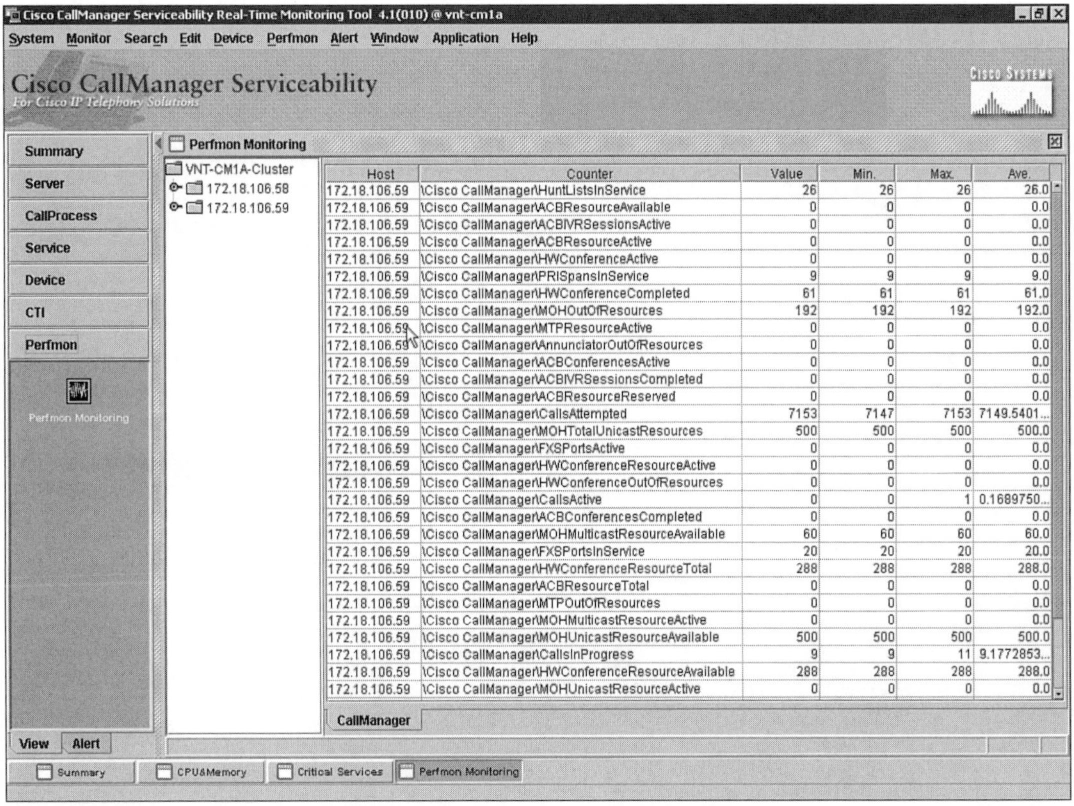

Note that CallManager-related statistics must be enabled for RTMT to collect data. These statistics are enabled by default in CallManager and can be turned on or off in the Service Parameters Configuration screen in CallManager Administration (**System > Service Parameters >** *select a server* **> Cisco CallManager >** *StatisticsEnable parameter set to **True** to enable or **False** to disable statistics*).

RTMT Alert Tab

The Alert tab in RTMT has only one category (Alert) with one subcategory (Alert Central). Alert Central provides two tables:

■ A list showing the status of all configured alerts

■ An alert history showing any alerts that have been previously triggered

Figure 6-12 shows the Alert Central window in RTMT.

Figure 6-12 *Alert Central in RTMT*

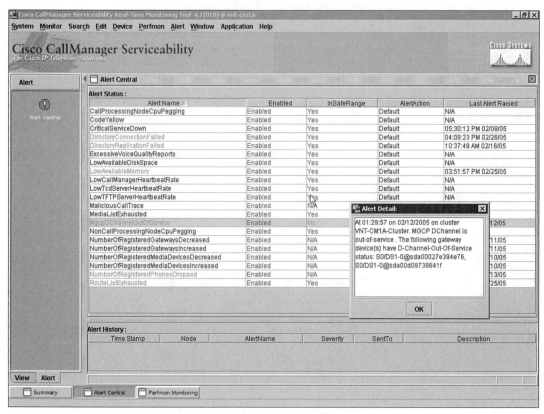

The alert status table shows the name of each alert, whether it is enabled, whether the alert is currently active, the action to take if the alert is triggered, and the date and time the alert was last triggered.

If the current value for the monitored counter is outside the configured threshold, the InSafeRange column will show No. Being outside the safe range might trigger an alert if the counter remains outside the configured threshold for a specified amount of time (the duration is user-configurable). You can get additional details about the alert by selecting **Alert Event Details** from the Alert menu. Figure 6-12 shows the alert details for the MgcpDChannelOutOfService alert. The alert details shows the list of gateways that have the D-channel out of service.

You can configure various alert actions in RTMT, which will send an e-mail of the alert to one or more configured e-mail addresses. You can set different actions for each alert if you want a different set of people to be notified based on the type of alert.

In addition to the preconfigured alerts, you can create an alert based on any performance counter. For example, if you want to be notified any time a call is rejected because a location has no more available bandwidth to allow that call, you can set an alert for the **LocationOutOfResources** counter in the Cisco CallManager performance object. To do this, add the counter to either a graph or table view in the Performance category of RTMT, and then right-click the counter and choose **Alert/Threshold....** You can then configure the level of the alert, a note that you want added to the e-mail any time the alert is sent, and the criteria under which the alert should trigger. The trigger criteria can be any of the following:

■   The value is over or under a specified limit

■   The value has changed by a certain amount or percentage since the last sampling interval

You can also choose to trigger the alert immediately or only when the threshold is exceeded for a certain number of seconds. You can also define during what times of the day the alert can be triggered.

Learn More About Real-Time Monitoring Tool

Detailed information about Real-Time Monitoring Tool is available at the following location or search Cisco.com for "Real-Time Monitoring Tool":

http://www.cisco.com/univercd/cc/td/doc/product/voice/c_callmg/4_1/service/serv413/ccmsrva/sartmt.htm

Microsoft Performance

Microsoft Performance is a Windows 2000 administrative tool that monitors and logs resource counters from CallManager nodes in the network. Performance shows CallManager-specific status information and Windows 2000 system information in real time. The CallManager system gathers statistical information about the Cisco IP Telephony deployment and feeds it into Performance by way of objects and counters. For example, you can monitor the number of calls in progress at any time, or the number of calls currently passing through a specific Cisco gateway. Data for non-CallManager-specific objects and counters are gathered by the respective services or the operating system itself. For example, the World Wide Web Publishing service feeds information to Performance about the various web pages served on a CallManager server.

Performance can collect data from multiple CallManager servers at once and compile it into a single log file. You can view the logged information in Performance and then export it into tab-separated value (TSV) or CSV file format that can you can view with most spreadsheet applications. Performance enables you to view statistical data in graphical, histogram, and report form. You can access Performance by clicking **Start > Programs > Administrative Tools > Performance**.

Customizing Microsoft Performance

Like the Real-Time Monitoring Tool, you can use Performance to monitor various real-time conditions in a CallManager system. For example, you can discover the number of calls in progress on a particular CallManager node at any time, or the number of calls currently being attempted in a CallManager cluster. This information is useful for capacity planning, network planning and design, load balancing, and troubleshooting, among other uses.

Each object includes counters that keep track of statistics such as the number of registered MGCP gateways or the number of registered hardware phones. These counters define current conditions within groups of related information. Each group of related information is called an object; each object contains one or more counters, such as Cisco CallManager or Cisco Software Conference Bridge, and each of these objects can have more than one instance of the object. Objects and counters are automatically added when CallManager or the related component (such as Conference Bridge) is installed. Using objects and counters, you can retrieve detailed, relevant, and timely system information. Performance can also be customized to track Cisco applications such as the IP IVR or Windows 2000 system objects and counters. This additional information can be useful to correlate system events with CallManager events. For example, if you notice a surge in CPU utilization, you might also notice that there is a surge in call volume which would explain the higher-than-expected CPU utilization.

Just as with RTMT, ensure that statistics are enabled in CallManager Administration for Performance to collect data. Statistics are enabled by default. You can stop CallManager from sending data to Performance and the Real-Time Monitoring Tool by setting the **Statistics Enabled** parameter to False in the Service Parameters Configuration page in CallManager Administration (**System > Service Parameters >** *select a server* **> Cisco CallManager**).

Learn More About Microsoft Performance

Detailed information about Performance is available in Microsoft Windows 2000 documentation.

Trace Collection Tool

The Trace Collection Tool (TCT) is a client plug-in (**Application > Install Plugins**) that you can install on a Windows PC to facilitate collecting trace data from a CallManager cluster. Before you can use TCT you must enable traces as described in the section "Cisco CallManager Serviceability."

You can collect traces for one or more services and one or more nodes of the cluster.

TCT collects traces for the following services:

- Cisco CallManager

- Cisco CDR Insert

- Cisco Certificate Authority Proxy Function

- Cisco CTI Manager

- Cisco CTL Provider

- Cisco Database Layer Monitor

- Cisco Extended Functions

- Cisco Extension Mobility

- Cisco IP Manager Assistant

- Cisco IP Voice Media Streaming App

- Cisco Messaging Interface

- Cisco MOH Audio Translator

- Cisco RIS Data Collector

- Cisco Telephony Call Dispatcher

- Cisco TFTP

- Cisco WebDialer

TCT also enables you to collect traces for the following CallManager applications:

- BAT

- CAR

- Cisco Serviceability Reporter

- Cisco Tomcat

- Installation Log Files

- Multilevel Administration (MLA)

- Quality Reporting Tool (QRT)

- Tool for Auto-Registered Phone Support

Finally, TCT enables you to collect the following system traces:

- Event Viewer logs (application, security, and system)

- Dr. Watson logs (crash dumps created by the Windows operating system)

- Internet Information Server (IIS) logs

- Microsoft SQL Server 2000 logs

- Directory logs

- System performance logs

- ProgLogs (includes system information from CallManager startup)

Figure 6-13 shows the trace selection screen. TCT enables you to collect all traces for the services selected or only those that fall within a specific timeframe. TCT can also optionally compress the collected files into a Zip archive to save hard drive space on the PC where you are collecting the traces.

Time-based collection can prove useful for diagnosing a problem where you know approximately the time of the problem. For example, if a user complains that a call was cut off, you can collect traces for the time period in which the dropped call occurred (say, yesterday morning between 7:45 a.m. and 8:15 a.m.).

Figure 6-13 *Trace Collection Tool*

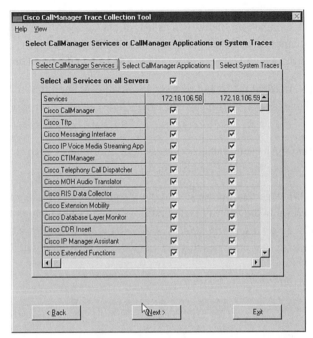

Learn More About the Trace Collection Tool

Detailed information about the Trace Collection Tool is available at the following location or search Cisco.com for "Trace Collection Tool":

http://www.cisco.com/univercd/cc/td/doc/product/voice/c_callmg/4_1/service/serv413/ccmsrva/satracec.htm

Event Viewer

Microsoft Event Viewer helps identify problems at the system level. For example, a group of users cannot make calls in a system with one gateway. You can use Event Viewer to look for events about the gateway (such as registration or unregistration events) to pinpoint the problem. Event Viewer starts automatically when Windows 2000 is started and records events in three kinds of logs:

- **Application log**—Contains events logged by applications or programs, such as CallManager.

- **System log**—Contains events logged by the Windows 2000 system components, such as the failure of a system component.

- **Security log**—Contains records of security events such as login failures.

Event Viewer displays the following types of events:

■ **Error**—A significant problem, such as loss of data or loss of functionality. For example, if a problem occurs with a device that is registered with CallManager, an error event provides device information and error details to help you isolate the problem.

■ **Warning**—An event that is not necessarily significant but might indicate a possible future problem. For example, warning events can include CallManager services that have stopped or started.

■ **Information**—An event that describes system information, such as host name or IP address and the version of the database layer in use.

By default, CallManager alarms are sent to the Event Viewer at the Error level. You can change the alarm event level in the Alarm Configuration screen in CallManager Serviceability (**Alarm > Configuration >** *select a server > select a service*). Figure 6-14 shows the details of an information message that indicates that the gateway has registered with CallManager.

Figure 6-14 *Event Viewer Information Message*

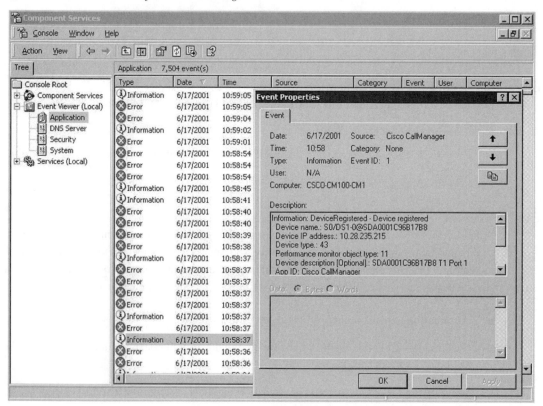

You can access Event Viewer by clicking **Start > Programs > Administrative Tools > Event Viewer**.

Learn More About Event Viewer

Detailed information about Event Viewer is available in Microsoft Windows 2000 documentation.

Terminal Services Client

Terminal Services Client, part of Windows 2000 Server, enables you to export a remote desktop to your PC. It is particularly useful because it allows you access to the remote PC as though you were local to the machine. You must know an administrator-level password on the remote server to access it via Terminal Services. After you have accessed a server using the Terminal Services client or Microsoft Remote Desktop client, you can perform tasks such as system administration, viewing log files or event logs, and so on.

Installing and Accessing Terminal Services Client

Installing the Terminal Services client is possible using a variety of methods. Cisco recommends using the latest Microsoft Remote Desktop Connection (RDC) client available from Microsoft.com.

Windows XP comes bundled with the RDC client and is available from the Start menu (**Programs > Accessories > Communications**). If you are not running Windows XP, you can obtain the RDC client from Microsoft.com for Windows 2000 or Mac OS X.

If you would like to install the older Terminal Services client instead of the RDC client or do not have Internet access, you must first create floppy disks containing the application. From the CallManager server, click **Start > Programs > Administrative Tools > Terminal Services Client Creator**. Use the Terminal Services Client Creator to create floppy disks; then install Terminal Services on any PC using the floppy disks. When installed on the PC, you can use Terminal Services by clicking **Start > Programs > Terminal Services Client** and designating the IP address or host name of the remote server you want to access.

> **NOTE** You must have the Terminal Services service started on the CallManager node to which you want to connect.

> **NOTE**   Cisco installs Terminal Services so that administrators and the Cisco Technical
> Assistance Center (TAC) can perform remote administration and troubleshooting tasks. Cisco
> does not support upgrades through Terminal Services. You can use VNC Viewer to perform
> remote upgrades.

Virtual Computer Networking (VNC) Viewer

Virtual Network Computing (VNC) Viewer is a remote display system that enables you to view a
remote desktop environment, similar to Terminal Services. VNC allows you to use one computer
to drive actions on a target computer, but differs from Terminal Services because with VNC, any
actions performed by you that occur on the target computer can be seen equally by the local user.
Unlike Terminal Services, you can use VNC to install, upgrade, or apply patches to CallManager.

You can access the VNC application and documentation files on the operating system (OS) version
2000.2.2 and later installation disc or download. If you're running an older version of the OS, run
the OS upgrade for version 2000.2.2 or later to gain access to the VNC files. OS upgrades are
available at the following link (requires Cisco.com login):

http://www.cisco.com/cgi-bin/tablebuild.pl/cmva-3des

> **CAUTION**   Using VNC can expose you to a security risk. Review the "Security Best
> Practices" section in the Cisco-produced document for installing VNC, which is available on the
> OS 2000 version 2.2 and later installation disc or at the download link previously shown. Use a
> complex alphanumeric password for VNC. VNC does not have a username/password structure;
> it uses only a single password, and VNC limits the password to eight characters, so make sure
> the password you choose is difficult to crack. A good password includes numbers, upper- and
> lowercase letters, and special characters, and does not use any known word. For example:
> 123eye67 is not as good a password choice as 4hW9Lv#g.

CiscoWorks IP Telephony Environment Monitor

CiscoWorks is the network management system (NMS) of choice for all Cisco devices, including
the CallManager system. CiscoWorks IP Telephony Environment Monitor (ITEM) adds additional
functionality to the base CiscoWorks package, which provides the capability to continuously
evaluate and report the operational health of your Cisco IP Telephony implementation and
provides some diagnostic tools to help troubleshoot problems that occur in the IP Telephony
network. ITEM provides specialized operations and security tools beneficial to large and small IP
telephony implementations. ITEM is not bundled with CallManager and must be purchased
separately.

Using CiscoWorks, you can configure and produce reports on log messages collected from
CallManager nodes and other IP telephony devices. CiscoWorks provides a common system log

for applications in the multiple-host and multiple-platform Cisco IP Communications environment. ITEM uses SNMP and CallManager's AXL SOAP interface to provide additional information on each device from which the log messages originate.

Each time a device is added to the ITEM device inventory, a new database entry is created. After the device is added to the list, ITEM gathers some device information over SNMP. You can read and use this information for system maintenance and problem solving.

ITEM includes five components.

- **CiscoWorks IP Telephony Monitor (ITM)**—Monitors Cisco voice elements in the network to alert operations personnel to potential problems and to help minimize downtime. This component also includes CiscoWorks Common Services, a common foundation for data storage, login, access privileges, and navigation and launch management for all CiscoWorks applications.

- **CiscoWorks IP Phone Information Utility (IPIU)**—Provides operational status and implementation details about an individual IP phone. This component also provides security reports that document IP phone "moves, adds, and changes" as well as information about the physical and logical connections of every Cisco IP Phone installed in a given network.

- **CiscoWorks IP Phone Help Desk Utility (IPHDU)**—Reports operational status and implementation details about individual IP phones. This component works in conjunction with the IPIU to make read-only access to Cisco IP Phone installation details available to help desk personnel.

- **CiscoWorks ITEM Gateway Statistics Utility (GSU)**—Collects performance and behavior statistics about CallManager-controlled and Cisco IOS Software-based IP telephony gateways, which can be processed by third-party software to produce utilization and capacity management reports.

- **CiscoWorks WAN Performance Utility (WPU)**—Measures the performance, latency, and availability of multiprotocol IP networks on an end-to-end and hop-by-hop (router-to-router) basis.

In addition to ITEM, the CiscoWorks family of web-based products supports maintenance of Cisco enterprise networks and devices. The products include Resource Management Essentials and Campus Manager, which provide syslog analysis, topology services, path analysis, user tracking, fault management, and other network management services.

System Log Management

The syslog analysis tools are Syslog Collector and Syslog Analyzer. They are offered with CiscoWorks as part of the Resource Management Essentials package. Syslog output from

CallManager can alternatively be adapted for use with other NMSs that support the standard syslog format:

- The Syslog Collector keeps common system logs that record messages reported to the CallManager system.

- The Syslog Analyzer controls and displays all events so they can easily be read, interpreted, and used for system maintenance and problem solving.

Using the reporting and managing capabilities of these tools, you can monitor and manage a wide range of events and error messages concurrently on each CallManager node and other Cisco devices.

Cisco Syslog Collector

Syslog Collector gathers log messages from a CallManager cluster or node at any network installation. The service collects a wide range of significant event messages that reflect system status. After validating the events or error messages collected, Syslog Collector passes them to the Syslog Analyzer. When this process is complete, you can use Syslog Analyzer to analyze the log messages.

Cisco Syslog Analyzer

Syslog Analyzer, which resides on a CiscoWorks server, receives the messages collected from multiple applications by the Syslog Collector. When a collection of data is received, the Syslog Analyzer parses and stores the results in the CiscoWorks database. This interface enables you to access and manage whatever data is collected from the system's managed devices.

With Syslog Analyzer, you can examine the event log reports from each Cisco CallManager system, including the description and recommended actions for each log message. In addition to a cluster of Cisco CallManagers, a network installation can also have some voice equipment, routers, gateways, and other devices generating log messages. After you have set up your system, you can access all of this information through one server.

Learn More About CiscoWorks and ITEM

You can find detailed information about CiscoWorks at the following locations:

http://www.cisco.com/en/US/products/sw/cscowork/ps2433/index.html

http://www.cisco.com/en/US/customer/products/sw/cscowork/ps2425/index.html

SNMP MIBs

A *Management Information Base* (MIB) is a structured set of data variables, called objects, in which each variable represents some resource to be managed. Simple Network Management Protocol (SNMP) MIB conceptual tables organize and distribute the information gathered from your IP telephony system.

SNMP allows CallManager to be managed with standard network management applications, such as CiscoWorks or HP OpenView. Windows 2000 Server provides an extensible SNMP agent that can be installed and run as a service. Cisco extension agents (dynamic link library, or DLL) support Cisco MIBs, which provides support for CallManager-specific data.

HP Insight Agent

For CallManager nodes that run on HP servers, the network management application can get system information from the HP Insight Agent MIB. No trap is provided in this MIB, so the management application needs to poll the information that it is interested in periodically and generate its own trap when it reaches a certain threshold value. You can obtain platform-specific information such as hard disk array and power-supply status from the HP Insight Agent. ITEM uses the HP Insight Agent to provide platform-specific alerts for your IP telephony servers.

IBM Director Agent

For CallManager nodes that run on IBM servers, the network management application can get system information from the IBM Director Agents. The IBM Director Agents are similar to the HP Insight Agent in that they provide platform-specific information. The IBM Director Agent can be used by ITEM to monitor the IP telephony server platform or can be used with IBM Director Server and Console to monitor the platform.

CCM MIB Extension Agent

SNMP objects and traps are defined in CISCO-CCM-MIB. The CCM MIB extension agent implements the Cisco CallManager MIB. This MIB exports the data in the CallManager database and in other data sources. A *trap* is an unsolicited message sent by an agent to a management station in an asynchronous manner. The purpose is to notify the management station of some unusual event. The traps are sent to trap-receiving hosts configured in the Windows 2000 SNMP service. Network management applications such as ITEM can gather data that can be used for fault management and analysis purposes. Although the design of the MIB and trap is tied to CiscoWorks applications, it does not limit you from developing network management applications by using third-party software. The SNMP extension agent for the CISCO-CCM-MIB is packaged as a DLL file and bundled in the CallManager installation.

CDP MIB Extension Agent

The CDP MIB extension agent implements all of the variables related to the tell side of Cisco Discovery Protocol (CDP). The MIB variables implemented are cdpInterfaceTable, cdpGlobalRun, cdpGlobalMessageInterval, and cdpGlobalDeviceId. This is the minimum CDP SNMP support that network management applications such as CiscoWorks need to discover the CallManager server. The variable cdpGlobalDeviceId is of type DisplayString (meaning an alphanumeric string) and will return the same value that CDP reports in its CDP advertisement messages.

Updating the CISCO-CCM-MIB Information

The Cisco RIS Data Collector is primarily responsible for updating the information used by the SNMP agents, and it buffers the CISCO-CCM-MIB information that the agents process. At startup, the Cisco RIS Data Collector updates all of the relevant information by periodically fetching data from CallManager or the CallManager database. This updated information is based on interaction with CallManager and other CallManager-associated services.

Updating the CISCO-CDP-MIB Information

At startup, the CDP SNMP extension agent interacts with the CDP driver, fetching and buffering CDP-related information.

Downloading the Latest MIBs

New features and bug fixes cause the CISCO-CCM-MIB to be routinely updated. You can download the latest MIB from the following location:

ftp.cisco.com/pub/mibs

This site provides detailed information about hundreds of MIBs, including CISCO-CDP-MIB and other MIBs that may be of interest to you.

Cisco Discovery Protocol (CDP)

CDP allows CallManager to advertise itself to other Cisco devices on the network by sending periodic messages to a well-known Multicast address monitored by other neighbor devices. Network operators and analysts use this information for configuration monitoring, topology discovery, and fault diagnosis purposes.

With CDP support, CallManager periodically sends out CDP messages or protocol data units (PDU) on the active physical interfaces. These messages contain CallManager information such as the device ID, interface name, system capabilities, and so on. Any Cisco devices with CDP support can discover CallManager by listening to these periodic messages.

Voice Log Translator (VLT)

CallManager provides a large amount of trace data to help you diagnose problems; however, analyzing trace logs can prove difficult for those unfamiliar with the formatting of the messages. In addition, much of the data in the traces appears in a numeric or hexadecimal format that you must decode to understand what is in the trace. For example, if a call going through a PRI gateway is disconnected, a cause code is sent indicating the reason for the disconnect, but the value in the CCM trace appears in hex, such as 0x8090. You need a way to convert this value into human-readable format—in this case "Normal call clearing." To facilitate this type of trace decoding, use the Voice Log Translator (VLT) tool.

VLT enables you to open a CCM (SDI) trace file and decode its contents. Figure 6-15 shows the output of the VLT tool. You can see that it is decoding the Q.931 Disconnect cause code of 0x8090 to "Normal call clearing."

Figure 6-15   *Voice Log Translator Tool*

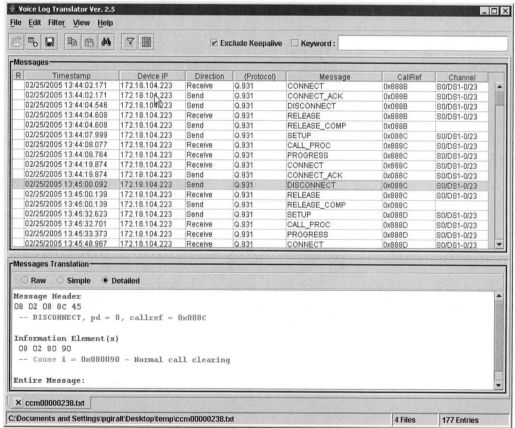

VLT supports the decoding of the following protocols/interfaces:

- SCCP

- Q.931

- H.225

- H.245

- MGCP

- JTAPI

In addition to decoding these protocols/interfaces, VLT also enables you to perform advanced searching and filtering of trace data to help you find the root cause of a problem. For example, if you know the called party number for a call that failed, you can do a search for that phone number and VLT will display only those messages that contain that phone number. You can then tell VLT to filter by the call reference for that call to see all the messages related to the call.

VLT will work only with text-based CCM (SDI) trace files and will not work with XML traces, which is another reason why Cisco recommends using the default text-based traces. VLT is available at the following URL or search Cisco.com for "Cisco Voice Tool":

> http://www.cisco.com/cgi-bin/tablebuild.pl/voice-tool

Summary

This chapter provided information about two applications to assist with managing your network, BAT and CAR. The important thing to consider is whether the tools described can help in your daily operations. In most cases, either BAT or CAR (or both tools) can save you considerable time (and, therefore, money) in configuring, managing, and diagnosing your CallManager system.

This chapter also covered several monitoring applications, including CallManager Serviceability and the Real-Time Monitoring Tool, which can assist in monitoring your system. You should understand how to use the features in CallManager Serviceability because these will help you troubleshoot the system.

Call Detail Records

Cisco CallManager produces two types of records which store call history and diagnostic information, as follows:

- **Call detail records (CDR)**—Data records that contain information about each call that was processed by CallManager.

- **Call management records (CMR)**— Data records that contain quality of service (QoS) or diagnostic information about the call. Also referred to as diagnostic records.

Both CDRs and CMRs together are referred to as *CDR data*. CDR data provides a record of all calls that have been made or received by users of the CallManager system. CDR data is useful primarily for generating billing records; however, it can also be used for tracking call activity, diagnosing certain types of problems, capacity planning, and evaluating the QoS of calls through the system.

This chapter includes a general overview of the CDR facilities provided in release 4.1 of CallManager. Most of this information applies to earlier versions of CallManager, too. The first three sections give a general understanding of the CDR data, the facilities provided for controlling the generation and usage of the data, and a description of what happens to CDR data in failure scenarios. The first three sections are as follows:

- Overview of CDR Data
- Creation and Usage of CDR Data
- Storage and Maintenance of CDR Data

The remaining sections offer more detailed information that you'll find useful if you are writing or integrating post-processing packages for CDR data, or simply interested in the details. The remaining sections are as follows:

- Understanding Field Data in CDRs
- Understanding Field Data in CMRs
- Identifying CDR Data Generated for Each Call Type
- Accessing CDR Data in the Central CDR Database
- Hints on Processing CDR Data
- Troubleshooting CDR Data Generation and Storage

Figure 7-1 shows the block structure of CallManager. CDRs are generated in the Call Control Layer of CallManager. CMRs are generated in the Station and Media Gateway Control Protocol (MGCP) components within the Device Layer. The shaded blocks are the CallManager components that generate CDR data. You can learn more about the various blocks and layers of CallManager in Chapter 1, "Cisco CallManager Architecture."

Figure 7-1 *CallManager Block Structure Diagram*

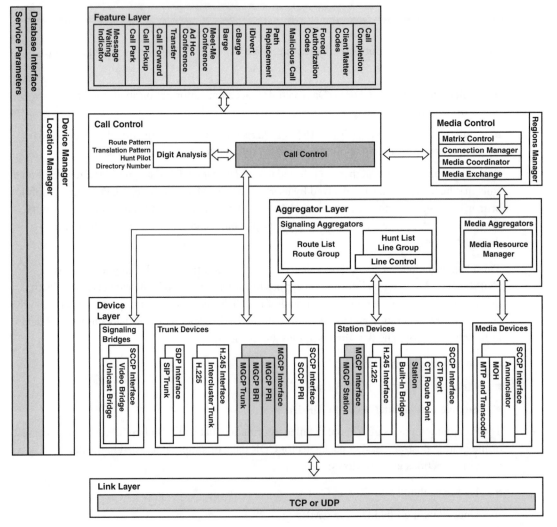

Overview of CDR Data

CDRs contain information about call origination, call destination, the date and time the call was started, the time it actually connected, and the time it ended. A call is considered started or originated when the caller goes off-hook. The call is considered ended when either the caller or the called party goes on-hook. CMRs contain information about the amount of data sent and received, jitter, latency, and lost packets.

CDR data is written when significant changes occur to a given call, such as the following:

- Ending a call

- Transferring a call

- Parking a call

- Creating a conference

- Joining a conference

- Barging into a call

- Holding a call

CDR data is stored in a central CDR data store. It can be retrieved by billing software or viewed by an administrator as soon as it has been written into the central data store. The process of gaining access to the data is described later in this chapter in the section "Accessing CDR Data in the Central CDR Database." The Call Control Layer generates CDRs from data that is collected from other layers of software during normal call processing. Most of the CDR data comes from the Device Layer, and some come from the Supplementary Services Layer.

Contents and Generation of CDRs

A CDR for a call contains information about the call origination, destination, and duration. It also indicates whether the call has been forwarded, and it contains information used to link all CDRs and CMRs related to a given call. CallManager writes only one CDR for each basic call that CallManager processes. A basic call is one in which a user calls another user directly and does not use any features. If a user invokes any features during the call, such as call park, transfer, or conference, CallManager might generate more than one CDR for that call. CallManager is a highly distributed system, which means that more than one CallManager node in the cluster can be involved in processing a single call. More than one CallManager node is involved, for example, when a call is placed from a phone that is registered on one CallManager node to a phone that is registered on another CallManager node. One CallManager node is always in charge of a call and is responsible for generating the CDRs as soon as a significant change happens to the call. The CallManager node in charge of a call is usually the CallManager node where the phone or device that originated the call is registered. However, this rule has several exceptions, including the following:

- If the phone has a shared line appearance, the first phone with the shared line to successfully register with CallManager determines the CallManager node that will be the controlling CallManager for all calls originating from that shared line for all phones that share the line. In the event of a CallManager failure or restart, the controlling CallManager node might change (determined by which phone registers first).

- The same CallManager node that controls the conference controller's call controls all calls that are part of that conference.

- The same CallManager node that controls the original call during a transfer operation controls all call connections that are part of the transfer.

Contents and Generation of CMRs

CMRs contain media stream statistics (packet loss, jitter, and so forth) as well as other call diagnostic information supplied by the phones or gateways that were used in a call. You can use the data to evaluate the QoS for that call, gather information on network congestion, and discover network configuration problems, device errors, and device performance issues. Not all devices can provide CMRs. In CallManager releases through 4.1, only IP phones and MGCP-controlled gateways can supply CMRs. When a call ends, CallManager requests CMR data from each endpoint device in the call that supports CMRs, and combines that data with other data supplied by CallManager and then writes a CMR for that endpoint. If the endpoint device does not support CMRs, CallManager does not write a CMR. IP phone-to-IP phone calls cause two CMRs to be written for each call: one for each endpoint. If a call was transferred, CallManager might write three or four CMRs, depending on the type of transfer. When a conference call ends, CallManager writes a CMR for each party in the conference that supported CMRs (IP phones or calls through an MGCP-controlled gateway).

> **TIP**   CallManager writes CMRs only for IP phones and gateways that use MGCP to interface with CallManager. The number of CMRs written can be more than one per endpoint involved in a call. If you go off-hook on an IP phone and call another IP phone, for example, two CMRs are generated when the call disconnects. If you made the same call and then placed the call on hold, an extra CMR is generated for your IP phone each time you place the call on hold.
>
> The number is even more complicated for a conference because you have one CMR for the initial call, one for the call to the third participant when you talk to them before adding that participant to the conference, and three CMRs for the phones in the conference when the conference terminates.
>
> When a call involves other endpoints besides IP phones and MGCP-controlled gateways, the diagnostic data is not available so the number of CMRs written for a given call varies accordingly.

CMRs contain data from the perspective of the device that provided the data. Each CMR holds information on the amount of voice data sent and received in the form of packet counts and octet (or byte) counts. It also contains the number of packets lost and jitter, which can be used to determine QoS on a call. *Jitter* is the difference in time between a packet's expected arrival time and the time the packet actually arrives. A CMR also contains information that links it to the CDR for that call. If two CMRs exist, one for each endpoint in a given call, the CMRs have corresponding data. However, it's possible that one of the endpoints experienced problems with voice quality caused by jitter or lost packets, while the other endpoint did not. In those cases, the packet and octet counts in associated CMRs might not correspond exactly. CMRs also contain a field for latency, but it is currently not used because the devices do not compute this value.

Creation and Usage of CDR Data

You can enable and disable CDR and CMR processing via service parameters in Cisco CallManager Administration (**Service > Service Parameters** > *select a server* > *select a service*). Select the desired service parameters from the list in Table 7-1, set their values appropriately, and update them. When you modify the CDR-related service parameters, the specified CallManager node changes its processing accordingly within a short time, usually within a few seconds. Table 7-1 lists the service parameters that control and manage CDR data.

Table 7-1 *CDR and CMR Service Parameters*

Parameter—Service and Section	Description	Default	Valid Values
CDR Enabled Flag— Cisco CallManager service, System	Enables and disables the generation of CDR data for the specified CallManager only.	False	True—Generate CDRs False—Do not generate CDRs
Call Diagnostics Enabled— Cisco CallManager service, Clusterwide Parameters (Device – General)	Enables and disables the generation of CMRs for all CallManager nodes in the cluster.	False	True— Generate CMRs False— Do not generate CMRs
CDR Log Calls with Zero Duration Flag— Cisco CallManager service, System	Enables and disables the logging of CDR data for calls that were not connected or were connected for less than 1 second for the specified CallManager only.	False	True— Generate CDRs for unconnected calls False— Do not generate CDRs for unconnected calls
Max CDR Records— Cisco Database Layer Monitor service, System	Specifies the maximum number of CDRs to keep in the database. If the number of CDRs reaches this maximum number, the oldest records are deleted and an alarm is generated. This check occurs once a day.	1,500,000 records	1 to 2147483647 records

continues

Table 7-1 *CDR and CMR Service Parameters*

Parameter—Service and Section	Description	Default	Valid Values
Maintenance Time (hr)— Cisco Database Layer Monitor service, Clusterwide Parameters	Specifies the hour in military time (24-hour clock) to begin CDR database maintenance. Use this parameter in combination with the Maintenance Window parameter. For example, specifying 22 in this parameter means that the CDR maintenance would begin at 10 p.m. If the Maintenance Window parameter is set to 2, it means that CDR maintenance will run every hour from 10 p.m. to midnight. If both parameters are set to 24, CDR maintenance will run every hour all day long. During CDR maintenance, the system deletes the oldest CDRs and associated CMRs, so the maximum number of records, as specified in the Max CDR Records parameter, is maintained. Also during maintenance, the system issues an alarm if the CDR file count exceeds 200 and checks for replication links between servers that have been broken and tries to reinitialize them.	24th hour	1 to 24
Maintenance Window— Cisco Database Layer Monitor service, Clusterwide Parameters	This parameter specifies the window of time during which CDR maintenance is performed on an hourly basis. For example, if this parameter is set to 12, CDR maintenance will run every hour for 12 hours, starting at the time that is specified in the Maintenance Time parameter. For example, if the Maintenance Time parameter is set to 7, and this parameter is set to 12, CDR maintenance will begin at 7 a.m. and run every hour until 7 p.m. If both parameters are set to 24, CDR maintenance will run every hour all day long.	2 hours	1 to 24

Enabling and Disabling CDR Data Generation

The CDR Enabled Flag service parameter (**Service > Service Parameters >** *select a server >* Cisco CallManager) determines whether CDR data is generated. CDR data generation is disabled by default when the system is installed because some users do not need CDR data, do not have processing resources to handle it, and because CDRs consume disk space. The default setting prevents the creation of the CDR data (which saves processing time and disk space) unless you explicitly enable its generation. You must set this parameter to True if you want to have CDR data at your disposal.

> **NOTE**   When you change the setting of the CDR Enabled Flag parameter, it only applies to the CallManager node selected. You should configure it to be the same for all CallManager nodes in the cluster to get consistent and predictable results. If you set the configuration differently on different CallManager nodes, some CDR data is not logged.

Logging or Not Logging Calls with Zero Duration

The CDR Log Calls with Zero Duration Flag service parameter determines whether CDRs for calls that were never connected or were connected for less than a second are generated. The following are three common examples:

- When a user goes off-hook and then on-hook without completing a call.

- When a user completes a blind transfer. (The consultation call does not connect.)

- When a user calls a destination that does not return answer supervision. The most common cases of this are calls to Public Safety Answering Points (PSAP; 911 emergency operator centers in North America). Many of these calls do not return answer supervision and as a result the 911 calls are not logged.

CallManager distinguishes between calls that have a duration of 0 seconds and terminate normally and calls that do not connect because of an error condition. Calls that terminate normally are those that have one of the following termination cause codes:

- **0**—No error

- **16**—Normal call clearing

- **31**—Normal, unspecified

CallManager always generates CDR data for calls that have a duration of 0 seconds and terminate because of an error condition of some sort, regardless of the setting of the CDR Log Calls with Zero Duration Flag service parameter. Calls to busy destinations or bad phone numbers are examples of this type of call. The duration of these calls is 0 because they were never connected, but their CDRs are generated anyway.

CallManager does not generate CDRs for calls that terminate normally and have a duration of 0 seconds, unless the CDR Log Calls with Zero Duration Flag service parameter is set to True. When CDR generation is enabled, CallManager generates a CDR for each call that was connected for 1 second or more.

> **TIP** The CDR Log Calls with Zero Duration Flag service parameter is valid only when the CDR Enabled Flag service parameter is set to True. If CDR generation is disabled, the setting of the CDR Log Calls with Zero Duration Flag service parameter has no significance.

Enabling and Disabling CMR or Diagnostic Data Generation

You can enable and disable the generation of CMRs through the Service Parameters Configuration page in CallManager Administration (**Service > Service Parameters** > *select a server* > **Cisco CallManager**). You control CMR generation by enabling the Call Diagnostics Enabled service parameter. CMR generation is disabled by default when the system is installed. The system generates CMRs only when the Call Diagnostics Enabled service parameter is set to True. The system generates CDRs based solely on the CDR Enabled Flag setting, so if all you want is CDRs, you do not need to set the Call Diagnostics Enabled parameter to True. If you want CMRs, you must enable call diagnostics specifically.

Cisco recommends that if you enable CMRs, you should also enable CDRs. Several processes, including the purging of CDR data and the processing of CDR data by the CDR Analysis & Reporting tool, are dependent on the existence of CDRs that are associated with CMRs. Problems with CAR and CDR data purge can occur if you have orphan CMRs (CMRs that do not have associated CDRs). If you use a third-party billing application to process CDR data, be aware that some applications purge CDRs but might not purge CMRs. Even if you have both CDRs and CMRs enabled, problems can still occur if the third-party application is deleting only CDRs and not the associated CMRs. One such problem is that over time, the unpurged CMRs can consume all the space on the disk and eventually crash CallManager. Because the purge process keys off CDRs, when the CDRs are deleted, the CMRs remain on the disk. This problem will be fixed in a future CallManager release, but as of release 4.1(2), the possibility for this problem still exists. When you change the setting of Call Diagnostics Enabled, it applies to all CallManager nodes in the cluster.

Storage and Maintenance of CDR Data

The CallManager cluster stores all CDR data in a central location. This can be either a central CDR database, or in comma-separated values (CSV or simply comma-delimited) flat files stored in a central location. This is referred to as the *central CDR data store*. Normally the CDR data is inserted into a central CDR database. This section describes how the central data store collects and stores CDR data and how the architecture provides fault tolerance and redundancy. Topics include the following:

- Why use a central database?

- What happens when the central database is not available?

- What happens to CDR data when a CallManager node fails?

- How to control the transport and storage of CDR data?

Read this section to discover some of the design goals and history relating to the current architecture. Furthermore, this section describes what happens when a CallManager node loses its link to the central CDR database and how the system recovers the data and makes it available in the central CDR data store.

Why Use a Central Database?

All CallManager nodes in a cluster form what is essentially one large system. Therefore, it is essential that all CDR data is collected and treated as if it is a single system. This section reviews the design decisions and tradeoffs that were made and why.

In very early versions of the software, CallManager wrote CDR data into comma-delimited files and stored them on the local disks because the whole system was on a single server. One file contained each day's records. Each CallManager was a complete system, as clustering technology was not available in versions 2.x and before.

Cisco's design team decided to enhance the system to make it a distributed, fault-tolerant, and redundant system. They designed it to have a scalable architecture so that it could grow into very large systems. Based on the design goals of creating a distributed system that is fault-tolerant and redundant, the team decided that having CDR data scattered on different servers did not fit well into the architecture for the new system. The team considered four major design goals when creating the current architecture of the system:

- Prevent the loss or unavailability of CDR data

- Store the CDR data in a fault-tolerant, redundant facility

- Make the data accessible from a single location

- Make the system handle very high traffic volumes

The team decided that putting the CDR data into a central CDR data store was the best way to meet these design goals. The central data store is normally a central database, but it can also be a folder on a server that holds the CDR CSV files. Having a central storage location makes it easier to secure the data and control access to it. A central data store can be either backed up or replicated as required to create a fault-tolerant and redundant storage facility. The data store can be made as secure as requirements for a particular customer demand.

There are a number of advantages in using a central data store for CDR data, including the following:

■ When a CallManager node crashes and takes the server down also, it does not affect the accessibility of the CDR data unless the CallManager node is running on the Publisher, which is where the central data store is normally located.

■ The data store can be made redundant and secure by specifying an off-cluster CDR connection string, as described in Table 7-2.

■ Billing systems interface with a single point of contact.

■ The data store does not need to be part of the CallManager cluster.

As the number of phones and other endpoints increased on the system, the amount of CDR data also increased accordingly. CallManager release 4.1 again increased the size of the system so that it supports as many as 7500 endpoints on a single node with up to 4 active nodes. The CDR data is written in comma-delimited format in flat files on the local disk of each CallManager server in the cluster with an active CallManager node that generates CDRs.

Release 3.3 and all later releases provide two distinct forms for the CDR data. The CDR data is initially written in comma-delimited format in flat files on the local disk. The Cisco Database Layer Monitor service then transfers these files via a TCP/IP connection to a central CDR data store on the Publisher. The data can either be stored as a set of flat files in the data store, or inserted into a SQL database. This transport occurs on an interval specified by the CDR File Time Interval service parameter (default is 1 minute).

You can choose how you want to store the CDR data by setting the CDR Format enterprise parameter appropriately (see Table 7-2). Most deployments choose to insert the CDR data into a SQL database by setting CDR Format to **CDRs will be inserted into database**. This choice enables the CDR Insert service, which monitors the CDR directories for new CDR data files. When a new file is written into the directory, CDR Insert reads the file and the CDR data it contains is inserted into the CDR database. CDR Insert then deletes the file. Figure 7-2 shows a CDR flow through the system. The CDR subsystem scales very well with this design and handles traffic loads well in excess of the current system capabilities.

When a CallManager server crashes, it does not affect the accessibility of the CDR data for calls handled by that node because the CDR data is stored in a central data store.

Figure 7-2 *CDR Flow Through CallManager System*

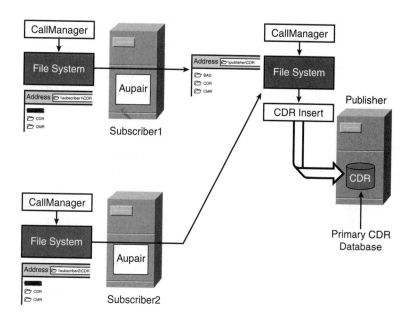

The clustering technology used in CallManager supports a significant number of CallManager nodes. Release 4.0 and later systems support a single cluster of eight CallManager nodes. As the number of nodes in a cluster grows, the collection and processing of CDR data becomes increasingly complex for a call management application, if the data must be collected and processed from each node in the cluster. In this architecture, the cluster looks and functions like a single system.

Storing the CDR data in a central data store provides a single location where all CDR data can be retrieved and processed. Software billing packages do not have to gather data from individual CallManager servers, and, therefore, they are not sensitive to the particular configuration of CallManager.

What Happens When the Central Database Is Not Available?

As in any distributed system, it's possible to lose a link between any of the nodes in the cluster and a central data storage facility.

The design team faced three major challenges in handling this contingency:

- How do you handle CDR data when the link between a CallManager node and the central database has been lost?

- How do you make the data secure on local drives in a cost-effective manner?

- How do you handle the CDR data when the amount of data during peak traffic periods from all CallManager nodes exceeds the capabilities of the database?

To resolve these challenges, the team decided to have all CDR data written as comma-delimited flat files on the local server as soon as data is generated. The data is then transferred to the central CDR data store in background mode. The directory where these files are stored on the local machine is monitored, and when a new CDR file closes (the system is finished writing data into it), the file is moved. After transferring the data successfully to the central CDR data store, the system removes the local copy.

If the link to the central data store is lost for any reason, CallManager stores CDR data on the local drives until the link is restored. The local drives on CallManager servers are mirrored drives so that no data is lost when a single drive fails. Mirrored drives minimize the potential loss of data until the link is restored. When the link is restored, the system transfers the CDR data in background mode to the central CDR data store. After transferring the data successfully, the local copy is removed.

Historical Background

The CDR processing design used in CallManager release 3.0 caused all CDR data to be written directly into the central database. Losing the link to the central database caused the Database Layer to write the CDR data into the local database on the CallManager server. When the link was recovered, the Database Layer transferred the CDR data to the central CDR database in background mode. After successfully transferring the data to the central database, the Database Layer removed the local copy.

During stress tests on CallManager release 3.0, the integration team discovered that the central database could not handle the volume of CDR data being generated within the cluster during peak traffic loads. This caused a design change in CallManager release 3.1 so that the Database Layer would write all CDR data to the local database on the CallManager server first.

As we scaled the cluster for CallManager release 3.2, we found that writes into the local database consumed more processor time than we desired, so we altered the design such that the system writes CDR data in comma-delimited flat files on the local disk, which is very fast. A background process called Aupair then transfers the CDR data to the CDR central data store. This design change enables handling the high traffic loads anticipated as we continue to scale the cluster.

What Happens to CDR Data When a CallManager Node Fails?

When a CallManager node fails, it loses all CDR data for all calls that it is controlling that are currently in progress but not completed. If call preservation is provided for the endpoints in question, the calls remain active even after CallManager fails, but there is no way to collect CDR data for those calls. Partial CDRs are never written.

When the CallManager node fails but the server hardware is working and Windows 2000 and the other services such as the database on the server platform that CallManager node is running on do not fail, the system continues transferring CDR data from the local disks to the central database until all local CDR data has been moved. If Windows 2000 crashes due to hardware failure or a system error or any other reason, the local CDR data is not accessible until the Windows 2000 server is brought back online and the system transfers the data to the main CDR data store.

How to Control the Storage and Transport of CDR Data

The two different aspects of CDR storage and processing that you can control are as follows:

- Where CDR data is stored

- How CDR data is stored

Where CDR Data Is Stored

You can control both the location of the central CDR data store, and in what form the CDR data is stored through the Enterprise Parameters page in CallManager Administration (**System > Enterprise Parameters**).

Table 7-2 identifies the enterprise parameters that control the storage of CDR data.

Table 7-2 *CDR Enterprise Parameters*

Parameter	Description	Default	Valid Values
Local CDR Path	Identifies the directory for local CDR files written by the CallManager node on the local server where CallManager is executing.	C:\Program Files\ Cisco\CallDetail	The local path CallManager uses to write CDR files.
CDR UNC Path	Identifies the central collection point for CDR files. If this parameter is blank, CDR files will not be moved from the local server.	Supplied during system installation.	Specifies a fully qualified Universal Naming Convention (UNC) path that is pointing to a read/write NT share for CDR file collection.

continues

Table 7-2 *CDR Enterprise Parameters (Continued)*

Parameter	Description	Default	Valid Values
Off Cluster CDR Connection String	Optional This parameter specifies the optional data set name (DSN) to use when you do not want CDRs inserted into the CDR database on the Publisher server. This string points to a central CDR data store on a server outside of the CallManager cluster. This server does not need to have CallManager installed, but it must point to an ODBC database server with matching CDR database schema. The DSN should include any necessary user and password information. Specifying a path in this parameter enables insertion of the CDRs into the specified off cluster database. It requires a trusted relationship between the Publisher and the external database. If this parameter is blank, CDRs are inserted into the CDR database on the Publisher using the path specified in the CDR UNC Path parameter.	N/A	Up to 255 alphanumeric characters.
CDR Format	Determines whether the files get inserted into the database.	CDRs will be inserted into database	CDRs will be inserted into database. CDRs will be kept in flat files. Note: Files will not be deleted.
CDR File Time Interval (min)	This parameter specifies the time interval for collecting CDR data. For example, if this value is set to 1, each file will contain 1 minute of CDR data or 1 minute of CMR data. CDR and CMR data is stored in separate files. The files will not be pushed to the CDR data store until the interval has expired, so consider how quickly you want access to the CDR data when you decide what interval to set in this parameter. For example, setting this parameter to 60 means that each file will contain 60 minutes worth of data, but that data will not be available until the 60-minute period has elapsed and the records are written to the CDR database.	1 minute	0 to 1440 minutes
Cluster ID	This parameter provides a unique identifier for this cluster. Because this parameter gets used in CDRs, collections of CDRs from multiple clusters can be traced to the sources.	StandAloneCluster	Up to 50 alphanumeric characters.

How CDR Data Is Stored

The CDR data is stored in one of two forms:

- Inserted into a SQL database

- Kept as CSV files in the specified CDR data store

The CDR Format enterprise parameter determines in which form the data is stored. See Table 7-2 for a definition of this parameter. If you use CDR data to create billing records, troubleshoot calls, or need to search the data for any particular reason, you might want the data inserted into a database. This makes the data more easily available for diagnostic, billing, or other such purposes.

On the other hand, if you just need to store the call records to fulfill either government or corporate requirements, you might consider leaving it in CSV files. These files can be compressed and stored in a much smaller space. CallManager is not designed to support storage of CDR data on the CallManager servers. This data must be moved to other servers for long-term storage.

> **TIP** If CDR data is stored as CSV files in the CDR data store, the files will not be deleted by the system. You need to establish proper file maintenance procedures and make sure the files are removed if appropriate.

Understanding Field Data in CDRs

The remainder of this chapter contains detailed information about the contents of each data record. Those who are interested in a general understanding of CDRs or are involved only as administrators on the system can skip the remainder of this chapter. If you use CDR data for diagnostic purposes, creating post-processing applications (such as billing systems or call management systems) or any other use that requires detailed information, the following sections are for you.

The topics in this section include the following:

- General information about the data types used

- Field data conversions

- Notes on other field types

- CDR field definitions

To understand and use the data from the CDRs, you need to understand both the type of the data as it is used in CallManager and the data type used to store the field value in the database. The two types are not always the same. The database field types are adequate to store the data, but the correct interpretation of the data must, in some cases, take into account the field types used by CallManager.

General Information About the Data Types Used

A fundamental difference exists in the data types used for handling and storing numeric data between CallManager and the Microsoft SQL database. CallManager always uses an unsigned integer as a type for all numeric CDR data fields, while the database always uses a signed integer field to store the data. The difference in the two data types causes the data in certain fields to appear inconsistent or even erroneous when viewed as a database record. The values displayed are sometimes negative and sometimes positive, but the real value is always a 32-bit positive number. You will notice this most often in fields that contain IP addresses. Always convert the value contained in a numeric database field to an unsigned integer value before interpreting the data.

> **TIP**   When processing field data values from CDR data, you must interpret or use the high-order bit, or sign bit, correctly because the value represented is a positive 32-bit number. All numeric fields contain 32-bit unsigned integer values but are stored in the CDR data as 32-bit signed integers. CDR data contains no negative numbers. The sign bit is part of the value contained in the field.

Default Values for Unused Fields

Not all fields contain valid data in every CDR or CMR. If the field is unused, the software sets it to its default value. The default values are as follows:

- Zero for numeric fields

- Blank for character fields

Field Data Conversions

The following sections define the conversion information for basic field types and explain what the types represent. Also covered is how to convert field types from their stored format to a more useful format that you can use when creating billing records and other reports.

Time Values

The database stores and displays all time values as signed integers, but the values are actually 32-bit unsigned integers. All time fields contain a value that is obtained from the Windows 2000 system routines. The value is the number of seconds since midnight (00:00:00) January 1, 1970, Greenwich mean time (GMT). The value is not adjusted for time zones or daylight savings time. All time values in a CDR are from the CallManager node that wrote the CDR. The ID of the CallManager node that wrote the CDR is found in the globalCallID_callManagerId field.

IP Addresses

IP addresses are normally written as four octets (8-bit groups) separated by periods, with each octet expressed as a decimal number. This is known as *dotted-decimal notation* (for example, 192.168.23.45). Because the database displays IP addresses as signed decimal integers, they sometimes appear as negative numbers. You can convert the signed decimal value to an IP address by first converting the value to an unsigned 32-bit hex (or binary) number.

A 32-bit number consists of four octets. Because the data is from an Intel-based machine, the four octets are in the reverse order of the four octets of an IP address. You must, therefore, reverse the order of the octets and then convert each octet to a decimal number. The resulting four octets are the four octet fields of the IP address. The following examples illustrate this conversion sequence.

> **TIP**   The database displays an IP address as a negative number when the low octet of the IP address has a value greater than or equal to 128.

Example: Conversion of an IP Address Displayed as a Negative Number

IP address value from CDR: –1139627840

> **TIP**   If you use a calculator to convert the value, enter the decimal number as a negative number, and then convert it to hex or binary.

Figure 7-3 illustrates how to convert a signed integer value to an unsigned integer value. Negative and positive values are essentially the same, but negative values have the high-order bit set. It is interpreted as a sign bit and displayed accordingly. Signed integers are 32-bit numbers and contain a 31-bit value plus a high-order sign bit. Unsigned integers are 32-bit numbers and contain a 32-bit value that is assumed to be a positive number.

Figure 7-3 *Convert Negative Signed Integer Value to Unsigned Integer Value*

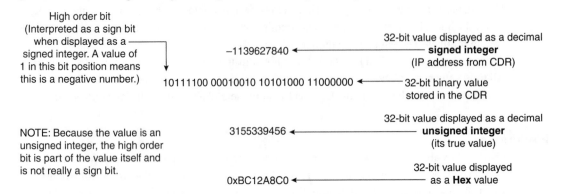

Figure 7-4 shows the steps needed to convert a 32-bit number into an IP address. As illustrated, the IP address from a CDR can be either a positive integer or a negative integer. When you look at it as a 32-bit binary value, it has four octets.

Figure 7-4 *How to Convert a 32-Bit Decimal Number to an IP Address*

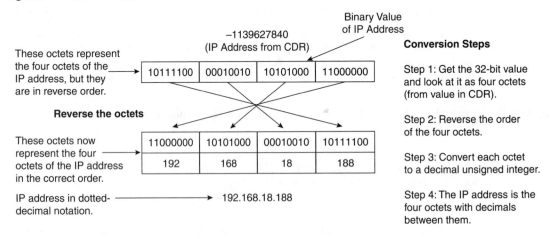

The following example illustrates the conversion process for a number that is positive.

Example: Conversion Example Using a Positive Number

IP address value from CDR: 991078592

Figure 7-5 illustrates how to convert a signed integer value to an unsigned integer value. Negative and positive values are essentially the same, but positive values have the high-order bit cleared. It is interpreted as a sign bit and displayed accordingly. Because this is a positive integer, it is the same in both signed and unsigned displays.

Figure 7-5 *Convert Positive Signed Integer Value to Unsigned Integer Value*

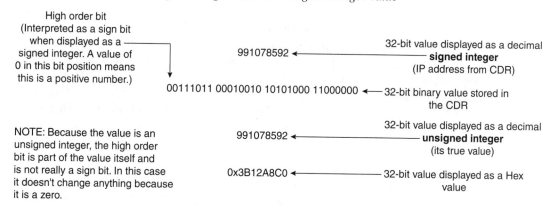

Figure 7-6 shows the steps needed to convert a positive integer number into an IP address. The IP address from a CDR can be either a positive integer or a negative integer. When you look at it as a 32-bit binary value, it has four octets.

Figure 7-6 *How to Convert a 32-Bit Positive Decimal Number to an IP Address*

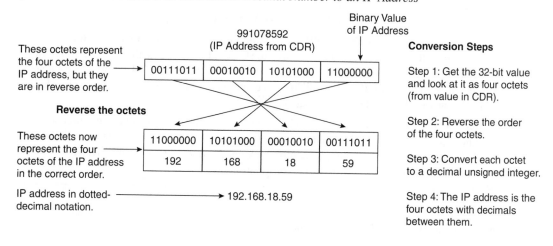

Notes on Other Field Types

This section contains useful information about some of the fields or types of fields contained in the CDRs that need explanation about their contents. This information should add to your understanding of how to use the data contained in these fields. In some cases, it might help to understand what the data actually represents and how it is used in CallManager.

Global Call Identifiers (GCID)

Historical Background

A global call identifier is usually referred to as a *global call ID* (GCID). GCIDs were originally created for use by the Computer Telephony Interface (CTI). The Java Telephony Application Programming Interface (JTAPI) dictated the requirement for GCID. The JTAPI call model requires a common identifier that identifies all call legs that are part of the same call. GCIDs have since been included in CDR data and are used to help identify CDRs related to a given call. Other fields also help identify the set of records that are needed.

CallManager uses a GCID to tag calls that are related to each other in some way and are logically part of the same call, as defined by CTI. The GCID does not tag all of the calls that are related from a CDR or billing perspective. The GCID in CDR data consists of two fields:

- **globalCallID_callManagerId**

- **globalCallID_callId**

GCID Structure Within CallManager

CallManager combines **globalCallID_callManagerId** and **globalCallID_callId** into a 64-bit unsigned integer structure that is known as the GCID. In CDR data, the GCID is stored in two separate numeric fields because the database cannot store a single 64-bit unsigned integer. The value in the **globalCallID_callId** field contains a 24-bit unsigned integer value that begins at 1 each time that CallManager is restarted.

Because the GCID resets each time CallManager is restarted, this value is not unique over time. Therefore, it is possible to have two sets of records in the CDR data store with the same GCID. To form a globally unique identifying value for a set of CDRs for a given call, you can combine these two fields with the call origination time.

The following examples illustrate the usage of GCIDs.

Example: GCID Usage in a Call Transfer

A call transfer creates three separate calls and therefore, three CDRs. If user A calls user B, and then user A transfers user B to user C, the calls created are as follows:

- **GCID 1**—Call from A to B

- **GCID 2**—Call from A to C to announce the transfer

- **GCID 1**—Call from B to C when the transfer is completed

In this case, CallManager assigns calls 1 and 3 the same GCID, and the second call is considered a separate call that is not necessarily related to the other two calls. Each call generates a CDR. In addition, the system logs four CMRs.

Example: GCID Usage in a Conference Call

A conference call consists of many separate but related calls. Each party that joins the conference is a separate call. In an Ad Hoc conference, when the conference controller presses the softkey to complete the conference, CallManager connects each of the three users to the same conference bridge and assigns each of their separate calls the same GCID. The calls created are as follows:

- **GCID 1**—Call from A to B, original call; conference always gets this GCID

- **GCID 2**—Call from A to C

- **GCID 1**—Call from A to conference bridge

- **GCID 1**—Call from B to conference bridge

- **GCID 1**—Call from C to conference bridge

- **GCID 1**—Call between last two parties when one hangs up; the conference bridge is dropped and the call between the remaining two parties is connected directly

The system generates six CDRs, and each CDR has the GCID as noted. CallManager also logs five CMRs. The section "Identifying CDR Data Generated for Each Call Type" later in this chapter identifies the set of records created for the illustrated call examples.

You can use GCIDs to help link all CDR data related to a given call. A GCID is unique across a cluster so long as you do not restart a CallManager node in that cluster. When you restart a CallManager node, the GCID restarts at the same value that it had when that CallManager node was originally started after installation. This is not a problem for online processing, because CallManager requires a GCID to be unique across all calls in the cluster for the duration of the call to which it is assigned. When you restart CallManager, the call signaling is lost for calls currently in progress. When new calls begin after the restart, they all have new GCIDs that are unique within the cluster at that point in time, even though they are duplicates of GCIDs previously used. Therefore, the GCIDs are not unique across time. Each time you restart a CallManager node, it creates the same set of GCIDs as the previous execution of the CallManager software.

Even though a CallManager node restart does not create any issues for online processing, it does create a problem for CDRs. CDR data that has the same GCID as the CDRs from the newly restarted CallManager node might exist. Thus, if a search is made in the database for all records with a given GCID, unrelated records might show up in the search results. When this occurs, the date and timestamps will differ and can be used to determine whether records are related.

Call Leg Identifiers

Call leg identifiers are usually referred to as call leg IDs. CallManager uses *call leg IDs* internally and includes them in the CDR data to help link CDR and CMR data records and CDRs related to the same call. You can also use call leg IDs in tracking call-related problems by using them as a hook into trace data generated by the system.

CallManager uses a call leg ID to identify a single call leg. Each complete call consists of two call legs. When you originate a call by going off-hook, the connection between your phone and CallManager is a *call leg*. When you dial a directory number that identifies a destination, the connection between CallManager and the destination is another call leg. Both call legs together form a complete call.

CallManager views each call as two separate call legs, and each call leg has a call leg ID that is unique within the cluster for the duration of that call. It is not unique across time, because when you restart a CallManager node for any reason, the call leg IDs start again with the same value that they had after the last restart of that CallManager node. The call leg ID is a 32-bit unsigned integer that consists of a 24-bit unsigned integer value, which begins at 1 each time CallManager is restarted, and the node ID for that CallManager.

Directory Numbers

CallManager applies translation patterns to digits that are dialed by a user. The translated number, and not the original dialed digits, is used to route the call, and is populated into the CDR. If the resulting translated number matches a route pattern, it is routed to a gateway. Gateways can also perform further modifications to a translated number before it is output through the gateway. The modifications made by the gateway (such as stripping leading or trailing digits, inserting additional digits) are not included in the CDR. For example, you might translate a call to 911 to 9-911 so that the caller does not need to dial an outside line in an emergency. 9911 is populated into the CDR.

If the dial plan allows callers to use the pound (#) key for terminating a dialed number, the # key is populated into the CDR when it is used. For example, the **finalCalledPartyNumber** field might contain a value such as 12087569174#.

Partitions

Directory numbers referenced within a CDR are identified uniquely by a combination of the directory number and its partition, if partitions are defined. When partitions exist, both values are required to fully identify a directory number because the same directory number might be used in more than one partition.

The **callingPartyNumberPartition** field might be empty when a call originates through a gateway. Certain types of gateways such as MGCP or SCCP-controlled FXS ports might have partitions assigned to them. If the gateway has a partition assigned, this field will contain a value. When a call terminates through a gateway, the **finalCalledPartyNumberPartition** field shows the partition associated with the route pattern that was used to access the gateway.

Duration

The duration field is an unsigned integer value that represents the number of seconds that the call was connected. The duration field is usually nonzero, except in two cases:

- The **CDR Log Calls with Zero Duration Flag** is enabled (True), the call duration is 0 seconds, and the call terminates normally. This happens mainly when a user took a phone off-hook and put it back on-hook without attempting a call.

- The call duration is 0 seconds, and one of the call termination cause codes in the CDR is not a normal termination code. This indicates that some error or special processing occurred.

CDR Field Definitions

Table 7-3 provides information about each field in a CDR. Each record consists of 67 individual fields. The information provided for each field is as follows:

- The field name or the column names from the database record

- The field data type

- The field definition

The fields are arranged here to facilitate an understanding of the information available and are not in the same order that they appear in the actual record.

All numeric fields in the CDR data are actually unsigned integers in CallManager. All character fields in CDR data are defined as 50-character fields with the following exceptions:

- **origDeviceName** and **destDeviceName** fields are 129-character fields.

- **callingPartyLoginUserID** and **finalCalledPartyUserID** fields are 250-character fields.

- **clientMatterCode** and **pkid** fields are 16-character fields.

- **comment** field is a 256-character field.

All character fields are of varying lengths in CallManager.

Table 7-3 *Field Definitions for a CDR*

Field Name	Field Type	Field Definition
cdrRecordType	Numeric	Specifies the type of this specific record. It will be set to End call record (1).
globalCallId_ClusterID	Character	The name assigned to this cluster. It will be unique so that if records are collected from multiple clusters, those from a given cluster can be identified.
globalCallID_callManagerId	Numeric	Half of the GCID. It represents the ID of the node that controlled the call corresponding to this record. This should be used with the second half of the GCID.
globalCallID_callId	Numeric	The second half of the GCID. It is a value that starts at 1 and is serially incremented for each GCID.
origDeviceName	Character	The name of the device from which this call originated. For IP phones and some other devices, the name contains the MAC address. The names are the device names from the CallManager Administration database. This field contains up to 129 characters.
origIpAddr	Numeric	Contains the IP address of the signaling connection on the device from which the call originated.
origIpPort	Numeric	This field is no longer used; it will contain zero by default.
callingPartyNumber	Character	The directory number of the device from which the call originated. For transferred calls, this is the transferred party.
callingPartyNumberPartition	Character	This field contains the partition associated with the directory number from which the call originated. If the call is an incoming call through an H.323 gateway, MGCP PRI gateway, or MGCP CAS trunk, the field is blank.
callingPartyLoginUserId	Character	The calling party's extension mobility user login ID.
origLegCallIdentifier	Numeric	The call leg ID for the origination leg of this call.

Table 7-3   *Field Definitions for a CDR (Continued)*

Field Name	Field Type	Field Definition
dateTimeOrigination	Numeric	Represents the time that the device originating the call went off-hook, or the time that an outside call was first recognized by the system. (It received the Setup message through a gateway.) The value is a GMT value and is the number of seconds since midnight (00:00:00) January 1, 1970.
origNodeId	Numeric	Represents the ID of the node within the CallManager cluster where the device that was used to originate the call was registered at the time of this call.
origSpan	Numeric	Contains the originator's port or span number if the call originated through a gateway. If the call originated through an H.323 trunk (H.225), this field contains the call leg ID of the corresponding call leg. If neither of these two cases is true, this field contains zero.
origCause_location	Numeric	Contains the ISDN location value from the cause information element for the originator's leg of the call. See Table 7-6 for a definition of the possible values for this field.
origCause_value	Numeric	Represents why the call leg to originating device was terminated. In the case of transfers, forwards, and so forth, the cause of call termination might be different for the originating device and the termination device. Thus, two cause fields are associated with each call. Usually, they will be the same. See Table 7-6 for a definition of the possible values for this field.
origPrecedenceLevel	Numeric	The Multilevel Precedence and Preemption (MLPP) precedence level for the call originator's call leg. See Table 7-9 for precedence levels.
origMediaTransportAddress_IP	Numeric	The destination IP address that the audio stream from the originator was connected to.
origMediaTransportAddress_Port	Numeric	The destination port to which the audio stream from the originator was connected.
origMediaCap_payloadCapability	Numeric	Contains the codec type that the originator used on the sending side during this call. It might be different from the codec type used on its receiving side. See Table 7-4 for a definition of possible values for this field.
origMediaCap_maxFramesPerPacket	Numeric	Contains the number of milliseconds of data per packet sent to the destination by the originator of this call. The actual data size depends on the codec type used to generate the data.
origMediaCap_g723BitRate	Numeric	Defines the bit rate to be used by G.723. There are two bit rate values: 1 for 5.3-kbps bit rate, and 2 for 6.3-kbps bit rate. (Not used in CallManager release 3.3.4 and later.)

continues

Table 7-3 *Field Definitions for a CDR (Continued)*

Field Name	Field Type	Field Definition
origVideoCap_Codec	Numeric	Identifies the video codec type used to create the video stream transmitted from the video call originator. See Table 7-4 for video codec values.
origVideoCap_Bandwidth	Numeric	Positive integer measured in kbps indicating the bandwidth used by the video stream transmitted from the video call originator.
origVideoCap_Resolution	Numeric	Identifies the video resolution of the video stream transmitted from the video call originator. See Table 7-10 for resolution values.
origVideoTransportAddress_Ip	Numeric	The video call originator's IP address where the video stream transmitted from the video call destination is received.
origVideoTransportAddress_Port	Numeric	The video call originator's port where the video stream transmitted from the video call destination is received.
origCallTerminationOnBehalfOf	Numeric	Identifies which feature or other entity caused the origination call leg to be terminated. See Table 7-7 for possible values.
lastRedirectDn	Character	The directory number of the last device that redirected this call. This field applies only to calls that were redirected, such as conference calls, call forwarded calls, and so forth, but is primarily used to identify who last forwarded the call.
lastRedirectDnPartition	Character	The partition of the last device that redirected this call. This field applies only to calls that were redirected, such as conference calls, call forwarded calls, and so forth, but is primarily used to identify who last forwarded the call.
lastRedirectRedirectOnBehalfOf	Numeric	Identifies which feature caused the last redirection. See Table 7-7 for possible values.
lastRedirectRedirectReason	Numeric	Contains the reason code identifying why the last redirect occurred. See Table 7-8 for possible code values.
joinOnBehalfOf	Numeric	Identifies the feature that caused the join to occur. See Table 7-7 for possible code values.
destDeviceName	Character	The device name of the device on which this call terminated. For IP phones and some other devices, the name contains the MAC address. The names are the device names from the CallManager Administration database. This field contains up to 129 characters.
destLegIdentifier	Numeric	The call leg ID for the destination leg of this call. The value is unique within a cluster at a given point in time.
destNodeId	Numeric	Contains the ID of CallManager node where the destination device was registered at the time of this call.

Table 7-3 *Field Definitions for a CDR (Continued)*

Field Name	Field Type	Field Definition
destSpan	Numeric	Contains the destination port or span number if the call was terminated through a gateway. If the call terminated through an H.323 trunk (H.225), this field contains the call leg ID of the corresponding call leg. If neither of these two cases is true, this field contains a zero.
destIpAddr	Numeric	Contains the IP address of the signaling connection on the device that terminated the call. For IP phones, this is the address of the IP phone. For PSTN calls or calls through a gateway, this is the IP address of the gateway. For intercluster calls, this is the IP address of the remote CallManager.
destIpPort	Numeric	This field is no longer used; it will contain zero by default.
destCallTerminationOnBehalfOf	Numeric	Identifies which feature or other entity caused the destination call leg to be terminated. See Table 7-7 for possible values.
destConversationId	Numeric	Contains the conversation ID associated with the destination side of this call. A conversation ID is sometimes referred to as the conference ID. Typically, this field will be filled in only for conference calls.
originalCalledPartyNumber	Character	Contains the directory number to which the call was originally extended, based on the digits dialed by the originator of the call. If the call completes normally (the call was not forwarded), this directory number must always be the same as the number in the finalCalledPartyNumber field. If the call was forwarded, this field contains the original destination of the call before it was forwarded.
originalCalledPartyNumberPartition	Character	Contains the partition associated with the originally called party number. If the call is outgoing through a gateway other than an MGCP FXS gateway, this field is the partition name associated with the route pattern associated with the gateway.
origCalledPartyRedirectReason	Numeric	Contains the reason code identifying why the call to the original called party was redirected. See Table 7-8 for redirect reason codes.
origCalledPartyRedirectOnBehalf Of	Numeric	Identifies the feature that caused the original call to be redirected. See Table 7-7 for possible values.

continues

Table 7-3 *Field Definitions for a CDR (Continued)*

Field Name	Field Type	Field Definition
finalCalledPartyNumber	Character	Contains the directory number to which the call was actually extended. If the call completes normally (the call was not forwarded), this directory number must always be the same as the number contained in the originalCalledPartyNumber field. If the call was forwarded, this field contains the directory number of the final destination of the call after all forwards were completed. For calls to a conference bridge, this field contains the internal, alphanumeric address of the conference bridge (for example, b0019901001).
finalCalledPartyNumberPartition	Character	Contains the partition associated with the destination to which the call was actually extended. In a normal call, this field should be the same as the partition contained in the originalCalledPartyNumberPartition field. If the call was forwarded, this field contains the partition of the final destination of the call after all forwards were completed. For outgoing calls through a gateway other than an MGCP FXS gateway, this field is the partition name associated with the route pattern associated with the gateway.
finalCalledPartyLoginUserID	Character	The final called party's extension mobility user login ID.
destCause_location	Numeric	The ISDN location value from the destination cause information element. See Table 7-5 for a definition of possible values in this field.
destCause_value	Numeric	This cause represents why the call to the termination device was terminated. In the case of transfers, forwards, and so forth, the cause of call termination might be different for the recipient of the call and the originator of the call. Thus, two cause fields are associated with each call, which usually are the same. When an attempt is made to extend a call to a busy device that is forwarded, the cause code reflects "Busy," even though the call was connected to a forward destination. See Table 7-6 for a definition of possible values in this field.
destPrecedenceLevel	Numeric	The MLPP precedence level for the call destination call leg. See Table 7-9 for precedence levels.
destMediaTransportAddress_IP	Numeric	The originator's IP address to which the audio stream from the destination was connected.
destMediaTransportAddress_Port	Numeric	The originator's port to which the audio stream from the destination was connected.
destMediaCap_payloadCapability	Numeric	Contains the codec type that the destination used on its sending side during this call. It might be different from the codec type used on its receiving side. See Table 7-4 for the definition of the possible values in this field.

Table 7-3   *Field Definitions for a CDR (Continued)*

Field Name	Field Type	Field Definition
destMediaCap_maxFramesPerPacket	Numeric	Contains the number of milliseconds of data per packet sent to the originator by the destination of this call. The actual data size depends on the codec type used to generate the data.
destMediaCap_g723BitRate	Numeric	Defines the bit rate to be used by G.723. There are two bit rate values: 1 for 5.3-kbps bit rate, and 2 for 6.3-kbps bit rate. (Not used in CallManager releases 3.3.4 and later.)
destVideoCap_Codec	Numeric	Identifies the video codec type used to create the video stream transmitted from the video call destination device. See Table 7-4 for video codec values.
destVideoCap_Bandwidth	Numeric	Positive integer measured in kbps indicating the bandwidth used by the video stream transmitted from the video call destination back to the originator.
destVideoCap_Resolution	Numeric	The video resolution of the video stream transmitted from the video call destination back to the originator. See Table 7-9 for resolution values.
destVideoTransportAddress_Ip	Numeric	The video call destination's IP address where the video stream transmitted from the video call originator is received.
destVideoTransportAddress_Port	Numeric	The video call destination's port where the video stream transmitted from the video call originator is received.
dateTimeConnect	Numeric	The date and time that the call was connected between the originating and terminating devices. The value is a GMT value and is the number of seconds since midnight (00:00:00) January 1, 1970. This field is zero if the call was not connected.
dateTimeDisconnect	Numeric	The time that the call was disconnected between the originating and terminating devices. The value is a GMT value and is the number of seconds since midnight (00:00:00) January 1, 1970. This field is zero if the call was not connected.
duration	Numeric	The number of seconds that the call was connected. It is the difference between the date/time of connect and the date/time of disconnect. It will be zero for all calls that were not connected, and also for calls that were connected for less than 1 second.
comment	Character	This field contains text strings from features to flag particular situations, such as malicious calls, and the conference controller on conference calls. See Table 7-11 for the definition of allowed text strings.
Pkid	Character	Text string used internally by the CDR database to uniquely identify each row in this table. This text string has no meaning to the call itself.

continues

Table 7-3 *Field Definitions for a CDR (Continued)*

Field Name	Field Type	Field Definition
authCodeDescription	Character	Description of the authorization code. For security purposes, the authorization code is not written to the CDR. The authorization description and level are written instead. The default value is an empty string " " or null.
AuthorizationLevel	Numeric	Positive integer indicating the level of the authorization code.
clientMatterCode	Character	The client matter code entered by the user before the call is extended.

Codec Types

Table 7-4 lists codecs used in the system. These are all the possible values for the **destMediaCap_payloadCapability** field and the **origMediaCap_payloadCapability** field.

Table 7-4 *Codec Types*

Value	Description
1	Nonstandard
2	G.711 A-law 64 kbps
3	G.711 A-law 56 kbps
4	G.711 μ-law 64 kbps
5	G.711 μ-law 56 kbps
6	G.722 64 kbps
7	G.722 56 kbps
8	G.722 48 kbps
9	G.7231
10	G.728
11	G.729
12	G.729AnnexA
13	Is11172AudioCap
14	Is13818AudioCap
15	G.729AnnexB
16	G.729 Annex AwAnnexB
18	GSM Full Rate
19	GSM Half Rate
20	GSM Enhanced Full Rate

Table 7-4 *Codec Types (Continued)*

Value	Description
25	Wideband 256 kbps
32	Data 64 kbps
33	Data 56 kbps
80	GSM
81	Active Voice
82	G.726_32 kbps
83	G.726_24 kbps
84	G.726_16 kbps
100	H.261 (video codec)
101	H.263 (video codec)
102	Cisco VT Advantage (video codec)
103	H.264 (video codec)
105	T.120 (Not currently supported)
106	H.224
257	Dynamic payload

Cause Location Definitions

Table 7-5 lists the possible values for the **origCause_location** and the **destCause_location** fields.

Table 7-5 *Cause Location Values*

Code	Description
0	User (U)
1	Private network serving the local user (LPN)
2	Public network serving the local user (LN)
3	Transit network (TN)
4	Public network serving the remote user (RLN)
5	Private network serving the remote user (RPN)
7	International network (INTL)
10	Network beyond interworking point (BI)

All other values are reserved.

Cause Code Definitions

Table 7-6 contains the definition of the cause code values for the **origCause_value** field and the **destCause_value** field. The clearing cause values are per ITU specification Q.850. For OnNet call legs, CallManager determines the cause value. For OffNet call legs, or those that pass through a gateway, the terminating switch or device determines the cause value.

Table 7-6 *Cause Code Definitions*

Code	Description
0	No error.
1	Unallocated (unassigned) number.
2	No route to specified transit network (national use).
3	No route to destination.
4	Send special information tone.
5	Misdialed trunk prefix (national use).
6	Channel unacceptable.
7	Call awarded and being delivered in an established channel.
8	Preemption; circuit not reserved for reuse.
9	Preemption; circuit reserved for reuse.
16	Normal call clearing.
17	User busy.
18	No user responding.
19	No answer from user (user alerted).
20	Subscriber absent.
21	Call rejected.
22	Number changed.
26	Nonselected user clearing.
27	Destination out of order.
28	Invalid number format (address incomplete).
29	Facility rejected.
30	Response to STATUS ENQUIRY.
31	Normal, unspecified.
34	No circuit/channel available.
38	Network out of order.
39	Permanent frame mode connection out of service.
40	Permanent frame mode connection operational.

Table 7-6 *Cause Code Definitions (Continued)*

Code	Description
41	Temporary failure.
42	Switching equipment congestion.
43	Access information discarded.
44	Requested circuit/channel not available.
46	Precedence call blocked: Not preemptable circuit or called user is busy with a call of equal or higher precedence level.
47	Resource unavailable, unspecified.
49	QoS not available.
50	Requested facility not subscribed.
53	Service operation violated.
54	Incoming calls barred.
55	Incoming calls barred within Closed User Group (CUG).
57	Bearer capability not authorized.
58	Bearer capability not presently available.
62	Inconsistency in designated outgoing access information and subscriber class.
63	Service or option not available, unspecified.
65	Bearer capability not implemented.
66	Channel type not implemented.
69	Requested facility not implemented.
70	Only restricted digital information bearer capability is available (national use).
79	Service or option not implemented, unspecified.
81	Invalid call reference value.
82	Identified channel does not exist.
83	A suspended call exists, but this call identity does not.
84	Call identity in use.
85	No call suspended.
86	Call having the requested call identity has been cleared.
87	User not member of CUG.
88	Incompatible destination.
90	Destination number missing and DC not subscribed or nonexistent CUG.
91	Invalid transit network selection (national use).
95	Invalid message, unspecified.

continues

Table 7-6 *Cause Code Definitions (Continued)*

Code	Description
96	Mandatory information element is missing.
97	Message type nonexistent or not implemented.
98	Message is not compatible with the call state, or the message type is nonexistent or not implemented.
99	An information element or parameter does not exist or is not implemented.
100	Invalid information element contents.
101	The message is not compatible with the call state.
102	The call was terminated when a timer expired and a recovery routine was executed recover from the error.
103	Parameter nonexistent or not implemented—passed on (national use).
110	Message with unrecognized parameter discarded.
111	Protocol error, unspecified.
122	Precedence level exceeded (this is a Cisco-specific code).
123	Device not preemptable (this is a Cisco-specific code).
124	Conference full (this is a Cisco-specific code).
125	Out of bandwidth (this is a Cisco-specific code).
126	Call split (this is a Cisco-specific code). It is used when a call is terminated during a feature operation indicating why the call leg was terminated. This occurs on transfers when the call leg was split off and terminated. (It was not part of the final transferred call.) This can help determine which calls were terminated as part of a feature operation.
127	Interworking, unspecified.
128	Conference drop any party or conference drop last party.
129	Precedence out of bandwidth.

Legend for the OnBehalfOf Fields

Table 7-7 defines the possible values of the OnBehalfOf fields. These fields are intended to help identify all records that are part of a feature call. These fields note the feature that is responsible for the call termination on each half of a call. They also note which feature caused the originator to be redirected, and which feature was the last feature to cause the call to be redirected. When a device terminates a call, the OnBehalfOf field is set to Device, which is the value that is used for all calls that do not involve a supplementary service.

Table 7-7 *Legend for the OnBehalfOf Fields*

Value	Feature
0	Unknown
1	CCtiLine
2	Unicast shared resource provider
3	Call park
4	Conference
5	Call forward
6	Meet-Me conference
7	Meet-Me conference intercepts
8	Message waiting
9	Multicast shared resource provider
10	Transfer
11	SSAPI manager
12	Device
13	Call control
14	Immediate divert
15	Barge

Reason for Redirect

Table 7-8 defines the possible values of the redirect reason codes. These codes are sent to the CTI interface to identify for third-party applications why a call has been redirected.

Table 7-8 *Reason for Redirect Codes*

Reason Code	Redirect Reasons
0	No reason
1	Call forward busy
2	Call forward no answer
4	Call transfer
5	Call pickup
7	Call park
8	Call park retrieve
9	Call customer premises equipment (CPE) out of order
10	Call forward

continues

Table 7-8 *Reason for Redirect Codes (Continued)*

Reason Code	Redirect Reasons
11	Call park reversion
15	Call forward all (unconditional)
Nonstandard	**Redirect Reasons**
18	Call deflection
34	Blind transfer
50	Call immediate divert
66	Call forward alternate party
82	Call forward on failure
98	Conference
114	Barge

MLPP Precedence Levels

Table 7-9 lists the precedence levels associated with a call leg. Each call has an originating call leg and a destination call leg. Each call leg has a precedence level associated with it.

Table 7-9 *MLPP Precedence Levels*

Precedence Level	Description
0	Flash override/executive override
1	Flash
2	Immediate
3	Priority
4	Routine

Video Resolution

Table 7-10 lists the video resolution of the originator's video output stream.

Table 7-10 *Video Resolution Values*

Resolution	Description
1	SQCIF—Sub-Quarter Common Interchange Format (128 × 96 pixel image size).
2	QCIF—Quarter Common Interchange Format. Produces a color image of 144 noninterlaced luminance lines, each containing 176 pixels to be sent at a rate of 30 frames per second (fps) with a 1.22:1 ratio of the image. QCIF requires one-fourths (π) of the bandwidth and delivers one-fourths (π) the resolution of CIF. QCIF is ideal for small-screen displays such as video phones.

Table 7-10 *Video Resolution Values (Continued)*

Resolution	Description
3	CIF—Common Interchange Format. Produces a color image of 288 noninterlaced luminance lines, each containing 352 pixels to be sent at a rate of 30 frames per second (fps) with a 1.22:1 ratio of the image. CIF is ideal for large-screen videoconferencing because of its greater resolution.
4	CIF4—4 times the resolution of CIF.
5	CIF16—16 times the resolution of CIF.
6	Custom Picture Format.

Comment Field in CDRs

Table 7-11 lists the comment strings and values that may be present in the comment field of a CDR.

Table 7-11 *Defined Text Strings for the Comment Field*

Tag	Value
CallFlag	MALICIOUS
ConfControllerDn=	Directory number of the conference controller
ConfControllerDeviceName=	Device name of the conference controller

Understanding Field Data in CMRs

This section lists all the fields contained in a diagnostic record. The field definitions include some basic information about the QoS fields, such as jitter and latency.

The topics covered are as follows:

■   Fields contained in the CMR

■   How to identify the CDR associated with a CMR

Fields Contained in the CMR

Table 7-12 provides information about each field in a CMR. Each record consists of 17 individual fields. The information provided about each field is as follows:

■   The field name or the column names from the database record

■   The field type

■   The field definition

The fields in Table 7-12 are arranged to facilitate understanding of the data that is available in the CMR. They are not in the same order as the actual database record.

NOTE All numeric fields in the CMR data are actually unsigned integers in CallManager. All character fields in CMR data are defined as 50-character fields, except the **deviceName** field. All character fields are of varying lengths in CallManager.

Table 7-12 *Field Definitions for a CMR*

Field Name	Field Type	Field Definition
cdrRecordType	Numeric	Specifies the type of this specific record. It is set to CMR record (2).
globalCallId_ClusterID	Character	The name assigned to this cluster. It is unique so that if records are collected from multiple clusters, those from a given cluster can be identified.
deviceName	Character	The name of the device from the CallManager Administration database. This field contains up to 129 characters.
globalCallID_callManagerId	Numeric	Half of the GCID. It represents the ID of the node that controlled the call corresponding to this record. This should be used in conjunction with the second half of the GCID.
globalCallID_callId	Numeric	The second half of the GCID. It is a value that starts at 1 and is serially incremented for each GCID.
nodeId	Numeric	The ID of the node within the CallManager cluster where the device from which these diagnostics were collected was registered.
callIdentifier	Numeric	A call leg ID that identifies to which call leg this record pertains. (This field is also used to map the CMR record back to the CDR record as noted below.)
directoryNum	Character	The directory number of the device from which these diagnostics were collected.
directoryNumPartition	Character	The partition of the directory number in this record.
dateTimeStamp	Numeric	Represents the approximate time that the device went on-hook. The time is put into the record when the device responds to a request for diagnostic information. The value is a GMT value and is the number of seconds since midnight (00:00:00) January 1, 1970. (It is not always the same as the date and time the call was disconnected; it may be a few seconds later.)

Table 7-12 *Field Definitions for a CMR (Continued)*

Field Name	Field Type	Field Definition
numberPacketsSent	Numeric	The total number of RTP data packets transmitted by the device since starting transmission on this connection. If the connection mode was "receive only," the value is zero.
numberOctetsSent	Numeric	The total number of payload octets (not including header or padding) transmitted in RTP data packets by the device since starting transmission on this connection. If the connection mode was "receive only," the value is zero.
numberPacketsReceived	Numeric	The total number of RTP data packets received by the device since starting reception on this connection. If the connection mode was "send only," the value is zero.
numberOctetsReceived	Numeric	The total number of payload octets (not including header or padding) received in RTP data packets by the device since starting reception on this connection. If the connection mode was "send only," the value is zero.
numberPacketsLost	Signed Integer	The total number of RTP data packets that have been lost since the beginning of data reception on this connection. This number is defined to be the number of packets expected less the number of packets actually received, where the number of packets received includes any that are late or duplicates. Thus, packets that arrive late are not counted as lost, and the loss might be negative if there are duplicates. The number of packets expected is defined to be the extended last sequence number received less the initial sequence number received. If the connection mode was "send only," the value is zero.
jitter	Numeric	An estimate of the statistical variance of the RTP data packet interarrival time measured in milliseconds and expressed as an unsigned integer. The interarrival jitter is defined to be the mean deviation (smoothed absolute value) of the difference in packet spacing at the receiver compared to the sender for a pair of packets. If the connection mode was "send only," the value is zero.
latency	Numeric	This field is currently unused and will contain a zero.
Pkid	Character	Text string that is used by the CDR database to uniquely identify each row in this table. This text string has no meaning to the call itself.

You can find more information in RFC 1889, including detailed computation algorithms for number of packets lost, jitter, and latency.

How to Identify the CDR Associated with a CMR

You cannot use any set of CDR data fields to guarantee a positive link between CMR and CDR data if you depend on an exact match between corresponding fields. You can, however, figure it out by using the combination of the GCID, call leg IDs, **globalCallId_ClusterID**, and the date/time fields that exist in each of the records. The **globalCallId_ClusterID** field was added to make the records unique across multiple clusters. The combination of the GCID fields and the call leg ID is not unique across time on the same cluster because their values are reset whenever a CallManager node is restarted. If you also consider the **dateTimeDisconnect** field in the CDR and the **dateTimeStamp** field in the CMR, it will make a positive match. The date/time field in a CMR might not match exactly the date/time of disconnect in the CDR because they are written separately.

Before the CMR can be written, CallManager must request the data for the CMR from the endpoint device. Some time lapse exists during this request cycle, and if the system clock ticks over a second boundary, the times will differ by a second. If the records have the same GCIDs and call leg IDs and the specified date/time values are within a few seconds of each other, the records are definitely related. It takes CallManager more than 20 seconds to come online after a restart, and it usually takes much longer, depending on the number of devices that are in the database for that system. Given that the IDs match, and the time is not off by more than 10 seconds, the records are related to the same call.

Identifying CDR Data Generated for Each Call Type

Each type of call creates a set of CDR data records. This section identifies the records that form the set for each type of call. Many types of calls produce multiple CDRs and CMRs. It helps to identify the expected set of records for a given call before processing the data for that call. This section does not provide an exhaustive set of call types and examples. It does, however, contain a representative sample of different types of calls and the records produced. The assumption is made that CDR generation is enabled, and the **CDR Log Calls with Zero Duration Flag** service parameter is disabled.

Calls Between Two Endpoints

A standard call is a call between two endpoints that does not involve any features. The endpoints can be either phones or gateways. These calls generate one CDR and two CMRs if they are between IP phones or between IP phones and MGCP-controlled gateways. If an endpoint involved in a call is not an IP phone or an MGCP-controlled gateway, no CMR data is written for that endpoint. This section covers the following two topics:

- CDR data for a call between two IP phones

- CDR data for calls involving a gateway

> **NOTE**   The **originalCalledPartyNumber** field always contains the same directory number as the **finalCalledPartyNumber** field in a normal call.

CDR Data for a Call Between Two IP Phones

Each normal call between two IP phones logs one CDR at the end of the call. Each CDR contains all fields identified in Table 7-3. Not all fields in a CDR or CMR are used for a given call. If the field is not used, it contains the default value for that field type. CallManager also writes one CMR per endpoint that is involved in the call. In a standard call between two parties that are each using an IP phone, the system writes two CMRs, one each for the originator and the destination of the call. In this case, the call will have a duration greater than 0 seconds, and the **originalCalledPartyNumber** field and the **finalCalledPartyNumber** field both contain the same information.

CDR Values for Calls Involving a Gateway

When a call involves a gateway as one of the endpoints, the IP address for that endpoint is the IP address of the gateway, even though the call might not actually terminate there. The call can pass through the gateway to a real endpoint on the PSTN. Calls that involve a gateway have a nonzero value for a span number in one or both of the span fields (**origSpan** or **destSpan**). The fields **origDeviceName** or **destDeviceName** contain the device names of the terminating devices. Thus, you have the name of the gateway through which the call passed. When you both originate and terminate a call through a gateway, the software writes a nonzero number into both span fields. The span is normally the port or channel on that gateway used for that call. In the case of an H.323 trunk call, the span fields contain the call leg ID for the call leg going through that gateway.

Abandoned Calls

An abandoned call is defined as any call that terminates before it actually connects to a destination. Abandoned calls will always have a duration of 0 seconds, and the **origCause_value** field indicates why the call was terminated. If the call has any cause termination value that is not a normal call termination (that is, not 0, 16, or 31), the CDR is logged for that call. Abandoned calls do not generate a CMR.

Some ways you can create abandoned calls include the following:

- Take a phone off-hook and place it back on-hook without dialing any digits. (CDR is not normally logged for this call type.)

- Take the phone off-hook and dial a partial or invalid number and then hang up. (CDR is logged.)

- Call a phone where the user did not answer and it was not forwarded. (CDR is logged.)

- Call a busy phone that did not forward on busy. (CDR is logged.)

CallManager does not distinguish between calls that you abandon on purpose and calls that do not connect because of some network or system error condition. If the cause of termination is anything but a normal call termination, the CDR is logged.

Short Calls

A short call is a call with a duration of less than 1 second. It appears as a zero duration call in the CDRs. These can be differentiated from failed calls by the **dateTimeConnect** field, which shows the actual connect time of the call. For failed calls (which have never connected), this value is zero. If you want to see these calls, you need to enable CDR Log Calls with Zero Duration Flag.

IP Phone Failures During a Call

When an IP phone is unplugged, there is no immediate physical indication to CallManager. CallManager relies on a TCP-based KeepAlive signaling mechanism to detect when an IP phone is disconnected. The KeepAlive interval is normally set to 30 seconds, and for this discussion, it is assumed that the interval is set at its default value.

Every 30 seconds, each IP phone sends a KeepAlive message to CallManager, and CallManager responds with an acknowledgment. Both parties then know that the other is functioning properly. When an IP phone is unplugged, it fails to send this KeepAlive message. CallManager waits for three KeepAlive intervals (by default, this is about 90 seconds) from the time of the last KeepAlive message before assuming that the IP phone is no longer functioning. The implication to billing is that when an IP phone is unplugged, the duration of the call reflected in the CDR can be up to 3 KeepAlive intervals (about 90 seconds) longer than the actual speech time experienced by the user. This value, 90 seconds, is worst-case, assuming that the default KeepAlive interval of 30 seconds is not changed. When two KeepAlives are missed, the call is terminated at the next KeepAlive interval. Calls that fail in this manner might be identified by a cause value of 41 (Temporary Failure). It is possible for this cause value to occur in other circumstances because external devices such as gateways can also generate this cause value.

Forwarded or Redirected Calls

The fields in the CDRs for both forwarded calls and redirected calls are the same as those for normal calls, except for the **originalCalledPartyNumber** field and the **originalCalledPartyNumber Partition** field. These two fields contain the directory number and partition of the original destination for this call. When you forward a call, the **finalCalledPartyNumber** and the **finalCalledPartyNumberPartition** fields are updated to contain the directory number of the final destination of the call. The **lastRedirectDn** and **lastRedirectDnPartition** fields contain the directory number and partition of the last phone that forwarded or redirected this call, and the **lastRedirectRedirectOnBehalfOf** field identifies which feature or entity caused the call to be redirected. In the case of forwarding, the **lastRedirectRedirectReason** field identifies why the call was forwarded. Features such as conference and call pickup redirect calls to implement the feature operation.

> **TIP**   If the call is forwarded more than one hop, the intermediate forwarding parties are not recorded in the CDR.

Precedence Calls (MLPP)

The fields in the CDRs for precedence calls are basically the same as for all other calls of the same type (normal calls, forwarded calls, transferred calls, and so forth). The difference is that the **destPrecedenceLevel** field or the **origPrecedenceLevel** field is set. If a call is preempted by a precedence call, the cause codes indicate the reason for the preemption. If a precedence call is preempted by a higher-level precedence call, the cause codes also indicate the reason for the preemption.

Malicious Calls

A malicious call is one where the called party feels threatened in some way. Users identify a call as a malicious call by pressing the **MCID** softkey. When a call is identified as malicious, CallManager flags the call by including the following string in the Comment field:

```
callFlag=MALICIOUS
```

Video Calls

Video calls appear the same as other voice calls of the same type except that the additional video fields contain the video data.

Immediate Divert (to Voice Mail)

CDRs for calls that have been diverted to voice mail using the immediate divert feature (via the **iDivert** softkey) appear the same as forwarded calls. The **origCalledPartyRedirectOnBehalfOf** field and the **lastRedirectRedirectOnBehalfOf** field indicate that a call was redirected on behalf of the immediate divert feature.

Transferred Calls and Examples

Calls that are transferred have additional records logged for them. The three calls that are logged are as follows:

- Original call from party A to party B

- Call from the transferring party (party A or B) to the transfer destination (party C)

- Call from the transferred party (party A or B) to the destination (party C)

If the transfer is a blind transfer—in which the user did not wait for the transfer destination to answer before completing the transfer—the record logged has a duration of 0 seconds and the **origCause_Value** and **destCause_Value** fields set to 126 (Call Split).

The following examples are not an exhaustive set and are intended to illustrate the records that are generated under the stated circumstances. The examples help clarify what records are generated on transferred calls, parked calls, and conference calls. These examples assume that you did not enable the **CDR Log Calls with Zero Duration Flag** service parameter.

Transferred Call Example 1: A Calls B, A Transfers B to C

The call scenario is as follows:

1. A calls B.
2. B answers the call.
3. A presses **Transf…**.
4. A calls C.
5. C answers the call.
6. A presses **Transf…** again.
7. When B and C are done talking, one or both hang up.

Three CDRs and four CMRs are generated for this call:

- **CMR for A**—Logged when A initiates the transfer.

■ Three records are logged when A completes the transfer (second softkey press):

— **CDR for call from A to B**—Original call

— **CDR for call from A to C**—Consultative call, where A announces the transfer of B to C

— **CMR for A**

■ Three records are logged when either B or C hangs up:

— **CDR for call from B to C**—Active call after transfer is complete

— **CMR for B**

— **CMR for C**

This call is a consultation transfer because the call from A to C was actually connected. The **originalCalledPartyNumber** and **finalCalledPartyNumber** field values are the same in the CDRs for this call.

Transferred Call Example 2: A Calls B, B Transfers A to C

The call scenario is as follows:

1. A calls B.

2. B answers the call.

3. B presses **Transf...** softkey.

4. B calls C.

5. C answers the call.

6. B presses **Transf...** softkey again.

7. When A and C are done talking, one or both hang up.

Three CDRs and four CMRs are generated for this call. The records logged are

■ **CMR for B**—Logged when B presses the **Transf...** softkey.

■ Three records are logged when B presses the **Transf...** softkey the second time:

— **CDR for call from A to B**—Original call

— **CDR for call from B to C**—Consultative call where B announces the transfer of A to C

— **CMR for B**

- Three records are logged when either A or C hangs up:

  — **CDR for call from A to C**—Active call after transfer is complete

  — **CMR for A**

  — **CMR for C**

Transferred Call Example 3: A Calls B, A Transfers B to C on a Blind Transfer

The call scenario is as follows:

1. A calls B.

2. B answers the call.

3. A presses **Transf...**.

4. A calls C.

5. C does not answer yet.

6. A presses **Transf...** again.

7. C answers the call.

8. When B and C are done talking, one or both hang up.

Three CDRs and four CMRs are generated for this call:

- **CMR for A**—Logged when A pressed the **Transf...** softkey.

- Three records are logged when A presses the **Transf...** softkey the second time:

  — **CDR for call from A to B**

  — **CMR for A**

  — **CDR for call from A to C** (zero duration and termination cause of 126 [Call Split])

- Three records are logged when either B or C hangs up:

  — **CDR for call from B to C**

  — **CMR for B**

  — **CMR for C**

Because the call was a blind transfer, the call from A to C has a duration of 0 seconds and the **origCause_Value** and **destCause_Value** set to 126 (Call Split). The call is logged because of the Call Split cause code.

Transferred Call Example 4: A Calls B, B Transfers A to C on a Blind Transfer

The call scenario is as follows:

1. A calls B.

2. B answers the call.

3. B presses **Transf...**.

4. B calls C.

5. C does not answer yet.

6. B presses **Transf...** again.

7. C answers the call.

8. When A and C are done talking, one or both hang up.

Three CDRs and four CMRs are generated for this call:

- **CMR for B**—Logged when B pressed the **Transf...** softkey.

- Three records are logged when B presses the **Transf...** softkey the second time:

  — **CDR for call from A to B**

  — **CMR for B**

  — **CDR for call from B to C** (zero duration and termination cause of 126 [Call Split])

- Three records are logged when either A or C hangs up:

  — **CDR for call from A to C**

  — **CMR for A**

  — **CMR for C**

Because the call was a blind transfer, the call from B to C has a duration of 0 seconds and the **origCause_Value** and **destCause_Value** set to 126 (Call Split).

Transferred Call Example 5: A Calls B, B Transfers A to C on a Blind Transfer, and C Is Forwarded to D

The call scenario is as follows:

1. Set Call Forward All on phone C to phone D.

2. A calls B.

3. B answers the call.

4. B presses **Transf...**.

5. B calls C (C is forwarded to D).

6. D does not answer yet.

7. B presses **Transf...** again.

8. D answers the call.

9. When A and D are done talking, one or both hang up.

Three CDRs and four CMRs are generated for this call:

- **CMR for B**—Logged when B pressed the **Transf...** softkey.

- Three records are logged when B presses the **Transf...** softkey the second time:

  — **CDR for call from A to B**

  — **CMR for B**

  — **CDR for call from B to C** (which was forwarded to D)

- Three records are logged when either A or D hangs up:

  — **CDR for call from A to D**

  — **CMR for A**

  — **CMR for D**

This call was a blind transfer, and the call from B to C has a duration of 0 seconds and the **origCause_Value** and **destCause_Value** set to 126 (Call Split). Because the destination C was forwarded to D, the call logged from A to D will have the **originalCalledPartyNumber** field set to C, and the **finalCalledPartyNumber** field set to D.

Parked Call Example: A Calls B, A Parks B, and C Picks Up B

The call scenario is as follows:

1. A calls B.

2. B answers the call.

3. A presses **Park** (call was parked on a park number).

4. C calls B's park number.

5. When B and C are done talking, one or both hang up.

Two CDRs and three CMRs are generated for a parked call:

- **CMR for A**—Logged when A pressed the **Park** softkey

- **CDR for call from A to B (original call)**—Logged when A pressed the **Park** softkey

- Three records are logged when either B or C hangs up:

    — **CDR for call from C to B** (the final call when C picked it up)

    — **CMR for B**

    — **CMR for C**

Conference Calls and Examples

CallManager allows two types of conferences—Ad Hoc and Meet-Me. CallManager creates a different set of records for each of these conference types.

Ad Hoc Conference Calls

You can identify the Ad Hoc conference controller by examining the Comment field in the CDR. When a call is involved in more than one conference, it contains multiple sets of conference controller information. This happens, for example, when a conference is reduced to two parties, and one of them starts another conference. When multiple sets exist, the last conference controller information in the CDR identifies the conference controller for the call.

When an Ad Hoc conference call is reduced to two parties, the two parties are connected directly and the conference bridge is released. This results in an additional CDR and up to two additional CMRs for the directly connected call.

Ad Hoc Conference Example: A Calls B, A Calls C, A Sets Up Conference Among A, B, and C

The call scenario is as follows:

1. A calls B.

2. B answers the call.

3. A presses **Confrn** softkey.

4. A calls C.

5. C answers the call.

6. A presses **Confrn** again.

7. When A, B, and C are done talking, two or more hang up.

Six CDRs and five CMRs are generated for a three-party Ad Hoc conference:

- **CMR for A**—Logged when A pressed the **Confrn** softkey.

- **CDR for call from A to B**—Logged when A pressed the **Confrn** softkey.

- **CDR for call from A to C**—Logged when A pressed the **Confrn** softkey the second time.

- **CMR for A**—Logged when A pressed the **Confrn** softkey the second time.

- Six records are logged when the conference is terminated. The CDRs are logged in the order that the participants hang up:

  — **CDR for call from A to conference bridge**

  — **CDR for call from B to conference bridge**

  — **CDR for call from C to conference bridge**

  — **CDR for call between last two parties when one of the three hangs up**

  — **CMR for A**

  — **CMR for B**

  — **CMR for C**

TIP The last CDR shown in the preceding list is normally generated. The only time it is not generated is when two or more of the last three parties in a conference hang up at the same time. When that occurs, the system terminates the conference without generating the last CDR because the call between the last two parties would not exist in that case.

You can identify the conference controller (*A*) for this conference call because the **Comment** field in the CDR contains a string with the following format:

```
ConfControllerDn=A;ConfControllerDeviceName=A's device name
```

If *A*'s DN were 1000 and *A's Device Name* were SEP0003E333FEBD, the **Comment** field would contain the following:

```
ConfControllerDn=1000;ConfControllerDeviceName=SEP0003E333FEBD
```

Calls that are connected to the conference bridge will have the **finalCalledPartyNumber** field set to a value similar to **b0019901001**.

In an Ad Hoc conference, each additional participant added causes four additional records to be generated. In this case, the call scenario to add another participant is as follows:

1. A presses **Confrn** softkey.

2. A calls D.

3. D answers the call.

4. A presses **Confrn** softkey again (D joins the conference).

Two CDRs and three CMRs would be logged:

- CMR for A when A pressed the **Confrn** softkey to begin the conference addition

- CDR for call from A to D logged when A pressed the **Confrn** softkey the second time

- CMR for A when A pressed the **Confrn** softkey the second time to rejoin the conference

- CDR for call from D to conference bridge logged when the conference is terminated

- CMR for D logged when conference was terminated

Meet-Me Conference Example: A Sets Up Meet-Me Conference, B and C Call into Conference

The call scenario is as follows:

1. A goes off-hook.

2. A presses **MeetMe** softkey.

3. A dials Meet-Me number (A is connected to the conference).

4. B calls Meet-Me number (B is connected to the conference).

5. C calls Meet-Me number (C is connected to the conference).

6. When A, B, and C are done talking, they hang up.

Three CDRs and three CMRs are generated for a three-party Meet-Me conference. The CDR and CMR for each call into the conference are logged when that participant hangs up. The records are as follows:

- CDR for call from A to Meet-Me conference

- CMR A

- CDR for call from B to Meet-Me conference

- CMR B

- CDR for call from C to Meet-Me conference

- CMR C

For each additional participant in a Meet-Me conference, one CDR is logged and one CMR is logged.

Held Calls Example

This section illustrates what happens when calls are placed on hold and resumed again.

The call scenario is as follows:

1. A calls B.

2. A presses **Hold**.

3. A presses **Resume**.

4. A presses **Hold**.

5. A presses **Resume**.

6. B presses **Hold**.

7. B presses **Resume**.

8. A presses **Hold**.

9. A presses **Resume**.

10. B presses **Hold**.

11. B presses **Resume**.

12. A or B hangs up.

Held calls create one CMR for each time you put a call on hold. They also create only one CDR for the entire call, which includes the talk time and hold time from the time the call originally connected to the time of the final disconnect. CMRs are generated in order each time a user presses the **Hold** softkey, and two CMRs are generated at the end of the actual call:

- **CMR for A** — B placed on hold

- **CMR for A** — B placed on hold again

- **CMR for B** — A placed on hold

- **CMR for A** — B placed on hold

- **CMR for B** — A placed on hold

- **CDR for call from A to B** when A or B hangs up

- **CMR for A**

- **CMR for B**

Calls with Busy or Bad Destinations

A call with a busy or bad destination is logged with all relevant fields containing data. Which fields contain data depends on what caused the call to terminate. The **destCause_value** field contains a cause code indicating why the call was not completed. One CDR is logged and possibly one CMR is logged for each of these calls.

If you abandoned the call without dialing any digits, the cause will be NO_ERROR (0), and the duration will always be 0 seconds. These calls are not logged unless the **CDR Log Calls with Zero Duration Flag** service parameter is enabled. If the call is logged, one CDR is logged and possibly one CMR is logged.

Accessing CDR Data in the Central CDR Database

CallManager stores all CDR data in the central CDR database. It is not the same database as the CallManager Administration database. You can access the CDR database in a read/write fashion.

When you are processing CDR data, you might want to read other tables in the CallManager Administration database to obtain information about the type of device for which this CDR was written. The device name is provided in the CDR, but the device type and other information is not. CallManager uses the Microsoft SQL 2000 database. You can gain direct access to the database with Open Database Connectivity (ODBC).

Gaining Access to Database Tables

The easiest way for an external application to read data from the SQL database is to use ODBC. To access the Publisher's CDR or CallManager database, an NT user account must be used that is authenticated on both the external application server and the CallManager Publisher. It is easier if the NT user for the external application is an NT user, and not a domain user.

You must add the NT user that the application uses to the CallManager Publisher, which will allow the application to gain access. You also need to add matching user accounts to the SQL Server and CDR database and grant them either read or write access as needed.

The following example illustrates what a good connection string looks like:

For Windows NT authentication:

```
Driver=SQL Server;SERVER=pubname;DATABASE=CDR;Trusted_Connection=yes
```

The registry on servers hosting a database can also be checked. Look at the following registry key for DBConnection0:

\\HKEY_LOCAL_MACHINE\Software\Cisco Systems Inc.\DBL

The DBConnection0 string item contains a connection string similar to the preceding with the machine name and database name of the primary database. Also, the CDR database name is stored in a local registry key.

\\HKEY_LOCAL_MACHINE\Software\Cisco Systems Inc.\DBL\PrimaryCdrServer

You will need access to both the configuration database and CDR database to properly resolve the CDR information.

Performance Issues Related to Processing and Removing CDR Data

Keep the following performance guidelines in mind when you consider how to process CDR data. If the database is on the same server as CallManager, CDR processing during normal to heavy call activity might have a significant impact on system performance. Cisco recommends that no CDR processing should be done on the data in the CDR table except to move the data to a separate machine. This is the best way to ensure that CDR analysis will not impact system performance. The following are additional tips for processing CDR data:

■ Partner's software and databases should never reside on the MCS platform and should be placed on a separate physical system.

■ Do not use database triggers on CallManager tables.

■ Do not use database-stored procedures on CallManager tables.

■ If a partner does not want CDR data written to the CallManager Publisher database, a Data Source Name (DSN) entry on CallManager can be changed so that CDR data is written to the separate server. If a large memory cache is made available on the separate server, these actions should improve CallManager performance.

■ If bulk pulling CDR data from the database, a rule of thumb is to pull no more than 10,000 records at a time.

Maintaining CDR/CMR Data in the Database

CallManagers within the cluster generate CDR data and write it into the database. In general, the system does not make any attempt to process the data or remove the data when it has been processed except those actions necessary to preserve system integrity. The section "System Actions and Limits on Record Storage" covers the actions taken to preserve system integrity.

Administrator's Responsibility

The administrator has the responsibility either to ensure that the post-processing software removes the CDR data when all processing of the data has been completed, or to establish and execute other procedures to remove the data. CallManager removes data as necessary to enforce a limit on disk usage if the data store grows too large. This preserves system integrity, but it can result in lost CDR data if it has not been processed.

The Database Layer creates a protective shield around the database to prevent altering configuration data except through CallManager Administration. You must have write access into the database to remove data, because this involves modifying the database.

When CDR data is removed from the database after analysis is completed, all related CMRs should also be removed. If either CMR data or CDR data is not removed when the corresponding records have been removed in the other table, no particular harm is done, except that the data is not available and takes up disk space. It is recommended that you do regular backups on your CDR database. If you do regular backups, no further action is needed.

System Actions and Limits on Record Storage

The CallManager server platforms ship with sufficient disk storage to safely store approximately 10 million CDRs and their associated CMRs. Once a day, the system checks the number of CDRs currently stored in the database against the maximum number of records allowed as defined by the Cisco Database Layer Monitor service parameter Max CDR Records. If the number of records contained in the CallDetailRecord table exceeds this maximum value, the system takes the following actions to ensure that sufficient disk space is maintained to safely operate the cluster:

- If CDRs accumulate to a configured maximum, the oldest CDRs are removed, along with related CMRs, once a day. The CDR data count is reduced back to the configured maximum.

- When records are removed from the database, an alarm is generated that says "Local CDR tables grew too large. Records were deleted." This alarm is routed to the Event Viewer and to trace files.

> **NOTE**   The configured maximum number of CDRs is set to 1.5 million when the system is shipped. CallManager makes no attempt to intelligently remove data, so if CallManager is required to remove CDR data, it is possible to remove part of the CDR data for a given call but not all of it.

> **NOTE**   You should remove records more often than once a day or per week in large systems. Queries to remove records consume CPU time and transaction log space relative to the size of the table. The smaller the table, the quicker your query runs. Removing significant quantities of records from the database during normal system operation might have a severe performance impact on CallManager.

Hints on Processing CDR Data

There are issues with the CDR data that CallManager generates. The CallManager database contains all configuration information needed to operate the system, but it does not contain enough information to satisfy all requirements from third-party call accounting software packages. This section identifies the known problem areas and gives a few suggestions on how you might resolve these issues.

Additional Configuration Data Needed

The CDR data contains IP addresses and device names for the endpoints of a call. This provides the necessary information for most endpoints; however, in the case of gateways, the post-processing software must collect some additional configuration data when the post-processing system is installed or configured. Some typical configuration data that the post-processing software might need are as follows:

- Identification of gateways by name or IP address

- Gateway physical location

- Gateway span configuration

- Gateway type or usage

- Billing rates

Only directory numbers assigned to devices on CallManager are in the database. You will have to make processing assumptions when the directory number is not found in the database. The following section provides clues about some typical assumptions you might need to make.

OnNet Versus OffNet

This is a really thorny issue when trying to generate accurate billing information, because it is difficult to determine whether the call stayed completely on the IP network or was terminated on the public network. One clue you can use is to check the device type on both ends of the call. If both are phones that are defined in the database, you can assume that it stayed OnNet. If the call terminated on a gateway, it is more difficult.

You might have different types of gateways configured on the system. Cisco VG248 gateways might have station ports with standard analog phones attached to them. Typically, these devices are considered OnNet. The Cisco VG248 gateway might be connected to analog phone lines and used as an access into the PSTN. Calls terminating on those ports went OffNet. Other gateways have similar situations that must be accounted for. You can also look at the called party number to see whether the number dialed is defined in the CallManager database. If you do not find it there, or it does not match a dial plan for OnNet calls, it likely went OffNet.

To process calls that terminate in the PSTN, you need to have information about the physical location of the gateway. A given directory number can be either local or long distance, depending on where the gateway is located.

Gateway Directory Number Processing

If you make a call that routes through a gateway and terminates on the PSTN somewhere, the digits you dialed to get to the gateway might not be the digits that were actually sent to the PSTN. The gateways have the capability of modifying the directory number further by stripping digits or adding additional digits and so forth. Whether the gateway modifies numbers or not depends on how you configure the gateway. The gateways can modify both incoming and outgoing digit strings. In either case, the Call Control process does not know about any modifications that are made to the digit strings by the gateways themselves. On the incoming side, the modified directory number is received from the gateway, but Call Control does not know whether any modifications were made by the gateway, or whether the number was just received by the gateway and passed through to Call Control. CDR data reflects any changes made by a gateway on the incoming side because that is the number that was processed by Call Control. The CDR data does not reflect any changes that are made by the gateways on the outgoing side because that information is not returned to Call Control.

Troubleshooting CDR Data Generation and Storage

Table 7-13 documents some common problems and errors and suggests possible solutions with regard to CDR data generation and storage. This is not an exhaustive list.

Table 7-13 *Recognizing and Resolving Common CDR Data Generation and Storage Problems*

Problem	Possible Cause	Solution
No CDRs are written to the central data store.	CallManager is shipped with CDR data generation disabled. The most common problem is that you have not enabled CDR data generation.	Set the CDR Enabled Flag service parameter to True on all CallManager nodes in the cluster. If you also want CMR data, you should set the Call Diagnostics Enabled service parameter to True also.
CDR data is logged for some calls, but not for others.	If you enable CDR data generation by setting the CDR Enabled Flag service parameter to True on some CallManager nodes in the cluster but not on other nodes, the system logs CDR data only from the CallManager nodes where you enabled CDR data generation.	Set the CDR Enabled Flag service parameter to True on all CallManager nodes in the cluster.
No CMRs are written to the central data store.	The system does not generate CMR data unless the Call Diagnostics Enabled service parameter is enabled.	Set the Call Diagnostics Enabled service parameter to True on all CallManager nodes in the cluster.
CMR data is logged for some IP phones and MGCP gateways, but not for others.	The current setting of the Call Diagnostics Enabled service parameters is not the same on all CallManager nodes in the cluster.	Set the Call Diagnostics Enabled service parameter to True on all CallManager nodes in the cluster.
CDR flat files get copied into the "BAD" directory on the Publisher.	The most common reasons are these: The flat file has been corrupted. There is one or more bad characters in a CDR entry in the file. The CDR Insert service does not have database access.	The corrupted file will have to be cleaned up or repaired. If there is one or more bad characters in a CDR entry in the flat file, that CDR was not be inserted into the database but the remainder of the entries were inserted.

Summary

Two record types are included in CDR data:

- **CDRs**—Contain information needed to create billing records

- **CMRs**—Contain information that can be used to evaluate the QoS for a given call

Together, CDRs and CMRs can be used for tracking call activity, diagnosing certain types of problems, and evaluating the QoS of calls through the system. Both records are stored in a central SQL database in separate tables.

With CallManager release 4.1, device names and other important information is now available directly from the CDR data and no longer requires additional external processes to obtain this information.

Calls such as transfers and conference calls produce a set of records that must be identified and processed as a set to properly bill for the calls. Extensive field data information and examples have been provided in the hope of being useful in the development of billing packages, call activity tracking, and other reporting tools.

With this information, you should have a good understanding of the CDR facilities that CallManager provides and be able to manage and control those facilities, obtain access to CDR data, and process the CDR data.

Feature List

This appendix provides a list of Cisco CallManager features. Features that are new to CallManager with release 4.*x* are indicated.

Both phone and CallManager features are detailed in this appendix. Features include the functions of the softkeys or buttons on a Cisco IP Phone in addition to administration functions for CallManager.

Cisco CallManager Feature List

The following features are available in CallManager release 4.1:

- Abbreviated Dialing (AbbrDial)

- Annunciator

- Answer/Release

- Application Programming Interfaces (API)

    — Call Detail Records (CDR) and Call Management Records (CMR) API

    — Computer Telephony Integration (CTI) API

    — AXL SOAP Database API

    — LDAP Directory Integration API

    — IP Phone Services API

- Audible Indicator of Ringing Phone

- Authentication/Encryption

- Auto Answer/Intercom

- Automated Alternate Routing (AAR)

- Automated Change Notification/Database Replication

- Automated Installation and Recovery

- Automated Systemwide Software and Feature Upgrades

- Automatic Attenuation/Gain Adjustment

- Automatic Bandwidth Selection

- Automatic Number Identification (ANI)

- Auto-Registration

- Backup and Restore System (BARS)

- Barge/Conference Barge (cBarge)

- Broadcast Paging Support (with third-party integration)

- Bulk Administration Tool (BAT)

- Call Admission Control (CAC)

- Call Back

- Call Connection

- Call Coverage

- Call Detail Records (CDR) and Call Management Records (CMR)

- Call Forwarding

- Call Forwarding Support for Third-Party Applications

- Call Park

- Call Pickup/Group Call Pickup (PickUp/GPickUp)

- Call Preservation for Active Calls During CallManager Server Outage

- Call Status per Line

- Call Waiting/Retrieve

- Calling Line Identification (CLID or Caller ID)

- Calling Line ID Restriction (CLIR) on a Per-Call Basis

- Calling Party Name Identification (CNID)

- Calling Party Display Restriction

- Certificate Authority Proxy Function (CAPF) Report Generation

- CDR Analysis and Reporting (CAR) Tool (formerly Administrative Reporting Tool)

- Centralized System Administration, Monitoring, and Reporting

- Cisco ATA-186 2-Port Analog Gateway Support

- Cisco Bulk Trace Analysis

- Cisco CallManager Administration Enhancements for Large System Administration

- Cisco CallManager Attendant Console (formerly Cisco WebAttendant)

- Cisco CallManager Serviceability

- Cisco CallManager Trace Collection Tool

- Cisco CallManager User Options Web Page

- Cisco Conference Connection (CCC) Support

- Cisco CTL Client

- Cisco Discovery Protocol (CDP) Support

- Cisco Emergency Responder (CER) Support

- Cisco IP Manager-Assistant

- Cisco IP Phones 7971, 7970, 7961, 7960, 7941, 7940, Conference Stations 7936 and 7935, Wireless 7920, Expansion Module 7914, 7912, 7905, and 7902 Support

- Cisco IP Phone Services

- Cisco IP Software-Based Phone Support (IP SoftPhone and IP Communicator)

- Cisco Personal Address Book

- Cisco VG248 48-Port Analog Gateway Support

- CISCO-CCM-MIB

- Click to Dial/Click to Call

- Client Matter Codes

- Codec Support (Audio and Video)

- Closest Match Routing

- Clustering
- Computer Telephony Integration (CTI) Support
- Conference/Confrn
- Context-Sensitive Help
- Contrast/LCD Contrast
- CTI Redundancy with CTIManager
- Date/Time Zone Display Format Configurable per Phone
- Dependency Records
- Device Type-Based Information and Resets
- Device Downloadable Feature Upgrade
- Device Pool
- Device Search in Cisco CallManager Administration
- Device Wizard
- DHCP IP Assignment for Phones and Gateways
- Dial Plan Partitions and Calling Search Spaces
- Dialed Number Analyzer (DNA)
- Dialed Number Translation Table (Inbound and Outbound Translation)
- Dialed Number Identification Service (DNIS) and RDNIS
- Digit Analysis and Translation (Calling Party Number and Called Party Number)
- Digital Signal Processor (DSP) Resource Management
- Direct Inward Dial
- Direct Outward Dial
- Direct Transfer (DirTrfr)
- Directories Button on Cisco IP Phones
- Directory Dial from Cisco IP Phones
- Distinctive Ring—Internal Versus External

- Distinctive Ring Selection

- Distributed CallManager Server Architecture

- Distributed and Topologically Aware Resource Sharing

- DSP Resource Alignment

- Dual Tone Multi-Frequency (DTMF) Support

- Embedded Directory for User Data

- Emergency 911 Service (E911) Support

- EndCall

- Extension Mobility

- External Route Plan Wizard

- External/Internal Trunk Designation

- Failover

- FAX/Modem over IP Support

- Forced Authorization Codes

- FXO and FXS Support

- Group Call Pickup/GPickUp

- H.323 Client, Gateway, and Gatekeeper Support

- Hold/Resume

- HTTP Server Support

- Hunt Lists and Line Groups

- Inline Power Support on Cisco IP Phones

- Internationalization/Localization

- ISDN Basic Rate Interface (BRI) Support

- Join

- JTAPI Computer Telephony Interface (CTI)

- JTAPI Control of Analog (FXS) Gateway Ports

- LDAPv3 Directory Interface

- Least Cost Routing (LCR) Support

- Lightweight Directory Access Protocol (LDAP) Support

- Line

- Manager Assistant Services

- Mappable Softkeys

- Media Gateway Control Protocol (MGCP) Support

- Media Resource Group List Support

- Meet-Me Conference/MeetMe

- Messages Button on Cisco IP Phones

- Message Waiting Indicator

- Microsoft NetMeeting

- Multilevel Administration

- Multi-Level Precedence and Preemption (MLPP)

- Multiple Calls per Line

- Multiple Line Appearances per Phone

- Music on Hold

- Mute

- NewCall

- North American Numbering Plan (NANP) and Non-NANP Support

- Off-Premise Extension (OPX) Support

- On-Hook and Off-Hook Dialing

- Overlap Sending/Receiving

- Paperless Phone

- Performance Monitoring and Alarms

- Privacy

- Private Line Auto RingDown (PLAR) Support

- QSIG Support

- Quality of Service (QoS)

- Quality Reporting Tool (QRT)

- Redial/REDL

- Redirected Number Identification Service (RDNIS)

- Redundancy/Failover

- Remote Site Survivability for MGCP Gateways

- Scalability Enhancements through H.323 Gatekeeper (Beyond Ten Sites)

- Serviceability Enhancements Through SNMP, CDP, CiscoWorks

- Service URLs on Line Buttons

- Services on XML-Capable Cisco IP Phones

- Settings Button on Cisco IP Phones

- Single CDR Repository per CallManager Cluster

- Single Point for System/Device Configuration

- Simple Network Management Protocol (SNMP) Support

- Speakerphone/SPKR

- Speed Dial

- Supplementary Services

- Survivable Remote Site Telephony (SRST)

- Syslog Support for Debugging Output

- System Event Reporting

- T1/E1 PRI Support

- T1/E1-CAS Support

- Telephony Application Programming Interface (TAPI) and JTAPI Support

- Time of Day Routing

- Time Zone Configuration

- Toll Restriction/Toll Fraud Prevention

- Tone on Hold

- Tool for Auto-Registered Phone Support (TAPS)

- Transcoding and Media Termination Point (MTP) Support

- Transfer/XFER/Transf...

- Trivial File Transfer Protocol (TFTP) Support

- Turn off Phone Display

- Unicast Conference

- Video Telephony Support

- Virus Protection Certification

- Visual Indicator of Ringing Phone

- Voice Activity Detection (VAD)/Silence Suppression Support

- Voice Mail Support

- Volume Controls

- XML Support

- Zero Cost Automated Phone Adds and Moves

Abbreviated Dialing (AbbrDial)

> **NOTE**   This feature was introduced in CallManager release 4.0.

Abbreviated dialing enables users to quickly access up to 99 preconfigured speed dial numbers that they have associated with index numbers. While the phone is on-hook, users can dial an index number, 01 through 99, and then press the **AbbrDial** softkey to dial the phone number associated with the index number. Users define their speed dials via the Cisco CallManager User Options web page or via the MyFastDials XML service on the phone.

Annunciator

> **NOTE**   This feature was introduced in CallManager release 4.0.

The Cisco IP Voice Media Streaming App service, which also offers Music on Hold, software-based (G.711 only) conferencing, and software-based (G.711 only) media termination point (MTP) functions, has been enhanced in CallManager release 4.0(1) to include the capability to play prerecorded announcements (.wav files) and tones to Cisco IP Phones, gateways, and other configurable devices. The annunciator capability enables CallManager to audibly alert callers with the reason that a call has failed. Annunciator can also play tones for some transferred calls (ringback tones) and some conference scenarios (party joining/departing tones).

Table A-1 provides information about the CallManager annunciator service parameter that you can access on the Service Parameters Configuration page (**Service > Service Parameters >** *select a server* **> Cisco CallManager**) in CallManager Administration.

Table A-1   *Annunciator (CCM.exe) Service Parameter*

Service Parameter	Default	Valid Value
Duplex Streaming Enabled Determines whether Music on Hold (MOH) and annunciator use duplex streaming. True means that MOH and annunciator use duplex (two-way) streaming; False means that MOH and annunciator use simplex (one-way) streaming. Specifying True facilitates interoperability with certain firewalls and routers configured for Network Address Translation (NAT).	False	True or False

Table A-2 provides information about Cisco IP Voice Media Streaming App annunciator service parameters that you can access on the Service Parameters Configuration page (**Service > Service Parameters >** *select a server* **> Cisco IP Voice Media Streaming App**).

Table A-2 *Annunciator (IPVMSA.exe) Service Parameters*

Service Parameter	Default	Valid Values
Call Count Specifies the maximum number of simultaneous announcements that the annunciator supports. Increasing this value above the recommended default of 48 might cause performance degradation on a CallManager that is running on the same server. If you need to increase this value above the default, consider installing the Cisco IP Voice Media Streaming App service on a separate server.	48	0 to 400
Run Flag This service parameter determines whether the annunciator functionality is enabled.	True	True or False

Answer/Release

Answer/Release is used in conjunction with a headset and is available for all Cisco IP Phones that can use a headset and display softkeys. The following sections describe how Answer/Release works for each Cisco IP Phone.

Answer/Release on Cisco IP Phone Series 79*xx*

Answer is a softkey used to answer a ringing line. To release a call, you can press **EndCall** or toggle the **HEADSET** button on the phone if you're using a headset. On Cisco IP Phone series 79*xx*, the Answer and Resume softkeys are automatically available.

Answer/Release on Cisco IP Phones 12SP+ and 30VIP

Answer/Release is used in conjunction with a headset, so the user can press a button on the headset apparatus to answer and release (disconnect) calls. The phone's handset must be off-hook to use Answer/Release.

Answer/Release can be configured on the button template for Cisco IP Phones 12SP+ or 30VIP. To answer a call when using a headset, the user presses the **Answer/Release** button and is connected to the caller. To disconnect, the user presses the **Answer/Release** button again.

Application Programming Interfaces (API)

CallManager exposes many of its databases, directories, and telephony interfaces through APIs. In addition, developers can write applications to deploy sophisticated IP Communications applications through CallManager's support for open standards such as XML and TAPI/JTAPI.

You can find documentation on these APIs at the Cisco AVVID Developer Support Central website at the following link:

http://www.cisco.com/pcgi-bin/dev_support/access_level/product_support

Call Detail Records (CDR) and Call Management Records (CMR) API

CallManager releases 3.2 and earlier use a Microsoft SQL Server 7.0 database. CallManager releases 3.3 and later use Microsoft SQL 2000. Call accounting and billing applications can query the CDR tables via ODBC calls, direct SQL queries to the database, or via Microsoft ActiveX Data Objects (ADO). Read-only access is provided to all tables in the database; access to the CDR and CMR tables is read/write.

Computer Telephony Integration (CTI) API

CallManager exposes sophisticated control of many aspects of the complete Cisco IP Communications telephony platform via its Computer Telephony Integration (CTI) APIs. These APIs enable custom applications to register interest in CallManager device call events and take full control of those devices to make, take, transfer, bridge, join, or end calls. Applications can monitor or control Cisco IP Phones, create and register software-based phone ports (CTI ports) that provide media streaming capabilities, and manage CTI route points to queue and distribute high-volume incoming calls. The section "Computer Telephony Integration (CTI) Support" provides more information.

AXL SOAP Database API

The AVVID XML Layer (AXL) API provides a mechanism for inserting, retrieving, updating, and removing data from the CallManager SQL database using an Extensible Markup Language (XML) Simple Object Access Protocol (SOAP) interface.

The AXL SOAP API provides application developers with direct access to the CallManager database and allows them to add, remove, update, and retrieve phones, lines, users, device profiles, route plan information (route patterns, translation patterns, calling search spaces, partitions), login, logout, device resets, and more.

LDAP Directory Integration API

CallManager provides an embedded Lightweight Directory Access Protocol (LDAP)-compliant directory for storing user and device profiles, user preferences, passwords and PINs, and other information. The API provides a method for integrating the CallManager embedded directory into external directories such as Microsoft Active Directory and iPlanet Netscape Directory Server to take advantage of an enterprise's existing LDAP directory infrastructure.

IP Phone Services API

XML-capable Cisco IP Phones provide support for accessing and displaying XML-formatted web content and applications developed by customers or third-party integrators. The API provides details and examples for developers to use in creating their own applications.

See the section "XML Support" for more details.

Audible Indicator of Ringing Phone

All Cisco IP Phones provide configurable audible notification of an incoming call on a per-line basis. Cisco IP Phones 79xx provide the option to ring, beep, or have audible notification disabled. You can configure the type of indication (audible and visual, see the later section "Visual Indicator of Ringing Phone" for more information) using the following service parameters:

■ Ring Setting of Busy Station Policy

■ Ring Setting of Busy Station

■ Ring Setting of Idle Station

You can access these service parameters in CallManager Administration (**Service > Service Parameters >** *select a server* **> Cisco CallManager**). Users can configure notification on the Cisco CallManager User Options web page (choose the link to **Configure the Ring Settings for Your Phone**).

Authentication/Encryption

Cisco IP Communications comprises numerous security mechanisms for authenticating, and in some cases encrypting, administrative access, user access, device signaling, and media. This appendix discusses the following areas:

■ Administrative access to CallManager

■ Device (that is, phones, gateways, and other devices) authentication, signaling, and media encryption

The Cisco Press book, *Cisco CallManager Best Practices* (ISBN: 1-58705-139-7) offers an excellent chapter on security.

CallManager Administration Web Page Authentication

CallManager Administration and CallManager Serviceability web pages utilize the integrated authentication scheme of Microsoft Internet Information Server (IIS) by default (that is, when Multilevel Administration [MLA] is not enabled). Users who are defined in the Windows 2000

Administrators group are granted access to the CallManager Administration and CallManager Serviceability web pages.

Multilevel Administration

CallManager release 3.2 introduced a new feature called Multilevel Administration (MLA). When MLA is enabled, the usernames and passwords of administrators are authenticated via LDAP rather than via Microsoft IIS Integrated Password Authentication. The LDAP directory used for administrative access can be the embedded directory provided during CallManager installation, or an external LDAP-compliant directory such as Microsoft Active Directory or Netscape Directory Services. See the section "Lightweight Directory Access Protocol (LDAP) Support" for more information.

> **NOTE**   MLA was enhanced in CallManager release 4.1.

As of CallManager release 4.1, MLA supports UMX APIs for LDAP directory access. Prior to this enhancement, custom Java-based code implemented directory access. Release 4.1 removes the dependency on Microsoft Java (JVM).

Cisco CallManager User Options Web Page Authentication

The username and password used to access the Cisco CallManager User Options web page is authenticated via LDAP. The LDAP directory used to authenticate connections to this web page can be the embedded directory provided during CallManager installation, or an external LDAP-compliant directory such as Microsoft Active Directory or Netscape Directory Services. The section "Lightweight Directory Access Protocol (LDAP) Support" provides more information.

CallManager Web Page Encryption (HTTPS)

> **NOTE**   This feature was introduced in CallManager release 4.1(2).

CallManager release 4.1(2) changes most (not all) web page directories to Hypertext Transfer Protocol Secure (HTTPS). To maintain backward compatibility with some third-party applications and XML services, some web directories continue to use nonencrypted HTTP with the intent that as those applications also migrate to HTTPS. Future releases of CallManager will force the use of HTTPS on all virtual directories. The digital certificates used by the IIS and Tomcat web servers are created automatically during installation and are self-signed. You can also update these certificates to use root-signed certificates. For CallManager release 4.1(2), the following virtual directories have been modified to force the use of HTTPS:

- CallManager Administration (CCMAdmin)

- CallManager Serviceability (CCMService)

- Cisco CallManager User Options (CCMUser)

Some examples of directories that have not moved to HTTPS are as follows:

- XML service directories (extension mobility, Quality Reporting Tool [QRT], call back)

- AXL SOAP API

LDAP over SSL (LDAPS) Support

> **NOTE** This feature was introduced in CallManager release 4.1(2).

Secure Sockets Layer (SSL) encrypt the communication between the web server and the LDAP server (used when authenticating user access to CallManager Administration, CallManager Serviceability, and Cisco CallManager User Options web pages). The embedded directory is automatically configured to use SSL during installation, and support is also provided for using SSL if integrated with an external LDAP-compliant directory such as Microsoft Active Directory or Netscape Directory Services.

Extension Mobility Username/PIN Authentication

Users are prompted to enter their username and PIN when accessing the extension mobility login service (for more information, see the section "Extension Mobility"). These usernames and PINs are transported over HTTP and authenticated via LDAP. The LDAP directory used for storing these usernames and PINs can be the embedded directory provided during CallManager installation or an external LDAP-compliant directory such as Microsoft Active Directory or Netscape Directory Services. See the section "Lightweight Directory Access Protocol (LDAP) Support" for more information.

SQL Database Access Authentication

Applications attempting to gain access to the CallManager SQL database via ODBC, ADA, or SOAP APIs are given access based on the authentication method configured in SQL Server. CallManager releases prior to 4.0(1) use SQL authentication while CallManager releases 4.0(1) and later use Windows Integrated Authentication. See the "Call Detail Records (CDR) and Call Management Records (CMR) API" and "Database API" sections for more details.

TFTP Directory Access Restrictions

The Cisco TFTP service is an integrated service that is installed and configured automatically during CallManager installation, and is tightly synchronized with the database of the cluster so that changes to devices made in CallManager Administration are automatically propagated through the Database Layer and into the individualized configuration files in the TFTP directory (C:\Program Files\Cisco\TFTPPath). The TFTP service is configured to allow only read-only requests from clients (read/write permissions are permitted only through the Database Layer), and the directory cannot be browsed (meaning the TFTP request must specify the exact filename). See the section "Trivial File Transfer Protocol (TFTP) Support" for more details.

Phone File Authentication

> **NOTE** This feature was enhanced in CallManager release 4.0(1).

File authentication prevents tampering with the files that the phone retrieves from the TFTP server, such as the firmware load, configuration files, and so on, prior to loading them on the phone. CallManager release 3.3(4) introduced signed binary firmware images only. Configuration files are still unsigned in this release. Tampering with the file will be detected by the phone, causing it to reject the file. After a signed firmware image has been loaded onto the phone, the phone will never accept an unsigned image again, eliminating the risk of a hacker working around this security measure by loading an older phone firmware image into the phone. File authentication is supported on Cisco IP Phones 7902, 7905, 7910, 7912, 7940, 7941, 7960, 7961, 7970, and 7971.

CallManager release 4.0(1) extended the use of signed files to also include configuration files, ringlists, locale files, and Certificate Trust List (CTL) files.

Device Authentication

> **NOTE** This feature was introduced in CallManager release 4.0(1).

Device authentication is composed of several components that work together to establish a mutual authentication between the IP Phone and CallManager:

- Each CallManager server has an x.509v3 certificate created and stored on its hard disk.

- On Cisco IP Phones 7940, 7941, 7960, 7961, 7970, and 7971, an x.509v3 digital certificate is also downloaded and stored in non-volatile random-access memory (NVRAM).

■ A Certificate Trust List (CTL) file (CTLFile.tlv) is created and stored in the TFTP server, and is downloaded by the phones. This CTL file contains the list of known servers so that the phones have a list of legitimate, trusted hosts to which they can communicate.

■ With all three of the preceding items in place, the phones use SSL to create a mutually authenticated TCP session over which to transmit all signaling messages.

Support is also extended to Cisco Unity voice mail and Cisco IOS voice gateways. Like the phones, Unity uses a self-signed or root-signed certificate and SSL to create a mutually authenticated TCP session over which to communicate with CallManager. Cisco IOS voice gateways also use self-signed or root-signed certificates, but manually configured IPSec tunnels instead of SSL. These IPSec tunnels are used to carry all MGCP, H.323, or SIP signaling messages between CallManager and the gateway. IPSec tunnels are configured either directly in each CallManager server, or a separate IPSec concentrator (such as a Cisco IOS router, PIX Firewall, or 3000 series VPN concentrator) can be used to front end the CallManager servers and offload the burden of managing large numbers of IPSec connections.

Signaling Encryption

> **NOTE**   This feature was introduced in CallManager release 4.0(1) and enhanced in CallManager release 4.1(2).

Leveraging the device authentication mechanisms described in the preceding section, "Device Authentication," all signaling messages transmitted over the SSL connection between the IP phone and CallManager can optionally be encrypted using Advanced Encryption Standard (AES) 128-bit encryption. CallManager Administration makes this optional to provide you with granular choices of how secure you want the network to be. Encrypting the signaling makes it more difficult to capture and troubleshoot with a sniffer, for example, so you have the option of configuring the phone for authentication only or for encryption. When the phone is set to encrypted mode, the media is also automatically encrypted (meaning you cannot configure the phone to encrypt only its signaling but not its media), and media encryption requires that the signaling also be encrypted (you cannot encrypt your media without first encrypting the signaling).

In the case of Cisco IOS voice gateways, the IPSec configuration determines what encryption algorithm will be used for the signaling channel. Cipher support varies by the platform and IOS version deployed. Most support Triple Data Encryption Standard (3DES), which is 168-bit encryption; some platforms also support AES-128 and AES-256.

CallManager release 4.1(2) extends support for signaling and media encryption to Cisco IP Phones 7940, 7941, 7960, and 7961. Prior to this release, these models supported device authentication only, but not encryption. CallManager security is implemented through authentication and encryption. CallManager provides enterprise parameters (described in Table A-3) and service parameters (described in Table A-4) to control certain security settings. Table A-3 provides information about security-related enterprise parameters (**System > Enterprise Parameters**).

Table A-3 *Security-Related Enterprise Parameters*

Enterprise Parameter	Default	Valid Values
Device Security Mode Determines whether security is provided for devices that have been configured as Use System Default in the Device Security Mode field on the Phone Configuration page in CallManager Administration. If you configure encryption for Cisco IP Phones that support barge or cBarge, those encrypted devices cannot accept barge requests when they are participating in an encrypted call. When the call is encrypted, the barge attempt fails. See the section "Barge/Conference" for more information.	Non Secure	Non Secure (no device authentication, signaling authentication, or encryption) Authenticated (only device authentication and signaling authentication) Encrypted (device authentication, signaling authentication, and encryption)
Cluster Security Mode Indicates the security mode of the cluster. Because this parameter is read-only, to change the cluster security mode, you must run the CTL Client plug-in. Restart Cisco CallManager for the parameter change to take effect.	0	**0**—Non Secure (phones will register in nonsecure mode [no security]) **1**—Mixed (the cluster allows the registration of both secure devices and nonsecure devices; Auto-registration is disabled)
CAPF Phone Port Specifies the port that the Cisco Authority Proxy Function (CAPF) service listens to for requests from a phone for a certificate. You must restart the CAPF service for the parameter change to take effect.	3804	1023 to 55556
CAPF Operation Expires in (days) This parameter, which affects all phones that use CAPF, specifies the number of days in which any CAPF operation must be completed.	10 days	1 to 365 days

Table A-4 provides information about security-related service parameters (**Service > Service Parameters >** *select a server* **> Cisco CallManager**).

Table A-4 *Security-Related Service Parameters*

Service Parameter	Default	Valid Values
Packet Capture Enable Determines whether CallManager captures Skinny Client Control Protocol (SCCP) packets that are sent or received over Transport Layer Security (TLS) connections.	True	True or False
Packet Capture Service TLS Listen Port Specifies the TLS port that accepts requests from real-time debugging applications to capture the SCCP packets that are sent or received over TLS connections.	2446	1024 to 65535
Packet Capture Max Real-Time Client Connections Specifies the maximum number of real-time debugging application connections that can be accepted to capture the SCCP packets that are sent or received over TLS connections. A value of zero indicates that no connections will be allowed.	5	0 to 5
Packet Capture Max File Size (MB) Specifies the maximum size of each packet capture file created by CallManager for batch mode debugging. You specify Batch Processing Mode in the Signal Packet Capture Mode field on the device's Configuration page in CallManager Administration. A value of zero indicates that no packets will be captured even if the Signal Packet Capture Mode field is set to Batch Processing Mode.	2 MB	0 to 5 MB

Media Encryption

> **NOTE**   This feature was introduced in CallManager release 4.0(1).

Cisco IP Phones 7940, 7941, 7960, 7961, 7970, and 7971 can be configured to automatically encrypt their media using AES 128-bit encryption. Media encryption requires the device authentication and signaling encryption previously described. In other words, after all the aforementioned certificate and signaling encryption mechanisms are in place to establish a mutually authenticated and encrypted SSL session between the IP Phone and CallManager and the signaling messages have been encrypted, CallManager can instruct the phone to encrypt its media too. CallManager negotiates media encryption on a call-by-call basis based on CallManager's knowledge of the devices participating in the call. Media encryption requires that the signaling also be encrypted (you cannot encrypt your media without first encrypting the signaling).

Certain Cisco IOS voice gateways also provide AES 128-bit encryption of the media. As of mid-2005, support is offered only when using MGCP on Cisco 1800, 2600-XM, 2800, 3660, 3700, and 3800 series routers configured with Packetized Digital Voice Module 2 (PDVM2). H.323 and SIP can leverage the signaling encryption previously described, but cannot encrypt their media with CallManager. The media encryption/decryption keys are passed over MGCP to the gateway; therefore, the MGCP signaling path must be configured to use IPSec to protect the confidentiality of these messages.

Visual Indication of Device Authentication/Encryption

NOTE   This feature was introduced in CallManager release 4.0(1).

Cisco IP Phones display a visual indication to the user (in the form of a lock or shield icon) of the security status of the phone. A shield icon indicates that all parties involved in the call are authenticated (but not encrypted), and a lock icon indicates that all parties are encrypted. Similar icons also appear under the **settings** menu on the phone to indicate the security status of the phone's communication with CallManager. A shield icon means that the SCCP signaling channel is authenticated but not encrypted; a lock icon means that the signaling is encrypted.

Auto Answer/Intercom

Auto answer allows an incoming call to automatically answer, causing the phone to go off-hook when an incoming call is received. Use auto answer with a headset or the speakerphone of Cisco IP Phones 7940, 7941, 7960, 7961, 7970, and 7971. Auto answer with headset does not engage if the headset is not in use. Auto answer with either headset or speakerphone does not engage if the user is on an active call; instead, the phone rings as usual or plays the call waiting tone, providing the user with the choice of answering or allowing the call to roll to the call forward busy/no answer destination, if configured.

Table A-5 provides information about auto answer service parameters (**Service > Service Parameters** > *select a server* > **Cisco CallManager**).

Table A-5 *Auto Answer Service Parameters*

Service Parameter	Default	Valid Values
Auto Answer Timer Specifies the seconds to wait before the Cisco IP Phone auto answers an incoming call on an idle line. The value that this parameter specifies should be less than the value that is specified in the T301 Timer parameter. If it is not, the call does not get answered, and the caller receives a busy signal. Setting this value to the higher end of the allowable range could result in calls being rolled to the voice mail system, if configured, before the call gets auto answered.	1	1 to 500 seconds
Alternate Idle Phone Auto Answer Behavior Specifies the call conditions that will disable the auto answer feature. True disables auto answer when a call is connected, incoming, outgoing, or on hold. False disables auto answer when a call is incoming or outgoing.	False	True or False
Override Auto Answer If Speaker Is Disabled Indicates whether a call automatically terminates if the speaker for the called phone is disabled when the Auto Answer with Speakerphone option is selected on the called phone line (Directory Number Configuration page in CallManager Administration).	True	True or False

Auto Answer with Zip Tone

Auto answer allows the user to have an incoming call announced by a beep, also called a *zip tone*, and then automatically connected if the user is not already on an active call. This feature eliminates the time it takes to answer a call, which allows more calls to be handled. Auto answer with zip tone requires the use of a headset and is compatible with Cisco IP Phones 7940, 7941, 7960, 7961, 7970, and 7971.

> **NOTE** The CTI API also supports auto answer.

Hands-Free Intercom

You can use auto answer to build a hands-free intercom function on an IP Phone by having incoming calls automatically answered by speakerphone. This feature can be configured on a per-line basis and is applicable to multiple-line IP Phones that offer full-duplex speakerphones, such as the 7940, 7941, 7960, 7961, 7970, and 7971. The Cisco IP Conference Phone models do not support this feature. This intercom function can be used only in a point-to-point fashion between two IP Phones. For group paging or broadcast paging, a third-party solution is required. See the section "Broadcast Paging Support" for more details.

The auto answer feature can be enabled on a per-line basis. If enabled, the directory number is auto answered when the **SPEAKER** button is in use. Auto Answer does not engage if the **SPEAKER** button is not on or if the user is on an active call; instead, the phone rings as usual or plays the call waiting tone, allowing the user the choice of answering or allowing the call to roll to the call forward busy/no answer target, if configured.

> **NOTE**   The CTI API also supports auto answer.

Automated Alternate Routing (AAR)

AAR provides a mechanism to reroute calls through the Public Switched Telephone Network (PSTN) or other network by using an alternate number when CallManager blocks a call because of insufficient bandwidth at a given location. With AAR, the caller does not need to hang up and redial the called party. The AAR group represents the dialing area where the line/directory number (DN), the Cisco voice mail port, and the gateway are located. You can assign route patterns to gateways or to a route list that contains one or more route groups. Route groups determine the order of preference for gateway and port usage. Route groups allow overflow from busy or failed devices to alternate devices. Digit manipulation can be performed at any step along the route pattern -> route list -> route group -> gateway logical path.

Prior to CallManager release 3.3, AAR was available only for calls destined for a device off-cluster (that is, via a route pattern, route list, and route group). Calls between two IP phones within the cluster could not take advantage of AAR in the event that bandwidth between the two phones was unavailable. CallManager release 3.3 introduces AAR groups, allowing you to configure alternate routes for calls that exceed the bandwidth restrictions configured for the location of the calling or called phone.

Automated Change Notification/Database Replication

Any changes made in CallManager Administration cause a change notification request to be sent to all CallManager nodes in the cluster. Change notifications ensure that each CallManager in the cluster has the most current configuration. If the change affects the configuration of a client device (for example, IP phone, IP Communicator, and so on) or an MGCP gateway, the change notification process also alerts these devices to download their TFTP configuration file immediately to obtain the new configuration. See the section "Clustering" for more information on CallManager clusters.

Change notification is the process by which changes you make through CallManager Administration get applied to running Cisco IP Communications services. Different Cisco IP Communications services respond to database updates through CallManager Administration differently, but there are three basic approaches:

- **Automatic update**—Any changes to the database causes the service to update immediately. Depending on which service is impacted, this can also cause devices associated with that service to update immediately.

- **Polled update**—The service polls the database periodically and refreshes its settings.

- **Manual update**—The service requires manual intervention to update its settings. In some cases, this means restarting the service; in other cases, it means that you must initiate a reset of a component related to the service from CallManager Administration.

Table A-6 shows the types of change notification used by different Cisco IP Communications services.

Table A-6 *Change Notification by Service*

Service	Change Notification
Cisco CTIManager	Manual update
Cisco Database Layer Monitor	Polled update every 5 minutes
Cisco IP Voice Media Streaming App	Automatic update
Cisco Messaging Interface	Polled update every 5 minutes
Cisco MOH Audio Translator	Polled update every 5 minutes
Cisco RIS Data Collector	Automatic update
Cisco Telephony Call Dispatcher	Polled update every 3 minutes
Cisco TFTP	Polled update every 5 minutes

Changes with no user impact usually get applied automatically; changes that could affect a call require you to manually initiate a device reset so that you can choose a time when the disruption will be minimal. Most changes to devices in CallManager Administration require only a reset of that one particular device that received the change. CallManager does not need to be restarted for device changes to take effect. Table A-7 provides general guidelines about the type of change notification that different changes use.

Table A-7   *CallManager Change Notification Guidelines*

Type of Change	Change Notification
AAR group	Automatic
Annunciator device	Manual reset from CallManager Administration (CCMAdmin); changes update when streaming to the device is idle
Partition, route filter	Manual reset of all affected devices from CCMAdmin
Cisco CallManager groups	Automatic
Class of control setting (time schedule, time period)	Automatic
Client matter code	Automatic
Date-time devices	Manual reset of all affected devices from CCMAdmin
Device pool	Manual reset of all affected devices from CCMAdmin
Device profile	Log out and log in again to the device with the affected profile
Enterprise parameters	Automatic unless otherwise noted
Forced authorization code	Automatic
Gatekeeper settings	Manual reset from CCMAdmin
Gateway	Manual reset from CCMAdmin
Hunt list and line group	Automatic
Line settings	Automatic reset of all devices sharing that line
Locations	Automatic
Media resources (conference bridge, MOH audio source, MRG)	Automatic
Media resource group list	Manual reset of all affected devices from CCMAdmin
MLA access rights (functional groups, user groups, enterprise parameters)	Automatic
MOH server	Changes update when streaming to the device is idle
MTP	Changes update when streaming to the device is idle
Phone button template	Manual reset from CCMAdmin of all devices using that template
Phone settings	Manual reset from CCMAdmin
Regions	Manual reset of all affected devices from CCMAdmin
Route list and route group	Automatic
Route pattern	Automatic reset of devices associated with the pattern

continues

Table A-7   *CallManager Change Notification Guidelines (Continued)*

Type of Change	Change Notification
Service parameters	Automatic unless otherwise noted
Softkey template	Manual reset of all affected devices from CCMAdmin
SRST reference	Automatic
Transcoder	Manual reset from CCMAdmin
Translation pattern	Automatic
Trunk settings	Manual reset from CCMAdmin
Voice mail port	Automatic

Automated Installation and Recovery

The CallManager DVD set includes an automated deployment tool to guide you through the operating system and CallManager installation.

Also provided is an integrated system Backup and Restore System (BARS). BARS can automatically back up all CallManager and IP Communications application servers within a cluster, providing a convenient method of recovering an entire system in the event of a disaster.

Automated Systemwide Software and Feature Upgrades

CallManager controls the device load information and related features of all SCCP devices and some MGCP gateway devices. When you upgrade CallManager, new device revisions and features are automatically propagated to all devices in the network that utilize TFTP to download their device load and configuration settings. The following list of devices is an example of the types of devices that use TFTP in this manner:

- IP phones that use SCCP

- Transcoding resources (except those that run on IOS devices)

- Conference bridge resources (except those that run on IOS devices)

- SGCP gateways

- MGCP gateways (except those that run on IOS devices)

See the section "Trivial File Transport Protocol (TFTP) Support" for more details.

Automatic Attenuation/Gain Adjustment

Automatic attenuation and gain adjustment is supported on all Cisco IP Phones, gateways, and applications. On gateways, attenuation and gain adjustment can be done for both transmit and receive on a port-by-port basis.

Automatic Bandwidth Selection

CallManager automatically chooses the correct audio codec to use for a given call. This choice is made by configuring regions in CallManager Administration (**System > Regions**) and assigning devices or device pools to those regions. Codecs are chosen for intra-region calls (calls between devices residing in the same region) and inter-region calls (calls from one region to another).

In addition, if a particular device does not support the audio codec specified in the region configuration, CallManager can invoke the use of a transcoding resource for the duration of that call, enabling a call between devices capable of two dissimilar codecs to proceed successfully. See the section "Codec Support (Audio and Video)" for more information.

Automatic Number Identification (ANI)

CallManager supports delivering and receiving ANI information through MGCP gateway interfaces on PRI/ISDN trunks, PRI/QSIG trunks, or Centralized Automated Message Accounting (CAMA) trunks. CallManager also supports delivering or receiving ANI on FXO trunks using H.323 or SIP gateway interfaces. Calling Line ID Restriction (CLIR) is also supported on a trunk-by-trunk basis See the Calling Line ID Restriction (CLIR) on a Per-Call Basis section for more information.

Auto-Registration

Auto-registration (**System > Cisco CallManager**) automatically assigns directory numbers and calling permission settings to new devices when they register with CallManager for the first time. When used in combination with the Bulk Administration Tool (BAT) and the Tool for Auto-Registered Phone Support (TAPS), auto-registration is useful for bringing large numbers of new phones onto the network with administrative ease. Learn more about BAT and TAPS in Chapter 6, "Manageability and Monitoring."

Backup and Restore System (BARS)

CallManager includes an automated backup and restore software application called BARS that backs up the database and directory of CallManager and certain other IP Communications applications. There are two versions: the Cisco IP Telephony Applications Backup Utility and the newer Cisco IP Telephony Backup and Restore System (BARS). The former provides a GUI application while the latter offers a web-based user interface. Both versions back up all database, directory, and configuration information for the CallManager server. One server within a CallManager cluster is designated as the backup server, and other servers can be designated as target servers. The following auxiliary applications can also be backed up using either the Backup Utility or BARS:

- Cisco Emergency Responder

- Cisco CDR Analysis and Reporting Tool (CAR)

- Cisco Customer Response Applications/Solutions (CRA/CRS) such as IP IVR, IP AA and IP ICD

BARS should be used for CallManager releases 3.3(2) and later. Older versions of CallManager should use the IP Telephony Applications Backup Utility.

Barge/Conference Barge (cBarge)

The barge feature adds a user to a call already in progress (effectively, barging into a connected call) and is supported on shared lines only. Pressing the **Barge** softkey automatically adds the user (initiator) to the shared-line call (target), and the users currently on the call receive a notification tone when the Party Entrance Tone service parameter (**Service > Service Parameter >** *select a service* **> Cisco CallManager**) is enabled (it is enabled by default).

> **NOTE** If you have configured encryption for Cisco IP Phones via the Device Security Mode enterprise parameter (**System > Enterprise Parameters**), those encrypted devices cannot accept barge requests when they are participating in an encrypted call. When the call is encrypted, the barge attempt fails.

To use barge, configure the barge-related service parameters in Table A-8 and assign the Barge softkey to the softkey template of the Cisco IP Phone.

With **cBarge**, a barge call gets set up by using the shared conference bridge, if available. The original call gets split and then joined at the conference bridge, which causes a brief media interruption. The call information for all parties is changed to reflect a conference call ("To Conference") with the barge target device as the conference controller. It can add more parties to the conference or can drop any party.

When any party releases from the call, which leaves only two parties in the conference, the remaining two parties experience a brief interruption and then get reconnected as a point-to-point call, which releases the shared conference resource.

The cBarge softkey is available only in the remote-in-use call state. Standard softkey templates do not include the cBarge softkey, so you must add it to a softkey template and then assign the softkey template to a device for the cBarge softkey to be accessible by users.

Table A-8 provides information about the barge service parameters (which also apply to cBarge) (**Service > Service Parameters >** *select a server* **> Cisco CallManager**).

Table A-8 *Barge/cBarge Service Parameters*

Service Parameter	Default	Valid Values
Party Entrance Tone Determines whether a tone plays when a party joins or exits a call with more than two parties. The following features play a tone based on this parameter: barge, cBarge, conference, join, and Meet-Me conference. Only those device types that have a built-in bridge, such as the Cisco IP Phones 7960, 7970, and so on, can play a tone to all parties. When the controlling device is no longer present in the call or lacks the capability, the tone does not play to all parties even if this parameter is set to True.	True	True or False
Privacy Determines whether the Privacy feature is enabled for phones that use the Default value in the Privacy setting on the Phone Configuration page in CallManager Administration. Privacy removes the call information from all phones that share lines and blocks other shared lines from barging in on its calls.	True	True or False

Broadcast Paging Support (with Third-Party Integration)

Broadcast paging support is achieved through configuration of one or more Foreign Exchange Station (FXS) gateway ports configured within CallManager with specific directory numbers on each port. A third-party product attached to the FXS ports automatically answers the calls and distributes the audio to broadcast speakers.

In addition, several third-party applications se the Cisco IP Phone Services XML API to instruct the IP phones to go off-hook on their speakerphone and tune into an IP Multicast stream to receive the page. Check with your Cisco representative for more information on these third-party partners or visit the Cisco site on Hot Dispatch at the following link:

http://www.hotdispatch.com/cisco-ip-telephony

Bulk Administration Tool (BAT)

The Bulk Administration Tool (BAT), a web-based application, can be used to perform bulk add, update, and delete operations on the CallManager database (**Application > Install Plugins**). For large systems, BAT significantly reduces the manual labor involved in creating or maintaining the CallManager database.

BAT provides the following features:

- Support for users, user device profiles, managers/assistants, most Cisco IP Phones and some third-party phone models, speed dials, lines, phone services, forced authorization codes, client matter codes, CAPF configuration, resetting or restarting phones, Cisco VG200 gateways, FXS ports on Cisco Catalyst 6000 gateways, Cisco VGC phones, H.323 clients, and combinations such as adding phones and users all at once.

- An export utility that enables you to export phone, user, and user device profile records to a comma-separated values (CSV) file. You can then reinsert the file onto another CallManager database.

- Support for the Tool for Auto-Registered Phone Support (TAPS). See the section "Tool for Auto-Registered Phone Support (TAPS)" for more information, and refer to Chapter 6 and Appendix B, "Cisco Integrated Solutions," for more information about BAT.

Call Admission Control (CAC)

Voice quality can begin to degrade when there are too many active calls on a link and the amount of bandwidth is oversubscribed. Call admission control (CAC) regulates voice quality by limiting the number of calls that can be active on a particular link at the same time.

CallManager supports two types of call admission control:

- **Locations-based**—Use locations to implement CAC in a centralized call processing environment, where phones at remote locations register to a centralized CallManager or CallManager cluster.

- **H.323 gatekeeper-based**—Use the Cisco IOS H.323 gatekeeper, also known as a Cisco Multimedia Conference Manager (MCM), to provide CAC in a distributed call processing environment where a separate CallManager or CallManager cluster exists at each site.

For an in-depth discussion of CAC, refer to the Cisco CallManager Solution Reference Network Design (SRND) or the Cisco IP Video Telephony SRND, available at the following link or search Cisco.com for "SRND":

http://www.cisco.com/go/srnd

Call Back

Users can press the **CallBack** softkey when they dial an OnNet number that is either busy or unanswered, and then be notified when that party is available. The call back feature monitors the status of the line, and presents an audible and visual notification to the calling user when the destination line becomes available.

Call back works across QSIG-enabled intercluster trunks and QSIG trunks to other PBXs and is available on Cisco IP Phones that support softkeys.

You enable call back through the use of mappable softkeys. The default softkey template does not include the CallBack softkey. Mappable softkeys allow you to enable the CallBack softkey for a particular phone or group of phones.

Table A-9 provides information about call back service parameters provided in the Cisco Extended Functions service (**Service > Service Parameters >** *select a server* **> Cisco Extended Functions**).

Table A-9 *Call Back Service Parameters*

Service Parameter	Default	Valid Values
Call Back Enabled Flag Enables the CallManager call back feature. Set this parameter to False if you are using an external call back feature. Restart the Cisco CallManager service for the parameter change to take effect.	True	True or False
Call Back Notification Audio File Name Specifies the name of the audio file that Cisco IP Phones play when a called party that has been marked for call back becomes available. The default file contains a "twinkle" sound. This file must be located in the directory C:\Program Files\Cisco\TFTPPath. Audio Format: 64-kbps audio μ-law.	CallBack.raw	Up to 255 characters

continues

Table A-9 *Call Back Service Parameters (Continued)*

Service Parameter	Default	Valid Values
Connection Proposal Type Determines the connection type proposed in the call back request. For example, Herb calls Greta, but Greta doesn't answer. Herb presses the **CallBack** softkey to set a watch on Greta's phone. On behalf of Herb's phone, the call back feature makes a signaling-only call (no media) to Greta's phone; instead of the signaling-only call being answered by Greta's phone, it is answered by the call back feature. In this signaling-only call, the call back feature at Herb's phone monitors Greta's phone to determine when Greta is available. In this signaling-only call from Herb to Greta, you can either keep the signaling-only call up so that the same call can be used by Greta to tell Herb that Greta is available, or release the signaling-only call and Greta's phone will make a new signaling-only call to Herb's phone when Greta is available. When the signaling-only call is not released or is retained, the procedure is called *connection retention*; otherwise, it is *connection release*. In this example, when the call back feature for Herb's phone started the signaling-only call, it uses the value specified in this parameter to propose to Greta's phone the type of connection to be used for the signaling-only call. This parameter works in conjunction with the Connection Response Type parameter.	Connection Retention	**Connection Release**—Causes the release of the call independent signaling connection as soon as a feature instance is initiated and the establishment of further call independent signaling connections for subsequent phases of the service **Connection Retention**—Provides for the use of a single call independent signaling connection throughout the lifetime of a particular instance of the feature **No Preference**—Provides the ability to not specify a preference to the terminating end
Connection Response Type Specifies the connection response type if the originating side of the call back does not specify a value for the retain-sig-connection element (Connection Response Type). Using the example from the Connection Proposal Type parameter description in the preceding row of this table, when Greta's phone receives the proposed connection type from Herb's phone, Greta's phone uses either the value proposed by Herb's phone (the one specified in the Connection Proposal Type parameter) or the value specified in this parameter to determine which connection type will be used.	Default to Connection Retention	Default to Connection Retention Default to Connection Release

Table A-9 *Call Back Service Parameters (Continued)*

Service Parameter	Default	Valid Values
Call Back Request Protection T1 Timer Specifies a timer that is started when a QSIG call back feature is invoked, and stopped on receipt of a response from the far end. This parameter provides for feature termination/failure in the event the far end does not respond to the request.	10 seconds	10 to 30 seconds
Call Back Recall T3 Timer Specifies a timer that is started when Herb (continuing with the example from the Connection Proposal Type description) is notified that Greta is now available. If Herb does not invoke the call back feature during this period, the call back feature is cancelled. However, Herb still sees on the display the notification that Greta had become available and Herb can still use the **Dial** softkey to attempt to reach her.	20 seconds	10 to 30 seconds
Call Back Calling Search Space Specifies a calling search space that will be used only by the call back feature in connection-release mode from the Terminating feature.	N/A	Choose from calling search spaces configured in the system

Call Connection

CallManager provides phone-to-phone call connection.

Call Coverage

CallManager provides several call coverage mechanisms. Which method you use depends on the specific usage scenario you are trying to achieve, and which release of CallManager you are using. You can use these features in combinations for maximum flexibility.

First, CallManager provides integrated support for Call Forward on Busy (CFB) and No Answer (CFNA) status. You can configure different destinations for CFB and CFNA depending on whether the call is OnNet (internal) or OffNet (external). See the "Call Forwarding" section for more details.

Second, CallManager provides two integrated hunt group features for distributing calls to hunt group members:

- **Cisco Telephony Call Dispatcher (TCD)**—Predominantly used with Cisco CallManager Attendant Console

- **Native CallManager hunt groups**—Configured natively within CallManager Administration for simpler hunt group scenarios in which an Attendant Console is not used

Third, CallManager release 4.1(2) introduces enhancements to the two features just described, which, when combined, allow you to configure advanced call coverage paths as described in the following section.

Finally, Cisco also offers rich call distribution/call queuing solutions in the Cisco IP Integrated Call Distributor (IP ICD), the Cisco IP Contact Center Express (IPCC Express), and Cisco IP Contact Center Enterprise (IPCC).

Per-User Enhanced Call Coverage Paths

NOTE   This feature was introduced in CallManager release 4.1(2).

CallManager supports the capability to forward out of a hunt pilot after all hunt list members have been exhausted or the Maximum Hunt Timer is reached (**Route Plan > Route/Hunt > Hunt Pilot**). By setting the Call Forward Busy/No Answer destinations on the user's directory number (line) to a hunt group pilot number configured in CallManager Administration, you can have inbound calls to that DN hunt through a coverage path. If no user in the coverage path answers the call, the call can be forwarded back to the original called user's voice mailbox. The directory number Call Forward settings are enhanced in release 4.1(2) to specify different targets for internal or external calls. This feature can also be combined with Time of Day Routing for even greater customization and flexibility.

Call Detail Records (CDR) and Call Management Records (CMR)

CDRs provide billing information about calls. CMRs provide diagnostic information about calls. You can learn more about these features in Chapter 7, "Call Detail Records."

When CDR/CMR collection is enabled, CallManager writes CDRs and CMRs to flat files on the hard drive of the Subscriber server as calls are made. The records are periodically passed from the Subscriber server to the Publisher, and the Cisco CDR Insert service inserts the records into the Publisher's centralized SQL database.

You can use the optional plug-in application, CDR Analysis and Reporting (CAR), provided in CallManager Serviceability (**Tools > CDR Analysis and Reporting**) to analyze CDRs and CMRs. See the section "CDR Analysis and Reporting Tool" for more information.

Enterprise and service parameters pertaining to CDRs and CMRs are discussed in Chapter 7.

Call Forwarding

Calls placed to a phone that has a call forwarding designation are forwarded to the specified number. Calls can be forwarded on the following conditions:

■ **Call forward all (CFA)**—You or the user designate a number to which all calls should be forwarded.

■ **Call forward busy (CFB)**—You designate a number to which calls should be forwarded when the line is busy.

■ **Call forward no answer (CFNA)**—You designate a number to which calls should be forwarded when the phone is not answered.

■ **Call forward on failure (CFF)**—Used only for CTI applications and ports; you designate a number to which calls should be forwarded when there is an error with the destination device.

■ **Call forward no coverage (CFNC)**—You designate a number to which calls should be forwarded when no endpoint in the hunt list accepts the forwarded call.

Call forwarding is administered differently based on phone model. For example, for Cisco IP Phones 12SP+, 30VIP, or 7910, the feature is called Forward All; for all other Cisco IP Phones, the feature is called CFwdAll. Also, using JTAPI, you can execute the **Forward All** command in CTI applications. Consult the phone or system documentation for configuration details.

Forward All/CFwdAll

To forward all calls, the user presses the **Forward All** button or **CFwdAll** softkey, hears two tones, and then dials the number (internal, or external if permitted) to which the user wants all calls forwarded. If the dialed number is valid, two confirmation tones are heard. To disable call forwarding, the user presses the **Forward All** button or **CFwdAll** softkey again, hears two tones, and the forwarding request is cancelled. For phones that offer a CFwdAll softkey, the display shows the number to which all calls are being forwarded. The user can also configure this feature in the Cisco CallManager User Options web page (see "Cisco CallManager User Options Web Page" later in this appendix). The CFwdAll softkey is automatically available. When a user sets the call forwarding all directive, the user's permission level (that is, class of restriction) to forward all his or her calls is based on the Call Forward All Calling Search Space configured on the line.

Table A-10 provides information about call forwarding service parameters (**Service > Service Parameters >** *select a server* **> Cisco CallManager**). Table A-11 describes the enterprise parameter that applies to call forwarding. You can access enterprise parameters on the Enterprise Parameters Configuration page (**System > Enterprise Parameters**).

Table A-10 *Forward All/CFwdAll Service Parameters*

Service Parameter	Default	Valid Values
Forward Maximum Hop Count Specifies the maximum number of times that a single internal or QSIG call can be diverted. Both internal and QSIG call diversions are counted equivalently. CallManager terminates the call if the number of hops specified in this parameter is exceeded and the final destination is not available (for example, busy or not registered). CallManager allows the call to ring until the T301 Timer expires if the number of hops specified in this parameter is exceeded and the final destination is available but not answering.	12	1 to 15
Forward No Answer Timer Determines how long, in seconds, the call will ring to the destination before being forwarded to the CFNA destination, if specified. This value must be less than the value specified in the T301 Timer parameter; if it is not, the call does not get forwarded and the caller receives a busy signal.	12	1 to 300 seconds
Max Forward Hops to DN Specifies the maximum number of forwards that are allowed for a directory number (DN) at the same time. For example, a call to DN 1000, which is forwarded to DN 2000, can only traverse this forwarding loop (from 1000 to 2000 then back to 1000 to start the loop over again) the number of times specified in this parameter. Use this count to stop forward loops for all external calls, for example, intercluster IP phones and IP phone to PSTN where phones are forwarded to each other. CallManager terminates the call when the value specified in this parameter is exceeded.	12	1 to 60; if 1 or 2 is entered, it will be forced to 3

Table A-10   *Forward All/CFwdAll Service Parameters (Continued)*

Service Parameter	Default	Valid Values
Retain Forward Information Determines whether forwarding information displays to the called party after the party goes off-hook. For example Phone A calls Phone B, which has call forward all set to Phone C. The call immediately gets forwarded to Phone C. While Phone C is ringing, its display shows forward information such as "Forward A by B." If this parameter is set to False, when Phone C answers, the forward information is replaced by connect information (for example, "From A"). If this parameter is set to True, after Phone C answers, the forward information remains on the Phone C's display and is not replaced by the connected information.	False	True or False
Forward By Reroute Enabled Enables the QSIG forward by reroute feature, which strives to reduce the number of B-channels in use between intercluster calls or calls to/from a PBX. For example, three co-workers, Chris, Tara, and Hakim, all have phones on different CallManager clusters connected via QSIG trunks. Chris, on a CallManager cluster in Boulder, calls Tara whose phone is on a CallManager cluster in Hawaii. Tara's phone is forwarded to co-worker Hakim, who is on a CallManager cluster in Chicago. This scenario results in two B-channels is use: one from Chris to Tara, and another from Tara to Hakim. With forwarding by rerouting, the CallManager in Hawaii issues a request to connect Chris and Hakim directly, thereby eliminating one of the B-channels.	False	True or False
Transform Forward by Reroute Destination Determines whether the called number transformations are applied to the call forward destination and sent as the called address in the call reroute application protocol data unit (APDU). This parameter applies to QSIG calls that use the call diversion by reroute feature. If you choose False, all call forward destinations should contain numeric characters only; non-numeric characters in call forward destinations may result in call reroute failures for diverted calls.	True	True or False

continues

Table A-10 *Forward All/CFwdAll Service Parameters (Continued)*

Service Parameter	Default	Valid Values
Always Forward Switch Voice Mail Calls Determines whether a QSIG call being forwarded to voice mail is diverted using forward switching or call rerouting. Forward switching joins an incoming QSIG call with a new call to the diverted-to user. Call rerouting requires the originating CallManager or PBX to invoke a new call to the diverted-to user.	True	**True**— QSIG calls will divert to voice mail using forward switching **False**—The system defers to the setting specified in the Forward By Reroute Enabled service parameter. When this parameter is set to False and the Forward By Reroute Enabled parameter is set to False, all QSIG calls being forwarded to voice mail will be forward switched
Forward By Reroute T1 Timer Specifies the time that the system on which the forward operation was initiated waits for a call reroute return result message after requesting a reroute to the originating PINX (CallManager/PBX). If a response is not received before this timer expires, forwarding by rerouting does not occur. If this timer expires and no rerouting occurs, CallManager attempts to forward-switch the call.	10 seconds	10 to 30 seconds
Include Original Called Info for Q.SIG Call Diversions Determines when to include the original called name and original called number in the DivertingLeg2Information application protocol data unit (APDU) or CallReRoute.inv APDU for QSIG call diversions.	Only after the first diversion	**Only after the first diversion**—Only encode the original called name and original called number when the diversion counter is greater than 1. The first time the call is diverted, the original called information is the same as the diverting party information, and therefore the original called information is omitted **Always**—Always encode the original called name and original called number in the DivertingLeg2Information APDU. Even though it's the first time the call is diverted, encode the original called name and original called number in the DivertingLeg2Information or CallReRoute.inv APDU

Table A-11 *Forwarding Enterprise Parameter*

Enterprise Parameter	Default	Valid Value
Show Call Forwarding Determines whether users have the option to set call forwarding directives via the Cisco CallManager User Options web page (CCMUser).	True	True or False

Call Forward Busy

Call forward busy forwards calls only when the line is busy. This feature is available for all Cisco IP Phones and can only be configured by the system administrator. You can configure call forward busy in the Directory Number Configuration page in CallManager Administration (**Device > Phone >** *select phone > select line*). You can specify different forwarding destinations based on whether the call is internal (OnNet) or external (OffNet).

Per-Line Configurable Call Forward Busy Trigger

NOTE   This feature was introduced in CallManager release 4.0(1).

CallManager supports up to 200 calls per line appearance. When configuring the line, you can set the maximum calls allowed on the line and the call forward busy trigger. The busy trigger dictates when CallManager begins forwarding calls to the call forward busy destination. The busy trigger allows you to leave some number of calls available for outbound calls on the line. For example, you set the maximum number of calls to 10, and the busy trigger to 5. This configuration allows 5 inbound calls to that line; additional inbound calls roll to the call forward busy target, but the user can still place outbound calls on the line (up to 10 in this case).

Call Forward No Answer

Call forward no answer (CFNA) forwards calls when the phone is not answered. This feature is available for all Cisco IP Phones and can only be configured by the system administrator.

The default length of time before an unanswered call rolls over to the designated directory number is 12 seconds. You can change the time clusterwide by configuring the Forward No Answer Timer service parameter (see Table A-10), or on a per-line basis by specifying a duration in the No Answer Ring Duration field on the Directory Number Configuration page in CallManager Administration (**Device > Phone >** *select phone > select line*). You configure the call forward no answer number in the Directory Number Configuration page, where you can specify different forwarding destinations based on whether the call is internal (OnNet) or external (OffNet).

Call Forward on Failure (CFF)

Call forward on failure applies only to CTI route points and CTI ports, and specifies the forwarding treatment for calls to a CTI route point or CTI port if the CTI route point or CTI port has no coverage. If a CTI device is unregistered, CallManager uses the CFNA destination to forward the call. Call forward on failure is only used if a CTI application is registered and has an active call, but then the CTI application fails. When the CTI application fails, the call is transferred to the call forward on failure destination. This feature is automatically available and can be configured in the Forward On Failure Ext/Int field on the Directory Number Configuration page in CallManager Administration (**Device > Phone >** *select a port > select line*).

Call Forward No Coverage (CFNC)

Call forward no coverage is used in conjunction with call coverage. You can configure hunt pilots to divert calls by enabling the Use Personal Preferences check box on the Hunt Pilot Configuration page (**Route Plan > Route/Hunt > Hunt Pilot**). Checking this box sends the call to the CFNC destination for the device that originally sent the call to the hunt pilot. Calls are diverted to the number specified in the directory number's Coverage/Destination field when a call to the directory number first diverts to coverage, and coverage either exhausts or times out, and the associated hunt pilot for coverage specifies Use Personal Preferences for its final forwarding.

Configure this feature in the Forward No Coverage fields (Internal and External) on the Directory Number Configuration page in CallManager Administration (**Device > Phone >** *select a port >* *select a line*).

Call Forward Reason Codes

CallManager provides reason codes that describe whether the call forwarded unconditionally, because of no response, or because of a busy subscriber to the voice mail system. The following interfaces are supported:

- SCCP

- Cisco Messaging Interface (by simplified message desk interface [SMDI])

- ISDN

- QSIG

- SIP

- CTI devices (Telephony Application Programming Interface (TAPI)/Java TAPI (JTAPI))

- H.323

Call Forwarding Support for Third-Party Applications

Using JTAPI, you can execute the **Forward All** command in third-party applications.

Call Forward Number Expansion to Voice Mail

This feature allows the internal extension of the phone to be different (shorter, longer, or different digits) from the DN of that user's voice mailbox. This is configured through the use of a Voice Mail Box Mask in the Voice Mail Profile of the device.

Call Park

Call park allows a user to store a call on a specific directory number so that the call can be retrieved from any other phone on the system. You configure park in CallManager Administration and users can implement it on any Cisco IP Phone on the system. Figure A-1 illustrates the call park operation.

Figure A-1 *Call Park Operation*

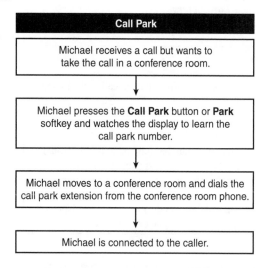

Configuring Call Park

To use call park, one or more directory numbers must be configured in CallManager Administration as call park numbers (**Feature > Call Park**). You can define either a single directory number or a range of directory numbers for use as call park extensions. Only one call at a time can be parked on each call park extension.

Call park, if configured, is available to the user during an active call on all Cisco IP Phones. For Cisco IP Phones 12SP+, 30VIP, or 7910, you must configure one **Call Park** button on the button template used by those phones. For all other Cisco IP Phones with a display, the Park softkey is automatically available. To use the feature, the user simply presses the **Call Park** button or **Park** softkey during an active call. The display indicates that the call is parked at the specified extension, and the call park reversion timer begins. The user has the length of time specified in the Call Park Reversion Timer service parameter to retrieve the call from any phone on the CallManager system that has access to the directory number to which the call is parked. To retrieve the call, the user goes off-hook and dials the extension at which the call was parked. The user is then connected to the parked party. If the call is not retrieved within the specified time, the call is automatically returned to the phone from which it was parked, and placed on hold.

You can configure up to 100 call park numbers at a time (for example, 35xx), or individually configure specific call park extensions (3500, 3501, and so on). The call park numbers must be unique; they cannot overlap between CallManager servers. Ensure that each CallManager server has its own call park number range. Table A-12 provides information about the call park service parameters, which can be set in the Service Parameters Configuration page in CallManager Administration (**Service > Service Parameters** > *select a server* > **Cisco CallManager**).

Table A-12 *Call Park Service Parameters*

Service Parameter	Default	Valid Values
Call Park Reversion Timer The number of seconds to wait before returning a parked call to the phone from which the call was parked.	60 seconds	30 to 1000 seconds
Call Park Display Timer The number of seconds that the call park number (and other notifications) display on the IP Phone. Specify a value that is less than or equal to the value that is specified for the Call Park Reversion Timer service parameter; if the value is not less, the call park display will be overwritten after the call park reversion time expires. A value of 0 causes the message to be displayed until it is overwritten by another message of equal or higher priority.	10 seconds	0 to 100 seconds

Call Pickup/Group Call Pickup (PickUp/GPickUp)

Call pickup and group call pickup enable users to answer a call that comes in on a directory number other than their own. When an incoming call rings on another nearby phone (within earshot), users can redirect the call to their phone by pressing the **PickUp** softkey or dialing the appropriate group number and then pressing the **GPickUp** softkey.

Call pickup/group call pickup is available for all Cisco IP Phones. On Cisco IP Phones 12SP+, 30VIP, and 7910, the buttons are called Call Pickup and Group Call Pickup and must be configured on the button template. For all other Cisco IP Phones, the softkeys are called PickUp and GPickUp and are automatically available.

For call pickup or group call pickup to be operational, you must configure the call pickup group in the Call Pickup Configuration page in CallManager Administration (**Feature > Call Pickup**). The call pickup group is composed of directory numbers. Only directory numbers that have a call pickup group designated in their line properties can use the call pickup feature. The appropriate call pickup group number must be configured in the Directory Number Configuration page in CallManager Administration (**Device > Phone >** *find and select phone > click line number*) for each directory number that should be able to use the call pickup feature. For users of one call pickup group to retrieve calls destined for members of another call pickup group, they must know the group number. After you have configured multiple call pickup groups, you should advise users of the call pickup group directory numbers.

To use call pickup/group call pickup, the user goes off-hook and presses the **Call Pickup** or **Group Call Pickup** button or **PickUp** or **GPickUp** softkey when the user hears an incoming call ringing on another phone. This causes the ringing call to be redirected to the user's phone. Figure A-2 illustrates the call pickup operation.

Figure A-2   *Call Pickup Operation*

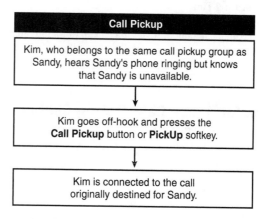

Figure A-3 illustrates the call pickup operation.

Figure A-3   *Group Call Pickup Operation*

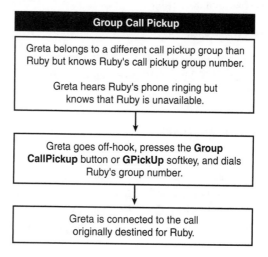

Table A-13 provides information about the call pickup service parameters (**Service > Service Parameters >** *select a server* **> Cisco CallManager**).

Table A-13 *Call Pickup Service Parameters*

Service Parameter	Default	Valid Values
Auto Call Pickup Enabled Determines whether the auto-pickup feature is enabled.	False	True or False
Call Pickup Locating Timer Specifies the maximum amount of time for a pickup to wait in order to get all alerting calls in the pickup groups from all of the nodes in the cluster.	1 second	1 to 5 seconds

Call Preservation for Active Calls During CallManager Server Outage

Call preservation ensures that active calls will not be interrupted if CallManager nodes fail or when communication between a device and its CallManager node fails. Calls are preserved even during failure if both parties are connected through one of the following devices:

■ Cisco IP Phones

■ Software conference bridge (Cisco IP Voice Media Streaming App service)

■ Software media termination point (Cisco IP Voice Media Streaming App service)

■ Hardware conference bridge

■ Hardware transcoding resources

■ Media Gateway Control Protocol (MGCP) gateways, including Cisco Catalyst 6000, Cisco Digital Access DT-24+ or DE-30+, and Cisco Analog Access gateways

■ Cisco IOS MGCP gateways

■ CTI devices (TAPI/JTAPI)

Active calls are maintained until the user hangs up or the devices can determine that the media connection has been released. When a CallManager node fails or communication fails between a device and the CallManager node that controls it, the call processing function for any calls that were set up through it is lost. Cisco IP Phones with an LCD display will display a text message stating that the CallManager server to which the phone was registered has gone down, and that all supplementary features for that call have been disabled. As soon as the active call disconnects, the phone automatically registers with the secondary or tertiary CallManager node and features are re-enabled for all subsequent calls.

Note that calls for H.323 devices are not preserved due to the connection-oriented nature of H.323 signaling.

Call Status per Line

All Cisco IP Phones that have a display provide basic call status on a per-line basis. The display indicates the connected state, the number, and a timer showing the call duration.

Call Waiting/Retrieve

When a call is received on the secondary line of the directory number currently in use, a tone sounds and the display shows the call information for the waiting call. The user can retrieve the new incoming call by disconnecting or placing the current call on hold. All Cisco IP Phones provide call waiting on each line, if enabled. Each single line appearance can accommodate up to 200 calls (see the "Line" section later in this appendix for more information). Call waiting service parameters were removed in CallManager release 4.0.

You or end users can configure the type of notification for incoming calls (audible and visual). See the sections "Audible Indicator of Ringing Phone" and "Visual Indicator of Ringing Phone" for more information.

Calling Line Identification (CLID or Caller ID)

Calling line identification (CLID or caller ID) provides the phone number of the calling party, either for inbound calls to IP phones from external locations or for outbound calls from IP phones and other devices to external locations. You can manipulate the CLID through the use of transformations on route patterns, route lists, and translation patterns, or through the use of the Calling Line ID Presentation field on the Gateway Configuration page (**Device > Gateway**) or Trunk Configuration page (**Device > Trunk**), and the External Phone Number Mask field on the Directory Number Configuration page (**Device > Phone >** *find and select a phone > click a line*) in CallManager Administration. You can set the number or text to display when the caller ID is not present in the call. The default text is "Unknown".

Table A-14 provides information about caller ID service parameters (**Service > Service Parameters >** *select a server* **> Cisco CallManager**).

Table A-14 *Caller ID Service Parameters*

Service Parameter	Default	Valid Values
Caller ID Provides a mask that formats the caller ID number for outbound calls. For example, if you set this service parameter to 214555XXXX and the directory number of the calling party is 1234, CallManager sends the string 2145551234 as the Caller ID field for outbound calls from that directory number. You can also use this parameter if you want all outbound calls to receive the same calling party number, such as a main phone number for the enterprise (2145551000). The value that is configured in this parameter applies to all calls on all gateways. **NOTE** You can achieve greater flexibility by configuring a calling party transformation on a route pattern or route list.	No default value	Up to 24 digits 0 through 9 (including the X wildcard)
Unknown Caller ID Provides the directory number to be displayed to called parties for inbound calls that have no caller ID information. This can be any numeric value representing a general number for your enterpise (if you want to provide caller ID functionality to called parties). For the number specified here to display to called parties, set the Unknown Caller ID Flag parameter to True.	No default value	Any valid telephone number, up to 82 digits
Unknown Caller ID Flag This parameter enables the Unknown Caller ID and Unknown Caller ID Text parameters. If this parameter is set to True, the information that is provided in the Unknown Caller ID and Unknown Caller ID Text parameters displays to called parties for inbound calls that are received without caller ID information. Cisco strongly recommends that you use the default setting.	True	True or False

Table A-14 *Caller ID Service Parameters*

Service Parameter	Default	Valid Values
Unknown Caller ID Text The text to be displayed to called parties for inbound calls that have no caller ID information; for example, Unknown Caller. For the text that is specified in this parameter to display to called parties, set the Unknown Caller ID Flag parameter to True.	No default value	Up to 23 characters. The first line allows 20 characters, and the second line allows up to 14 characters. The system breaks the text across lines based on a preconfigured algorithm that takes into account kerning and placement of spaces. To ensure the text looks good when broken across lines, use shorter words and frequent spaces between words. Newer Cisco IP Phones models such as the 7971 and 7970 do not wrap text, so this is no longer a consideration

Calling Line ID Restriction (CLIR) on a Per-Call Basis

CallManager allows you to set CLIR on or off on a per-call basis. You can create prefix patterns on gateways that allow users to enable CLIR on a call-by-call basis. This feature is required by law in some states in the United States, and allows users to place calls without fear of the called party learning the number from which the call was placed.

For example, you configure a prefix of *67 to restrict calling line ID. Users can then dial *67 followed by the number, and phones with caller ID capability will not transmit the originating number. Note that the calling line ID (CLID) is still present in the Q.931 signaling information fields, and is also recorded in any related CDRs for that call. The feature simply sets the Presentation bit to disabled, which instructs the receiving switch to not present the caller ID to the destination device.

Per-call CLIR is available on MGCP-controlled T1/E1 PRI trunks, as well as SIP trunks and H.323 gateways. See the "Media Gateway Control Protocol (MGCP) Support" section for more information.

Calling Party Name Identification (CNID)

CallManager provides the caller's name instead of or in addition to the number to the party receiving the call. See the "Calling Line Identification (CLID or Caller ID)" section for more information.

CNID over Q.931 Facility Information Element

CallManager supports caller identification by using Q.931 Facility Information Element (IE) for all incoming and outgoing calls on non-QSIG PRI trunks.

Calling Party Display Restriction

> **NOTE**   This feature was introduced in CallManager release 4.1(2).

CallManager allows you to choose the information that displays for calling and/or connected lines, depending on the parties involved in the call. By using translation patterns with calling and connected party restrictions configured, call display information can be presented or restricted for each call. To override this, the Phone Configuration page in CallManager Administration provides an Ignore Presentation Indicators (internal calls only) check box that, when set, ignores presentation settings of the remote party for internal calls. This feature is useful in locations such as hotel rooms, where the hotel operator wants to be able to see the CLID and CNID of the caller; but when the operator transfers the call to another hotel room guest, the CLID and CNID of the calling and called parties should be restricted so that the guests cannot see each others' information.

For incoming calls from an OffNet trunk, the system respects the received presentation indicators even if the check box is checked. The Ignore Presentation Indicators check box is also available on user device profiles and device default profiles so that the setting can be preserved or changed when the user logs in or out of Extension Mobility.

CAPF Report Generation

You can generate a Certificate Authority Proxy Function (CAPF) report (**Device > Device Settings > CAPF Report**) to view the certificate operation status, to view the authentication strings, or to view the authentication mode for listed devices. After you generate the CAPF report, you can view the report in a CSV file.

The Cisco Certificate Authority Proxy Function service provides several service parameters relating to CAPF configuration (**Service > Service Parameters >** *select a server* **> Cisco Certificate Authority Proxy Function**), as described in Table A-15.

Table A-15 *CAPF Service Parameters*

Service Parameter	Default	Valid Values
Certificate Issuer Determines the entity that issues the certificate to a phone. For changes to this parameter to take effect, you must run the Cisco CTL Client plug-in and restart the Cisco CallManager and Cisco TFTP services. Running the plug-in updates the certificates at C:\Program Files\Cisco\Certificates\Trustlist with the issuer certificate to all the nodes in the cluster.	Cisco Certificate Authority Proxy Function	Cisco Certificate Authority Proxy Function Microsoft Certificate Authority KEON Certificate Authority
Duration Of Certificate Validity Specifies the number of years a certificate issued by Cisco Certificate Authority Proxy Function remains valid. Restart the Cisco Certificate Authority Proxy Function Service for this parameter to take effect.	15 years	1 to 20 years
Key Size Specifies the key size that Cisco CAPF should use to generate its private and public keys. Restart the Cisco Certificate Authority Proxy Function service for this parameter to take effect.	1024 bits	512 bits 1024 bits 2048 bits
Maximum Allowable Time For Key Generation Specifies the length of time that Cisco Certificate Authority Proxy Function (CAPF) will wait for a phone to generate public and private keys. The connection between CAPF and the phone terminates when this timer expires. Restart the Cisco Certificate Authority Proxy Function service for this parameter to take effect.	30 minutes	10 to 60 minutes
Maximum Allowable Attempts for Key Generation Specifies the number of attempts that a phone can make to generate its public and private keys. Cisco CAPF will wait for the duration specified in the Maximum Allowable Time For Key Generation parameter for each attempt that the phone makes. By default, CAPF will wait for three sets of up to 30 minutes for the phone to generate keys. Restart the Cisco Certificate Authority Proxy Function service for this parameter to take effect.	3	3 to 10

continues

Table A-15 *CAPF Service Parameters (Continued)*

Service Parameter	Default	Valid Values
KEON Jurisdiction ID Specifies the KEON jurisdiction ID. This parameter is only used when the Certificate Issuer parameter specifies KEON Certificate Authority. Restart the Cisco Certificate Authority Proxy Function service for this parameter to take effect.	No default value	Up to 50 characters
SCEP Port Number Specifies the Simple Certificate Enrollment Protocol (SCEP) port number of the Certificate Authority server. Restart the Cisco Certificate Authority Proxy Function service for this parameter to take effect.	446	1 to 55556
Certificate Authority Address Specifies the IP address of the Certificate Authority server, which is the primary CallManager node. Restart the Cisco Certificate Authority Proxy Function service for this parameter to take effect.	No default value	Up to 255 characters

CDR Analysis and Reporting (CAR) Tool (formerly Administrative Reporting Tool)

The CDR Analysis and Reporting (CAR) tool, formerly known as Administrative Reporting Tool (ART), is a web-based application that provides reports to help simplify departmental billing, create reports based on CDRs and CMRs, and quality of service (QoS) and traffic monitoring, among other features. Refer to Chapter 6 for detailed information about CAR.

Centralized System Administration, Monitoring, and Reporting

CallManager Administration, a web-based application, provides centralized databases that can be accessed by CallManager nodes. CallManager cluster configuration is stored in a collection of multiple databases. One database is designated as the Publisher (master) database. All other databases in the cluster are designated as Subscriber databases. All CallManager nodes communicate to the database through an abstraction layer called the Database Layer. When you work in CallManager Administration, you are making changes to the configuration of the system. Those changes are immediately posted to the Publisher database. Replication services automatically synchronize the changes to the Subscriber databases. This design allows for improved system redundancy and enhances overall system availability. CallManager

Administration is essentially a collection of web pages that are connected through a web server with access to the Publisher database.

See the following related sections:

- Cisco CallManager Serviceability

- Bulk Administration Tool

- Syslog Support for Debugging Output

- Device Pool

- Device Search Filtering Criteria for Finding/Listing Devices in Large Environments

- External Route Plan Wizard

- HTTPD Server

- Performance Monitoring and Alarms

- Quality Reporting Tool (QRT)

- Call Detail Records (CDR) and Call Management Records (CMR)

- System Event Reporting

- Zero Cost Automated Phone Moves

- Zero Cost Automated Phone Adds

Cisco ATA-186 2-Port Analog Gateway Support

Cisco ATA-186 is a low-density, two-port FXS gateway running SCCP firmware. The ATA-186 is also available in MGCP, H.323, and SIP modes, although in these modes they do not benefit from all of the features that SCCP provides.

Cisco Bulk Trace Analysis

Cisco Bulk Trace Analysis tool, which is used for post-processing of large SDI/SDL trace files in XML format, provides parsing and filtering. Download, install, and operate the Bulk Trace Analysis tool on a client PC (not a CallManager server). Access the installation file from the Install Plugins page in CallManager Administration (**Application > Install Plugins**).

Cisco CallManager Administration Enhancements for Large System Administration

CallManager and BAT allow you to locate devices in a large system by finding and listing phones, gateways, and other devices using filtering criteria. Figure A-4 shows the results of a search for all phones in the system starting with "SEP."

Figure A-4 *Phone Search Results in CallManager Administration*

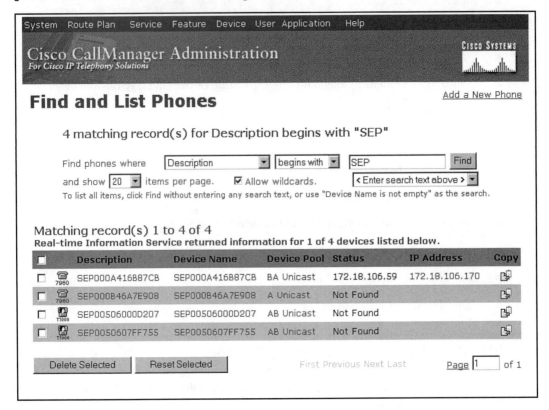

You can also control the number of items that display in list boxes, which directly affects how fast some pages display in CallManager Administration.

Table A-16 provides information about enterprise parameters relating to CallManager Administration (**System > Enterprise Parameters**).

Table A-16 *CallManager Administration Enterprise Parameters*

Enterprise Parameter	Default	Valid Values
Max List Box Items The maximum number of items that display in a list box in the pages in CallManager Administration and BAT (for example, partition, calling search space, and voice mail profile). For any value above the number that is specified in this parameter, only the default (such as None) and the currently selected items appear in the list box, and a lookup (…) button appears to the right of the list box. See Figure A-5 for an example of the lookup button. Click the lookup button to find and choose the desired item. Increasing the value above the default sends more items directly to the browser but results in slower page loads in a large system. Decreasing the value sends fewer items directly to the browser and results in faster page load for a large system. You need to close and reopen the browser for the change to take effect.	250	50 to 9999 items
Max Lookup Items This parameter specifies the maximum number of items that will be sent to the browser when doing a lookup (click the […] button) for a data entry field (list box). Using a higher value sends more items directly to the lookup browser window (results in slower page load but faster searching). Using a lower value sends fewer items directly to the lookup browser window (results in faster page load but slower search). You need to close and reopen the browser for the change to take effect.	1000	250 to 99999 items

Figure A-5 shows the Phone Configuration page with a lookup button on the fields Calling Search Space and AAR Calling Search Space.

Figure A-5 *Lookup (...) Button in CallManager Administration*

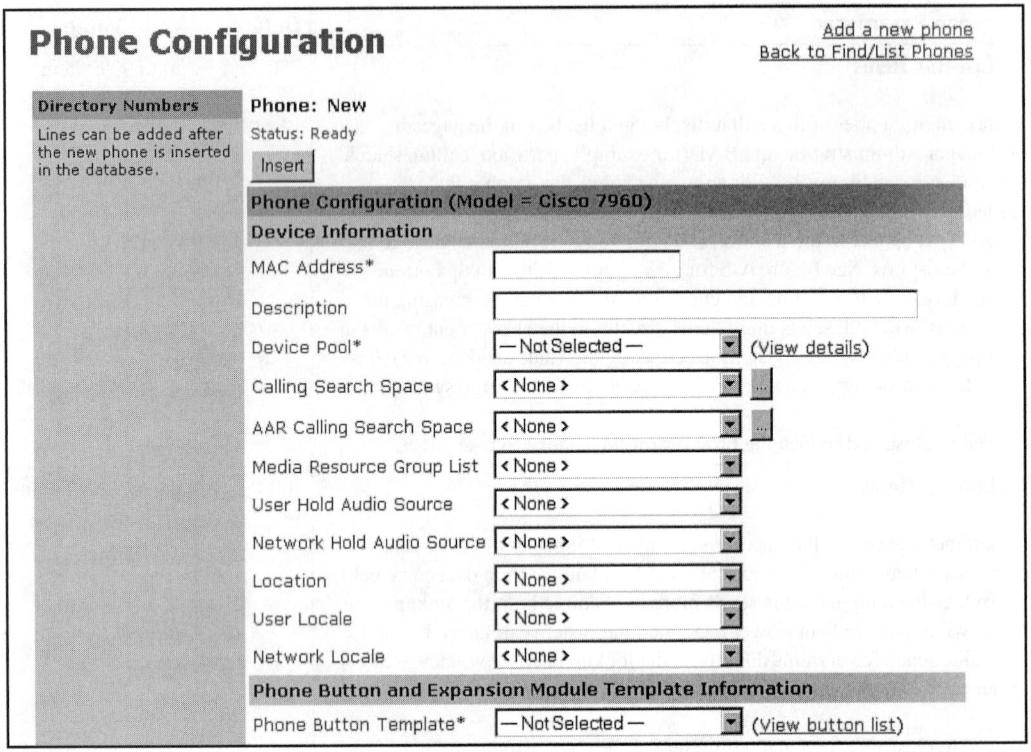

Cisco CallManager Attendant Console (Formerly Cisco WebAttendant)

> **NOTE** Cisco CallManager Attendant Console replaces the Cisco WebAttendant application. Attendant Console retains all of the features of Cisco WebAttendant plus introduces many new enhancements. Attendant Console is compatible with CallManager release 3.1(2c) and later. Support for Cisco WebAttendant was removed in CallManager release 3.3.

Cisco CallManager Attendant Console allows one or more live attendants to answer and handle inbound and outbound calls that are not serviced by Direct Inward Dial (DID), Direct Outward Dial (DOD), or automated attendant functions. Attendant Console is a client/server application consisting of Attendant Console, the client application used by the live attendant (receptionist), and Telephony Call Dispatcher (TcdSrv), the server application that extends telephony services to

Attendant Console clients and performs the hunt group routing function. Line state server (LSS) monitors line and device status in the cluster and is one of the functions of the Telephony Call Dispatcher.

Attendant Console provides the following features:

- Busy or available indication

- Call status (date, duration, number)

- Drag-and-drop transfer

- Call queuing

- Multiple call distribution algorithms

- Advanced directory search

- Accessibility support for visually impaired users

- Localization to all languages for which CallManager provides user locales

See Appendix B for more information about Cisco CallManager Attendant Console.

Table A-17 provides information about the Attendant Console service parameter that is configurable in the Cisco CallManager service (**Service > Service Parameters >** *select a server >* **Cisco CallManager**).

Table A-18 provides information about Attendant Console service parameters, which are configurable in the Cisco Telephony Call Dispatcher service (**Service > Service Parameters >** *select a server >* **Cisco Telephony Call Dispatcher**).

Table A-17 *Attendant Console-Related CallManager Service Parameter*

Service Parameter	Default	Valid Value
Line State Update Enabled Specifies whether the Line State Server can track the active/inactive states of each directory number. Restart the Cisco CallManager service or reregister the directory number for the parameter change to take effect.	True	True or False

Table A-18 *Cisco Telephony Call Dispatcher Service Parameters*

Service Parameter	Default	Valid Values
Allow Routing with Unknown Line State Determines whether calls get routed to a line in the hunt group even if the state of the line is unknown. Sometimes line states are not available for some devices; setting this parameter to True allows calls to be routed to devices with unknown line states. Set this parameter to True if you configure hunt groups that contain devices that do not have line states, such as FXO ports connected to analog voice mail ports.	False	True or False
Cisco CallManager Line State Port Designates the port number of the TCP/IP port in CallManager that is used by the line state server to register and receive line and device information.	3223	1024 to 65535 Cisco recommends that the default value be used; however, any port can be used as long as it has been properly configured on all clients and servers
Cisco Telephony Call Dispatcher Server Listening Port Specifies the UDP port that Attendant Console clients use to register with the Telephony Call Dispatcher server (TcdSrv) for call control. Keep this parameter set to the default value unless a Cisco support engineer instructs otherwise.	4321	1024 to 65535
CTI Request Timeout Specifies the time that Attendant Console will wait for the CTIManager to respond to a Redirect request. If a response is not received within the specified time, Attendant Console drops the call. **NOTE** ■ CTIManager must be up and running. ■ Restart the Cisco Telephony Call Dispatcher service for the parameter change to take effect.	15 seconds	15 to 60 seconds

Table A-18 *Cisco Telephony Call Dispatcher Service Parameters (Continued)*

Service Parameter	Default	Valid Values
Directory Sync Period Specifies the interval between synchronization of the Attendant Console server (TcdSrv) UserList with the CallManager DC Directory (any LDAP directory integrated with CallManager; for example, Active Directory). User information such as new users, deleted users, or modified user information does not get synchronized between TcdSrv and CallManager DC Directory until the time specified in this timer has elapsed, which triggers synchronization. A value of 0 disables directory synchronization.	3 hours	0 to 720 hours
Keep Original Called Party If Forwarded Determines whether the directory number of the original called party gets reset to the redirected number if the call is forwarded to the pilot point.	True	True or False
LSS Access Password Specifies the password that the line state server uses for authentication at registration time. The default is "private".	private	Any range of up to 7 alphanumeric characters. Cisco recommends you do not change the default value
LSS Listening Port Designates the UDP port that Attendant Console clients use to register with the Attendant Console server (TcdSrv) for line and device state information.	3224	1024 to 65535 Cisco recommends that the default value be used; however, any port can be used as long as it has been properly configured on all clients
Redirect With Directing Party CSS Specifies whether the redirecting party's (that is, the pilot point) calling search space (CSS) is used when the Attendant Console server (TcdSrv) redirects the call to its agent.	True	True or False
Reset Original Called Party on Redirect Determines whether to reset the directory number of the original called party during redirect to the redirected number. The Keep Original Called Party If Forwarded parameter can override the value that is specified in this parameter if the call was forwarded to the pilot point.	True	True or False

Cisco CallManager Serviceability

CallManager Serviceability, a web-based application, provides management and monitoring tools for the CallManager system, including the following:

- Detailed alarm definitions and configuration

- Trace configuration, analysis, and collection

- Control center and service activation, which provides start/stop and activate/deactivate services in the CallManager system

- QRT Viewer, which, if configured, enables you to view log files for IP phone problems reported by IP phone users

- Serviceability Reports Archive, which, if configured, provides auto-generated alert, call activity, and statistics reports

- Component version information (click **Help > Component Versions**) to see version numbers for the various components in the system on a server-basis

- Access to install the Real-Time Monitoring Tool, which monitors the performance of IP Telephony components in a CallManager cluster

CallManager Serviceability is available from CallManager Administration (**Application > Cisco CallManager Serviceability**). Chapter 6 provides detailed information about CallManager Serviceability.

Cisco CallManager Trace Collection Tool

The Trace Collection Tool collects traces for a CallManager cluster into a single .zip file. The collection includes all traces for CallManager and logs such as Event Viewer (Application, System, Security), Dr. Watson log, Cisco Update, Prog Logs, RIS DC logs, SQL and IIS logs. You can learn more about the Trace Collection Tool in Chapter 6.

Cisco CallManager User Options Web Page

The Cisco CallManager User Options (CCMUser) web page allows users to program various functions on their IP Phones, such as setting speed dial buttons (if applicable), changing their PIN (for extension mobility), changing their password, configuring IP phone services (if applicable), setting message waiting indicator and call forwarding directives, and more.

Table A-19 describes enterprise parameters (**System > Enterprise Parameters**) that control which options are provided on the CCMUser web page. Changes to these parameters take effect during the next login to the CCMUser web page. Only those options that are valid for each phone type can be displayed in CCMUser when these parameters are enabled. For example, a phone that does not support speed dial will not display speed dial settings even if the Show Speed Dial Settings parameter is enabled.

Table A-19 *Cisco CallManager User Options (CCMUser) Enterprise Parameters*

Enterprise Parameter	Default	Valid Values
Show Ring Settings Determines whether the option to change the ring settings on a phone appears on the CCMUser web page.	False	True or False
Show Call Forwarding Determines whether the option to set call forwarding on a phone appears on the CCMUser web page.	True	True or False
Show Speed Dial Settings Determines whether the option to add or update speed dial settings on a phone appears on the CCMUser web page.	True	True or False
Show Cisco IP Phone Services Settings Determines whether the option to view and change IP Phone XML services on a phone appears on the CCMUser web page.	True	True or False
Show Personal Address Book Settings Determines whether users can view and change Personal Address Book settings on the CCMUser web page.	True	True or False
Show Message Waiting Lamp Policy Settings Determines whether the option to view and change the message waiting lamp policy on a phone appears on the CCMUser web page.	True	True or False
Show Line Text Label Settings Determines whether the option to configure line text label for a phone appears on the CCMUser web page. If the user's current device has line(s) configured, the user can view and change the line text label for each line on that phone unless the line is the primary line.	False	True or False
Show Locale for Phone Settings Determines whether the option to change the locale for this phone appears on the CCMUser web page.	True	True or False

continues

Table A-19 *Cisco CallManager User Options (CCMUser) Enterprise Parameters (Continued)*

Enterprise Parameter	Default	Valid Values
Show Locale for Web Pages Settings Determines whether the option to change the locale for web pages appears on the CCMUser web page. If this parameter is enabled, users can view and change the user locale setting for extension mobility and the CCMUser web page.	True	True or False
Show Change Password Option Determines whether the option to change the password for a user appears on the CCMUser web page.	True	True or False
Show Change PIN Option Determines whether the option to change the PIN for a user appears on the CCMUser web page.	True	True or False
Show Download Plugin Option Determines whether the option to download and install plug-ins for a user appears on the CCMUser web page.	True	True or False
Show Online Guide Option Determines whether the option to display the online phone guide appears on the CCMUser web page.	True	True or False
Enable All User Search Determines whether to allow a search for all users (search with no last name/first name/directory number specified) when searching for users via the Corporate Directory from the phone. This parameter also applies to the directory search in CallManager Administration.	True	True or False
User Search Limit Specifies the maximum number of users to be retrieved from a search in the Corporate Directory feature on the phone. This parameter also applies to the directory search in CallManager Administration. Search does not apply when the Enable All User Search enterprise parameter is set to False and no criteria are set for the search.	64	1 to 500

The Cisco CallManager User Options web page, available in multiple languages, is password-protected and uses LDAP for password authentication. See Appendix B for more information about the Cisco CallManager User Options web page.

Cisco Conference Connection (CCC) Support

CallManager integrates with Cisco Conference Connection, which is a Meet-Me audio conferencing solution. Conferences are scheduled from an intuitive web-based conference-scheduling interface. Conference participants call in to a central number, enter a meeting identification number (and optionally a password), and are then placed into the conference. At the discretion of the conference organizer, conference participants using Cisco IP Phones 7940, 7941, 7960, 7961, 7970, and 7971 can join meetings at the touch of a button via the Cisco Conference Connection XML service.

Learn more about other conferencing options in Appendix B.

Cisco CTL Client

The CTL Client plug-in retrieves the CTL file from the Cisco TFTP server. It digitally signs the CTL file by using a security token and then updates the file on the Cisco TFTP server.

The Cisco CTL Provider service provides one service parameter relating to CTL configuration (**Service > Service Parameters >** *select a server* **> Cisco CTL Provider**), as described in Table A-20.

Table A-20   *Cisco CTL Provider Service Parameter*

Service Parameter	Default	Valid Values
Port Number Specifies the port number to use for opening a Transport Layer Security (TLS) connection between the Certificate Trust List (CTL) clients and the CTL provider. The CTL clients must connect using the port specified in this parameter.	2444	1027 to 32767

Cisco Discovery Protocol (CDP) Support

Cisco IP Phones 79*xx* utilize CDP upon initialization to negotiate with the upstream switch. This also allows the exact physical location of the phones (that is, to which switch port they are connected) to be auto-discovered by device tracking applications such as CiscoWorks and Cisco Emergency Responder. Phones also use CDP to negotiate power requirements with the switch as well as voice VLAN information.

In addition, CallManager and applications that run on Cisco MCS server platforms also use CDP so that CiscoWorks can auto-discover the servers in the network.

Cisco Emergency Responder (CER) Support

Cisco Emergency Responder is an emergency call routing and reporting solution that dynamically addresses the need to identify the location of 911 callers in the North American numbering plan

(NANP) in an emergency, with no administration required when phones and/or people move from one location to another. CER tracks the location of IP phones in real time through SNMP and CDP mechanisms.

Appendix B provides additional information on CER.

Cisco IP Manager-Assistant

See the "Manager Assistant Services" section later in this appendix for more information about Cisco IP Manager-Assistant.

Cisco IP Phone 7902, 7905, 7912, Expansion Module 7914, Wireless 7920, Conference Station 7936 and 7935, 7940, 7941, 7960, 7961, 7970, and 7971 Support

CallManager supports many different Cisco IP Phones, as covered in greater detail in Chapter 3, "Station Devices." You can also learn more about Cisco's phone product offerings at the following link or search Cisco.com for "Cisco IP Phones":

http://www.cisco.com/en/US/products/hw/phones/ps379/index.html

Table A-21 describes enterprise parameters (**System > Enterprise Parameters**) that specify URLs for Cisco IP Phones.

Table A-21 *Cisco IP Phone URL Enterprise Parameters*

Enterprise Parameter	Default	Valid Values
URL Authentication Specifies the URL that points to a web page that resides in one of the Cisco CallManager Cisco IP Phone (CCMCIP) webs in the cluster. This URL provides an authentication proxy service between Cisco IP Phones 7940, 7941, 7960, 7961, 7970, 7971 and the LDAP directory. This URL gets used to validate requests made directly to the phone. This URL is automatically configured at install time. If the URL is removed, the push capabilities to Cisco IP Phones will be disabled.	No default value	Up to 255 characters in the format of a well-formed URL (for example, http://myserver/myscript.asp) Test the URL in a separate browser window to make sure that it is valid

Table A-21 *Cisco IP Phone URL Enterprise Parameters (Continued)*

Enterprise Parameter	Default	Valid Values
URL Directories Specifies the URL that Cisco IP Phones 7940, 7941, 7960, 7961, 7970, and 7971 use when the **directories** button is pressed. This URL must return a CiscoIPPhoneMenu object even if no MenuItems are specified in the object. The MenuItems that are specified get appended to the directory list along with the three internal directories on the Cisco IP Phones. You can learn more about the CiscoIPPhoneMenu object in Appendix C, "Protocol Details."	No default value	Up to 255 characters in the format of a well-formed URL
URL Idle Specifies the URL that Cisco IP Phones 7940, 7941, 7960, 7961, 7970, and 7971 use to display information on the screen when the phone remains idle for the time that the URL Idle Time parameter specifies.	No default value	Up to 255 characters in the format of a well-formed URL
URL Idle Time Specifies the time that Cisco IP Phones 7940, 7941, 7960, 7961, 7970, and 7971 should remain idle before displaying the URL that the URL Idle parameter specifies. If the time is set to zero, the URL that the URL Idle parameter specifies will not display.	0 seconds (disabled)	0 to 604800 seconds
URL Information Specifies a URL that points to a page in the Cisco CallManager Cisco IP Phone (CCMCIP) webs and returns the requested help text to the display on Cisco IP Phones 7940, 7941, 7960, 7961, 7970, and 7971. This information displays when a user presses the **i** or **?** button on the phone.	No default value	Up to 255 characters in the format of a well-formed URL
URL Messages Specifies a URL that the Cisco IP Phones should load when the **messages** button is pressed. The URL must return a CiscoIPPhoneMenu object when called. The MenuItems that are returned get appended to the built-in items on Cisco IP Phones 7940, 7941, 7960, 7961, 7970, and 7971.	No default value	Up to 255 characters in the format of a well-formed URL

continues

Table A-21 *Cisco IP Phone URL Enterprise Parameters (Continued)*

Enterprise Parameter	Default	Valid Values
IP Phone Proxy Address Specifies a proxy server name or address and port (for example, proxy.cisco.com:8080). If the proxy server is specified, Cisco IP Phones use it to request all URLs. Leave this setting blank for the phones to attempt to connect directly to all URLs. If a name is used instead of an IP address, configure phones with valid DNS servers to allow name-to-IP resolution. Confirm that the proxy server is listening at the destination that is specified.	No default value	Proxy server name or address and port (for example, proxy.cisco.com:8080), up to 255 characters
URL Services Specifies the URL that Cisco IP Phones call when a user presses the **services** button. The initial request by the phone passes the device name as a parameter. The default page in the Cisco CallManager Cisco IP Phone (CCMCIP) web returns a CiscoIPPhoneMenu object with a list of services that are subscribed to the device. If no subscriptions exist, the return text indicates that no subscriptions exist for the device.	No default value	Up to 255 characters in the format of a well-formed URL

Cisco IP Phone Services

An XML application programming interface (API) works in conjunction with XML-capable Cisco IP Phones to offer custom-configured services. XML primitives include the ability to overwrite softkey set definitions, which allows for remapping of the existing functionality and labels to different keys and adding new keys with associated URLs for application control. A mechanism such as an icon is also provided to indicate to the user that an instant message has been received.

Appendix C provides more information about the XML functionality available in the form of an XML Software Development Kit (SDK).

Cisco IP Software-Based Phone Support (IP SoftPhone and IP Communicator)

CallManager provides support for Cisco IP SoftPhone and Cisco IP Communicator, virtual telephones that run on the user's desktop. Using virtual private networks (VPN), users can use any Internet connection while on the road to handle calls on their extensions as if they were in the office. The software-based IP phones have all of the features of a desktop business telephone, including hold, transfer, mute, Ad Hoc and Meet-Me conferencing, redial, caller ID display, voice mail integration, dial pad by keyboard or onscreen, context-sensitive online help, and more.

Cisco IP SoftPhone Support for Microsoft NetMeeting

Cisco IP SoftPhone can launch the following applications for Microsoft NetMeeting if a collaborative PC is configured:

- Application sharing

- Chat

- File transfer

- Video

- White board

Refer to Microsoft documentation for more information about each of these features.

Cisco Personal Address Book

Cisco Personal Address Book is an IP phone application that lets users store and retrieve their personal address book entries from their IP phone. Personal Address Book consists of two IP phone services to which users can subscribe. The PersonalAddressBook service allows users to search and view their address book entries and dial a corresponding directory number from the Cisco IP Phone. The PersonalFastDials service is similar to a speed dial button on the IP phone. When the user selects the service using the **services** button, a list of fast dial entries displays in menu format. The user can select a menu item by entering the index number on the IP phone's keypad. The corresponding directory number is then automatically dialed.

The Cisco IP Phone Address Book Synchronizer plug-in (**Application > Install Plugins**) allows users to synchronize their Microsoft Outlook and Outlook Express address book entries with Cisco Personal Address Book. The Cisco IP Phone Synchronizer performs the synchronization process on the user's desktop.

This feature works with Cisco IP Phones 7905, 7912, 7920, 7940, 7941, 7960, 7961, 7970, and 7971 and requires configuration in CallManager Administration. For users to have access to Personal Address Book, you must first configure the PersonalAddressBook and PersonalFastDials services in CallManager Administration (**Feature > Cisco IP Phone Services**). To allow users access to the Synchronization utility, you must download the plug-in (**Application > Install Plugins**) and post it to a location that users are aware of and can access.

Users can subscribe to Cisco Personal Address Book services on the Cisco CallManager User Options web page. They can also synchronize their contact information there, as well as configure their Personal Address Book.

Cisco VG248 48-Port Analog Gateway Support

The Cisco VG248 Analog Phone Gateway, a high-density, 48-port FXS gateway, enables you to integrate analog telephones, modems, and fax machines with the CallManager system. Because it runs SCCP, the connected POTS phones have traditional telephony features associated with them, which are accessible to the user through configurable feature codes. These features include blind transfer, hold/resume, MWI (stutter dial tone), calling line ID, Ad Hoc conferencing, call waiting, and call park. The VG248 represents an alternative to IP phones for simple POTS phone users who also require extended telephony features.

Using version 1.1(1) or later of the VG248 software, you can integrate legacy voice mail and PBX systems with CallManager using Simplified Message Desk Interface (SMDI) and analog FXS connections on the VG248.

CISCO-CCM-MIB Updates

Simple Network Management Protocol (SNMP) Management Information Base (MIB) tables organize and distribute the information gathered from your company site. Additional objects are routinely added to the CISCO-CCM-MIB tables. You can view the MIBs at the following locations:

http://tools.cisco.com/Support/SNMP/do/BrowseMIB.do?local=en&mibName=CISCO-CCM-MIB

http://www.cisco.com/public/sw-center/netmgmt/cmtk/mibs.shtml

ftp://ftp.cisco.com/pub/mibs/v2/CISCO-CCM-MIB.my

You can learn about MIB tools at the following location:

http://tools.cisco.com/ITDIT/MIBS/servlet/index

See the section "Simple Network Management Protocol (SNMP) Support" for additional information.

Click to Dial/Click to Call

CallManager supports click to dial/call in several forms:

■   Cisco IP Phones that provide directory access via the **directories** button offer one-touch dialing from available directories and call initiation from a list of missed, received, and placed calls. The Dial softkey allows users to dial the displayed directory listing or missed/placed/received call just by pressing the softkey. An EditDial softkey allows the user to modify the displayed number before dialing.

■ The WebDialer application offers click to dial services. See the "Cisco WebDialer Click-to-Dial Service" section for more information.

■ CTI integration via third-party software solutions offers click to dial services. See the "Computer Telephony Integration (CTI) Support" and the "Telephony Application Programming Interface (TAPI) and JTAPI Support" sections for more details.

Cisco WebDialer Click-to-Dial Service

Cisco WebDialer allows Cisco IP Phone users to place calls by clicking a hyperlink in web applications or other desktop applications (for example, click-to-call from within your Microsoft Outlook address book). In CallManager release 3.3(3), WebDialer is downloaded from Cisco.com and installed on your CallManager server. In CallManager release 3.3(4) and later, WebDialer is an integrated service of CallManager that you enable. Integrating with other applications is achieved using the publicly documented API, available at the following link:

http://www.cisco.com/univercd/cc/td/doc/product/voice/c_callmg/3_3/sys_ad/3_3_4/ccmfeat/fswbdlr.htm

The Cisco WebDialer service provides several service parameters relating to WebDialer configuration (**Service > Service Parameters >** *select a server* **> Cisco WebDialer**), as described in Table A-22.

Table A-22 *Cisco WebDialer Service Parameters*

Service Parameter	Default	Valid Values
List of WebDialers Specifies a space-separated list of IP addresses for all WebDialers in the enterprise; for example, one IP address in San Jose, one in Dallas, one in London, and so on. For multiple IP addresses, leave a space between each IP address (for example, 123.45.67.89 123.55.67.90). You need to use this optional parameter only if you are configuring a redirector. Restart the Cisco Tomcat service for the parameter change to take effect.	No default value	Up to 1024 characters Entry should contain a valid IP address (for example, 123.45.67.89). Separate IP addresses by space if specifying more than one WebDialer (for example, 123.45.67.89 123.45.67.90)
Primary Cisco CTIManager Specifies the IP address of the primary CTIManager. Restart the Cisco Tomcat service for the parameter change to take effect.	127.0.0.1	Up to 15 digits in the form of an IP address (for example, 123.45.67.89)

continues

Table A-22 *Cisco WebDialer Service Parameters (Continued)*

Service Parameter	Default	Valid Values
Backup Cisco CTIManager Specifies the IP address of the backup CTIManager. Restart the Cisco Tomcat service for the parameter change to take effect.	No default value	Up to 15 digits in the form of an IP address (for example, 123.45.67.89)
User Session Expiry Specifies the time after which the user session will expire. A value of 0 indicates that the session will never expire. Restart the Cisco Tomcat service for the parameter change to take effect.	0	0 to 168 hours
Duration of End Call Dialog Specifies the duration for which the End Call dialog displays. The End Call dialog allows users to end the call when they made the call in error. Restart the Cisco Tomcat service for the parameter change to take effect.	15 seconds	10 to 60 seconds
Apply Application Dial Rules on Dial Specifies whether application dial rules must be applied when the user presses the Dial button. WebDialer applies dial rules before displaying the Make Call screen. Setting this parameter to True causes WebDialer to apply the dial rules again when the user clicks the Dial button in the Make Call screen.	True	True or False

Learn more about WebDialer in Appendix B.

Client Matter Codes

Client matter codes (CMC) facilitate call accounting and billing for billable clients. The client matter codes feature forces the user to enter a code to identify calls that relate to a specific client.

To use the CMC feature, you enable CMC through route patterns, and then configure CMC (**Feature > Client Matter Code**). When a user dials a number that is routed through a CMC-enabled route pattern, a tone prompts the user to enter the client matter code. When the user enters a valid CMC, the call is routed to the dialed number. The CMC used on the call writes to the CDR so you can collect the information via the CDR Analysis and Reporting (CAR) tool or a third-party CDR application. If the user enters an invalid code, the call is not routed and the user hears reorder tone.

CMC can be used alone or in conjunction with forced authorization codes. See the "Forced Authorization Codes" section for more information.

Codec Support (Audio and Video)

CallManager supports numerous audio and video codec formats and is capable of selecting which codec should be used, on a call-by-call basis, through the use of regions and through the knowledge of what each device's codec capabilities are. See the "Automatic Bandwidth Selection" section for more information.

Tables A-23 and A-24 correlate CallManager releases to the supported codecs. However, in many cases, even though CallManager supports a particular codec, the endpoint device (phone, video terminal, transcoder, conference bridge, application, and so on) might not support it. For this reason, the codec that is chosen for a given call is a combination of the following:

- Which codecs each device participating in the call supports

- Which codecs CallManager supports

- What the region configuration dictates should be used

Table A-23 *Audio Codecs Supported per CallManager Release*

CallManager Release	G.711 A-law/ G.711 μ-law	G.722	G.722.1	G.728	G.729a/G.729b/ G.729ab	Cisco Wideband Audio (16-Bit/ 16 kHz)
3.0(x)	Yes	No	No	No	Yes	No
3.1(x)	Yes	No	No	No	Yes	Yes
3.2(x)	Yes	No	No	No	Yes	Yes
3.3(x)	Yes	No	No	No	Yes	Yes
4.0(x)	Yes	Yes	No	Yes	Yes	Yes
4.1(x)	Yes	Yes	No	Yes	Yes	Yes

Table A-24 *Video Codecs Supported per CallManager Release*

CallManager Release	H.261	H.263	H.264	Cisco Wideband Video
3.0(x)	No	No	No	No
3.1(x)	No	No	No	No
3.2(x)	No	No	No	No
3.3(x)	No	No	No	No
4.0(x)	Yes	Yes	No	Yes
4.1(x)	Yes	Yes	Yes[*]	Yes

[*]H.264 is supported only on SCCP endpoint devices in CallManager release 4.1(2)

Table A-25 describes service parameters (**Service > Service Parameters >** *select a server >* **Cisco CallManager**) that control media-related details.

Table A-25 *Media-Related Service Parameters*

Service Parameter	Default	Valid Values
Media Exchange Interface Capability Timer Specifies the maximum amount of time that CallManager will wait for media connection to be set up between two parties. This timer pertains to media connection that occurs at the device interface level.	8 seconds	0 to 300 seconds
Media Exchange Timer Specifies the maximum amount of time that CallManager will wait for a media connection to be established. If the media connection is not established within the specified time, the user will hear reorder tone. The default value normally provides sufficient leeway; however, for a heavily congested network, you can use a larger value.	12 seconds	0 to 300 seconds
Media Exchange Stop Streaming Timer Specifies the maximum amount of time that CallManager will wait to receive a response to a StopStreaming request. If the response is not received within the specified time, CallManager terminates the call.	8 seconds	3 to 300 seconds
Media Resource Allocation Timer Specifies the maximum amount of time that CallManager will wait for a media resource to be allocated. If a media resource is not allocated within the specified time, CallManager rejects the media resource allocation request. The default value normally provides sufficient leeway; however, for a heavily congested network, you can use a larger value.	12 seconds	0 to 60 seconds

Table A-25 *Media-Related Service Parameters (Continued)*

Service Parameter	Default	Valid Values
*Strip G.729 Annex B (Silence Suppression) from Capabilities Determines whether the system will advertise or negotiate Annex B for G.729 codecs. True means that the system will not advertise or negotiate Annex B for G.729 codecs, unless that is the only matching codec (G.729b or G.729ab). Annex B provides silence suppression. If you are using a device that only advertises G.729b and/or G.729ab, the potential exists for the call to fail due to a capabilities mismatch. If the system can detect the mismatch, it will try to connect the call with Annex B anyway; however, if the call involves an intercluster trunk, this may not be possible and a transcoder may be allocated or the call may fail. As the solution, reconfigure the device to support other capabilities (such as G.729 or G.729a) if possible. Also, remember that this service parameter works independently from the other systemwide parameters Silence Suppression and Silence Suppression for Gateways. Those parameters only determine whether silence suppression is enabled in SCCP and MGCP, but this setting does not affect the capabilities negotiation. Some devices will override the value of this parameter on the basis of the negotiated capability.	False	True or False
Enforce Millisecond Packet Size Determines whether an audio channel is allowed if it does not comply with the advertised millisecond packet size. True means that an audio channel is only allowed when its millisecond packet size is within the setting specified in the "Preferred G.7*xx* Millisecond Packet Size" parameters; False means that an audio channel is always allowed because its millisecond packet size is not being checked or enforced.	True	True or False
Preferred G711 Millisecond Packet Size Specifies the preferred size for delivering G.711 packets. To avoid adding latency, the valid values specify 10, 20, or 30 milliseconds.	20 milliseconds	10, 20, or 30 milliseconds
Preferred G723 Millisecond Packet Size Specifies the preferred size for delivering G.723 packets. To avoid adding latency, the valid values specify 30 or 60 milliseconds.	30 milliseconds	30 or 60 milliseconds

continues

Table A-25 *Media-Related Service Parameters (Continued)*

Service Parameter	Default	Valid Values
Preferred G729 Millisecond Packet Size Specifies the preferred size for delivering G.729 packets. To avoid adding latency, the valid values specify 10, 20, 30, 40, 50, or 60 milliseconds.	20 milliseconds	10, 20, 30, 40, 50, or 60 milliseconds
Preferred GSM EFR Bytes Packet Size Specifies the preferred number of bytes per 20-ms sample for the GSM EFR codec. Regardless of the total sample size, this parameter specifies whether each 20-ms sample will contain 31 bytes or 32 bytes.	31 bytes	31 or 32 bytes per 20-ms sample size

*The Strip G.729 Annex B (Silence Suppression) from Capabilities parameter must be set to the same value on every node in the cluster

Cisco Wideband Audio Codec Support

Cisco wideband audio codec is a Cisco-proprietary encoding method that provides 16-bit/16-kHz sampling. It is supported only on the following devices:

- Cisco IP Phone 7910, 7940, 7941, 7960, 7961, 7970, and 7971

- Cisco IP Voice Media Streaming App service (for Music on Hold)

Cisco Wideband Video Codec Support

Cisco wideband video codec is a Cisco-proprietary encoding method that provides 30 frames per second 320×240 resolution video at 7 Mbps. It is supported only on Cisco VT Advantage. See the "Video Telephony Support" section for more details.

GSM-EFR/FR Support Through Use of Hardware Transcoder

CallManager supports Groupe Speciale Mobile-Enhanced Full Rate/Full Rate (GSM-EFR/FR). Cisco IP Phones do not natively support the GSM-EFR/FR codecs so a hardware transcoder must be used. This feature also allows calls from a GSM phone (in conjunction with a third-party service provider) to a G.729 or G.711 endpoint.

H.261 and H.263 Video Codec Support

CallManager supports H.261 and H.263 codecs (for SCCP and H.323 devices only). See the "Video Telephony Support" section for more details.

H.264 Video Codec Support

> **NOTE** This feature was introduced in CallManager 4.1(2).

This release adds support for H.264 codec (for SCCP devices only). See the "Video Telephony Support" section for more details.

G.728 and G.722 Audio Codec Support

CallManager supports G.728 and G.722 audio codecs typically used by H.323 videoconferencing devices. See the "Video Telephony Support" section for more details.

Closest Match Routing

The closest match routing process routes a call using the route pattern that most closely matches the dialed number. When CallManager encounters a dialed number that matches multiple route patterns, it uses closest match routing to determine which route pattern most closely matches the number and directs the call using that route pattern.

You can learn more about closest match routing in Chapter 2, "Call Routing."

Clustering

A cluster consists of a set of CallManager nodes that share the same database and resources. This allows the load of processing calls and other functions to be distributed across multiple servers to achieve scalability. Each server in the cluster can be configured to perform one or more of the following functions:

- Publisher server

- TFTP server

- Application software server

- Primary call processing node

- Backup call processing node

- Music on Hold server

- Software conferencing server (for Ad Hoc conferences or Meet-Me conferences)

Chapter 1, "Cisco CallManager Architecture," provides more information about clustering, including the maximum number of IP phones per cluster and redundancy schemes.

Computer Telephony Integration (CTI) Support

CallManager provides CTI support through TAPI/JTAPI interfaces. Scalability and redundancy for CTI applications is provided by the CTIManager service, which runs on one or more CallManager nodes in a cluster.

Software Developer Kits (SDK) are provided for application programmers who want to integrate CTI applications into CallManager. See the "Telephony Application Programming Interface (TAPI) and JTAPI Support" section for more information.

Conference/Confrn

> **NOTE**   CallManager provides two types of conferences: Ad Hoc and Meet-Me. Ad Hoc conferences require the conference controller to include attendees to the conference by calling them individually. Meet-Me conferences allow attendees to dial in to the conference after the conference controller has established the conference. Ad Hoc conferences are identified simply by the term *conference*, while Meet-Me conferences are identified by the term *Meet-Me*. This section describes the Conference feature. Meet-Me is covered in this appendix in the section "Meet-Me Conference/MeetMe."

Conference allows a user to establish a conference, call individual attendees, and connect them to that conference. Conference is available for all Cisco IP Phones. On Cisco IP Phones that use buttons rather than softkeys, such as 12SP+, 30VIP, and 7910, the button is called Conference and must be configured on the button template. On Cisco IP Phones that have softkeys, such as 7971 and 7961, the softkey is called Confrn and is automatically available during an active call. The Conference button/Confrn softkey is not used to participate in a conference call, only to initiate one.

To establish a conference, the user, known as a *conference controller*, calls the first conference attendee. When connected to that party, the conference controller presses the **Conference** button or **Confrn** softkey. The called party is placed on hold, and the conference controller hears a dial tone. At the dial tone, the conference controller dials the next conference participant and, after connecting to that party, presses the **Conference/Confrn** button again to connect all three parties and establish the conference. The conference controller can continue to add attendees in this fashion until the maximum number of allowed participants is reached or until there are no more bridge ports available. Conference attendees and the conference controller can depart the conference at any time. As long as there are two conference attendees, the conference will remain in effect, but without the conference controller, no additional attendees can be added. Figure A-6 illustrates the conference operation.

Figure A-6   *Conference Operation (Ad Hoc)*

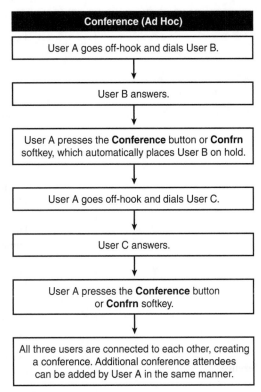

Table A-26 provides information about Ad Hoc conference service parameters (**Service > Service Parameters** > *select a server* > **Cisco CallManager**).

Table A-26   *Conference Service Parameters*

Service Parameter	Default	Valid Values
Suppress MOH to Conference Bridge Determines whether music on hold (MOH) plays to a conference when a conference participant places the conference on hold.	True	True or False

continues

Table A-26 *Conference Service Parameters (Continued)*

Service Parameter	Default	Valid Values
Drop Ad Hoc Conference **NOTE** This service parameter was introduced in CallManager release 3.3(4) and enhanced in release 4.1(2). Determines how an Ad Hoc conference terminates.	Never	**Never**—The conference remains active a) after the conference controller hangs, and b) after all OnNet parties hang up. Be aware that choosing this option means that if OnNet parties conference in OffNet parties and then disconnect, the conference stays active between the OffNet parties, which could result in potential toll fraud **When Conference Controller Leaves**—Terminate the conference when the conference controller hangs up or when the conference controller transfers, redirects, or parks the conference call and the retrieving party hangs up **When No OnNet Parties Remain in Conference**—Terminate the conference when there are no OnNet parties remaining in the conference
Maximum Ad Hoc Conference Specifies the maximum number of participants that are allowed in a single Ad Hoc conference. The value you specify in this field depends on the capabilities of the software/hardware conference bridge. The maximum number of conference bridge participants for typical conference bridges follow: Software Conference 64; Cisco Catalyst WS-X6608: 16; Cisco Catalyst 4000: 16; PVDM2-based IOS gateways: 8; and NM-HDV: 6. Setting this value above the maximum capacity of the conference will result in failed entrance to a conference bridge if you try to add more ports than the specific conference bridge configuration allows. Caution: CTI applications and the Drop Any Party feature (accessed via the ConfList softkey) do not support more than 16 participants. Although an Ad Hoc conference can support more than 16 participants, the participant list used by CTI applications and the Drop Any Party feature will display only the 16 most recent conference participants.	4	3 to 64

Table A-26 *Conference Service Parameters (Continued)*

Service Parameter	Default	Valid Values
Maximum MeetMe Conference Unicast Specifies the maximum number of participants that are allowed in a single Unicast Meet-Me conference. The value you specify in this field depends on the capabilities of the software/hardware conference bridge; for example, a software conference bridge conferences up to 128 participants. When a conference is created, the system automatically reserves a minimum of 3 streams, so specifying a value less than 3 allows a maximum of 3 participants.	4	1 to 128

You can learn more about the Ad Hoc conference feature in Chapter 5.

Drop Last Conference Party

The conference controller can remove the last party added to any Ad Hoc conference by pressing the **RmLstC** softkey.

List Conference Participants

Conference participants can view the list of conference participants by pressing the **ConfList** softkey. The conference controller can remove participants from the conference by scrolling to the participant's name and pressing the **Remove** softkey.

Drop Conference When Initiator Leaves

You can configure Ad Hoc conferences to terminate when the conference controller departs the conference by choosing the When Conference Controller Leaves value of the Drop Ad Hoc Conference service parameter described in Table A-26. The conference will also terminate when the controller transfers, redirects, or parks the conference call and the retrieving party hangs up.

Drop Conference When No OnNet Parties Remain

> **NOTE** This feature was introduced in CallManager release 4.1(2).

You can configure Ad Hoc conferences to terminate when only OffNet parties remain in the conference by using the When No OnNet Parties Remain in the Conference value of the Drop Ad Hoc Conference service parameter described in Table A-26. Choosing this value protects against the potential toll fraud case of OnNet parties conferencing in OffNet parties and then disconnecting, allowing the OffNet parties to continue the conversation at the enterprise's expense.

Release Conference Bridge When Only Two Parties Remain

CallManager terminates Ad Hoc conferences when only two conference participants remain in the conference. The call dynamically returns to being a point-to-point call, releasing the conference bridge resource.

Context-Sensitive Help

CallManager Administration provides context-sensitive help on all web pages.

Cisco IP Phones that have an **i** or **?** button provide help for phone features. Help displays on the screen. You can use the **i** or **?** button in three ways:

- Press the **i** or **?** button and then any other key about which you would like information.

- With a feature selected, press the **i** or **?** button twice in quick succession to display help for that feature. For example, press the **settings** button. A menu displays several options. If you press the **i** or **?** button twice quickly, the help for the selected option displays.

- Press the **i** or **?** button twice in quick succession during an active call to view network statistics about the call.

Contrast/LCD Contrast

The contrast feature in the **settings** menu on Cisco IP Phones allows the user to adjust the contrast of the display panel on the phone.

CTI Redundancy with CTIManager

The CTI API supports redundancy.

Because CTIManager is a separate service from CallManager, applications can connect to a single CTI to obtain access to resources and functionality of all CallManager nodes in the cluster. CTI provides recovery of failure conditions resulting from a failed CallManager node within a cluster that includes CallManager and the CTIManager service. Recovery and survivability are available for the following:

- CTI port/route point

- Cisco IP Phones

- CTIManager

- Applications

Date/Time Zone Display Format Configurable per Phone

Devices belong to a device pool that designates the appropriate date format and time zone. All Cisco IP Phones display the date and time according to their designated device pool.

Dependency Records

Dependency records show you which records in the CallManager database are dependent on other records in the database. For example, you can determine which devices (such as CTI route points or phones) use a particular calling search space or which device belongs to a specific device pool.

If you need to delete a device pool from CallManager, you can use dependency records to show which devices use that device pool and then reassign the affected devices to a new device pool. You must remove all dependent devices before deleting the device pool.

The capability to generate and display dependency records is controlled by an enterprise parameter, Enable Dependency Records (**System > Enterprise Parameters**). Close and reopen the web browser for the parameter change to take effect.

> **NOTE**   Displaying dependency records leads to high CPU usage and takes some time because it executes in a low-priority thread. If you monitor CPU usage, you might see high CPU usage alarms. To avoid possible performance issues, display dependency records only during off-peak hours or during the next maintenance window.

Device Type-Based Information and Resets

You can view and update load information, device pool, and phone template information for all devices in the system, grouped by device type. You can also reset all devices of the same type in the Device Defaults Configuration page in CallManager Administration (**System > Device Defaults**).

Device Downloadable Feature Upgrade

You can upgrade firmware by downloading a new version on device initialization. You can download upgrades for the following devices:

- Cisco IP Phones and IP conference phones

- Transcoder resources

- Conference bridge resources

- Cisco Catalyst 6000, Cisco Analog Access, and Cisco Digital Access gateways

Device Pool

Device pools (**System > Device Pool**) reduce administration time for a large system by allowing you to specify criteria that are common among many devices. The following criteria are specified in a device pool:

- Cisco CallManager group

- Date/time group

- Region

- Softkey template

- SRST reference

- Calling search space for auto-registration (optional)

- Media resource group list (optional)

- Network hold music on hold audio source (optional)

- User hold music on hold audio source (optional)

- Network locale (optional)

- User locale (optional)

- Connection monitor duration (optional)

- MLPP indication

- MLPP preemption

- MLPP domain (optional)

Device Search in CallManager Administration

CallManager Administration provides a device search by name, description, calling search space, device type, and more to make locating a specific device in a large system simpler. A complete list of all devices is also available by clicking the **Find** button without specifying any search criteria. See Figure A-4 for an example of a device search.

Device Wizard

CallManager Administration provides a Device Wizard (**Device > Add a New Device**) that makes adding individual new devices to CallManager a simple process. You can add single instances of devices such as the following using the Device Wizard:

■ CTI route point

■ Gatekeeper

■ Gateway

■ Phone

■ Cisco voice mail port

■ Trunk

Use BAT to add multiple devices at one time. See the section "Bulk Administration Tool (BAT)" for more information.

DHCP IP Assignment for Phones and Gateways

Cisco IP Phones, gateways, and media resources support the use of Dynamic Host Configuration Protocol (DHCP) for IP address assignment. In addition, the use of the Site Specific Option 150 allows the DHCP server to inform these devices of the address of the TFTP server they should use to retrieve their configuration file(s). See the "Trivial File Transfer Protocol (TFTP) Support" section for more information.

Dial Plan Partitions and Calling Search Spaces

Partitions and calling search spaces are an extremely powerful but complex pair of mechanisms by which you can customize dialing restrictions for individual users. Partitions and calling search spaces allow you to administer such policies as routing by geographic location, routing for multiple tenants, and routing by security level of the calling user. You can learn more about partitions and calling search spaces in Chapter 2.

Dialed Number Analyzer (DNA)

The Dialed Number Analyzer tool (DNA), an installable plug-in for CallManager, runs as a service on the server and it allows you to test a CallManager dial plan configuration prior to deploying it or to analyze dial plans after the dial plan is deployed. You can use the results to diagnose a dial plan, to identify potential problems, and to tune a dial plan.

Dialed Number Translation Table (Inbound and Outbound Translation)

CallManager can translate dialed or received digits.

Dialed Number Identification Service (DNIS) and RDNIS

CallManager supports receiving and passing the called party number/dialed number.

Redirected Number Identification Service (RDNIS)

Collectively, RDNIS support displays the last redirected number as well as the originally dialed number to and from configured devices and applications.

Outbound RDNIS to H.323 Gateways

CallManager supports passing the redirected number (RDNIS) to Cisco IOS H.323 gateways.

Digit Analysis (Calling Party Number and Called Party Number)

CallManager can analyze and process dialed or received digits for any call—both external or internal, inbound or outbound—on any route pattern, route group, gateway trunk, or translation pattern.

Digital Signal Processor (DSP) Resource Management

CallManager provides support for DSP devices. When a resource allocation for a device is required (that is, if a call needs a transcoder or initiates or joins a conference), CallManager checks to see whether the number of parties has exceeded the allowed limit. If not, CallManager allows the new party to join the conference if the DSP still has streaming capability. An error message is returned if the DSP is out of streams.

Direct Inward Dial

Direct Inward Dial (DID/DDI) allows a caller outside a company to call an internal extension directly, without the assistance of an operator or attendant.

Direct Outward Dial

Direct Outward Dial (DOD) allows a user to call an external phone number directly, without the assistance of an operator or attendant. Usually an access digit, such as 9, is dialed first to indicate an external call, followed by the external phone number. DOD is supported on all gateway trunk types.

Direct Transfer (DirTrfr)

The direct call transfer feature (DirTrfr softkey) directly transfers two parties on a user's line to each other without including the user. Prior to CallManager release 4.0(1), a user had to use either consultative transfer or blind transfer. Direct transfer works in conjunction with the multiple calls per line feature in which a user can make and/or receive multiple calls on a single line, and then directly transfer them together via the DirTrfr softkey. This action connects the two parties together while simultaneously dropping the party who performed the transfer.

The Block OffNet to OffNet Transfer service parameter discussed in Table A-48 applies to the direct transfer feature.

Directories Button on Cisco IP Phones

The **directories** button on Cisco IP Phones provides access to the following features as well as other administrator-configured directories:

- Missed Calls

- Received Calls

- Placed Calls

- Corporate Directory

The Corporate (Global) Directory is integrated with CallManager through CallManager Administration (**User > Global Directory**).

Missed Calls

Missed Calls displays a list of calls that have been received by the phone but not answered. Selecting a call from the list and pressing the **Dial** softkey automatically speed dials the telephone number of the missed call.

Received Calls

Received Calls displays a list of calls that have been answered by the phone. Selecting a call from the list and pressing the **Dial** softkey automatically speed dials the telephone number of the received call.

Placed Calls

Placed Calls displays a list of calls that have been made from the phone. Selecting a call from the list and pressing the **Dial** softkey automatically speed dials the telephone number of the previously placed call.

Corporate Directory

Corporate Directory provides a search feature for users based on first name, last name, or number. You can enter letters or numbers using the dial pad, and then press the **Search** softkey to return a list of users most closely matching the criteria you entered. You can then select a user in the list and press the **Dial** softkey to call that person. User information is pulled from your currently configured Lightweight Directory Access Protocol (LDAP) directory.

Directory Dial from Cisco IP Phones

Using the **directories** button, users can speed dial the number of a missed, placed, or received call on a Cisco IP Phone. See the section "Directories Button on Cisco IP Phones" for more information.

Distinctive Ring: Internal Versus External

All Cisco IP Phones provide a distinction in the ringer behavior for internal and external calls. Internal calls generate one ring, while external calls generate two rings with a very short pause between the rings. You can enable/disable this feature on a per-device basis via the Call Classification field on the Gateway Configuration page in CallManager Administration or systemwide via the Call Classification service parameter (**Service > Service Parameters** > *select a server* > **Cisco CallManager**).

Distinctive Ring Selection

Cisco IP Phone 79*xx* models provide multiple different ringer sounds, allowing the user to choose a preferred ring or to differentiate the phone from a neighboring user's ringer sound. Distinctive rings can be configured on a per-line basis for those phone models that support multiple line appearances. You can modify or limit the number of the available rings via the ringlist.xml file that is retrieved by the phone via TFTP during boot up. Users can choose their ringer sound by pressing **settings > Ring Type** on the phone.

Distributed CallManager Server Architecture

Multiple redundant CallManager servers can exist across one or more locations to create a distributed environment. You can learn more about this feature in Chapter 1.

Distributed and Topologically Aware Resource Sharing

CallManager provides a Media Resource Manager (MRM) that is responsible for maintaining a list of available and in-use resources. When a resource (for example, for a conference bridge, transcoder, MOH source) is required for a call, the MRM can allocate resources across the cluster as needed to complete various feature requests. These resources can be pooled using media resource groups (MRG) and media resource group lists (MRGL). You can then dictate which

MRGL a phone, gateway, or CTI device uses by defining the MRGL in the device pool or at the individual device level. Chapter 5 provides complete information about resource management.

Dual-Tone Multi-Frequency (DTMF) Support

> **NOTE**   SIP inband support was introduced in CallManager release 4.1(2).

All DTMF signals are treated as out of band, and digits can be passed in either direction to/from any device type. The following list shows the DTMF support for each device type:

- **SCCP**—Out of band

- **MGCP 0.1**—Out of band

- **TAPI/JTAPI**—Out of band

- **H.323**—H.245 alphanumeric out of band

- **SIP**—RFC 2833 inband

To interwork between SIP and the other protocols, CallManager inserts a media termination point (MTP) for all SIP calls. The MTP interprets the inband RFC2833 DTMF payloads used by the SIP endpoint and converts them to SCCP out-of-band messages to CallManager. CallManager then converts them to whatever protocol is used by the other endpoint (SCCP, MGCP, or TAPI/JTAPI). Conversely, CallManager interprets the out-of-band DTMF messages sent by SCCP, MGCP, and TAPI/JTAPI endpoints and sends them to the MTP via SCCP. The MTP then converts them to RFC 2833 inband payloads to the SIP endpoint.

Embedded Directory for User Data

CallManager servers provide an LDAP directory for user information.

Emergency 911 Service (E911) Support

CallManager and supporting components provide a complete E911 solution. CallManager provides a sophisticated and flexible solution for E911 call routing and reporting. Its partitioned dial plan allows multiple distributed sites to share a common dial pattern for emergency services (such as 911 in the United States) while allowing the calls to that pattern to be routed out through local site gateways. Call back information and information required by local E911 agents to resolve phone location in the event of an emergency services call is delivered through PRI ISDN trunks or Centralized Automatic Message Accounting (CAMA) trunks. The CAMA solution is achieved through a Cisco IOS-based FXS gateway and a third-party product that translates calling line ID information on the FXS ports to CAMA signaling. You can learn more about routing emergency numbers in Chapter 2.

EndCall

The EndCall softkey on Cisco IP Phones allows the user to disconnect a call with the touch of a softkey, which proves particularly useful when using a headset. The softkey is automatically available, and there are no configuration requirements.

Extension Mobility

Extension mobility allows a user to log in to any IP phone causing it to appear as that user's phone temporarily. By logging in to an IP phone, the user can temporarily convert the phone to adopt his or her line numbers, speed dials, services, and other user-specific properties of an IP phone. This feature is particularly useful in situations where users are not permanently assigned physical phones.

In the past, only system administrators could change phone settings using CallManager Administration. With extension mobility, users can achieve the same effect by way of a user login service on the phone. This service provides an interface by which applications can log users in and out. The login service enforces a variety of policies, including duration limits on phone configuration and authorization to log in to a particular phone. The login service is programmable so that system administrators or third parties can replace some of its components. For example, capabilities such as authenticating by smart card readers or automating the login process according to a desk-sharing web application could be added to the standard login service provided in CallManager. The Cisco Extension Mobility service is installed separately from CallManager, and can be co-resident (on the same server) with CallManager or on a standalone server for additional scalability in large clusters.

> **NOTE**   Phones that have a specific owner identified in the Owner User ID field on the Phone Configuration page in CallManager Administration cannot be used in conjunction with extension mobility. You need to remove the owner user ID before you configure the phone for extension mobility.

The Cisco Extension Mobility service provides several service parameters relating to extension mobility configuration (**Service > Service Parameters >** *select a server* **> Cisco Extension Mobility**), as described in Table A-27.

Table A-27   *Extension Mobility Service Parameters*

Service Parameter	Default	Valid Values
Enforce Maximum Login Time Determines whether the value specified in the Maximum Login Time parameter is enforced.	False	True or False

Table A-27 *Extension Mobility Service Parameters (Continued)*

Service Parameter	Default	Valid Values
Maximum Login Time Specifies the maximum time that a user is allowed to be logged in to a device, such as 8 hours (in the format 8:00) or 30 minutes (n the format :30). CallManager ignores this parameter if the Enforce Maximum Login Time parameter is set to False.	8 hours (8:00)	Up to 7 digits in the form hours:minutes
Maximum Concurrent Requests Specifies the maximum number of login or logout operations which can occur simultaneously. This maximum prevents the Extension Mobility service from consuming excessive system resources.	3	1 to 100
Multiple Login Behavior Specifies the behavior for multiple attempted logins by the same user on different devices.	Multiple Logins Not Allowed	**Multiple Logins Allowed**—The same user ID can be logged in to extension mobility on more than one device **Multiple Logins Not Allowed**—A user ID can only be logged into one device **Auto Logout**—If a user ID is logged into extension mobility on one device, and the same user ID attempts to login to extension mobility on a different device, the first device automatically logs out
Alphanumeric User ID Specifies whether the user ID to be used is alphanumeric or numeric. Restart the Cisco Tomcat service for the parameter change to take effect.	True	**True**—User ID is alphanumeric **False**—User ID is numeric
Remember the Last User Logged In Specifies whether the user ID of the last user logged in on a phone is remembered by the extension mobility application. The default value, False, provides greater security. Restart the Cisco Tomcat Service for the parameter change to take effect.	False	True or False

External Route Plan Wizard

CallManager Administration provides an External Route Plan Wizard that you can use to create a basic route plan for geographically dispersed locations. The wizard uses gateway device settings in CallManager Administration and information you provide, making adding route plans to CallManager a simpler process. You can learn more about this feature in Chapter 2.

External/Internal Trunk Designation

> **NOTE**   This feature was introduced in CallManager release 4.1(2).

The Call Classification field on the Gateway Configuration page for all gateway trunks enables you to designate whether the trunk should be treated as an internal connection (for example, a trunk to another internal PBX) or as an external connection (for example, a trunk to a central office switch). This designation then affects several aspects of calls to/from the trunk, such as distinctive ring tones, call detail records, and call transfer restrictions.

Failover

See the section "Redundancy/Failover" later in this appendix for information about failover.

FAX/Modem over IP Support

CallManager supports three methods to transmit fax traffic across the IP network and two methods to transmit modem traffic:

- Cisco Fax Relay

- Fax Pass-Through

- T.38 Fax-Relay

- Modem Pass-Through

- Cisco Modem-Relay

Cisco Fax Relay mode is the preferred method to transmit fax traffic. However, if a specific gateway does not support Cisco Fax Relay, the gateway supports Fax Pass-Through.

Cisco Fax Relay

Cisco Fax Relay does not involve CallManager; it is a gateway-controlled fax mode. In fact, most of the fax processing occurs in the digital signal processors (DSP), requiring only packet switching from the main processor (CPU) and some limited signaling to switch to fax mode. Therefore, the CPU overhead is very similar to a normal voice call.

Initially, a voice call is established. When the V.21 preamble is detected at the terminating gateway, the originating and the terminating gateway negotiate the codec type. If the two sides cannot negotiate on a common codec and speed, the fax fails. If negotiation succeeds, the fax transmission begins.

Cisco Fax Relay is supported using MGCP, H.323, or SCCP depending on the specific gateway type. The Cisco voice gateways support as many concurrent fax calls as G.711 voice calls.

The voice gateway demodulates the fax data before crossing the IP network. The voice gateway at the other end of the IP network demodulates it again for transmission to the receiving fax machine.

Fax Pass-Through

In Fax Pass-Through mode, some call modifications occur. Namely, voice activity detection (VAD) is automatically disabled, the echo canceller might be disabled in some cases, the call may "upspeed" to G.711 if a lower bandwidth codec is in use, and the jitter buffers are increased.

T.38 Support

> **NOTE**   This feature was introduced in CallManager release 4.1(2).

In addition to Cisco Fax Relay and Fax Pass-Through, some of the Cisco voice gateway platforms also support T.38 fax relay. The T.38 fax relay is a standards-based protocol supported on H.323 gateways. Because the T.38 fax relay protocol is standards-based, these gateways can interoperate with third-party T.38-enabled gateways and gatekeepers in a mixed-vendor network.

Forced Authorization Codes

The forced authorization codes feature regulates the types of calls that certain users can place by requiring users to enter a valid authorization code prior to extending calls that are routed through FAC-enabled route patterns. You can enable or disable FAC through route patterns. When a user dials a number that is routed through a FAC-enabled route pattern, a tone plays, prompting the user to enter the authorization code.

You can configure multiple levels of authorization. If the user's authorization code does not meet or exceed the level of authorization required to route the dialed number, the user hears reorder. If the authorization is accepted, CallManager extends the call. The authorization code name is written to the CDR so the information can be collected in the CDR Analysis and Reporting (CAR) tool, which allows you to generate reports for accounting and billing.

This feature can be used for colleges, universities, or any business or organization for whom limiting access to specific classes of calls would be beneficial. Also, by assigning unique authorization codes, you can determine which users placed calls.

For each user, you specify an authorization code and then enable FAC on the relevant route patterns (**Route Plan > Route Pattern**) by selecting the **Require Forced Authorization Code** check box and specifying the minimum authorization level for calls through that route pattern. Any user who attempts to dial a number that is routed through that route pattern must have at least the authorization level specified or higher. To implement FAC, you need to devise a list of arbitrary authorization levels and their meanings.

FAC can be used alone or in conjunction with client matter codes. See the "Client Matter Codes" section for more information.

FXO and FXS Support

CallManager supports Foreign eXchange Office (FXO)/Foreign eXchange Station (FXS) ports on essentially any H.323, MGCP, or SIP Cisco voice gateway that offers that type of physical interface.

Group Call Pickup/GPickUp

Group call pickup allows users who belong to one call pickup group to answer incoming calls in other groups. See the section "Call Pickup/Group Call Pickup (PickUp/GPickUp)" for more information.

H.323 Client, Gateway, and Gatekeeper Support

CallManager provides an H.323v2-compliant interface to H.323 clients, gateways, multipoint conference units (MCU), and gatekeepers. As of release 4.1(2), CallManager does not support the T.120 protocol.

H.323v2 Gatekeeper Support

Support is provided for registering multiple CallManager servers in a cluster with a gatekeeper. This provides a scalable way of configuring intersite trunks, and is also used for call admission control. See the "Call Admission Control (CAC)" section for more details.

Multiple Gatekeepers per Cluster

CallManager supports the definition of multiple gatekeepers. This provides the flexibility to configure routes to different gatekeepers for different purposes, such as an internal gatekeeper within the enterprise and another to connect to a service provider's network.

H.323 Call Scalability Improvements

Each CallManager server can handle 1,000 H.323 calls, which means that a cluster with 4 active CallManager servers can support 4000 simultaneous H.323 calls.

H.323 Trunks and Scalability Improvements

CallManager provides H.323 interface support and added enhancements to support administrative scalability, dial plan management, and solution redundancy. Enhancements include the following features:

- Alternate gatekeeper

- Alternate endpoints

- Multiple gatekeepers per clusters

- Simple Bandwidth Resolution Query (BRQ) support

- Adherence to H.323v2 specification of Registration, Admission, and Status (RAS) retries and timers

- Call-by-call automated selection of intercluster trunk (ICT) signaling protocols

- CanMapAlias support (for called party number only)

- Gatekeeper serviceability enhancements (new performance monitor counters and the option of taking a gatekeeper offline for maintenance).

Microsoft NetMeeting Support

All Cisco IP Phones can call Microsoft NetMeeting devices that have been configured in CallManager Administration as an H.323 client, or are reachable through an H.323 gatekeeper.

Videoconferencing Support

CallManager supports H.261 and H.263 video codecs and other necessary mechanisms to fully support H.323 videoconferencing clients. See the "Codec Support (Audio and Video)" section for more details.

H.323 FastStart Signaling Support

> **NOTE**   This feature was introduced in CallManager release 3.3(3) and enhanced in 4.1(2).

CallManager supports receiving H.323 FastStart calls, and release 4.1(2) adds support for initiating H.323 FastStart calls on H.323 trunks and gateways. CallManager uses media termination points for making an H.323 outbound FastStart call. The called endpoint can refuse the H.323 Fast Connect procedure by not returning the FastStart element in any of the messages up to and including the CONNECT message. In this case, CallManager handles the call as a normal call and uses the MTP for subsequent media cut-through. If an MTP is not available when the call is set up, the call continues without FastStart and without supplementary services. If you want all calls to use FastStart only, you can set the Fail Call If MTP Allocation Fails service parameter, which, when enabled, configures the system to reject calls when no MTP is available.

Hold/Resume

Hold allows a user to store a call at his or her extension. It is automatically available for most Cisco IP Phones. The Cisco IP Phone 12SP+ requires a button template with the Hold button configured.

Pressing the **Resume** softkey allows a user to retrieve a call placed on hold. It is automatically available for all Cisco IP Phones that have softkeys. There are no configuration requirements.

Hold on Cisco IP Phone Model 12SP+

Hold is a programmable feature button on Cisco IP Phone 12SP+. To place an active call on hold, the user presses the **Hold** button. The display indicates the held call. To retrieve the call, the user presses the **Hold** button again and is reconnected with the held call.

Hold on Cisco IP Phones 7902, 7910, and 30VIP

Hold is a static button on Cisco IP Phones 7902, 7910, and 30VIP. To place an active call on hold, the user presses the **Hold** button. The light for the line with the call on hold remains lit. To retrieve the call, the user presses the line button and is reconnected with the held call.

Hold/Resume on Cisco IP Phones

Hold and Resume are softkeys on Cisco IP Phones. To place an active call on hold, the user presses the **Hold** softkey. To retrieve the call from hold, the user selects the line on which the call is being held and presses the **Resume** softkey. The caller is reconnected to the held call. Hold and Resume softkeys are automatically available with no configuration required on Cisco IP Phones that support softeys.

Table A-28 provides information about Hold and Resume service parameters (**Service > Service Parameters** > *select a server* > **Cisco CallManager**).

Table A-28 *Hold/Resume Service Parameters*

Service Parameter	Default	Valid Values
Hold Type In the case where two different legacy Cisco IP Phones, models 12SP+ or 30VIP, share the same directory number, this parameter determines whether the hold light flashes more rapidly for the user who placed the call on hold.	False	**True**—rapid flashing **False**—normal flashing also known as winking
Tone on Hold Timer Determines the number of seconds between every 2 hold tones that are played when a call is put on hold. For non-MGCP-based devices, if this value is 0, the held device plays the hold tone only one time when the caller is put on hold; if the value is 200000, no hold tone plays; otherwise, the held device plays the hold tone every so many seconds (specified by this value) repeatedly. If the specified value is between 1 and 4 seconds, the device raises it to 5 seconds automatically. For MGCP-based devices, the hold tone is disabled if this value is 0 or 200000; any other value enables the hold tone on MGCP-based devices when the caller is put on hold.	10 seconds	0 to 200000 seconds
Maximum Hold Duration Timer Specifies the maximum duration that one or both parties on a call can remain on hold before CallManager clears the call. A value of 0 disables the timer.	360 minutes	0 to 35791 minutes
Default Network Hold MOH Audio Source ID Specifies the clusterwide network hold (hold initiated by features such as transfer, conference, call park, and so on) audio source ID. The system uses this audio source when no higher levels (device pool, device, and directory number levels) of audio source ID are defined/chosen.	1	1 to 51
Default User Hold MOH Audio Source ID Specifies the clusterwide user hold (hold initiated by the user) audio source ID. The system uses this audio source when no higher levels (device pool, device, and directory number levels) of audio source ID are defined/chosen.	1	1 to 51

continues

Table A-28 *Hold/Resume Service Parameters (Continued)*

Service Parameter	Default	Valid Values
Disable Resume from Shared-Line MGCP FXS Port Determines whether a call on hold can be resumed on a line that an MGCP FXS port shares. Cisco does not recommend that you configure the system with shared lines with IOS-based MGCP FXS port. If this parameter is set to False, the system allows the MGCP FXS port to resume one hold call. Currently, CallManager does not support MGCP FXS port capability to resume with multiple hold calls. It's best to leave this to the default value, True. If this parameter is set to False, a port malfunction could occur if an IP phone that shares the line with the FXS port invokes supplementary services such as hold, transfer, and so on. The port malfunction can only be cleared by resetting the port or gateway.	True	True or False Keep this parameter set to the default value (True) unless a Cisco support engineer instructs otherwise

Hookflash/Hookflash Transfer

CallManager provides hookflash detection on Cisco MGCP and SCCP voice gateways that offer analog FXS interfaces. The hookflash timer can be configured on a per-port basis.

CallManager supports receiving hookflash transfer on calls from the Cisco WS-X6608-T1 gateway. After the call is transferred, CallManager releases the unused channel of the T1 line, which frees up the trunk for additional calls.

HTTP Server Support

Cisco IP Phones, Cisco Digital Access DT-24+, DE-30+, and Cisco Catalyst 6000 gateways support HTTP server functionality. This functionality is referred to as the HTTP Daemon, or HTTPD. The daemon can run on a variety of platforms using the operating system on the Cisco IP Phone.

Hunt Lists and Line Groups

CallManager provides an integrated logic for hunting for an available line. After directory numbers are added to hunt lists, CallManager can distribute calls in circular, broadcast, linear, or longest-idle order. You can configure directory numbers into a line group, then add one or more line groups to a hunt list, and then configure a hunt pilot to route calls to the hunt list. Route groups can also be configured as members of a hunt list, allowing call distribution through MGCP, H.323, or SIP gateways and trunks. See Chapter 2 for more information about hunt lists.

> **NOTE** CTI devices do not support hunt list functionality.

Inline Power Support on Cisco IP Phones

Cisco IP Phones 79*xx* support the Cisco-proprietary method of receiving inline power from Cisco Catalyst and IOS inline powered line cards.

Inline power enables the phone to operate independent of an AC power source. If the inline powered switch that the phone is connected to utilizes an uninterruptible power supply (UPS) system, the phones remain powered even in the event of a power failure to the building.

IEEE 802.3af Inline Power Support

Cisco IP Phones 7941, 7961, 7970, and 7971 support 802.3af inline power. Cisco plans to ensure that newer Catalyst switch ports that support the 802.3af standard will be backward compatible with older Cisco IP Phones that do not support the standard, and that newer Cisco IP Phones that support the 802.3af standard will be backward compatible with older Catalyst switch ports that do not support the standard.

Internationalization/Localization

Client-facing audio user interfaces and graphical user interfaces are available in U.S. English and a variety of other languages, including Greek, Russian, Spanish, Japanese, and many more. New languages are regularly being added.

The language and locale can be administered on a server-wide basis, on a device pool basis, or on an individual phone level. The user locale dictates the language that displays on the IP Phone's LCD screen, and the network locale dictates the network sounds that are heard by the user, such as off-hook, ringback, and busy tones as well as the locale-specific tones and cadences on Cisco voice gateways.

In addition, the Cisco CallManager User Options web pages, Tool for Auto-Registered Phone Support (TAPS) prompts, and system and end-user documentation are available in a variety of languages.

You can use the Cisco IP Telephony Locale Installer to add new language support directly to a CallManager server. The English_United_States locale is installed by default. You can obtain other locales at the following link or search Cisco.com for "CallManager localized":

http://www.cisco.com/kobayashi/sw-center/telephony/callmgr/locale-installer.shtml

Table A-29 provides information about localization enterprise parameters (**System > Enterprise Parameters**).

Table A-29 *Localization-Related Enterprise Parameters*

Enterprise Parameter	Default
Default Network Locale Specifies the default network locale for tones and cadences. The chosen network locale applies to all gateways and phones that do not have the network locale set at the device level or device pool level. Make sure that the chosen network locale is installed and supported for all gateways and phones. Refer to product documentation, if necessary. Reset all devices for the parameter change to take effect.	United States
Default User Locale Specifies the default user locale for language selection. Reset all devices for the parameter change to take effect.	English United States

International Dial Plan

CallManager international dial plan provides country-specific dialing functionality for countries outside the North American numbering plan (NANP). The international dial plan includes route pattern wildcards, special characters, calling party transformation settings, and called party transformation settings that non-NANP dial plans use. It also describes the Discard Digit Instructions (DDI) and tags that dial plans of specific countries use. The NANP is installed by default. You can obtain other country-specific dial plans at the following link or search Cisco.com for "CallManager IDP":

> http://www.cisco.com/cgi-bin/tablebuild.pl/IDP

ISDN Basic Rate Interface (BRI) Support

> **NOTE** This feature was enhanced in CallManager release 4.1(2).

Prior to CallManager release 4.1(2), BRI ISDN connections required H.323 or SIP gateways. Release 4.1(2) introduces support for ISDN BRI interfaces on MGCP gateways. Note that this release provides support only for ETSI BRI basic-net3 (user side only), which means that it can only be used as a trunk-side interface (that is, to the PSTN or a PBX).

MGCP-controlled ISDN BRI is supported on all Cisco IOS gateway platforms that support the VIC-2BRI-NT/TE or VIC-2BRI-S/T-TE voice interface cards on the NM-2V module. See the following link for more information:

> http://www.cisco.com/univercd/cc/td/doc/product/software/ios123/123cgcr/vvfax_c/callc_c/ccm_c/int_bri.htm

Join

Cisco IP Phones 79*xx* provide a Join softkey that allows users to join multiple parties on a line into an Ad Hoc conference. Using the Join softkey, users can conference two or more incoming calls together into a conference. This feature works in conjunction with the multiple calls per line feature in which a user can make and/or receive multiple calls on a single line, and then join them together via the Join softkey, creating an Ad Hoc conference.

The Drop Ad Hoc Conference service parameter described in Table A-26 applies to the join feature.

JTAPI Computer Telephony Interface (CTI)

An SDK is available for third-party developers. Learn more about JTAPI in Appendix C.

JTAPI Control of Analog (FXS) Gateway Ports

JTAPI applications can control analog phones that are connected to Cisco ATA186, Cisco ATA-188, or Cisco VG248 model gateways.

LDAPv3 Directory Interface

Support is provided for Microsoft Active Directory and Netscape Directory Services.

Least Cost Routing Support

CallManager supports least cost routing through the use of dial plan partitioning, route lists, and route groups. Using these route plan tools, you can configure CallManager to utilize gateways in preferential order, whether that preference is based on geography or cost.

Lightweight Directory Access Protocol (LDAP) Support

CallManager provides an LDAPv3 compliant interface. You can use the embedded directory that comes with the CallManager installation, or use an external directory.

Table A-30 provides information about LDAP service parameters (**System > Service Parameters >** *select a server* **> Cisco Database Layer Monitor**).

Table A-30 *LDAP Service Parameters*

Service Parameter	Default	Valid Values
LDAP Number of Notifications Controls the number of LDAP notifications that are processed before LDAP "sleeps" and relinquishes the CPU for other activities. Use this parameter in combination with the LDAP Sleep Time parameter. For example, if this parameter is set to 50 and LDAP Sleep Time is set to 600, the Cisco Database Layer Monitor service will sleep for 600 milliseconds after processing 50 notifications. Sleeping yields processor resources so that other services can utilize the CPU.	0	0 to 999
LDAP Sleep Time Designates the time to yield CPU after the value specified in the LDAP Number of Notifications value is met. A value of zero indicates no sleep time, which works successfully for sites that do not perform bulk add or delete operations, which can create a strain on the CPU during production hours. If you routinely perform bulk add or delete operations during production hours and notice the CPU spiking in the Cisco Database Layer Monitor service, specify nondefault values in this parameter and the LDAP Number of Notification parameter to ensure that the LDAP change notifications get processed and made available to applications.	0 milliseconds	0 to 999 milliseconds
Maximum AXL Writes Allowed per Minute Specifies the maximum number of updates that can be performed by using the AVVID XML Layer (AXL) API, per minute, to the CallManager database and the LDAP user directory.	20	0 to 999

Embedded Directory

CallManager servers provide an embedded LDAP directory for user information. The embedded directory is installed automatically during CallManager installation, and all servers in the cluster automatically participate in LDAP directory synchronization.

External LDAP Directory Support

Support is provided for Microsoft Active Directory and Netscape Directory Server. Configuration of these directories is done via the Cisco Customer Directory Configuration Plugin available in CallManager Administration (**Application > Install Plugins**).

Line

A line allows a user to access incoming calls or place outgoing calls. At least one line must be configured in CallManager Administration for each IP phone in the system (**Device > Phone >** *find and click phone* **>** *click line*). Each line on an IP phone can support up to 200 calls on one directory number per line. The default is a maximum of 4 calls with a busy trigger of 2. (See the section "Shared-Line Appearances/Bridged-Line Appearances" for more information.)

To use an IP phone, one or more lines must be configured. Each line on a given phone must have a directory number assigned to it; two lines on the same phone cannot have the same directory number assigned unless they're configured in separate partitions; the same directory number can be configured on multiple phones. Configuration and use of line buttons differs depending on the phone model. The myriad ways of accessing a line include lifting the handset, pressing the **HEADSET** or **SPEAKERPHONE** buttons, pressing the **NewCall** softkey or **messages** button, or pressing a line button on the phone.

Line buttons on Cisco IP Phones 7940, 7941, 7960, 7961, 7970, and 7971 can be configured as speed dial buttons, XML service URLs, or as a Privacy button. See the following sections for more information:

- Speed Dial

- Service URLs on Line Buttons

- Privacy

Table A-31 provides information about service parameters that affect lines or directory numbers on IP phones. You can access service parameters in the Service Parameters Configuration page in CallManager Administration (**Service > Service Parameters >** *select a server* **> Cisco CallManager**).

Table A-31 *Line-Related Service Parameters*

Service Parameter	Default	Valid Values
Always Use Prime Line Specifies whether the primary line on an IP phone will be selected, if available, when the user goes off-hook.	False	**True**—When a phone goes off-hook, the primary line gets chosen and becomes the active line. Even if a call is ringing on the user's second line, going off-hook makes only the first line active; it does not answer the ringing call on the second line. In this case, the user must choose the second line to answer the call **False**—The IP phone automatically chooses an available line as the active line
Always Use Prime Line for Voice Message Determines whether the primary line gets chosen and becomes the active line when the **messages** button is pressed.	False	**True**—The phone automatically dials the voice messaging system from the primary line **False**—The phone automatically dials the voice messaging system from whichever line has a voice message (not always the primary line)
Builtin Bridge Enable Determines whether the bridge that is built in to Cisco IP Phones 7940, 7941, 7960, 7961, 7970, and 7971 is enabled. A device with a built-in bridge can mix streams, which is required for the barge feature. The only codec that the built-in bridge supports is G.711. CallManager uses this parameter for phones that have Default chosen in the Built In Bridge field on the Phone Configuration page in CallManager Administration. If you configure encryption for Cisco IP Phones 7940, 7941, 7960 and 7961, those encrypted devices cannot accept barge requests when they are participating in an encrypted call. When the call is encrypted, the barge attempt fails. Reset or restart the corresponding IP phones for the parameter change to take effect.	Off	On or Off

Table A-31   *Line-Related Service Parameters (Continued)*

Service Parameter	Default	Valid Values
Auto Answer Timer Specifies the amount of time to wait before the Cisco IP Phone auto answers an incoming call on an idle line. The value in this parameter should be les than the value that is specified in the T301 Timer parameter. If the value in the Auto Answer Timer parameter is greater than the value that is specified in the T301 Timer parameter, the call does not get answered and the caller receives a busy signal. Setting this value to the higher end of the allowable range could result in calls being rolled to the voice mail system, if configured, before the call auto answers.	1 second	1 to 500 seconds
Alternate Idle Phone Auto Answer Behavior Specifies the call conditions that disable the auto answer feature.	False	**True**—Auto answer is disabled when a call is on hold, a call is incoming or outgoing, or a call is connected **False**—Auto answer is disabled when a call is incoming or outgoing
Line State Update Enabled Specifies whether the Line State Server (which Attendant Console and other services use) can track the active/inactive states of each directory number. You must restart the Cisco CallManager service or reregister the directory number for the parameter change to take effect.	True	True or False
Off-Hook to First Digit Timer Specifies the maximum amount of time that CallManager waits to receive the first digit that the user dialed. If a digit is not received before this timer expires, CallManager terminates the call.	15000 milliseconds	0 to 150000 milliseconds
Override Auto Answer If Speaker Is Disabled Indicates whether a call automatically disconnects if the speaker for the called phone is disabled when the Auto Answer with Speakerphone option is selected on the called phone line (Directory Number Configuration page in CallManager Administration).	True	**True**—Extend the call **False**—Terminate the call automatically

continues

Table A-31 *Line-Related Service Parameters (Continued)*

Service Parameter	Default	Valid Values
Out-of-Bandwidth Text Specifies the text that displays on the phone when the call cannot be placed because of lack of bandwidth.	Not Enough Bandwidth	Up to 23 characters
AAR Network Congestion Rerouting Text Designates the text that displays on the phone when the call is rerouted through an alternate route because of network congestion.	Network Congestion. Rerouting.	Up to 31 characters
Always Use Inside Dial Tone Determines whether CallManager always plays inside dial tone, even for calls that are destined for OffNet.	False	**True**—No distinction between inside and outside dial tone **False**—Outside dial tone can differ from inside dial tone

Multiple Line Appearances per Phone

Cisco IP Phones with more than one line/feature button can have multiple line appearances.

Shared-Line Appearances/Bridged-Line Appearances

The same directory number can be configured on multiple phones, providing a shared-line appearance. This feature is also known as *bridged-line appearances*. Devices with shared lines support multiple calls. This allows users on shared-line phones to make or receive a call while the remote phone is in use. Call information (such as calling party or called party) displays on all devices that are sharing a line. If the Privacy feature is enabled on one of the devices, other devices that are sharing the line will not see active calls made from the device that turned privacy on.

Devices with shared-line appearances support the Call Forward Busy Trigger and the Maximum Number of Calls fields. You can configure Call Forward Busy Trigger per line appearance, but the configuration cannot exceed the maximum number call setting for that directory number.

Cisco IPMA with shared-line support allows managers and assistants to share lines. See the "Manager Assistant Services" section for more information.

Unassigned Directory Numbers

When you remove a directory number from a phone, the number still exists in CallManager. Unassigned DNs allow customers to continue forwarding to the voice messaging system or another destination for DNs that are no longer assigned to devices. This can happen when employees are reassigned or terminated. Prior to CallManager release 4.0, the system automatically deleted directory numbers when a device was deleted. Because line group support is a feature of release 4.0, you can now keep unassigned DNs.

To see a list of directory numbers that are not associated with phones, search in the Route Plan Report page (**Route Plan > Route Plan Report >** *select* **Unassigned DN** *in the* **Find** *drop-down list > click* **Find**).

Manager Assistant Services

> **NOTE** This feature was enhanced to supported shared-line appearances in CallManager release 4.0(1).

The Cisco IP Manager Assistant (IPMA) service allows managers and assistants to handle phone calls more effectively. Each assistant can support up to five manager lines. Managers can enable features such as do not disturb (DND), send-all-calls (SAC), immediate divert, transfer to voice mail, call intercept, and set watch from the softkeys on IP Phones. Assistants can use the Assistant Console application to answer calls for their managers and themselves and to configure manager and assistant preferences. As of CallManager release 4.0(1), IPMA supports shared-line appearances.

The Cisco IP Manager Assistant service provides service parameters relating to IPMA configuration (**Service > Service Parameters >** *select a server >* **Cisco IP Manager Assistant**), as described in Table A-32.

Table A-32 *Cisco IPMA Service Parameters*

Service Parameter	Default	Valid Values
CTI Manager (Primary) IP Address Specifies the IP address of the primary CTIManager that this Cisco IPMA server uses for call control. Restart the Cisco Tomcat service for changes to this parameter to take effect.	No default value	Up to 15 characters in the form of an IP address (for example, 123.45.67.89)
CTI Manager (Backup) IP Address Specifies the IP address of the backup CTIManager that this Cisco IPMA server uses for call control. Restart the Cisco Tomcat service for changes to this parameter to take effect.	No default value	Up to 15 characters in the form of an IP address

continues

Table A-32 *Cisco IPMA Service Parameters (Continued)*

Service Parameter	Default	Valid Values
Route Point Device Name for Proxy Mode Specifies the device name of the route point that this Cisco IPMA server uses to intercept all calls to managers' primary lines for intelligent routing. Cisco recommends that you use same route point device for all servers. You must configure this parameter if any manager or assistant will be configured to use proxy mode. Restart the Cisco Tomcat service for changes to this parameter to take effect.	No default value	The route point's device name
Clusterwide Parameters		
Cisco IPMA Server (Primary) IP Address Specifies the IP address of the primary Cisco IPMA server. Restart the Cisco Tomcat service for the changes to this parameter to take effect.	No default value	Up to 15 characters in the form of an IP address
Cisco IPMA Server (Backup) IP Address Specifies the IP address of the backup (secondary) Cisco IPMA server. Restart the Cisco Tomcat service for changes to this parameter to take effect.	No default value	Up to 15 characters in the form of an IP address
Cisco IPMA Server Port Specifies the TCP/IP port on the Cisco IPMA server to which the desktop client will open socket connections. Restart the Cisco Tomcat service for changes to this parameter to take effect.	2912	1025 to 65535
Desktop Heartbeat Interval Specifies the interval at which the Cisco IPMA server sends KeepAlive messages (heartbeat) to the desktop client. Clients initiate failover if they do not receive a heartbeat before this interval expires. Restart the Cisco Tomcat service for changes to this parameter to take effect.	30 seconds	10 to 300 seconds

Table A-32 *Cisco IPMA Service Parameters (Continued)*

Service Parameter	Default	Valid Values
Desktop Request Timeout Specifies the time that the desktop clients wait to receive a response to a request sent to the Cisco IPMA server. Restart the Cisco Tomcat service for changes to this parameter to take effect.	30 seconds	10 to 300 seconds
Cisco IPMA RNA Forwarding Flag Determines whether Cisco IPMA ring no answer (RNA) forwarding is enabled or disabled. If this parameter is set to True (enabled), the system forwards the unanswered call to next available assistant when the duration specified in the Cisco IPMA RNA Timeout parameter expires. Restart the Cisco Tomcat service for changes to this parameter to take effect.	False	True or False
Cisco IPMA RNA Timeout Specifies the amount of time that the Cisco IPMA server waits before forwarding an unanswered call to the next available assistant. Restart the Cisco Tomcat service for changes to this parameter to take effect.	10 seconds	5 to 300 seconds
Clusterwide Parameters (Softkey Templates)		
Assistant Softkey Template Specifies the softkey template that gets assigned to assistant devices during IPMA assistant automatic configuration.	Standard IPMA Assistant	Standard IPMA Assistant Other softkey templates already configured in the system
Manager Softkey Template for Proxy Mode Specifies the softkey template that gets assigned to manager devices during IPMA manager automatic configuration when the manager is configured to use proxy mode.	Standard IPMA Manager	Standard IPMA Manager Other softkey templates already configured in the system
Manager Softkey Template for Shared Mode Specifies the softkey template that gets assigned to manager devices during IPMA manager automatic configuration when the manager is configured to use shared mode.	Standard IPMA Shared Mode Manager	Standard IPMA Shared Mode Manager Other softkey templates already configured in the system

continues

Table A-32 *Cisco IPMA Service Parameters (Continued)*

Service Parameter	Default	Valid Values
Clusterwide Parameters (IPMA Device Configuration Defaults for Proxy Mode)		
Manager Partition Specifies the partition that is assigned to lines on an IPMA-controlled manager device when the Cisco IPMA Configuration Wizard is run. The partition specified in this parameter must be configured in CallManager Administration prior to selecting it in this parameter. This parameter only applies if the manager is configured to use proxy mode.	No default value	Up to 50 characters
All User Partition Specifies the partition that is assigned to proxy line(s) and intercom line on assistant devices, as well as the intercom line on manager devices, when the Cisco IPMA Configuration Wizard is run. The partition specified in this parameter must be configured in CallManager Administration prior to selecting it in this parameter. This parameter only applies if the manager or assistant is configured to use proxy mode.	No default value	Up to 50 characters
IPMA Calling Search Space Specifies the calling search space that is assigned to line(s) and the intercom line on manager devices, as well as the assistant intercom line on assistant devices for IPMA-controlled manager and assistant devices when the Cisco IPMA Configuration Wizard is run. The calling search space specified in this parameter must be configured in CallManager Administration prior to selecting it in this parameter. This parameter only applies if the manager or assistant is configured to use proxy mode.	No default value	Up to 50 characters
Manager Calling Search Space Specifies the calling search space that is assigned to proxy line(s) on assistant devices when the Cisco IPMA Configuration Wizard is run. The calling search space specified in this parameter must be configured in CallManager Administration prior to selecting it in this parameter. This parameter only applies if the assistant is configured to use proxy mode.	No default value	Up to 50 characters
IPMA Phone Service Specifies the IP phone service to which manager devices are subscribed when the Cisco IPMA Configuration Wizard is run. This parameter only applies if the manager is configured to use proxy mode.	No default value	

Table A-32 *Cisco IPMA Service Parameters (Continued)*

Service Parameter	Default	Valid Values
Clusterwide Parameters (Proxy Directory Number Range for Proxy Mode)		
Starting Directory Number Specifies the starting (the first) directory number for automatic generation of proxy directory number(s) during IPMA assistant configuration. Configuration will display the next available number. The last number that is used gets remembered. This parameter applies only if the assistant is configured to use proxy mode.	No default value	Up to 8 digits
Ending Directory Number Specifies the ending (the last) directory number for automatic generation of proxy directory number(s) during IPMA assistant configuration. Configuration will stop at this number. This parameter applies only if the assistant is configured to use proxy mode.	No default value	Up to 8 digits
Clusterwide Parameters (Proxy Directory Number Prefix for Proxy Mode)		
Number of Characters to be Stripped from Manager Directory Number Specifies the number of characters to be stripped from the manager IPMA directory number (DN) in the process of generating the proxy DN. Generation of a proxy DN might involve stripping some number of digits from a manager DN. For example, a manager DN is 2002, the number of characters to be stripped is 2, and the prefix to be added is 30. The resulting proxy DN is 3002. This parameter applies only if the assistant is configured to use proxy mode.	0	0 to 24
Prefix for Manager Directory Number Specifies the prefix to be added to a manager directory number (DN) in the process of generating the proxy DN. For example, a manager DN is 1001, the number of characters to be stripped is 0, and the prefix is *. The resulting proxy DN is *1001. This parameter applies only if the assistant is configured to use proxy mode.	No default value	Up to 24 characters, including numbers and * or # characters

Mappable Softkeys

You can create softkey templates (**Device > Device Settings > Softkey Template**) that define features and associate softkeys for every call state, and map these features to the softkeys based on call usage patterns. Apply these templates to individual phones or to groups of phones to create special templates for managers, assistants, and other special users.

Media Gateway Control Protocol (MGCP) Support

CallManager supports the use of MGCP on various gateway models. MGCP provides enhanced ease of administration compared to H.323 because all the configuration of the gateway is done in CallManager Administration, and the gateways then download their configuration from CallManager. In addition, MGCP provides enhanced redundancy and call preservation support.

MGCP Gateway Fallback to H.323

MGCP gateway fallback support allows an MGCP gateway at a remote site to fallback to H.323 mode when the WAN connection to the remote site is lost. Falling back to H.323 mode enables the gateway to be used by the Survivable Remote Site Telephony (SRST) services that provide local call control for the phones at that site during a WAN failure.

MGCP ISDN T1/E1 PRI and T1-CAS with Q.931 Backhaul

MGCP gateways backhaul (tunnel) the ISDN Layer 3 and above to CallManager. The ISDN lower-layer information (Q.921 and below) is terminated and processed on the gateway. The Layer 3 information (Q.931 and above) is transported over TCP to CallManager (MGCP call agent).

MGCP support extends to many gateways and TDM signaling protocols: T1-CAS, T1-PRI and E1-PRI to the Cisco 2600, 3600, 3700, and 3800 series multiple-service routers, the Cisco Communication Media Module (CMM), the VG200 VoIP gateway, and the Cisco 1760 Modular Access Router. In addition, T1-CAS support over MGCP extends to the Catalyst 6000-series voice services card (WS-6608-T1).

MGCP support provides for centralized gateway administration, supplementary services to FXS gateways (hookflash/transfer), as well as call preservation in the event of CallManager service disruption.

Network-Specific Facilities (NSF) Support

CallManager supports outbound call-by-call delivery of AT&T Network-Specific Facilities, including Software-Defined Network (SDN) and Megacom services. Support extends to 4ESS and 5ESS switches on MGCP-controlled T1/E1 PRI interfaces.

Media Resource Group List Support

Within a cluster, devices can be grouped together and associated with transcoder and conference bridge resources using the media resource group list (MRGL). You can learn more about MRGLs in Chapter 5.

Meet-Me Conference/MeetMe

> **NOTE** CallManager provides two types of conferences: Ad Hoc and Meet-Me. Ad Hoc conferences require the conference controller to include attendees individually to the conference by calling them. Meet-Me conferences allow attendees to dial in to the conference after the conference controller has established it. This section covers the Meet-Me Conference feature. The Ad Hoc Conference feature is covered in this appendix in the section "Conference/Confrn."

Meet-Me conference allows a user to establish a conference that attendees can direct dial in to. Meet-Me conference is available for all Cisco IP Phones. On Cisco IP Phones 12SP+, 30VIP, and 7910, the button is called Meet Me Conference and must be configured on the button template. On other Cisco IP Phones such as 7940, 7960, and 7970, the softkey is called MeetMe and is automatically available when the phone is off-hook. For the Meet-Me conference feature to function, you must install a Unicast conference bridge and then establish one or more directory numbers to be used for Meet-Me conferences. You can do this in the Meet Me Number/Pattern Configuration page in CallManager Administration on a conference bridge that has already been configured (**Service > Conference Bridge > Meet Me Number/Pattern Configuration**). You do not need a Meet-Me softkey to participate in a conference call, only to initiate one.

Figure A-7 illustrates the Meet-Me conference operation.

Figure A-7 *Meet-Me Conference Operation*

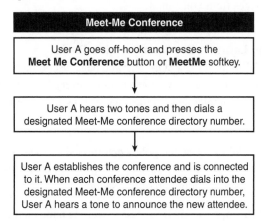

You can learn more about this feature in Chapter 5.

Messages Button on Cisco IP Phones

The **messages** button on Cisco IP Phones provides one-touch speed dial access to a voice mail system, if the voice mail system is integrated with CallManager.

Message Waiting Indicator

The message waiting indicator provides visual notification that a message is waiting in the user's voice mailbox. The indicator is available for all Cisco IP Phones, but implementation differs depending on model. For the feature to work in conjunction with your voice mail system, the voice mail system must be configured to work with CallManager and the **messages** or Message Waiting button must be programmed to connect directly to the voice mail system.

Message Waiting Indicator on Legacy Cisco IP Phones 12SP+ and 30VIP

Message Waiting is a programmable feature button on Cisco IP Phones 12SP+ or 30VIP. For this feature to be available, the Cisco IP Phone button template must have a Message Waiting button assigned. The light next to the Message Waiting button remains lit when there is a new message in the user's voice mailbox.

Message Waiting Indicator on Cisco IP Phones

Message waiting indicators appear on the handset and body of most Cisco IP Phones including 7910, 7940, 7941, 7960, 7961, 7970, and 7971. The indicator is lit in the color red when there is a message waiting. See the section "Messages Button on Cisco IP Phones" for information about retrieving messages from voice mail.

Set Message Waiting Lamp Policy on a Per-Line Basis

Via the Cisco CallManager User Options web page, users can specify how they want the message waiting light to indicate they have voice mail for every line on a phone. Previously, only system administrators could implement the message waiting indicator policy. Options include the following:

- **Use System Policy**—Use the policy determined by the system administrator. The system policy is defined by the CallManager service parameter Message Waiting Lamp Policy, described in the last paragraph of this section.

- **Light and Prompt**—Light the message waiting lamp on the phone and display a text prompt such as "You have voice mail" on the phone's display.

- **Prompt Only**—Display a text prompt such as "You have voice mail" on the phone's display; do not light the message waiting lamp on the phone.

- **Light Only**—Light the message waiting lamp on the phone; do not display a text prompt.

- **None**—Do not light the lamp or display a text prompt.

The system policy is controlled by the service parameter Message Waiting Lamp Policy (**Service > Service Parameters >** *select a server* **> Cisco CallManager**).

Microsoft NetMeeting

All Cisco IP Phones can call Microsoft NetMeeting devices that have been configured with CallManager.

Multilevel Administration (MLA)

Multilevel administration access provides multiple levels of security to CallManager Administration. MLA permits granting only the required privileges for a selected group of users and limits the configuration functions that users in a particular user group can perform.

Using a combination of functional groups (based on the menu structure in CallManager Administration) and user groups, access to the different parts of CallManager Administration can be controlled. Each functional group can have different access levels, such as no access, read-only access, and full access, to different user groups. MLA access also provides audit logs of user logins and access and modifications to CallManager configuration data.

You can learn more about MLA in Chapter 9, "Using Multilevel Administration" of the book *Cisco CallManager Best Practices* (ISBN: 1-58705-139-7).

Multilevel Precedence and Preemption (MLPP)

> **NOTE**   This feature was introduced in CallManager release 4.0(1) and enhanced in release 4.1(2).

The Multilevel Precedence and Preemption (MLPP) feature allows placement of priority calls. CallManager's MLPP implementation complies with ANSI T1.619/T1.619a and Generic Switching Center Requirements (GSCR). MLPP plays a tone to indicate to users on an IP-to-IP phone call that their call is being preempted. A user with higher precedence can also preempt a call with lower precedence that is made through a gateway. MLPP also provides Alternate Party Diversion (APD), which allows CallManager to route the priority call to a different phone if the target party does not answer the call.

You configure precedence patterns within route patterns and translation patterns. As of CallManager release 4.1(2), six precedence levels exist:

■ Executive Override

■ Flash Override

■ Flash

■ Immediate

■ Priority

■ Routine

As of CallManager release 4.1(2), the following user devices support MLPP: Cisco IP Phones 7905, 7912, 7940, 7941, 7960, 7961, 7970, 7971, and SCCP-controlled ISDN BRI gateways. The following trunk-side devices are also supported: MGCP-controlled T1 PRI, MGCP-controlled T1-CAS, and H.323 intercluster trunks.

For a call between two user devices, the target of the precedence call receives appropriate visual and/or audible notification of the precedence level of the call, and any lower-precedence call that might be active on the target user's phone is preempted. For a call between a user device and a trunk-side device, if the target gateway is fully subscribed, the precedence of other calls on the route group gets sampled for precedence level and a call with lower precedence gets selected and preempted. For T1 PRI and T1-CAS gateways, the determination is based on all DS-0s being in use. For H.323 intercluster trunks (ICT), the determination is based on CallManager's locations-based call admission control mechanism. Precedence levels are also passed over the T1 PRI, T1-CAS, or H.323 ICT trunk to the remote PBX so that the precedence level of the call can be preserved across PBX domains.

Provisions also exist for optionally configuring an alternate party diversion target on user devices in the event that the target phone does not answer the precedence call. If no alternate party target is defined, normal call forward no answer (CFNA) and call forward busy (CFB) paths are followed.

Table A-33 provides information about MLPP service parameters (**Service > Service Parameters >** *select a server* **> Cisco CallManager**).

Table A-34 provides information about MLPP enterprise parameters (**System > Enterprise Parameters**).

Table A-33 *MLPP Service Parameters*

Service Parameter	Default	Valid Values
Locations-based MLPP Enable Determines whether to enable locations-based MLPP. Locations-based MLPP ensures that bandwidth is allocated for precedence calls when using locations-based call admission control.	False	True or False
Executive Override Call Preemptable Determines whether a call marked as Executive Override can preempt another call that is also marked as Executive Override.	False	**True**—The new Executive Override call preempts the existing Executive Override call, and the existing call hears a tone or announcement indicating that the call has been preempted **False**—The existing Executive Override call is not preempted when another Executive Override call arrives, and the new caller hears a tone or announcement indicating that the new precedence call cannot be established

Table A-34 *MLPP Enterprise Parameters*

Enterprise Parameter	Default	Valid Values
MLPP Domain Identifier Specifies the service domain used by MLPP. The MLPP service applies to an MLPP domain only. Connections and resources that belong to a call from an MLPP subscriber get marked with a precedence level and MLPP domain identifier that only calls of higher precedence from MLPP users in the same MLPP domain can preempt. Reset all devices for the change to take effect. You can reset all devices by resetting every device pool in the system.	0	Hex values only (value must start with 0x): 0 to 16777215
MLPP Indication Status Determines whether the device should apply MLPP services such as tones, special displays and sending of MLPP/precedence-related Precedence information element (IE) and values in Signal and Cause IEs.	MLPP Indication turned off	MLPP Indication turned off MLPP Indication turned on

continues

Table A-34 *MLPP Enterprise Parameters (Continued)*

Enterprise Parameter	Default	Valid Values
MLPP Preemption Setting Determines whether a device should apply preemption and preemption signaling (preemption tones/information elements) to accommodate higher-precedence calls. Reset all devices for the parameter change to take effect. You can reset all devices by resetting every device pool in the system.	No Preemption Allowed	**No Preemption Allowed** **Forceful Preemption**— Lower-precedence calls terminate when a higher-precedence call arrives that, to complete the call, needs the resource that the lower-precedence call currently uses
Precedence Alternate Party Timeout Specifies the maximum time to wait before diverting a call to the predetermined alternate party when the called party has MLPP Alternate Party Settings specified in the Directory Number Configuration page in CallManager Administration and the called party does not acknowledge preemption or does not answer a precedence call before this timer expires.	30 seconds	4 to 60 seconds
Use Standard VM Handling for Precedence Calls Determines whether a precedence call is forwarded to the voice mail system, such as when no answer or busy signal occurs. For MLPP, Cisco recommends that a voice mail system does not answer precedence calls; rather, configure the system so that MLPP calls forward to an operator.	False	True or False

Multiple Calls per Line

CallManager supports multiple calls on the same line. Depending on the phone model, some phones can display up to 200 calls on a single line. The user scrolls to view each call. The multiple calls per line feature eliminates the need to create multiple instances of the same directory number in different partitions to allow users to share a line and still be able to receive and place multiple calls out of the same line. To easily manage more than one call on the line and to view calling name and number of the calls on the line, a new user-interaction model exists on the phone display.

In the Directory Number Configuration page, configure the following multiple call/call waiting line parameters on each line of the phone:

- **No Answer Ring Duration**—Used in conjunction with Call Forward No Answer Destination, this field sets the timer for how long the phone rings before the call gets forwarded. Leave this setting blank to use the value specified in the Forward No Answer Timer service parameter (detailed in Table A-10).

- **Maximum Number of Calls**—You can configure up to 200 calls for a line on a device, with the limiting factor being the total number of calls that are configured on the device. As you configure the number of calls for one line, the calls that are available for another line decrease.

- **Call Forward No Answer**—This field forwards calls when the phone is not answered after the configured No Answer Ring Duration.

- **Busy Trigger**—This setting, which works in conjunction with Maximum Number of Calls and Call Forward Busy fields, determines the maximum number of calls that can be offered to the line before additional incoming calls roll to the Call Forward Busy destination, if configured.

Multiple Line Appearances per Phone

Cisco IP Phones provide multiple line appearances. See the section "Line" for more information.

Music on Hold

The integrated Music on Hold (MOH) feature provides the ability to place OnNet and OffNet users on hold with music from a streaming source. MOH sources can be either Unicast or Multicast, and can be configured separately for user hold and network hold. User hold occurs when the user places a caller on hold. Network hold occurs when CallManager places a call on hold, such as during call park, conference, or transfer operations. OnNet devices include Cisco IP Phones and applications placed on any form of hold by an Integrated Voice Response (IVR) system or call distributor. OffNet users include those connected through MGCP or SCCP-based gateways, Cisco IOS H.323 gateways, and Cisco IOS MGCP gateways.

Up to 51 different audio sources are supported by each Cisco MCS 7815, 7825, or 7835 server. The audio sources include the following:

- Fifty continuously looping .wav file sources stored on the hard disk drive of the server

- One real-time encoding source from a sound card installed in the server

Server capabilities and processing load are some of the factors that determine how many streaming sessions a server can provide. By way of example, each Cisco MCS 7835 server supports a maximum of 250 simultaneous on-hold streaming sessions when the server is a dedicated MOH server, and up to 25 simultaneous streams when the MOH service is configured on the same server (that is, co-resident) as other CallManager services. You can install multiple MOH servers per cluster for application scalability, server load balancing, and redundancy. Other servers will have different limitations; check your product documentation for details.

CallManager MOH service supports the following compression formats:

- G.711 (μ-law and A-law)

- G.729a

- Cisco wideband audio codec

Each .wav file stored on the hard disk drive of the server is automatically translated to each of the preceding codec formats using an audio translation utility.

Chapter 5 provides complete information about music on hold. See also the section "Tone on Hold."

Table A-35 provides information about MOH CallManager service parameters that you can access on the Service Parameters Configuration page (**Service > Service Parameters >** *select a server >* **Cisco CallManager**).

Table A-36 provides information about MOH IP Voice Media Streaming App service parameters that you can access on the Service Parameters Configuration page (**Service > Service Parameters >** *select a server >* **Cisco IP Voice Media Streaming App**).

Table A-35 *Music on Hold (CCM.exe) Service Parameters*

Service Parameter	Default	Valid Values
Suppress MOH to Conference Bridge Determines whether MOH plays to a conference when a conference participant places the conference on hold.	True	True or False
Default Network Hold MOH Audio Source ID Specifies the clusterwide network hold (hold initiated by features such as transfer, conference, call park, and so on) audio source ID. The system uses this audio source when no higher levels (device pool, device, and directory number levels) of audio source ID are defined/chosen.	1	1 to 51
Default User Hold MOH Audio Source ID Specifies the clusterwide user hold (hold initiated by the user) audio source ID. The system uses this audio source when no higher levels (device pool, device, and directory number levels) of audio source ID are defined/chosen.	1	1 to 51

Table A-35 *Music on Hold (CCM.exe) Service Parameters (Continued)*

Service Parameter	Default	Valid Values
Duplex Streaming Enabled Determines whether MOH and annunciator use duplex streaming.	False	**True**—MOH and annunciator use duplex (two-way) streaming. Choosing True facilitates interoperability with certain firewalls and routers configured for Network Address Translation (NAT) **False**—MOH and annunciator use simplex (one-way) streaming

Table A-36 *Music on Hold (IPVMSA.exe) Service Parameters*

Service Parameter	Default	Valid Values
Supported MOH Codecs Specifies the codec (compression/decompression) types that the MOH system should support. Choose one or more codec types by pressing the Ctrl key and clicking the codecs you want to select. G.729a is optimized for speech, and, when used for music, the audio quality is very marginal. G.729 Annex A is compatible with G.729.	G.711 μ-law	G.711 μ-law G.711 A-law G.729 Annex A—This codec is optimized for speech so the audio fidelity of music is marginal Wideband
Default TFTP MOH IP Address Specifies the computer name or IP address of the default MOH TFTP server. This server should contain the configured MOH audio source files for the MOH system to transfer to the local machine on request by using the TFTP server. If the name of the TFTP server used by MOH is changed, you must update this parameter with the new TFTP server name.	No default value	Up to 63 characters

Mute

Many Cisco IP Phones allow the user to disconnect the handset or speakerphone microphone so the other party cannot hear the user. The Mute button toggles on and off.

NewCall

The NewCall softkey on Cisco IP Phones allows the user to access an available line without lifting the handset. The line is accessed automatically by speakerphone, unless a headset is attached. The softkey is automatically available on Cisco IP Phones that provide softkeys and there are no configuration requirements.

North American Numbering Plan (NANP) and Non-NANP Support

CallManager supports the use of NANP and non-NANP route plans. A built-in macro file is provided during installation that supports any number sequence used in the NANP. This macro is invoked by using the @ wildcard when configuring an external route pattern. When the @ wildcard is used, CallManager matches any number dialed in the NANP against that route pattern (for example, 9.@ allows the user to dial 9 as an access code, receive a secondary dial tone, and then dial any number recognized by the NANP).

Further manipulation of the NANP in CallManager is provided through the use of route filters, where you can filter on any combination of area codes, access codes, country codes, and so on. This makes it easy to configure a single route pattern (9.@, for example) for reaching any destination in the NANP, but filtering out certain number sequences, such as 900 numbers; or for filtering on known area codes to least-cost route a call out a remote gateway.

Non-NANP Support

See the "International Dial Plan" section for information.

On-Hook and Off-Hook Dialing

All Cisco IP Phones provide a dial tone automatically when the phone goes off-hook (user lifts the handset or presses a line button, a speakerphone button, or the **NewCall** softkey, and so on). Users of Cisco IP Phones 79*xx* can also dial a number while on-hook, and then lift the receiver or press the **Dial** softkey to have the phone go off-hook to the speakerphone or headset and dial the number automatically. Entering a pause character is not supported.

Overlap Sending/Receiving

CallManager supports Q.931 overlap sending procedure for E1 PRI in both User and Network modes. Overlap sending procedure is a part of the International Telecommunication Union (ITU) standard. With this procedure, the route plan for a CallManager system can be simplified in the environments where route patterns with various lengths and patterns are required. See Chapter 2 for more information about overlap sending or receiving.

Paperless Phone

Cisco IP Phones 79xx provide LCD button labels directly on the phone's display, eliminating the need for printed button labeling that was required with earlier models or legacy phones such as the 12SP+ and Cisco IP Phone 7910 when the default template is used.

Performance Monitoring and Alarms

You can monitor the performance of the CallManager system by way of SNMP statistics from applications to the Real-Time Monitoring Tool (RTMT), the SNMP manager, or Microsoft Performance (a Microsoft monitoring application). Nearly every aspect of the CallManager cluster has a counter associated with it, and you can choose which counters to monitor. You can configure alarms to monitor a particular counter and generate an alert when a given threshold is reached. Learn more about monitoring in Chapter 6.

The Cisco Serviceability Reporter service provides two service parameters relating to RTMT configuration (**Service > Service Parameters >** *select a server* **> Cisco Serviceability Reporter**), as described in Table A-37.

Table A-37 *Cisco Serviceability Reporter Service Parameters*

Service Parameter	Default	Valid Values
RTMT Report Generation Time Specifies the number of minutes after midnight (00:00) when Real-Time Monitoring Tool reports are generated. To reduce any impact to call processing, run non-real-time reports during non-production hours.	30 minutes	0 to 1439 minutes
RTMT Report Deletion Age Specifies the number of days that must elapse before reports are deleted. For example, if this parameter is set to 7, reports that were generated seven days ago get deleted on the eighth day. A value of 0 disables report generation, and any existing reports get deleted.	7 days	0 to 30 days

Privacy

In a shared-line appearance situation, the user who first goes off-hook on the shared-line appearance has privacy on the line. Privacy controls whether other users who share a line with the first user can see call information and have the ability to barge or cBarge into a call on the first user's station. See the "Barge/cBarge" section for more details.

Privacy can be configured at the device level, line level by assigning a Privacy button, or at the system level via the service parameter described in Table A-38.

Table A-38 provides information about the privacy service parameter (**Service > Service Parameters >** *select a server* **> Cisco CallManager**).

Table A-38 *Privacy Service Parameter*

Service Parameter	Default	Valid Value
Privacy Setting Determines whether the Privacy feature is enabled for phones that use the Default value in the Privacy setting on the Phone Configuration page in CallManager Administration. Privacy removes the call information from all phones that share lines and blocks other shared lines from barging in on its calls.	True	True or False

Private Line Automatic RingDown (PLAR) Support

CallManager can be configured to support the PLAR phone feature for virtually any device (IP phone, POTS phone, gateway trunk, application, and so on) by using partitions and calling search spaces. You can configure the calling search space of the phone so that when it goes off-hook it can only dial a single destination. This destination would become the best match, and would immediately connect to that number without the user having to dial any digits. See Chapter 2 for more information about PLAR.

QSIG Support

> **NOTE**   This feature was introduced in CallManager release 3.3(2) and enhanced in releases 3.3(3), 4.0(1), and 4.1(2).

CallManager supports QSIG signaling on MGCP-controlled T1 and E1 PRI trunks. The implementation of QSIG in CallManager is compliant with the International Standards Organization (ISO) I-ETS 300-170 specification. For compatibility with older ECMA variants of the QSIG protocol, CallManager release 4.1(2) introduces service parameters in which the ASN.1 ROSE OID encoding and QSIG variant values can be configured. See Table A-39 for details.

Table A-39 *QSIG Variant Service Parameters*

Service Parameter	Default	Valid Values
ASN.1 ROSE OID Encoding Specifies how to encode the Invoke Object ID (OID) for remote operations service element (ROSE) operations. Keep this parameter set to the default value unless a Cisco support engineer instructs otherwise.	Use Local Value	**Use Local Value**—Supported by most telephony systems and should be used when the QSIG Variant service parameter is set to ISO (Protocol Profile 0x9F) **Use Global Value (ISO)**—Use only if the connected PBX does not support Local Value **Use Global Value (ECMA)**—Use if the QSIG Variant service parameter is set to ECMA (Protocol Profile 0x91)
QSIG Variant Specifies the protocol profile that is sent in outbound QSIG facility information elements when the trunk is configured for QSIG. If this service parameter is set to ECMA (Protocol Profile 0x91), the ASN.1 Rose OID Encoding service parameter should be set to Use Global Value (ECMA). If this parameter is set to ISO (Protocol Profile 0x9F), the ASN.1 Rose OID Encoding service parameter should be set to Use Local Value. Keep this parameter set to the default value unless a Cisco support engineer instructs otherwise. **CAUTION** CallManager does not support ECMA when using intercluster trunks with the Tunneled Protocol field set to QSIG on the Trunk Configuration page in CallManager Administration. If you set this service parameter to ECMA (Protocol Profile 0x91), all intercluster trunks must have the Tunneled Protocol field set to None.	ISO (Protocol Profile 0x9F)	**ECMA (Protocol Profile 0x91)**—Typically used with ECMA PBXs that only use Protocol Profile 0x91 **ISO (Protocol Profile 0x9F)**—The current ISO recommendation

Although compatibility depends on the model and version of PBX, in general CallManager supports the following QSIG identification services:

- Calling Line Identification Presentation (CLIP)

- Calling Name Identification Presentation (CNIP)

- Connected Name Identification Presentation (CONP)

- Calling/Connected Line Identification Restriction (CLIR)

- Calling/Connected Name Identification Restriction (CNIR) (added in release 4.0(1))

- Alerting Name (added in release 4.1(2))

CallManager supports QSIG only on MGCP-controlled T1/E1 PRI gateway trunks. CallManager release 4.1(2) introduced support for H.323 Annex M.1, which allows the tunneling of QSIG over H.323 intercluster trunk and H.323 gateway connections. Annex M.1 is only compatible with the ISO variant of QSIG, so if ROSE encoding values are configured to interoperate with an older QSIG PBX, you cannot use Annex M.1 over your H.323 intercluster trunks. In addition, prior to CallManager release 3.3(3), QSIG trunks and non-QSIG trunks cannot be configured as members of the same route list or route group in CallManager.

Support for QSIG and Non-QSIG Devices in Route Lists

CallManager supports route lists that contain both a route group with QSIG devices and a route group with non-QSIG devices in the same configuration. This provides greater flexibility in configuring alternate routes when a QSIG span is down or when the span is oversubscribed.

Message Waiting Indication Support

CallManager supports sending and receiving message waiting indication (MWI) QSIG application protocol data units (APDU) to allow voice mails on one side of a QSIG trunk to light the message waiting lamp of subscribers on the other side of the QSIG trunk.

Call Diversion (Also Known as Call Forward)

> **NOTE**   This feature was introduced in CallManager release 4.0(1) and enhanced in release 4.1(2).

CallManager release 4.0(1) implemented call diversion by using forward switching. Additionally, release 4.0(1) protects calls from going into forwarding loops by using call diversion counters. APDUs carry the call diversion information. CallManager 4.1(2) introduced call diversion by reroute. CallManager supports the following supplementary services:

- Call Forward Unconditional (SS-CFU)

- Call Forward Busy (SS-CFB)

- Call Forward No Reply (SS-CFNR)

Call Completion (Also Known as Call Back)

> **NOTE**   This feature was introduced in CallManager release 4.1(2).

You can activate the Cisco Extended Functions service for a destination phone that is on a remote Private Integrated Network Exchange (PINX, which for the purposes of this discussion, is a term that represents CallManager or a PBX) over QSIG trunks or QSIG-enabled intercluster trunks, and vice versa.

Path Replacement

> **NOTE**   This feature was introduced in CallManager release 4.1(2).

In a QSIG network, a switch such as CallManager or other PBX represents a PINX. After a call is transferred or forwarded to a phone in a third PINX, multiple connections through at least three PINXs can exist for the call. When the call connects, the path replacement feature drops the connection to the transit PINX(s) and establishes a new, more direct call connection to the terminating PINX. CallManager initiates path replacement for calls that are transferred by joining and for calls that are diverted by forward switching only. See Table A-40 for service parameters relating to the path replacement feature.

Table A-40 *Path Replacement Service Parameters*

Service Parameter	Default	Valid Values
Path Replacement Enabled Enables the QSIG path replacement feature. Path replacement is used in a QSIG network to optimize the call path between two edge PINXs (CallManagers or PBXs) involved in a call to minimize the number of B-channels in use when users are not located in the same cluster or on the same system (such as when CallManager is interacting with a PBX). For example, A calls B and B transfers the call to C, resulting in the use of two B-channels (one from A to B and another from B to C). With path replacement, CallManager is able to reduce the number of B-channels in use from two to one in the same scenario, so that only a B-channel between A and C is in use (provided that a meshed network topology is implemented). **NOTE** Enabling this parameter could affect the functionality of applications that were released before CallManager release 4.1. Be sure to check version compatibility of all applications installed in your IP Communications network. Disabling the companion parameter, Path Replacement on Tromboned Calls, eliminates the scenarios that can adversely impact older applications.	False	True or False
Path Replacement on Tromboned Calls Determines whether path replacement occurs on tromboned connections. A *tromboned connection* is one in which two parties on a CallManager cluster are connected via QSIG trunking. Path replacement interferes with backward compatibility for some CTI applications; if you discover a problem with a CTI application, try disabling this parameter to resolve the problem.	True	True or False
Start Path Replacement Minimum Delay Time Specifies the minimum amount of time to wait after call connection before proposing a path replacement. Choosing a value of zero means that path replacement will be proposed as soon as the call is in a connected state.	0 seconds	0 to 30 seconds
Start Path Replacement Maximum Delay Time Specifies the maximum amount of time to wait after call connection before proposing a path replacement. If the value in this parameter is less than or equal to the value specified in the Start Path Replacement Minimum Delay Time parameter, the value in this parameter will be ignored. If this value is larger than the Start Path Replacement Minimum Delay Time, a random value between Start Path Replacement Minimum Delay Time and Start Path Replacement Maximum Delay Time will be used. You can specify an exact number of seconds to wait before proposing a path replacement by setting the Minimum and Maximum values to the same number. For example, if you set both the Start Path Replacement Minimum Delay Time parameter and the Start Path Replacement Maximum Delay Time parameter to 5, the path replacement proposal will occur exactly 5 seconds after the call is connected.	0 seconds	0 to 30 seconds

Table A-40 *Path Replacement Service Parameters (Continued)*

Service Parameter	Default	Valid Values
Path Replacement T1 Timer Specifies the time that CallManager waits for a SETUP message from the far-end PINX (CallManager or PBX) after proposing a path replacement. When this timer expires, CallManager no longer responds to messages about path replacement for this call instance.	30 seconds	30 to 60 seconds
Path Replacement T2 Timer Specifies the time that CallManager waits for a DISCONNECT message for the original call reference from the far-end PINX (CallManager or PBX) after sending a CONNECT message on the new call reference. If this timer expires before a DISCONNECT message is received from the far end, CallManager sends the DISCONNECT message.	15 seconds	15 to 30 seconds
Path Replacement PINX ID Specifies the path replacement PINX ID, up to 20 digits in length. There are two modes in which to do path replacement: Use the user's directory number (DN) as the rerouting number for the path replacement or use a PINX ID (a DN which is unique in your network to represent this CallManager cluster) as the rerouting number. If this parameter is blank, the user's DN is used in the rerouting. If this parameter is not blank, the number specified in this parameter is used as the rerouting number for the path replacement. If you specify a number in this parameter, you must create a call pickup group with a DN of the same number. This call pickup group should remain empty; do not use it as an actual call pickup group.	N/A	Up to 20 characters using digits 0 through 9
Path Replacement Calling Search Space Specifies the calling search space that CallManager (as the cooperating PINX) uses when sending a SETUP message to the system that requested path replacement (the requesting PINX) for completion of path replacement.	N/A	N/A

QSIG over H.323 (Annex M.1)

> **NOTE**   This feature was introduced in CallManager release 4.1(2).

The Annex M.1 feature uses intercluster trunks to transport (tunnel) non-H.323 protocol information in H.323 signaling messages between CallManager nodes. Annex M.1 supports QSIG calls and QSIG call independent signaling connections.

QSIG tunneling supports the call completion, call diversion, call transfer, identification services, message waiting indication, and path replacement features.

Quality of Service (QoS)

QoS is an integral part of the Cisco IP Communications architecture. CallManager, IP phones, gateways, and network resources (conference bridges, transcoders, music on hold servers, and so on) all support QoS.

Differentiated Services (DiffServ) and IP Precedence (ToS)

Support is provided for the Differentiated Services Code Point (DSCP), as well as the older IP Precedence method, in the IPv4 header. By default, the ICCP protocol link (in other words, the signaling channel) is marked as follows:

- **Signaling channel**—DSCP = Conversational services (CS)3/IP Precedence = 3

The marking of the voice bearer channel depends on whether the call is a video call or voice-only call. By default for a voice-only call the voice bearer channel is marked as follows:

- **Audio call**—DSCP = Expedited Forwarding (EF)/IP Precedence = 5

In a video call both the voice bearer and video bearer channels are marked as follows, by default:

- **Video call**—DSCP = Assured Forwarding (AF41)/IP Precedence = 4

DSCP values can be modified via the CallManager service parameters described in Table A-41. However, Cisco strongly recommends that you do not modify these values.

Table A-41 provides information about DSCP-related service parameters (**Service > Service Parameters >** *select a server* **> Cisco CallManager**).

Table A-41 *DSCP Service Parameters*

Service Parameter	Default	Valid Values
DSCP for Audio Calls Specifies the Differentiated Service Code Point (DSCP) value for audio calls. Keep this parameter set to the default value unless a Cisco support engineer instructs otherwise.	EF DSCP (101110)	AF11 DSCP (001010) AF12 DSCP (001100) AF13 DSCP (001110) AF21 DSCP (010010) AF22 DSCP (010100) AF23 DSCP (010110)

Table A-41   *DSCP Service Parameters (Continued)*

Service Parameter	Default	Valid Values
DSCP for Audio Calls *Continued*		AF31 DSCP (011010)
		AF32 DSCP (011100)
		AF33 DSCP (011110)
		AF41 DSCP (100010)
		AF42 DSCP (100100)
		AF43 DSCP (100110)
		CS1(precedence 1) DSCP (001000)
		CS2(precedence 2) DSCP (010000)
		CS3(precedence 3) DSCP (011000)
		CS4(precedence 4) DSCP (100000)
		CS5(precedence 5) DSCP (101000)
		CS6(precedence 6) DSCP (110000)
		CS7(precedence 7) DSCP (111000)
		default DSCP (000000)
		EF DSCP (101110)
DSCP for Video Calls Specifies the DSCP value for video calls. This is used for both the voice and video bearer channel. Keep this parameter set to the default value unless a Cisco support engineer instructs otherwise.	EF DSCP (100010)	Same values as for DSCP for Audio Calls parameter

continues

Table A-41 *DSCP Service Parameters (Continued)*

Service Parameter	Default	Valid Values
DSCP for ICCP Protocol Links Specifies the DSCP IP classification for the Intracluster Communication Protocol (ICCP) protocol links. Keep this parameter set to the default value unless a Cisco support engineer instructs otherwise. Restart the Cisco CallManager service for the parameter change to take effect.	CS3(precedence 3) DSCP (011000)	Same values as for DSCP for Audio Calls parameter

Table A-42 provides information about DSCP-related enterprise parameters (**System > Enterprise Parameters**).

Table A-42 *DSCP Enterprise Parameters*

Enterprise Parameter	Default	Valid Values
DSCP for SCCP Phone-based Services Specifies the DSCP IP classification for IP phone services on SCCP-based phones, including any HTTP traffic. Restart SCCP-based phones for this parameter change to take effect.	DSCP (000000)	AF11 DSCP (001010) AF12 DSCP (001100) AF13 DSCP (001110) AF21 DSCP (010010) AF22 DSCP (010100) AF23 DSCP (010110) AF31 DSCP (011010) AF32 DSCP (011100) AF33 DSCP (011110) AF41 DSCP (100010) AF42 DSCP (100100) AF43 DSCP (100110) CS1(precedence 1) DSCP (001000) CS2(precedence 2) DSCP (010000)

Table A-42 *DSCP Enterprise Parameters (Continued)*

Enterprise Parameter	Default	Valid Values
DSCP for SCCP Phone-based Services *Continued*		CS3(precedence 3) DSCP (011000)
		CS4(precedence 4) DSCP (100000)
		CS5(precedence 5) DSCP (101000)
		CS6(precedence 6) DSCP (110000)
		CS7(precedence 7) DSCP (111000)
		default DSCP (000000)
		EF DSCP (101110)
DSCP for SCCP Phone Configuration Specifies the DSCP IP classification for any SCCP-based phone configuration, including any TFTP, DNS, or DHCP access that is necessary for phone configuration. Restart SCCP-based phones for this parameter change to take effect.	CS3(precedence 3) DSCP (011000)	Same values as for DSCP for DSCP for SCCP Phone-based Services parameter
DSCP for Cisco CallManager to Device Interface Specifies the DSCP IP classification for protocol control interfaces that are used in CallManager-to-device communications. Restart CallManager servers and associated devices for this parameter change to take effect.	CS3(precedence 3) DSCP (011000)	Same values as for DSCP for DSCP for SCCP Phone-based Services parameter

802.1p Class of Service (CoS)

Cisco IP Phones 79*xx* support the use of the 802.1p field in the IEEE 802.3 Ethernet frame header. Using Cisco Discovery Protocol between the phones and the upstream switch, the switch is able to "trust" the phone to set its Layer 2 CoS. This provides a scalable and dynamic way of ensuring the correct QoS for voice packets as they enter into the edge of the network. See the section "Cisco Discovery Protocol (CDP) Support" for additional information.

In addition, Cisco IP Phones that offer a secondary Ethernet interface for connecting to a downstream PC will automatically rewrite the Layer 2 CoS value of frames entering the PC port, thereby eliminating the PC user's ability to accidentally or maliciously override the QoS values that the PC's applications should receive.

QoS Statistics

You can view QoS statistics in real time by accessing the built-in HTTPD interface on Cisco IP Phones 79*xx* and various hardware transcoding/conferencing resources such as the Cisco Catalyst 6000 (WS-6608-x1) eight-port module. Access lists and/or firewalls can be used to restrict access to the built-in HTTPD server on these devices, which in turn might restrict your access to QoS statistics.

In addition, some Cisco IP Phones (such as 7971, 7961, but not 7920, 7912, or 7905) provide QoS statistics on the phone itself. During an active call, press the **i** or **?** button twice in quick succession. QoS statistics for the active call are shown on the phone's display.

Finally, all Cisco IP Phones and various hardware transcoding/conferencing resources send these QoS statistics to the CallManager server for inclusion into the CDR files stored in the database of the cluster. You can view these QoS statistics using CAR to capture trends (for example, every time a certain gateway is used to connect a call, the QoS statistics show negative results). See the "CDR Analysis and Reporting (CAR) Tool" section for more details.

Quality Reporting Tool (QRT)

QRT allows users to report phone-related problems to you by pressing the **QRT** softkey on any softkey-supporting Cisco IP Phone. After pressing the **QRT** softkey, the user is prompted to select one of the predefined problem definitions, such as "poor audio quality" or "phone rebooted." The report is sent via XML to the QRT web service running on one or more CallManager nodes in the cluster. This data is stored and you can run reports on the IP Phone Problem Reporting page in CallManager Serviceability (**Tools > QRT Viewer**).

You can choose to provide additional prompts for the user and configure other details for the QRT service by using the service parameters in the Cisco Extended Functions service (**Service > Service Parameters >** *select a server* **> Cisco Extended Functions**), as described in Table A-43.

Table A-43 *QRT Service Parameters*

Service Parameter	Default	Valid Values
Display Extended QRT Menu Choices Determines whether additional menu choices are presented to the user after the QRT softkey is pressed during an active call. The extended menu provides a list of choices that the user can select to explain the quality problem that is occurring, such as "I hear echo."	False	True or False

Table A-43 *QRT Service Parameters (Continued)*

Service Parameter	Default	Valid Values
Streaming Statistics Polling Duration Specifies the time during which streaming statistics can be captured from the IP phone when the user presses the **QRT** softkey during an active call. The information includes statistics such as jitter and packet loss. A duration of −1 means that polling continues until the call ends. A duration of 0 disables polling. Any positive value represents the number of seconds to allow polling; polling stops when the call ends. This parameter works in combination with the Streaming Statistics Polling Frequency parameter: This parameter specifies the length of time polling can occur, and the polling frequency determines how many seconds to wait before polling again. For example, this parameter is set to 90 seconds and the Streaming Statistics Polling Frequency parameter is set to 10 seconds. For a call that lasts 120 seconds, the call will be polled 9 times (poll when the user presses the **QRT** softkey and then poll every 10 seconds until the call ends or, in this case, until the Streaming Statistics Polling Duration of 90 seconds expires).	−1 seconds	−1 to 10000 seconds
Streaming Statistics Polling Frequency Designates the seconds to wait between each poll for statistics on an active call. This parameter works in combination with the Streaming Statistics Polling Duration parameter: This parameter specifies how long to wait before polling again and the Streaming Statistics Polling Duration specifies the length of time that polling is allowed. For example, this parameter is set to 15 seconds, and the Streaming Statistics Polling Duration parameter is set to 40 seconds. For a call that lasts 120 seconds, the call will be polled 3 times (poll when the user presses the **QRT** softkey and then poll every 15 seconds, which means that polling occurs at the 0-, 15-, and 30-second marks after the softkey is pressed).	30 seconds	30 to 3600 seconds
Log File Specifies the absolute path where QRT report files are stored.	Default: C:\Program Files\Cisco\QRT\QRT.xml	255 characters
Maximum No. of Files Specifies the maximum number of files that QRT collects before restarting the file count and overwriting old files.	250 files	1 to 100000 files
Maximum No. of Lines Per File Specifies the maximum number of lines in each QRT file before the next file is started.	2000 lines	100 to 2000 lines

Redial/REDL

Redial allows the user to automatically speed dial the last number dialed on a line. If the Cisco IP Phone has multiple lines, the user can press a specific line button and then press **Redial** to redial the last number dialed on the selected line. If a specific line is not selected before pressing **Redial**, the phone automatically redials the last number dialed on Line 1. Redial is automatically available for all Cisco IP Phones except 12SP+ and 7910, where it can be configured on the button template (**Device > Phone Button Template**). No configuration is necessary for other Cisco IP Phone models.

Redirected Number Identification Service (RDNIS)

See the section "Dialed Number Identification Service (DNIS) and RDNIS."

Redundancy/Failover

CallManager provides several forms of redundancy:

- **Database redundancy**—CallManager servers in a cluster maintain backup copies of their shared SQL database. This database is kept in constant sync between the Publisher and Subscriber servers. In addition, CDRs are written to flat files that are stored locally on each Subscriber in the cluster, and then replicated to the Publisher database at fixed intervals. If the Publisher is down, CDRs build up on the Subscribers until the Publisher comes back online, so CDRs are not lost for the time that the Publisher is down.

- **Directory redundancy**—CallManager servers in a cluster maintain backup copies of their shared LDAP directory. This directory is kept in constant sync between all servers in the cluster.

- **Call processing redundancy**—Using Cisco CallManager groups, you can designate backup CallManagers to handle call processing for a disabled CallManager in a form of redundancy known as device failover. All SCCP devices and MGCP gateways receive a list of up to three CallManager servers, ordered according to the priority they will be used in (that is, primary, secondary, tertiary) in their TFTP configuration download. CTI applications and H.323 gateways can be preconfigured with this list.

- **Media resource redundancy**—Multiple transcoding and conferencing resources can be configured to provide redundancy, and these resources take advantage of the call processing redundancy previously described in the event of a CallManager server failure.

- **CTI redundancy**—CTI application servers can be configured redundantly and the applications can take advantage of the call processing redundancy previously described in the event of a CallManager server failure.

- **Gateway/route redundancy**—Multiple gateway trunks can be configured in route groups and route lists which allows CallManager to connect to the first available trunk in the list and roll to the next available trunk if the first one is busy or out of service. The list of trunks in a route group and route groups in a route list can be configured in priority order (designate which should be used first, second, and so on).

- **Voice mail redundancy**—Multiple ports can be connected in CallManager to access the voice mail system, whether it is SCCP-based or you use H.323, MGCP or SCCP gateway ports to connect to it. The ports can be configured in priority order (designate which should be used first, second, and so on).

CallManager Failover Interoperability with Cisco IOS H.323 Gateways

Cisco IOS gateways using release 12.1(2)T support redundant CallManager servers. The command **h225 tcp timeout** *seconds* specifies the time it takes for the Cisco IOS gateway to establish an H.225 control connection for H.323 call setup. If the Cisco IOS gateway cannot establish an H.225 connection to the primary CallManager, it tries a second CallManager defined in another dial-peer statement. The Cisco IOS gateway shifts to the dial-peer statement with next highest preference setting.

This does not provide call preservation of active calls in the event of a CallManager failure because call preservation is not available on H.323 gateways. See the "Call Preservation for Active Calls During CallManager Server Outage" section for more details.

CTI Redundancy

The CTI API supports redundancy. See the "CTI Redundancy with CTIManager" section for details.

Remote Site Survivability for MGCP Gateways

MGCP gateway fallback support is provided on nearly all Cisco IOS gateways. Fallback support provides remote offices a low-cost fallback solution when the WAN connection to CallManager fails.

MGCP gateways connect a Cisco IP Communications network to traditional telephone trunks or analog devices. The trunks can be connected to the PSTN or existing PBX systems. The gateways communicate with CallManager using MGCP or H.323 version 2 network. This fallback support allows the default H.323 protocol to be used for basic call handling for FXS, FXO, and T1-CAS interfaces during the fallback period.

Scalability Enhancements Through H.323 Gatekeeper (Beyond Ten Sites)

Support is provided for registering multiple CallManager servers in a cluster with a gatekeeper.

Serviceability Enhancements Through SNMP, CDP, CiscoWorks

Serviceability enhancements are available through SNMP, Cisco Discovery Protocol (CDP), and CiscoWorks. Refer to Chapter 6 for more information about serviceability.

Service URLs on Line/Feature Buttons

CallManager extends the use of line buttons on Cisco IP Phones 7940, 7941, 7960, 7961, 7970, 7971, and the 7914 Expansion Module to include the ability to assign an XML service to the line. The name of the XML service appears next to the line on the phone, and when the user presses the line button the phone immediately accesses the URL associated with that service.

Services on Cisco IP Phones

The **services** button on Cisco IP Phones provides access to Cisco- and customer-created XML services. Services integrate with CallManager through CallManager Administration (**Feature > Cisco IP Phone Services**).

Personal Directory

The Personal Directory feature in the Cisco CallManager User Options web page allows users to create their own personal directory, containing the contacts they add. They then subscribe to the My Address Book service and can retrieve directory information via the **services** button on their phone. Using the Cisco IP Phone Address Book Synchronizer (PABSynch), users can synchronize their Microsoft Outlook and/or Outlook Express address book entries with the personal directory in Cisco CallManager User Options. You must download the plug-in and then post it to a location that end users can access, so they can utilize the PABSynch application. Use the Personal Address Book service to look up entries, make a selection, and press the **Dial** softkey to dial the selected number.

Settings Button on Cisco IP Phones

The **settings** button on Cisco IP Phones provides access to the following features and information, depending on the phone model:

- Contrast

- Ring type

- Network configuration such as DHCP server, MAC address, and more

- Model information such as model number, load file, CTL file, and more

- Status including firmware versions

- Device configuration such as URLs, locales, security configuration, Ethernet configuration, and more

- User preferences such as ring tones, brightness, viewing angle, and more

Contrast/LCD Contrast/Viewing Angle

Contrast allows the user to adjust the contrast of the display panel on the phone. Cisco IP Phones 7971G-GE and 7970G allow the user to adjust the viewing angle, as well as the contrast for any attached Cisco IP Phone 7914 Expansion Modules.

Ring Type

Ring type allows the user to select the type of ring tone used by the phone.

Network Configuration/Network Settings

Network Configuration displays configuration information for the phone. Only a system administrator can unlock the phone and make changes. Refer to your Cisco IP Phone or the end-user documentation for a list of configuration items that can be viewed or modified in Network Configuration. The available configuration items vary depending on the phone model.

Model Information

Model Information displays hardware and software information about the phone such as the MAC address, the various load IDs, serial number, CTL file, and more.

Status/Phone Info

Status displays status messages, network statistics, firmware version information (application load ID and boot load ID), and expansion module statistics (if applicable) for the phone.

Device Configuration

The Device Configuration menu encapsulates all the configuration information provided by CallManager. On phones that provide a Device Configuration menu, you cannot modify any of the device configuration settings locally on the phone. You must use CallManager Administration to make changes.

Device Configuration displays configuration information such as user and network locale, headset, speaker, and video capability, power save settings, Ethernet settings, security information such as whether web access is enabled, the security mode used by the phone, and more.

Single CDR Repository per CallManager Cluster

In a CallManager cluster, a single CallManager server (the Publisher) becomes the collection point for all CDRs, providing a central point for accessing clusterwide call usage statistics and CDRs. You can learn more about this feature in Chapter 7.

Single Point for System/Device Configuration

CallManager Administration provides a single point for all system and device configuration. Because it operates as a collection of web pages, you can administer systems anywhere in the world from a web browser.

Simple Network Management Protocol (SNMP) Support

CallManager provides SNMPv2 support. During CallManager installation, the SNMP service is enabled and you are prompted to change the default SNMP community string. See the "CISCO-CCM-MIB Updates" section for additional information.

Speakerphone/SPKR

Speakerphone-capable Cisco IP Phones such as 12SP+, 30VIP, 7940, 7941, 7960, 7961, 7970, and 7971 provide hands-free communication. Users can press a speaker button to place and answer calls without using the handset. Cisco IP Phone 7910 uses the Speaker and Mute button combination to provide hands-free dialing only.

Speed Dial

Speed dial allows a user to dial a designated phone number with the press of a single button. This feature is available for all Cisco IP Phones, if configured.

Speed dial buttons can be configured on the button templates for all Cisco IP Phones. You can program as many speed dial buttons as there are line/feature buttons on the phone, except for line 1, which must always be a line button. After you designate speed dial buttons on the button template, the user can specify the speed dial numbers in the Cisco CallManager User Options web page. Users can also use abbreviated dialing or the My Fast Dials and Personal Directory XML services to program up to 99 speed dial entries on the phone. See the "Abbreviated Dialing (AbbrDial)" section for more information.

Supplementary Services

CallManager provides support for most types of supplementary services, such as hold or transfer. These features can be invoked by virtually any type of phone (IP phones, POTS phones using MGCP or SCCP gateways, CTI applications, and so on). A gateway trunk port, such as an FXS connection from a PBX, can also invoke supplementary services (via hookflash).

In addition, CallManager provides a service called media termination point (MTP), which allows IP phones to invoke supplementary services for calls that go through an H.323v1 or v2 device that does not support the use of the TerminalCapabilitiesSet=Null (also known as empty capabilities set) function. The MTP can be enabled/disabled on a per-H.323 client, gateway, or trunk basis.

Supplementary Services to Cisco IOS H.323 Gateways Without Media Termination Point (MTP)

Prior to CallManager release 3.1, an MTP was required to offer supplementary services, such as hold and transfer, to calls through an H.323 gateway. Now supplementary services are available during calls routed through Cisco IOS H.323 gateways (includes Cisco gateway models 1760, 26*xx*, 36*xx*, 37*xx*, 38*xx*, 53*xx*, 65*xx*, and 7*xxx*), because of implementation of H.323 version 2 empty capabilities set.

Survivable Remote Site Telephony (SRST)

SRST provides continuous IP telephony services to branch offices via numerous SRST-capable Cisco IOS routers. You can learn more about SRST in Appendix B.

Table A-44 describes the SRST-related enterprise parameter (**System > Enterprise Parameters**).

Table A-44 *SRST Enterprise Parameter*

Enterprise Parameter	Default	Valid Value
Connection Monitor Duration Specifies the duration that a Cisco IP Phone 7940, 7941, 7960 or 7961 currently registered to the SRST router will monitor a link to CallManager before attempting to register with CallManager. This parameter helps prevent the possibility of a flapping WAN interface causing phones to loop back and forth between CallManager and the SRST router. The phone monitors the link to CallManager for 2 minutes (by default) to ensure that a constant connection exists. After this duration expires, the phone unregisters from the SRST reference and registers with CallManager. Reset all devices for the parameter change to take effect. **NOTE** It's likely that a future firmware image will add this capability for Cisco IP Phones 7970G and 7971G-GE.	120 seconds	0 to 2592000 seconds

Syslog Support for Debugging Output

Trace and alarm data can be generated in syslog format and output to a syslog interface, where it can be collected and processed. In CallManager Serviceability, click **Alarm > Configuration >** *click a server > click a service > check the box for* **Syslog Trace**.

System Event Reporting

CallManager reports system events to a common syslog or Windows Event Viewer.

T1/E1 PRI Support

CallManager supports the use of T1/E1 PRI on many Cisco IOS and non-IOS gateways. Support differs on each gateway model depending on whether H.323 or MGCP is used between CallManager and the gateway.

T1/E1-CAS Support

CallManager supports the use of T1/E1-CAS on many Cisco IOS and non-IOS gateways. Support differs on each gateway model depending on whether H.323, MGCP, or SIP is used between CallManager and the gateway.

> **NOTE**   While T1-CAS is supported on MGCP, H.323, and SIP gateways, E1-CAS is only supported on H.323 and SIP gateways.

Telephony Application Programming Interface (TAPI) and JTAPI Support

CallManager provides TAPI 2.1- and JTAPI 1.3-compliant interfaces for CTI applications integration. An SDK is available for third-party developers. You can learn more about TAPI and JTAPI in Chapter 3 and Appendix C.

TAPI/JTAPI Redundancy Support

Cisco JTAPI supports redundancy across CallManager clusters by way of the CTIManager service. CTIManager communicates with all CallManager nodes in the cluster. JTAPI applications communicate with CTIManager instead of a specific CallManager node. If a CallManager node fails, the devices rehome to the next CallManager node in the group, as defined by the prioritized list of CallManager nodes contained in the device pool configured for each device. JTAPI abstracts this transition to the applications.

Time-of-Day Routing

> **NOTE**   This feature was introduced in CallManager release 4.1(2).

Enhancements to partitions and calling search spaces allow you to build time-of-day routing rules (**Route Plan > Class of Control**). You define individual time periods and group them into time schedules. Then associate partitions with these time schedules so that the partitions are made available/unavailable based on the calling search space of the device, the time zone the calling device is in, and what time schedule the partition is in that contains the dialed number.

You can learn more about time-of-day routing in Chapter 2.

Time Zone Configuration

Devices can be configured with the appropriate time zone using CallManager Administration (**System > Device Pool**).

Toll Restriction/Toll Fraud Prevention

CallManager supports toll restriction through the use of dial plan partitioning and route filtering. See the "Dial Plan Partitions and Calling Search Spaces" section for more information.

Tone on Hold

When a user places a caller on hold, CallManager can provide an intermittent tone if MOH is not configured or is out of resources. Table A-45 provides information about the Tone on Hold service parameter (**Service > Service Parameters > *select a server* > Cisco CallManager**).

Table A-45 *Tone on Hold Service Parameter*

Service Parameter	Default	Valid Value
Tone on Hold Timer Determines the number of seconds between every 2 hold tones that are played when a call is put on hold. For non-MGCP-based devices, if this value is 0, the held device plays the hold tone only one time when the caller is put on hold; if the value is 200000, no hold tone plays; otherwise, the held device plays the hold tone every so many seconds (specified by this value) repeatedly. If the specified value is between 1 and 4 seconds, the device raises it to 5 seconds automatically. For MGCP-based devices, the hold tone is disabled if this value is 0 or 200000; any other value enables the hold tone on MGCP-based devices when the caller is put on hold.	10 seconds	0 to 200000 seconds

Tool for Auto-Registered Phone Support (TAPS)

TAPS is a plug-in application (**Application > Install Plugins**) that lets you or users automatically download a predefined user profile to a phone simply by plugging the phone into the auto-registration-enabled network and dialing in to a predefined TAPS directory number. TAPS can be used to update auto-registered phones with existing configurations, or to update auto-registered phones with dummy Media Access Control (MAC) addresses that have been added to the CallManager database using BAT.

Using BAT, you bulk-add phones using dummy MAC addresses, which saves you the labor of manually entering valid MAC addresses for each phone in the bulk operation. You can then use TAPS to update the dummy MAC address automatically in the CallManager database with the phone's actual MAC address. After the phones with dummy MAC addresses have been added to the CallManager database using BAT, either you or the phone's end user can plug the phone into the data port, apply power, and dial the TAPS directory number to initialize the IP phone. TAPS provides voice prompts to walk the user through the short initialization process.

Learn more about TAPS in Appendix B.

Transcoding and Media Termination Point (MTP) Support

CallManager uses the DSP resources in various Cisco IOS and non-IOS devices to provide transcoding between different codecs as needed.

In addition, CallManager and DSP resources provide MTP functionality, which is necessary to provide supplementary services to some H.323 clients. See the "Supplementary Services" section for more information.

Table A-46 provides information about the MTP service parameter (**Service > Service Parameters >** *select a server* **> Cisco CallManager**).

Table A-46 *MTP Service Parameter*

Service Parameter	Default	Valid Value
Fail Call If MTP Allocation Fails Determines whether a call that requires an MTP will be allowed to proceed if no MTP resource is available.	False	**True**—The call will fail if no MTP resource is available **False**—The call stays up and supplementary services are disabled

Table A-47 provides information about the transcoder service parameter (**Service > Service Parameters >** *select a server* **> Cisco CallManager**).

Table A-47 *Transcoder Service Parameter*

Service Parameter	Default	Valid Value
Intercluster Trunk Capabilities Mismatch Timer Specifies the amount of time that CallManager waits to receive updated capabilities from the other CallManager when there is a capability mismatch during an intercluster call; if this timer expires before receiving updated capabilities, CallManager will allocate a local transcoder. This (local) CallManager server uses the updated capabilities information received from the other CallManager to determine whether the local CallManager or the CallManager across the cluster should allocate the transcoder. In addition to this timer expiring, the following two cases will also cause CallManager to automatically allocate a transcoder locally: • If the endpoint on this cluster does not support any capabilities that are compatible with the region specified on this CallManager. • If the far end reports having capabilities compatible with the region on this cluster *and* the endpoint on this cluster has capabilities compatible with the region *and* those capabilities do not overlap, then this cluster will allocate a transcoder if the bandwidth used by this cluster's compatible codec is larger than the bandwidth used by the remote cluster's compatible codec.	1000 milliseconds	100 to 60000 milliseconds

Transfer/XFER/Transf...

Transfer allows a user to send a call to another extension. It is automatically available for any Cisco IP Phone on the system except the Cisco IP Phone 12SP+, where the Transfer button must be configured on the button template. For all other models, there are no configuration requirements. Transfer is also provided in Cisco CallManager Attendant Console. On Cisco IP Phone 30VIP, transfer is a static button called **XFER**. On all other Cisco IP Phones, transfer is a softkey called **Transf...**.

There are two types of transfer:

■ **Blind transfer**—The user transfers a call to another extension.

■ **Consultation transfer**—The user discusses the transferred call with the intended recipient before completing the transfer.

A consultation transfer allows the person receiving the transferred call to be apprised of the situation before connecting with the caller. Figure A-8 illustrates the blind transfer operation.

Figure A-8 *Blind Transfer Operation*

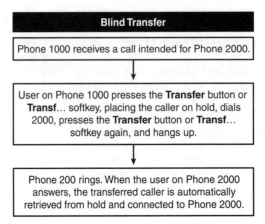

Figure A-9 illustrates the consultation transfer operation.

Figure A-9 *Consultation Transfer Operation*

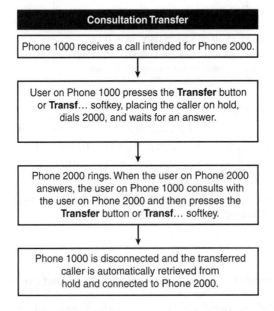

Transfer is available during an active call. To transfer a call, the user presses the **Transf...** softkey and dials the directory number to which the user wants to transfer the call. To complete the transfer, the user presses the **Transf...** softkey again, before or after discussing the call with the intended recipient. A service parameter, Transfer On-hook Enabled, allows users to skip the second step so that the transfer completes when they go on-hook after pressing the **Transf...** softkey. Refer to Figures A-6 and A-7 for more information about blind transfer and consultation transfer. See the "Direct Transfer (DirTrfr)" section for information about that feature.

Table A-48 provides information about transfer service parameters (**Service > Service Parameters >** *select a server* **> Cisco CallManager**).

Table A-48 *Transfer Service Parameters*

Service Parameter	Default	Valid Values
Transfer On-hook Enabled Determines whether a call transfer completes as a result of the user going on-hook after initiating a transfer operation.	False	**True**—The user presses the **Transf...** softkey, dials the number to which the call should be transferred, and then presses the **Transf...** softkey again or simply goes on-hook to complete the transfer operation **False**—The user presses the **Transf...** softkey, dials the number to which the call should be transferred, and then presses the **Transf...** softkey again to complete the transfer operation
Block OffNet to OffNet Transfer **NOTE** This service parameter was introduced in CallManager release 3.3(4) as Block External to External Transfer and renamed in release 4.1(2). Determines whether transfers between external (OffNet) parties are blocked (not allowed). Allowing external transfers could result in toll fraud issues. See the section "External Transfer Restrictions (to Reduce Toll Fraud)" for more information.	False	True or False

External Transfer Restrictions (to Reduce Toll Fraud)

NOTE   This feature was introduced in CallManager release 3.3(4) and enhanced in 4.1(2).

The Block OffNet to OffNet Transfer service parameter described in Table A-48 allows you to prevent users from transferring external calls to another external number. When set to True, CallManager blocks OffNet calls from being transferred to another external device. This clusterwide service parameter affects all types of trunks. In CallManager Administration, you can designate on a trunk-by-trunk basis whether the trunk should be considered an external or internal device. The default is external.

Trivial File Transfer Protocol (TFTP) Support

The Cisco TFTP service builds and serves files consistent with the Trivial File Transfer Protocol, which is a simplified version of the File Transfer Protocol (FTP). Cisco TFTP builds configuration files and serves embedded component executables, ringer files, and device configuration files.

A configuration file contains a prioritized list of CallManager servers for a device (phones and gateways), the TCP port on which the device connects to those CallManager servers, and an executable load identifier. Configuration files for Cisco IP Phones also contain URLs for the phone buttons: messages, directories, services, and information. Configuration files for gateways contain all their configuration information.

Configuration files can be in .cnf format or .cnf.xml format, depending on the device type and your TFTP service parameter settings. When you set the Build CNF Files service parameter to Build All, the TFTP server builds both .cnf.xml and .cnf format configuration files for devices. When you set the parameter to Build None, the TFTP server builds only .cnf.xml files for devices. A third option, Build Selective, lets you build CNF files for legacy devices that do not support XML.

The Cisco TFTP service provides several service parameters relating to TFTP configuration (**Service > Service Parameters >** *select a server* **> Cisco Tftp**), as described in Table A-49.

Table A-49 *Cisco TFTP Service Parameters*

Service Parameter	Default	Valid Values
Alternate File Location 1 The Alternate File Location parameters specify the first through tenth alternate file paths. These locations get searched when a file is not found in the primary TFTP path location of the TFTP server (as specified in the File Location parameter). The Alternate File Location parameters offer an easy method to manage Cisco TFTP options in a multiple-CallManager cluster and multiple-VLAN environment.	No default value	Up to 255 characters
Alternate File Location 2 through **Alternate File Location 10** These parameters specify the second through tenth alternate file path. See the help for Alternate File Location 1 for more information.	No default value	Up to 255 characters
File Delete Determines whether unused configuration files are deleted from the TFTP server. If this parameter is set to True, the TFTP server checks for old files that are no longer used (such as configuration files for devices that have been removed from the database) and deletes them when it starts building configuration files.	True	True or False

Table A-49   *Cisco TFTP Service Parameters (Continued)*

Service Parameter	Default	Valid Values
File Location Specifies the primary TFTP path for caching, building, and serving device configuration and firmware files. When configuring this parameter for use in a multiple-CallManager cluster environment, Cisco recommends that you use UNC configurations (\\IPAddress\path).	C:\Program Files\Cisco\TFT Ppath	Up to 255 characters
Server IP Track Determines whether the local IP address is used. Use this parameter and the TFTP IP Address together if the TFTP server has multiple NIC cards. In that case, set this parameter to False and set the TFTP IP Address parameter to the IP address of the NIC card to use for serving files via TFTP.	True	**True**—Use the local IP address **False**—Use the IP address that the TFTP IP Address parameter specifies
TFTP IP Address Specifies the IP address of the NIC card to use for serving files via TFTP. If your TFTP server has multiple NIC cards, use this parameter in combination with the Server IP Track parameter: set this parameter to the IP address of the NIC card to use for serving files via TFTP and set the Server IP Track to False.	127.0.0.1	Up to 15 characters
Maximum Serving Count Specifies the maximum number of client requests to accept and to serve files at a time. Specify a low value if you are serving files over a low bandwidth connection. You can set it to a higher number if you are serving small files over a large bandwidth connection and when CPU resources are available, such as when no other services run on the TFTP server. Use the default value if the TFTP service is run along with other CallManager services on the same server. Use the following suggested values for a dedicated TFTP server: 1500 for a single-processor system and 3000 for a dual-processor system. If the dual-processor system is running Windows 2000 Advanced Server, the serving count can be up to 5000.	200	1 o 5000

continues

Table A-49 *Cisco TFTP Service Parameters (Continued)*

Clusterwide Parameters (Parameters that apply to all servers)		
Service Parameter	**Default**	**Valid Values**
Build CNF Files Determines whether CNF files are generated in addition to XML files. XML files always get built by default. Consider resource constraints before choosing Build All because this setting consumes more disk space, more memory, and requires additional time to build both XML and CNF files. For the best performance, choose Build None or Build Selective if you have legacy devices.	Build Selective	**Build None**—Build only XML configuration files for all devices) **Build Selective**—Also build CNF configuration files for legacy devices that do not support XML **Build All**—Build both XML and CNF configuration files for all devices
Enable Caching of Constant and Bin Files at Startup Determines whether the TFTP server caches firmware binary files, locale files, and constant files such as ringlist.xml at startup. During CallManager installation, device firmware binary files, locale files, and constant files get installed in the TFTP path.	True	True or False
Enable Caching of Configuration Files Determines whether device configuration files (CNF and XML) are built and kept only in memory (cached). Keeping configuration files in memory cache significantly improves performance. If this parameter is set to False, the TFTP server writes all the CNF and XML files to the TFTP Path on the disk (specified in the File Location service parameter). Writing these files to the disk can take a long time if a large number of devices exist in the network.	True	**True**—Configuration files are kept only in memory **False**—Configuration files are written only to disk

Turn off Phone Display

On Cisco IP Phones 7970 and 7971, you can configure the display to turn off on specific days of the week and the time the display should turn on again. By default, the displays turn off on Sundays. You can also configure phones to turn off the display when the phone has been idle for a specified length of time. The default is one hour of inactivity.

Unicast Conference

Conferences are provided in conjunction with software on CallManager. You can learn more about the Unicast conference feature in Chapter 5.

Video Telephony Support

> **NOTE**   This feature was introduced in CallManager release 4.0(1) and enhanced in release 4.1(2).

CallManager release 4.0(1) added support for video calls by enhancing SCCP and H.323 signaling and call processing with CallManager to allow video calls to be placed using the same model as audio calls. Three types of SCCP video devices exist:

■ **Cisco VT Advantage** — A low-cost PC camera and software application that, when used in conjunction with a Cisco IP Phone 7940, 7941, 7960, 7961, 7970, or 7971, allows the user to make and receive video calls just like they would an ordinary phone call. CallManager release 4.0(1)sr2 or later supports Cisco VT Advantage.

■ **Cisco IP Phone 7985** — A personal desktop audio/video phone that supports H.264, H.263+, H.263, and H.261 video standards. Learn more about Cisco IP Phone 7985 in Chapter 3.

■ **Tandberg SCCP video endpoints** — Tandberg has implemented SCCP on several of their videoconferencing endpoint models. These endpoints mimic, in almost every way, the user experience of a Cisco IP Phone 79*xx*. See the following link for more information:

http://www.tandberg.net/products/video_telephony.jsp

■ **SCCP on Cisco IP/VC 3500 series MCUs** — By implementing SCCP on the IP/VC 3500 series (3511 and 3540 models) multipoint conference units (MCU), video-capable SCCP endpoints can invoke Ad Hoc multiple-party conferences with the touch of a button.

In addition, support is provided for controlling calls made to/from H.323 videoconferencing devices, including H.323 clients, MCUs, and H.323/H.320 gateways. CallManager can either integrate with an H.323 gatekeeper to reach these devices, or the devices can be configured directly in CallManager Administration.

H.281-compliant far-end camera control (FECC) is also provided for SCCP and H.323 clients that offer a pan-tilt-zoom camera.

CallManager also provides a complete set of serviceability features for monitoring and maintaining these video telephony devices, including CDRs accessible through the CDR Analysis and Reporting (CAR) tool, real-time performance monitor statistics and alarms accessible through the Real-Time Monitoring Tool (RTMT) and Microsoft Performance, and detailed call processing trace files accessible through the Trace feature in CallManager Serviceability.

CallManager release 4.1(2) introduced the following video enhancements:

- **SCCP H.264**—Users can place an H.264 video call from an SCCP device. This action assumes that both the calling and called SCCP device support H.264.

- **Mid-call video for Cisco VT Advantage**—Users who turn on Cisco VT Advantage during an active audio call get video if the other party is also using video.

- **Video display mode**— Cisco IP Phones provide a VidMode softkey that toggles the video display mode from Voice Activated to Continuous Presence during a video conference. This feature is available for video conferences that are on a SCCP video bridge that supports this feature.

- **Participant information**—User information displays in the video during a video conference. This feature is available for video conferences that are on a SCCP video bridge that supports this feature.

- **H.323-client integration improvements**—H.323 clients can be configured as gatekeeper-controlled and CallManager will query the gatekeeper to resolve the client's IP address each time a call is placed to the client's directory number. This feature eases the complexity of integrating with third-party H.323 clients.

For an in-depth study of CallManager's video telephony capabilities, refer to the IP Video Telephony Solutions Reference Network Design (SRND) at the following link or search Cisco.com for "Video SRND":

> http://www.cisco.com/go/srnd

Also refer to the "Codec Support (Audio and Video)" section in this appendix for details on which audio and video codecs are supported per endpoint type.

Virus Protection Certification

CallManager has been tested to support certain third-party virus protection software applications. Search Cisco.com for "CallManager virus protection" for details.

Visual Indicator of Ringing Phone

All Cisco IP Phones provide configurable visual notification of an incoming call on a per-line basis. Cisco IP Phones 79xx provide an indicator on the handset and the phone body itself. An incoming call is signaled by the indicator, which strobes in the color red. You can configure the type of indication (audible and visual), or disable it, using the service parameters Ring Setting of

Busy Station Policy, Ring Setting of Busy Station, and Ring Setting of Idle Station in CallManager Administration; and users can configure or disable it on the Cisco CallManager User Options web page (choose the link to **Configure the Ring Settings for Your Phone**).

Table A-50 provides information about the ring policy service parameters (**Service > Service Parameters >** *select a server* **> Cisco CallManager**).

Table A-50 *Ring Policy Service Parameters*

Service Parameter	Default	Valid Values
Ring Setting of Busy Station Policy Specifies the ring setting policy for a busy station when the busy station (phone) changes states from busy to idle to busy again. This parameter works in conjunction with the parameter Ring Setting of Busy Station.	Only Apply Ring Setting of Busy Station When Incoming Call Arrives	**Always Apply Ring Setting of Busy Station**—Regardless of a state change, the busy station always receives the notification that is specified in the Ring Setting of Busy Station parameter **Only Apply Ring Setting of Busy Station When Incoming Call Arrives**—A busy station with an incoming call only provides the ring setting notification that is specified in the Ring Setting of Busy Station parameter when the station is initially in the busy state (for example, if the station changes from busy to idle state by placing a call on hold, and then switches back to busy state by retrieving the call, all while the same call is incoming; then, the busy station no longer receives notification of the same incoming call regardless of the setting that is specified in the Ring Setting of Busy Station parameter)
Ring Setting of Busy Station Determines the kind of notification that is provided when a phone is busy (in use) and an incoming call is received.	Beep Only	Disable—No ring or flash Flash Only Ring Once Ring—Ring until the call is answered, forwarded, or disconnected Beep only
Ring Setting of Idle Station Determines the kind of notification that is provided when a phone is idle (not in use) and an incoming call is received.	Ring	Disable—No ring or flash Flash Only Ring Once Ring—Ring until the call is answered, forwarded, or disconnected

Voice Activity Detection (VAD)/Silence Suppression Support

Cisco IP Phones and gateways provide Voice Activity Detection (VAD). VAD can be enabled/disabled on a systemwide basis in CallManager Administration. VAD is disabled by default.

When VAD is enabled, Cisco IP Phones and gateways provide comfort noise.

Voice Mail Support

CallManager interacts with voice messaging and unified messaging systems using the following types of interfaces:

■ **SCCP**—Cisco Unity uses SCCP to communicate with CallManager to make and receive calls, and send message waiting indicator (MWI) messages.

■ **Analog FXS interfaces and SMDI**—Legacy voice mail systems are supported by connecting one or more analog FXS ports to an MGCP or SCCP gateway and then using an SMDI serial interface to pass calling party/called party and MWI messages between the voice mail system and CallManager. Using an MGCP gateway, the SMDI serial cable is attached directly to a serial port on one of the CallManager servers in the cluster. This CallManager server must be configured to run the Cisco Messaging Interface (CMI) service. The drawback to this approach is that if the CallManager server that the SMDI serial cable is connected to goes down or the CMI service is stopped, voice mail access terminates. Using a Cisco VG248 SCCP gateway, the SMDI serial cable is attached to the VG248, and the VG248 translates SMDI messages into SCCP messages to CallManager. Multiple VG248 gateways can be used for redundancy of the SMDI serial cable connection, and the SCCP connection between the VG248 and CallManager takes advantage of cluster redundancy. In addition, the VG248 actually provides two SMDI interfaces: one to connect to the voice mail system, and one to connect to a legacy PBX (that is, provides an MWI passthrough connection). This allows the voice mail system to be shared between CallManager and a legacy PBX. This method works with any voice mail system and legacy PBX that provide a serial SMDI connection.

■ **Digital interfaces**—Octel voice mail is also supported by connecting the digital trunk from the voice mail system into a Cisco Digital Port Adapter (DPA) 76*xx* series voice mail gateway. The DPA mimics the proprietary protocol of the voice mail system and makes the voice mail system think that it is still talking directly to a PBX. The DPA is then connected to the PBX via the second digital interface (that is, provides a pass-through connection) and to CallManager via SCCP. The pass-through connection to the PBX makes the PBX think that it is still directly connected to the voice mail system. This allows the voice mail system to be shared between CallManager and a legacy PBX. This method only works with select versions of Octel voice mail system that utilize a digital connection.

You can configure the MWI light behavior on a per-line basis, so that if users have more than one line appearance on their phone, they can set the MWI setting on or off per line. Users achieve this in the Cisco CallManager User Options web page.

Voice mail profiles ensure that voice mail settings can be easily applied to multiple phones/users. If a user has multiple line appearances, each line appearance can be assigned a different voice mail profile so that when users press the **messages** button, they will be connected to the voice mail system for that line appearance.

The voice mailbox can be configured with a longer directory number than what is configured on the phone (for example, extension 5000 on the phone, voice mailbox DN of 555-5000). This is useful in multiple-tenant environments or in corporations where overlapping dial plans are present. You can send the expanded DN to the voice mail system so that it can accurately decide which mailbox the call is destined for. The Call Forward Number Expansion mask can be applied in the voice mail profile.

Table A-51 provides information about voice mail-related service parameters in the Cisco CallManager service (**Service > Service Parameters >** *select a server* **> Cisco CallManager**). The Cisco Messaging Interface service also offers other service parameters relating to SMDI configuration.

Table A-51 *Voice Mail-Related Service Parameters*

Service Parameter	Default	Valid Values
SMDI Call Delay Timer Represents the duration by which the call to external voice mail system is delayed.	0 seconds	0 to 10 seconds
Multiple Tenant MWI Modes Determines whether to apply translation patterns to voice mailbox numbers.	False	**True**—CallManager uses translation patterns to convert voice mailbox numbers into directory numbers when your voice messaging system issues a command to set a message waiting indicator **False**—CallManager does not translate the voice mailbox numbers that it receives from your voice messaging system

Volume Controls

All Cisco IP Phones provide volume control for one or more of the following:

- Handset

- Speakerphone

- Ringer

- Headset

XML Support

Cisco IP Phones are capable of launching eXtensible Markup Language (XML) applications that enable the display of interactive content with text and graphics on the phone's LCD display.

When the user presses the **services** button on Cisco IP Phones, the phone uses its HTTP client to load a specific URL that contains a menu of services to which the user has subscribed for the phone. When the user chooses a service from the menu, the URL is requested via HTTP and a server provides the content, which then updates the phone display.

CallManager uses XML to provide certain built-in services, such as extension mobility, the Quality Reporting Tool (QRT), and callback. In addition, the Cisco AVVID Partner Program has hundreds of applications written by Cisco partners and resellers for enabling robust, feature-rich applications to increase productivity, gain a competitive advantage, and even generate revenue. Deployment of Cisco IP Phone services occurs using HTTP from standard web servers, such as the Microsoft Internet Information Server (IIS).

The "Application Programming Interfaces (API)" section provides additional information about the IP Phone Services API. You can also learn more in Chapter 3 and Appendix C. The Cisco Press book *Developing Cisco IP Phone Services* (ISBN: 1-58705-060-9) provides detailed information about building your own custom services and directories.

Zero-Cost Automated Phone Adds and Moves

Cisco IP Phones can auto-register with the system without incurring any cost for doing so, as long as there are available directory numbers and the phones are on the same subnet or have DHCP enabled. See the "Auto-Registration" section earlier in this appendix for more information.

Cisco IP Phones, legacy Skinny Gateway Control Protocol (SGCP) gateways, and MGCP gateways automatically reregister with the same device information (directory number and other settings) when moved from one Ethernet port to another, as long as they are on the same subnet or have DHCP enabled. This results in zero cost for unlimited moves.

Cisco Integrated Solutions

Cisco offers many solutions that you can integrate with Cisco CallManager to enhance the capabilities of the Cisco IP Communications solution. Some solutions are already integrated into CallManager, such as CallManager Serviceability, and other solutions are available as plug-ins in Cisco CallManager Administration (**Application > Install Plugins**). Other solutions detailed in this appendix are external to CallManager and must be installed or integrated separately. Little or no emphasis is placed on integrated solutions that are discussed elsewhere in the book, such as Cisco IP Wireless Phones, Cisco IP Voice Media Streaming App, CTIManager service, and so on, and those services or solutions that are integral to CallManager functionality, such as Cisco TFTP, Cisco CTL Client, CallManager Administration, and more. You can find additional information about each of the solutions at Cisco.com.

> **NOTE** In addition to Cisco offerings, many third-party products are available. This appendix focuses on Cisco-offered solutions. You can learn more about third-party products on the IP Communication partner program web page at the following links or search Cisco.com for "technology developer CallManager" or "partner program CallManager":
>
> ■ http://www.cisco.com/en/US/partner/partners/pr46/tdp/index.shtml
>
> ■ http://www.cisco.com/en/US/partner/partners/pr46/pr13/partners_pgm_concept_home.shtml
>
> ■ http://www.cisco.com/en/US/partner/partners/pr46/pr13/partners_program_solution 09186a00800a3807.html

The four main components that constitute a Cisco IP Communications system are as follows:

■ **Infrastructure**—Devices that provide media transport and connect the enterprise IP Communications networks to the Public Switched Telephone Network (PSTN) and to other private telephone systems, such as Private Branch Exchange (PBX). Infrastructure solutions include telephony service-enabled switches, routers, conference bridges, transcoders, and router-based, switch-based, and standalone voice over IP (VoIP) gateways (learn more about switches and gateways on Cisco.com; all models are not addressed in this appendix), and video packet to time-division multiplexing (TDM) video gateways. This appendix describes the following infrastructure solutions:

— Cisco Analog Telephone Adaptors (ATA)

— Cisco DPA Voice Mail gateways

— Cisco VG248 FXS or Voice Mail Gateway

— Cisco IP Videoconferencing (Cisco IP/VC)

— Cisco Survivable Remote Site Telephony (SRST)

You can learn detailed information about conference bridges and transcoders in Chapter 5, "Media Processing." Chapter 4, "Trunk Devices," provides information about the various gateways Cisco offers. You can also get information about all the switches, phones, gateways, and servers that integrate with CallManager at the following link or search Cisco.com for "voice and IP communications":

http://www.cisco.com/en/US/partner/products/sw/voicesw/
tsd_products_support_category_home.html

- **Telephony services**—Provides the services required for call processing, management, directory, database, application, and other features. Telephony services include CallManager (call processing), CiscoWorks, Lightweight Directory Access Protocol (LDAP) directory support, configuration database, and computer telephony application programming interfaces (API). This appendix describes the following telephony services solutions:

  — AXL SOAP API

  — Bulk Administration Tool (BAT)

  — Cisco EGW/PGW

  — CDR Analysis and Reporting (CAR) (formerly Administrative Reporting Tool)

  — Cisco CallManager Express (formerly Cisco IOS Telephony Services)

  — Cisco CallManager Serviceability

  — Cisco CallManager User Options web page

  — Cisco Messaging Interface (CMI)

  — LDAP Support

  — Real-Time Monitoring Tool (formerly Admin Serviceability Tool [AST])

  — Tool for Auto-Registered Phones Support (TAPS)

- **Clients**—Multimedia, client-facing endpoints including hardware-based Cisco IP Phones which are discussed in Chapter 3, "Station Devices," software-based IP phones such as the Cisco IP Communicator, and video phones. This appendix describes the following client solutions:

  — Cisco IP Communicator (predecessor: Cisco IP SoftPhone)

  — Cisco VT Advantage

■ **Applications**—Software applications and tools that provide extended multimedia services to clients and administrators. Applications include IP Interactive Voice Response (IP IVR), IP Contact Centers (IPCC), Meet-Me (scheduled and reservationless) conferencing, Cisco CallManager Attendant Console, and others. Development tools include TAPI, JTAPI, Cisco IP Phone Services Software Development Kit (SDK), and configuration database APIs. This appendix describes the following application solutions:

— Cisco Applications SDK—TAPI, JTAPI

— Cisco CallManager Attendant Console (formerly Cisco WebAttendant)

— Cisco Emergency Responder

— Cisco IP Contact Center (IPCC)

— Cisco IP Manager Assistant (IPMA)

— Cisco IP Phone Address Book Synchronizer

— Cisco IP Phone Services SDK

— Cisco MeetingPlace

— Cisco MeetingPlace Express

— Cisco Personal Assistant

— Cisco Unity

— Cisco Unity Express

— Cisco WebDialer

In addition, many system tools help you configure, analyze, diagnose, and troubleshoot the IP Communications system. This appendix describes the following system tools:

■ Cisco CallManager Trace Collection Tool

■ Cisco Dialed Number Analyzer

■ Cisco IP IVP and Cisco IP Queue Manager (IP QM)

■ Cisco Security Agent (CSA)

■ CiscoWorks Internet Telephony Environment Monitor (ITEM) and CiscoWorks QoS Policy Manager (QPM)

You can find documentation for many of the products discussed in this appendix on the Cisco IP Communications and Voice Products page on Cisco.com (shown in Figure B-1) at the following link:

http://www.cisco.com/univercd/cc/td/doc/product/ipcvoice.htm

Figure B-1 *Cisco IP Communications and Voice Products Page on Cisco.com*

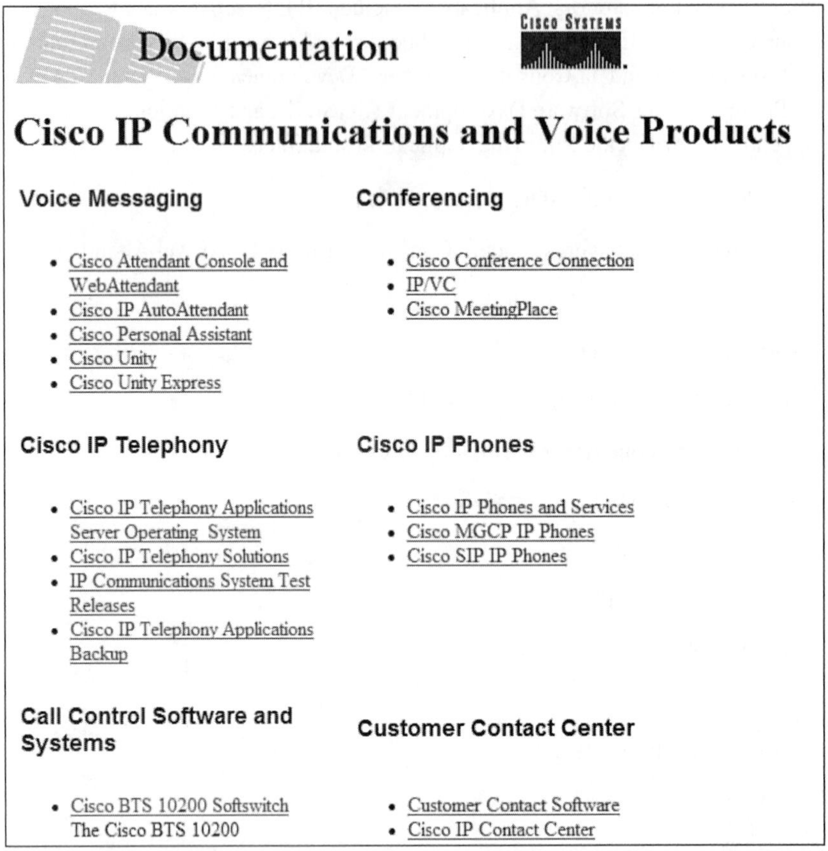

You can learn about the many gateways and phones on Cisco.com at the following link:

http://www.cisco.com/en/US/partner/products/sw/voicesw/
tsd_products_support_category_home.html

Infrastructure Solutions

Infrastructure solutions include devices that provide media transport and manipulation, and connect the enterprise IP telephony networks to the PSTN and to other private telephone systems, such as PBX.

Cisco Analog Telephone Adaptors (ATA)

The Cisco ATA 186 and 188 Analog Telephone Adaptors are desktop hardware devices that interface legacy analog devices such as telephones, fax machines, and conference telephones to IP-based telephony networks. The Cisco ATA enables organizations to protect their investment in analog devices and to migrate to IP telephony at their own pace. Using a Cisco ATA, you can turn traditional telephone devices into IP devices that can take advantage of the many new and exciting IP telephony applications.

The Cisco ATA is installed at the end user's premises. Both the Cisco ATA 186 and 188 support two voice ports, each with its own independent telephone number. The Cisco ATA 186 has a single Ethernet port for upstream IP connectivity; the Cisco ATA 188 provides a second switched Ethernet port that supports a downstream device such as a PC. By turning any analog telephone into an IP phone, the Cisco ATA addresses the needs of the emerging market of "second-line" residential VoIP services as well as the needs of enterprise organizations that want to protect their investment in legacy analog equipment.

You can learn more about Cisco ATA models at the following link or search Cisco.com for "ATA":

http://www.cisco.com/en/US/products/hw/gatecont/ps514/index.html

Cisco DPA Voice Mail Gateways

Cisco DPA 7630 and 7610 are voice mail gateways that enable legacy voice mail equipment to connect to a Cisco IP Communications network. If you have an existing Octel 2xx or 3xx with digital line cards, you can use a Cisco DPA gateway to connect to CallManager without any changes to the voice mail system. The Cisco DPA 7630 allows the voice mail system to be used solely by CallManager or to be shared between CallManager and the PBX. Figure B-2 shows the Cisco DPA gateway integrated with a legacy PBX.

Cisco DPA gateways communicate with CallManager by emulating IP phones using an auto-sensing 10/100 Ethernet port. Cisco DPA gateways communicate with the PBX and voice mail system using 24 digital station lines, and they are easily configured using a simple menu system accessed by Telnet. On the CallManager side, configuration is performed in CallManager Administration or automatically using auto-registration.

You can learn more about Cisco DPA voice mail gateways on Cisco.com at the following location or search Cisco.com for "Cisco DPA":

http://www.cisco.com/en/US/products/hw/gatecont/ps821/index.html

Figure B-2 *Using Cisco DPA 7610/7630 with a Legacy PBX*

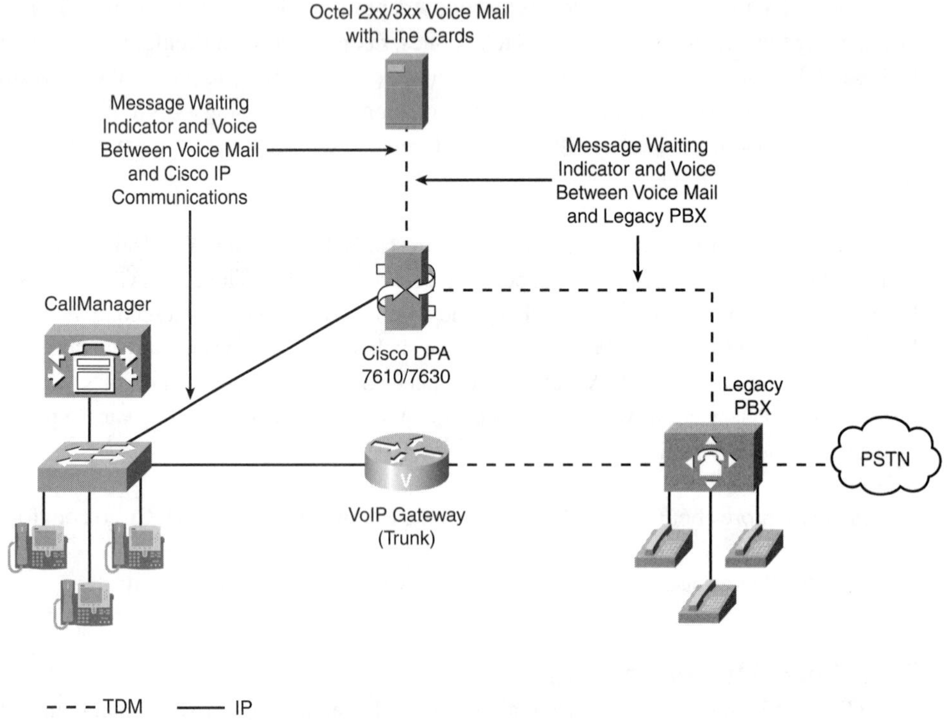

Cisco VG248 FXS or Voice Mail Gateway

The Cisco VG248 is a high-density gateway for using analog phones, fax machines, modems, voice mail systems, and speakerphones with a CallManager-based phone system. The Cisco VG248 provides supplementary services for analog phones, including hold, transfer, and conference. Using the Cisco VG248 Analog Phone Gateway, you can integrate your existing analog voice mail systems (which are compatible with Simple Message Desk Interface [SMDI], MCI, or Ericsson voice mail protocols) and legacy PBX systems with CallManager. The VG248 gateway provides voice mail systems with the information needed to intelligently process incoming calls, supply calling and called party identification, and set and clear message waiting indicators (MWI) through an EIA/TIA-232 serial connection.

The VG248 generates call information for all calls coming into any of the voice mail-enabled ports. The VG248 provides advantages to other methods used for integrating CallManager with analog voice mail systems, including the following:

■ Reliability for voice mail links using CallManager failover

■ Scalability by linking VG248 devices

■ Flexibility to use multiple voice mail systems on a single cluster by using one VG248 per voice mail system, or use a single voice mail system on multiple clusters by using one VG248 per cluster, or a single voice mail system to be shared between CallManager and a legacy PBX

You can learn more about the Cisco VG248 at the following links or search Cisco.com for "VG200":

http://www.cisco.com/en/US/products/hw/gatecont/ps2250/index.html

http://www.cisco.com/univercd/cc/td/doc/product/voice/c_access/apg/index.htm

Cisco IP Videoconferencing (Cisco IP/VC)

The Cisco IP Videoconferencing (Cisco IP/VC) product family offers a flexible videoconferencing solution supporting the ITU H.323 standard and Skinny Client Control Protocol (SCCP). The Cisco IP/VC series includes audio and video bridges, also called multipoint conference units (MCU), which enable interactive collaboration between three or more endpoints. When used in a CallManager release 4.0 environment, these MCUs also provide bridging for videoconferences initiated by the **Confrn** or **MeetMe** softkeys on an IP phone equipped with a VT Advantage camera or a Tandberg SCCP endpoint. The IP/VC series also includes gateways that enable video calls between networks of IP-based video endpoints and ISDN-based H.320 videoconferencing systems. In addition, the T.120 data collaboration servers expand the capability of any videoconference to include application sharing, cooperative white boarding, and file transfer.

Cisco IP/VC products, and the solutions they enable, are developed for organizations that want a reliable, easy-to-manage, and cost-effective network infrastructure for videoconferencing applications deployment. Figure B-3 shows the Cisco IP/VC solution at work.

You can learn more about Cisco IP/VC in the Cisco IP Video Telephony Solutions Reference Network Design (SRND) guide, at the following links, or search Cisco.com for "IP/VC" or "SRND":

http://www.cisco.com/en/US/products/hw/video/ps1870/index.html

http://www.cisco.com/univercd/cc/td/doc/product/ipvc/index.htm

http://www.cisco.com/go/srnd

> **NOTE**   If you already have substantial investments in H.320 videoconferencing, be aware that the H.323 standard enables interoperation with H.320-based systems. Furthermore, CallManager provides the protocol conversion to allow SCCP-based video endpoints, such as the Cisco VT Advantage solution and Tandberg SCCP video endpoints to also interoperate with H.320-based systems via the Cisco IP/VC H.320 gateways. Cisco IP/VC products enable an enterprise that has already experienced the benefits of videoconferencing over ISDN to leverage and protect its original investment while implementing new IP-based solutions.

Figure B-3 *Cisco IP/VC Solution*

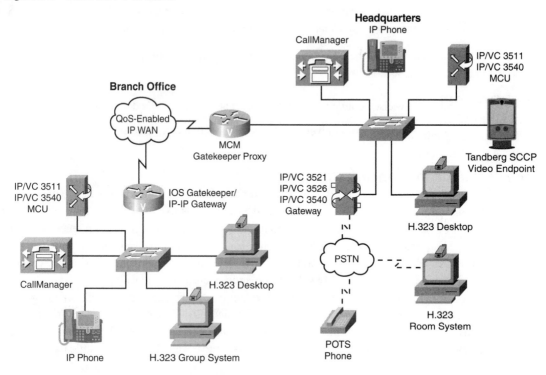

Cisco Survivable Remote Site Telephony (SRST)

SRS Telephony provides a cost-effective, reliable mechanism for providing feature-rich call processing redundancy to enterprise branch offices while leveraging the existing branch office infrastructure. SRST comprises network intelligence integrated into Cisco IOS Software, which acts as the call processing engine for IP phones located in the branch office during a WAN outage. SRST is available on the Cisco 175x, 1760, 1800, 2600, 2800, 3600, 3700, 3800, and 7200 series multiple-service access routers and the Communication Media Module (CMM) on the Catalyst 6000, with more platforms continually being added.

You can learn more about SRST at the following links or search Cisco.com for "SRS Telephony":

http://www.cisco.com/en/US/products/sw/voicesw/ps2169/index.html

http://www.cisco.com/univercd/cc/td/doc/product/voice/srst/index.htm

Telephony Service Solutions

Telephony services provide the services required for call processing, management, directory, database, application, and other features. The sections that follow cover the individual telephony service solutions in more detail.

AXL SOAP API

The AVVID XML Layer (AXL) API provides a way for an experienced programmer to interact with and manipulate the CallManager database in ways not possible using CallManager Administration. Using an Extensible Markup Language (XML) Simple Object Access Protocol (SOAP) interface, the AXL SOAP API allows a programmer to access CallManager provisioning services using XML and exchange data in XML form, instead of using a binary library or DLL.

Brian Sedgley, a technical leader in the CallManager development group at Cisco System, runs the Alpha deployment for Cisco IP Communications on the Richardson, Texas campus. He regularly uses the AXL SOAP API to effect changes to the database that cannot be achieved through existing CallManager Administration functionality or to perform common changes in a faster way. The following list provides some examples of scripts from Brian's bag of AXL SOAP tricks:

- A display prompt script that allows the system administrator to flash a message on the IP phone display of all or selected devices, such as "You will be logged out of this phone in 30 minutes to allow for device updates. We apologize for the inconvenience."

- Phones that are currently logged in to extension mobility cannot receive line updates (such as audio source changes, updates to forwarding directives, and so on). A logout script allows Brian to logout all phones from extension mobility so that he can make the necessary changes.

- Scripts for advanced bulk functions not currently possible in BAT. For example, the Richardson campus recently switched from five-digit extensions to eight-digits. An XML SOAP script made this dial plan change quick and painless.

- A script that gathers a list of all registered devices and their dates and times of registration to aid with performance monitoring.

- A script that allows the system administrator to check the message waiting indicator status of all phones.

- A script that allows the system administrator to add phones to CallManager quickly and completely: configuring all aspects of the new phone such as device profile, user account and device association, extension mobility configuration, and more all at once.

The AXL API methods, known as requests, are performed using a combination of HTTP and SOAP. SOAP is an XML remote procedure call protocol. Users perform requests by sending XML data to the CallManager server. The server then returns the AXL response, which is also a SOAP message.

Programmers using the AXL SOAP API should have some experience with C++, Java, Perl, or equivalent language, as well as knowledge or experience in the following areas:

- TCP/IP

- HTTP

- Socket programming

- XML

A strong background with the XML Schema, which was used to define the AXL requests, responses, and errors, is also required. You can learn more about the XML Schema at the following link or search Google.com for "W3C XML schema":

http://www.w3.org/TR/xmlschema-0/

Learn more about the AXL SOAP API on Cisco.com (login may be required) at the following links or search for "AXL SOAP API":

http://www.cisco.com/cgi-bin/dev_support/access_level/product_support

http://www.cisco.com/en/US/partner/products/sw/voicesw/ps556/products_ programming_reference_guides_list.html

Bulk Administration Tool (BAT)

The Bulk Administration Tool (BAT), a web-based application, helps you perform bulk modifications to the CallManager database. With BAT, you can create templates and comma-separated value (CSV) files that can be reused for future bulk modifications. You can use BAT for database changes (including add, update, or delete, depending on the device type) for users, user device profiles, managers/assistants, most Cisco IP Phone models and some third-party phone models, speed dials, lines, IP phone services, forced authorization codes, client matter codes, CAPF configuration, resetting or restarting phones, Cisco VG200 gateways, FXS ports on Cisco Catalyst 6000 gateways, and combinations such as adding phones and users all at once. With BAT, you minimize the amount of time you spend manually adding, updating, or deleting users and devices in CallManager Administration. You can also use BAT to export selected information about specific phones or all phones in the CallManager database.

You can learn more about BAT in Chapter 6, "Manageability and Monitoring," or at the following location or search Cisco.com for "BAT":

http://www.cisco.com/en/US/products/sw/voicesw/ps556/products_user_guide_list.html

Cisco EGW/PGW

The Cisco EGW 2200 Enterprise Gateway (EGW) is a media gateway controller that serves as a migration tool for optimizing the transition from existing Digital Private Network Signaling System (DPNSS) PBX enterprises to CallManager. The Cisco EGW also introduces Cisco Unity into existing DPNSS or QSIG PBX enterprises and supports toll bypass for QSIG and DPNSS PBXs. In these deployment scenarios, the Cisco EGW acts as an adjunct to CallManager and Unity to complete a connection to the PSTN.

The Cisco EGW targets the enterprise market and the Cisco PGW supports the worldwide service provider and large enterprise markets.

The Cisco PGW 2200 Softswitch is a flexible multiple-protocol media gateway controller that provides a bridge between the Public Switched Telephone Network (PSTN) and packet networks.

In conjunction with Cisco media gateways, the PGW 2200 Softswitch acts as a PSTN gateway that allows service providers to deploy and operate multiple packet-based network applications while maintaining a stable interconnect with the PSTN. At the heart of the product is its Universal Call Model, which allows the PGW 2200 to support interoperability between multiple legacy TDM interfaces and Internet protocols, including Signaling System 7 (SS7/C7), PRI, DPNSS, ITU QSIG, MGCP, SIP, and ITU H.323 protocols.

You can learn more about Cisco EGW/PGW at the following links or search Cisco.com for "Cisco EGW" or "Cisco PGW":

> http://www.cisco.com/en/US/products/ps5938/index.html
>
> http://www.cisco.com/en/US/products/hw/vcallcon/ps2027/index.html

CDR Analysis and Reporting (CAR)

CDR Analysis and Reporting (CAR), formerly known as the Administrative Reporting Tool (ART), provides call and billing information; usage reporting; and performance information on the CallManager system via a web-based application, including end-to-end management information for voice quality and quality-of-service (QoS) metrics.

Calls are grouped into a voice-quality category based on the call information provided by call detail records (CDR), the diagnostic call management records (CMR), and QoS parameters you specify. Information that is not present in CDRs and CMRs, but that is required for various reports, is retrieved from LDAP or must be supplied by the CAR administrator. After this information is retrieved, it is stored in a CAR database. CAR can then use this information to generate billing, usage, forced authorization code, client matter code, traffic summary, voice quality, and other reports for the CallManager system.

Chapter 6 provides additional information about CAR. You can view the user guide for CAR at the following location (then follow these navigation instructions: *choose your release* > **Serviceability** > *the serviceability guide for your release*) or search Cisco.com for "CDR Analysis and Reporting":

> http://www.cisco.com/univercd/cc/td/doc/product/voice/c_callmg/index.htm

Cisco CallManager Express

Cisco CallManager Express (CME), formerly called Cisco IOS Telephony Services, is an optional software feature in Cisco IOS-based routers designed for customers looking to deploy IP Communications solutions for the small/medium business or branch office. The solution supports 240 phones or fewer and provides customers with a choice of distributed call processing that works with CallManager at the central site. Whether offered through a service provider's managed services offering, positioned in a retail environment, or purchased directly by a corporation, CallManager Express offers many of the core telephony features required in the small office as well as many advanced features not available on traditional telephony solutions.

CallManager Express offers the following benefits:

■ Interoperability with CallManager 3.3(3) and higher (H.323 or SIP trunking)

■ A cost-effective IP communications solution for retail customers with numerous independent sites

■ A converged solution for voice, data, and IP communications services on a single Cisco Integrated Services Router platform

■ A risk-free protected initial investment in Cisco IP Communications for customers migrating to a CallManager and SRST deployment

■ Multiple voice mail integration options including Unity Express, Unity, or third-party system

■ Support for XML-based Cisco IP Phone services

You can learn more about CallManager Express at the following link or search Cisco.com for "CallManager Express":

> http://www.cisco.com/en/US/products/sw/voicesw/ps4625/index.html

Cisco CallManager Serviceability

CallManager Serviceability is bundled with CallManager Administration and provides alarm and trace configuration, as well a number of tools including Service Activation; a Control Center for starting and stopping services; QRT Viewer for retrieving problem reports logged by IP phone users; the Serviceability Reports Archive which, if configured, provides auto-generated alerts, call activity, and statistics reports; and real-time monitoring information about CallManager, Cisco IP Phones, gateways, applications, and infrastructure components within the IP Communications network. CallManager Serviceability monitors status and alarm information from these devices and can be configured to relay this information to service managers through SNMP and HTTP/XML via tools such as syslog and Event Viewer. CallManager Serviceability is automatically installed with CallManager and is accessible from the **Application** menu in CallManager Administration.

CallManager Serviceability provides alarm configuration and detailed alarm definitions as well as simplified tracing with the option to display trace results in easy-to-read XML format. The tradeoff with using an XML format is that less data is displayed. You can check version information for components installed in the CallManager system and monitor system and device status and alarms in real time using the Real-Time Monitoring Tool.

> **TIP** CallManager Serviceability provides access to the Q.931 Translator (**Trace > Q931 Translator**), which translates ISDN trace files into familiar Cisco IOS-equivalent messages, and also helps you troubleshoot problems with hardware that does not use the Q.931 protocol, such as the WS-X6624 analog FXS card, T1 CAS on the WS-X6608 card, and calls to and from an H.323 gateway. Although the Q.931 Translator allows you to quickly observe Q.931 and H.225 events, its functionality is somewhat limited. An adroit Cisco TAC engineer, Paul Giralt (read his book *Troubleshooting Cisco IP Telephony* [ISBN: 1-58705-075-7]) wrote a completely new version of Q.931 Translator. You can learn more about Q.931 Translator version 2.2.1 in Chapter 6.
>
> Another useful tool is the TripleCombo, written by Cisco TAC engineer Murat Tiryakioglu, which can parse SCCP, SIP, MGCP, Q.931/H.225, and H.245 messages found in CCM traces. You can access the TripleCombo tool at the following link:
>
> http://www.employees.org/~tiryaki/tc/

You can learn more about CallManager Serviceability in the online help (**Help > Contents and Index**).

Cisco CallManager User Options Web Page

The Cisco CallManager User Options web page allows users to configure various phone-related options. Some options are standard for all phone models, such as forwarding calls, changing the phone's locale, changing the locale for your device profile, changing password and PIN, while the availability of additional features depend on the phone model in use. For example, users of some Cisco IP Phone models such as 7970G, 7960G, and 7940G can also set speed dial numbers, change the message waiting indicator policy for the phone, change the phone's ring settings, manage Cisco IP Phone service subscriptions, configure Service URLs on their phone buttons, and configure Cisco Personal Address Book, as shown in Figure B-4.

Figure B-4   *Cisco CallManager User Options Web Page for Cisco IP Phone 7960G*

To have access to the Cisco CallManager User Options web page, users must be configured in the Global Directory of CallManager Administration. To use the features in the web page, users need to have a phone associated with them. The Cisco CallManager User Options web page is available by default, but you can turn off access to the various configuration items (such as speed dials, phone services, locales, and more) in the CCMUser Parameters area on the Enterprise Parameters Configuration page (**System > Enterprise Parameters**). Learn more about these parameters in the section "Cisco CallManager User Options Web Page" in Appendix A, "Feature List." Also, for security reasons, you can disable external call forwarding so that users cannot set a call forwarding directive for a number that is outside of the CallManager system.

Forwarding All Calls

Users can enter the number to which they want all calls forwarded on a per-line basis or to cancel an existing call forwarding directive, as well as set or cancel call forwarding using the **CFwdAll** softkey on their phone (affects primary line only). The number to which calls should be forwarded must be entered exactly as it would need to be dialed from the system, including any access number (such as a 9 for external calls or another number for internal calls). You can prevent users from forwarding calls to numbers outside the CallManager system for security reasons by allowing them to forward only to internal numbers.

Only system administrators can set Call Forward Busy and Call Forward No Answer directives using CallManager Administration. For secondary lines on an IP phone, CallManager Administration provides the only means to configure call forward destinations.

Configuring Speed Dials/Abbreviated Dialing

Users can enter the speed dial number and display text for each line/feature button assigned to their phone. The phone's template determines the number of line/feature buttons available. Users of Cisco IP Phone model 7910 can enter the speed dial number and then print a button template that displays the text for each line and feature button.

The lower half of the speed dial page allows users to specify abbreviated dialing numbers. These function similarly to speed dial entries except that while on-hook, users dial an index number associated with a speed dial number and then press the **AbbrDial** softkey. The phone accesses a line and speed dials the number associated with the abbreviated dialing index number that the user entered. Chapter 3 covers abbreviated dialing in more detail.

Configuring IP Phone Services

Users can subscribe to a list of available services, see a list of services to which they are subscribed, and unsubscribe from services. Services can be custom-configured by your company; see Chapter 3 and the section "Cisco IP Phone Productivity Services (by XML API)" in Appendix A for more information. After the user subscribes to the services, the user can press the **services** button on his or her phone to access the subscribed services, or access the service from a line/feature button that has had the service assigned via the Service URL feature.

Configuring Service URLs

Service URLs allow users to assign an IP phone service to a line/feature button, providing one-touch access to any IP phone XML service available on the system. For users to have access to Service URLs, you must configure Service URL on buttons on the button template (**Device > Device Settings > Phone Button Template**).

Configuring the Cisco Personal Address Book

Cisco Personal Address Book allows users to create a personal address book that can be accessed from the Cisco CallManager User Options web page or from some Cisco IP Phone models, such as the 7960G or 7940G. A Synchronization utility enables users to import contacts from Microsoft Outlook or Outlook Express directly into the Cisco Personal Address Book. Two services, PersonalAddressBook and PersonalFastDials, enable users to access the information from their phone.

Changing the Message Waiting Indicator Policy

Users can choose the behavior of the message waiting lamp on their phone's handsets. A number of options are available, including not lighting the lamp at all.

Changing the Ring Settings

Users can choose the behavior of the phone when a new call arrives for both idle and in-use states. A number of options are available, including ringing, flashing, beeping, and not ringing or lighting the lamp at all.

Changing the Phone Locale

Users can choose the user locale for their phones, which determines the language on the phone's display. Users can choose from the locales that you have installed.

Changing the Device Profile Locale

Users can choose the user locale for their device profile, which means that phones to which they log on will display the specified locale. The profile also determines what language the Cisco CallManager User Options web page displays in. Users can choose from the locales that you have installed.

Changing the Password

Users can update the password they use to access IP phone services and the Cisco CallManager User Options web page. Passwords must be a minimum of 5 and a maximum of 20 alphanumeric characters (no spaces or quote marks).

Changing the PIN

Users can update their personal identification number (PIN), which is used to access extension mobility. PINs must be a minimum of 5 and a maximum of 20 numerals.

Viewing the User Guide for the Phone

Users can click the link to **View the User Guide for your phone** and the phone's user guide will display in a new browser window.

Cisco Messaging Interface (CMI)

Cisco Messaging Interface enables you to use an external voice mail system with CallManager. The voice mail system must meet the following requirements:

- Have a simplified message desk interface (SMDI) accessible with an EIA/TIA-232 cable and an available serial port

- Use analog ports or digital T1/E1 ports with CAS or PRI protocols for connecting voice lines

You also need a Cisco Catalyst 6000 24-port FXS gateway, Cisco VG248 gateway, Cisco Catalyst 6000 8-port T1 or E1 gateway, or any MGCP-controlled IOS gateway installed and configured to interface with the voice mail system.

The SMDI-compliant voice mail system is connected to CallManager in two ways:

- Using a standard serial connection to CallManager

- Using plain old telephone service (POTS) line connections to a Cisco Catalyst 6000 24-port FXS gateway, Cisco VG248 gateway, Cisco Catalyst 6000 8-port T1 or E1 gateway, or any MGCP-controlled IOS gateway

You can learn more about CMI in the CallManager documentation at the following link (follow these navigation instructions: *choose your release* > **System Administration and Features and Services** > *choose the guide for your release* > **Cisco CallManager System Guide**):

http://www.cisco.com/univercd/cc/td/doc/product/voice/c_callmg/index.htm

LDAP Support

CallManager uses an LDAP directory to store authentication and authorization information about telephony application users as well as phone numbers and user information such as first name, last name, department number, manager's name, and so on. Authentication establishes a user's right to access the system; authorization identifies the telephony resources that a user is permitted to use, such as a specific telephone extension.

The CallManager LDAP directory infrastructure supports Secure Sockets Layer (SSL) connections, allowing applications to securely transmit data/information between CallManager and the LDAP directory server.

You can integrate CallManager with an external LDAP directory by running the Cisco Customer Directory Configuration Plugin (**Application > Install Plugins**). This plug-in serves the following purposes:

■ Extends the corporate directory schema to accommodate the application-specific objects and attributes

■ Populates the "Cisco" subtree with the configuration objects that CallManager needs

■ Configures CallManager to use the corporate directory and disables the embedded directory

■ Allows you to configure LDAP over SSL. If configured, the SSL port number and the path to the server certificate gets requested each time data is passed to and from the directory

You can learn more about LDAP support in the Cisco IP Communications system in the CallManager Administration Guide at the following link:

http://www.cisco.com/univercd/cc/td/doc/product/voice/c_callmg/index.htm

Real-Time Monitoring Tool (RTMT)

The Real-Time Monitoring Tool (RTMT), formerly known as the Admin Serviceability Tool (AST), provides real-time information about your CallManager system for management and monitoring purposes. As of CallManager release 4.0, RTMT is a separate application from CallManager Serviceability, a move that offers greater speed and enhanced performance. After you install the Cisco CallManager Serviceability Real-Time Monitoring Tool plug-in (**Application > Install Plugins**), you access RTMT from your desktop.

Like Microsoft Performance, RTMT uses performance objects and counters to allow you to monitor and troubleshoot the enterprise IP telephony system. RTMT also provides alerting capability so that you can be advised with server messages or e-mails when specified conditions occur.

You can learn more about RTMT in Chapter 6, as well as at the following link (*then click on your CallManager release* > **Serviceability** > *the serviceability guide for your release*), or search Cisco.com for "CallManager Serviceability RTMT":

http://www.cisco.com/univercd/cc/td/doc/product/voice/c_callmg/index.htm

Tool for Auto-Registered Phones Support (TAPS)

The Tool for Auto-Registered Phones Support (TAPS) is a plug-in application (**Application > Install Plugins**) that enables you or users to automatically download a predefined user profile to a phone simply by plugging the phone into the network and dialing into a predefined TAPS directory number. TAPS can be used to update auto-registered phones with existing configurations, or to update auto-registered phones that received dummy Media Access Control (MAC) addresses when they were added to the CallManager database using BAT. TAPS requires that auto-registration be enabled in CallManager Administration (**System > Cisco CallManager**). TAPS can be used in conjunction with a Cisco Customer Response Solutions (CRS) server; TAPS requires the Cisco IP IVR application that runs on the Cisco CRS server for the user interface and prompts. Alternatively, for a four-port solution, TAPS can be used with Extended Services which you can download from Cisco.com.

Using BAT, you bulk-add phones using dummy MAC addresses which saves you the labor of manually entering valid MAC addresses for each phone in the bulk operation. You can then use TAPS to update the dummy MAC address automatically in the CallManager database with the phone's actual MAC address. After the phones with dummy MAC addresses have been added to the CallManager database using BAT, either you or the phone's end user can plug the phone into the data port, apply power, wait for the phone to auto-register with CallManager, and dial the TAPS directory number to re-initialize the IP phone. TAPS provides voice prompts to walk the user through the short initialization process.

TAPS provides a secure feature that prevents important directory numbers from being overwritten. For security reasons, you should disable auto-registration and stop the TAPS service when TAPS is no longer needed.

You can learn more about TAPS by searching Cisco.com for "TAPS."

Client Solutions

Client solutions include multimedia, client-facing endpoints as described in further detail in the following sections.

Cisco IP Communicator (Predecessor: Cisco IP SoftPhone)

Cisco IP Communicator, whose predecessor was the Cisco IP SoftPhone, is a desktop application that turns a computer into a full-featured IP telephone. IP Communicator is designed for use as a supplemental telephone when traveling or as a telecommuting device. When using IP Communicator remotely, users aren't just taking their office extension with them, they also have access to the same familiar phone services they have in their office. When registered to CallManager, IP Communicator has the features and functionality of a Cisco IP Phone, including the capability to transfer calls, forward calls, and conference additional participants to an existing call. This also means that you can provision IP Communicator just like any other Cisco IP Phone, greatly simplifying IP phone administration. Figure B-5 shows the IP Communicator user interface.

Figure B-5 *Cisco IP Communicator*

Learn more about IP Communicator at the following link or search Cisco.com for
"IP Communicator":

http://www.cisco.com/en/US/products/sw/voicesw/ps5475/index.html

Cisco VT Advantage

Cisco VT Advantage enables you to add video to your existing Cisco IP Phone models 7940G,
7941G, 7960G, 7961G, 7970G, and 7971G-GE, in effect turning the phones into videophones.
Cisco VT Advantage application software, coupled with the Cisco VT Camera, allows a PC
connected to a Cisco IP Phone to add video to phone calls without requiring any extra button
pushing or mouse clicking.

Cisco VT Advantage works so well that video telephone calls are just like regular phone calls.
Features such as call forward, transfer, conference, and hold, are available with video and are all
initiated through the IP Phone. IP telephony and IP video telephony are delivered to every
employee using a unified dial plan and a common directory through CallManager. When a user
places a call to another IP Phone with video capability, the call proceeds as a video call seamlessly.
If the other party does not have video capability, the call proceeds as a voice-only call. In addition,
because Cisco VT Advantage utilizes standards-based video protocols such as H.263, it can
interoperate with H.323- and H.320-based videoconferencing devices.

Learn more about Cisco VT Advantage in the Cisco IP Video Telephony Solutions Reference Network Design (SRND) guide, at the following links, or search Cisco.com for "VT Advantage" or "SRND":

> http://www.cisco.com/en/US/products/sw/voicesw/ps5662/index.html

> http://www.cisco.com/go/srnd

Application Solutions

Application solutions are software-only applications and tools that provide extended multimedia services to clients and administrators as described in the sections that follow.

Cisco TAPI Software

Cisco provides Telephony Application Programming Interface (TAPI) software as plug-in applications (**Application > Install Plugins**). You can use the SDK to develop applications to use in conjunction with CallManager. TAPI is the set of classes and principles of operation that constitute a telephony application programming interface. TAPI implementations are the interface between computer telephony applications and telephony services. The Cisco TAPI implementation uses the Microsoft TAPI v2.1 specification and supplies extension functions to support Cisco IP Communications solutions.

CallManager provides the TAPI Service Provider (Cisco TSP). Cisco TSP allows developers to create customized IP telephony applications for Cisco users, for example, voice mail with other TAPI-compliant systems, automatic call distribution (ACD), and caller ID screen pops. Cisco TSP enables the Cisco IP Communications system to understand commands from the user-level application, such as Cisco IP SoftPhone, with the operating system.

The Cisco TSP is a TAPI-based application programming interface that allows applications to communicate with CallManager using a standard set of functions. Cisco TSP is a plug-in application available in CallManager Administration (**Application > Install Plugins**). TAPI implementation consists of a Cisco TSP client that resides on all client machines running Cisco TAPI applications. Installation of the Cisco TSP is necessary before Cisco or partner-developed TAPI applications will function correctly. The Cisco TSP software is installed on the machine where applications reside.

Cisco TSP Processes

Cisco TSP supports a variety of features in TAPI. Initialization and security are processes that are generally invisible to the application but are important components of Cisco TSP. They are specific to the device with which Cisco TSP is communicating.

Initialization in Cisco TSP must cover connection to CallManager, authenticating the user, and device and line enumeration. Cisco TSP also has to handle failures at any point in the process and provide recovery options. Security has been added to provide a mechanism for administering lines to users. To configure security, the user must enter a username and password on the TSP configuration screen. This username and password must match the username and password entered in CallManager Administration.

Cisco Wave Driver

The Cisco wave driver is used by third-party applications and IVR applications that use TAPI. To use first-party call control, you must install the Cisco wave driver; you should do this even if you are performing your own media termination.

You can learn more about TAPI development at the following link or search Cisco.com for "TAPI" or "CallManager programming guide":

> http://www.cisco.com/en/US/products/sw/voicesw/ps556/products_programming_
> reference_guides_list.html

Cisco JTAPI Software

CallManager provides Java Telephony Application Programming Interface (JTAPI) software as a plug-in application (**Application > Install Plugins**). You can use the SDK to develop applications to use in conjunction with CallManager. JTAPI is an object-oriented API for telephony applications written in Java. JTAPI is an abstract telephony model capable of uniformly representing the characteristics of a wide variety of telecommunication systems. Because it's defined without direct reference to any particular telephony hardware or software, JTAPI is well suited to the task of controlling or observing nearly any telephone system. For instance, a computer program that makes telephone calls using an implementation of JTAPI for modems might work without modification using the Cisco JTAPI implementation.

JTAPI implementation consists of a Cisco JTAPI Service Provider (also referred to as Cisco JTAPI) client that resides on all client machines running Cisco JTAPI applications. Installation of Cisco JTAPI is necessary before Cisco JTAPI applications will function correctly. Cisco JTAPI is a plug-in application available in CallManager Administration (**Application > Install Plugins**). The Cisco JTAPI software is installed on the machine where JTAPI applications reside.

After you install and configure the Cisco JTAPI plug-in, the JTAPI framework connects to the Cisco CTIManager service to initialize the CTI connection. JTAPI sends the configured authentication information during initialization. CTIManager performs authentication for the user and authorization to determine which devices the user has the privilege to control.

You can learn more about JTAPI development at the following link or search Cisco.com for "JTAPI":

> http://www.cisco.com/en/US/products/sw/voicesw/ps556/products_programming_
> reference_guides_list.html

Cisco CallManager Attendant Console (formerly Cisco WebAttendant)

Cisco CallManager Attendant Console, formerly Cisco WebAttendant, is an affordable and scalable solution that replaces the traditional PBX manual attendant console.

Attendant Console works in conjunction with a Cisco IP Phone to allow the attendant to quickly accept and dispatch calls to enterprise users. An integrated directory service provides traditional busy lamp field (BLF) and direct station select (DSS) functions for any line in the system. One of its primary benefits over traditional attendant console systems is its ability to monitor the state of every line in the system and to efficiently dispatch calls. The absence of a hardware-based line monitor device offers a much more affordable and easily distributed manual attendant solution than traditional consoles. Figure B-6 shows the Attendant Console interface.

Figure B-6 *Attendant Console Interface*

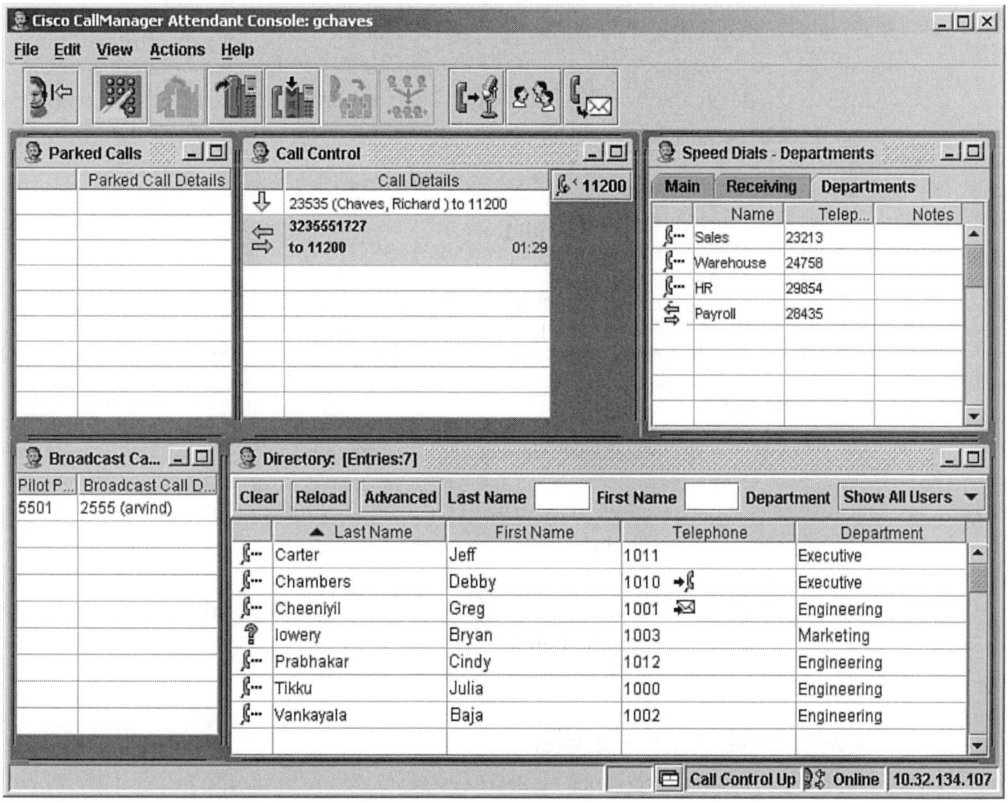

Call distribution groups can be assigned to any pilot number, which can in turn be assigned to an Attendant Console hunt group. The hunt group represents answerable lines in a multiple attendant system. Calls are queued to an online attendant group, thereby allowing scale and distribution among multiple operators. Multiple Attendant Consoles can be configured to monitor the same lines, affording scale to multiple operators when conditions require.

Attendant Console provides the following features, among others:

■ Queuing can be enabled on each of the pilot points, with queue size and queue hold time specified in seconds

■ New call distribution algorithms are supported, including broadcast (call is offered to all attendants simultaneously), circular (call is offered to each attendant consecutively), first available, and longest idle

■ Advanced directory search on attributes such as first name, last name, job title, department, building, site, email address, business telephone, home telephone, mobile number, and pager

■ Attendant Console client can import customer-generated user lists, which allow nearly live update of directory listings. For example, in a hospitality setting, the Attendant Console client can receive updated directory information to keep up-to-date records of guests who have checked in/checked out

■ Support for shared lines

■ Accessibility support for visually handicapped users:

— Optional screen reader that verbalizes the Attendant Console screen

— Shortcut keys allowing exclusive use of the keyboard (no mouse required)

— Audible alerts

■ Localization of the Attendant Console client in 25 languages as of CallManager release 4.1(2)

You can learn more about Attendant Console at the following links or search Cisco.com for "Attendant Console":

http://www.cisco.com/univercd/cc/td/doc/product/voice/c_callmg/attendnt/index.htm

http://www.cisco.com/en/US/products/sw/voicesw/ps555/index.html

Cisco Emergency Responder (CER)

Cisco Emergency Responder enables emergency agencies to identify the location of 911 callers (the emergency services number in the North American Numbering Plan) and eliminates the need for any administration when phones or people move from one location to another. Enhancing the existing E9-1-1 functionality in CallManager, Emergency Responder's real-time location-tracking database and improved routing capabilities direct emergency calls to the appropriate Public Safety Answering Point (PSAP) based on the caller's location.

Emergency Responder provides the following features:

- Automatically locates phones and users

- Dynamically routes emergency calls and provides real-time location information

- Provides real-time alerts

- Provides auditing and reporting

To ensure smooth operation, be sure to test your CER configuration prior to deployment. For best practice reasons, confirm that the information your system sends through the PSTN is accurately communicated to the PSAP.

You can learn more about Cisco Emergency Responder at the following links or search Cisco.com for "Cisco Emergency Responder":

> http://www.cisco.com/en/US/partner/products/sw/voicesw/ps842/
> tsd_products_support_series_home.html

> http://www.cisco.com/en/US/partner/products/sw/voicesw/ps842/index.html

Cisco IP Contact Center (IPCC)

Cisco IPCC is an IP-based, high-function contact center for use with CallManager. IPCC comes in three editions:

- IPCC Express, principally used for branch sites or small to medium-size companies planning to deploy an entry-level or mid-market contact center solution

- IPCC Enterprise, for full-scale enterprise deployments

- IPCC Hosted, for service provider environments

Using Cisco Customer Response Solutions technology, the suite of IPCC products provides the following functionality:

- IP IVR

- Automatic call distribution (ACD)

- IP Queue Manager

The IPCC uses JTAPI to control IP phones and to convey call control messages to CallManager. IPCC can be internetworked to other vendors' call centers and PBXs through a Cisco proprietary protocol. Through internetworking, a large, distributed, feature-transparent call center network can be constructed where each node has access to telephony and data information for every call. Sophisticated agent interaction is available through a software-based agent application.

You can learn more about IPCC at the following links or search Cisco.com for "IPCC":

> http://www.cisco.com/en/US/products/sw/custcosw/ps1844/index.html
>
> http://www.cisco.com/en/US/products/sw/custcosw/ps1846/index.html
>
> http://www.cisco.com/en/US/customer/products/sw/custcosw/ps5053/index.html

Cisco IP Manager Assistant (IPMA)

The Cisco IP Manager Assistant (IPMA) feature enables managers and their assistants to work together effectively. IPMA provides a call routing service and desktop interfaces for both the manager and the assistant. The IPMA service intercepts calls that are destined for managers and routes them to selected assistants, managers, or other targets based on preconfigured call filters. Managers can change the call routing dynamically. For example, by pressing a softkey on the phone, the manager can instruct the service to route all calls to the assistant and can receive status on these calls.

The IPMA Configuration Wizard is run once at the initial setup of the CallManager cluster. The server on which the Bulk Administration Tool is installed should be the server on which the wizard is run. The wizard utilizes pregenerated partitions and calling search spaces and improves the initial configuration experience for IPMA. While improving the configuration capability, the wizard gives you full control of the configuration. After you verify the data and click the **Submit** button, the wizard populates the database with all the data necessary for IPMA to function as configured.

The IPMA Assistant desktop user interface is consistent with the Attendant Console user interface. A status bar provides online/offline status as well as status of the connection to the server. Call control icons offer improved control over the call features. Call handling for the assistant incorporates double-clicks, drag and drop, right-click menus, menu bar, and call control buttons. The Cisco IPMA configuration is linked from the User Configuration page in CallManager Administration (**Global Directory >** *find and select a user* **> Cisco IPMA**) and allows you to configure manager information and specify the lines that IMPA will control.

You can learn more about IPMA at the following links or search Cisco.com for "IP Manager Assistant":

> http://www.cisco.com/en/US/products/sw/voicesw/ps5015/tsd_products_support_series_home.html

http://www.cisco.com/en/US/products/sw/voicesw/ps5015/products_data_
sheet09186a00801f8e4c.html

Cisco IP Phone Address Book Synchronizer

Cisco IP Phone Address Book Synchronizer allows users to synchronize Windows Address Book
(**Start > Programs > Accessories > Address Book**) with the Cisco Personal Address Book
service. From a Cisco IP Phone, a user can use the Personal Address Book service to look up
entries, make a selection, and press a softkey to dial the selected number.

The Synchronizer provides two-way synchronization between Microsoft and Cisco products. You
must download the plug-in and then post it to a location that end users can access so they can
utilize the Cisco IP Phone Address Book Synchronizer application.

You can learn more about the IP Phone Address Book Synchronizer at the following link or search
Cisco.com for "IP Phone Address Book Synchronizer":

http://www.cisco.com/en/US/products/hw/phones/ps379/
products_administration_guide_chapter09186a00801d66cc.html

Cisco IP Phone Services Software Development Kit (SDK)

The Cisco IP Phone Services SDK makes it easier for web developers to format and deliver
content to Cisco IP Phone models such as 7971G-GE, 7970G, 7960G, 7940G, 7920, 7912, and
7905 by providing web server components for LDAP directory access, web proxy, and graphics
conversion. Access to these services is provided through an XML API into the phone. An
embedded XML parser within the phone is able to parse selected XML tags. The SDK also
contains several sample applications that illustrate the use of the various XML tags that the phone
supports. The SDK includes the following items:

- Utilities, such as LDAP Search, which can perform queries on any LDAP-compliant directory
  server and return the output in the Cisco IP Phone services XML data format; URL Proxy, a
  proxy service required by the sample services in the SDK; a CallManager simulator; graphics
  conversion tools; and more

- Sample applications, including a touch screen keyboard application for use on touch screen–
  enabled IP Phones such as the 797x, color or black-and-white slideshow viewer application,
  photo directory, extension mobility controller that allows you to query and control extension
  mobility login status for users and phones, intercom, graphic image converter, and much more

- Documentation, including the Cisco IP Phone Services Application Development Notes, the
  Cisco URL Proxy Guide, and Programming Guides for the included ActiveX components

See the section "Cisco CallManager User Options Web Page" in this appendix for more information about how users subscribe or unsubscribe to services you create or install from the SDK. You can learn more about creating and coding Cisco IP Phone services in the Cisco Press book *Developing Cisco IP Phone Services* (ISBN: 1-58705-060-9). You can learn more about the SDK at the following links or search Cisco.com for "Cisco IP Phone Services SDK" or "Applications Central":

http://www.cisco.com/en/US/products/hw/phones/ps379/products_data_sheet09186a0080092 5a8.html

http://www.cisco.com/go/apps

http://www.cisco.com/go/developersupport/

Cisco MeetingPlace

Cisco MeetingPlace provides a fully integrated rich-media conferencing solution, including voice-, web-, and videoconferencing capabilities. MeetingPlace resides on the network and offers unmatched security, reliability, scalability, application integration, and cost-efficiency.

When integrated with a Cisco IP Communications network, MeetingPlace takes advantage of voice and data networks to greatly reduce or eliminate substantial ongoing monthly service charges, transport tolls, and recurring conferencing charges. You can also access MeetingPlace from the display on a Cisco IP Phone. MeetingPlace integrates with Cisco IP/VC multipoint control units (MCU) to enable scheduling of video conferences.

You can purchase a MeetingPlace solution outright and manage it yourself. You can also purchase hosted or on-premise services that are managed by Cisco or a certified MeetingPlace Service Provider. MeetingPlace Managed Solutions combines the benefits of a dedicated on-network conferencing solution with the convenience of an outsourced, pay-per-use conferencing service.

You can learn more about MeetingPlace at the following link or search Cisco.com for "MeetingPlace":

http://www.cisco.com/en/US/products/sw/ps5664/ps5669/index.html

Cisco MeetingPlace Express

Cisco MeetingPlace Express is the next-generation low-end audio and web-conferencing solution designed to provide many of the benefits offered in MeetingPlace for the commercial, workgroup, and small enterprise markets. MeetingPlace Express improves corporate productivity, reduces costs using OnNet capabilities, and enhances the user's meeting experience. MeetingPlace Express will be available in late 2005 and will offer Cisco Conference Connection (CCC) customers a strong migration path to a rich-media conferencing solution.

For more information, search Cisco.com for "MeetingPlace Express."

Cisco Personal Assistant

Cisco Personal Assistant is an application that plays the role of a virtual personal assistant. Personal Assistant can be used by anyone in your company to redirect incoming calls based on rules that individual users create. Incoming calls can be handled differently based on caller ID, date and time of day, and the user's meeting status based on the user's calendar. Personal Assistant can also selectively route calls to other telephone numbers so that an incoming call to a desk phone can be routed to a cell phone, home phone, or other phone based on the call routing rules created by the user. An incoming call can even generate an e-mail-based page. For example, if you are in a meeting from 2 to 3 p.m., you can configure Personal Assistant to send your calls to voice mail and page you with details of the call except if it is caller Y. In that case, you can direct Personal Assistant to forward the call to your cell phone.

Personal Assistant includes speech recognition as well. By simply speaking to Personal Assistant, users can access their voice mail and perform directory dialing and conferencing. Speech-enabled features are described in the following list:

- **Speech-enabled directory dialing**—Allows a user to pick up the phone and speak a person's name to reach that person, instead of having to dial an extension

- **Speech-enabled voice mail browsing**—Provides a speech interface to Cisco Unity whereby a user can perform common voice mail operations by speaking to Personal Assistant

- **Simple speech-enabled Ad Hoc conferencing**—Allows a user to initiate a conference with several parties simply by speaking to Personal Assistant

You can learn more about Personal Assistant at the following links or search Cisco.com for "Personal Assistant":

>   http://www.cisco.com/en/US/products/sw/voicesw/ps2026/index.html

>   http://www.cisco.com/univercd/cc/td/doc/product/voice/assist/index.htm

Cisco Unity

Cisco Unity provides voice mail and unified messaging so you can access voice, fax, and e-mail messages using your desktop PC, a touch-tone telephone, or the Internet. With simplified message management, you can have all voice, fax, and e-mail messages delivered to your Microsoft Outlook inbox. Unity provides a self-enrollment conversation that is so easy to use, new employees can personalize their voice mailboxes and begin using Unity within minutes. Users can choose between full menu options or brief menus for faster system navigation. Text-to-speech capability exists, enabling users to listen to e-mail messages, numerous configurable personal greetings, and many more features.

Cisco Unity supports CallManager as well as leading traditional telephone systems, even simultaneously, to help you transition to IP telephony at your own pace and protect the investment you have in existing infrastructure. Unity integrates with CallManager using a software-only solution, requiring no additional hardware.

You can learn more about Unity at the following links or search Cisco.com for "Unity":

> http://www.cisco.com/en/US/products/sw/voicesw/ps2237/index.html
>
> http://www.cisco.com/univercd/cc/td/doc/product/voice/c_unity/index.htm

Cisco Unity Express

Cisco Unity Express provides voice mail and automated attendant services for small and medium branch offices with either CallManager or CallManager Express. Unity Express integrates into the broad range of Cisco Access routers including the Cisco 2600XM series, Cisco 2800 series, Cisco 3700 series, and Cisco 3800 series providing design options and flexibility. Unity Express integrates with CallManager using JTAPI and supports typical voice mail features such as message composition, message save, forward, reply, delete, undelete, and tagging for urgency or privacy. You can easily customize the standard automated attendant for Unity Express with the time of day, day of week, holiday schedules, and multiple menu levels to meet the specific needs of your organization. Cisco Unity Express also supports Voice Profile for Internet Mail (VPIM) for voice mail message networking interoperability.

You can learn more about Cisco Unity Express at the following links or search Cisco.com for "Unity Express":

> http://www.cisco.com/en/US/products/sw/voicesw/ps5520/index.html
>
> http://www.cisco.com/univercd/cc/td/doc/product/voice/unityexp/index.htm

Cisco WebDialer

Cisco WebDialer works in conjunction with CallManager to allow IP Phone users to make calls from web and desktop applications. For example, an online company directory uses WebDialer to provide hyperlinked telephone numbers that enable users to initiate a call on their IP Phone by clicking the telephone number of the person they want to call. Another example is an Outlook Add-in that enables users to make calls from their Outlook contacts.

Two Java servlets—WebDialer servlet and Redirector servlet—used together or independently of each other based on your application interface, comprise WebDialer.

The WebDialer servlet interacts with CallManager to allow call origination and termination as well as phone configuration. The WebDialer servlet supports two types of application interfaces:

- **SOAP over HTTP**—Use this interface to develop desktop applications such as the Microsoft Outlook Add-in and SameTime Client plug-in. Developers can use the isClusterUserSoap interface to design multiple cluster applications that require functionality similar to a Redirector servlet.

- **HTML over HTTP**—Use this interface to develop web-based applications such as the CallManager directory search page (directory.asp). Developers who use this interface can use the Redirector servlet for designing multiple cluster applications.

The Redirector servlet locates the relevant CallManager cluster to fulfill a request that a WebDialer user makes. The servlet then redirects that request to the specific WebDialer server located in that user's CallManager cluster. The Redirector servlet is only involved for multiple cluster applications that are developed using HTML over HTTP interfaces.

You can learn more about WebDialer at the following link or search Cisco.com for "WebDialer":

http://www.cisco.com/en/US/products/sw/voicesw/ps556/
products_programming_reference_guide09186a008042be75.html

System Tools

System tools include applications that help you configure, analyze, diagnose, and troubleshoot your IP Communications system, as described in the sections that follow.

Cisco CallManager Trace Collection Tool

The CallManager Trace Collection Tool is a plug-in to CallManager (**Application > Install Plugins**) that collects traces for a CallManager cluster into a single .zip file. The collection includes all traces for CallManager and logs such as those sent to Event Viewer, Dr. Watson, Internet Information Server (IIS), Structured Query Language (SQL), ProgLogs, and Directory logs. You can select traces based on date/time criteria, and you can choose the compression factor when zipping the resulting trace files.

Learn more about the Trace Collection Tool by searching Cisco.com for "Trace Collection Tool."

Cisco Dialed Number Analyzer

Use the Cisco Dialed Number Analyzer, a plug-in to CallManager (**Application > Install Plugins**), to test a CallManager dial plan prior to deploying it, or to analyze dial plans after implementation. You can also use the tool to trace the path of a specific string of digits, which can help you identify problems with the dialed digits or with the dial plan itself. The tool applies the complex permutations of the dial plan to inbound and outbound calls, such as calling search spaces, calling and called party transformations, features such as call park and more, to analyze the dialed digits and show details of the call.

You can learn more about the Cisco Dialed Number Analyzer by searching Cisco.com for "Dialed Number Analyzer."

Cisco IP Interactive Voice Response (IP IVR) and Cisco IP Queue Manager (IP QM)

The Cisco IP IVR uses Cisco Customer Response Solutions technology to allow you to develop speech-enabled, self-service, menu-driven applications that callers use to navigate your database to acquire information from or enter data into the database. Examples of IVRs include the automated flight arrival and departure times offered via toll-free telephone number by most airlines, and automated account information from banks and credit card companies. With Cisco IP IVR, you can direct customer access to data by processing user commands entered through touch-tone or speech recognition.

The Cisco IP IVR is written entirely in Java and designed and constructed by Cisco to facilitate concurrent multimedia communication processing. The Cisco IP IVR architecture is open and extensible, allowing you to incorporate voice XML applications and custom-developed Java classes to extend the Cisco IP IVR solution to meet your unique business needs.

Cisco IP Queue Manager (IP QM) is a subset of the Cisco IP IVR available for IPCC Enterprise customers, providing call treatment and queuing with IPCC Enterprise, allowing callers to select routing options and wait on hold until an agent is available. Cisco IP QM call treatment messages can be prerecorded announcements or dynamic announcements tailored to specific caller interests. Like a website that displays content based on a user's previous visits, IP QM can provide dynamic content to queued callers, delivering unique messages tailored to each caller's needs, the route selected, the caller's place in the queue, or other associated values.

You can learn more about IP IVR and IP Queue Manager at the following links or search Cisco.com for "IP IVR" or "IP Queue Manager":

> http://www.cisco.com/en/US/products/sw/custcosw/ps3651/index.html
>
> http://www.cisco.com/en/US/products/sw/custcosw/ps1844/ps3653/index.html

Cisco Security Agent (CSA)

Cisco Security Agent provides proactive and adaptive threat protection for servers and desktop computing systems. CSA brings together multiple levels of security functionality by combining host intrusion prevention, distributed firewall, malicious mobile code protection, operating system integrity assurance, and audit log consolidation all within a single agent package.

CSA technology is composed of several elements:

- **Cisco Security Agent**—Free, standalone agent with a static security policy and the same policy in an XML formatted .export file that can be used with the Management Center for Cisco Security Agents. The free agent provides core endpoint software that resides on servers such as CallManager, Cisco Unity, Cisco Unity Bridge, Cisco Emergency Responder, Cisco IP IVR, Cisco IP Queue Manager, Cisco Personal Assistant, and Cisco IPCC Express, which autonomously enforces local policies that prevent attacks. This standalone agent, based on CSA release 4.0(1), represents one aspect of a comprehensive system-level security approach that takes into account best practices available in the SAFE Blueprint for Voice. You have the option of upgrading from the free, standalone agent to the fully managed CSA agent for a fee.

- **CiscoWorks Management Center for Cisco Security Agents**—Core management software that provides a central means of defining and distributing policies, providing software updates, and maintaining communications to the agents.

You can learn more about CSA at the following links or search Cisco.com for "Cisco Security Agent" or "SAFE IP Telephony Blueprint":

> http://www.cisco.com/en/US/products/sw/secursw/ps5057/index.html

> http://www.cisco.com/en/US/products/sw/cscowork/ps5212/index.html

> http://www.cisco.com/en/US/netsol/ns340/ns394/ns171/ns128/
> networking_solutions_package.html

CiscoWorks Internet Telephony Environment Monitor (ITEM) and CiscoWorks QoS Policy Manager (QPM)

CiscoWorks ITEM is a powerful suite of applications and tools that continuously evaluates and reports the operational health of your IP telephony system. CiscoWorks ITEM provides specialized operations and security tools beneficial to large and small IP telephony implementations. CiscoWorks ITEM provides the following:

- Proactive health and fault monitoring of converged IP networks and IP telephony implementations

- Tools to effectively manage the day-to-day customer care responsibilities of help desk personnel

- Capability to capture performance and capacity management data

The CiscoWorks family of web-based products also includes the CiscoWorks QoS Policy Manager (QPM), which provides centralized QoS monitoring, policy control, and automated reliable policy deployment across network infrastructures for converged voice, video, and data applications. CiscoWorks QPM enables you to do the following:

- Validate QoS settings and results with traffic analysis

- Get real-time and historical reports for QoS troubleshooting

- Control roles and privileges for policy view, modification, and deployment

- Deploy QoS for IP telephony across the entire network using a step-by-step wizard and templates based on Cisco design recommendations

- Use IOS Network-based Application Recognition (NBAR) for extended QoS differentiation

- Use a rules-based policy wizard to ensure consistent QoS across different switches and routers as well as various IOS and Catalyst OS versions

You can learn more about CiscoWorks ITEM and CiscoWorks QPM at the following links or search Cisco.com for "CiscoWorks IP Telephony Environment Monitor" or "CiscoWorks QoS Policy Manager":

> http://www.cisco.com/en/US/products/sw/cscowork/ps2433/index.html
>
> http://www.cisco.com/en/US/products/sw/cscowork/ps2064/index.html

Protocol Details

This appendix covers call signaling protocols and application protocols included in Cisco CallManager. Call signaling protocols support communication with trunks and endpoints, and application protocols enable the development of additional applications that complement CallManager functionality.

CallManager uses the following signaling protocols to communicate with its devices:

- H.323

- QSIG

- SIP (Session Initiation Protocol)

- Skinny Client Control Protocol (SCCP)

Signaling protocols provide an agreed-upon set of rules that define the format of messages used to transmit information and commands between devices.

This chapter addresses each of the signaling protocols in detail in the following sections:

- "H.323 Signaling" presents message details for Registration, Admission, and Status (RAS) and H.225 signaling described in Chapter 4, "Trunk Devices."

- "QSIG" presents message details for the QSIG feature-to-feature messages that CallManager uses for feature transparency. Chapter 4 provides an overview of QSIG.

- "SIP Signaling" presents the message headers that CallManager sends and receives over its SIP trunk interface, which is described in Chapter 4.

- "SCCP Call Signaling" presents an example message flow that CallManager uses when establishing calls to a Cisco IP Phone. Chapter 3, "Station Devices," describes Cisco IP Phones in more detail.

H.323 Signaling

H.323 operates using three main protocols, discussed at length in Chapter 4:

■   Registration, Admission, and Status (RAS) for interaction with H.323 gatekeepers

■   H.225 for the call signaling phase of a call

■   H.245 for the media control phase of a call

RAS Messaging Details

The RAS protocol supported by CallManager includes specific message types and information elements. The RAS message support provided by CallManager is the H.225 version 2 protocol. Tables C-1 through C-7 describe the specific fields. The tables are arranged alphabetically by message type. Table C-1 shows the fields that an H.323 entity uses to discover the gatekeeper. CallManager does not currently support RAS discovery messages, but they are included here for completeness.

Table C-1   *H.225 RAS Terminal and Gateway Discovery Message Details: User-User Information Element (UUIE) Fields*

Message	Field Name	Comments
GRQ (Gatekeeper Request) to GK (Gatekeeper)	requestSeqNumber	Not used in CallManager 4.1
	protocolIdentifier	
	nonStandardData	
	rasAddress	
	endpointType	
	gatekeeperIdentifier	
	callServices	
	endpointAlias	
	alternateEndpoints	
	tokens	
	cryptoTokens	
	authenticationCapability	
	algorithmsOIDs	
	integrity	
	integrityCheckValue	

Table C-1   *H.225 RAS Terminal and Gateway Discovery Message Details: User-User Information Element (UUIE) Fields (Continued)*

Message	Field Name	Comments
GCF (Gatekeeper Confirmation) from GK	requestSeqNumber	Allowed, but ignored when received
	protocolIdentifier	
	nonStandardData	
	gatekeeperIdentifier	
	rasAddress	
	alternateGatekeeper	
	authenticationMode	
	tokens	
	cryptoTokens	
	algorithmsOIDs	
	integrity	
	integrityCheckValue	
GRJ (Gatekeeper Reject) from GK	requestSeqNumber	Allowed, but ignored when received
	protocolIdentifier	
	nonStandardData	
	gatekeeperIdentifier	
	rejectReason	
	altGKInfo	
	Tokens	
	cryptoTokens	
	integrityCheckValue	

CallManager uses registration messages to register with the gatekeeper that the manual or automatic discovery process identifies. CallManager attempts to register with the gatekeeper and, if not successful, retries the registration at configurable intervals.

Table C-2 shows the fields that CallManager uses to register with the gatekeeper.

Table C-2 *H.225 RAS Registration Message Details: UUIE Fields*

Message	Field Name	Comments
RRQ (Registration Request) to GK	requestSeqNumber	Unique sequence number that is incremented for each new request
	protocolIdentifier	Set to v2
	nonStandardData	Not used
	discoveryComplete	Set to false
	callSignalAddress	Set to the IP and port of the call signaling address
	rasAddress	Set to the IP and port of the RAS signaling address
	terminalType	Set to indicate terminal or gateway device
	terminalAlias	No alias set
	gatekeeperIdentifier	Gatekeeper ID set
	alternateEndpoints	Set to transport addresses of alternate CallManager nodes
	timeTolive	Set to configuration value; defaults to 60
	tokens	Not supported
	cryptoTokens	Not supported
	integrityCheckValue	Not supported
	keepAlive	Set to true if this is a refresh registration
	endpointIdentifier	Endpoint ID set
	willSupplyUUIEs	Defaults to false
RCF (Registration Confirmation) from GK	requestSeqNumber	Unique sequence number
	protocolIdentifier	CallManager does not screen this field
	nonStandardData	Not used
	callSignalAddress	CallManager sends H.225 signaling to this address
	terminalAlias	Not used

Table C-2 *H.225 RAS Registration Message Details: UUIE Fields (Continued)*

Message	Field Name	Comments
RCF (Registration Confirmation) from GK *(continued)*	gatekeeperIdentifier	Identifies the H.323 zone
	endpointIdentifier	Endpoint identifier
	alternateGatekeeper	Defines gatekeepers to contact if registering gatekeeper is unavailable
	timeToLive	CallManager periodically reregisters according to this timer
	tokens	Not supported
	cryptoTokens	Not supported
	integrityCheckValue	Not supported
	willRespondToIRR	Ignored
	pregrantedARQ	Not used
RRJ (Registration Reject) from GK	requestSeqNumber	Unique sequence number
	protocolIdentifier	Not screened
	nonStandardData	Not used
	rejectReason	Reject reason
	gatekeeperIdentifier	Indicates the zone of the rejecting gatekeeper
	altGKInfo	Indicates an alternate gatekeeper with which to register
	tokens	Not supported
	cryptoTokens	Not supported
	integrityCheckValue	Not supported

CallManager uses unregistration messages to unregister from the gatekeeper when a gatekeeper-registered device is stopped. Table C-3 shows the fields that CallManager uses to unregister from the gatekeeper.

Table C-3 *H.225 RAS Unregistration Message Details: UUIE Fields*

Message	Field Name	Comments
URQ (Unregister Request) to GK	requestSeqNumber	Unique sequence number that is incremented for each new request

continues

Table C-3   *H.225 RAS Unregistration Message Details: UUIE Fields (Continued)*

Message	Field Name	Comments
URQ (Unregister Request) to GK *(continued)*	protocolIdentifier	Not screened
	callSignalAddress	Set to the IP and port of the call signaling address
	endpointAlias	Not set
	nonStandardData	Not used
	endpointIdentifier	Indicates the identifier of the unregistering request
	alternateEndpoints	Not used
	gatekeeperIdentifier	Not set
	tokens	Not supported
	cryptoTokens	Not supported
	integrityCheckValue	Not supported
	reason	CallManager sets no reason and ignores the reason when receiving a URQ
UCF (Unregister Confirm) from GK	requestSeqNumber	Allowed, but ignored when received
	nonStandardData	
	tokens	
	cryptoTokens	
	integrityCheckValue	
URJ (Unregister Reject) from GK	requestSeqNumber	Allowed, but ignored when received
	rejectReason	
	nonStandardData	
	altGKInfo	
	tokens	
	cryptoTokens	
	integrityCheckValue	

CallManager uses call admission control to discover routes to other CallManager clusters and gateways and to determine whether enough bandwidth exists for CallManager to place or receive a call.

Table C-4 shows the fields that CallManager uses to exchange call admission control messages with the gatekeeper.

Table C-4 *H.225 RAS Admission Message Details: UUIE Fields*

Message	Field Name	Comments
ARQ (Admission Request) to GK	requestSeqNumber	Unique sequence number that is incremented for each new request
	callType	Set to point to point
	callModel	Not set
	endpointIdentifier	Set to endpoint ID
	destinationInfo	Up to 16 E.164 addresses
	destCallSignalAddress	IP address, if set by CallManager
	destExtraCallInfo	Not set
	srcInfo	If present, a list of up to 16 E.164 addresses
	srcCallSignalAddress	Set to the IP and port of the call signaling address
	bandwidth	Requested bandwidth to be used
	callReferenceValue	Set to call reference value for this call
	nonStandardData	Not used
	callServices	Set to None
	conferenceId	Unique conference identifier
	activeMC	Set to false for no multipoint controller (MC)
	answeredCall	Set to true if call is incoming, false on outgoing
	canMapAlias	Set to true
	callIdentifier	Unique call identifier
	srcAlternatives	Set to None
	gatekeeperIdentifier	Not set
	tokens	Not supported
	cryptoTokens	Not supported
	integrityCheckValue	Not supported

continues

Table C-4   *H.225 RAS Admission Message Details: UUIE Fields (Continued)*

Message	Field Name	Comments
ARQ (Admission Request) to GK (continued)	transportQOS	Not supported
	willSupplyUUIEs	Defaults to false
ACF (Admission Confirm) from GK	requestSeqNumber	Unique sequence number
	bandWidth	Not used
	callModel	CallManager always acts as if the response is direct
	destCallSignalAddress	Uses the IP address to specify the call signaling address; used if configured for anonymous device; ignored otherwise
	irrFrequency	Used to specify the Information Request Response (IRR) frequency in seconds while on the call
	nonStandardData	Not used
	destinationInfo	Not used
	destExtraCallInfo	Not used
	destinationType	Not used
	remoteExtensionAddress	Not used
	alternateEndpoints	Transport address of associated H.323 trunks
	tokens	Not supported
	cryptoTokens	Not supported
	integrityCheckValue	Not supported
	transportQOS	Not supported
	willRespondToIRR	Not used
	uuiesRequested	Not used

Table C-4   *H.225 RAS Admission Message Details: UUIE Fields (Continued)*

Message	Field Name	Comments
ARJ (Admission Reject) from GK	requestSeqNumber	Unique sequence number
	rejectReason	Used only for ARJ trace display
	nonStandardData	Not used
	altGKInfo	If provided, CallManager contacts the alternate gatekeeper
	tokens	Not supported
	cryptoTokens	Not supported
	callSignalAddress	Not used
	integrityCheckValue	Not supported

CallManager does not use bandwidth control messages by default. Bandwidth control messages are used if you set the service parameter to enable bandwidth control. Table C-5 shows the bandwidth message fields.

Table C-5   *H.225 RAS Bandwidth Message Details: UUIE Fields*

Message	Field Name	Comments
BRQ (Bandwidth Request) from GK	requestSeqNumber	CallManager returns a BRJ (Bandwidth Reject)
	endpointIdentifier	
	conferenceID	
	callReferenceValue	
	callType	
	bandWidth	
	nonStandardData	
	callIdentifier	
	gatekeeperIdentifier	
	tokens	
	cryptoTokens	
	integrityCheckValue	
	answeredCall	

continues

Table C-5   *H.225 RAS Bandwidth Message Details: UUIE Fields (Continued)*

Message	Field Name	Comments
BRQ (Bandwidth Request) to GK	requestSeqNumber	Unique sequence number
	endpointIdentifier	Endpoint identifier
	conferenceID	Unique conference identifier
	callReferenceValue	Call reference value
	callType	Point to point
	bandWidth	New bandwidth
	nonStandardData	Not used
	callIdentifier	Unique call identifier
	gatekeeperIdentifier	Not supported
	tokens	Not supported
	cryptoTokens	Not supported
	integrityCheckValue	Not supported
	answeredCall	True on terminating side
BCF (Bandwidth Confirm) from GK	requestSeqNumber	Unique sequence number
	bandWidth	Bandwidth granted
	nonStandardData	Not used
	tokens	Not used
	cryptoTokens	Not used
	integrityCheckValue	Not used
BRJ (Bandwidth Reject) from GK	requestSeqNumber	Unique sequence number
	rejectReason	Reason bandwidth change was disallowed
	allowedBandWidth	Amount of bandwidth allowed
	nonStandardData	Not used
	altGKInfo	ID of alternate gatekeeper
	tokens	Not used
	cryptoTokens	Not used
	integrityCheckValue	Not used

Gatekeepers use disengage messages to force a call to be dropped. CallManager uses disengage messages to indicate that an endpoint is being dropped.

Table C-6 shows the fields that CallManager uses to exchange disengage messages with the gatekeeper.

Table C-6 *H.225 RAS Disengage Message Details: UUIE Fields*

Message	Field Name	Comments
DRQ (Disengage Request) to or from GK	requestSeqNumber	Unique sequence number
	endpointIdentifier	Endpoint identifier
	conferenceID	Unique conference identifier
	callReferenceValue	Call reference value
	disengageReason	If sent, set to reason; if received, used to set the release complete reason
	nonStandardData	Not used
	callIdentifier	Unique call identifier
	gatekeeperIdentifier	Not used
	tokens	Not supported
	cryptoTokens	Not supported
	integrityCheckValue	Not supported
	answeredCall	Supported
DCF (Disengage Confirm) to or from GK	requestSeqNumber	Unique sequence number
	nonStandardData	Not used
	tokens	Not supported
	cryptoTokens	Not supported
	integrityCheckValue	Not supported
DRJ (Disengage Reject) from GK	requestSeqNumber	Unique sequence number
	rejectReason	CallManager ignores
	nonStandardData	Not used
	altGKInfo	Not supported
	tokens	Not supported
	cryptoTokens	Not supported
	integrityCheckValue	Not supported

The gatekeeper sends Information Request (IRQ) messages to request status information. CallManager responds to information request messages from the gatekeeper with Information

Request Response (IRR) messages, but CallManager does not send unsolicited IRQ messages to the gatekeeper. IRR messages are sent at the intervals specified by the irrFrequency field in the ACF message.

Table C-7 shows the fields that CallManager uses to exchange information request messages with the gatekeeper.

Table C-7   *H.225 RAS Information Request Message Details: UUIE Fields*

Message	Field Name	Comments
IRQ (Information Request) from GK	requestSeqNumber	Unique sequence number
	callReferenceValue	Call reference value
	nonStandardData	Not used
	replyAddress	Not used
	callIdentifier	Not used
	tokens	Not supported
	cryptoTokens	Not supported
	integrityCheckValue	Not supported
	uuiesRequested	Not used
IRR (Information Request Response) to GK	nonStandardData	Not used
	requestSeqNumber	Unique sequence number
	endpointType	Set to terminal or gateway
	endpointIdentifier	Endpoint identifier
	rasAddress	Set to the IP address and port of the RAS signaling address
	callSignalAddress	Not present
	endpointAlias	Not present
	perCallInfo	See the following perCall fields
	perCallInfo.nonStandardData	Not used
	perCallInfo.callReferenceValue	Call reference value
	perCallInfo.conferenceId	Unique conference ID
	perCallInfo.originator	Set to false
	perCallInfo.audio	Not set
	perCallInfo.video	Not set
	perCallInfo.data	Not set

Table C-7 *H.225 RAS Information Request Message Details: UUIE Fields (Continued)*

Message	Field Name	Comments
IRR (Information Request Response) to GK	perCallInfo.h245	Set to false
	perCallInfo.callSignaling	Not present
	perCallInfo.callType	Point to point
	perCallInfo.bandwidth	Set to 1280 for a G.711 call; 480 for a G.729 call
	perCallInfo.callModel	Set to direct
	perCallInfo.callIdentifier	Call ID
	perCallInfo.tokens	Not supported
	perCallInfo.cryptoTokens	Not supported
	perCallInfo.substituteConfIDs	Not supported
	perCallInfo.pdu	Not supported
	tokens	Not supported
	cryptoTokens	Not supported
	integrityCheckValue	Not supported
	needResponse	Not supported
IACK (Information Request Acknowledgement) from GK	requestSeqNumber	Allowed, but ignored when received
	nonStandardData	
	tokens	
	cryptoTokens	
	integrityCheckValue	
INAK (Information Request Negative Acknowledgement) from GK	requestSeqNumber	Allowed, but ignored when received
	nonStandardData	
	nakReason	
	altGKInfo	
	tokens	
	cryptoTokens	
	integrityCheckValue	

continues

H.225 Messaging Details

H.323 messages, including the call signaling messages, follow the ITU-T Q.931 recommendation as specified in H.323. In H.323, the user-user information element (UUIE) conveys the H.323-related information. The H.323 user information protocol data unit (PDU) is ASN.1-encoded. The ASN.1 is encoded using the basic aligned variant of the packed encoding rules as specified in X.691. The ASN.1 structure begins with H323-UserInformation.

H.225 is the call signaling protocol that is supported in the H.323 protocol umbrella. H.225 includes the call signaling messages and the RAS messages. This section covers the specific details of the H.225 call signaling messages.

Table C-8 lists each H.225 message and provides the specific UUIE fields of the H.225 call signaling messages that CallManager exchanges with an H.323 gateway or CallManager H.323 trunk (gateway in table).

Table C-8   *H.225 Call Signaling Message Details: UUIE Fields*

Message	Field Name	Comments
Alerting from gateway	protocolIdentifier	Assumes version 2 (v2); only v2 fields are processed
	destinationInfo	Used
	h245Address	Used if present
	callIdentifier	Unique call identifier
	h245SecurityMode	Not supported
	tokens	Not supported
	cryptoTokens	Not supported
	fastStart	Supported
Alerting to gateway	protocolIdentifier	Set to v2
	destinationInfo	Endpoint type terminal
	h245Address	If present at alerting, contains the IP address and port of the CallManager H.245 transport address
	callIdentifier	Unique call identifier
	h245SecurityMode	Not supported
	tokens	Not supported
	cryptoTokens	Not supported
	fastStart	Supported

Table C-8 *H.225 Call Signaling Message Details: UUIE Fields (Continued)*

Message	Field Name	Comments
CallProceeding from gateway	protocolIdentifier	Assumes v2; only v2 fields are processed
	destinationInfo	Used
	h245Address	Used if present
	callIdentifier	Unique call identifier
	h245SecurityMode	Not supported
	tokens	Not supported
	cryptoTokens	Not supported
	fastStart	Supported
CallProceeding to gateway	protocolIdentifier	Set to v2
	destinationInfo	Endpoint type terminal
	h245Address	If present at CallProceeding, contains the IP address and port of the CallManager H.245 transport address
	callIdentifier	Unique call identifier
	h245SecurityMode	Not supported
	tokens	Not supported
	cryptoTokens	Not supported
	fastStart	Supported
Connect from gateway	protocolDiscriminator	Assumes v2; only v2 fields are processed
	h245Address	Used if present; required if not present in previous message
	destinationInfo	Used
	conferenceId	Required
	callIdentifier	Unique call identifier
	h245SecurityMode	Not supported
	tokens	Not supported
	cryptoTokens	Not supported
	fastStart	Supported

continues

Table C-8 *H.225 Call Signaling Message Details: UUIE Fields (Continued)*

Message	Field Name	Comments
Connect to gateway	protocolDiscriminator	Set to v2
	h245Address	Contains the IP address and port of the CallManager H.245 transport address
	destinationInfo	Endpoint type terminal
	conferenceId	Unique conference identifier
	callIdentifier	Unique call identifier
	h245SecurityMode	Not supported
	tokens	Not supported
	cryptoTokens	Not supported
	fastStart	Supported
Facility from and to gateway	protocolDiscriminator	Set to v2
	alternativeAddress	Not used
	alternativeAliasAddress	Not used
	conferenceID	Not used
	reason	Used
	callIdentifier	Unique call identifier
	destExtraCallInfo	Not used
	remoteExtensionAddress	Not used
	tokens	Not used
	cryptoTokens	Not used
	conferences	Not used
	h245Address	Not used
UserInformation from gateway	protocolIdentifier	Assumes v2; only v2 fields are processed
	callIdentifier	Not used
UserInformation to gateway	protocolIdentifier	Set to v2
	callIdentifier	Unique call identifier

Table C-8 *H.225 Call Signaling Message Details: UUIE Fields (Continued)*

Message	Field Name	Comments
Progress from gateway	protocolIdentifier	Assumes v2; only v2 fields are processed
	destinationInfo	Not used
	h245Address	Used if present; required if not present in previous message
	callIdentifier	Unique call identifier
	h245SecurityMode	Not supported
	tokens	Not supported
	cryptoTokens	Not supported
	fastStart	Supported
Progress to gateway	protocolIdentifier	Set to v2
	destinationInfo	Endpoint type terminal
	h245Address	Contains the IP address and port of the CallManager H.245 transport address
	callIdentifier	Unique call identifier
	h245SecurityMode	Not supported
	tokens	Not supported
	cryptoTokens	Not supported
	fastStart	Supported
ReleaseComplete from gateway	protocolIdentifier	Assumes v2; only v2 fields are processed
	reason	Reason for disconnect
	callIdentifier	Unique call identifier
ReleaseComplete to gateway	protocolIdentifier	Set to v2
	reason	Reason for disconnect
	callIdentifier	Unique call identifier

continues

Table C-8   *H.225 Call Signaling Message Details: UUIE Fields (Continued)*

Message	Field Name	Comments
Setup from gateway	protocolIdentifier	Assumes v2; only v2 fields are processed
	h245Address	Contains the IP address and port of the CallManager H.245 transport address
	sourceInfo	Not used
	sourceAddress	Source address if provided
	destinationAddress	Not used; E.164 address is in the Q.931 called party number IE (information element)
	destCallSignalAddress	Not used
	destExtraCallInfo	Not used
	destExtraCRV	Not used
	activeMC	Used
	conferenceId	Unique conference identifier
	conferenceGoal	Used
	callServices	Not used
	callType	Used
	sourceCallSignalAddress	Used
	remoteExtensionAddress	Not used
	callIdentifier	Unique call identifier
	h245SecurityCapability	Not supported
	tokens	Not supported
	cryptoTokens	Not supported
	fastStart	Supported
	mediaWaitForConnect	Used if present; defaults to false if not present
	canOverlapSend	Not used

Table C-8 *H.225 Call Signaling Message Details: UUIE Fields (Continued)*

Message	Field Name	Comments
Setup to gateway	protocolIdentifier	Set to v2
	h245Address	Contains the IP address and port of the CallManager H.245 transport address
	sourceInfo	Endpoint type terminal
	sourceAddress	Source address as E.164 address, H.323 alias, or both
	destinationIAddress	E.164 address present here and also included in the Q.931 called party number IE (information element)
	destinationCallSignalAddress	Not used
	destExtraCallInfo	Not used
	destExtraCRV	Not used
	activeMC	Used
	conferenceId	Unique conference identifier
	conferenceGoal	Set to create
	callServices	Not used
	callType	Point to point
	sourceCallSignalAddress	Used
	remoteExtensionAddress	Not used
	callIdentifier	Unique call identifier
	h245SecurityCapability	Not supported
	tokens	Not supported
	cryptoTokens	Not supported
	fastStart	Supported
	mediaWaitForConnect	Set to true
	canOverlapSend	Set to false

QSIG

Chapter 4 covers QSIG, a messaging framework that fosters feature transparency between Private Branch Exchanges (PBX). For CallManager, QSIG is almost a protocol within a protocol within a protocol—the QSIG feature messages wrapped in ISDN signaling communicated to MGCP gateways.

QSIG messages are called application protocol data units (APDU). They tend to contain a handful of fields at most. CallManager uses QSIG APDUs to implement the following features:

- Call completion

- Call diversion

- Call transfer

- Name services (calling name presentation and restriction, alerting name presentation and restriction, connected name presentation and restriction)

- Message waiting indicator

- Path replacement

The sections that follow describe the APDUs required for each of these features and the encoding rules that CallManager uses for the fields within the messages.

> **NOTE**   You'll notice frequent use of the term PBX. In the QSIG section, PBX is used interchangeably for CallManager clusters as well as legacy PBXs.

Call Completion

The QSIG call completion feature allows a user who calls a destination that is busy or that does not answer to set a watch over the called party. When the called party becomes available, The IP phone prompts the calling user to redial the destination.

Call completion relies on the following APDUs:

- **ccnrRequest and ccbsRequest**—Communicate from one PBX to another that a user wants to start monitoring the called party.

  The ccnrRequest and ccbsRequest APDUs contain the following fields:

  — **numberA**—Indicates the number of the monitoring party.

  — **numberB**—Indicates the number of the party to be monitored.

- **ccExecPossible**—Communicates the availability of the called user to the PBX that set the watch.

  The ccExecPossible APDU contains the following fields:

  — **numberA**—Indicates the number of the monitoring party.

  — **numberB**—Indicates the number of the party to be monitored.

- **ccCancel**—Indicates the caller's or the PBX's desire to cancel the callback.

  The ccExecPossible APDU contains the following fields:

  - **numberA**—Indicates the number of the monitoring party.

  - **numberB**—Indicates the number of the party to be monitored.

- **ccRingout**—Indicates that an incoming call is the result of a callback attempt; contains no APDU fields.

- **ccSuspend**—Pauses the watch when the calling user is busy at the time of the called party's availability; contains no APDU fields.

- **ccResume**—Resumes the watch when the caller is idle; contains no APDU fields.

Call Diversion

The QSIG call diversion feature causes the displays of the calling and called parties to update when a call is forwarded from one user to another.

Call diversion relies on the following APDUs:

- **divertingLegInformation1**—Communicates diversion information from the forwarded phone to the caller while the call diversion is being processed.

  The divertingLegInformation1 APDU contains the following fields:

  - **diversionReason**—Indicates why the diversion occurred (for example, the destination was busy or failed to answer).

  - **subscriptionOption**—Determines whether to deliver number or name to the user.

  - **nominatedNr**—Indicates the call forwarding target to the caller.

- **divertingLegInformation2**—Communicates diversion information from the forwarded phone to the forward target while the call diversion is being processed.

  The divertingLegInformation2 APDU contains the following fields:

  - **diversionCounter**—Indicates the number of times that the call has been previously diverted, to minimize the effect of call forwarding loops.

  - **diversionReason**—Indicates why the diversion occurred.

  - **originalDiversionReason**—In the case of multiple diversions, indicates why the original called party diverted the call.

  - **divertingNr**—Indicates the number of the device that diverted the call.

> — **originalDivertingNr**—In the case of multiple diversions, indicates the number associated with the original target of the call.

> — **redirectingName**—Indicates the display name associated with the diverting user.

> — **redirectingName**—In the case of multiple diversions, indicates the display name associated with the original target of the call.

■ **divertingLegInformation3**—Communicates diversion information from the forward target to the caller when the call forward has completed.

The divertingLegInformation3 APDU contains the following fields:

> — **presentationAllowedIndicator**—Indicates whether the caller is permitted to see the name of the forward target.

> — **redirectionName**—Indicates the display name associated with the user to whom the call was diverted.

Call Transfer

The QSIG call transfer feature causes the displays of the transferred and transfer destination to update when a user transfers a call from one party to the other.

Call transfer relies on the following APDUs:

■ **ctComplete**—Communicates information about the transferred party to the transfer destination upon completion of the transfer.

The ctComplete APDU contains the following fields:

> — **redirectionNumber**—Indicates the transferred-to number if sent to the calling party. If sent to the transferred-to user, it represents the calling party number.

> — **redirectionName**—Indicates the transferred-to name if sent to the calling party. If sent to the transferred-to user, it represents the calling party name.

■ **ctActive**—Communicates when a ringing transfer destination answers the call.

The ctActive APDU contains the following fields:

> — **connectedAddress**—Is sent to the calling party and indicates the transferred-to number.

> — **redirectionName**—Is sent to the calling party and indicates the transferred-to name.

■ **ctUpdate**—Communicates display information about the transferred party to the transfer destination and vice versa, once the transfer is complete.

The ctUpdate APDU contains the following fields:

— **redirectionNumber**—Indicates the transferred-to number if sent to the calling party. If sent to the transferred-to user, it represents the calling party number.

— **redirectionName**—Indicates the transferred-to name if sent to the calling party. If sent to the transferred-to user, it represents the calling party name.

Message Waiting Indicator

The QSIG message waiting feature allows a voice mail system attached to one PBX to deliver message waiting indications to users connected to another PBX.

QSIG message waiting relies on the following APDUs:

- **mwiActivate**—Communicates the number of the phone whose message waiting indicator must be lit from the system hosting voice mail to the system hosting the phone. This APDU contains the servedUserNr field, which indicates the number of the party whose lamp state needs to be altered.

- **mwiDeactivate**—Communicates the number of the phone whose message waiting indicator must be extinguished from the system hosting voice mail to the system hosting the phone. This APDU contains the servedUserNr field, which indicates the number of the party whose lamp state needs to be altered.

Name Services

The QSIG name services features ensure that a caller can see the name of the called party (when permissible) and that a called party can see the name of the calling party (when permissible).

QSIG name services features include the following:

- Calling name presentation and restriction

- Alerting name presentation and restriction

- Connected name presentation and restriction

QSIG name services APDUs communicate two main pieces of information:

- The name of the calling, alerting, or called party

- The presentation indicator associated with that party, which determines whether the recipient of the message can see the name of the sender

Path Replacement

The QSIG path replacement feature permits PBXs that have been involved in a call diversion or call transfer to optimize the signaling path after the diversion or transfer completes. This process can free up trunk circuits when a call has hairpinned through the network.

QSIG path replacement relies on the following APDUs:

- **prPropose**—Allows one PBX to propose to another PBX that the path be optimized.

  The prPropose APDU contains the following fields:

  — **callIdentity**—Provides a numeric key that the receiving PBX should encode in the replacement call so that the sending PBX can identify the new incoming call.

  — **reroutingNumber**—Indicates the number that the receiving PBX should use when placing the replacement call. This number is not the number of the actual party involved in the call but is instead a number associated with the CallManager node that is hosting the party.

- **prSetup**—A PBX embeds this APDU in a call setup attempt to the target PBX to indicate that the incoming call is not a new call but is an optimized call attempt that should replace the incoming leg of the original call. This APDU contains the callIdentity field, which indicates the numeric key that will be provided in the prPropose sent by the initiating PBX of the path replacement operation.

SIP Signaling

This section describes CallManager support for SIP methods and header fields. Chapter 4 provides an overview of CallManager support for SIP trunks.

SIP defines messages into requests and responses. Request messages are named; response messages are numbered. Table C-9 lists the request messages.

Table C-9 *SIP Request Messages*

Request	Supported by CallManager?	Comments
INVITE	Y	Establishes a session; CallManager originates and receives this message.
ACK	Y	Acknowledges the establishment of a session; CallManager sends and receives this message.
OPTIONS	Y	Queries a User Agent (UA) about its capabilities; CallManager never sends this message but does respond to it.

Table C-9   *SIP Request Messages (Continued)*

Request	Supported by CallManager?	Comments
BYE	Y	Terminates an established session. CallManager sends and receives this message.
CANCEL	Y	Rescinds an INVITE before the session is established.
REGISTER	N	Registers SIP addresses with a registrar. CallManager never sends this message and responds with a 405 Method Not Allowed if it receives it.
PRACK	Y	Acknowledges the receipt of a provisional response (such as 180 Alerting) by the UA; used only when reliable provisional responses are in effect.
UPDATE	Y	Allows session parameters for an unestablished session to be changed. CallManager never sends this message but can accept it.

Response messages are numbered in the range 1xx to 6xx. Each group of a hundred represents a specific class of responses to the requests. Table C-10 lists the message classes and describes CallManager support for specific messages in the class.

Table C-10   *SIP Response Messages*

Request	Supported by CallManager?	Comments
1xx messages indicate events that occur as a session is being established		
100 Trying	Y	Indicates that the Proxy or UA has been able to resolve an address and continue routing. CallManager supports sending and receiving this message.
180 Ringing	Y	Indicates the target UA is ringing. CallManager sends and receives this message.
181 Call Forward	N	CallManager cannot send or receive this message.
182 Call Queued	N	CallManager cannot send or receive this message.
183 Progress	Y	CallManager can receive and send this message. CallManager may connect media on receipt of this message.
2xx messages confirm the establishment of a session		
200 OK	Y	Confirms that a session has been established.
3xx messages indicate that the session being established should be established to or via a different SIP entity		
300–302, 305, 380	Y	CallManager never sends these messages. When it receives this class of message, CallManager attempts to re-establish the session to the contacts listed in the message.

continues

Table C-10 *SIP Response Messages (Continued)*

Request	Supported by CallManager?	Comments
4xx messages are definitive, final failure responses from the target of the request		
4xx	Y	CallManager sends and receives this message. CallManager initiates a call disconnect upon receiving this message.
5xx messages indicate that an unexpected condition was encountered that prevented the establishment of the session		
5xx	Y	CallManager sends this message. Upon receiving this message, CallManager issues a new request if the response contains an alternate contact. Otherwise, CallManager ends the call.
6xx messages indicate that the target of the request was busy and cannot accept the incoming call		
6xx	Y	CallManager never sends this message. CallManager disconnects the call upon receiving this message.

SIP requests and responses contain header fields. CallManager support for header fields is fairly consistent from message to message.

Table C-11 lists the header fields that CallManager sends in requests it originates.

Table C-11 *SIP Response Messages*

Header	Appears in Requests	Example with Comments
From	All	From: *callerName* <sip:*cgpn*@*CCM_IP_addr*> *callerName* is the caller's display name; *cgpn* is the caller's number; *CCM_IP_addr* is the IP address of CallManager.
To	All	To: *calledName* <sip:*cdpn*@*destIP*;user=*phone*> *calledName* is the name of the call target, if available; *cdpn* is the number of the called party; *destIP* is the resolved IP address of the target of the SIP trunk.
Via	All	Via:SIP/2.0 *IPaddr*:*port*;branch=*number* *IPaddr* is the IP address of CallManager; *port* is the port assigned to CallManager's SIP trunk; branch is a unique *number* that identifies each branch of an outgoing forked call. CallManager SIP trunks don't support forking, which means CallManager issues only a single request with a single branch identifier.

Table C-11 *SIP Response Messages (Continued)*

Header	Appears in Requests	Example with Comments
Call-ID	All	Call-ID: *number@IPaddr* *number* is a unique call identifier determined by CallManager; *IPaddr* is the IP address of CallManager.
Contact	All	Contact: <sip:*cgpn@IPaddr:localPort*;user=*phone*> *IPAddr* is the IP address of CallManager; *cgpn* is the calling number; *localPort* is the incoming port assigned to the issuing SIP trunk.
Cseq	All	Cseq: *number method* *number* is a number that increments for each subsequent outgoing request; *method* is the name of the request (INVITE, ACK, and so on).
Max-Forwards	All	Max-Forwards: *number* *number* indicates the maximum number of times that the message can propagate from call agent to call agent before the request expires. CallManager sets this value to 6 for originated SIP calls.
Remote-Party-Id	INVITE	Remote-Party-Id: *calledName* <sip:*cdpn@called_ IP_ address*;user=*phone*>;party=calling;screen=no;privacy=off Indicates the display information for the party issuing the response. user indicates the class of responding device; party indicates the role of the responder in the call; screen indicates whether an intermediary entity has validated the display information; privacy indicates whether the information should be displayed to the requestor.
Diversion	INVITE	Diversion: <sip:*divertingNumber @diverting_IP_address* >;reason=no-answer Indicates the prior history of the call. If the call has been previously diverted, this information must be communicated to the downstream voice mail server. reason indicates the reason for the diversion.

Table C-12 lists the header fields that CallManager sends in responses to requests that it receives.

Table C-12 *SIP Response Messages*

Header	Appears in Message Classes	Example with Comments
From	All	From: <sip:*cgpn@CCM_IP_Addr*>;tag=16777234 *cgpn* is the number of the caller; *CCM_IP_Addr* is the address that issued the request; tag is part of a unique call identifier.

continues

Table C-12   *SIP Response Messages (Continued)*

Header	Appears in Message Classes	Example with Comments
To	All	To: <sip:*cdpn@destIP*>;tag=*xxyyzz* *cdpn* is the number of the responder; *destIP* is the IP address of the responder; tag is part of a unique call identifier.
Via	All	Via: SIP/2.0/TCP *CCM_IP_Addr* :*localPort*;received=*CCM_IP_Addr* ;branch=z9hG4bKfe8d27ec The Via chain—this header often occurs multiple times in a SIP request—indicates the path that the request took. branch is a unique identifier that indicates which fork of a branching call is issuing the response.
Contact	All	Contact: <sip:*cdpn@destIP:calledPort*> The Contact represents the address of the specific entity that is responding to the message.
Remote-Party-Id	18X 2XX	Remote-Party-Id: *calledName* <sip:*cdpn*@destIP;user=*phone*>;party=called; screen=no;privacy=off Indicates the display information for the party issuing the response. user indicates the class of the responding device; party indicates the role of the responder in the call; screen indicates whether an intermediary entity has validated the display information; privacy indicates whether the information should be displayed to the requestor.

SCCP Call Signaling

The Skinny Client Control Protocol (SCCP) is a simple stimulus interface between the Cisco IP Phone and CallManager. Communication takes place over a TCP/IP connection that the phone establishes to CallManager on port 2000 by default (port number is configurable). Secure connections communicate on port 2443. Once established, the connection remains as long as the phone is capable of initiating or accepting calls.

SCCP provides a means of receiving stimulus events from the phone such as off-hook, on-hook, and button press events (including keypad digits, fixed keys, softkeys, and line keys). SCCP also provides a means of sending control information to the phone to drive the specific behavior required for the phone to provide the user with the correct information as calls are made and features are handled. You can review the details of SCCP in this appendix.

Figure C-1 illustrates calls made between Cisco IP Phones.

Figure C-1 *Making a Call Between IP Phones*

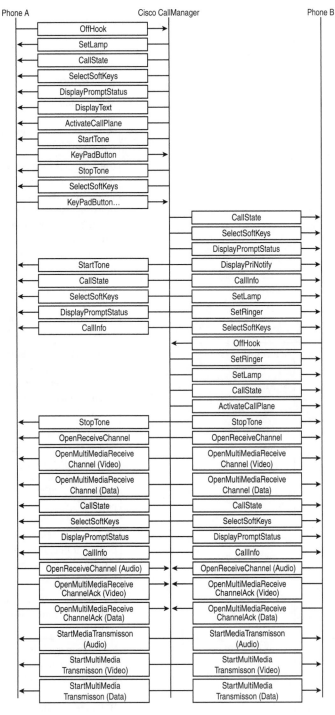

Table C-13 provides a step-by-step description of calls placed between two Cisco IP Phones.

Table C-13   *Making a Call (Audio, Video, and Data) Between IP Phones that Are Each Connected to Cisco IP Communicator*

Phone A	Cisco CallManager	Phone B	Description
OffHook -->			When you perform any number of off-hook actions, such as lifting the handset of IP Phone A or pressing the **NewCall** softkey, the phone reports off-hook to CallManager.
	SetLamp <--		CallManager sends this message for several possible reasons. SetLamp has a lineInstance field. When the lineInstance field is 0, it lights or extinguishes the MWI lamp. If the lineInstance is other than 0, it turns on the envelope icon next to the line button on which a message is waiting. If the line button can be lit, it will be lit as well.
	CallState <--		CallManager sends the CallState information, which the Cisco IP Phones 79*xx* series use to update the icon of the appropriate line as a visual indication of call state.
	SelectSoftKeys <--		CallManager sends SelectSoftKeys to activate a set of softkeys and a mask to select which softkeys are enabled and which keys are disabled. Cisco 79*xx* series IP Phones use softkeys.
	DisplayPrompt Status <--		CallManager sends the DisplayPromptStatus to update the prompt line, which is the display line just above the softkey text line on Cisco 79*xx* series IP Phones. This initial prompt for off-hook state is "Enter number." For idle state, the phone displays "Your current options." The prompt message is associated with a particular line. If a different line is selected, the prompt changes to the prompt associated with the selected line.
	DisplayText <--		CallManager sends the text to update the display of a limited-display phone, such as the 30VIP.
	ActivateCallPlane <--		CallManager sends ActivateCallPlane to activate the call plane for the specified line. In this case, the call is line 1 as the default because no specific line was selected. Cisco 79xx series IP Phones use the ActivateCallPlane command.

Table C-13   *Making a Call (Audio, Video, and Data) Between IP Phones that Are Each Connected to Cisco IP Communicator (Continued)*

Phone A	Cisco CallManager	Phone B	Description
	StartTone <--		CallManager directs the phone to play an inside dial tone. The phone internally generates a dial tone.
KeyPad Button -->			As you enter the number of the desired destination—Phone B in this case—the phone sends a KeyPadButton for each digit dialed. The KeyPadButton messages continue until CallManager determines that you have entered the required number of digits to reach your destination. When CallManager determines the called party—Phone B in this case— CallManager initiates the message sequence to Phone B to extend the call to Phone B.
	StopTone <--		CallManager directs the phone to stop playing dial tone after you enter the first digit.
	SelectSoftKeys <--		CallManager sends SelectSoftKeys to activate the next set of softkeys and the mask to select which softkeys are enabled and which softkeys are disabled. Cisco 79*xx* series IP Phones use softkeys.
	CallState -->		CallManager sends CallState information, which Cisco 79*xx* series IP Phones use to update the call state information and the icon of the appropriate line as a visual indication of call state. In this case, the call state indicates an incoming call.
	SelectSoftKeys -->		CallManager sends SelectSoftKeys to Phone B to activate the appropriate softkeys.
	DisplayPrompt Status -->		CallManager sends DisplayPromptStatus to Phone B to update the display associated with the particular line of the incoming call. This display persists for the selected line until it is changed by another DisplayPromptStatus message of an equal or higher priority.

continues

Table C-13 *Making a Call (Audio, Video, and Data) Between IP Phones that Are Each Connected to Cisco IP Communicator (Continued)*

Phone A	Cisco CallManager	Phone B	Description
	DisplayPriNotify -->		CallManager sends DisplayPriNotify to Phone B to indicate an incoming call. DisplayPriNotify, which has an associated timeout that defaults to 10 seconds, updates the display immediately and is not associated with a particular line. The priority of the incoming call is included with the notification.
	CallInfo -->		CallManager sends CallInfo to the station to provide the specific information about the call, which includes calling and called party name and number, the line number for the call, and the type of call (inbound, outbound, or forwarded). In this case, the call type is inbound. The name might not be provided in all cases. A gateway call, for example, might not provide calling party name.
	SetLamp -->		CallManager sends this message for several possible reasons. SetLamp has a lineInstance field. When the lineInstance field is 0, it lights or extinguishes the MWI lamp. If the lineInstance is other than 0, it turns on the envelope icon next to the line button on which a message is waiting. If the line button can be lit, it will be lit as well.
	SetRinger -->		CallManager sends the SetRinger to Phone B to cause the phone to ring, indicating an incoming call. The ring type is InsideRing, as distinguished from OutsideRing, because this is an internal call from Phone A to Phone B.
	StartTone <--		CallManager sends StartTone to Phone A to initiate the ringback tone to the caller at Phone A. The tone is generated internally by Phone A.
	CallState <--		CallManager updates the call state of Phone A to indicate that Phone B is now ringing.
	SelectSoftKeys <--		CallManager sends SelectSoftKeys to Phone A to activate the appropriate softkeys for the ringing call.

Table C-13 *Making a Call (Audio, Video, and Data) Between IP Phones that Are Each Connected to Cisco IP Communicator (Continued)*

Phone A	Cisco CallManager	Phone B	Description
	DisplayPrompt Status <--		CallManager sends DisplayPromptStatus to Phone A to display the prompt appropriate for the updated softkeys.
	CallInfo <--		CallManager sends CallInfo to Phone A to provide the specific information about the call, which includes calling and called party name and number, the line number for the call, and the type of call. Because Phone A originated the call, the call is outbound.
		OffHook <--	When you perform any number of off-hook actions, such as lifting the handset of Phone B or pressing the **Answer** softkey, the phone reports off-hook to CallManager.
	SetRinger -->		CallManager turns off the ringer because the call has been answered.
	SetLamp -->		CallManager uses this message to set the line lamp of the line answered on Phone B.
	CallState -->		CallManager updates the call state information for the call because it has changed from ringing to answered.
	ActivateCallPlane -->		CallManager activates the call plane for the line that was answered.
	StopTone <-- -->		CallManager stops the ringback tone on Phone A and the ringer tone on Phone B.
	OpenReceive Channel (audio) <-- -->		CallManager sends OpenReceiveChannel to both Phone A and B to cause the phone to begin receiving audio sent from the other phone. This is only half of the audio path, and because neither phone is transmitting at this point, the connection is not yet fully established.

continues

Table C-13 *Making a Call (Audio, Video, and Data) Between IP Phones that Are Each Connected to Cisco IP Communicator (Continued)*

Phone A	Cisco CallManager	Phone B	Description
	OpenMultiMedia ReceiveChannel (video) <-- -->		CallManager sends OpenMultiMediaReceiveChannel (video) to both Phone A and B to cause the phone to begin receiving video sent from the other phone. This is only half of the video path, and because neither phone is transmitting at this point, the connection is not yet fully established.
	OpenMultiMedia ReceiveChannel (data) <-- -->		CallManager sends OpenMultiMediaReceiveChannel (data) to both Phone A and B to cause the phone to begin receiving data sent from the other phone. This is only half of the data path, and because neither phone is transmitting at this point, the connection is not yet fully established.
	CallState <-- -->		The call state is updated to connected for both Phone A and B.
	SelectSoftKeys <-- -->		The softkeys are updated on both Phone A and B.
	DisplayPrompt Status <-- -->		The prompt line is updated on both Phone A and B.
	CallInfo <-- -->		The call info is updated for both Phone A and B.
Open Receive Channel Ack (audio) -->		Open Receive Channel Ack (audio) <--	Both phones have responded with an OpenReceiveChannelAck (audio), indicating that they are ready to receive audio transmission.

Table C-13 *Making a Call (Audio, Video, and Data) Between IP Phones that Are Each Connected to Cisco IP Communicator (Continued)*

Phone A	Cisco CallManager	Phone B	Description
Open MultiMedia Receive Channel Ack (video) -->		Open MultiMedia Receive Channel Ack (video) <--	Both phones have responded with an OpenMultiMediaReceiveChannelAck (video), indicating that they are ready to receive video transmission.
Open MultiMedia Receive Channel Ack (data) -->		Open MultiMedia Receive Channel Ack (data) <--	Both phones have responded with an OpenMultiMediaReceiveChannelAck (data), indicating that they are ready to receive data transmission.
	StartMedia Transmission (audio) <-- -->		CallManager sends StartMediaTransmission (audio) to both Phone A and B to cause the phone to begin sending audio to the other phone. Because both phones are transmitting and receiving audio at this point, the audio connection is now fully established.
	StartMultiMedia Transmission (video) <-- -->		CallManager sends StartMultiMediaTransmission (video) to both Phone A and B to cause the phone to begin sending video to the other phone. Because both phones are transmitting and receiving video at this point, the video connection is now fully established.
	StartMultiMedia Transmission (data) <-- -->		CallManager sends StartMultiMediaTransmission (data) to both Phone A and B to cause the phone to begin sending data to the other phone. Because both phones are transmitting and receiving data at this point, the data connection is now fully established.

Application Protocols

CallManager provides support for application development. The protocols to support applications include TAPI, JTAPI, and XML for application development. TAPI is not covered in this appendix; you can learn about TAPI in Chapter 3.

JTAPI Package Support

JTAPI supports call control and primitive media support. JTAPI consists of a set of packages. A package is a means of grouping the functionality used by applications. Telephony server implementations choose the functionality that they support in each of the packages to leverage the underlying capabilities offered to the application. Applications can query to discover what packages and functionality is provided. The Core package support is the central functionality and the surrounding JTAPI packages include Call Center, Call Control, and Media packages, described in the tables that follow.

Core Package

Table C-14 lists each JTAPI interface in the JTAPI Core Package, all of which are supported in the Cisco JTAPI implementation.

Table C-14   *JTAPI Core Package Support*

Class Name	Method Name	Comments
Address	addCallObserver	
	addressObserver	
	getAddressCapabilities	
	getCallObservers	
	getCapabilities	
	getConnections	
	getName	
	getObservers	
	getProvider	
	getTerminals	
	removeCallObserver	
	removeObserver	
AddressObserver	addressChangedEvent	
Call	addObserver	
	connect	A CallObserver must exist for the terminal or address originating the call.
	getCallCapabilities	
	getCapabilities	
	getConnections	
	getObservers	
	getProvider	
	getState	
	removeObserver	

Table C-14 *JTAPI Core Package Support (Continued)*

Class Name	Method Name	Comments
CallObserver	callChangedEvent	
Connection	disconnect	
	getAddress	
	getCall	
	getCapabilities	
	getConnectionCapabilities	
	getState	
	getTerminalConnections	
JtapiPeer	getName	
	getProvider	
	getServices	
JtapiPeerFactory	getJtapiPeer	
Provider	addObserver	
	createCall	
	getAddress	
	getAddressCapabilities()	
	getAddressCapabilities(Terminal)	
	getAddresses	
	getCallCapabilities()	
	getCallCapabilities(Terminal, Address)	
	getCalls	This method returns calls only when there are CallObservers attached to addresses or terminals, when a RouteAddress is registered for routing, or when a CiscoMedia Terminal is registered.
	getCapabilities	
	getConnectionCapabilities()	
	getConnectionCapabilities(Terminal, Address)	
	getName	
	getObservers	
	getProviderCapabilities()	
	getProviderCapabilities(Terminal)	
	getState	
	getTerminal	
	getTerminalCapabilities()	

continues

Table C-14 *JTAPI Core Package Support (Continued)*

Class Name	Method Name	Comments
Provider *(continued)*	getTerminalCapabilities(Terminal)	
	getTerminalConnectionCapabilities()	
	getTerminalConnectionCapabilities (Terminal)	
	getTerminals	
	removeObserver	
	shutdown	
ProviderObserver	providerChangedEvent	
Terminal	addCallObserver	
	addObserver	
	getAddresses	
	getCallObservers	
	getCapabilities	
	getName	
	getObservers	
	getProvider	
	getTerminalCapabilities	
	getTerminalConnections	
	removeCallObserver	
	removeObserver	
TerminalConnection	answer	
	getCapabilities	
	getConnection	
	getState	
	getTerminal	
	getTerminalConnectionCapabilities	
TerminalObserver	terminalChangedEvent	

Call Center Package

Table C-15 lists each JTAPI interface in the JTAPI Call Center Package and the support provided by the Cisco JTAPI implementation.

Table C-15   *JTAPI Call Center Package Support*

Class Name	Method Name	Cisco JTAPI Support
ACDAddress	getACDManagerAddress	No
	getLoggedOnAgents	No
	getNumberQueued	No
	getOldestCallQueued	No
	getQueueWaitTime	No
	getRelativeQueueLoad	No
ACDAddressObserver		No
ACDConnection	getACDManagerConnection	No
ACDManagerAddress	getACDAddresses	No
ACDManagerConnection	getACDConnections	No
Agent	getACDAddress	No
	getAgentAddress	No
	getAgentID	No
	getAgentTerminal	No
	getState	No
	setState	No
AgentTerminal	addAgent	No
	getAgents	No
	removeAgents	No
	setAgents	No
AgentTerminalObserver		No
CallCenterAddress	addCallObserver	No
CallCenterCall	connectPredictive	No
	getApplicationData	No
	getTrunks	No
	setApplicationData	No
CallCenterCallObserver		No
CallCenterProvider	getACDAddresses	No
	getACDManagerAddresses	No
	getRouteableAddresses	No

continues

Table C-15   *JTAPI Call Center Package Support (Continued)*

Class Name	Method Name	Cisco JTAPI Support
CallCenterTrunk	getCall	No
	getName	No
	getState	No
	getType	No
RouteAddress	cancelRouteCallback	Yes
	getActiveRouteSessions	Yes
	getRouteCallback	Yes
	registerRouteCallback	Yes
RouteCallback	reRouteEvent	Yes
	routeCallbackEndedEvent	Yes
	routeEndEvent	Yes
	routeEvent	Yes
	routeUsedEvent	Yes
RouteSession	endRoute	Yes
	getCause	Yes
	getRouteAddress	Yes
	getState	Yes
	selectRoute	Yes

Call Center Capabilities Package

Table C-16 lists each JTAPI interface in the JTAPI Call Center Capabilities Package and the support provided by the Cisco JTAPI implementation.

Table C-16   *JTAPI Call Center Capabilities Package Support*

Class Name	Method Name	Cisco JTAPI Support
ACDAddressCapabilities	canGetACDManagerAddress	No
	canGetLoggedOnAgents	No
	canGetNumberQueued	No
	canGetOldestCallQueued	No
	canGetQueueWaitTime	No
	canGetRelativeQueueLoad	No

Table C-16   *JTAPI Call Center Capabilities Package Support (Continued)*

Class Name	Method Name	Cisco JTAPI Support
ACDConnectionCapabilities	canGetACDManagerConnection	No
ACDManagerAddressCapabilities	canGetACDAddresses	No
ACDManagerConnectionCapabilities	canGetACDConnections	No
AgentTerminalCapabilities	canHandleAgents	No
CallCenterAddressCapabilities	canAddCallObserver	No
CallCenterCallCapabilities	canConnectPredictive	No
	canGetTrunks	No
	canHandleApplicationData	No
CallCenterProviderCapabilities	canGetACDAddresses	Yes
	canGetACDManagerAddresses	Yes
	canGetRouteableAddresses	Yes
RouteAddressCapabilities	canRouteCalls	Yes

Call Center Events Package

Table C-17 lists each JTAPI interface in the JTAPI Call Center Events Package and the support provided by the Cisco JTAPI implementation.

Table C-17   *JTAPI Call Center Events Package Support*

Class Name	Method Name	Cisco JTAPI Support
ACDAddrBusyEv		No
ACDAddrEv	getAgent	No
	getAgentAddress	No
	getAgentTerminal	No
	getState	No
	getTrunks	No
ACDAddrLoggedOffEv		No
ACDAddrLoggedOnEv		No
ACDAddrNotReadyEv		No
ACDAddrReadyEv		No
ACDAddrUnknownEv		No
ACDAddrWorkNotReadyEv		No

continues

Table C-17 *JTAPI Call Center Events Package Support (Continued)*

Class Name	Method Name	Cisco JTAPI Support
ACDAddrWorkReadyEv		No
AgentTermBusyEv		No
AgentTermEv	getACDAddress	No
	getAgent	No
	getAgentAddress	No
	getAgentID	No
	getState	No
AgentTermLoggedOffEv		No
AgentTermLoggedOnEv		No
AgentTermNotReadyEv		No
AgentTermReadyEv		No
AgentTermUnknownEv		No
AgentTermWorkNotReadyEv		No
AgentTermWorkReadyEv		No
CallCentCallAppDataEv	getApplicationData	No
CallCentCallEv	getCalledAddress	No
	getCallingAddress	No
	getCallingTerminal	No
	getLastRedirectedAddress	No
	getTrunks	No
CallCentConnEv		No
CallCentConnInProgressEv		No
CallCentEv	getCallCenterCause	No
CallCentTrunkEv	getTrunk	No
CallCentTrunkInvalidEv		No
CallCentTrunkValidEv		No
ReRouteEvent		Yes
RouteCallbackEndedEvent	getRouteAddress	Yes
RouteEndEvent		Yes

Table C-17   *JTAPI Call Center Events Package Support (Continued)*

Class Name	Method Name	Cisco JTAPI Support
RouteEvent	getCallingAddress	Yes
	getCallingTerminal	Yes
	getCurrentRouteAddress	Yes
	getRouteSelectAlgorithm	Yes
	getSetupInformation	Yes
RouteSessionEvent	getRouteSession	Yes
RouteUsedEvent	getCallingAddress	Yes
	getCallingTerminal	Yes
	getDomain	Yes
	getRouteUsed	Yes

Call Control Package

Table C-18 lists each JTAPI interface in the JTAPI Call Control Package and the support provided by the Cisco JTAPI implementation.

Table C-18   *JTAPI Call Control Package Support*

Class Name	Method Name	Cisco JTAPI Support	Comments
CallControlAddress	cancelForwarding	Yes	Only for Call Forward All.
	getDoNotDisturb	No	
	getForwarding	Yes	Only for Call Forward All.
	getMessageWaiting	No	
	setDoNotDisturb	No	
	setForwarding	Yes	Only for Call Forward All.
	setMessageWaiting	No	
CallControlCall	addParty	No	
	conference	Yes	In a consultation conference scenario where the conference controller speaks with the potential conference participant prior to adding the participant to the conference, only OriginalCall.conference (ConsultCall) is supported. ConsultCall.conference (OriginalCall) is not supported.

continues

Table C-18   *JTAPI Call Control Package Support (Continued)*

Class Name	Method Name	Cisco JTAPI Support	Comments
CallControlCall	consult(TerminalConnection)	Yes	
	consult(TerminalConnection, String)	Yes	
	drop	Yes	
	getCalledAddress	Yes	
	getCallingAddress	Yes	
	getCallingTerminal	Yes	
	getConferenceController	Yes	
	getConferenceEnable	Yes	
	getLastRedirectedAddress	Yes	
	getTransferController	Yes	
	getTransferEnable	Yes	
	offHook	Yes	
	setConferenceController	Yes	
	setConferenceEnable	Yes	
	setTransferController	Yes	
	setTransferEnable	Yes	
	transfer(Call)	Yes	In a consultation transfer scenario, only OriginalCall.transfer (ConsultCall) is supported. ConsultCall.transfer (OriginalCall) is not supported.
	transfer(String)	Yes	
CallControlCallObserver		Yes	
CallControlConnection	accept	Yes	
	addToAddress	Yes	
	getCallControlState	Yes	
	park	Yes	
	redirect	Yes	Redirect allows a connection in the state, CallControlConnection. ESTABLISHED, to be redirected.
	reject	Yes	

Table C-18   *JTAPI Call Control Package Support (Continued)*

CallControlForwarding	getDestinationAddress	No	
	getFilter	No	
	getSpecificCaller	No	
	getType	No	
CallControlTerminal	getDoNotDisturb	No	
	pickup (Address, Address)	No	
	pickup (Connection, Address)	No	
	pickup (TerminalConnection, Address)	No	
	pickupFromGroup(Address)	No	
	pickupFromGroup(String, Address)	No	
	setDoNotDisturb	No	
CallControlTerminal Connection	getCallControlState	Yes	
	hold	Yes	
	join	No	
	leave	No	
	unhold	Yes	
CallControlTerminal Observer		No	

Call Control Capabilities Package

Table C-19 lists each JTAPI interface in the JTAPI Call Control Capabilities Package, all of which are supported in the Cisco JTAPI implementation.

Table C-19   *JTAPI Call Control Capabilities Package Support*

Class Name	Method Name
CallControlAddressCapabilities	canCancelForwarding
	canGetDoNotDisturb
	canGetForwarding
	canGetMessageWaiting
	canSetDoNotDisturb
	canSetForwarding
	canSetMessageWaiting

continues

Table C-19 *JTAPI Call Control Capabilities Package Support (Continued)*

Class Name	Method Name
CallControlCallCapabilities	canAddParty
	canConference
	canConsult
	canConsult(TerminalConnection)
	canConsult(TerminalConnection, String)
	canDrop
	canOffHook
	canSetConferenceController
	canSetConferenceEnable
	canSetTransferController
	canSetTransferEnable
	canTransfer
	canTransfer(Call)
	canTransfer(String)
CallControlConnectionCapabilities	canAccept
	canAddToAddress
	canPark
	canRedirect
	canReject
CallControlTerminalCapabilities	canGetDoNotDisturb
	canPickup
	canPickup(Address, Address)
	canPickup(Connection, Address)
	canPickup(TerminalConnection, Address)
	canPickupFromGroup
	canPickupFromGroup(Address)
	canPickupFromGroup(String, Address)
	canSetDoNotDisturb
CallControlTerminalConnectionCapabilities	canHold
	canJoin
	canLeave
	canUnhold

Call Control Events Package

Table C-20 lists each JTAPI interface in the JTAPI Call Control Events Package and the support provided by the Cisco JTAPI implementation.

Table C-20   *JTAPI Call Control Events Package Support*

Class Name	Method Name	Cisco JTAPI Support
CallCtlAddrDoNotDisturbEv	getDoNotDisturbState	No
CallCtlAddrEv		No
CallCtlAddrForwardEv	getForwarding	Yes
CallCtlAddrMessageWaitingEv	getMessageWaitingState	No
CallCtlCallEv	getCalledState	Yes
	getCallingAddress	Yes
	getCallingTerminal	Yes
	getLastRedirectedAddress	Yes
CallCtlConnAlertingEv		Yes
CallCtlConnDialingEv	getDigits	Yes
CallCtlConnDisconnectedEv		Yes
CallCtlConnEstablishedEv		Yes
CallCtlConnEv		Yes
CallCtlConnFailedEv		Yes
CallCtlConnInitiatedEv		Yes
CallCtlConnNetworkAlertingEv		Yes
CallCtlConnNetworkReachedEv		Yes
CallCtlConnOfferedEv		Yes
CallCtlConnQueuedEv	getNumberInQueue	Yes
CallCtlConnUnknownEv		Yes
CallCtlEv	getCallControlCause	Yes
CallCtlTermConnBridgedEv		No
CallCtlTermConnDroppedEv		Yes
CallCtlTermConnEv		Yes
CallCtlTermConnHeldEv		Yes
CallCtlTermConnInUseEv		No
CallCtlTermConnRingingEv		Yes
CallCtlTermConnTalkingEv		Yes

continues

Table C-20   *JTAPI Call Control Events Package Support (Continued)*

Class Name	Method Name	Cisco JTAPI Support
CallCtlTermConnUnknownEv		Yes
CallCtlTermDoNotDisturbEv		No
CallCtlTermEv		No

Capabilities Package

Table C-21 lists each JTAPI interface in the JTAPI Capabilities Package, all of which are supported by the Cisco JTAPI implementation.

Table C-21   *JTAPI Capabilities Package Support*

Class Name	Method Name
AddressCapabilities	isObservable
CallCapabilities	canConnect
	isObservable
ConnectionCapabilities	canDisconnect
ProviderCapabilities	isObservable
TerminalCapabilities	isObservable
TerminalConnectionCapabilities	canAnswer

Events Package

Table C-22 lists each JTAPI interface in the JTAPI Events Package and the support provided by the Cisco JTAPI implementation.

Table C-22   *JTAPI Events Package Support*

Class Name	Method Name	Cisco JTAPI Support
AddrEv	getAddress	Yes
AddrObservationEndedEv		Yes
CallActiveEv		Yes
CallEv	getCall	Yes
CallInvalidEv		Yes
CallObservationEndedEv	getEndedObject	Yes
ConnAlertingEv		Yes
ConnConnectedEv		Yes

Table C-22   *JTAPI Events Package Support (Continued)*

Class Name	Method Name	Cisco JTAPI Support
ConnCreatedEv		Yes
ConnDisconnectedEv		Yes
ConnEv	getConnection	Yes
ConnFailedEv		Yes
ConnInProgressEv		Yes
ConnUnknownEv		Yes
Ev	getCause	Yes
	getID	Yes
	getMetaCode	Yes
	getObserved	Yes
	isNewMetaEvent	Yes
ProvEv	getProvider	Yes
ProvInServiceEv		Yes
ProvObservationEndedEv		Yes
ProvOutOfServiceEv		Yes
ProvShutdownEv		Yes
TermConnActiveEv		Yes
TermConnCreatedEv		Yes
TermConnDroppedEv		Yes
TermConnEvgetTerminalConnection		Yes
TermConnPassiveEv		No
TermConnRingingEv		Yes
TermConnUnknownEv		Yes
TermEv	getTerminal	Yes
TermObservationEndedEv		Yes

Media Package

Table C-23 lists each JTAPI interface in the JTAPI Media Package and the support provided by the Cisco JTAPI implementation.

Table C-23 *JTAPI Media Package Support*

Class Name	Method Name	Cisco JTAPI Support
MediaCallObserver		Yes
MediaTerminalConnection	generateDtmf	Yes
	getMediaAvailability	No
	getMediaState	No
	setDtmfDetection	Yes
	startPlaying	No
	startRecording	No
	stopPlaying	No
	stopRecording	No
	useDefaultMicrophone	No
	useDefaultSpeaker	No
	usePlayURL	No
	useRecordURL	No

Media Capabilities Package

Table C-24 lists each JTAPI interface in the JTAPI Media Capabilities Package, all of which are supported by the Cisco JTAPI implementation.

Table C-24 *JTAPI Media Capabilities Package Support*

Class Name	Method Name
MediaTerminalConnectionCapabilities	canDetectDtmf
	canGenerateDtmf
	canStartPlaying
	canStartRecording
	canStopPlaying
	canStopRecording
	canUseDefaultMicrophone
	canUseDefaultSpeaker
	canUsePlayURL
	canUseRecordURL

Media Events Package

Table C-25 lists each JTAPI interface in the JTAPI Media Events Package and the support provided by the Cisco JTAPI implementation.

Table C-25 *JTAPI Media Events Package Support*

Class Name	Method Name	Cisco JTAPI Support
MediaEv	getMediaCause	Yes
MediaTermConnAvailableEv		No
MediaTermConnDtmfEv	getDtmfDigit	Yes
MediaTermConnEv		Yes
MediaTermConnStateEv	getMediaState	No
MediaTermConnUnavailableEv		No

XML Data Types

This section provides the details of the XML support provided by the Cisco IP Phones to support the development of IP phone services described in Chapter 3.

Several of the XML data types described here have optional Title and Prompt fields. These fields behave identically, so this section describes them and the remainder of this chapter does not repeat the description.

Text defined in the Title field appears at the top of the page. If the data page specifies no Title field, the IP phone displays the Name field of the last selected MenuItem in the Title field.

The Prompt field defines text to appear at the bottom of the display page. If the data page specifies no Prompt parameter, the prompt area of the display is cleared.

Menu

The XML type CiscoIPPhoneMenu simply lists text items, one per line. Users select individual menu items either by using the scroll and entry selector or by number from the numeric keypad. The XML format allows you to specify a menu Title and Prompt, followed by up to 100 MenuItems. Each MenuItem has a name and an associated URL. After the user selects a menu option, the phone sends an HTTP request based on the URL associated with the menu item selected. Example C-1 shows the CiscoIPPhoneMenu XML type.

Example C-1 *CiscoIPPhoneMenu XML Type*

```
<CiscoIPPhoneMenu>
  <Title>Title text goes here</Title>
  <Prompt>Prompt text goes here</Prompt>
```

continues

Example C-1 *CiscoIPPhoneMenu XML Type (Continued)*

```
   <MenuItem>
     <Name>The name of each menu item</Name>
     <URL>The URL associated with the menu item</URL>
   </MenuItem>
   <SoftKeyItem>
     <Name>Name of softkey</Name>
     <URL>URL or URI of softkey</URL>
     <Position>Position information of the softkey</Position>
   </SoftKeyItem>
 </CiscoIPPhoneMenu>
```

IconMenu

Icon menus, like text menus, enable you to select a URL from a list. The icon menu allows you the additional capability to display visual information, such as item state or category, for each item in the list. Example C-2 shows the IconMenu XML type.

Example C-2 *CiscoIPPhoneIconMenu XML Type*

```
<CiscoIPPhoneIconMenu>
   <Title>Title text goes here</Title>
   <Prompt>Prompt text goes here</Prompt>
   <MenuItem>
     <IconIndex>Indicates what IconItem to display</IconIndex>
     <Name>The name of each menu item</Name>
     <URL>The URL associated with the menu item</URL>
   </MenuItem>
   <SoftKeyItem>
     <Name>Name of softkey</Name>
     <URL>URL or URI of softkey</URL>
     <Position>Position information of the softkey</Position>
   </SoftKeyItem>
   <IconItem>
     <Index>A unique index from 0 to 9</Index>
     <Height>size information for the icon</Height>
 </CiscoIPPhoneIconMenu>
```

Text

The XML type CiscoIPPhoneText displays text on the phone display. The text should contain no control characters other than carriage return, line feed, or tab. The phone provides pagination and word-wrap to fit the text to the phone display. Plain text can be delivered either through this XML type or as plain text through HTTP. Text delivered as type text/HTML behaves the same as type

CiscoIPPhoneText, except for the inability to include a Title or Prompt. Example C-3 shows the CiscoIPPhoneText XML type.

Example C-3 *CiscoIPPhoneText XML Type*

```
<CiscoIPPhoneText>
  <Title>Title text goes here</Title>
  <Prompt>The prompt text goes here</Prompt>
  <Text>The text to be displayed as the message body goes here</Text>
  <SoftKeyItem>
    <Name>Name of softkey</Name>
    <URL>URL or URI of softkey</URL>
    <Position>Position information of the softkey</Position>
  </SoftKeyItem>
</CiscoIPPhoneText>
```

Image

The Cisco IP Phones 7960 and 7940 have a bitmapped display that is 133 by 65 pixels. Each pixel has four grayscale settings. The CiscoIPPhoneImage is used to render graphics on the Cisco IP Phone 7960 or 7940 display. The CiscoIPPhoneImage objects will display on the 7971, 7970, 7961, 7941, and IP Communicator phones, and the image size is doubled to compensate for the difference in screen resolution. The values specified by parameters LocationX and LocationY control the position of the graphic. These values specify the location, in pixels, of the upper-left corner of the graphic. The values 0, 0 position the graphic at the upper-left corner of the display. The values −1, −1 instruct the phone to center the graphic in the display area.

Width and Height, used to control those two dimensions, must be matched up properly with the pixel stream in the Data field to produce the desired results. Depth specifies the number of bits per pixel, which currently can be set to 1 for black and white image support or 2 bits per pixel grayscale yielding white, light gray, dark gray, and black.

The Data tag delimits a string of hexadecimal digits that contain the packed value of pixels in the display. In the Cisco IP Phones 7960 and 7940, each pixel has only three possible states, allowing 4 pixels packed per byte. Each byte is specified as 2 hex digits.

Table C-26 shows how the hex digits are packed to specify the pixel values, 2 bits per pixel. A contiguous stream of hex digits, with no separators or spaces, specifies the entire display. The stream is (width × height + 3)/4 characters in length. The phone display is cleared at the time the graphic is displayed. For a single pixel depth of 1 (black and white), the pixels are packed 8 pixels per byte.

Table C-26 *Data Tag Digits*

Pixels	1	3	2	0
Binary Value	01	11	10	00
Reordered Pairs	00	10	11	01
Hex Digits	2		D	
Packed Value	2D			

Example C-4 shows the CiscoIPPhoneImage XML type.

Example C-4 *CiscoIPPhoneImage XML Type*

```
<CiscoIPPhoneImage>
  <Title>Image title goes here</Title>
  <Prompt>Prompt text goes here</Prompt>
  <LocationX>Position information of graphic</LocationX>
  <LocationY>Position information of graphic</LocationY>
  <Width>Size information for the graphic</Width>
  <Height>Size information for the graphic</Height>
  <Depth>Number of bits per pixel</Depth>
  <Data>Packed Pixel Data</Data>
  <SoftKeyItem>
    <Name>Name of softkey</Name>
    <URL>URL or URI of softkey</URL>
    <Position>Position information of the softkey</Position>
  </SoftKeyItem>
</CiscoIPPhoneImage>
```

ImageFile

Because the latest generation of Cisco IP Phones—7971, 7970, 7961, and 7941, for example—have higher-resolution displays with more color depth, the ImageFile object has been added to allow the use of color Portable Network Graphics (PNG) images. The PNG image can either be palletized or RGB. The maximum image size and the color depth differ for the various Cisco IP Phone models. For the best display results, the number of colors in the image should be matched to the capabilities of the Cisco IP Phone. Table C-27 lists the resolution and color depth supported in each of the phone models.

Table C-27 *Display Size and Color Depth*

Model	Resolution Width × Height	Color/Grayscale	Color Depth (Bits)
7905/7912	Does not support DisplayImage	N/A	1
7920	128 × 59	Grayscale	1

Table C-27   *Display Size and Color Depth*

Model	Resolution Width × Height	Color/Grayscale	Color Depth (Bits)
7940/7960	133×65	Grayscale	2
7941/7961	298×144	Grayscale	4
7970/7971	298×168	Color	12
IP Communicator	298×168	Color	24

Example C-5 shows the CiscoIPPhoneImageFile XML type.

Example C-5   *CiscoIPPhoneImageFile XML Type*

```
<CiscoIPPhoneImageFile>
  <Title>Image title goes here</Title>
  <Prompt>Prompt text goes here</Prompt>
  <LocationX>Position information of graphic</LocationX>
  <LocationY>Position information of graphic</LocationY>
  <UR>Points to the PNG image</URL>
</CiscoIPPhoneImageFile>
```

GraphicMenu

Graphic menus, like text menus, enable a user to select a menu item. The graphic menu allows a graphic to be used rather than text for the menu items. The menu item is presented as a bitmapped graphic. The user enters a menu selection by using the keypad to enter a number that selects the menu item. The XML tags for GraphicMenu are identical to the tag definitions for CiscoIPPhoneImage and CiscoIPPhoneMenu. Example C-6 shows the CiscoIPPhoneGraphicMenu XML type.

Example C-6   *CiscoIPPhoneGraphicMenu XML Type*

```
<CiscoIPPhoneGraphicMenu>
  <Title>Menu title goes here</Title>
  <LocationX>Position information of graphic</LocationX>
  <LocationY>Position information of graphic</LocationY>
  <Width>Size information for the graphic</Width>
  <Height>Size information for the graphic</Height>
  <Depth>Number of bits per pixel</Depth>
  <Data>Packed Pixel Data</Data>
  <Prompt>Prompt text goes here</Prompt>
  <MenuItem>
    <Name>The name of each menu item</Name>
    <URL>The URL associated with the menu item</URL>
  </MenuItem>
  <SoftKeyItem>
```

continues

Example C-6 *CiscoIPPhoneGraphicMenu XML Type (Continued)*

```
      <Name>Name of softkey</Name>
      <URL>URL or URI of softkey</URL>
      <Position>Position information of the softkey</Position>
    </SoftKeyItem>
</CiscoIPPhoneGraphicMenu>
```

GraphicFileMenu

The GraphicFileMenu enables you to leverage the pointer devices available on some of the Cisco IP Phones, including the touch-screen overlay of the Cisco IP Phone 7971 and 7970 and the standard Windows mouse pointer for Cisco IP Communicator. The GraphicFileMenu behaves similarly to the GraphicMenu but defines touch areas for the selection rather that the keypad. Example C-7 shows the CiscoIPPhoneGraphicFileMenu XML type.

Example C-7 *CiscoIPPhoneGraphicFileMenu XML Type*

```
<CiscoIPPhoneGraphicFileMenu>
  <Title>Image title goes here</Title>
  <Prompt>Prompt text goes here</Prompt>
  <LocationX>Horizontal position of graphic</LocationX>
  <LocationY>Vertical position of graphic</LocationY>
  <URL>Points to the PNG background image</URL>
  <MenuItem>
    <Name>Same as CiscoIPPhoneGraphicMenu</Name>
    <URL>Invoked when the TouchArea is touched</URL>
    <TouchArea X1="left edge" Y1="top edge" X2="right edge" Y2="bottom edge"/>
  </MenuItem>
</ CiscoIPPhoneGraphicFileMenu >
```

Directory

CiscoIPPhoneDirectory XML data type is used for directory-type operations. The directory entry is selected just like menu items. Up to 32 directory entries can be included in the directory. In addition, the Cisco IP Phones 7971, 7970,, 7961, 7960, 7941, 7940, 7912, and 7905 display the appropriate softkeys that are needed to initiate a call to the selected number. One softkey is **EditDial**, which allows the user to insert an access code or other necessary digits before dialing. The DirectoryEntry field is repeated as many times as is necessary to send all the entries to the phone. Example C-8 shows the CiscoIPPhoneDirectory XML type.

Example C-8 *CiscoIPPhoneDirectory XML Type*

```
<CiscoIPPhoneDirectory>
  <Title>Directory title goes here</Title>
  <Prompt>Prompt text goes here</Prompt>
  <DirectoryEntry>
    <Name>The name of the directory entry</Name>
```

Example C-8   *CiscoIPPhoneDirectory XML Type (Continued)*

```
    <Telephone>The telephone number for the entry</Telephone>
  </DirectoryEntry>
  <SoftKeyItem>
    <Name>Name of softkey</Name>
    <URL>URL or URI of softkey</URL>
    <Position>Position information of the softkey</Position>
  </SoftKeyItem>
</CiscoIPPhoneDirectory>
```

Input

In response to a CiscoIPPhoneInput, the phone builds and displays the input form. The input form prompts the user for specific data. When the user enters the data, the phone collects that data according to the input form specifications and sends the data to the target URL. The URL tag specifies the URL to receive the results. The HTTP request sent to the server is the URL with a list of parameters appended as a query string. The parameters are name/value pairs, one pair for each input item.

> **NOTE**   Cisco IP Phones do not support the HTTP POST method. POST is an HTTP method for submitting data to a web server.

The InputItem tag delimits each of the lists of input items. Each item has a DisplayName, a QueryStringParam, a DefaultValue, and a set of InputFlags. The DisplayName specifies the prompt that is written to the display for the input list item. The QueryStringParam provides the parameter name used in the URL that is returned to the server when the input is complete. The DefaultValue tag, if specified, denotes the default value to be displayed. The set of InputFlags controls the input to be used for the input item. The input types include

- **A**—Plain ASCII text. The dual-tone multifrequency (DTMF) keypad is used to enter text consisting of uppercase and lowercase letters, numbers, and special characters.

- **T**—Telephone number. DTMF digits are the only acceptable input for this field. This includes numbers, the pound key (#), and the asterisk key (*).

- **N**—Numeric. Numbers are the only acceptable input.

- **E**—Equation. This includes numbers and special math symbols.

- **U**—Uppercase. This is only uppercase letters.

- **L**—Lowercase. This is only lowercase letters.

■ **P**—Password field. Individual characters are displayed as they are keyed in using the standard keypad-repeat entry mode. As soon as each character is accepted, it is converted to an asterisk, allowing for privacy of the entered value. The password type is always a modifier to one of the other types and not used by itself. AP, for example, is valid and uses the Password field to modify the plain ASCII text field.

Example C-9 shows the CiscoIPPhoneInput XML type.

Example C-9   *CiscoIPPhoneInput XML Type*

```
<CiscoIPPhoneInput>
  <Title>Directory title goes here</Title>
  <Prompt>Prompt text goes here</Prompt>
  <URL>The target URL for the completed input goes here</URL>
  <InputItem>
    <DisplayName>Name of the input field to display</DisplayName>
    <QueryStringParam>The URL query parameter</QueryStringParam>
    <DefaultValue>Value</DefaultValue>
    <InputFlagsThe default display name></InputFlags>
  </InputItem>
  <SoftKeyItem>
    <Name>Name of softkey</Name>
    <URL>URL or URI of softkey</URL>
    <Position>Position information of the softkey</Position>
  </SoftKeyItem>
</CiscoIPPhoneInput>
```

Softkeys

During the entry of the text, as shown in Example C-9, the Cisco IP Phones 7971, 7970, 7961, 7960, 7941, and 7940 display softkeys that are intended to help the data-entry process. The following softkeys are used:

■ **Select**—Select an item for action.

■ **OK**—Leave the current page, committing any value changes made on the page.

■ **Cancel**—Leave the current page, and cancel any value changes made on the page.

■ **Exit**—Exit the current menu page.

■ **Next**—Use to move to the next item or page.

■ **Back**—Use to go back to the previous item or page.

■ **Update**—Reload and update the current page.

■ **Dial**—Initiate a call to the current entry selected.

- **EditDial**—Open an edit screen for the current entry selected.

- **Submit**—Indicates that the form is complete and the resulting URL should be sent by HTTP.

- **<<**—Backspace within a field.

Field-to-field navigation can be performed with the navigation control (vertical scroll bar or 4-way control) used to navigate menus.

IPPhoneStatus

Status is a displayable object that enables you to display information on the call plane of a Cisco IP Phone. The display object is typically used by CTI applications to present status updates to the user, which can be refreshed or replaced as needed.

Example C-10 shows the CiscoIPPhoneStatus XML type.

Example C-10 *CiscoIPPhoneStatus XML Type*

```
<CiscoIPPhoneStatus>
  <Text>This is the text area</Text>
  <Timer>Timer seed value in seconds</Timer>
  <LocationX>Horizontal alignment</LocationX>
  <LocationY>Vertical alignment</LocationY>
  <Width>Pixel width of graphic</Width>
  <Height>Pixel height of graphic</Height>
  <Depth>Color depth in bits</Depth>
  <Data>Hex binary image data</Data>
</CiscoIPPhoneStatus>
```

IPPhoneExecute

Use the Execute object to push a request to the phone via the web server using the HTTP POST method, providing HTTP authentication information with the POST. You can include up to three ExecuteItems in a single POST composed of URIs and URLs. You can include one URL or none in a POST, and the rest of the items, up to the maximum, are URIs as needed. The optional Priority attribute determines when the requested action is performed by the phone.

- **0**—Execute immediately (default priority). The URL executes regardless of the state of the phone.

- **1**—Execute when idle. Delay the URL execution until the phone is idle.

- **2**—Execute if idle. Execute the URL if the phone is idle; otherwise do not execute.

Example C-11 shows the CiscoIPPhoneExecute XML type.

Example C-11 *CiscoIPPhoneExecute XML Type*

```
<CiscoIPPhoneExecute>
  <ExecuteItemPriority ="the priority" ExecuteItem URL="the URL or URI to be executed"/>
</CiscoIPPhoneExecute>
```

IPPhoneResponse

You receive a response item for every ExecuteItem sent to the phone. The URL attribute identifies the URL or URI that you sent with the request. Data contains any special data and the Status attribute returns the status code. A status code of zero indicates no error; if an error occurs, the CiscoIPPhoneError object described below is returned. Example C-12 shows the CiscoIPPhoneResponse XML type.

Example C-12 *CiscoIPPhoneResponse XML Type*

```
<CiscoIPPhoneResponse>
  <ResponseItem Status="the success or failure of the action"
  Data="the information returned with the response" URL="the URL or
  URI specified in the Execute object"/>
</CiscoIPPhoneResponse>
```

IPPhoneError

The error response provides a means of returning an error status to an execute request. Example C-13 shows the CiscoIPPhoneError XML type.

Example C-13 *CiscoIPPhoneError XML Type*

```
<CiscoIPPhoneError Number="X"/>
```

The error response values are as follows:

- **Error 1**—Error parsing CiscoIPPhoneExecute object. There is a syntax error in the executed code. You should correct the syntax of the object and rerun.

- **Error 2**—Error framing CiscoIPPhoneResponse object. There is a problem rendering the object data. Review the rendering that the object attempted and make the required changes to allow it to be properly framed and rerun.

- **Error 3**—Internal file error. You should correct the file problems encountered and rerun.

- **Error 4**—Authentication error. You should correct the improper authentication issues and then rerun.

Phone-Supported URIs

Table C-28 and the sections that follow describe the URIs that you can use in conjunction with the XML objects with support provided by the various Cisco IP Phone models.

Table C-28   *URIs Supported*

Phone Model URI	7905/7912	7920	7940/7960	7941/7961	797x/IP Communicator
Key	X	X	X	X	X
SoftKey	X	X	X	X	X
Init		X	X	X	X
Dial, EditDial	X	X	X	X	X
Play	X	X	X	X	X
QueryStringParam		X	X	X	X
Unicast RTP (RTPRx,RTRTx)	v parameter not supported	v parameter not supported; single stream in/out	X	X	X
Multicast RTP (RTPMRx,RTRMTx)	v parameter not supported		X	X	X

Key URI

With the Key URI, you are able to send an event that a key has been pressed and have the same effect as if the button had been pressed on the phone. Just as with actual keypress events, the keypress must be valid at the time of the keypress to have the desired effect.

Key:*n*

where *n* = one of the following key names:

- Key:Line1 to Key:Line36

- Key:KeyPad0 to Key:Keypad9

- Key:Soft1 to Key:Soft4 or Soft5 (to Soft5 for 7971/7970/IP Communicator only)

- Key:KeyPadStar

- Key:KeyPadPound

- Key:VolDwn

- Key:VolUp

- Key:Headset

- Key:Speaker

- Key:Mute

- Key:Info

- Key:Messages

- Key:Services

- Key:Directories

- Key:Settings

- Key:NavUp

- Key:NavDwn

- Key:NavLeft

- Key:NavRight

QueryStringParam URI

The QueryStringParam URI enables you to collect more user information with less interaction. You can, for example, append a query string parameter to a highlighted menu item or apply the query string parameter from the menu item to the URL of the softkey.

> QueryStringParam:*d*

where *d* = the data to be appended to a corresponding URL.

RTP Streaming Control URIs

The RTP Streaming Control URIs are a collection of URIs that control media to and from the Cisco IP Phones, enabling you to instruct the phone to start or stop sending or receiving a Unicast or Multicast RTP stream. These URIs are as follows:

- **RTPRx:i:p:v**—Receive Unicast RTP stream

- **RTPRx:Stop**—Stop Unicast RTP stream receive

- **RTPTx:i:p**—Transmit Unicast RTP stream

- **RTPTx:Stop**—Stop Unicast RTP stream transmit

- **RTPMRx:i:p:v**—Receive Multicast RTP stream

- **RTPMRx:Stop**—Stop Multicast RTP stream receive

- **RTPMTx:i:p**—Transmit Multicast RTP stream

- **RTPMTx:Stop**—Stop Multicast RTP stream transmit

where:

- **i**—the Unicast or Multicast IP address for the transmit or receive.

- **p**—the Unicast or Multicast TCP port number. If specified, make sure the port number is an even number in the decimal range 20480 to 32768.

- **v**—optional volume setting that specifies a percentage of the max volume level of the phone on the range 0–100.

Init URI

The init URI allows you to initialize a feature or data:

Init:*o*

where *o* is the object name and can take on the following values:

- **CallHistory**—Used to clear the call history logs and initialize missed calls, received calls, and placed calls.

- **AppStatus**—Used to clear the application status window, which is the window above the status line of the phone.

Dial URI

The Dial URI enables you to initiate a new call to the specified number. The URI is contained in a menu item and is invoked when the menu item is highlighted and the phone goes off-hook:

Dial:*n*

where *n* is the number to be dialed.

EditDial URI

The EditDial URI is identical in functionality to the Dial URI except that it allows the user the option of editing the number prior to placing the call:

EditDial:*n*

where *n* is the number to be dialed.

Play URI

With the Play URI, you can direct the Cisco IP Phone to download and play an audio file from the TFTP server:

Play:*f*

where *f* is the filename of a raw audio file in the TFTP path.

This glossary lists terms and abbreviations applicable to *Cisco CallManager Fundamentals*. You can find additional information at the following location:

http://www.cisco.com/univercd/cc/td/doc/product/voice/evbugl4.htm

A

AA   Auto Attendant; an application designed to permit a switchboard attendant to efficiently distribute calls received by an enterprise.

ACD   Automatic call distribution; a call routing application whose primary function is to deliver calls that arrive at an enterprise to an available user. This application is commonly used to deliver calls to call centers or groups of attendants.

ACF   Admission Confirm; an H.323 gatekeeper sends this RAS message when it permits an H.323 endpoint to make a call.

ACK   Acknowledgement.

Ad Hoc   A type of conference in which a controlling station manually adds conferees one at a time. Contrast with Meet-Me conference.

AES-CM   Advanced Encryption Standard Counter Mode; an encryption algorithm.

ALI   Automatic Location Identification; information about the physical location of a caller that emergency response centers use when handling E911 calls.

annunciator   A Cisco IP Voice Media Streaming App device that plays various pre-recorded announcements and tones to a single party, a conference, or an MTP.

ANSI   American National Standards Institute; an American organization chartered with the development of standards in the United States.

APDU   Application protocol data unit; in QSIG, a message with associated parameters that is sent from the feature layer in one PINX to the feature layer in another PINX by tunneling the message in the QSIG generic functional protocol.

API   Application programming interface; usually a set of libraries with accompanying header files that application programmers can use in their programs to interact with a third-party application.

ARJ   Admission Reject; an H.323 gatekeeper sends this RAS message when it denies an H.323 endpoint's request to place a call.

ARQ   Admission Request; H.323 endpoints that rely on a gatekeeper to route their calls send this RAS message, which requests permission from the gatekeeper for the endpoint to place a call.

ART   Administrative Reporting Tool; a web-based application used to generate various reports about the CallManager system.

ASN1   Abstract Syntax Notation One; an ITU-T language designed for the description of data types. H.323 defines certain parts of certain messages in ASN.1.

ASP   Active Server Page; a web page that uses ActiveX scripting to dynamically control the content of the web page. Cisco CallManager Administration relies on Active Server Pages.

AST   Admin. Serviceability Tool; a CallManager Serviceability tool that can be used to view performance information for the CallManager cluster.

AUCX   Audit Connection; an MGCP message that the call agent sends to the gateway to audit the specified connection on an endpoint.

AUEP   Audit Endpoint; an MGCP message that the call agent sends to the gateway to audit a specified gateway.

authentication   A security process whereby one network component (for instance, CallManager) validates the identity of another, such as a gateway or IP phone. Authentication can be one-way, in which case one component can trust the identity of the other but not vice versa, or two-way, in which case both components can be confident as to the identities of each other.

authorization   A security process whereby a network component defines what types of services that an authenticated component can access. For example, you can configure CallManager routing to provide long distance calls for certain valid users but not for other valid users.

AVC   Advanced Video Coding.

AVVID IP Telephony   Cisco Architecture for Voice, Video, and Integrated Data; a suite of applications that is designed to handle enterprise voice networks and which processes user calls over an enterprise's IP network.

B

B2BUA   Back-to-back user agent; a call agent that maintains two independent sessions, one from the originator to the call agent and one from the call agent to the target.

B-channel   Bearer channel; one of 23 or 30 timeslots of information that can carry a user's voice or data content over an ISDN interface. See also *D-channel*.

backhaul   The practice of passing signaling information from PSTN ports transparently through a gateway to a call agent, rather than relying on the gateway to process the signaling information itself.

bandwidth   A measurement of the amount of data per unit of time that a communications interface can send or receive.

BAT   Bulk Administration Tool; a web-based application used to bulk-add, bulk-update, or bulk-delete large numbers of devices and users in the CallManager database.

BCF   Bandwidth Confirm; an H.323 gatekeeper sends this RAS message when it honors an H.323 endpoint's request to change the bandwidth of the media stream that the endpoint is using.

BHCA   Busy hour call attempts; a call attempt is a transaction that begins when a caller goes off-hook and immediately dials four digits. The transaction completes when the originator returns to an idle state, whether call setup completed to the target phone or an error condition was encountered. BHCA is the number of these transactions, at a sustained rate, that a CallManager or cluster of CallManagers can process within one hour. However, Cisco bases CallManager performance metrics on BHCC, a statistic that focuses of the number of successful calls.

BHCC   Busy hour call completion; call completion is a transaction that begins when a caller goes off-hook, immediately dials four digits, and rings a target phone, which immediately answers. The transaction completes when the endpoints negotiate and exchange media, terminate their session, and return to the idle state. BHCC is the number of these transactions that a CallManager or cluster of CallManagers can process in one hour, with the assumption that all call transactions are evenly spaced.

blade   Cards that are the width of the chassis that they are going into and contain the DSPs for transcoding, conferencing, and media termination. See also *VICs*.

BLF   Busy Lamp Field; an indicator at a station that displays the busy or idle status of other users in the enterprise.

BRI   Basic Rate Interface; a version of ISDN designed for phones that uses two B-channels for media and one D-channel for signaling.

bridged line appearance   See *shared line appearance*.

BRJ   Bandwidth Reject; an H.323 gatekeeper sends this RAS message when it denies an H.323 endpoint's request to change the bandwidth of the media stream that the endpoint is using.

BRQ   Bandwidth Request; a gatekeeper-enabled H.323 endpoint sends this RAS message when it wants to change the codec (and thus the bandwidth) that it is using for a particular media session.

BSD   Berkeley Software Distribution; an open source code distribution originated at the University of California at Berkeley.

built-in bridge   A DSP inside Cisco IP Phones that acts as a small conference bridge.

C

call admissions control (CAC)   Mechanisms that prevent an IP network from becoming clogged with voice and video traffic to the point of unusability by rejecting new call attempts when the network path is saturated with calls. CallManager currently supports two forms of CAC: gatekeeper-controlled and locations-based.

call appearances   A configuration of CallManager whereby the administrator makes it appear as if the same line appearance occurs multiple times on an individual phone.

call hunting constructs   Mechanisms that allow CallManager to intelligently route a single call to several devices—either simultaneously or serially. Route lists and hunt lists are call hunting constructs.

call leg ID   A value appearing in call detail records (CDR), unique among all CallManager nodes in a cluster, that identifies each participant in a call.

call preservation   The process by which a Cisco IP Communications network maintains the media exchange of a call in progress when a network error or server failure interrupts the signaling and media control for the call.

caller ID   The calling number of a station that places a call.

calling search space Along with partitions, a call routing concept that allows CallManager to provide individualized routing to users for purposes of routing by class of calling user, geographic location, or organization.

CAMA Centralized Automatic Message Accounting; a system in a central location capable of collecting data, usually call accounting-related, on behalf of multiple switches.

CAS Channel Associated Signaling; a scheme for transmission of call signaling information that relies on interleaving the call signaling within the media information that the interface transmits.

CCM Cisco CallManager; a Cisco IP Communications service whose primary function is the control and routing of calls from voice-enabled IP devices.

CCS Common Channel Signaling; in circuit-switched communications, a system in which one channel of a multiple-channel link is reserved to handle the call signaling for all other channels, which can then be dedicated solely to media.

CDP Cisco Discovery Protocol; a device discovery protocol that runs on Cisco devices and allows devices to advertise their existence to other devices on a LAN or WAN.

CdPN Called party number.

CDR Call detail record; a record that CallManager logs after a call completes to permit billing or auditing of system use.

CDR data The grouping together of call detail records (CDR) and call management records (CMR).

central CDR data store A single location where CallManager stores all CDR data, either in flat files or in a common CDR database.

centralized call processing A cluster deployment model whereby a cluster in a campus provides IP telephony service across the IP WAN for phones and gateways in branch offices that lack a CallManager.

CFA Call Forward All; a CallManager feature that allows all calls placed to a given directory number to be forwarded to a different directory number.

CFB   Call Forward Busy; a CallManager feature that allows calls placed to a given directory number to be forwarded in the event that the directory number is busy.

CFNA   Call Forward No Answer; a CallManager feature that allows calls placed to a given directory number to be forwarded in the event that they are not answered.

CFNC   Call Forward No Coverage; a CallManager feature that allows calls that have forwarded to a hunt list with personal final forwarding enabled to route to the CFNC destination configured on the original endpoint if no endpoint in the hunt list accepts the forwarded call.

CFF   Call Forward on Failure; a CallManager feature that allows calls to a directory number associated with a CTI application to forward when the CTI application is no longer associated with CallManager because of a failure such as an application server crash or disconnected link.

CgPN   Calling party number.

CIF   Common Intermediate Format.

circuit switching   A process of completing calls whereby a call agent manages the transport of the media from one endpoint to another through commands to switch cards that form an actual end-to-end analog or digital circuit.

Cisco CallManager server   A Cisco-certified Windows 2000 server that is running CallManager software.

Cisco Unity   A voice mail system that integrates with CallManager. Formerly known as Active Voice.

CiscoWorks   A family of web-based products used to manage Cisco enterprise networks and devices.

Class 5 switch   A switch in a national telephone system operated by a local telephone company. Class 5 switches directly handle residential and commercial subscribers.

CLI   Command line interface; an interface to Cisco switches and routers running the IOS operating system in which a user types text commands to provision a device.

clipping   The loss of speech during the initial moments of a conversation due to delay in setting up an end-to-end media path after the called party answers.

CLID   Calling line ID; the calling number of a station that is placing a call.

closest match routing   A system of resolving conflicts between multiple matched dial patterns that prioritizes patterns of lower expressivity (that is, patterns that match the fewest number of input dial strings) over patterns of greater expressivity (patterns that match a greater number of input dial strings). With closest match routing, the dial string 1234 would select pattern 1X34 instead of 12XX in a configuration that included both patterns.

clustering   A process by which CallManager nodes cooperatively processes an enterprise's calls with such tight integration that users cannot detect which CallManager nodes are processing their calls. Clustering relies on direct communication among CallManager nodes in a cluster.

clustering over the WAN   Separation of CallManager cluster members into different geographic areas.

CMF   Common Management Framework; the Cisco management foundation on which CiscoWorks network management application suites run.

CMI   Cisco Messaging Interface; a Windows 2000 service that is part of Cisco IP Communications and that coordinates SMDI communications with legacy voice mail systems.

CMR   Call management record; also known as a diagnostic record, a record that CallManager logs that provides information about the media session on which a device participated.

CNID   Calling party name identification; a feature that permits CallManager to present the calling user's display name to the called party.

CO   Central office; a switch in the PSTN, usually Class 5, that handles calls on behalf of residential and commercial subscribers.

codec   Coder-decoder; a media-encoding scheme by which an end device encodes speech or visual information into a digital representation for transmission across a media connection. It decodes the digital representation into speech or visual information for playback by the recipient.

COM   Component Object Model; a Microsoft framework used in many companies' applications that is designed to permit the interoperation of software objects running in separate tasks in a computer network.

comfort noise   Background noise that is meant to make the user feel more comfortable that the call is still active while the endpoint with which he or she is conversing is suppressing audio. Also called *white noise* or *background noise*.

community   In the context of SNMP, a relationship between an agent and a set of SNMP managers that defines security characteristics.

conference controller   A conference controller is the user who initiates a conference. For Ad Hoc conferences, the conference controller calls each conference participant and individually connects each participant to the conference. For Meet-Me conferences, the conference controller sets up the directory number that conference participants dial into.

conference device   A media device that mixes multiple signals from different stations or gateways and sends the combined signals to all the conference participants.

CoS   Class of service; a method of classifying the data that a network routes to provide preferential packet routing treatment to data related to certain types of media: voice, data, and video, for example.

CPU   Central processing unit; the chip or chips inside a computer that execute the instructions that permit applications to function.

CRCX   Create Connection; an MGCP message the call agent sends to gateway to create a new connection on an endpoint.

CSV   Comma-separated value; a type of file in which commas are used to separate individual fields of a complex data record and new lines indicate the end of an individual record.

CTI   Computer Telephone Integration or Computer Telephony Interface; for the purposes of this book, CTI most commonly means Computer Telephony Interface. This is an interface exported by CallManager that allows application developers to create programs that work with the telephone system.

D

D-channel   Data channel; one timeslot on an ISDN interface that is dedicated to handling the call signaling related to the bearer channels that the interface manages. See also .

DBL   Database Layer; a set of software components that provide a programming interface to the SQL database containing all the CallManager configuration information.

DCF   Disengage Confirm; an H.323 gatekeeper sends this RAS message when it wants to honor an H.323 endpoint's request to terminate a call.

default technology prefix   A Cisco gatekeeper feature that, when configured, instructs the gatekeeper to look for endpoints that have registered with the specified technology prefix and choose one of these endpoints to route the call to.

DES   Data Encryption Standard; an encryption algorithm.

DHCP   Dynamic Host Control Protocol; a network service whose primary purpose is to automatically assign IP addresses to new devices that connect or existing devices that reconnect to the network.

diagnostic record   See *CMR*.

dialing transformations   Any CallManager setting that permits CallManager to modify the calling or called number as the call is being established.

DID   Direct Inward Dial; a type of central office trunk that provides additional routing information on incoming calls. This allows trunk calls to be routed directly to a specific directory number, instead of being routed to a common attendant.

distributed call processing   A CallManager cluster deployment model whereby independent CallManager clusters, possibly gatekeeper-enabled, handle the call routing and call establishment for an enterprise and its branch offices.

DLCX   Delete Connection; an MGCP message the call agent sends to gateway to delete a connection on the endpoint.

DLL   Dynamic link library; a software component used by a larger program that the operating system on which the program runs includes only when the program requires the functionality provided by the software component. Dynamic link libraries allow large programs to use less RAM because they only take up memory when the larger program actually executes them.

DN   Directory number; the numeric address assigned to phones within an enterprise.

DNS   Domain Name System; a network service whose primary function is to convert fully qualified domain names (textual) into numeric IP addresses, and vice versa.

DOD   Direct Outward Dial; a service that permits a device in the enterprise to place calls directly to the public network.

DoS attacks   Denial-of-service attacks; this is a form of attack that can be launched against various network systems. In general, a DoS attack is performed by launching a flood of network requests to a computer, thereby monopolizing its resources.

dotted-decimal notation   A formatting convention for an IP address whereby each octet of a 4-octet IP address is converted to a decimal value from 0 to 255 and delimited by periods.

DPA   Digital PBX Adapter; Cisco DPAs provide Lucent Octel voice mail integration with CallManager.

DRJ   Disengage Reject; an H.323 gatekeeper sends this RAS message when it wants to deny an H.323 endpoint's request to terminate a call.

DRQ   Disengage Request; a gatekeeper-enabled H.323 endpoint sends this RAS message to the gatekeeper when it wants to terminate a call.

DSP   Digital signal processor; a specialized type of CPU used for computationally intensive tasks. CallManager has DSP resources that are typically used to process voice streams. For example, DSPs are used to transcode voice and conference multiple streams.

DSS   Direct Station Select; a telephony feature that permits a user to dial a destination by pressing a single button.

DTD   Document Type Definition; a specific definition that describes the structure of documents that conform to the Standard Generalized Markup Language (SMGL)—for example, HTML and XML—through the insertion of tags within the documents themselves. Programs interpret the tags and use them to render the document context.

DTMF   Dual Tone Multifrequency; a common tone signaling method used by touchtone phones in which two pure frequencies are superimposed.

duplex   Two-way.

E

E1   A digital trunk specification that permits the transfer of 2.048 Mbps of information per second.

E164 address   A fully qualified numeric address for a device attached to a national network. The ITU-T specification E.164 defines the framework in which nations manage their national numbering plans.

early media   To prevent clipping, a set of procedures that establishes a full or partial end-to-end media path between calling and called parties before the called party actually answers.

ECMA   European Computer Manufacturing Association; an association of European manufacturers that develops standards related to telecommunications.

EDS   Event Distribution System; the event distribution of the Cisco Management Framework (CMF).

EFR   Enhanced Full Rate; a codec optimized for speech primarily used in digital wireless networks.

E&M   Ear and Mouth; an analog trunk interface that carries signaling information over a different pair of wires (called "ear" and "mouth") than audio information.

empty capabilities set support   An H.323 requirement that endpoints suspend sending media when they receive a mid-call request to select a new codec from an empty list of codecs. CallManager uses this capability to affect features such as hold and transfer.

endpoint   A device or software application that provides real-time, two-way communication for users.

ESN   Emergency Service Number; a numeric address that the North American national network uses to identify emergency response centers.

Extended Superframe (ESF) formatting   A framing strategy that groups frames of voice channels into groups of 24.

F

failover   The process whereby devices on a Cisco IP Communications network seek out backup CallManager nodes if they lose their connection to their primary CallManager.

fallback   The process of offering a call to a less-desirable gateway after all desirable gateways have been exhausted.

FastStart   Also called *fast connect*; a provision of H.323, version 2, which permits an endpoint to embed media control information in the call signaling phase of a call, thus dramatically speeding up the rate at with an end-to-end media connection can be established.

feature transparency   The ability of a communications system to provide users served by different call agents the same number and quality of features as users served by a single call agent.

firewall A computer system placed at the junction between a private computer network and other computer networks. It is designed to protect users of a private network from users in the other networks.

first-party call control A method of application control by which the application controls an endpoint as if it were a user at that endpoint.

flashhook On a POTS phone, the process of temporarily interrupting the circuit to gain access to network features; on a digital phone, a brief depression of the hookswitch to gain access to network features.

forwarding A process whereby a call agent can divert a call from the dialed destination to an alternate destination, either unconditionally or if the called user is busy or does not respond within a specified period of time.

fps Frames per second.

framing bit Signaling bits that synchronize the clocks of the transmitter and receiver.

FR Full Rate; a codec optimized for speech primarily used in digital wireless networks.

fully-meshed topology A topology in which every node in a network maintains a communications channel with every other node in a network. CallManager clustering relies on a fully meshed topology.

FXO Foreign Exchange Office; a VoIP gateway providing analog access to central office's line termination.

FXS Foreign Exchange Station; a VoIP gateway providing analog access to a POTS station.

G

G.711 A simple codec used to encode voice communications that requires 64-kbps bandwidth.

G.723 A codec used to encode voice communications that requires either 5- or 6-kbps bandwidth.

G.729 A codec used to encode voice communications that requires 8-kbps bandwidth.

gatekeeper   An H.323 entity that provides address resolution, controls access to the network, and can terminate calls. In a Cisco IP Communications network, H.323 gatekeepers provide call routing and admissions control functions only.

gateway   A device that provides real-time, two-way communications between the packet-based network and other stations on a switched network.

GCF   Gatekeeper Confirm; an H.323 gatekeeper sends this RAS message to an H.323 endpoint's search for gatekeepers on a network if it wants to advertise its existence.

GCID   Global call identifier; a common identifier that identifies all calls that are related to each other in some way. Used in CDR data.

glare   A signaling problem that occurs on telephony interfaces when both sides of the wire simultaneously go off-hook and attempt to compete for the same media channel.

GMT   Greenwich mean time.

grep   General Regular Expressions Parser; a text-matching capability originally developed for the UNIX operating system. It permits a user to determine whether a particular text string conforms to a user-specified structure.

GRJ   Gatekeeper Reject; an H.323 gatekeeper sends this RAS message to an H.323 endpoint's search for gatekeepers on a network if it wants to prevent the H.323 endpoint from registering with it.

ground-start signaling   A system of call signaling over an analog circuit that relies on both ends temporarily grounding the wires to coordinate seizure of the circuit.

GRQ   Gatekeeper Request; a gatekeeper-enabled H.323 endpoint sends this RAS message when it needs to find out which gatekeepers it can register with.

GSM   Groupe Speciale Mobile; a voice codec commonly used in wireless devices that requires 13-kbps bandwidth.

H

H.225   A protocol that forms the call signaling portion of the ITU-T H.323 protocol.

H.245   A protocol that forms the media control portion of the ITU-T H.323 protocol.

H.320   An ITU-T recommendation that covers videoconferencing in a circuit-switched environment.

H.323   An umbrella ITU-T specification that describes terminals, gateways, and other entities that provide communication services over packet-based networks. It references other specifications for the call signaling, media control, and coding and decoding control specifications.

H.450   A protocol that defines feature transparency for the ITU-T H.323 protocol.

hairpinning   In circuit-switched communications, the introduction of unnecessary circuits into an end-to-end signaling and media path, usually as the result of feature operation. In packet-switched communications, the introduction of additional unnecessary signaling or media hops into an end-to-end path, also usually as the result of feature operation.

hotline   A call routing feature whereby a call agent immediately places a call to a specified destination when certain phones are taken off-hook.

HP-UX   Hewlett-Packard's version of UNIX.

HTML   Hypertext Markup Language; a document type definition (DTD) used by web pages and browsers on the World Wide Web that tells a web browser how to render the content of a web page.

HTTP   Hypertext Transfer Protocol; a method by which applications can exchange multimedia files on the World Wide Web.

hub   A nexus in a network where data arriving from one endpoint can select multiple routes of egress.

I

IACK   Information Request Acknowledgement; a RAS message.

ICCS   Intracluster Control Signaling; proprietary signaling that CallManager nodes in a cluster exchange to cooperatively manage calls.

ICD   Integrated Contact Distribution.

ICM   Intelligent Contact Manager; an application that manages distribution of voice, web, and e-mail across an enterprise of automatic call distribution (ACD), Private Branch Exchange (PBX), Interactive Voice Response (IVR), database, and desktop applications.

ICMP   Internet Control Message Protocol; a message control and error reporting protocol carried over an IP network.

IE   Information Element; an individual field in an ISDN message.

IETF   Internet Engineering Task Force; a standards body that issues recommended protocols for applications that interact over the Internet.

I-frame   The link layer message that the ITU-T Q.921 standard defines for the purpose of encapsulating user data.

IIS   Internet Information Server; a Microsoft service designed to permit users to create and manage Internet services such as web servers.

INAK   Information Request N Acknowledgement; a RAS message.

intercluster   Commonly used in the term intercluster trunks, this term refers to any interaction that occurs between CallManager nodes that are not members of the same cluster.

intercluster trunk   IP-based signaling and media control connections between clusters used for the purposes of call establishment. Intercluster trunks run a variant of the H.323 protocol.

interdigit timeout   An event that causes CallManager to cease collecting a dialing user's dialed digits (and to route based on the entered digits) when CallManager detects that no digits have been entered for a specified period of time.

IOS   Internetwork Operating System; the operating system used by many Cisco routers and switches, including the gateways used by CallManager.

IP   Internet Protocol; a method by which one computer can communicate packets of information to another computer on a network.

IPCC   IP Contact Center; a software package that works with CallManager to perform call distribution and the management functions needed by call centers.

IPSec   A set of protocols developed by the IETF to support the secure exchange of IP packets. IPSec both allows CallManager and the Cisco gateway to mutually authenticate each other and to ensure the privacy of the signaling stream via DES.

IP Centrex   A business model whereby a service provider sells IP telephony connectivity to the PSTN to different subscribers.

IP Telephony   The establishment of primarily voice, but also video and data communications over the same type of data network that makes up the Internet.

IP/VC   Internet Protocol/Videoconferencing; a family of Cisco videoconferencing devices.

IRQ   Information Request; a RAS message that H.323 gatekeepers often use to monitor the status of H.323 terminals for which they maintain registrations.

IRR   Information Request Response; a RAS message that H.323 terminals send in response to a RAS Information Request message.

ISDN   Integrated Services Digital Network; a digital circuit-switched-based telephony protocol that relies on interfaces that consist of a single D-channel for signaling and multiple B-channels for media.

ISUP   Integrated Services User Part; a component of the SS7 telephony standard that handles call signaling. SS7 is a protocol widely used in the PSTN.

ITU-T   International Telecommunication Union Telecommunication Standardization Sector; the branch of an international standards body that develops and publishes standards related to telecommunications.

IVR   Interactive Voice Response; a voice application that provides a telephone user interface and that is capable of retrieving data and redirecting calls.

IXC   Interexchange carrier, or long distance company; a company whose chief responsibility is the interconnection of local exchange carriers.

J

---

jitter   The difference in time between a packet's expected arrival time and the time the packet actually arrives. Also called *variable delay*.

JMF   Java Media Framework; an application programming interface (API) that enables audio, video, and other time-based media to be added to Java applications and applets.

JTAPI   Java Telephony Application Program Interface; an API that enables the development of Java applications that work with CallManager.

JTSP   Java TAPI Service Provider; a library that makers of telephony systems provide to permit third parties to control the telephony system over JTAPI.

K

kbps   Kilobits per second.

KBps   Kilobytes per second.

key system   Small-scale telephone system designed to handle telephone communications for a small office of 1 to 25 users.

L

LAN   Local-area network; a group of independent computers and network appliances within a small geographic area that access common resources and each other over communications protocols.

LATA   Local Access and Transport Area; in North America, geographical regions within the same LATA can generally place unmetered calls.

LCD   Liquid crystal display.

LCF   Location Confirm; an H.323 gatekeeper sends this RAS message, which provides the network address of an H.323 endpoint, to a requesting H.323 gatekeeper when the requesting H.323 gatekeeper needs to discover the endpoint's network address.

LDAP   Lightweight Directory Access Protocol; an API that defines a programming interface that can be used to access computer-based directories. LDAP directories are a specialized format of database that is often used to hold user information in large organizations.

LEC   Local exchange carrier, or local telephone company; a company whose chief responsibility is providing PSTN connectivity to residential and commercial subscribers.

LED   Light emitting diode; a semiconductor device that emits light when an electric current passes through it.

legacy   Using established, possibly outdated, methods.

line appearance   A logical entity on a phone capable of terminating calls; often associated with a particular button on a phone. Line appearances have addresses called DNs.

logical channel   A network pathway that carries a streaming data connection between two endpoints.

longest match routing   A system of resolving conflicts between multiple matched dial patterns that prioritizes patterns that begin with the longest sequence of specific digits over patterns that begin with shorter sequences. With longest match routing, the dial string 1234 would select pattern 12XX instead of 1X34 in a configuration that included both patterns.

loop-start signaling   A signaling type most commonly used in residential service; when the phone goes off-hook, the circuit is closed, and the central office detects the change in current. The central office then inserts tone detectors to collect the digits, which are sent as tones on the wire.

LRJ   Location Reject; an H.323 gatekeeper sends this RAS message to a requesting H.323 gatekeeper when it does not know the network address of the device that the requesting H.323 gatekeeper is seeking.

LRQ   Location Request; an H.323 gatekeeper might send this RAS message to find out from other gatekeepers the network address associated with a particular E.164 or endpoint alias.

M

managed device   A device containing a network management agent implementation. The media server, MCS-7835-1000, is a managed device.

mask   A mechanism commonly used by the call routing component of CallManager to enable you to change a number substantially while retaining some of the original number's digits.

Mbps   Megabits per second.

MBps   Megabytes per second.

MCL   Media Control Layer; the layer within CallManager responsible for coordinating the media control phase of call establishment.

MCS   Media Convergence Server; a Cisco-certified server that comes pre-installed with the components that make up Cisco IP Telephony.

MDCX   Modify Connection; an MGCP message that the call agent sends to the gateway to modify the specified connection on an endpoint.

media stream   A one-way flow of media from one participant in a conversation to another. VoIP media streams are always encapsulated in RTP.

MGC   Media Gateway Controller; the call signaling and media control signaling intelligence for gateway devices.

MGCP   Media Gateway Control Protocol; an IETF standard protocol, defined in RFCs 2705 and 3435 among others, that uses a text-based protocol to permit a Media Gateway Controller—a function that CallManager fulfills—to establish and tear down calls.

MIB   Management Information Base; a virtual information store that is used with network management protocol and network management application to provide information on a managed object.

Management Information Base; a single specification (an MIB), the union of all specifications implemented (the MIB), or the actual values of management information in a system.

MIME   Multipart Internet Mail Extensions; a set of methods described in RFC 2045 that allows binary information such as pictures and sounds to be converted to text and encoded in such a way that the recipient can reconstruct the original information.

MOH   Music On Hold; a CallManager feature that streams music to callers who have been placed on hold.

MOH audio source   A file on a disk or a fixed device from which a source stream obtains the streaming data, which it provides to all connected streams.

MOH data source   A file on a disk or a fixed device from which a source obtains the streaming data that it provides to all connected streams.

MOH group   MOH audio sources having the same filename and content. Usually spans multiple MOH servers. The MOH group is implemented as MRG in CallManager release 3.1.

MOH group session   One or more streams connected to an MOH audio source on an MOH server.

MOH server   Software application that provides MOH audio sources and connects an MOH audio source to a number of streams.

MPEG   Moving Picture Experts Group; a set of ISO and ITU standards for the compression of video.

MRG   Media Resource Group; a logical grouping of media servers that can be used to provide geographically specific, class of service, or class of user access to a set of media resources.

MRGL   Media Resource Group List; a list that consists of prioritized MRGs. An application can select required media resources among the available ones according to the priority order defined in the MRGL.

MRM   Media Resource Manager; software component in CallManager that allocates and de-allocates media resources based on a provided MRGL.

MTP   Media termination point; a device that terminates a media stream for the purpose of allowing the stream to be redirected. CallManager can insert an MTP into a call to insulate endpoints from incompatibilities between each other's media control processing, to provide DTMF relay, and to provide call progress tones.

multiple tenant   Also *multitenant*. A type of CallManager installation in which one administrator manages a Cisco IP Communications network on behalf of a group of different enterprise or residential customers. This type of deployment is smaller in scale than IP Centrex.

N

NAK   Negative Acknowledge; a message sent by the remote end of a Transmission Control Protocol (TCP) connection that indicates failure of the connection's establishment.

NANP   North American numbering plan; the set of valid dialable addresses on the North American PSTN.

network hold   The hold action that is initialized by system as the result of a feature invocation such as transfer or conference.

NMS   Network management station; a server where SNMP management applications run.

node   Servers in a CallManager cluster that are running the CallManager service.

NTFY   Notify; an MGCP message indicating certain requested event has occurred on the gateway.

NT registry   A repository of configuration data maintained by the Windows NT operating system. All applications on a computer can access the registry to store and retrieve configuration information.

Nyquist's theorem   A theory that suggests that to accurately encode an analog audio signal into a digital system and then accurately resynthesize the analog version, the frequency with which one must sample the signal must be at least twice the highest frequency present in the original analog signal.

O

object   In the context of SNMP, a data variable that represents some resource or other aspect of a managed device.

object type   Defines a particular kind of managed object. The definition of an object type is therefore a syntactic description.

octet   An 8-bit binary number corresponding to values 0 to 255 in the decimal system.

ODBC   Open Database Connectivity; a vendor-independent standard that enables applications to interact with different databases.

off-hook   The action whereby a user initiates a call or accepts an incoming call.

OffNet   A term applied to calls between the enterprise and another telephone network (generally the PSTN).

on-hook   The action whereby a user returns a station to an idle state.

OnNet   A term applied to calls that are placed and received within the same enterprise.

operator   One of a set of three tests (EXISTS, DOES-NOT-EXIST, ==) that route filters apply when determining which route patterns in the national numbering plan should be included as part of CallManager's expansion of the @ wildcard.

orphan timeout   A CallManager setting that dictates how long a media resource device, such as Cisco IP Voice Media Streaming App, waits until it tears down resources relating to a conversation. This happens when the Cisco IP Voice Media Streaming App has lost its connection to CallManager and it has detected no voice activity from an endpoint in the conversation.

OS   Operating system; a set of services running on a hardware platform that provide other applications with access to the resources (such as processor, memory, network interfaces) that the hardware platform provides.

outside dial tone   A high-pitched audio indication that CallManager applies during dialing to alert a calling user that the entered address may cause the call to route to a public network.

overlapped dialing   The process whereby CallManager collects dialed digits one at a time from a user. See also *overlapped sending*.

overlapped sending   The process whereby CallManager collects dialed digits one at a time from a user.

The process whereby CallManager passes dialed digits from a calling user to switches in connected networks that actually manage the address.

P

PA   Personal Assistant; an application that works with CallManager. This application is designed to permit a user to customize call forwarding behavior based on who is calling and to track a user down given multiple possible destinations.

package   A means of grouping the JTAPI functions used by applications.

packet switching   A process of completing calls whereby a call agent manages call signaling and media control of two endpoints in a call but in which the media is streamed directly from one device to the other over a network of routers.

In a peer-to-peer network, a process of completing calls whereby two endpoints negotiate their call signaling, media control, and media session directly with each other over a network of routers.

partition   Along with calling search spaces, a call routing concept that allows CallManager to provide individualized routing to users for purposes of routing by class of calling user, geographic location, or organization.

PBX   Private Branch Exchange; a small phone system located at a customer premise site. The PBX is used to supplement or replace functionality that might normally be provided by a central office (CO).

PC   Personal computer.

PCM   Pulse Code Modulation; the standard for voice encoding in the circuit-switched world.

PDU   Protocol data unit; a unit of information that peer entities in a network exchange for control purposes.

picocell   A transmission and reception area for wireless devices less than 100 meters in radius.

PIN   Personal identification number.

PINX   Private Integrated Services Network Exchange; vendor call agents, such as a CallManager cluster or a PBX, in QSIG.

pink noise   Background noise that resembles the background sounds from the current call. See also *comfort noise*.

PISN   Private Integrated Services Network; in QSIG, a privately owned network of PINXs.

PLAR   Private Line Automatic Ringdown; see *hotline*.

POTS   Plain old telephone service.

power cycle   To reset a device by interrupting and restoring power to the device.

PR   Path replacement; a QSIG feature that eliminates hairpins by optimizing the call signaling and media path between two participants in a conversation.

PreDot   The section of a route pattern that corresponds to all matched digits before the . wildcard's position in the route pattern.

presentation bit   A field in an ISDN information element that specifically indicates whether a call recipient is permitted or forbidden from viewing the calling number.

presentation settings   Configuration settings that dictate whether the users involved in a call are permitted to view the calling or called name or number.

PRI   Primary Rate Interface; an ISDN interface containing 24 or 32 channels for the communication of media and signaling information.

primary line   The first line appearance on a station device.

privacy   A process whereby communications between network components is secured from the scrutiny of unauthorized intruders. Privacy prevents intruders from eavesdropping on conversations or capturing information such as dialed numbers from call attempts.

PSAP   Public Safety Answering Point; an emergency response center dedicated specifically to handling emergency calls from subscribers on the PSTN. Emergency response centers have special facilities for contacting public safety and health officers.

PSTN   Public Switched Telephone Network; the international phone system we all know and love. Typically displayed on block diagrams as a puffy, friendly looking cloud. Appearances can be deceiving.

Publisher   The master database for CallManager.

Q

Q.921   Layer 2 protocol for ISDN telephony.

Q.931   Layer 3 protocol for ISDN telephony.

QBE   Quick Buffer Encoding; commonly pronounced "cube."

QCIF   Quarter Common Intermediate Format (QCIF).

QoS   Quality of service; the traffic management mechanisms of a distributed multimedia system that permit it to guarantee the transmission of coherent information. Such mechanisms include traffic classification, traffic prioritization, bandwidth management, and admissions control.

QSIG   A messaging framework defined by ECMA and ISO that fosters feature transparency between PBXs.

QSIG tunneling   The process of encapsulating the QSIG protocol within other call signaling protocols. H.323 defines a method (which CallManager supports) for tunneling QSIG in H.323 in Annex M1.

R

RAID   Redundant Array of Independent Disks; a device containing a set of disks that appears as a single disk to an operating system. RAIDs store copies of the same piece of data in different physical locations, thus providing security against component failure and possibly improving disk performance, because information can be written simultaneously to two different disks.

RAS   Registration, Admission, and Status; part of the ITU-T H.323 protocol that defines how H.323 endpoints and gatekeepers communicate.

redundancy   The process whereby backup systems assume responsibility for providing network services if primary components fail or become unreachable.

reorder tone   A fast, cyclical tone that CallManager uses to indicate some sort of problem during call establishment.

requests   In the context of AVVID XML Layer (AXL) application programming interface (API), requests are AXL API methods that allow a programmer to interact with and manipulate the CallManager database.

RFC   Request For Comments; a document that proposes Internet standards and is produced for public review by the Internet Engineering Task Force (IETF). RFCs that are accepted become official Internet standards.

RIS   Real-Time Information Server; a Cisco IP Communications service that collects serviceability information for multiple CallManager nodes in a cluster.

RME   Resource Manager Essentials; a suite of web-based network management solutions for Cisco switches, access servers, and routers. Essential features include configuration management, change auditing, software image management, inventory, availability, and syslog analysis, while also allowing integration with other Cisco web management tools and third-party applications.

route filter   A textual clause composed of tags, operators, and values that CallManager uses to restrict which route patterns it includes when performing a macro expansion of the @ wildcard.

route list   A CallManager feature that allows CallManager to search serially for and extend a call to an available gateway from among the gateways that the route list contains.

route pattern   An expression that describes a numeric address (telephone number) or range of addresses; also, this expression as assigned to a gateway or route list.

RQNT   Request Notify; a Media Gateway Control Protocol (MGCP) message that a call agent sends to a gateway to request the gateway to inform the call agent when a particular event (such as dialed digits) occurs.

RR   Receiver Ready; an ITU-T Q.921 message that a message recipient sends when it is ready to receive a transmission from its peer.

RRQ   Registration Request; a gatekeeper-enabled H.323 endpoint sends this RAS message to an H.323 gatekeeper when it wants the gatekeeper to maintain the address information (and possibly route calls for) the endpoint.

RS-232   A recommendation published by Electronic Industries Association (EIA) that defines the physical and signaling characteristics of serial data communications.

RSIP   Restart In Progress; a Media Control Gateway Protocol (MGCP) message that a gateway sends to a call agent to indicate that an endpoint or group of endpoints is being brought into or taken out of service.

RTCP   Real-Time Control Protocol; Internet-standard protocol for the transport of control data relating to data transmitted by Real-Time Transport Protocol (RTP).

RTP   Real-Time Transport Protocol; Internet-standard protocol for the transport of real-time data, including audio and video.

RTSP   Real-Time Streaming Protocol; a protocol used in streaming media systems that allows a client to remotely control a streaming media server, issuing VCR-like commands such as play and pause, and allowing time-based access to files on a server. Developed by the IETF and published in 1998 as RFC 2326.

RUDP   Reliable User Datagram Protocol; a simple packet-based transport protocol that is layered on the UDP/IP protocols and provides reliable in-order delivery for virtual connections.

S

SA   Syslog Analyzer; one of the CiscoWorks features that provides reports and analysis of syslog messages from the Cisco devices.

SABME   Set Asynchronous Balanced Mode (Extended); a link layer control message requesting the establishment of a connection over which numbered I-frames can be sent.

SCCP   Skinny Client Control Protocol; a protocol used by CallManager and devices to provide signaling and media control functions for Cisco IP Phones.

SDI   System Diagnostic Interface; a trace interface that is used in CallManager.

SDK   Software Development Kit; a set of programming interfaces and documentation provided to programmers seeking to interface to a given operating system, application, or other product.

SDL   Signal Distribution Layer; an application framework that provides all of the components required to implement a state-machine-based application. It provides for creation of state machines and the interprocessor communication of signals between those state machines.

Specification and Description Language; an ITU-T language defined in specification Z.100 that describes a notation for state-machine-based systems.

SDP   Session Description Protocol; a protocol that allows SIP- and MGCP-based VoIP endpoints to negotiate IP addresses and ports for media communications using specific codecs.

secondary line   Any line appearance on a station other than the first.

service parameters   Settings for Cisco IP Communications services that take effect on a service-wide basis.

SGCP   Skinny Gateway Control Protocol; a protocol used by devices to communicate with CallManager.

shared line appearance   A directory number that appears on two or more devices. Phones with shared line appearances ring simultaneously when a call arrives at the shared directory number. A phone with a shared line appearance receives status information related to calls that other devices are managing on the shared directory number. (In CallManager, to be shared, directory numbers must also reside in the same partition.)

signaling protocols   An agreed-upon set of rules that define the format of messages used to transmit information and commands between devices.

signed integer   32-bit numbers that contain a 31-bit value plus a high-order sign bit.

silence suppression   The process whereby, to save network bandwidth, a voice-enabled IP device ceases transmitting media when the volume level of the speaker drops below a certain threshold.

simplex   One-way.

SIP   Session Initiation Protocol; an IETF standard related to HTTP and defined in RFC 3261 among many others that uses a text-based protocol for both signaling and, via SDP bodies, media control.

SMDI   Simplified Message Desk Interface; an RS-232 protocol that can be used to integrate a voice mail system with a PBX. CallManager provides an interface to voice mail systems with the Cisco Messaging Interface service, also known as *CMI*.

SMI   Structure of Management Information; specifications that define the model of management information, the allowed data types, and the rules for specifying classes (or types) of management information.

SNMP   Simple Network Management Protocol; a protocol designed to permit monitoring and management of devices on a computer network.

softkey   Context-sensitive digital display buttons on the bottom row of the display of XML-capable Cisco IP Phones, such as models 7905, 7912, 7920, 7940, 7941, 7960, 7961, 7970, 7971, and 7985.

software Unicast bridge   A server-based conference mixer capable of mixing G.711 and wideband audio streams and rebroadcasting them to conference participants.

source   A connection point on an MOH server where streams can be connected. It provides the audio-streaming data to all connected streams.

SQL   Structured Query Language; a standard language defined to permit reading from and writing to databases.

SS7   Signaling System 7; a protocol used on the Public Switched Telephone Network (PSTN) that uses a separate packet-switched network for the carriage of signaling information between switches in the PSTN.

state machine   Small event-driven processes within the layers of the CallManager architecture that handle small bits of the responsibility of placing calls in a CallManager network. These small state-machine tasks are managed by the SDL application engine.

station   Any device that provides a user with a direct interface to a voice network.

steering code   An initial sequence of digits used to direct calls to a particular set of gateways.

stream   A one-way, active media session connected through a simplex logical channel from an MOH server to a device.

Subscriber   One or more duplicate databases serving the CallManager system. Subscriber databases are updated with information from the Publisher database.

subscriber   A user of a (usually public) telephone network.

Superframe (SF) formatting   A framing strategy that groups frames of audio information into groups of 12.

switchback   The process whereby devices unregister with one CallManager node and reregister with a higher-priority CallManager node.

switchover   A process whereby where a secondary call agent can assume control of the call signaling and media control for a call that was earlier controlled by a different call agent.

T

T.120   An ITU standard composed of a suite of communication and application protocols. Using these protocols, developers can create compatible products and services for real-time, multipoint data connections and conferencing.

T1   A digital trunk interface that provides twenty-four 64-kbps timeslots for a total of 1.544 Mbps of bandwidth.

T3   A digital trunk interface that provides 44.736 Mbps of bandwidth.

TAC   Cisco Technical Assistance Center; a customer support organization.

tag   A text string that characterizes a meaningful portion of one or more route patterns in a dial plan file. Route filters rely on tags to classify numbers within a dial plan.

TAPI   Telephony Application Programming Interface; a Microsoft API that permits programmers to create telephony applications on Windows systems.

TcdSrv   Cisco Telephony Call Dispatcher Service; the server-side process from which Cisco WebAttendant clients obtain their call control services.

TCP   Transmission Control Protocol; a connection-oriented protocol that provides for the reliable end-to-end, ordered delivery of IP packets.

TDM   Time division multiplexing; a method of transporting information for multiple endpoints across a single interface that relies on assigning each endpoint a specific window of time when it has exclusive access to the interface.

technology prefix   A routing-related setting on the gatekeeper configuration that allows a gatekeeper to differentiate between groups of endpoints in the same zone.

TFTP   Trivial File Transfer Protocol; a User Datagram Protocol (UDP)-based protocol that permits the transmission of files between network devices.

third-party call control   A method of application control by which the application controls one or more endpoints and simultaneously maintains a view of all controlled endpoints.

TLA   Telealue, a geographical routing prefix in the Finnish national numbering plan.

toll restriction   A configuration whereby an enterprise routes calls between geographical regions over its own IP network instead of the PSTN, thereby avoiding any charges that the PSTN levies for placing the call.

ToS   Type of service; a method of classifying the data that a network routes to provide preferential packet routing treatment to data related to certain types of media: voice, data, and video, for example.

traffic prioritization   The process of assigning preferential routing treatment to media streams based on the type of information they contain.

transcode   To convert a voice data stream from one codec type to another codec type.

transcoder   A hardware or software device that provides a means of allowing devices that do not have a matching set of capabilities for the allowed bandwidth to communicate. Transcoders convert one media stream type into a different media stream type to allow devices to communicate.

translation pattern   A CallManager call routing feature that permits you to define aliases for route patterns.

trap   A trap is an unsolicited message sent by an agent to a management station in an asynchronous manner. The purpose is to notify the management station of some unusual event. The traps are sent to trap-receiving hosts configured in the Windows 2000 SNMP Service. With this enhancement, network management applications such as Voice Health Manager (VHM) can gather more data that can be used for fault management and analysis purpose.

trunk   A circuit between a station and the network that serves it or between two networks.

TSP   TAPI Service Provider or Telephony Service Provider; a library that makers of telephony systems provide to permit third parties to control the telephony system over Microsoft's Telephony Application Program Interface (TAPI).

TSV   Tab-separated values; a file format in which individual data fields of a record are separated by a tab character and records are separated by new lines.

TTL   Time-to-live; a piece of information embedded in broadcast and multicast packets that dictates how many router hops a packet is permitted to traverse.

U

UA   User agent; in SIP, an entity that includes the functions of both a UAC and a UAS.

UAC   User agent client; the originator of a SIP method.

UAS   User agent server; the originator of SIP responses.

UDP   User Datagram Protocol.

UMS   Unified messaging system; a system that provides a unified way of accessing voice mail, e-mail, and fax.

Unicast conference bridge   A hardware or software device that receives multiple media streams from parties on a conference, sums the information contained within, and rebroadcasts the summed information to each conference participant.

unsigned integer   32-bit numbers that contain a 32-bit value that is assumed to be a positive number.

URI   Uniform Resource Identifier; an Internet naming format. URLs are a type of URI.

URJ   Unregister reject; an H.323 gatekeeper sends this RAS message to an H.323 endpoint when it denies the endpoint's request that the gatekeeper purge registration information related to the endpoint.

URL   Uniform Resource Locator; an Internet addressing format.

URQ   Unregistration Request; a gatekeeper-enabled H.323 endpoint sends this RAS message to an H.323 gatekeeper to ask the gatekeeper to purge registration information related to the endpoint.

user   A person or software application that makes use of a system.

user hold   A hold action that is initialized by an end user who presses the hold button on a phone.

UUIE   User-User Information Element; a field defined by ITU-T Q.931. H.323 messages use this field to encapsulate H.323-specific values.

V

v2   In the H.225 protocol, v2 refers to version 2.

VAD   Voice activity detection; see *silence suppression*.

varbind   Variable binding; in Simple Network Management Protocol (SNMP), a pairing of an object instance name and its associated value.

VCEG   Video Coding Experts Group.

VHM   Voice Health Manager; a CiscoWorks application that provides proactive fault management and root cause analysis for Cisco IP Communications system. It was also previously known as Voice Health and Fault Manager (VHFM).

VICs   Voice interface cards; typically small trunk interface modules that are inserted into IOS gateways to allow for OffNet communication.

video codec   See *codec*.

video data stream   A compressed stream of data packets of a specific format supported by a specific video codec. This series of data packets is then routed to the other endpoint through a previously established logical channel.

voice codec   See *codec*.

VoIP   Voice over IP; the process of routing voice communications over a network running Internet Protocol.

W–Z

WAN   Wide-area network.

wildcards   Elements within route patterns that describe a range of matching digits, cause a previous wildcard to match multiple digits, delimit portions of the route pattern, or direct CallManager to perform a macro expansion.

Index

Symbols

Numerics

A

F

Cisco Press

Learning is serious business.

Invest wisely.

3 STEPS TO LEARNING

STEP 1

First-Step

STEP 2

Fundamentals

STEP 3

Networking
Technology Guides

STEP 1   **First-Step**—Benefit from easy-to-grasp explanations.
No experience required!

STEP 2   **Fundamentals**—Understand the purpose, application,
and management of technology.

STEP 3   **Networking Technology Guides**—Gain the knowledge
to master the challenge of the network.

NETWORK BUSINESS SERIES

The Network Business series helps professionals tackle the
business issues surrounding the network. Whether you are a
seasoned IT professional or a business manager with minimal
technical expertise, this series will help you understand the
business case for technologies.

Justify Your Network Investment.

Learning is serious business.   **Invest wisely.**

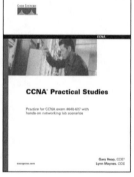

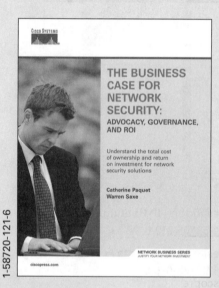

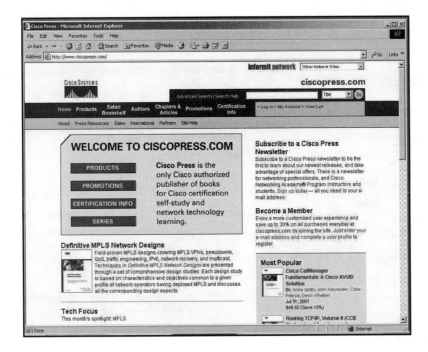
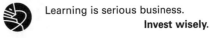

SEARCH THOUSANDS OF BOOKS FROM LEADING PUBLISHERS

Safari® Bookshelf is a searchable electronic reference library for IT professionals that features thousands of titles from technical publishers, including Cisco Press.

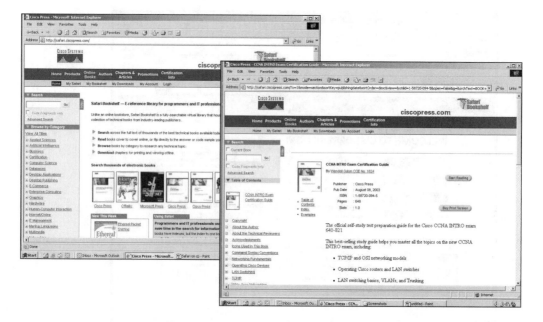

With Safari Bookshelf you can

- **Search** the full text of thousands of technical books, including more than 130 Cisco Press titles from authors such as Wendell Odom, Jeff Doyle, Bill Parkhurst, Sam Halabi, and Dave Hucaby.

- **Read** the books on My Bookshelf from cover to cover, or just flip to the information you need.

- **Browse** books by category to research any technical topic.

- **Download** chapters for printing and viewing offline.

With a customized library, you'll have access to your books when and where you need them—and all you need is a user name and password.